European Politics in the Age of Globalization

European Politics in the Age of Globalization

Howard J. Wiarda
University of Massachusetts–Amherst
(Editor)

HARCOURT COLLEGE PUBLISHERS
Fort Worth Philadelphia San Diego New York Orlando Austin San Antonio
Toronto Montreal London Sydney Tokyo

Publisher	Earl McPeek
Executive Editor	David Tatom
Market Strategist	Laura Brennan
Developmental Editor	Stacey Sims
Project Manager	Barrett Lackey

Cover design courtesy John Ritland

ISBN: 0-15-507388-5
Library of Congress Catalog Card Number: 00-104251

Copyright © 2001 by Harcourt, Inc.

All rights reserved. No part of this publication may be reproduced or transmitted in any form or by any means, electronic or mechanical, including photocopy, recording, or any information storage and retrieval system, without permission in writing from the publisher.

Requests for permission to make copies of any part of the work should be mailed to: Permissions Department, Harcourt, Inc., 6277 Sea Harbor Drive, Orlando, Florida 32887-6777.

Copyrights and acknowledgments begin on page 479, which constitutes a continuation of the copyright page.

Address for Domestic Orders
Harcourt College Publishers, 6277 Sea Harbor Drive, Orlando, FL 32887-6777
800-782-4479

Address for International Orders
International Customer Service
Harcourt College Publishers, 6277 Sea Harbor Drive, Orlando, FL 32887-6777
407-345-3800
(fax) 407-345-4060
(e-mail) hbintl@harcourtbrace.com

Address for Editorial Correspondence
Harcourt College Publishers, 301 Commerce Street, Suite 3700, Fort Worth, TX 76102

Web Site Address
http://www.harcourtcollege.com

Printed in the United States of America

0 1 2 3 4 5 6 7 8 9   066   9 8 7 6 5 4 3 2 1

Harcourt College Publishers

*To the New Europeans
and to our students who
seek to understand them.*

PREFACE

It is time for a new book on European politics. Older texts are badly out of date—both factually and in the ideas and concepts they convey. They were largely written during the Cold War and often show the old, Iron Curtain–era divide between Western and Eastern Europe. In some cases the older texts focus exclusively on the domestic politics of the several countries, largely ignoring the trends toward deeper regional integration and globalization of recent years that have blurred the lines between domestic and international politics. When these texts are revised, they often pay lip service to the newer changes by adding some new pages or an appendix, usually without re-thinking or re-conceptualizing the underlying themes of the book.

This book offers a fresh approach, containing country-by-country analyses of the major nations and regions of Europe while also recasting the treatment in the light of the broader themes of greater European integration and the impact of globalization. It employs the most recent conceptual approaches while also breaking down the old Cold War divisions of Europe. It is current, up to date both factually and conceptually, and offers new, younger, well-informed authors. It is a text for the twenty-first century.

The reasons for a new text on Europe at this time are compelling:

- The collapse of the Soviet Union and the halting, partial reintegration of a democratic Russia into Europe.
- The unification of Germany, its emergence as Europe's most powerful nation, and its energetic foreign policy toward Central and Eastern Europe.
- The movement in Central and Eastern Europe toward democracy and free markets, along with the consolidation of democracy in Southern Europe (Greece, Portugal, and Spain), so that for the first time virtually all of Europe is under democratic rule.
- The movement within Europe toward a common currency, common financial policy, and perhaps even a common foreign and defense policy.
- The new financial and political pressures on Europe's advanced welfare states, and the alternative plans for handling the recent economic crisis.
- Fighting and conflict in Bosnia, Kosovo, and Southeast Europe, which is forcing Europe to initiate new military and foreign-policy measures.
- New issues throughout Europe of the relations between the state and internal interest groups, of privatization and state downsizing, and of new public-private partnerships.
- New issues internally, across the Mediterranean, and to the east: immigration (legal and illegal), drugs, pollution, public health, law enforcement, and societal pluralism.

- The decline of political parties and ideologies, new questioning of established institutions, and new forms of public-private partnerships.
- New issues involving lifestyle changes, women in politics, and rights for homosexuals.
- New racial, ethnic, and regional sentiments that are surfacing, sometimes exploding, across Europe.

All of these are provocative and fascinating themes. And because the countries of Europe are leaders in so many areas and often models for other countries, Europe's experiences with these issues may offer lessons for the United States, Japan, as well as the developing nations.

Many of these large themes are raised in the provocative introduction to the book, which wrestles with such major and controversial themes as where Europe begins and ends; what it means these days to be "European"; whether political parties, parliament, trade unions, and ideologies are becoming less important in the new modern Europe; and what the hot new issues are. The Introduction provides background for understanding European or "Western" history; the changing economics, sociology, and politics of the continent; and Europe's changing international and global position. The Introduction also sets forth the main themes, ideas, and conceptual framework for the book.

The major countries covered are Great Britain, France, Germany, and Russia. These are the biggest countries, with the largest gross national products (GNP), and are the major powers. These are still the main countries treated in both introductory comparative politics and European politics courses. The focus on the large countries gives students a country-specific peg on which to hang their scholarly and reading hats, a factual basis of knowledge from which to develop broader comparisons as well as theoretical ideas.

A specific feature of the book is treatment of most of the other European countries through a regional focus. Full-length treatment is given to Scandinavia (Denmark, Finland, Iceland, Norway, and Sweden), Southern Europe (Greece, Italy, Portugal, and Spain), and Central and Eastern Europe (Poland, the Czech Republic, Slovakia, Hungary, Romania, Bulgaria, Albania, Croatia, Slovenia, Bosnia, and Serbia). These regional areas are treated in an explicitly comparative manner that serves to stimulate discussion; for both the large countries and the regional chapters a common outline is used that facilitates genuine comparisons and conceptual thinking. In these ways, too, teachers have maximum flexibility either to concentrate on the "Big Four" countries, to introduce a regional analysis, or to focus comparatively on some big issues, such as comparative democratization and development in Southern and Eastern Europe.

Another special feature of the book is its focus on European regional integration, as well as the effects on Europe of globalization. By integration we mean not just the deepening of the European Union through a common economic and foreign policy, but also the expansion of the Union, as well as NATO, to include, currently or potentially, countries in the South and East of Europe, and conceivably one day including Russia. By globalization we have in mind not only the impact in Europe of such global trends as democratization and free market economics but also the power of global television, culture, and ways of behaving. In addition, we deal with the rise of new global issues, such as drugs, terrorism, immigration, and the environment, and their effects on Europe.

One of the features of the book is that all the chapters and the country/regional studies strongly emphasize these new, post–Cold War, front-burner issues and trends. The book is therefore not only up to date, but in the forefront of contemporary comparative politics analysis. An especially attractive feature is that the book includes a separate, full-length section detailing the history, institutions, and politics of the European Union and the implications of these developments. For example (and it is an intriguing forerunner of things to come), Denmark's foreign policy is approximately

80% determined by broader European common foreign policy and only 20% by specific Danish interests—a loss of sovereignty that carries far-ranging implications.

The book is designed to be used as a text in introductory courses in comparative politics, in junior–senior level courses on European politics, and in other courses in comparative politics, in state-society relations, comparative democratization, processes of integration, and the future of already developed or postindustrial nations. Even after several decades of often path-breaking experimentation by faculty members with teaching other countries and areas, Europe still leads the way to the future and offers a model for other nations. We have much to learn from the European experiences of modernization, national development, and now regional unity and integration.

Special thanks in the preparation of this volume go to Executive Editor David Tatom who helped conceive the plan of the book; to Doris Holden of Amherst, Massachusetts, who labored heroically with the production of a complex and multifaceted manuscript; and to my fellow authors who produced (and on time) well-written, provocative, stimulating chapters. There are probably some remaining errors of fact and assessment in the book that ultimately are the fault of the authors and editor and for which we invite your suggestions and comments; however, we also hope that the book—even in its most controversial sections—will stimulate debate, discussion, and an interest in comparative politics.

Howard J. Wiarda
Amherst and Washington, D.C.
Winter 2001

About the Authors

Howard J. Wiarda

Howard J. Wiarda, the editor of this volume, is Professor of Political Science and the Leonard J. Horwitz Professor of Iberian and Latin American Studies at the University of Massachusetts/Amherst. He is also Senior Associate of the Center for Strategic and International Studies (CSIS) and a Senior Scholar of the Woodrow Wilson International Center for Scholars in Washington, D.C. He is editor of the Harcourt Series "New Directions in Comparative Politics" and author or editor of *Introduction to Comparative Politics, Non-Western Theories of Development, Latin American Politics,* and *Comparative Transitions to Democracy,* all published by Harcourt College Publishers.

Andrew M. Appleton

Andrew M. Appleton is Professor of Political Science at Washington State University. A longtime resident and student of France, he is a specialist in comparative political parties. His publications include *Party Politics, State Party Politics,* and comparative studies of political parties in France and the United States.

Steve D. Boilard

Steve D. Boilard has had a long career, both as a scholar and a government official, most recently as Legislative Analyst with the California State Assembly. He is the author of *Reinterpreting Russia, Moscow and the New World Order,* and the best-selling contemporary text on Russia published by Harcourt, *Russia at the Twenty-First Century: Politics and Social Change in the Post-Soviet Era.*

Gerald Braunthal

Gerald Braunthal is Professor of Political Science Emeritus at the University of Massachusetts. A specialist in comparative political parties, labor movements, and social democracy, in 1999 he was awarded the Commander Cross of the Order of Merit, Germany's highest honor. His many books include *The Federation of German Industry in Politics, Parties and Politics in Modern Germany, German Social Democrats,* and *Political Loyalty and Public Service in West Germany.*

David Gress

David Gress is professor at Aarhus University in Denmark and an associate at the Danish Institute of International Affairs in Copenhagen. Classically trained, he is a specialist in European history, the history of ideas, and Scandinavian politics and foreign policy. His best-selling book *From Plato to NATO: The Idea of the West and Its Opponents* is superb reading.

Dale Herspring

Dale Herspring, after a long career at the highest levels of the Department of State, is Professor of Political Science and Head of the Department of Political Science at Kansas State University. A specialist in Central and Eastern Europe, Germany, and Russia, he is the author of *Russian Civil-Military Relations, The Soviet High Command, Requiem for an Army: The Demise of the East German Military,* and *Soldiers, Commissars, and Chaplains.*

John McCormick

John McCormick is Professor of Political Science at Indiana University. A specialist in European politics, a former journalist, and a superb writer, he is the author of *Acid Rain, European Union, Reclaiming Paradise: The Global Environmental Movement,* as well as the best-selling text, *Comparative Politics in Transition,* published by Harcourt College Publishers.

Amy G. Mazur

Amy G. Mazur is Professor in the Department of Political Science/Criminal Justice System at Washington State University. She is a specialist in women's politics as well as a longtime student and resident of France. Her books include *Making Democracy Work for Women, Gender Bias and the State, Comparative State Feminism,* and *Gender, Policy, and Comparative Theory: Intersections Between Feminist Analysis and Political Science.*

CONTENTS

1. AN INTRODUCTION TO EUROPE AND EUROPEAN POLITICS: CHANGING DYNAMICS IN THE AGE OF INTERDEPENDENCE AND GLOBALIZATION 1
Howard J. Wiarda

   Europe: An Introduction 2
   - What is Europe? 9
   - Europe's Place in Comparative Politics 12

   Why Study Europe? 13

   The Grand Sweep of European History and Background 15
   - Geography, Climate, and Topography 15
   - European History: The Western Tradition 17

   The End of the Cold War and the New Vision of Europe 26

   NATO and the EU: Regionalization in the Face of Globalization 30

   Comparative Transition to Democracy 38

   Europe in a Comparative Politics Context 42

   The Book: A Look Ahead 50

2. BRITAIN: CHANGING YET STEADFAST 52
John McCormick

   Introduction 54

   Background and History 56
   - The Romans and Their Legacy (55 B.C.–1066) 56
   - The End of Feudalism (1215–1689) 57
   - Economic Revolutions (Seventeenth–Nineteenth Centuries) 57
   - The Imperial Era (Eighteenth Century–Early 1960s) 58
   - Postwar Adjustment and the Welfare State (1945–1975) 58
   - The Thatcher "Revolution" 59
   - Britain Today 60

   Political Culture 62
   - Pragmatism 62
   - Faith in the Political System 62
   - Social Liberalism 63
   - A Closed Society 63

Representation and Participation 64
  Social and Class Structure 64
  Elections and the Electoral System 65
  Political Parties 67
  Interest Groups 70
  The Media 72

Political System 72
  The Constitution 73
  The Monarchy 74
  The Executive: Prime Minister and Cabinet 75
  The Legislature: Parliament 78
  The Judiciary 81
  Subnational Goverment 82

Policies and Policymaking 82
  Economic Policy 83
  Social Policy 86
  Foreign Policy 86

Conclusions 89

3. FRANCE AT THE CROSSROADS: AN END TO FRENCH EXCEPTIONALISM? 92
Amy G. Mazur and Andrew Appleton

Introduction 94

The Best of French History 95

The Social Bases of Politics 105
  Race and Immigration 105
  Religion 111

Political Parties and Interests 113
  The State-Society Nexus in Politics 113
  Political Party System and Political Parties 115

Political Institutions and Public Policy Formation 123
  Executive Legislative Relations: The Semi-Presidential System 124
  The Bureaucracy and the Upper Civil Servants 127
  Territorial Division of Power and Decentralization Since 1982 128
  The Constitutional Council and the Code Law System 130
  French Public Policy Formation in Action: Policy Styles and Women's Rights Legislation 131

Current Trends in Public Policy 133

France at a Global Crossroads 136

4. GERMANY: FROM BONN REPUBLIC TO BERLIN REPUBLIC 138
Gerald Braunthal

Introduction 140

History, Geography, Background, and Political Culture 142
  History 142
  Geography, Background, and Political Culture 150

Social and Ethnic Groups, Class Structure, Interest Groups, and Political Parties 152
    Social and Ethnic Groups 152
    Class Structure 154
    Interest Groups 154
    Political Parties 155

Political Institutions, Law and Legal System, Role of the State, and the Bureaucracy 158
    Political Institutions 158
    Law and Legal System 161
    Role of the State and the Bureaucracy 162

Public Policy, Major Domestic and Foreign Policy Issues, and Policymaking 164
    Public Policy 164
    Major Domestic and Foreign Policy Issues 166

Conclusions, Prospects, Problems, and Future Directions 173

5. Russia: Joining the West, But Slowly 176
Steve D. Boilard

Introduction 178

History, Geography, Background, and Political Culture 179
    Establishing the Russian State 179
    Imperial Russia 179
    The Russian Revolution 181
    The Soviet Union 182
    The Cold War and Superpowerdom 182
    Gorbachev's Reforms 183
    The Demise of the Soviet Union 185
    The Reemergence of Russia 185
    Democratization and Political Culture 185

Social and Ethnic Groups, Class Structure, Interest Groups, and Political Parties 187
    Ethnic and National Groups 188
    Development of Parties and Interest Groups 191

Political Institutions, Law and Legal System, Role of the State, and Bureaucracy 199
    The Presidency 201
    Elections 202
    The Government 203
    The Legislature 204
    Lawmaking 205
    Legal System 206
    Role of the State 209

Public Policy, Major Domestic and Foreign Policy Issues, and Policymaking 210
    Foreign Policy 212
    Institutions 213

Conclusions, Prospects, Problems, and Future Directions 214

6. The Nordic Countries 218
David Gress

    Nordic Temperaments, Nordic Values 220

    Basic Issues and Patterns 226

    The Nordic Model 230

    Geography, Peoples, Languages, and Historical Legacies 234

    Foundations of Modern Scandinavia 243

    Parties and Constitutions 248

    From "The People's Home" to the "Strong Society" 259

    From Faith to Fear 269

    Crisis or Transformation of the Nordic Model 274

    Economy and Society at the Turn of the Century 280

    Culture, Education, Religion, Values 285

    Foreign and Security Policy 291

7. Southern or Mediterranean Europe: Politics and the Political System of Greece, Italy, Portugal, and Spain 304
Howard J. Wiarda

    Introduction: The Importance of Southern Europe 306

    History, Geography, Background, and Political Culture 308
        Political Culture 315

    Socioeconomic Background, Class Structure, and Interest Groups 321
        Socioeconomic Background 322
        Classes and Social Structure 323

    Political Parties and Elections 331
        Greece 333
        Portugal 335
        Spain 336

    Decision Making and the Role of the State 338
        Origins 338
        State-Society Relations 340
        Bureaucratic Politics 342
        Government Institutions 343

    Public Policy, Domestic and Foreign 348
        Domestic Policy 348
        Foreign Policy 354

    Regionalism and Globalization 361

    Conclusion 363

8. WHITHER EASTERN EUROPE? 368
Dale Herspring

> *Introduction 370*
>
> *History, Geography, Background, and Political Culture 372*
>
> *Ethnicity 380*
>> The Importance of Language 380
>> Gypsies 382
>> Hungarians in Romania 384
>> Hungarians in Slovakia 385
>> Turks in Bulgaria 386
>> Greeks in Albania 386
>> Albanians in Macedonia 387
>> Bosnia and Kosovo 387
>
> *The Challenge of Creating Democratic Political Institutions 391*
>> Interest Groups 391
>> Political Parties 392
>> Personalizing Power 393
>> Writing Constitutions 394
>> Corruption 394
>> Separation of Powers 395
>> The Media 395
>> Poland 396
>> The Czech Republic 397
>> Slovakia 399
>> Hungary 400
>> Romania 401
>> Bulgaria 402
>> Albania 404
>> Former Yugoslavia 407
>
> *Policy Concerns 409*
>
> *Conclusion 410*

9. THE EUROPEAN UNION 412
John McCormick

> *Introduction 414*
>
> *Background and History 416*
>> Opening Moves: 1951–1958 417
>> Widening and Deepening: 1960–1987 419
>> Maastricht and Further Enlargement: 1987–1995 420
>> The Single Currency and Beyond: 1997–Present 421
>
> *Political Culture 422*
>> A Tension Between Intergovernmentalism and Supranationalism 423
>> Elitism and the Democratic Deficit 423
>> The Knowledge Deficit 424
>
> *Representation and Participation 424*
>> Elections and the Electoral System 425
>> Political Parties 427

Interest Groups 429
The Media 431

Political System 432
The Constitution 433
The European Commission 433
The Council of Ministers 436
The European Parliament 438
The European Court of Justice 439
The European Council 440
Other Institutions 441

Policies and Policymaking 442
Economic Policy 442
The Single Market 443
Effects of the Single European Act 445
Toward a Single Currency 446
Foreign and Security Policy 447

Conclusions 451

Appendix A 456
Index 461
Credits 479

1

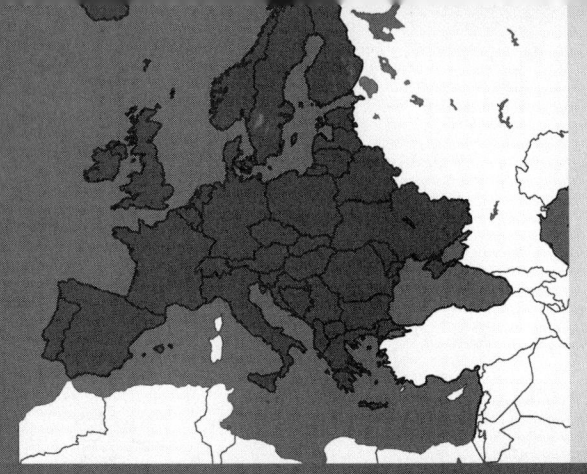

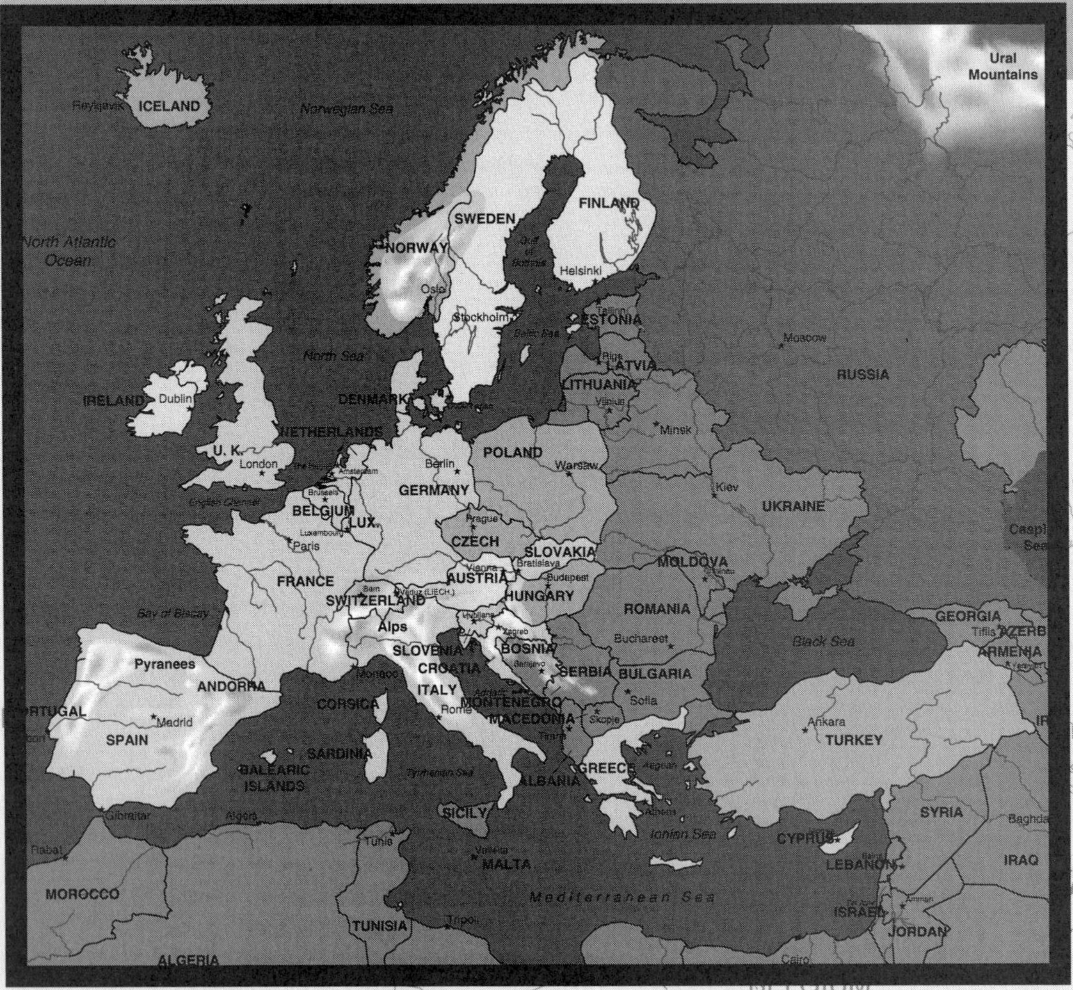

= EU countries
= EU and NATO countries
= Russia
= NATO countries

An Introduction to Europe and European Politics
Changing Dynamics in the Age of Interdependence and Globalization

Howard J. Wiarda

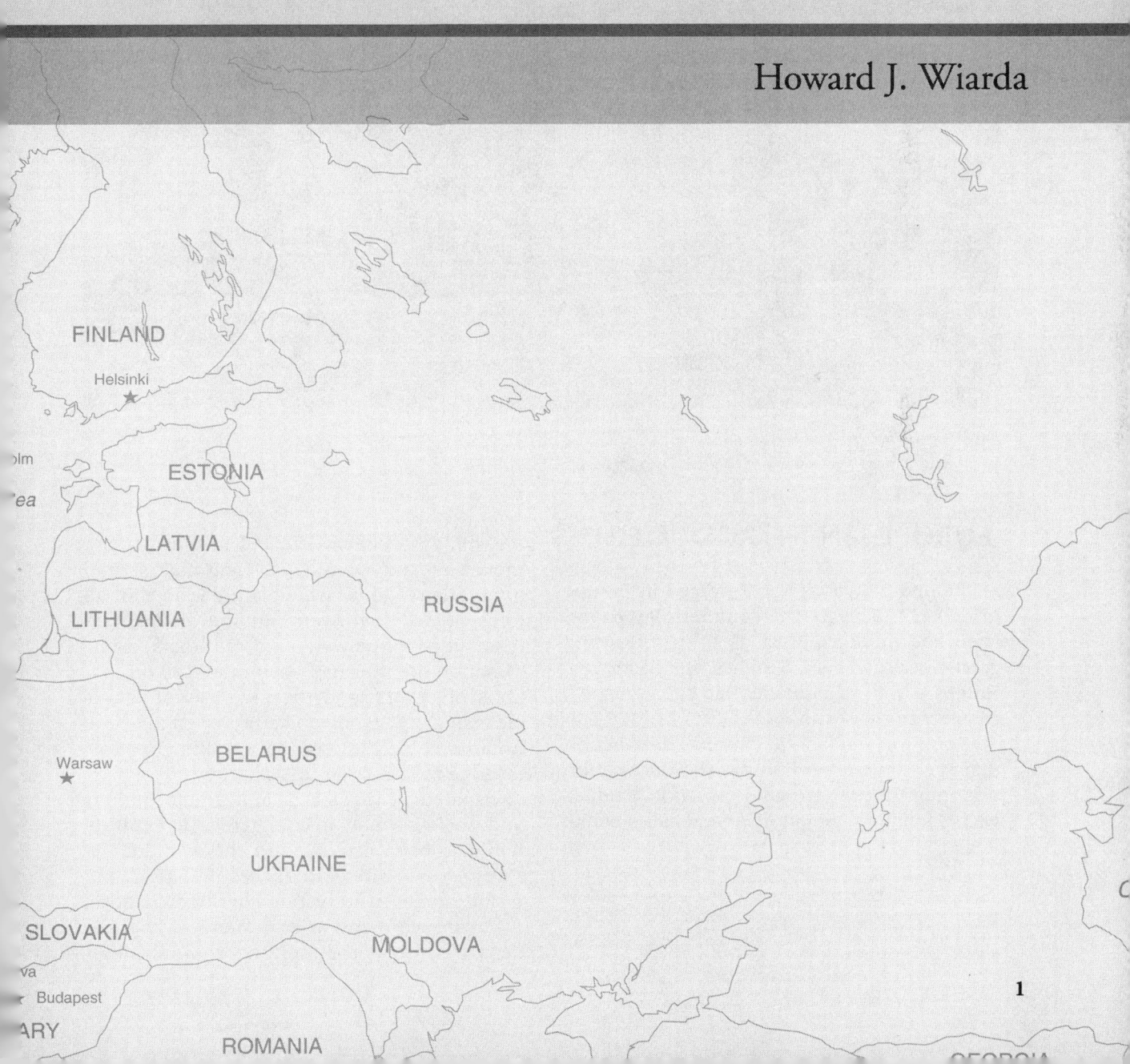

Europe devastated by World War II.

EUROPE: AN INTRODUCTION

At the end of World War II, waged in Europe from 1939 to 1945, the continent lay devastated and in ruins. Most of its factories and great cities[1] had been flattened and destroyed. Homes as well as industries had been crushed; rubble was everywhere.

But it was not just the physical destruction that had devastated Europe; the devastation was moral, cultural, and psychological as well. Germany's Adolph Hitler and Italy's Benito Mussolini had been defeated in the war, but the scars and wounds of their fascist and totalitarian regimes were plainly visible for all to see. More than twenty million people had been killed in the war; abhorrent racial extermination theories had been practiced on millions of others; and the practices of ethnic cleansing and genocide had reached new and unfathomable dimensions. Families had lost loved ones; entire groups of peoples had been eliminated or displaced; and whole nations and societies had disintegrated. Agriculture had also been destroyed in the war, and for several years afterwards mass privation, suffering, and even starvation continued to beset the European countries.[2] Many Europeans despaired that the continent would *ever*

---

[1] Prague, the capitol of the Czech Republic, was an exception. It was largely untouched by the wartime bombings and hence, its spectacular inner city with its medieval heritage remained intact. Now, with its restoration, Prague has become one of Europe's major tourist attractions.

Modern European beachfront.

recover from the devastation wreaked on them and their countries; the damage and destruction were so extensive that they tried men's and women's souls as well as their bodies. At the time it seemed unlikely that Europe, which had long been the world's leader in culture, industry, and civilization, would ever be able to pull itself up and together again.

In fact, not only has Europe pulled itself together, but it has also now emerged as the world's most prosperous continent. Americans are always shocked to discover that they are second best in anything, but at least five of the European countries have a higher per capita income than the United States; Europe is also ahead of the United States in literacy, health care, and life expectancy. European cities are generally safer, cleaner, and more livable than American cities; corruption is at a far lower level than in the United States; crime is far less; and European social welfare provides for virtually cradle-to-grave health care, education, and social security. Americans who travel to Europe, especially for the first time, are often amazed that Europe is so livable, its people are so healthy and happy, and that in so many areas Europe has forged ahead of the United States. The European recovery since World War II is such that Europe has again taken its place as one of the great economic, commercial, and trading areas in the world, the others being the United States and North America and Japan and Asia-Pacific.

To make these changes and the comparisons indicated more specific, examine Tables 1.1 and 1.2. Table 1.1 shows the rank ordering of the world's countries, from poorest to

---

[2]One of my earliest memories as a young boy in 1946–1947 growing up in Michigan was my mother, who never complained about anything, complaining to my father that he was sending so much food and clothing back to needy and starving relatives in "the old country"—in our case, The Netherlands—that it was depriving our own family of necessities.

TABLE 1.1 Size of the Economy

Economy	Population Millions 1998	Surface area Thousands of sq. km 1996	Population density People per sq. km 1998	Gross national product (GNP) Billions of Dollars 1998[b]	Rank 1998	Avg. annual growth rate (%) 1997-98	GNP per capita Dollars 1998[b]	Rank 1998	Avg. annual growth rate (%) 1997-98	GNP measured at PPP[a] Billions of dollars 1998	Per capita Dollars 1998	Rank 1998
Albania	3	29	123	2.7	137	—	810	144	—	—	—	—
Algeria	30	2,382	13	46.5	50	7.3	1,550	116	5.0	131.4[c]	4,380[c]	104
Angola	12	1,247	10	4.1	121	7.9	340	178	4.8	10.1[c]	840[c]	197
Argentina	36	2,780	13	324.1	17	4.0	8,970	55	2.7	368.5	10,200	64
Armenia	4	30	135	1.8	156	—	480	162	—	—	—	—
Australia	19	7,741	2	380.6	14	3.8	20,300	24	2.6	377.5	20,130	25
Austria	8	84	98	217.2	21	3.4	26,850	12	3.2	183.9	22,740	16
Azerbaijan	8	87	91	3.9	125	9.4	490	161	8.1	14.3	1,820	157
Bangladesh	126	144	965	44.0	52	5.0	350	175	3.4	137.7	1,100	188
Belarus	10	208	49	22.5	61	—	2,200	102	—	—	—	—
Belgium	10	33	311	259.0	19	2.9	25,380	15	2.7	239.7	23,480	12
Benin	6	113	54	2.3	142	4.5	380	173	1.5	7.5	1,250	182
Bolivia	8	1,099	7	7.9	94	4.7	1,000	138	2.3	22.4	2,820	140
Botswana	2	582	3	5.6	107	5.5	3,600	82	3.5	13.0	8,310	70
Brazil	166	8,547	20	758.0	8	0.0	4,570	72	−1.4	1,021.4	6,160	88
Bulgaria	8	111	75	10.1	84	—	1,230	131	—	—	—	—
Burkina Faso	11	274	39	2.6	140	6.3	240	196	3.8	11.0[c]	1,020[c]	191
Burundi	7	28	256	0.9	173	4.6	140	206	2.2	4.1[c]	620[c]	207
Cambodia	11	181	61	3.0	135	−0.1	280	191	−2.3	13.3	1,240	184
Cameroon	14	475	31	8.7	89	6.7	610	156	3.8	25.9	1,810	158
Canada	31	9,971	3	612.2	9	6.1	20,020	26	5.1	735.6	24,050	9
Central African Republic	3	623	6	1.0	170	4.5	300	186	2.6	4.5[c]	1,290[c]	181
Chad	7	1,284	6	1.7	160	—	230	197	—	—	—	—
Chile	15	757	20	71.3	42	8.0	4,810	71	6.5	191.1	12,890	53
China	1,239	9,597[d]	133	928.9	7	7.4	750	149	6.5	3,983.6	3,220	129
Hong Kong, China	7	1	6,755	158.3[c]	24	−5.1	23.670[c]	21	−7.8	147.1	22,000	18
Colombia	41	1,139	39	106.1	35	5.6	2,600	95	3.7	306.0	7,500	76
Congo, Dem. Rep.	48	2,345	21	5.3	108	4.0	110	209	0.7	36.4[c]	750[c]	200
Congo, Rep.	3	342	8	1.9	151	11.9	690	153	8.9	4.0	1,430	174
Costa Rica	4	51	69	9.8	85	4.7	2,780	93	3.1	23.3	6,620	86
Cote d'Ivoire	14	322	46	10.1	83	5.7	700	152	3.6	25.0	1,730	161
Croatia	5	57	82	20.7	63	—	4,520	73	—	—	—	—
Czech Republic	10	79	133	51.8	48	—	5,040	69	—	—	—	—
Denmark	5	43	125	176.4	23	3.0	33,260	6	2.6	126.4	23,830	11
Dominican Republic	8	49	171	14.6	78	6.5	1,770	109	4.6	38.8	4,700	99
Ecuador	12	284	44	18.6	70	2.1	1,530	119	0.2	56.3	4,630	100
Egypt, Arab Rep.	61	1,001	62	79.2	40	5.1	1,290	127	3.3	192.5	3,130	132
El Salvador	6	21	292	11.2	81	3.6	1,850	107	1.4	17.3	2.850	139
Eritrea	4	118	38	0.8	176	−4.0	200	202	−6.7	3.7	950	193
Estonia	1	45	34	4.9	112	—	3,390	87	—	—	—	—
Ethiopia	61	1,104	61	6.1	104	−0.8	100	210	−3.2	30.8	500	208
Finland	5	338	17	124.3	30	5.2	24,110	19	4.8	104.5	20,270	23
France	59	552	107	1,466.2	4	3.2	24,940	17	2.9	1,312.0	22,320	17
Georgia	5	70	78	5.1	109	—	930	139	—	—	—	—
Germany	82	357	235	2,122.7	3	−0.4	25,850	13	−0.4	1,708.5	20,810	20
Ghana	18	239	81	7.2	98	4.6	390	171	1.9	29.8[c]	1,610[c]	168
Greece	11	132	82	122.9	31	3.7	11,650	47	3.4	137.2	13,010	52
Guatemala	11	109	100	17.7	72	4.8	1,640	115	2.1	44.0	4,070	107
Guinea	7	246	29	3.8	127	4.3	540	159	1.9	12.5	1,760	160
Haiti	8	28	277	3.1	134	3.0	410	167	1.1	9.6[c]	1,250[c]	182
Honduras	6	112	55	4.5	117	3.9	730	151	1.0	13.2	2,140	154
Hungary	10	93	110	45.6	51	—	4,510	74	—	—	—	—
India	980	3,288	330	421.3	11	6.1	430	165	4.2	1,660.9	1,700	163
Indonesia	204	1,905	112	138.5	28	−14.8	680	154	−16.2	568.9	2,790	141
Iran, Islamic Rep.	62	1,633	38	109.6	33	—	1,770	109	—	—	—	—
Ireland	4	70	53	67.5	43	9.0	18,340	27	8.5	67.5	18,340	30
Israel	6	21	290	95.2	36	1.9	15,940	32	−0.4	103.4	17,310	33
Italy	58	301	196	1,166.2	6	2.3	20,250	25	2.2	1,163.4	20,200	24
Jamaica	3	11	238	4.3	118	−1.1	1,680	113	−1.9	8.3	3,210	130

Europe: An Introduction

TABLE 1.1 Size of the Economy—Cont'd.

Economy	Population Millions 1998	Surface area Thousands of sq. km 1996	Population density People per sq. km 1998	Gross national product (GNP) Billions of Dollars 1998[b]	Rank 1998	Avg. annual growth rate (%) 1997-98	GNP per capita Dollars 1998[b]	Rank 1998	Avg. annual growth rate (%) 1997-98	GNP measured at PPP[a] Billions of dollars 1998	Per capita Dollars 1998	Rank 1998
Japan	126	378	335	4,089.9	2	−2.6	32,380	7	−2.8	2,928.4	23,180	14
Jordan	5	89	51	6.9	100	0.3	1,520	120	−2.5	14.8	3,230	128
Kazakhstan	16	2,717	6	20.6	64	−2.6	1,310	126	−2.0	53.4	3,400	126
Kenya	29	580	51	9.7	86	1.5	330	180	−0.9	33.1	1,130	187
Korea, Rep.	46	99	470	369.9	15	−6.3	7,970	59	−7.1	569.3	12,270	55
Kuwait	2	18	105	—	—	—	—[f]	—	—	—	—	—
Kyrgyz Republic	5	199	24	1.6	162	4.2	350	175	2.8	10.3	2,200	152
Lao PDR	5	237	22	1.6	163	4.0	330	180	1.4	6.5[c]	1,300[c]	180
Latvia	2	65	39	5.9	105	—	2,430	98	—	—	—	—
Lebanon	4	10	412	15.0	77	4.3	3,560	84	2.7	25.9	6,150	89
Lesotho	2	30	68	1.2	168	−3.1	570	158	−5.4	4.8[c]	2,320[c]	147
Lithuania	4	65	57	9.0	88	5.6	2,440	97	5.9	15.9	4,310	105
Macedonia, FYR	2	26	79	2.6	139	2.9	1,290	127	2.2	7.4	3,660	116
Madagascar	15	587	25	3.8	128	4.8	260	193	1.6	13.1	900	194
Malawi	11	118	112	2.1	144	1.8	200	202	−0.7	7.7	730	203
Malaysia	22	330	68	79.8	39	−6.3	3,600	82	−8.4	155.1[c]	6,990[c]	79
Mali	11	1,240	9	2.6	138	5.3	250	194	2.2	7.7	720	204
Mauritania	3	1,026	2	1.0	171	5.2	410	167	2.4	4.2[c]	1,660[c]	165
Mexico	96	1,958	50	380.9	13	4.8	3,970	76	3.0	785.8[c]	8,190[c]	71
Moldova	4	34	130	1.8	158	—	410	167	—	—	—	—
Mongolia	3	1,567	2	1.0	172	4.9	400	170	3.2	3.9	1,520	170
Morocco	28	447	62	34.8	56	0.8	1,250	130	−1.0	86.8	3,120	133
Mozambique	17	802	22	3.6	130	11.3	210	199	9.2	14.5[c]	850[c]	196
Myanmar	44	677	68	—	—	—	—[g]	—	—	—	—	—
Namibia	2	824	2	3.2	131	1.2	1,940	106	−1.2	8.2[c]	4,950[c]	94
Nepal	23	147	160	4.8	114	2.2	210	199	−0.1	24.9	1,090	189
Netherlands	16	41	463	388.7	12	3.3	24,760	18	2.7	339.3	21,620	19
New Zealand	4	271	14	55.8	46	1.4	14,700	36	0.5	60.1	15,840	40
Nicaragua	5	130	40	—	—	—	—	—	—	8.6[c]	1,790[c]	159
Niger	10	1,267	8	1.9	150	4.3	190	204	0.8	8.4	830	198
Nigeria	121	924	133	36.4	55	1.1	300	186	−1.7	99.7	820	199
Norway	4	324	14	152.1	25	2.4	34,330	4	1.8	107.6	24,290	8
Pakistan	132	796	171	63.2	44	5.0	480	162	2.5	204.9	1,560	169
Panama	3	76	37	8.5	91	3.8	3,080	90	2.0	19.2	6,940	81
Papua New Guinea	5	463	10	4.1	120	2.3	890	140	0.0	12.4[c]	2,700[c]	142
Paraguay	5	407	13	9.2	87	0.2	1,760	111	−2.1	19.0	3,650	117
Peru	25	1,285	19	61.1	45	—	2,460	96	—	—	—	—
Philippines	75	300	252	78.9	41	0.1	1,050	135	−2.1	265.6	3,540	122
Poland	39	323	127	150.8	26	5.4	3,900	79	5.4	260.7	6,740	83
Portugal	10	92	109	106.4	34	3.9	10,690	51	3.8	143.1	14,380	45
Romania	22	238	98	31.3	58	−5.6	1,390	125	−5.3	89.3	3,970	109
Russian Federation	147	17,075	9	337.9	16	−6.6	2,300	101	−6.3	579.8	3,950	110
Rwanda	8	26	329	1.9	155	9.9	230	197	7.1	5.6	690	206
Saudi Arabia	21	2,150	10	—	—	—	—[h]	—	—	—	—	—
Senegal	9	197	47	4.8	115	6.0	530	160	3.1	15.4	1,710	162
Sierra Leone	5	72	68	0.7	181	−0.7	140	206	−2.9	1.9	390	210
Singapore	3	1	5,186	95.1	37	1.5	30,060	9	−0.4	90.5	28,620	5
Slovak Republic	5	49	112	20.0	66	—	3,700	80	—	—	—	—
Slovenia	2	20	99	19.4	67	—	9,760	52	—	—	—	—
South Africa	41	1,221	34	119.0	32	0.6	2,880	92	−1.2	288.7[c]	6,990[c]	79
Spain	39	506	79	553.7	10	3.7	14,080	39	3.7	631.5	16,060	38
Sri Lanka	19	66	290	15.2	76	—	810	144	—	—	—	—
Sweden	9	450	22	226.9	20	3.5	25,620	14	3.5	172.5	19,480	27
Switzerland	7	41	180	284.8	18	2.1	40,080	3	1.8	189.1	26,620	7
Syrian Arab Republic	15	185	83	15.6	75	4.4	1,020	136	1.8	45.8	3,000	136
Tajikistan	6	143	43	2.1	143	—	350	175	—	—	—	—
Tanzania	32	945	36	6.7[i]	101	3.2	210[i]	199	0.6	15.9	490	209
Thailand	61	513	120	134.4	29	−7.7	2,200	102	−8.5	357.1	5,840	91
Togo	4	57	82	1.5	164	−1.0	330	180	−3.5	6.2	1,390	176
Tunisia	9	164	60	19.2	69	5.5	2,050	105	3.9	48.3	5,160	93
Turkey	63	775	82	200.5	22	—	3,160	89	—	—	—	—
Turkmenistan	5	488	10	—	136	—	—[g]	—	—	—	—	—
Uganda	21	241	105	6.7	102	5.8	320	185	2.9	24.5[c]	1,170[c]	185

TABLE 1.1 Size of the Economy—*Cont'd.*

Economy	Population Millions 1998	Surface area Thousands of sq. km 1996	Population density People per sq. km 1998	Gross national product (GNP) Billions of Dollars 1998[b]	Gross national product (GNP) Rank 1998	Gross national product (GNP) Avg. annual growth rate (%) 1997-98	GNP per capita Dollars 1998[b]	GNP per capita Rank 1998	GNP per capita Avg. annual growth rate (%) 1997-98	GNP measured at PPP[a] Billions of dollars 1998	GNP measured at PPP[a] Per capita Dollars 1998	GNP measured at PPP[a] Per capita Rank 1998
Ukraine	50	604	87	42.7	53	—	850	142	—	—	—	—
United Kingdom	59	245	244	1,263.8	5	2.0	21,400	22	1.9	1,218.6	20,640	22
United States	270	9,364	29	7,921.3	1	3.7	29,340	10	2.8	7,922.6	29,340	3
Uruguay	3	177	19	20.3	65	6.6	6,180	67	5.8	31.2	9,480	67
Uzbekistan	24	447	58	20.9	62	3.0	870	141	1.2	69.8	2,900	138
Venezuela	23	912	26	81.3	38	−0.4	3,500	85	−2.4	190.4	8,190	71
Vietnam	78	332	238	25.6	60	4.0	330	180	2.8	131.0	1,690	164
Yemen, Rep.	16	528	31	4.9	110	7.3	300	186	4.6	12.1	740	202
Zambia	10	753	13	3.2	132	−1.8	330	180	−4.0	8.3	860	195
Zimbabwe	12	391	30	7.1	99	−0.4	610	156	−2.2	25.2	2,150	153
World	5,897 s	133,567 s	45 w	28,862.2 t		1.5 w	4,890 t		0.1 w	36,556.8 t	6,200 w	
Low income	3,515	42,695	85	1,843.7		3.8	520		2.1	7,475.1	2,130	
Excl. China & India	1,296	29,810	45	493.5		−3.9	380		−5.9	1,821.3	1,400	
Middle income	1,496	58,789	26	4,419.6		−0.4	2,950		−1.5	8,315.8	5,560	
Lower middle income	908	36,729	25	1,557.4		−1.5	1,710		−2.6	3,709.4	4,080	
Upper middle income	588	22,060	27	2,862.1		0.2	4,860		−1.1	4,606.3	7,830	
Low and middle income	5,011	101,484	50	6,263.3		1.0	1,250		−0.5	15,790.8	3,150	
East Asia & Pacific	1,817	16,384	114	1,801.6		−1.1	990		−2.2	6,179.5	3,400	
Europe & Central Asia	473	24,208	20	1,038.8		—	2,190		—	2,005.5	4,240	
Latin America & Carib.	502	20,462	25	1,977.6		2.5	3,940		0.8	3,401.5	6,780	
Middle East & N. Africa	285	11,000	26	585.6		—	2,050		—	1,203.3	4,220	
South Asia	1,305	5,140	273	555.5		5.9	430		3.9	2,100.4	1,610	
Sub-Saharan Africa	628	24,290	27	304.2		2.2	480		−0.4	900.6	1,430	
High income	885	32,082	29	22,599.0		1.6	25,510		1.1	20,766.0	23,440	

Note: For data comparability, and coverage, see the Technical Notes. Figures in italics are for years other than those specified. Rankings are based on 210 economics, including the 78 listed in Table 1a. See Technical Notes.

Source: World Bank.

a. Purchasing power parity; see the Technical Notes. b. Preliminary World Bank estimates calculated using the World Bank *Atlas* method. c. Estimate based on regression: others are extrapolated from the latest International Comparison Programme benchmark estimates. d. Includes Taiwan, China. e. GNP data refer to GDP. f. Estimated to be high income ($9,361 or more). g. Estimated to be low income ($760 or less). h. Estimated to be upper middle income ($3,031 to $9,360). i. Data refer to mainland Tanzania only.

richest. Of all the European countries, only proverbially poor Albania is still considered a low-income country—and it is close to middle-income status. In the middle-income category, all of the European countries represented are in Eastern Europe, which not only lagged economically for many centuries behind the rest of Europe but was also under Soviet domination for approximately forty years. Now look at the high-income economies: *All* of the other European countries fall into this category; several of them are ranked ahead of the United States; and Switzerland tops the list as the wealthiest country in the world. It is clear that the Western European countries are doing very well indeed.

A second way to look at these rankings is provided in Table 1.2, which classifies countries by income and region. Note that the only poor or low-income countries in Europe and Central Asia (not part of Europe) are Albania and some new countries that were formerly a part of the Soviet Union. Similarly, the middle-income countries are all located in Eastern Europe or again were part of the Soviet Union. Now look at the column of high-income countries: *No* Eastern European country has yet made it to that category, but *every* Western European country can be found at this high level. Table 1.2 reinforces the argument of how wealthy and prosperous the Western European countries have become.

TABLE 1.2   Classification of Economies by Income and Region, 1998

Income group	Subgroup	Sub-Saharan Africa		Asia		Europe and Central Asia		Middle East and North Africa		Americas
		East and Southern Africa	West Africa	East Asia and Pacific	South Asia	Eastern Europe and Central Asia	Rest of Europe	Middle East	North Africa	
Low-income		Angola Burundi Comoros Congo, Dem. Rep. Eritrea Ethiopia Kenya Lesotho Madagascar Malawi Mozambique Rwanda Somalia Sudan Tanzania Uganda Zambia Zimbabwe	Benin Burkina Faso Cameroon Central African Republic Chad Congo, Rep. Cote d'Ivoire Gambia, The Ghana Guinea Guinea-Bissau Liberia Mali Mauritania Niger Nigeria São Tomé and Principe Senegal Sierra Leone Togo	Cambodia China Indonesia Korea, Dem. Rep. Lao PDR Mongolia Myanmar Solomon Islands Vietnam	Afghanistan Bangladesh Bhutan India Nepal Pakistan	Armenia Azerbaijan Kyrgyz Republic Moldova Tajikistan Turkmenistan		Yemen, Rep.		Haiti Honduras Nicaragua
Middle-income	Lower	Djibouti Namibia South Africa Swaziland	Cape Verde Equatorial Guinea	Fiji Kiribati Marshall Islands Micronesia, Fed. Sts. Papua New Guinea Philippines Samoa Thailand Tonga Vanuatu	Maldives Sri Lanka	Albania Belarus Bosnia and Herzegovina Bulgaria Georgia Kazakhstan Latvia Lithuania Macedonia, FYR[a] Romania Russian Federation Ukraine Uzbekistan Yugoslavia, Fed. Rep.[b]		Iran, Islamic Rep. Iraq Jordan Syrian Arab Republic West Bank and Gaza	Algeria Egypt, Arab Rep. Morocco Tunisia	Belize Bolivia Colombia Costa Rica Cuba Dominica Dominican Republic Ecuador El Salvador Guatemala Guyana Jamaica Paraguay Peru St. Vincent and the Grenadines Suriname
	Upper	Botswana Mauritius Mayotte Seychelles	Gabon	American Samoa Korea, Rep Malaysia Palau		Croatia Czech Republic Estonia Hungary Poland Slovak Republic	Isle of Man Turkey	Bahrain Lebanon Oman Saudi Arabia	Libya	Antigua and Barbuda Argentina Barbados Brazil Chile Grenada Guadeloupe Mexico Panama Puerto Rico St. Kitts and Nevis St. Lucia Trinidad and Tobago Uruguay Venezuela
Subtotal:	157	26	23	23	8	26	3	10	6	34

TABLE 1.2 Classification of Economies by Income and Region, 1998—*Cont'd.*

| Income group | Subgroup | Sub-Saharan Africa | | Asia | | Europe and Central Asia | | Middle East and North Africa | | Americas |
		East and Southern Africa	West Africa	East Asia and Pacific	South Asia	Eastern Europe and Central Asia	Rest of Europe	Middle East	North Africa	
High-income	OECD			Australia Japan New Zealand			Austria Belgium Denmark Finland France Germany Greece Iceland Ireland Italy Luxembourg Netherlands Norway Portugal Spain Sweden Switzerland United Kingdom			Canada United States
	Non-OECD	Réunion		Brunei French Polynesia Guam Hong Kong, China[c] Macao New Caledonia N. Mariana Islands Singapore Taiwan, China		Slovenia	Andorra Channel Islands Cyprus Faeroe Islands Greenland Liechtenstein Monaco	Israel Kuwait Qatar United Arab Emirates	Malta	Aruba Bahamas, The Bermuda Cayman Islands French Guiana Martinique Netherlands Antilles Virgin Islands (U.S.)
Total: 211		27	23	37	8	27	27	14	6	44

a. Former Yugoslav Republic of Macedonia.
b. Federal Republic of Yugoslavia (Serbia/Montenegro).
c. On July 1, 1997, China resumed its sovereignty over Hong Kong.
Source: World Bank data.

In recent years Europe has moved beyond the confines of the nation-state to practice a kind and degree of unity and integration not found in any other area. European integration is no longer limited primarily to economic integration but now includes unprecedented levels of social, political, and even strategic integration as well. Europe is moving toward not only a common financial system and a common currency but toward a common foreign and defense policy as well. Virtually no passport regulations or other controls exist among the Western European countries anymore; the police from one country may pursue criminals into another without judicial or other permission; and European foreign ministries now spend most of their time adjusting their policies to the common European policy rather than pursuing independent policies of their own. More recently, with the tumbling of the Iron Curtain and the collapse of the Soviet Union, European integration has expanded eastward as well. The Czech Republic, Hungary, and Poland have been accepted into the North Atlantic Treaty Organization (NATO); these same countries are petitioning to join the European Union (EU); and other countries are likely to be included in one form or another as well. It is not far-fetched, now that the Cold War is over, to envision Russia and other parts of the former Soviet Union becoming integrated into Europe, too. All of these themes receive more detailed treatment later in the book.

Of course, cost and tradeoffs are involved in all of these European transformations as well. Thus, although many European countries have a higher per capita income than the United States, because of high taxes in Europe, Americans actually have on average more disposable (after-tax) income than do Europeans. American houses are bigger and the housing generally better than European housing; Americans have more cars (but less and poorer public transportation) than do Europeans; and the American middle class generally has more goods—appliances, TVs, computers, VCRs, and so forth—than their European counterparts. In contrast, European social and welfare programs are far more generous and universal than U.S. programs, but Americans have not yet been willing to pay taxes on the scale Europeans do (often 50–65 percent of earned income) to pay for all of these services. Europeans argue that their public policy programs are better than the American counterparts, but Americans tend to be more individualistic than Europeans and may not want to give up their individualism and differences for a more homogenized European-like society; nor are Americans as convinced as Europeans about the value of economic integration: witness the mixed U.S. attitudes toward closer ties and a free-trade agreement (North American Free Trade Agreement—NAFTA) with Mexico. In other words, although some tout Europe as more "advanced" than the United States (and in some areas it undoubtedly is), that assessment often involves value judgments, political choices, and deep-rooted cultural differences between the two areas that may never be erased. The United States is a fundamentally different country than those of Europe (although both are part of the Western tradition), and the choices that people in the different countries make reflect these immense differences. That is what the study of comparative politics is all about: examining the similarities as well as differences among countries and culture areas.

What Is Europe?

Europe as seen on a global map looks like a large, irregular peninsula jutting out of the great Eurasian land mass toward the West and the Atlantic. Europe is the second smallest continent (ahead only of Australia) with about 7 percent of the world's total land area. The EU countries are home to approximately 370 million people; non-EU but still European countries add approximately 200 million more. For many centuries Europe was the world's leader in science, technology, industry, and global power; and even today Europe constitutes the world's largest, most prosperous, and most powerful market. Europe's wealth and importance are clearly far greater on a global scale than its physical size or population alone would indicate.

But where precisely are Europe's borders and how does one define which countries are in or out of Europe? Is Turkey, with its Islamic tradition, a European country, for example? The question is controversial both in Turkey as well as in the rest of Europe. Are Russia and the main western areas of the former Soviet Union (the Ukraine, Belarus) part of Europe or are they something else? How about the Baltic states (Estonia, Latvia, Lithuania), which used to be part of the Soviet Union but are now independent? Or, on the other side of the continent, what about Iceland, which is geographically closer to North America but, as a former Danish colony, considers itself a part of Europe culturally, historically, and economically? All of these questions are not only complex, but they also carry important political, economic, and psychological implications for the countries affected.

The problem is complicated—and high stakes are involved—because Europe can be defined in several different ways. Using a geographic definition, Europe generally consists of everything west of Russia's Ural Mountains and north of the Mediterranean and the Black and Caspian seas (see Map A.3, p. 458). The Urals have long been considered to divide Europe from Asia. Using that definition would mean that all of Eastern Europe, the Baltics, and large parts of Russia, Ukraine, and Belarus are all part of Europe. But not everyone is convinced that they want to see all of these countries included in "Europe."

If we use economic criteria, according to the European Economic Community (EEC), which was recently renamed the European Union (EU), the definition of which countries are included is somewhat more restrictive. Historically the EEC was limited to the Western, capitalistic, or mixed economies. The EEC had six original members (Belgium, France, Italy, Germany, Luxembourg, and The Netherlands), and then added Denmark, Great Britain, and Ireland in 1973 and included Greece in 1981 and Spain and Portugal in 1986. But now seven other countries that were previously neutral, did not want to join the EEC, and had their own European Free Trade Association (EFTA)—Austria, Finland, Iceland, Liechtenstein, Norway, Sweden, and Switzerland—are either in the market already or are seriously considering joining the EU. Since the collapse of communism, the Baltic states and the countries of Eastern Europe and Russia are clamoring to be included as well. The fall of the Iron Curtain has erased the old East-West divide in Europe—physically, if not yet economically and psychologically.

Now let us consider political and strategic criteria. Here the principal "European" organization has been the Atlantic alliance or NATO. But NATO also includes the United States and Canada—Western but definitely *not* European countries. It also includes, for strategic reasons, Turkey, which sits astride the Bosporus and right on the border of the former Soviet Union, and thus was a major strategic asset in the Cold War; but on other geographic, cultural, and religious grounds, Turkey fits uncomfortably in to the "European" category. At the same time, now that the Iron Curtain has been torn down and the Cold War is over, Eastern Europe or Russia should not be automatically excluded. Hungary, the Czech Republic, and Poland have already been voted into NATO; the Baltic states are clamoring to join; other countries have their applications in; and Russia may want "in" as a full member (it is already a partial member) as well.

A fourth definition of Europe is cultural and religious. Europe may thus be identified as "Western" (the Judeo-Christian tradition, heir of Greco-Roman civilization, of German individualism, the Renaissance, the Enlightenment, democracy, and the Industrial Revolution) and predominantly "Christian" (historically at least including Protestant, Catholic, and Eastern Orthodox). That definition seems to exclude Turkey (predominantly Muslim), which is also on the margins of Europe geographically, but what about Albania, Bosnia, or Kosovo, which are predominantly Muslim but inside Europe geographically? And what about those areas, like Russia, that are only partly and incompletely Western? Or how about all those immigrant workers and political refugees from other countries who presently make Europe appear more multicultural than just white and Christian? The culture/religion definition is fraught with dangers of racial, ethnic, and religious prejudice and stereotyping, but it has clearly been used to keep Turkey out of the EU.

Europe, too, has become diverse and multicultural.

Moreover, as we see in the following paragraphs, there is *something* to this idea of a common, Western, European culture and civilization.

The end of the Cold War has complicated and simultaneously simplified our efforts to define Europe. Previously, with the Iron Curtain stretched across Europe from the Baltic to the Adriatic, Western Europe was identified with "The West," whereas the Soviet Union and Eastern Europe were part of "The East" or "The Soviet Bloc." The former countries were democratic (excepting Greece, Portugal, and Spain) and part of the "free world," whereas the latter were communist or totalitarian. Similarly, using economic criteria, Western Europe was primarily identified with the First World of modern, industrialized, capitalistic, or mixed economies, whereas Eastern Europe and the U.S.S.R. constituted the Second World of Marxist-Leninist or command economies. But when the wall between East and West crumbled, so did many of the differences between the two sectors. Now Russia and Eastern Europe also want to be democratic, to enjoy free-market prosperity, to join Europe in all its dimensions, and to become more like the West. Although the Cold War seemed as if it lasted a long time (forty to forty-five years), in terms of the long stretch of history, it represented a short, often artificial dividing line across Europe. Now, with that line erased, we can again study Europe in its full dimensions.

For the purposes of this book, we use all four of the definitions of Europe set forth here, even while recognizing that in some countries the definition of being European is ambiguous, varies from country to country, and may change over time. That approach means Russia is treated at length here, as well as (briefly) its former territories of Ukraine and Belarus—even while recognizing that these countries are still torn by their degrees of "Westernness." The major core European countries of Great Britain, France, and Germany also receive detailed treatment. The text treats the three major subregions of Europe: Northern or Scandinavian Europe, Southern or Mediterranean Europe, and Eastern or former communist Europe. We are also interested, in terms of globalization and interdependence, in NATO, the EEC, the EU, and other pan-European movements, as well as their expansion to include new countries. Using all four definitions also means that, for purposes of this book, Turkey is excluded as is Central Asia and the former Soviet republics in the trans-Caucasus: Armenia, Azerbaijan, and Chechnya.

Europe's Place in Comparative Politics

For a long time, from the beginning of political science as a discipline until the dawn of the 1960s, Europe was the main and virtually only focus of Comparative Politics. The first country studied was usually Great Britain, a fellow English-speaking country, a democracy, and the source of many of our own American political ideas and institutions. So, it made sense to study Great Britain initially and to develop comparisons with the United States. Next, the typical introductory Comparative Government course moved across the English Channel to study France, with its more divisive and polarized (since the French Revolution of 1789) history and parliamentary system. The third country studied was almost always Germany, with its more authoritarian tradition culminating in Hitler and Naziism. Fourth was the Soviet Union, with its bolshevism and communism—the last of the "Great European Powers."

Several factors operated to limit the study of Comparative Government to these four countries and not others. First, these were the largest and, arguably, most important countries, the source and origin of most Americans' backgrounds as well as political experiences. Second, these were the only countries about which large numbers of books and studies were readily available. Third, this was the period (pre-1960) before modern jet travel and global television (no CNN!); if instructors in Comparative Government courses had traveled or researched abroad at all, it was usually in these countries. And fourth, in those days most Political Science departments had rules governing the introductory comparative course that *forced* professors to teach about these four countries and no others. Of course, there were always a handful of instructors who did research on Scandinavia, the Benelux (Belgium, Netherlands, Luxembourg) countries, Italy, Iberia (Spain and Portugal), Latin America, or the British Commonwealth (Australia, Canada, New Zealand) countries; but the overwhelming majority of Comparative Politics courses was devoted to Europe and, within Europe, to the "Big Four."

In the mid- to late 1950s, the focus of research and teaching began to shift away from Europe. Several factors were involved in this shift as well. First, within Political Science, it began to be considered narrow-minded and ethnocentric (seeing the world only through our own or European eyes) to focus in Comparative Politics courses only on these four European countries; there were some devastating critiques of the field beginning in the mid-1950s that made precisely that point. Second, in the late 1950s and early 1960s, a host of new and developing nations appeared on the world scene that not only vastly expanded the number of countries for Comparative Politics to study but also changed its focus from government *institutions* to more informal processes: social movements, revolutions, military coups d'etat, and so on. Third, the focus of the Cold War and of U.S. foreign policy shifted as well, away from Europe and toward these developing nations; and the study of Comparative Politics mirrored that shift. Fourth, modern jet air travel coming into widespread use precisely during this period enormously facilitated the ability of scholars to conduct research abroad, not just in Europe but in the developing areas as well. Henceforth, almost no area of the globe would be more than one day's travel time away. And fifth, Political Science departments became less restrictive in stating what the introductory Comparative Politics course could cover, enabling instructors (and textbook writers) to incorporate such previously not covered countries as Japan, China, Mexico, Nigeria, and others.

During the 1960s and 1970s, the focus of attention in Comparative Politics was far more on the developing countries of Africa, Asia,

Latin America, and the Middle East than on the developed European ones. That was where the excitement was in terms of revolutions and guerrilla movements; the Cold War was centered there (Vietnam, Central America, southern Africa); the Peace Corps and U.S. foreign aid were concentrated there; and that was where the fellowships were for aspiring graduate students. In addition, within Comparative Politics, the most exciting new theories in the field came from these new areas: developmentalism, dependency theory, corporatism, bureaucratic-authoritarianism, and transitions to democracy. Another measure is the size of these distinct areas' associations of scholars: for example, the Latin American Studies Association membership grew from the 1960s to the 1980s to a size *ten times* that of the European Studies Association: five thousand versus five hundred members.

Now that focus has begun to change again. Europe is coming back to the fore. It is one of the most prosperous and advanced areas in the world and a "living laboratory" of modern social and economic innovation. More young students are studying in and about Europe than ever before. Europe is being rediscovered. In the next section we explore why this change has taken place.

WHY STUDY EUROPE?

There are many good reasons, both personal and scholarly, to study Europe these days; here we list only some of these:

1. *Our roots are there.* Although the United States is becoming a more diverse, multiracial, and multicultural society, most Americans still trace their origins to Europe and to the countries and cultures our forebears left behind.
2. *Our political, social, and economic ideas and institutions come from there.* America is a New World society with indigenous as well as imported institutions; nevertheless, most of our political, social, religious, and economic ideas came from Europe—democracy, representative government, human rights, separation of powers, and free markets, to name just a few.
3. *The United States and Europe share a common Western heritage.* Although the United States is becoming more culturally diverse, our main heritage is that of the West: the Judeo-Christian tradition, Greece, Rome, the Middle Ages, the Renaissance, the Enlightenment, the Industrial Revolution, ideas of social justice, and so on.
4. *The United States and Europe are partners*—in NATO, the Atlantic Alliance, the Group of Seven, and a host of other international organizations.
5. *We travel there.* Americans, including tourists, students, businessmen, and government officials, travel mainly to Europe. If you are a student, then Europe is probably where your parents want you to go to study abroad.
6. *Europe is developed and modern.* Along with the United States, Canada, Japan, and a handful of other countries (Australia, New Zealand)—all of which except Japan were formed by Europe—Europe is the most developed area in the world. This is the First World of modern, industrialized countries. *All* the countries of Western Europe occupy high places in the previously mentioned Table 1.1; Eastern Europe and Russia are now striving to catch up; and most of the rest of the world would similarly like to imitate and enjoy European living standards.
7. *Europe is a developmental model.* Europe has among the world's highest standards of living, well-developed democracies, and the world's most advanced welfare system. As such, it serves as a model to much of the Third World and an inspiration to American social reformers as well.

8. *European integration is going forward.* The EU is moving toward even greater economic and financial as well as political and foreign policy integration; it is a fascinating process to examine and study and contains many lessons for Asian and Western hemisphere integration.
9. *Europe is clean, efficient, and progressive.* It also has relatively safe streets, low crime, and little pollution. Europe has much that it can teach us.
10. *Europe has achieved significant equity.* The gaps in Europe between rich and poor are far less than in the United States; at the same time, class lines in Europe are often more rigid and harder to cross than in the United States. Americans can profitably study Europe to get a clearer idea of the tradeoffs involved: high taxes and advanced welfare versus low taxes and limited social welfare; greater equity and more conformity versus less equity and more individualism, and so on.
11. *Europe's foreign policy is often parallel to yet diverges from ours.* Although the United States and Europe are allies, Europe's foreign policies—on the Middle East, Russia, Latin America, and a host of other issues—diverge from America's. Can these differences be merged? Are such differences inevitable in a world of independent nation-states? Will the differences become larger rather than narrower now that the Cold War is over? If globalization is the wave of the future, is Europe farther advanced along that path than the United States?
12. *Europe represents the future*—not only a model to the Third World but perhaps to other advanced, industrial nations as well. Europe (along with the United States) is currently carrying out some of the world's most exciting social, economic, and political experiments: reform of the state, welfare reform, changes in state-society relations, regionalism and decentralization, and greater democratization. Are some of these experiments in store for us as well? What can we learn from Europe?
13. *Europe is a "living laboratory"*—of virtually every social, economic, cultural, religious, and political trend and process since the dawn of time. Here we have approximately twenty (the number keeps changing) nations all with certain common *Western* values and institutions, and yet with enormous variations among them. What a perfect laboratory for studying the change processes of national development, both institutions and public policies, where we can hold some variables of culture, religion, history, and background constant while we examine other variables to determine distinct political outcomes and policies.
14. *Europe is presently at the forefront of modern social and political experimentation and change.* Should Europe try to emulate the free-market successes of the United States by moving toward lower taxes, privatization, state downsizing, and reduced welfare state (Great Britain currently)? Or should it keep its hallowed cradle-to-grave welfare in place and, consequently, be willing to accept lower economic growth (France)? Or are there ways to have both the incentives and stimuli of a free market and the benefits of an advanced welfare state (Germany, The Netherlands)? These questions are exciting and at the forefront of current policy debates in the United States as well as Europe.

So Europe is an exciting area these days. It is not just some stodgy, ancient, irrelevant "Old World." Rather, it is at the forefront of change, among or perhaps *the* most prosperous and advanced area in the world, with important lessons from which America, Japan, and the Third World can learn.

THE GRAND SWEEP OF EUROPEAN HISTORY AND BACKGROUND

Geography, Climate, and Topography

Let us now take the geographic definition of Europe, that Europe includes the area west of the Ural Mountains in Russia and north of the Mediterranean, Black, and Caspian seas. As can be seen from the map (Map A.3, p. 458), that region includes the land areas roughly between ten and sixty degrees longitude (plus Iceland) and between forty and seventy degrees latitude (plus the southern parts of Portugal, Spain, Italy, and Greece).

That means that the bulk of the European land mass is north of the United States, closer to Canada in latitude; however, Europe is warmed by the Gulf current and, therefore, has a climate and temperature, with variations, close to that of the United States: cold in the north, warm in the south, but generally moderate throughout.

Europe lies in what we have come to call the *temperate zone*. Its temperatures are generally moderate and healthy and with abundant rainfall. There are no deserts or tropical areas in Europe, and extreme cold is largely confined to northern Scandinavia and Russia, where few people live. Winter temperatures are sufficiently cold to kill most of the diseases that thrive in tropical climes, and summers are sufficiently mild in most areas to encourage outdoor farming and labor. Historically, these geographic factors help explain why progress and civilization thrived in Europe more than in other areas.

Farming is blessed not just by moderate temperatures and adequate rainfall but also by an abundance of good agricultural land in the west of Europe. All of western and northern France, the "low countries" of Holland and Belgium, much of southern England, northern Germany, and all of Denmark, southern Sweden, virtually all of Poland, and much of Russia, Belarus, and Ukraine contain rich agricultural lands amenable, eventually, to mechanized agriculture. The rich lands enabled many of these countries to produce agricultural surpluses, which not only fed their own people but also would eventually provide surpluses to pay for industrialization and modernization.

In contrast, mountains and high plateaus tend to dominate in Spain, northern Portugal, Italy, Switzerland, Austria, Yugoslavia, Greece, Slovakia, the Czech Republic, Norway, Ireland, and the Balkans. It is probably no accident that most of these countries, less blessed in terms of farmland, lagged behind the development of the northern and central countries. In the absence of rich agricultural lands, olive trees and grapevines have long been cultivated along the Mediterranean Coast, with Greece, Italy, and Spain producing 75 percent of the world's olive oil.

Europe is also blessed by many, usually gently flowing rivers that have greatly facilitated internal commerce and transportation. The Rhine, Rhone, Seine, Loire, Garonne, Elbe, Danube, Vistula, Dnieper, Dan, and Volga are only some of the main rivers navigable for long distances and providing water for drinking and irrigation as well. Canals now connect many of these rivers, providing a network of inland waterways by which one can travel throughout much of Europe. Such inland seas as the Baltic, Mediterranean, Adriatic, Aegean, Black, Ionian, and Caspian have also been main sources of commerce and transportation and avenues for the spread of civilization.

Europe has been blessed with an abundance of minerals for modern industrial use, which also helps explain the continent's early development compared to other areas. The countries have rich deposits of iron ore, coal, bauxite (aluminum), oil, and natural gas. These resources are unevenly distributed,

Nuclear power is used in Europe far more frequently than in the United States, but it it also under attack from enviromentalists and others.

however, and over the centuries have triggered fierce competition and wars among the European nations. Russia is especially rich in all of these resources, but historically it has seldom been well enough organized to exploit them fully; Great Britain and Norway have been enriched recently by major oil discoveries in the North Sea.

Forests blanketed 80 percent of Europe thirty-five hundred years ago; now only one-third of the continent is forested, most of it in northern Scandinavia and Russia. Seventy-five percent of Europeans now live in urban areas, but the less-developed countries of Eastern Europe and Russia tend to be more rural. European farmers grow two-thirds of the world's potatoes and oats, 40 percent of the world's wheat, and one third of the world's meat. Cropland and pasture account for half the continent's land area.

Europe is rich in major industries as well as natural resources. Machinery, electronics, steel, energy, chemicals, textiles, automobiles, forest products, fish processing, and construction are among Europe's major industries. Recently, high-tech electronic, computer, and service industries have grown up alongside these other sectors. Europe now competes with the United States and Japan in virtually all commercial and industrial areas.

Although Europe is the second smallest continent in size, it is, with more than 500 million persons, second largest (behind Asia) in population. Europe is densely populated; heavy emphasis is placed on using space fully and wisely. But with high population and heavy industry, Europe's environment requires intensive care. Pollution attacks forests in Central Europe; the burning of fossil fuels in Scandinavia is destroying fish supplies; oil spills in the North Sea threaten coastlines; acid rain is eroding historic structures throughout Europe; and Venice is slowly slipping underwater as the aquifer under the city is drained. Urban industrial centers and coastal cities have been discharging metals and sewage in toxic amounts.

Historic inland seas such as the Baltic, Adriatic, Caspian, Black, and Mediterranean are now threatened, prompting international action in which some countries cooperate and pay for the damage more than others. Environmental conditions are especially bad in Eastern Europe and Russia, where decades of industrialization under communist rule, with no safeguards and no accountability or responsibility, have proven disastrous. Dozens of aging and poorly built nuclear plants threaten another Chernobyl; nuclear waste often mixes with town and village water supplies; farmland is contaminated with lead and other heavy metals, and in Poland 90 percent of the river water is too toxic to drink. Although Western Europe is pursuing often vigorous actions to clean up the air, land, and water, far poorer Eastern Europe lags far behind both economically and environmentally.

European History: The Western Tradition

Both America and Europe are part of what is called "Western civilization." We are both, predominantly, part of "The West," and we share, historically and to a large extent at present, certain characteristics and traditions of culture, religion, politics, ideology, economics, and society. These characteristics make us different from other civilizations, such as the Confucian, the Hindu, or the Islamic, even while many elements from these cultures are being integrated into the Western countries. But what precisely do we mean by the term "civilization"? What exactly is "Western civilization"? What common traditions in this age of pluralism, multiculturalism, and greater racial and ethnic diversity do we still share, and how are these traditions now changing?

If we go back to the ancient world that flourished for roughly one thousand years, approximately 500 B.C. to A.D. 500, three major influences helped shape the Western world. These influences were the Judeo-Christian tradition, the world of ancient Greece and the Greek city-states, and then the vast Roman empire that encompassed the entire circum-Mediterranean area.

Judaism gave us the story of creation, a monotheistic (one God) religion, the captivity into Egypt, the wandering in the desert and the Ten Commandments, the prophets, and the moral injunctions that still undergird much of our law and behavior. With Christianity, this religion spread far beyond the confines of the Holy Land where it had begun, reached into all of Europe and beyond, gave us notions of salvation and redemption, and provided an institutional and organizational structure centered in Rome that the early church had lacked. Christianity provided the message of not only a just (Old Testament) but also a loving (New Testament) God who suffered, was crucified, and was resurrected for the sake of his people; it also injected the idea of human equality, at first in a spiritual sense, later in a political sense as well, in a highly stratified ancient society.

The early Greeks provided us with philosophy, political science, culture, geometry, astronomy, and rigorous logic. More than that, the Greeks were champions of the human mind and spirit, who set forth a secular understanding of the world that was internally consistent without God or gods, and who developed many of the ideals that we still hold true today: balance, moderation, and the dignity of the individual.

Although the Greeks achieved cultural magnificence, their constantly feuding, warring city-states left them divided and unable to hold off the encroaching power of Rome. The Romans established central authority around the entire circum-Mediterranean, conquered east as far as the Persian Gulf and north through France (then called Gaul) and southern Britain, but not Germany north of the Danube, Scandinavia, or Russia (although even in these latter areas the finding of Roman coins indicates commercial relations with Rome). The empire also provided—once Christianity was accepted as the official state religion—an avenue for the enormous spread of Christendom throughout the then-known world. The Romans introduced a common law, language, culture, administrative and military structure, and social hierarchy in its vast empire that in many respects persist to this day. For example, the Portuguese, Spanish, French, Romanian, and Italian languages all derive from Roman Latin.

Note from Map A.1 (Appendix A, p. 456) that two thousand years ago, at the height of Rome's power, "Western civilization," as we now know it, was centered in and around the Mediterranean. It included North Africa as well as Turkey and large parts of what we now call the Middle East. But with the rise of Islam in the eighth century A.D., all of North Africa, Turkey, the Middle East, Spain (for a time), and even parts of southeast Europe (Bosnia, Kosovo, and Albania) became predominantly Muslim. Eventually, the Muslim advances into Europe would be stopped in fierce battles in the valleys of Austria as well as in Iberia and, with the exception of those small enclaves noted previously, driven back over time across the straits of Gibraltar into North Africa and across the Bosporus into Turkey. In this way, the *religious-cultural* boundaries of Europe were established, encompassing (nearly) everything north of the Mediterranean and northwest of the Bosporus.

On its northern border, we have said, the Roman empire largely stopped at the Danube and Rhine rivers. South of that line was considered *civilization* (and still is, in some quarters!), whereas north of it was wild, uncivilized, and barbarian. (My own ancestors in The Netherlands, for example, are supposed to have eaten Saint Boniface when he came to try to Christianize them.) So there we have another north-south border in Europe that still persists. That border was reinforced or reappeared once again in the sixteenth century when during the Reformation most of the area north of that line became Protestant, whereas south of it remained Roman Catholic. And, with what was called "the Protestant ethic" that accompanied the rise of Protestantism, the North came to be viewed (or saw itself) as more energetic, ambitious, capitalistic, efficient, prosperous, and righteous, whereas the South was often viewed as slothful, less ambitious, less capitalistic and poorer, and less efficient. Some of these prejudices that have long divided Northern from Southern Europe (and sometimes carry racial overtones as well—remember the south was invaded and occupied for a time by Islamic "Moors" from North Africa) are still with us today, including the problem that the northern countries still tend to be wealthier than the southern and often to look down on them as well.

So much (for now) for the North-South divide; how about the East-West one—and not just that caused by the recent (and recently torn down) Cold War–era iron curtain across Europe? Historically, even greater East-West divides existed than that brought on by the Cold War. Again, take a look at the map. Note that, while the Roman empire included some parts of Eastern Europe (Thrace, Pannonia, Illyria, Dacia—what we now know as Hungary, Yugoslavia, Romania, and Bulgaria), it did not include the Czech Republic, Slovakia, Poland, or present-day Belarus, Ukraine, or Russia. So there is another important divide, and a sense that these latter areas were never quite as "civilized" as those that fell within the Roman Empire. These areas are also different ethnically, consisting mainly of Slavs as distinct from Germans or Anglo-Saxons.

But then, after the fall of the Roman Empire, the religious unity that Rome had imposed on its vast territories was lost as well.

Italy and the lands to the west remained Roman Catholic throughout the Middle Ages (until the Protestant Reformation introduced a further divide), but to the east in Greece, present-day Yugoslavia, and Russia, the Eastern Orthodox Church prevailed. The East refused to recognize the supremacy of the Pope and introduced changes in the liturgy and theology that Roman Catholicism refused to recognize. The Eastern Church was centered at Constantinople (now Istanbul) in Turkey. But when these and other lands were overrun by Islam in the eighth century, the Christian Orthodox churches (in Turkey, Egypt, Syria, Iraq, Lebanon, and Jordan) became minority churches within a predominantly Islamic culture; however, in the Ukraine, Belarus, Serbia, and Russia (and in part to hold off the expansionism of Islam), the Orthodox religion became the official state church. So from west to east in Europe there is a profound religious, ethnic, and cultural divide as well as the more familiar (now erased) political one.

The Roman Empire collapsed in A.D. 476 as a result of economic stagnation, internal decay, and outside pressures. The outside pressures came mainly from the "barbarian" Germanic tribes north of the Danube who, in fact, had been launching raids against the Empire for centuries and now, finally, were able to topple it completely. The Germanic tribes conquered not only Italy but also Switzerland, parts of France, and most of Spain and Portugal. Although the *Western* Empire thus fell into Germanic hands and under Germanic influence, the *Eastern* half, now known as the Byzantine Empire and dominated by Eastern Orthodoxy, lasted another one thousand years until it was finally conquered by the Turks in A.D. 1453. East and West were then divided by a mammoth religious (Christian versus Islamic) wall of separation with little contact between the two sides. In effect, the East was lost to the West and the West to the East for centuries; the histories of these two areas would now diverge radically.

In the West, the complete collapse of the Roman Empire in the decades following A.D. 476 paved the way for reversion to a more primitive form of existence. Population declined; cities and urban life all but disappeared; trade declined drastically; farm production decreased; illiteracy rose dramatically; and civilization was all but eliminated. In addition, social and political order all but disappeared; economic life declined; little government or political and military authority was exerted; virtually all of the institutions (except the Church) that were built up painstakingly over one thousand years of Greek and Roman history disappeared. This was the Middle Ages, often referred to as the "Dark Ages," and this period, too, would last approximately one thousand years (A.D. 500 to 1500). Other than the Church and some cities in the south, what had heretofore constituted Western civilization was all but submerged.

Although the Middle Ages may indeed have been "dark," they were not entirely devoid of bright spots. Christianity now spread among the Germanic tribes as well and eventually reached all the way to Scandinavia; whereas in the East, Orthodoxy spread into Russia as well and by the ninth century had become one of the main foundations of the emerging Russian state. In the West, the monastic movement helped preserve literature, learning, and civilization, the monasteries constituting island of culture and continuity in a sea of chaos and disintegration. In France, Charlemagne made heroic efforts to restore the glory and unity of the Roman Empire but ultimately failed. In Spain, under Moorish rule from A.D. 711 to 1492, culture flourished in a context of religious tolerance (Jewish, Christian, Muslim), and the vast learning of Greek civilization (Aristotle, Plato, and Ptolemy)—lost in the West for centuries—was revived and then channeled back into Europe. One of the places where it was channeled was the University of Paris in the thirteenth century, where the great Catholic theologian Thomas Aquinas achieved a massive and powerful synthesis of Christian theology and Greek logic.

Although the Middle Ages are often looked on as a long, thousand-year setback in the march of Western and European civilization, that view is not entirely accurate. Western civilization was not forged just in terms of a cultural narrative encompassing Greece, Rome, Christianity, the Renaissance, the Enlightenment, and so on—from Plato to NATO, as it is sometimes called. It was also forged in actual practice, in the pull and push of rival German tribes, in the struggle between gradually expanding and encroaching central authority (kings, princes, and nation-states) *and* the effort of local entities—towns, groups, families, and individuals—to maintain autonomy and independence. In other words, Western civilization, including freedom and democracy, has to be looked at not just as a single, unfolding, progressive chain of ideas throughout history but as a result of real-life struggles, compromises, half-way houses, and political deals among central states and local power centers that are the warp and woof of real history.

It is conventional to divide the Middle Ages into two periods of roughly five hundred years each. The first, usually called the Low Middle Ages, from A.D. 500 to 1000, did represent a low point or nadir: Social, economic, and political institutions declined; most of Europe reverted to a more primitive form of existence. But during the second period, the High Middle Ages, A.D. 1000 to 1500, society began to recover somewhat. Towns grew and many new ones were founded; trade increased; European populations grew; new universities were founded; prosperity increased; and new states emerged and many old ones were gradually consolidated. The notion of limited, representative government and of a society based on law emerged in England and other areas and provided a base for the later growth of democracy. At the end of this period, the Renaissance provided an intellectual spark that stimulated culture, learning, science, and a more modern outlook. Indeed, many of the changes previously identified could more accurately be identified with the modern age rather than the medieval one. The line between medieval and modern is not quite so clearcut as we might think.

The modern period in European history and Western civilization is conventionally said to have begun around A.D. 1500. But why then? What is it that marks the period after 1500 as "modern"?

First, Columbus's discovery of America in 1492 vastly expanded the then-known universe, led to important new discoveries, immensely increased Europe's wealth, and produced great leaps forward in navigation, anthropology, trade, and commerce. It also began the Europeanization and Westernization of the globe that have continued to the present. In some cases, native peoples suffered negative consequences from this globalization, but their lives were not always idyllic before the Europeans arrived and, in most cases, Europeanization also meant greater prosperity, a higher standard of living, better health and education, and a chance to join in the modernization that otherwise would not have been possible.

Second, in the political sphere, systems of absolutist, authoritarian, top-down rule began gradually, varying from country to country, to give rise to systems that were more democratic, limited, representative, and based on the rule of law. This process had begun in England, but it eventually spread to the continent as well and, in our time and for the first time, encompassed Southern Europe, Eastern Europe, and Russia. This "revolution" in government also led to a modern, secular view of politics in such writers as Machiavelli, Hobbes, and Locke rather than the purely religious basis on which political systems had been based in the past.

Third, the year 1500 marks a turning point because only seventeen years after that date Luther nailed his famous theses to the church

TABLE 1.3 — Europe: Medieval and Modern, Circa 1500

	Medieval (pre-1500)	Modern (post-1500)
International	Closed, parochial	Expansionist, Europeanization of globe
Political	Absolutist, authoritarian, top-down	Limited, representative government; rule of law, democracy
Religious	Catholic Orthodoxy	Religious freedom and pluralism
Economic	Feudal, mercantilist	Capitalist, progressive
Social	Two-class, feudal, rigid, hierarchical	Multi-class, social change
Educational	Revealed truth, rote memorization, deductive, scholastic	Empirical, scientific, inductive

doors at Wittenberg in Germany and thus began the Protestant Reformation. Not only did the Reformation divide the Christian world, but it also stimulated the rise of individualism by emphasizing each Christian's right and duty to read and interpret the Bible in her or his own way. In addition, the movement stressed that each person was equal before God. The Reformation gave rise to a religious pluralism that, as in America, eventually produced political pluralism, too, but it also redrew the north-south line across Europe, again roughly corresponding to the frontiers of the old Roman Empire, between the Catholic South and a Protestant North.

Economically, fourth, this was approximately the period when capitalism began, first in the Italian city-states and then, especially after the Reformation, concentrating in the northern countries of Holland and England. Trade and commerce were stimulated, and Europe began the steady rise that would soon carry it far past China, India, and the Middle East as the most developed of the world's areas and civilizations.

With gradually expanding economic development, fifth, came accelerated social change. Cities increased in size; people lived longer and were more prosperous; and societies became more dynamic and change-oriented. Specifically, a middle class or *bourgeoisie* emerged in the cities, inserting itself into what heretofore had been a predominantly two-class (lord and peasant) society, growing more prosperous, insisting on stability, becoming the more dynamic element in society, and eventually serving as a strong base for democracy and moderation.

A sixth change took place in the intellectual sphere. To this point, knowledge had been based on scholasticism: rote memorization mainly of the Church fathers, Aristotelian logic as employed by Thomas Aquinas, and a deductive (top-down) method of arriving at truth. But now, with Galileo, Newton, and Copernicus, knowledge came to be based more on science, experimentation, observation, and an inductive (bottom or facts-up) methodology. The new science often challenged traditional, God-given religious and political beliefs and led to greater secularism and humanism in European thinking.

Now, if we add all these changes up, whose combined impact was considerably greater than the sum of their individual parts, we can see (in Table 1.3) that A.D. 1500 marked a sharp turning point in Western civilization. Before that date, European society was closed, parochial, unitary, monolithic, absolutist (religiously as well as politically), pre-capitalist, two-class, hierarchical, feudal, and scholastic. But after that date, European society was more internationalist, globalist, democratic, religiously diverse and pluralist, capitalist, multi-class, and scientific. These latter traits help us define the modern age. They also provide the foundation on which the British and Dutch colonies of North America were based, but not Spain's or Portugal's colonies in Latin America, which were formed on the pre-1500 or feudal-medieval basis. These differences also explain why North America, founded on and in modernity, was destined to forge ahead, whereas Latin America, founded on and long dominated by a feudal and medieval tradition, was destined to lag behind.

The characteristics listed previously and in Table 1.3 are what social scientists call *ideal types;* they are a simplification and an approximation of reality to help us better understand the changes underway, but they are not an exact mirror of reality itself, which is always much more complicated. They apply to some countries and regions more than to others. But the table also helps us explain comparatively the differences (foundations that are either pre- or post-1500) among countries that still often apply to this day.

The change to modernization outlined previously began in the core countries of The Netherlands and England. The change to capitalism, a middle-class society, greater enlightenment, religious pluralism, and the rule of law and representative democracy initially began in these countries. Then the modernizing trends spread, unevenly and over a long period, to the heartland of Europe: present-day Belgium, France, and Germany. It is no accident that these countries remain among the leaders in Europe even today, with higher per capita income, excellent social programs, and stable, functioning democracies.

Note that some countries and some whole areas of Europe have not yet been mentioned; they lagged behind and experienced rapid modernization only later and, often, in quite different form. For example, Scandinavia remained rural, more backward, and primitive for a long time; it only began to industrialize late in the nineteenth century and developed modern social democracy (now the world's most advanced) in the twentieth century.

Southern Europe also lagged behind socially, economically, and politically; never having experienced the Protestant Reformation or a sharp break with the past, it continued right into the twentieth century to exhibit a conflicting mixture of pre-1500 and post-1500 traits.

Eastern Europe remained similarly traditional, agricultural, backward, and pre-modern. When Eastern Europe finally began to modernize, it was torn by conflict, and its industrialization and democratization were perverted by nearly half a century of communist control. Then there is Russia: the farthest country from Europe's core area, the slowest to develop, endemically torn by its Europeanizing versus its Slavophile tendencies, governed for long centuries by a backward-looking Czarist regime, and eventually falling prey to a communist dictatorship that for seventy years warped and postponed its modernization. Already in these early, sixteenth-century differences, we can see the patterns of variations that will constitute the main subject areas of European Comparative Politics; why did some countries forge ahead; why did others lag behind, and what explains the main differences?

Subsequent developments in the seventeenth and eighteenth centuries tended to reinforce and perpetuate these differences rather than ameliorate them. For example, in the sixteenth century, Spain and Portugal were Europe's foremost colonizing nations, exploring and opening up vast new territories in Africa, Asia, and Latin America. But Spain and Portugal retained an older, mercantilist (not capitalist) economic conception and, hence, instead of benefiting these two countries, the gold and silver of the Americas and Asia flowed through these countries and on to Holland and England, from which Spain and Portugal purchased arms and supplies to defend Catholic orthodoxy and hegemony in Europe (the counter-Reformation), which ultimately proved a failure. Based on this new-found wealth, the industrial revolution, hence, began in England and the low countries (Holland, Belgium) and not in Iberia. Similarly, with the Enlightenment and the scientific revolution: they were concentrated in the core countries of France, England, and (somewhat later) Germany and only reached Southern Europe, Eastern Europe, and Russia tardily, if at all.

One of Europe's key turning points was the French Revolution of 1789. Unlike Britain, France, although modernizing economically and socially, had not democratized its political system; France was also torn by class and religious conflicts. These conflicts exploded in the French Revolution, which resulted in the destruction of both the old ruling class and the old order based on feudalism, tradition, hierarchy, and Catholicism. Soon the revolution's ideals of liberty, equality, and fraternity spread—often accompanying Napoleon's conquering armies—to other countries where they similarly provoked violent conflict. Indeed, much of Europe's nineteenth-century history can be written in terms of the ongoing and virtually constant conflict between the continent's traditional conservative forces (the Church, the landed oligarchy, monarchy, and the nobility) and their efforts to hang onto their power, *and* the rising newer forces (the middle class, urban dwellers, and modernizing elements) to wrest power from them and gain a share of it for themselves.

In 1791, the French Revolution abolished the system of feudal privilege left over from the Middle Ages; early in the nineteenth century most other European countries followed suit. That meant an end to the privileges that such specially favored groups as the Church, the nobility, the landed elites, or the guilds had enjoyed. But these people constituted some of the most powerful groups in society; their special place and power could not be abolished so easily. So while in law and constitution most European countries formally abolished feudal privilege, in actual practice many countries failed to implement these laws. The laws or constitutions proclaimed liberty, fraternity, and equality, but the reality was that in many countries the traditional wielders of power continued to retain their perks and privileges.

The result of this dichotomy was a series of upheavals, revolts, and even revolutions occurring periodically throughout the nineteenth century and into the twentieth. Many of these rebellions were not just political revolts but also took on the form of social revolutions or class warfare, pitting the traditional wielders of power against the rising, aspiring new classes. Thus, the French Revolution of 1789 was soon followed in the early nineteenth century by a conservative reaction; a series of revolutions broke out anew in 1830, followed once more by a conservative reaction; then revolutions and popular uprisings followed again in 1848 and in 1870. The Russian Revolution of 1917 and other revolts in Europe around the same time of World War I could be said to be renewed expressions of that same revolutionary impulse.

Revolutionary fervor and class conflict were stimulated by the industrial revolution and the vast social changes it inspired. The industrial revolution and the response by governments and different social groups to it was the anvil on which much of the structure of the modern state and society was hammered out. In England, the industrial revolution began around 1780 and continued through the nineteenth century; in the other main countries of Europe, France and Germany, the industrial revolution began several decades later but was in full swing from the mid-nineteenth century on. The industrial revolution stimulated urbanization, drew people out of the countryside and into the factories, and helped create both a new middle class and, eventually, an organized working class. It also perpetrated some horrible working conditions (long hours, child labor, unsafe factories, and woefully low wages), as documented both by economist Karl Marx and novelist Charles Dickens. The new groups began to demand political power, better working conditions, and a larger share of the profits of capitalism—or its destruction!

Early in the nineteenth century, the response of the more traditional groups to these changes and to the new demands thrust on them was to try to go back to the *status quo ante,* to restore the privileges, authority, and hierarchy of the pre-1789 period. This stance was reactionary and often involved the deployment and bloody use of police and military forces against the clamoring new groups. But in England in 1832, and then again in 1868, the franchise and other political rights were extended to some of these new groups, thus defusing the potential for upheaval and resulting in greater democracy. After the European revolutions of 1848, other countries also began to reassess their attitudes toward the emerging middle class and organized labor.

Three major, more or less forward-looking options presented themselves in the last decades of the nineteenth century, although the fourth option—complete reaction and repression, as in Russia under the last of the czars—was also present. The first of these options might be called the English model or *liberalism*: gradual, evolutionary, incremental change that expands participation and democratization and leads eventually to a more socially just society. The second model was called *corporatism;* it had both Catholic (Italy, Austria, France, Spain, Portugal, and southern Germany) and Protestant (The Netherlands, Scandinavia, and northern Germany) variants, and it involved the gradual incorporation of the middle and working classes into national life but under—through the creation of official trade unions and other interest groups—state (which meant the dominant elites) control and auspices. The third model was *socialism* (defined as workers' control of the means of production and distribution), which took many forms: anarchism, anarcho-syndicalism, communism, democratic socialism, and bolshevism. These distinct reformist tendencies vied for dominance in the late nineteenth century and into the twentieth, not only with the traditional wielders of power—the elites, the oligarchies, religious institutions, monarchs, and often the military—but also with each other.

Meanwhile, other changes were occurring in Europe that also demand our attention. Italy and Germany, long fragmented into feuding principalities and city-states, now came together after the mid-nineteenth century to form unified nation-states. In addition, the vast social changes mentioned earlier associated with industrialization and modernization accelerated, thus gradually tipping the balance of power away from the traditional elites and toward the newer forces. In Britain under Queen Victoria and in Germany under Otto von Bismarck, a long period of stability after earlier instability enabled economic growth to proceed at an unprecedented pace. These two countries, as well as Belgium, France, and Denmark, entered into a renewed race for colonies not seen since the sixteenth and seventeenth centuries, which brought much of Africa, Asia, and the Middle East under their control. At the same time, the late-modernizing countries of Eastern, Southern, and Northern Europe belatedly began the process of industrialization but still lagged behind the core countries and, at least in the cases of Eastern and Southern Europe, in ways that often produced turbulence and the potential for revolutionary upheaval.

World War I was another one of those momentous events in European history—like the French Revolution of 1789—that produced profound transformations in society, politics, and economics. It was a military conflict, but its implications were actually far broader. For one thing, Russia's disastrous performance in the war, plus the Romanov royal family's blindness and opposition to change, helped lead to the Communist Revolution of 1917. Indeed, all over Europe, what historian Barbara Tuchman called the "Proud Tower" of pre–World War I European society (elitist, aristocratic, hierarchical, and nonegalitarian) came crashing down in the war or its aftermath, replaced often by instability and uncertainty. In Germany in 1918, and in other countries besides, uprisings and revolutionary movements served as warnings of future, larger upheavals. As a direct result of the war, finally, some of Europe's historic empires collapsed: the Ottoman Empire centered in Turkey, which led to the independence of the Balkan states, and the Austro-Hungarian Empire in central Europe, which, coupled with the defeat in the war of both Germany and Russia, led to the independence of Eastern Europe and the rest of the Balkans.

The 1920s were a period, in general, of peace and prosperity in Europe, of a return (as in the United States) to "normalcy." In 1922, however, Benito Mussolini came to power in Italy, a regime that represented a combination of corporatism (state-controlled interest groups), fascism (totalitarian rule), and one-man dictatorship. In Germany, too, under the Weimar Republic, there was bitterness at the country's defeat in World War I, immense social tensions left over from the pre-War years, and cultural excesses that reflected Germany's search for self-identity. In other countries there were many signs of social tensions, which were often "brushed under the rug" by the prosperity and reckless abandon of those times.

But in 1929 the stock market crashed; by 1930 a *worldwide* depression set in that lasted through most of the decade until World War II. In Europe, the Depression, coupled with social and political tensions already present, produced a disastrous decade that led to a renewed world war whose effects are still with us. The Depression led to the fear that capitalism was doomed and that a whole series of Bolshevik revolutions would follow. As Italy fell under Fascist dictatorship and Hitler and the National Socialists (Nazis) took power in Germany in 1933, it began to appear that liberalism and democracy might be doomed as well. As many societies polarized, liberalism seemed to be squeezed between Marxism or Marxism-Leninism, on the one hand, and fascism on the other. It was a time of fear and foreboding because the center failed to hold in many countries and gave way to the extremes. France, the Benelux countries, Britain, and Scandinavia remained democratic, but in much of Southern and Eastern Europe, weak, divided, and unstable democratic regimes gave way to corporatist, bureaucratic, authoritarian, and quasi-fascist regimes. Nazi atrocities, the Holocaust, and the ensuing war left as many as forty million people dead.

After the War, Europe was divided once again, in not entirely unfamiliar ways. There was, of course, the Cold War divide and the East-West divide, with the Iron Curtain drawing a line across Europe stretching from the Baltic to the Adriatic. The East was occupied by Soviet armies, whereas the West was organized into NATO and the EEC. The East had always been poorer than the West, but now these differences were magnified: by the 1990s much of the West (see Table 1.1) had reached a per capita income of $30,000 per year and was *the* most prosperous area in the world; whereas the East, after forty-five years of Soviet mismanagement and totalitarianism, had a per capita income only *one-tenth* that of the West, less than $3,000 per person in most countries, and at the level of such Third World developing countries as Mexico and Colombia. Only after the Soviet Union collapsed and the Iron Curtain fell in 1989–1991 did it become clear how poor, polluted, and underdeveloped Eastern Europe was. It will take decades, if not generations for the region to catch up.

In Southern Europe, the conditions and prospects were considerably better. Italy rejoined the democratic fold after World War II, became an active member of NATO and the EEC, and enjoyed new-found prosperity even while its political system often seemed precarious. Spain and Portugal, however, remained under the pre–World War II corporatist and quasi-fascist regimes of Franco and Salazar, respectively; whereas Greece was torn by civil war, instability, and eventually in the 1960s and 1970s military dictatorship. But in the mid-1970s, all three of these regimes underwent transitions to democracy, then in the 1980s joined the EEC and—after lagging for so long—over the course of the next two decades achieved a standard of living approximately 70–80 percent of the European average. A major issue in European Comparative Politics today is to explain why Southern Europe has been so successful in its transitions to democracy but Eastern Europe—and Russia—are still both so backward and so precarious.

The most successful, by almost all measures, of Europe's historically peripheral areas is Scandinavia. Therefore, a key comparative politics question to answer is: Why? Is it climate and natural resources; is it religion (historically Lutheran) and the common values and national unity that entailed; is it institutions; or is it Scandinavia's advanced social programs? Here we have an area that started its industrialization later than the core areas of Europe, and yet during the course of the twentieth century developed as among the globe's most modern, most egalitarian, most progressive areas. Look once more at Table 1.1, where Norway and Denmark are ranked numbers three and four, respectively, among the world's nations in terms of per capita income, and Sweden is number ten and Finland, thirteen. Many American social scientists have been attracted to Scandinavia, both because of its impressive record of achievements and because they view these countries as "about as good as we can do" and perhaps able to provide a model or lessons for the United States. But we also need to ask whether, given the different histories, political cultures, values, and institutions between Scandinavia and the United States, the Scandinavian experience and successes are really exportable or are they unique to those countries? These are some of the intriguing questions that a study of comparative politics raises.

In the core of Europe, too, several countries have been doing very well. They, too, have their ups and downs, their malaises, their periods of what is called "Euro-pessimism." But once again we are drawn back to the statistics in Table 1.1. Note that Switzerland is number one in the world in per capita income; Germany, seven; Austria, eight; Belgium, nine; France, eleven; and the Netherlands, twelve. In other words, *all* of the core European countries are at the highest levels of the prosperity chart. All of them are wealthy, with high standards of living, little poverty, clean and safe streets and cities, advanced social programs, and new environmental programs to improve the quality of life. America and others could clearly learn from Western Europe, even while we recognize—the heart of Comparative Politics—the many differences that exist. Meanwhile, through its economic integration efforts and now its common financial and foreign policy agendas, Europe is taking new and exciting steps toward an even more advanced state. We return to this topic in greater detail later in the book.

THE END OF THE COLD WAR AND THE NEW VISION OF EUROPE

For most students of Europe, the Cold War has been one of the (maybe *the*) most important and salient features of modern times. The Cold War divided Europe in half, West and East; the Iron Curtain was like a jagged scar running north to south through the heart of Europe. Most scholars failed to foresee the collapse of the Soviet Union, the breakup of the Warsaw pact (the Soviet Union's and Eastern Europe's answer to NATO), or the end of communism. We tended to assume that the division of Europe between West and East, between First World (liberal, democratic, developed, and capitalistic states) and Second World (developed

The wall comes down.

communist states), was likely to be permanent. But now all this has changed.

The Cold War–era division of Europe between East and West evoked some powerful metaphors. Eastern Europe under communist rule was referred to as the "enslaved areas," the "captive nations," or the "Soviet Bloc"; it was usually portrayed in red and under Soviet domination in the Cold War–era maps that adorned school classrooms (see Map A.2, p. 457). Meanwhile, the West was referred to as the "Free World," a not entirely inaccurate description but one that included such not-very-democratic countries for long periods as Spain, Portugal, and Greece. The Western countries joined NATO and were members of the Atlantic Alliance, whereas the Eastern countries were part of the Soviet-dominated "Comintern." The West was open to travel and research, whereas the East was often closed off to scholars for long periods or else limits were put on what could be studied. Our knowledge of developments in the West was far more extensive than our knowledge of the East.

Meanwhile, the economic differences between West and East were also widening. Eastern Europe had long lagged behind the level of development of Western Europe, but now these gaps became a chasm. Please refer to Table 1.1 once more: The standard of living of the Western countries is by now ten times that of Eastern Europe. At some points only fifty or sixty years ago, Southern Europe, the other historically peripheral area of Europe, was roughly equal to Eastern Europe in living standards; but now Southern Europe has also forged ahead and has a per capita income *six or seven times* that of Eastern Europe. Literacy, life expectancy, and environmental degradation have also fallen to abysmally low levels in Eastern Europe. Forty-five years of Soviet domination and Marxist-Leninist economics have dragged Eastern Europe steadily downhill. It is a mistake to call Eastern Europe a part of the Second World of *developed* states; instead, much of Eastern Europe plus Russia are closer to the Third World of underdeveloped nations. One does not expect to see high illiteracy, disease, and malnutrition in Europe, but there it is, in the East, plainly (and painfully) present.

During the 1989–1991 period, in a dramatic chain of events that forever changed the course of history and the face of Europe, the Iron Curtain, the Berlin Wall, the Soviet Union, and the Warsaw Pact all came tumbling down. Suddenly, we were presented with a large group of newly freed nations that wanted to join "the West" and to enjoy Western living standards. For many long years prior to the crashing of the Iron Curtain, many Easterners had been envious of the West and had tried—often braving Soviet barbed wire, tanks, and machine guns—to reach it; many failed or lost their lives in the process. Now, vast new opportunities opened to the Easterners. But few realized at the time just how poor and underdeveloped the East was, how extensive were its problems, how painful and difficult the postcommunist transition would prove to be. The East would have to transition all at once from communism to capitalism, from dictatorship to democracy, from backwardness to modernization. But unlike Southern Europe during its transition to democracy two decades earlier, Eastern Europe had almost no base on which to build: no democratic political parties, no democratic interest groups, no democratic institutions of any kind, no or few markets, no stock exchanges, no banks, no functioning bureaucracy, no experienced leadership cadres, few entrepreneurs besides a handful of robber barons, and no solid currencies.

In retrospect, it is now clear that the Western nations, including the United States, misread Russia and Eastern Europe and woefully underestimated the problems there and the time it would take to resolve them. For these were not, it bears repeating, developed albeit communist countries; rather, they were woefully underdeveloped, closer to the Third World than to the First, and so lacking in modern economic and political institutions that the manifold problems would take decades and two or three generations to solve. It was not a matter of a "few years" and a "little pump-priming," as many Western officials believed. Russia and Eastern Europe would be long-term "projects" and not ones that could be dealt with easily or quickly. Moreover, many of these nations are also torn by *internal* ferment and discord, by shifting alliances and international loyalties, which complicate enormously their efforts both to join and to acquire equality with the West.

Let us try to briefly trace these shifting borders, alliances, and aspirations, recognizing that a more detailed treatment is reserved for later in the book. Our analysis proceeds generally from west to east.

First, the German Democratic Republic (GDR) or East Germany has now been reunited with West Germany to form a single, populous (over eighty million, the most populous country in Europe), potentially powerful (both economically and strategically) nation. To symbolize these changes, the capital has also moved east, from Bonn to Berlin, Germany's historic capital, with the Bundestag (parliament) and Chancellor's (prime minister's) office right in the heart of Berlin where the now-demolished Wall once stood. But the former East Germany is far less developed and lacking in institutions than previously thought, and it is proving far more difficult and expensive than expected to integrate the East with the West. These tensions will likely continue, causing severe stresses in Germany internally as well as in its international position.

Second, with the collapse of the Iron Curtain, all of Eastern Europe has been liberated from Soviet dominance; Eastern Europe (although in varying degrees) now wishes to join the West both economically (free markets) and politically (democracy). Several points need to be made about this issue: (1) Although Eastern Europe is still Eastern Europe (referring to the region as a whole), the more-developed parts of it—Poland, the Czech Republic, Hungary, and Slovakia—prefer to be called "Central Europe," both for geographic regions and to distinguish themselves from the less-successful states of the Balkans. (2) As with East Germany's integration into West Germany, Eastern Europe's problems are far greater than expected, and the time and costs for integration into Western Europe will be far greater than earlier thought. (3) Some parts of Eastern Europe—Poland, the Czech Republic, and Hungary—are more modern, prosperous, and readier for integration into Europe than others. They have already been voted into NATO and are hopeful of being admitted to the EU early in the twenty-first century.

Third, several Eastern European countries—Romania, Bulgaria, the former Yugoslavia, as well as some of those already named—are torn by tension, violence, and ethnic and religious strife. Both the former Yugoslavia and the former Czechoslovakia have split up into smaller, often feuding and warring (in the case of Yugoslavia) entities over these issues. In Eastern Europe, there is fear that a new "Iron Curtain," separating the more affluent countries that are being integrated into Europe from the poorer, less successful ones, is descending over the area and forcing us to draw a new line on the map between those countries that are making it and those that are not.

Fourth, there are the Baltic countries: Estonia, Latvia, and Lithuania. All three of these countries think of themselves as part of the West; all three want to maintain their autonomy and independence from Russia; all three are hoping to join NATO and the EU. Yet for hundreds of years these territories were pawns traded among the larger European powers, gaining their independence briefly in the inter-war period, before being swallowed up by the Soviet Union. However, they kept their ethnic, cultural, and linguistic identity, think of themselves as Western or Scandinavian countries rather than Eastern ones, and when the time came as the Soviet Union disintegrated, declared their independence. With Russia as their large and sometimes overbearing neighbor and with upwards of 40 percent of their populations Russian, the Baltic states have a sometimes precarious future. Yet they have carefully cultivated the West, and several of their Scandinavian Baltic neighbors (Denmark, Finland, and Sweden) are presently assisting the Balts and seeking to integrate them into an expanded Europe. It is a close call; only time will tell whether the Balts can maintain their independence and become integrated into the West or if they will again be pushed back into the Russian orbit.

Moving still farther east, fifth, we come to the newly independent states of Belarus and the Ukraine. These areas, like the Baltic states, were part of the Union of Soviet Socialist Republics; but when the U.S.S.R. disintegrated, they also went their separate, independent ways. They became part of the Commonwealth of Independent States (CIS), independent but still linked to Russia with whom they have long been a part. Although some in the West have sought to pull Belarus and the Ukraine closer into the Western orbit and to further detach them from Russia, in fact these new states have limited economic and political links to the West. None of the three have well-established democratic institutions or open and free markets, and under the CIS arrangements their foreign and defense policies are still mainly handled by Russia.

Finally, sixth, there is Russia itself, or at least European Russia, that part of Russia west of the Urals. Russia, although now diminished and degraded since the end of the Cold War, is nevertheless still the world's largest nation and a force (including nuclear) with which to be reckoned. Yet even that part of Russia that is geographically a part of Europe has never been entirely sure whether it wants to be part of the West, or Europe, or not. It has waxed hot and cold on the subject, has often been torn apart by the dispute, and even now is deeply culturally divided between its European and its Slavophile tendencies. Clearly, Russia wants the economic benefits of the West and wants to be respected among nations, but it lacks the political institutions that would ensure stable democracy and the economic institutions for a dynamic, prospering free-market system. Meanwhile, we have also discovered that Russia, like Eastern Europe, was not a *developed* communist country but, in fact, a very poor one and closer to the level of the Third World. Furthermore, since the demise of communism, life expectancy, literacy, health care, and standards of living have all fallen quite drastically. It will take a long time—several generations—to catch up. So Russia, like Belarus and the Ukraine, may or may not join the West and become integrated with it. Several European governments (such as Austria and Germany), as well as many investors, have all but given up on it, pulling out the investments and terminating the assistance programs initiated in the early 1990s when the old Soviet Union collapsed and Russia still looked hopeful, and concentrating on Eastern Europe, which is not only closer to their borders but at this stage looks like a more hopeful possibility.

As we think about Europe's opening to the East, therefore, several points need to be made. First, all of these areas are far poorer and less developed in terms of economic and political institutions than our earlier understanding of the Second World of "developed" communist countries would lead us to expect. Second, democratic, social, institutional, and economic modernization will take far longer than expected; we are talking about two or three *generations* for change to take place, not a few years as some officials thought earlier. Third, degrees and gradations of proximity to the West exist and, therefore, the expectation of being integrated into it varies. At present, Poland, Hungary, and the Czech Republic look like the best prospects for early integration; they are followed by Slovakia, Slovenia, and Croatia; and then Bulgaria, Romania, the Baltic states, and perhaps (if peace and stability can be restored) Bosnia and Serbia. It seems unlikely that Belarus, the Ukraine, and Russia will be fully integrated into the West anytime soon; indeed, in the security and foreign policy fields and perhaps the political and economic ones as well, Belarus and the Ukraine may move to the East, toward *re*integration with Russia rather than integration into the West. On these as well as on other controversial issues raised here, we refer the reader to the more detailed country and regional chapters that follow.

NATO AND THE EU: REGIONALIZATION IN THE FACE OF GLOBALIZATION

The dream of unity has a long history in Europe. The Roman Empire had unified all of the then-known world; after its fall, the hope of *re*unifying Europe under new and changed auspices lived on. Charlemagne, the German Holy Roman Empire, the "Catholic sovereigns" Charles I and Phillip II of Spain, Napoleon, and Hitler have all sought, in one form or another, to bring Europe back together under a single banner. The European Economic Community (EEC)—later shortened to the European Community (EC) and now referred to as the European Union (EU)—and more recent steps toward a common currency (the *euro*) and a common foreign and defense strategy, are only the most recent of a long history of efforts to forge unity—a "Europe whole and free," as the recent rallying cry states—in a continent long dominated by feuding, warring nation-states. Indeed, this continent originally gave birth to such concepts as "national sovereignty" and the "nation-state."

These most recent efforts to achieve European unity, in fact, emerged out of the previous attempt by Hitler and the Nazis to impose unity by force of arms and a totalitarian state.

Determined to prevent fascism from happening again, appalled by Stalin's totalitarianism in the Soviet Union, and traumatized by two world wars in a century not yet half over, many Europeans began to plan how a new, strong, prosperous, and reunified Europe could be brought into existence in the aftermath of World War II. The goals included steps to rebuild the European economies devastated by the war, to keep Germany under control and prevent it from launching another conflagration, and to build strength through unity as a means of keeping Stalin's armies—already in Eastern Europe—out of the West. Right from the beginning, therefore, the goals of a unified Europe were as much political and strategic as economic. Hence, the creation both of a European *economic* community (the EEC) aimed at rebuilding the shattered European economies as one way of defending Europe against the Soviet Union and a European *strategic* community (NATO), which provided an explicitly military defense against the U.S.S.R.

The post–World War II movement toward a united Europe should not be seen as an inevitable process involving necessarily foreordained progress toward some teleological, higher goal. There is nothing inevitable about European unity, and even today the principles of how and to what degree to achieve a unified Europe are hotly debated. At every step, hard choices were made that involved conflicting interests and strong arguments on all sides. Still today Europe and the various countries within the EU have different views about the euro, about deepening and widening the community, about surrendering parts of national sovereignty to a pan-European bureaucracy located in Brussels, and about who mainly pays and who benefits from the community. Although Europe has by now taken major steps toward integration, these steps remain as controversial now as they were when the community was first organized. This is not necessarily an heroic story with a happy ending, but rather a political process involving many close calls and, even now, great uncertainty about the outcome.

Now that the Iron Curtain has come down, the community faces a whole new series of choices. Should the newly liberated states of Eastern Europe now be included? If so, who should pay to bring their underdeveloped economies up to Western levels? Should the Baltic states be included? How about Belarus and the Ukraine? How about Russia: Should it now be brought into Europe? How about Turkey, which desperately wants to join? As can be seen, these questions raise again the age-old issue of where Europe begins and ends; which countries are in it and which are not and why; and for the countries that are already in the EU, they face serious questions about whether a single currency and a single, common monetary policy can possibly work on a continent of diverse nations and diverse economies; whether German unification and the powerful German economy will throw the entire notion of "community" out of whack; where and how far to extend the community (Cyprus? North Africa? and so on); and how much sovereignty over foreign policy, defense forces, and internal social and economic programs to cede to European bureaucrats who may not be sympathetic to local or national interests.

The idea for a new, postwar European community began even while World War II was still being fought; a concrete proposal took shape in the late-1940s era of reconstruction. In 1946 British wartime leader Winston Churchill called for a "United States of Europe"; in 1948 and 1949 a "Council of Europe" was organized. The Council did little more than exchange ideas and information on cultural, social, and legal matters, but it did serve as a forerunner to the later EEC.

The main issue at the time was still the reconstruction of war-ravaged Europe; that goal took priority over attempts at union. But in the late 1940s, it began to be seen that a European *economic* community or common market could also revive and harmonize Europe's still-sluggish economies. The principal architects of the plan that emerged in 1950 were the Frenchmen Jean Monnet and Robert Schuman and the German Walter Hallstein. Monnet was the main driving force, using his political skills to shepherd the proposal through the several, often suspicious national bureaucracies and eventually earning the title "Mr. Europe."

The proposal that emerged in 1950 was for a European Coal and Steel Community (ECSC) and, later, a European Atomic Energy Community and, eventually, the European Economic Community (EEC). Note how limited this initial agreement was: coal and steel; it was not by any means a full common market—yet. The initial agreement included only six states ("The Six"): France, Germany, Italy, Belgium, The Netherlands, and Luxembourg. Note that Great Britain was not represented among the original members; nor were any members from Scandinavia, Eastern Europe (the emerging Communist Bloc), or Southern Europe (except Italy) included.

At the core of the original common market agreement were the two biggest countries of the continent, France and Germany. What made the agreement work—and this has implications for other, recent free-trade areas—is that their economics were complementary. Germany was a highly industrialized, technological, manufacturing economy temporarily devastated by the war; whereas France had rich mineral and agricultural resources. Each had resources, natural and otherwise, that the other could use. It was a "natural" progression for these two countries to trade with each other because both would benefit. That scenario is unlike the situation of some free-trade areas in Latin America, for example: If *all* of the member countries produce only coffee or bananas, what is the sense of their trading with each other? But in the case of France and Germany, the complementarity of the two main economies, including initially and especially the coal and steel industries, made the entire system work. Structuring the agreement as a coal-and-steel pact was also useful because that approach helped remove the tension between the two countries over long-disputed territories be-tween them (the Ruhr and Rhineland) where the coal and the steel industries were concentrated. The United States would also be supportive of the pact because (1) it brought two of the main protagonists in World War II—France and Germany—together and defused the tension between them; (2) it helped stimulate the economic recovery of Europe, which the United States was also supporting through the Marshall Plan; and (3) it provided European solidarity in the face of the Cold War Soviet threat.

Despite these advantages, the Community was controversial from the start. Not all counties (especially Britain) wanted to surrender even a limited part of their sovereignty to it. Austria, Switzerland, and the Scandinavian countries either wanted or were forced by postwar circumstances to remain neutral, which included not joining the Community. We have already remarked about how the Community's initial area of responsibilities was limited to coal and steel. But more than that, even the limited proposal for the ECSC brought to the surface the dispute between federalists and unionists that had been simmering for many years and that is still a catalyst of today's disputes about the euro. Federalists wanted to have a true federation, a "United States of Europe," in which the member states would truly surrender national sovereignty to a central, pan-European parliament or commission. Unionists in contrast preferred a loose organization in which the *member states* would make all major decisions; the central European bureaucracy would be small and limited; and it would make decisions only after *all* of the member states had agreed. The unionist position won out initially, but now, with the agreement over a common currency and a common foreign and defense policy, *and* with the European parliament and the EU's central administration in Brussels making many and important decisions, the federalist position may be winning. And once again this issue has provoked controversy and opposition from member states and their voters who may or may not want to see their national sovereignty eroded.

Despite these doubts and controversies, the ECSC and its successor, the EEC, proved during the 1950s to be a huge success. Europe recovered; France and Germany cooperated; an economic boom took place within the member countries; and the Soviets were kept at bay. Of course, not all of these accomplishments were the direct result of Community activities, but the Community certainly contributed to them. The success of the Community and the high praise it received enabled it to expand its functions and responsibilities and to become a true common market.

When General Charles de Gaulle came to power in France in 1958 and during much of the 1960s, the Community went into the doldrums. De Gaulle, in other words, resurrected the Unionist position against the increasing Federalist tendencies within the EEC. But meanwhile, during the 1960s, the economies of The Six, especially Germany's, continued to boom. Hence, when de Gaulle left office in 1968, the Community resumed its forward march.

The main development of the early 1970s was the expansion of the EEC to include three new members: Great Britain, Denmark, and Ireland. The Six now became The Nine. Norway had also applied for admission, but, after a bitterly contested political campaign that polarized public opinion, the Norwegian electorate turned down membership by a 53.5 percent to 46.5 percent margin. Only in the late 1980s, when the pull of the single market made membership look more attractive, would Norway reapply. For Denmark and Great Britain, the decision to join the Community was also difficult; both countries took pride in their distinctiveness and independence, and Great Britain also wanted to retain its "special relationship" with the United States. For these countries, joining the EEC was mainly pragmatic; they saw the trade advantages of being "inside the tent," and they realized that they would only be hurt financially by staying outside the Community.

But immediately after this enlargement, Europe in the mid-1970s went into a severe economic slump. The immediate cause of the recession was the two great oil crises of 1974 and 1979, when world oil prices doubled and then doubled again. Europe (except for Great Britain, Norway, and Russia, which have their own supplies) is even more dependent on imported oil, mainly from the Middle East, than is the United States, so when the oil crises hit, everything became more costly; inflation accelerated; the European economies went into a slump; and the price of gasoline shot up to about four dollars a gallon (compared with one dollar in the United States). European integration, we now know, proceeds faster and works better in prosperous times than in slump times, so as the European economies slowed down, so did the urge to move forward on integration. The late 1970s and early 1980s, therefore, came to be known for their "Euro-pessimism" and "Euro-skepticism."

The coming to power in Great Britain of Prime Minister Margaret Thatcher also slowed the integration process (and drove the European bureaucrats in Brussels crazy). Mrs. Thatcher was a strong skeptic of further integration, did not want to sacrifice Britain's autonomy to a supernational organization like the EEC, and, similar to Charles de Gaulle two decades earlier, wanted to retain Britain's autonomy and freedom of action. In a famous speech, Mrs. Thatcher argued that she had not deregulated, privatized, and freed-up the now-booming British economy only to see these controls, bigness, and bureaucratization reimposed by a faceless European bureaucracy.

As the European economies began to recover again in the 1980s, so, too, did the movement for integration. Two large steps were taken: (1) a second enlargement that brought in Greece, Portugal, and Spain, and (2) the movement toward a single market, which carried with it the adoption of a single currency. Both of these carried major political as well as economic implications.

Until the mid-1970s, Greece, Portugal, and Spain had been governed by dictatorships; now they were beginning their transitions to democracy. So part of the reason for admitting them to the EEC was to secure their fragile democracies, to prevent a reversion to dictatorship, and (a Cold War theme) to keep their strong domestic communist parties from coming to power. At the same time, considerable rivalry and maneuvering occurred *among* these countries to be the first into the Community and thus to qualify for the largest Community subsidies, which in fact proved to be enormously helpful in bringing these less-developed Southern European economies closer to the general European level. Finally, the existing EEC members voiced a lot of dissatisfaction because many of them did not want to pay these subsidies, especially France, (which saw Spain as a cheaper competitor that might undersell its own agricultural products.) As a result, Greece came into the Community in 1981, but Spain and Portugal were not admitted until 1986.

The movement toward a single market and a common currency was also interesting. The movement was led by another Frenchman, Jacques Delors, whose determination to move the Community ahead and political skills at getting the task accomplished matched those of the Community's founder Jean Monnet in the 1950s. The single market concept meant that *all* tariffs would be removed, all barriers to trade eliminated, and that Europe would operate as a single, large economy. In fact, when combined, it would be the world's largest economy, able to compete evenly with such other economic powerhouses as the United States and Japan. The single market concept also implied that all border restrictions would be eliminated, passports would not be needed (except when traveling outside the Community, in which case an EU passport would be used), there would be full movement of labor as well as of goods and services, and a single, new currency, the *euro*, would replace the separate national currencies. The single market also carried the implications of a common, unified foreign policy as well as a common defense policy for the European states.

Delors was skillful at winning allies and political support, and his frequent pronouncements that the single market was "inevitable" helped make this vision seem feasible. At the same time, the professional EU bureaucrats in Brussels, by now skilled and seasoned practitioners of their art, elaborated such a vast web of rules, regulations, and propaganda that it proved virtually impossible to stop the steamroller. The member countries were all but presented with a *fait accompli;* if they now objected, they would be deeply resented by their fellow members and ostracized in the court of European public opinion. By this point, approximately fifty years after the common market had begun, it seemed that the federalists who stood for a single Europe had emerged triumphant and that the unionists who wanted to maintain separate national sovereignties but within a common market context were in full retreat.

But the differences continued and could not be easily "papered over." Some countries, worried about crime, drugs, and illegal immigrants, were not eager to eliminate passport controls and border restrictions. Great Britain, as usual, was divided on the issues, both among the major parties and within them. Conservative Margaret Thatcher continued to oppose any loss of British sovereignty; her successor John Major softened the rhetoric somewhat, and Labor Prime Minister Tony Blair gave off stronger, pro-European vibes. The big surprise (to Delors and the EC bureaucrats, who could not conceive of any rational person being opposed) came when Denmark voted down the agreement. Sentiment in the key core countries of France and Germany was also deeply divided, whereas Portugal, Spain, Belgium, and The Netherlands remained strongly pro–single market. So, at one level, the single market issue is a highly arcane technical issue, but at another it is also intensely political.

Then, unexpectedly, the Soviet Union collapsed; the Eastern European countries threw off their communist regimes, and the Iron Curtain and the Berlin Wall came crashing down. These momentous events added new complications to the European single market debate.

Prior to the demolition of the Iron Curtain, the Eastern European communist countries had tried to match the EEC by creating their own common market. Called COMECON (Community of Eastern European Countries), this organization was a strange mixture. Often labeled a "common market," it had no real marketplace in a capitalist sense; it also served as a propaganda device for the Soviet Union, which wanted its Eastern European puppet states to *appear* to be as forward-looking as their Western counterparts; and it functioned in the context of a command or communist economy that was always subordinate to Soviet interests. COMECON, therefore, *never* functioned as a real common market; worse than that, under Soviet and communist domination, the economies of Eastern Europe not only lagged *far* behind Western Europe but also continued to slide downhill. Today, although newly liberated and beginning to make a comeback, most of Eastern Europe has living standards that have slipped to Third World levels. In traveling to Africa and Latin America, however sad it is, seeing poverty and malnutrition there is common; but to see similar poverty, illiteracy, malnutrition, malnutrition-related diseases (TB, dysentery), cancer-causing pollution, and dramatically lowered life expectancy (fifty-five years) in *Europe* is shocking. That problem provides an interesting *comparative* perspective on Eastern Europe: countries that fifty or sixty years ago were at the same level as Greece, Portugal, and Spain (Southern Europe) have now fallen *far* behind that level and are at the same underdeveloped level as the middle-level Latin American countries.

When the Soviet Union collapsed and the Iron Curtain was torn down, COMECON also collapsed. Most of the Eastern European nations quickly petitioned for membership in the EC, assuming that the act of joining the Community would quickly ensure their immediate prosperity, too. But a host of questions and political issues soon arose. Germany, Europe's most powerful economy and closer in proximity than other countries to Eastern Europe, initially showed a strong interest in expanding its trade and assistance to the East; but as the costs of its own unification with former East Germany mounted, Germany showed less and less interest in pouring its resources into other countries. Second, the other EEC members—once the costs of Eastern European modernization became apparent (earlier, the poverty and misery of these countries had been largely hidden by totalitarian controls)—were similarly not eager to spend scarce resources to build up Eastern Europe. Third, Spain, Portugal, and Greece were particularly opposed because, as the poorest members of the EU, they had been receiving European subsidies for many years, and now they anticipated the subsidies being redirected away from them and toward the East. Finally, the question of *which* Eastern European countries would be admitted was critical: *all* of them or only those that were already beginning to prosper or had the beginnings of a free-market system (Poland, the Czech Republic, and Hungary). Currently, only these three countries plus Slovenia are in a position to be admitted; but then what about the Balkans (Bulgaria, Romania, and the other countries of the former Yugoslavia); how about the Baltics (Estonia, Latvia, and Lithuania); what of Belarus and the Ukraine; and finally what about Russia? The entry of these countries into the EU will be slower and more difficult.

A few words should be said about another organization that is parallel to the EC, the European Free Trade Association (EFTA). EFTA consists of seven countries—Austria, Finland, Iceland, Liechtenstein, Norway, Sweden, and Switzerland—that wanted to be neutral in the Cold War and saw the EC as too linked to NATO and the Western alliance to be truly neutral. So these countries formed their own free-trade group, which was supposedly neutral between the U.S. and the U.S.S.R., even though approximately 60 percent of their trade was and is with the EU. But with the collapse of the Soviet Union and the Cold War over, this neutral stance may now be outmoded: What is there to be neutral about, and neutral between which countries? Neutrality may no longer make much sense for most of these countries; in fact, several of them are moving away from their earlier neutrality and closer to the EU. But that would require them also to conform to all of the economic and technical criteria of the EU and to the requirements of the single market, the euro, and the movement toward a common foreign and defense policy, steps that not all of the EFTA countries are so far willing to undertake.

Now, what about NATO? The North Atlantic Treaty Organization came into existence during the same period (the early Cold War) as the EEC, and to the American officials involved it had many of the same purposes. The United States saw the EEC and NATO as serving parallel and complementary purposes: The EEC was to be the agent of European recovery and prosperity and thus deter the Soviet Union by demonstrating Europe's economic strength, whereas NATO would be the Western Alliance's strategic and military arm. One major difference between the EEC and NATO, however, was that the United States and Canada were members of the latter but not of the former and, as we have just seen, given NATO's explicitly Cold War and military purpose, many of Europe's neutrals did not want to be members of NATO and, to the extent that organization was also part of the Western Alliance, of the EEC either—although both EFTA members Iceland and Norway were NATO members.

A popular aphorism says that the purposes of NATO were to keep the Americans *in* Europe, the Soviets *out,* and the Germans divided—so as to prevent a repeat of World Wars I and II. To a large extent these purposes have been accomplished: The United States has maintained its commitment to a strong European defense and has long kept its own troops there, and the Soviet Union was prevented from making any further gains in Europe after the drawing of the Iron Curtain. The only purpose not fulfilled was to keep Germany divided, but, notwithstanding the fears of some statesmen concerning the future of a stronger, larger, more nationalistic Germany, once the Berlin Wall fell and the Soviet Union collapsed, Germany's reunification was inevitable. Hence, because the main purposes of NATO have been accomplished, in many ways dramatically so—the West won the Cold War!—the question now becomes, what purpose or purposes (if any) should the Alliance now serve?

Immediately after the Soviet Union collapsed and the Cold War ended, many people discussed abolishing NATO or radically restructuring it. After all, its major purpose had been accomplished. There was serious discussion (mainly by the Europeans) of replacing NATO with a purely European defense alliance, which would exclude the United States and give Europe a truly *European* defense alliance, or perhaps, to please the Americans, to have *both* NATO and a separate European defense arrangement, such as the Western European Union (WEU), of which the United States is not a member. But then came civil war in Yugoslavia to which Europe was slow to react and in the pacification of which NATO seemed to be the only institution capable of acting. In addition, a separate European defense force would be enormously expensive and, many Europeans reasoned, as long as the United States was still willing to pay for NATO, why not let the Americans continue to pay for Europe's defense arrangements instead of Europe itself footing a larger share of the bill? Then, too, NATO continued to have an enormously powerful lobby in Washington, where it was known as "the most successful alliance ever." NATO is sacrosanct; no one can tamper with it or its budget. Finally, domestic politics had to be considered: Many Eastern Europeans consti-

The European Community is headquartered in Brussels, Belgium, where both NATO headquarters and the EU are centered.

tute decisive ethnic constituencies in important American swing states, and in the 1996 election, *both* presidential candidates promised NATO membership to Eastern Europe with the hope of winning the support of those constituencies.

The result is that not only has NATO been continued even though its main reason for existence (containing the Soviet Union) has ended, but it is now in the process of being expanded. Poland, the Czech Republic, and Hungary have all been admitted to NATO even though everyone recognizes that it will be enormously expensive to bring them up to NATO standards. The problem is that not only must these countries' militaries be modernized but, as basically Third World countries, all of their internal *systems* need to be rebuilt as well: the educational system, health care, communication, transportation, electricity and power, public administration, roads, infrastructure, the economy, *everything*. All of this modernization will cost tremendous amounts of money, which neither the countries involved nor the other Europeans nor the Americans have available. But if it will be expensive for these, the best-off Eastern European countries to meet NATO standards, it will be even more expensive for the other less-developed Eastern European countries. All of these countries do want to join both NATO and the EU to serve as a bulwark against what they see as eventually a reassertive Russia *and* because these memberships are seen by them as a badge of approval for the progress they have made so far and a symbol that they are actually a part of the West.

But NATO, it must be recalled, is a military defense or collective security arrangement: an attack on one member *requires* all the others to come to its defense. Are Americans and Europeans (mainly the former) ready to come *automatically* to the defense of those Eastern European countries whose borders on virtually all sides are still disputed and where ongoing ethnic, religious, and nationality conflicts (as with former Yugoslavia, but that is just the tip of the iceberg of a regionwide set of such problems in eastern Europe) may drag the United States and Europe into a series of endemic, almost unsolvable conflicts in which we have few interests? And is it worthwhile to antagonize Russia, with its twenty thousand nuclear weapons, by expanding NATO's European defense perimeter (a new Iron Curtain?), which Russia sees as targeted against it, right up to the borders of Russia itself?

To these questions American policymakers have responded that NATO is changing, that it's now more like a political club than a military alliance, and that Russia need not worry because it's not really aimed at them—and indeed Russian members have been invited to sit on some NATO committees. But it is precisely because NATO *is* a collective security agreement that Eastern Europe wants to join, as a defense against what they see as a still or future threatening Russia. Well, it has to be either a "political club" or a military defensive alliance; only by a great stretch of imagination, definition, and word play can it be considered both. Meanwhile, NATO has been updating its mission statement to indicate not just common defense but also military intervention in nonmember states (the former Yugoslavia) to serve humanitarian purposes. It seems likely, therefore, that the debate over NATO's role and purpose, as well as the question of how membership in NATO and the EU helps the boundaries of Europe, will go on.

At the same time, we need to raise a series of questions concerning the relation of these *regional* organizations to the larger trends toward *globalization* in which Europe now is also involved. Parallel questions can be asked about other regional arrangements such as Japan and its trade bloc in Asia or the United States and Canada/Mexico (NAFTA). Those questions include: To what extent does this long European emphasis on *regional* union detract from Europe playing a larger *global* role? Is Europe's trade to be concentrated almost exclusively within Europe itself or will Europe join the trend toward global markets? Does Europe's expanding internal trade and accompanying exclusion of outside products help it or hurt it in long-term worldwide trade? Is NATO as in the past to be confined to the European continent or might it be used in out-of-area peace-making, peace-keeping, and counterterrorism as well? As Europe has focused on building a common market and the euro, has it become too inward-looking, too ethnocentric, too narrow and parochial? Can a more unified Europe, but one still with numerous problems as outlined here, compete with the United States, Japan, China, and other rising countries in the emerging global marketplace?

These questions are critical not just for Europe but also for the world. These questions lie at the heart of the analysis in this book. We return to these themes repeatedly in the discussions that follow.

COMPARATIVE TRANSITION TO DEMOCRACY

Prior to 1989, most Comparative Politics texts divided the world's political systems into three major categories: a First World of developed, industrialized, democratic nations; a Second World of developed, industrialized, communist nations; and a Third World of developing countries. But now with the collapse of communism in Eastern Europe and Russia, that categorization has been rendered moot. The Second World of supposedly developed communist states has disappeared, and the Third World—encompassing everything from China and India to Africa, the Middle East and Latin America, and therefore too broad a category to be useful—has been further subdivided into Newly Industrialized Countries (NICs, such as South Korea or Singapore), Middle-Income Economies, and Low-Income Economies. But the changes are not just economic, they are also political. Nowadays, everyone wants to be democratic.

While the Cold War was still on, countries had a choice in selecting their route to development and the endpoint at which they hoped to arrive. Once again, three main possibilities existed, with variations. The democratic route to development was exemplified by the United States, Canada, much of Western Europe, and a handful of other nations; a Marxist-Leninist route to development was exemplified by the Soviet Union, Eastern Europe, China, and Cuba; and an authoritarian route to development was exemplified by the Spain of Francisco Franco, the Portugal of Antonio Salazar, and a variety of Third World authoritarian regimes. But now two of these three possibilities—Marxism-Leninism and authoritarianism—have all but disappeared, certainly in Western Europe and in many developing nations as well. No more Marxist-Leninist regimes are left in Western Europe and no more authoritarian ones can be found there either. In virtually all countries, support for extreme left-wing (communist) and extreme right-wing (authoritarian) political parties is diminished; public opinion surveys also tell us that almost no one wants to be known as a Marxist-Leninist or an authoritarian either anymore. Once again, democracy appears to be the only system left, the only one that enjoys legitimacy, and certainly so in modern Europe. Not only is democracy the only form of political system that enjoys near-universal legitimacy, but it is the only one that seems capable of handling the problems of change, adaptation, succession, pluralism, and effective, participatory, decision making so necessary in the modern world.

But—and this is the main point of this section—the European countries have democratized at different points in history, in different contexts, from different starting points, with different assumptions, and with different cultural, social, economic, and institutional foundations. Just because Europe is now democratic does not mean that democracy is everywhere the same—far from it. Hence, in this section we introduce some of the themes that help account for the distinct kinds of democracy that exist in Europe, focusing particularly on the strengths, weaknesses, and variations of democracy in the various countries. What we find is that the transitions to democracy in Southern Europe (Greece, Italy, Spain, and Portugal) are very different from the transitions to democracy in Eastern Europe, which are also very different from the considerably earlier transitions to democracy in Scandinavia as well as in the core countries of Central/Western Europe. Not only is this theme of transitions to democracy one of the most exciting in current Comparative Politics, but it also helps us understand why Russia and many parts of Eastern Europe are presently having such a difficult time in their transitions.

Great Britain was the first country to democratize, beginning in the thirteenth century with the Magna Carta, continuing in subsequent centuries to develop the rule of law, expanding the participatory nation in the seventeenth century, extending the suffrage in the nineteenth century, and becoming a full-fledged social democracy in the twentieth century. Three facets stand out particularly about British democratization: (1) how long and gradual the process was; (2) how strong Great Britain's democratic institutions and political culture are; and (3) that Britain was able to take all of these steps toward modernization in sequence (political first, economic later), so that the system would not be overloaded by trying to do everything at once. That is, Great Britain was already an established democracy before the industrial revolution and its accompanying rapid social change occurred, so it could handle all these earth-shaking changes sequentially and without provoking chaos and instability. Contrast that scenario with present-day Russia, for example, which is having to deal with vast social, economic, cultural, and political changes suddenly and simultaneously. Russia's circuits, in contrast to Great Britain's, are vastly overloaded, and one can readily understand, therefore, why Russia's present prospects look so uncertain and unstable.

The next countries to democratize include the core continental countries of The Netherlands and France. The Netherlands, similar to Great Britain, democratized fairly smoothly and over a considerable period, but in France democracy seemed more uncertain and threatened. Rather than a smooth path to democracy as in Britain and Holland, France seemed to oscillate after the Revolution of 1789 and for much of the nineteenth century between sudden, often violent, explosions of almost anarchic democracy on the one hand, and reversions to authoritarianism on the other. But France has been a solid democracy now for more than a century, and it would be unthinkable for the country to revert to any other system. Belgium, Switzerland, and the Scandinavian countries have followed similar trajectories: starting somewhat later than Great Britain but nevertheless developing over a long period into stable, effective, functioning democracies. The issue for these countries at present is often social or economic democracy and the degree of this conversion because political democracy is already stable and well institutionalized.

The same cannot be said for Germany and Italy. These two countries unified later than most other European countries and on a more unstable base. Italy was volatile and often unstable from the time of unification in the 1860s through World War I and beyond, and in

1922 Mussolini and the fascists seized power. Hence, it was only after the defeat of fascism in World War II that Italy, in 1946, experienced an extended, more than fifty-year period of democracy. Democracy in Italy now appears to be well-established, but it is still relatively recent, often chaotic, and with several still-powerful centrifugal forces: the rebaptized (in the wake of the Cold War) Communist Party, strong right-wing movements, and the sharp split verging on secession between North and South.

Germany is similarly a relative latecomer to democracy and sometimes still harbors sentiments that students of German history find potentially worrisome. Germany had a long authoritarian tradition, was one of the instigators if not *the* instigator of two world wars in this century, and, as the largest (now unified), richest, and most powerful country in Europe, still manages to frighten its smaller neighbors by its occasional outbursts. Germany's only experience with democracy came right after World War I; that regime, the Weimar Republic, was also known for its excesses and paved the way for Hitler and the Nazis in 1933. Hitler and the Nazis plunged Europe into darkness and war, slaughtered millions of helpless peoples (Jews, gypsies, homosexuals, and foreign nationals), and enslaved most of the European continent under totalitarianism. So Germany's democracy also dates only from after World War II, but, by this time, it seems stable, affluent, contented, and middle class, all of which are usually good indicators of democratic permanence. But Germany also has the skinheads, powerful (including racist) anti-immigration sentiment, extreme left- and right-wing movements, a renewed sense of nationalism (now that it is unified) that leads some Germans to arrogance and the sense that they are better than other peoples, and sometimes bizarre behavior that reminds some observers of the Weimar period. So, although Germany's democracy seems stable and assured, there may be enough worrisome currents that Germany bears future watching.

In the mid-1970s, it was the Southern European countries' turn to democratize: Greece and Portugal beginning in 1974 and Spain in 1975. All three of these countries had powerful authoritarian traditions in the nineteenth century and into the twentieth, unstable politics, and (like Italy and Germany) unhappy experiences with democracy during those brief interludes when it was tried. In addition, all three countries industrialized later than their neighbors, were late in producing a middle class on which stable democracy could be based, experienced long periods of polarized politics, class struggle, and civil war, and failed until quite recently to produce a value system or political culture supportive of democracy. Given these conditions, it is no accident that these countries democratized later than any of the others discussed here and that, unlike Italy or Germany, their authoritarian regimes (Franco in Spain, Salazar in Portugal; military authoritarianism was restored in Greece from 1967–1974) survived World War II and lasted all the way to the mid-1970s. All three of these countries, however, have been democratic now for more than twenty-five years, their democratic regimes look stable, and, although their transitions to democracy are still incomplete in certain particulars (see the following section,) they have also developed the social, cultural, and economic underpinnings of democracy.

The same cannot be said, however, for Eastern Europe and Russia. That is why the study of Southern European democratization provides such an interesting comparison with Eastern Europe (including now Russia) and why the Southern European experience offers important lessons from which Eastern Europe can learn. For even though Southern European democracy still looks a little shaky, wobbly, and incomplete sometimes, its underpinnings are *much* stronger than are those of Eastern Europe. Hence, once again the value of comparative analysis: understanding Southern Europe's experience with democratization offers important insights into why the process in Eastern Europe and Russia has been so difficult. Such an analysis has important foreign policy implications as well.

Immediately after the communist regimes in Russia and Eastern Europe fell (between 1989 and 1991), several Comparative Politics scholars offered the Southern European experience with post-authoritarian democratization as a model to follow. That model implied a relatively smooth and peaceful transition to democracy, a relatively rapid (four to five years) transition, and above all a *successful* transition to democracy. But now, a decade or so later, we have come to realize that these transitions are not so easy; that Eastern Europe (and, of course, we need to distinguish among individual countries) and Russia are not at all like Southern Europe; and that the transition from communism to democracy is *much* more difficult than the transition from authoritarianism to democracy.

So what went wrong? What are the differences? Why was the Southern European experience so much easier than the Eastern Europe/Russia experience? Here are some preliminary thoughts on an issue with enormous policy consequences, which also shows the value of using the Comparative Method to understand truly world-shaking events:

1. By the 1970s, Southern Europe—even though authoritarian and with significant portions of the economy dominated by the state—was experiencing robust economic growth, had a large private economy, and understood and had much of the machinery of a market system. By contrast, Russia and much of Eastern Europe in the 1980s had no real market system, none of the institutions required to operate a private economy, and declining economic figures. The Czech Republic, Hungary, and Poland did have at least the beginnings of these institutions in place, and it is no accident that among the Eastern European countries these three have done the best and show the most promise in the post–Cold War era.

2. Greece, Portugal, and Spain, although authoritarian, nevertheless at the time of their transitions to democracy had a functioning, although limited, civil society: the Church, interest groups, community and neighborhood associations, and the like. This civil society served as the base for the democratic pluralism that emerged after these countries' dictators fell. By contrast, Russia and Eastern Europe (except perhaps for Poland and Hungary) had almost no civil society and no base on which democracy and pluralism could be built.

3. The Southern European countries either had a nascent political party system already in place even under authoritarianism (in the form of "study groups," exile organizations, or underground movements) or an understanding of how political parties function in a democracy. By contrast, Russia and Eastern Europe had nothing except the Communist Party and a totalitarian apparatus that snuffed out all other dissenting movements. Either democracy had never existed, or it had existed so long ago that almost no one knew how political parties or elections worked.

4. At the time of their transitions, the Southern European countries had a political culture that was strongly supportive of democracy and a powerful desire to live, behave, act, and so forth, just like the rest of Europe (which stood for democracy, human rights, social justice, and modernity) from which they, as semi-peripheral nations, had long been cut off. By contrast, in Russia and much of Eastern Europe, although many people were supportive of democracy, they had little idea what it meant or how it worked. Others were pulled in the opposite direction, away from the West and democracy and toward older, often authoritarian Russian and Eastern European traditions. The consensus to go in a democratic direction was often weak and lacked institutions to support that transition.

5. By the 1970s, Southern Europe had numerous cadres of leaders (governmental, military, economic and bureaucratic) who were experienced in European institutions, the EEC, NATO, and so on, who could facilitate these countries' rejoining Europe. In contrast, Russia and Eastern Europe not only had no experience in the EEC and NATO, but for many decades they had also been entirely cut off from the *myriad* of European agencies that had multiplied over the years. So not only were Russia and parts of Eastern Europe ambivalent about Europe's democracy and open markets, but they also had almost no leaders who knew how to operate in this new (to them) environment.

6. When Greece, Portugal, and Spain undertook democratization, they already had in place functioning ministries and bureaucracies, many (although limited) social welfare programs, and much of the apparatus of a modern state. Russia and Eastern Europe, in contrast, had few effectively functioning government agencies; they were often dominated by corruption, absenteeism, and incredible inefficiencies; and the notion that these agencies should actually serve the public was all but unheard of. In addition to all of their problems (no markets, no civil society, no parties, few leaders, etc.), the entire Russian and Eastern European state or governmental system would have to be reorganized and reoriented as well.

7. Finally, in this list of difficulties making Russia's and Eastern Europe's transitions to democracy harder than Southern Europe's, is the international environment. In the 1970s, other Western countries were willing to massively assist Southern Europe and to subsidize their economies for many years. By contrast, in the 1990s, for Eastern Europe foreign aid has been greatly reduced; few subsidies are available, and private investors have often been unwilling to risk capital in an environment that looks so unstable.[3]

The previous analysis suggests that Russia and Eastern Europe's democratization will be more difficult and take longer than that of Southern Europe. Russia and Eastern Europe are starting from a lower social and economic base; they lack the institutions Southern Europe had at the time it began its democratization; and Russia and Eastern Europe must undergo reform of all of their institutions—social, political, cultural, and economic—at once rather than gradually and in sequence as Southern Europe did. These differences also mean that the models that scholars and policy analysts used to interpret Southern European democratization are of limited utility when applied to Russia and Eastern Europe. Instead, we will need two models: one for Southern Europe, and a second to provide guidelines for studying post-communism. From these two, quite distinct experiences, it may be possible in the future to extract some general ideas about transitions to democracy that are common to both areas. At the same time, the expressed *goals* in both regions are remarkably parallel: democracy, a modern market/mixed economy, and integration with the West. The communist "Second World" has now disappeared from Europe; only the "First World" is left.

EUROPE IN A COMPARATIVE POLITICS CONTEXT

Because this text is about Comparative European Politics, our goal is *not just* to understand

---

[3]Right after the Soviet Union and the Iron Curtain fell, several Western European socialist and social-democratic governments rushed to aid Russia, arguing that Russia got socialism "wrong" (Leninist and Stalinist) at first in 1917, and now they, the Western Europeans, could help Russia get it "right." But as the Russian economy drifted downward, many of these Western countries withdrew their "ideological" aid and investment and redirected it closer to home (the Baltics, the Czech Republic, Poland, and Hungary), where they concluded it would do more good *and* give them a return in the form of trade and influence.

the European countries individually and on their own terms (although that is also a worthy goal) but also to develop comparisons between and among them. For Comparative Politics is not only interested in individual country analyses but also in analyzing patterns, trends, and comparisons: Why some countries are more developed and/or democratic than others; why some have forged ahead while others have lagged behind; why some have stable institutions and others do not.

To facilitate such comparisons, a common outline is used in each of the country and regional chapters contained in the book. The outline used here is one that scholars of Comparative Politics often use in their studies of foreign countries. The use of such a common outline and of common terms and categories helps us to think comparatively about the different countries, to identify trends and patterns, and to see commonalties as well as differences. At the same time, the use of a common outline falls short of being a full-scale "model" of European politics and change. The authors of this text are not sure that a full-fledged model of European politics to which all countries correspond yet exists. So, short of having a model, we use a common out-line that helps us to identify trends and patterns that may in the future become a full model. Our outline is, therefore, a teaching and analytic device for thinking about and organizing our understanding of European politics. As such, it is subject to change, rethinking, and reorganization—pragmatically, as Europe itself changes. We use this outline, therefore, to advance our knowledge and understanding, but not to elevate it in importance to a position it does not have. Indeed, we urge students and scholars alike to constantly rethink and refashion the outline provided here to bring it closer into line with European realities.

The outline we employ for each country and area chapter builds in dynamic change factors and borrows from modern systems (input-decision making-output-feedback) theory. It encompasses the following categories:

I. History, Background, and Political Culture
II. Socioeconomic Background, Class Structure, and Interest Groups
III. Political Parties and Elections
IV. Government, Bureaucracy, and Decision Making
V. Public Policies and Programs
VI. The New Globalism and Its Effects

Let us discuss each of these main subject areas in turn, so that we will have a basis on which to examine the individual countries and regions, and to measure the changes and new trends occurring in each. Our goal here is not to provide a complete overview of European politics—that is for our individual authors and chapters to do—but to raise questions, offer provocations, and stimulate discussion as a way of exploring some of the key issues and controversies in European politics.

Our first category is History, Background, and Political Culture. Here we are obviously interested in the differing histories and backgrounds of the several countries and regions. Why did Great Britain develop constitutional government ahead of other countries? Why has French politics been so divisive? Why were Germany and Italy so late in consolidating as nation-states and how did that delayed unification affect their political development? What is there about Russian history that produced the Bolshevik Revolution in 1917? Why did both Southern Europe and Eastern Europe remain on the periphery of Europe for so long, often lagging behind developments occurring in the core countries? These are just some of the questions that our historical analysis seeks to answer.

This first category also deals with the subject of political culture. Political culture refers to the basic values, beliefs, and behavioral patterns that are characteristic of different countries and regions. Political culture seeks to avoid national stereotyping and recognizes that within a given country, several, often competing, changing, and overlapping values may exist, and that political culture is a *contested* issue and may involve a struggle over which political-cultural values will be dominant. Nevertheless, political culture, particularly when based on careful public opinion or survey research, is valuable in analyzing trends and patterns. Is Germany still more authoritarian than Great Britain or Scandinavia, and, if so, what are the implications of that? Are class attitudes stronger in Southern Europe than in Northern Europe, and, if so, why? What is the influence of different religions—Catholicism in the south of Europe, Protestantism in the north, orthodoxy to the east—on politics, and is that religious influence now in decline as much of Europe becomes more secular? Are Russians less committed to democratic, liberal values and a democratic political system than other countries, and is that why both democracy and a free-market system are having such a difficult time there? These are only some of the questions that an exploration of political culture factors provides.

The next subject in each of our chapters concerns the socioeconomic background of the various countries and their class and interest-group structures. In terms of socioeconomic background, we will want to know the per capita income of all of the European countries (see Table 1.1), how that wealth is distributed (equitably or inequitably), and some of the main social characteristics (literacy, life expectancy) of these countries. Note that Switzerland, at more than $40,000 income per person per year, is not only the richest country in Europe but the richest in the world. Austria, Belgium, France, Germany, Great Britain, Italy, The Netherlands, and the Scandinavian countries are all in the top ranks (along with the United States and Japan) of the world's wealthiest countries. But note that Ireland and Southern Europe (Greece, Portugal, and Spain) are poorer, at a level only roughly two-thirds to three-quarters of the European average; nevertheless, these countries still rank among the world's top thirty countries.

Note the sharp dropoff in per capita income, however, when we get to Eastern Europe and Russia. Most of these countries have per capita incomes about one-tenth those of the Western European countries. In economic terms, Eastern Europe and Russia are closer to the Third World of developing countries than to the First World of modern, industrialized nations. In terms of social indicators, they also lag behind with higher levels of illiteracy, more pollution, more disease, and lower life expectancy. To achieve modernity, Eastern Europe and Russia must also rebuild and reform their infrastructures, all of which are woefully underdeveloped: schools, transportation, public administration, communications, banking, finance, and so on. One of the consistent findings of Comparative Politics research over the years is that wealthier countries are likely to be more supportive of democracy than poor countries; and looking over these figures for Eastern Europe, it becomes easy to see why, with their poverty and depressed social conditions, Eastern Europe and Russia have had a hard time establishing democracy and open markets following the fall of communism. Much of Eastern Europe and Russia lack the social base to support democracy. At the same time, as the Eastern Europe chapter makes clear, we need to distinguish between the more developed and more democratic countries of Northeast and Central Europe (the Baltics, Poland, Hungary, and the Czech Republic) and the poorer, less democratic countries (Albania, Bulgaria, Romania, and the countries of the former Yugoslavia) of southeast Europe.

In this section, we will also look at the class structure of the various countries and the relations of that structure to democracy and development. For example, Great Britain, France, and the countries of Southern Europe still have some pronounced class structures, whereas Scandinavia is more egalitarian. Does that egalitarianism help explain the extent and popularity of Scandinavia's advanced social welfare system? In contrast, although Russia and Eastern Europe, because of their earlier communist backgrounds, have a commitment to egalitarianism, they lack a strong middle class to provide support for democracy and a strong entrepreneurial sector to provide their countries with a more solid economic base.

In this section of their chapters, building on this socioeconomic background, we have asked each of our authors to discuss interest groups. Several intriguing issues arise here. Are interest groups stronger in some countries than in others, and why? In the new era of integration and globalization, are business groups becoming more powerful? At the same time, are labor unions becoming less influential? How about other social and political groups, students, professional associations, defense establishments, environmental groups, or greens? How pluralist are these societies? Are some groups more powerful and influential and some weaker? Which groups—immigrants, peasants, gypsies, and others—are effectively excluded from the political process? Which groups are rising and which are falling in influence?

At the same time, if we look at the interest group *system,* some large changes are occurring as well. The major change seems to be a shift away from a free, independent, autonomous, laissez faire, interest-group struggle as in the United States, toward an interest-group system where the state or government licenses and regulates the interest groups and often incorporates them into the state's deliberations on public policy and its regulatory roles. Such a system of state-sponsored and state-regulated interest groups is called *corporatism,* as distinct from the pluralism of U.S. interest groups; and we will want to know which countries have more or lesser corporatism versus pluralism, or which have mixed—corporatist and liberal-pluralist—systems at the same time. By way of contrast, again because of their communist backgrounds, both Eastern Europe and Russia lack a strong system of well-organized interest groups or of "civil society," which almost all political scientists believe to be a strong underpinning for democracy.

The third part of each of our authors' chapters deals with political parties and elections. On this subject, too, many interesting questions may be asked. Why are political parties stronger in some countries than in others? Is Europe electorally now headed toward the left, the right, or what is often called the "Third Way," between capitalism and socialism and with a mix of both? Actually, at present (Spring 2000), thirteen of the EU countries, all except Ireland and Spain, are governed by parties of the left or in coalitions where the left is the major party. But how much difference does that make now that the left in much of Europe has moved closer to the center, forsaking its old Marxist rallying cries in favor of a pro-business stance? The European left presently feels reborn, but the many differences among the several left parties in the countries of the region leave plenty of room for disagreement.

With the increasing importance of European integration and globalization, are center and business-oriented parties likely to fare better in the future? Or, contrarily, will the left parties be seen as the defenders of social welfare and the weak against the unfettered inequality of the marketplace? Now that the Cold War is over, does that also mean that the political parties associated with Cold War positions, such as communists, socialists, and the ultra-right wing, will also go into decline? What will happen to the historic Christian-Democratic parties of Europe, especially in Germany and Italy, as religious beliefs and sentiments become less pervasive? And what are we to make of some of the newer parties: the "Greens" or environmental parties often on the left and the anti-immigration parties often associated with the right?

Most of the European countries have parliamentary rather than presidential (as in the United States) systems, so we will want to know the differences between these two types of systems. In those countries such as Germany or Portugal that do have presidents, the president is usually the ceremonial head of government, whereas real day-to-day power is exercised by the prime minister. Moreover, within these predominantly parliamentary systems, we will see both two- as well as multi-party systems. Most Americans are familiar with two-party systems, but we are often unfamiliar with multi-party systems. So we need to know how these party systems operate, how governing coalitions are built when no one party has an absolute majority, and how cabinet and government positions may be divided up among the parties in return for their support on crucial parliamentary votes. We will also want to know, in the separate countries, how the balances in these governing coalitions are shifting: more toward the left, the right, or the center.

Once again, Russia and Eastern Europe provide the exceptions. Because of long communist rule, the new democratic parties tend to be weak, poorly organized, underfunded, with thin leadership, and often without strong organizations outside the capital cities. At the same time, in many of these countries, the old communist parties, now with new names, are making a comeback. So, we will want to know not just the ideologies and platforms of these parties but also how well organized they are and how deeply they have set down roots in the new democracies (if that's what they are) of Russia and Eastern Europe.

An even bigger question affects political parties. In many countries, political parties and party systems are in decline. They devise party platforms and present candidates at election time, but between elections the parties are almost dead. In the realm of ideas and political influence, the parties are being supplanted—if not replaced—in the United States as well as Western Europe by think tanks, political action committees (PACs), and interest groups with their own research arms that funnel their ideas directly into the policy arena without going through the intermediary of political parties and parliament. Ironically, while political parties appear to be declining in the West of Europe, these same countries are encouraging and often financing the growth of political parties in Russia and Eastern Europe as a way of helping to stabilize democracy in these countries.

In the next part of our authors' outlines, we look at the role of government, bureaucracy, and decision making. In examining distinct government systems, we will want to know if they are parliamentary or presidential and the various mixes of both. We will want to know if the country is unitary or federal, centralized or decentralized. Portugal, for instance, has been moving to create a new decentralized system of regional government, but it is not clear whether this system would improve democracy and efficiency or if it is just another layer of bureaucracy that will mainly provide the government with more patronage positions.

Next, we will want to look at the role of bureaucracy. Here the issue is not just whether the government civil service is efficient, responsible, and honest, although those are all crucial issues; we will also want to know if the political system itself is becoming more bureaucratic. Once again the issue is, with globalization, is bureaucracy gradually replacing politics? That is, when business and global trade are on the rise, with the Cold War over, and with political parties and some interest groups (organized labor) in decline, is the bureaucracy now replacing the party and parliamentary arenas as the main focus of national life? Are the European states becoming what we call administrative or bureaucratic states rather than party or even democratic states? For when the realm of administration, licensing, regulation, government permits, and so on, replaces ideology as the main force in politics, then the administrative state is usually on the rise. To the extent that the European states have become bureaucratic states, does that also mean they are becoming less democratic?

We will also want to look at government decision making in this section. How do decisions get made? What interests or groups are consulted before a government makes a decision? What constituencies need to be satisfied? In an era of globalization and regional integration, to what extent do decisions represent *national* decisions versus to what extent must the Europeans now take the larger community into account?

The fifth part of each country or region chapter deals with public policies and programs. We are interested in both foreign policy and domestic policy, and, in this new global age, the connections between foreign and domestic policy. We will want to know the present and future directions of these countries' foreign policies: with the United States, with each other, and with the outside world—North Africa, Asia, the Middle East, and Latin America, for example. With the Cold War over, we will want to know how the European countries have reoriented their foreign policies, no longer to contain the Soviet Union and the Warsaw Pact, for instance, but to assist Russia and Eastern Europe with democracy and economic growth. We will want to know which country or countries have taken the lead, primarily Germany because it borders on Eastern Europe, but also Austria and the Scandinavian countries, which similarly have strong interests there. Perhaps most important, we will want to know the relations of the European nations with each other, through NATO, the EU, and now the common currency of the euro. Now that Germany is united, we will want to know the changing balance of power within Europe, the shifting alliances, the fears, and the new interests that are surfacing. To what extent are these nations following a common European foreign policy; how had that policy helped or hindered Europe in dealing with such aggressor nations as Serbia; and what is the balance between a sovereign or *national-interest*-based foreign policy *versus* one subordinated to a common *European* policy?

Domestic politics and policy making are no less interesting. The key questions involve economic policy and social welfare policy. All of the countries require a robust, growing economy to help support their prosperity (recall the wealthiest area in the world with the highest living standards), as well as their extensive social programs. At the same time, the extensive social programs that many Europeans favor require ever-higher taxes—to the point where the high taxes begin to discourage initiative that chokes off growth and may stimulate a taxpayer revolt. The famed European welfare state, which has been growing and expanding over the decades and which many American intellectuals and policymakers have looked to as a model for the United States, is now in crisis. What to do about this crisis is one of the key issues of our time.

On the one hand, most Europeans like and want to continue their extensive social welfare programs, including free education, free health care, housing assistance, long vacations, subsidized public transportation, a strong social safety net, elaborate pension plans, and so forth. On the other hand, most objective observers believe that the system has now become inefficient, wasteful, and too expensive. Taxes in Scandinavia, for example, even for middle-class persons, may now reach 70 percent, and for working-class persons it may be 50 percent, which does not include the 15 percent Value Added Tax (VAT), which is like a U.S. sales tax. Those rates are exceedingly high; they leave people with excellent public services (clean streets, good public transportation, etc.) but very little disposable income.

Now many Europeans are discovering (as in the United States) that their pension plans may not be able to pay fully for their retirement. Yet their incomes after taxes are insufficient in buy private pension plans and to support the lifestyles to which they have become accustomed. In addition, as in the United States, Europe's population is aging, meaning that over time proportionately fewer and fewer younger working people are paying taxes and more and more older persons are drawing benefits from the system. Something will have to give.

The issue is complicated, and different countries and people have taken distinct positions on the issues. First, although many Europeans lament the high taxes they must pay, they are also immensely proud of their vast social welfare systems and are loathe to give them up. Riots, strikes, and protest movements have been sparked in France and other countries over government proposals to trim social welfare. Second, although advanced social welfare programs have usually been championed by socialist and social-democratic parties in Scandinavia and elsewhere, even conservative parties and coalitions have been reluctant to roll them back, usually contenting themselves with arguments that they can manage them better. The reason for this reluctance to curtail social welfare, third, is electoral logic: in countries like Sweden and other advanced social-welfare states, up to 80 to 85 percent of the population may be getting a subsidy or entitlement of one kind or another from the government; and, therefore, no party that wants to get elected can afford to tamper overly with social programs that have such a large constituency.

Currently, three main approaches or models of social welfare are predominant in Europe. The British model (which is close to that of the United States), a product of earlier Conservative Party governments and of the conclusion that Great Britain could no longer afford the costs of the welfare state, involves government downsizing, privatization, and a reduction of the welfare rolls. In contrast, France and the Scandinavian countries, headed by socialist or social-democratic governments, have been reluctant to cut back on welfare spending and may even be expanding some programs. A third model is that of The Netherlands, which, with modifications, is also followed by dynamic and powerful Germany. This third model involves limited privatization and state downsizing, and a variety of incentives for private business, combined with high taxes on the profits made. In this way, private business and entrepreneurship are encouraged, but the high taxes imposed *after* the profits are made help to pay for elaborate social welfare systems. *All* of the countries of Western Europe are now facing a crisis of their vast social programs, mainly in the form of not enough money to pay for them all; yet reflecting national values as well as voter volatility, the countries have arrived at different balances in dealing with the issue.

Meanwhile, in Russia and Eastern Europe, the problem is not elaborate social welfare programs but the absence of funds to afford *any* kind of social safety net. Russia and Eastern Europe have always been poor—far poorer than Western Europe—but under communism the state maintained at least a minimum level of welfare programs and subsidies. But now with the collapse of communism and the move to an unfettered market system, many of these safety nets have withered away; few if any private programs are available; and the post-communist governments of these countries can seldom afford to pay social welfare costs. Indeed, that is one reason why Russia and Eastern Europe wish to be admitted to the EU because they hope that European subsidies will help pay some of the welfare costs they cannot afford.

Finally, in the last section of each chapter, we have asked our authors to consider the impact of regionalism and globalization on their individual countries and regions. Reflecting its importance, we have also dedicated Chapter 9 to the same topic.

In Europe, international (regional and global) events are driving social, economic, and political policy almost as much as (maybe more than) domestic forces. When a country joins the EU, for example, it now needs to keep its budget under control, exercise financial prudence, and conform to certain *common, European* social and economic requirements. Its products need to conform to the standards set by the European community; its monetary and fiscal policies need to be in accord with the community's policies; and it now must accept the euro as a common currency. It is not allowed to "dump" products on the European market, thus lowering the price; it must accept the production quotes on various goods and products that the Community sets for it; and it must accept the regulatory standards that are now common to all EU members. EU countries are required to give preferential treatment to the products of other Community members and cannot—except in special circumstances—maintain special trade or commercial relationships with other non-EU countries: for example, Britain with America, Spain with Latin America, or France with

French-speaking Africa. The complex and detailed rules and regulations that govern all of these EU relationships are now voluminous; both countries and individual companies within them must conform but often only after considerable grumbling and even protests.

The EU's offices are headquartered (along with NATO) in Brussels, Belgium; the European Parliament meets in plush new surroundings in Strasbourg, France, close to the German border. These headquarters are elaborate: the EU bureaucracy in Brussels has expanded significantly and now, in numbers of personnel and buildings, resembles the *governments* of many EU countries. The power of these EU bureaucrats is enormous; the regulations that they issue have the force of law, and in many sensitive social and economic areas supercede national law. Individual countries and their business firms *must* conform to these regulations, which are often stiff and difficult. At the same time, elections to the European Parliament are becoming almost as important as elections to the national parliament. Much of sovereignty and decision making on social and economic policy has clearly by now been ceded to these European institutions, often at the expense of national sovereignty.

The next steps—at the same time that even closer social and economic policy coordination goes forward—involve foreign and strategic policy. The European Union is not just an economic common market anymore, but, in some quarters, involves the prospects for political union as well, which means a common foreign and defense policy as well as a common currency. One of the key reasons that NATO was slow to act in Bosnia and Kosovo against Serbian atrocities and aggression is precisely this need to negotiate a common foreign policy toward the former Yugoslavia by all the EU member states. For one thing, all of these negotiations take time to hammer out; for another, such key countries as France, Great Britain, and Germany have different goals and interests in that region, which cannot always be easily harmonized.

The movement toward a common European foreign and defense policy now has such momentum that a small country like Denmark says that fully 80 percent of its foreign policy is in conformity with a common European foreign policy. That is, on almost all issues, Denmark and the rest of Europe are in fundamental agreement on what policies they should pursue; that leaves only 20 percent of Danish foreign policy—mainly concentrated in the North Atlantic and the Baltic—for Denmark itself to decide. But that balance raises serious questions about sovereignty: is Denmark really a sovereign nation if it has ceded so much of its foreign and defense policy to Europe, or does it still retain autonomy to act on its own? This question is difficult in Europe at present where the divisions are between federalists (those who favor a single, centralized, *European* foreign and defense policy coming out of Brussels) and unionists (those favoring a looser union, more like the federation of the American Articles of Confederation of 1781, with each individual country still pursuing its own independent foreign policy). In the meantime, with borders being erased, passport controls being eliminated, the police in one country able to pursue and arrest criminals in other countries, and a whole *host* of other steps being taken, the movement toward European integration—politically as well as economically—continues to move forward.

Europe is continuing to integrate and unify on a regional level at the same time that the world is experiencing globalization. So the question becomes: Are these two trends compatible or incompatible? Can countries maintain regional unity and a regional trading bloc at the same time that cultural currents, trade patterns, and money flows are becoming increasingly global in character? Europe thinks so, but the adjustments are not always easy. Just as Europe is now reaching the apex of its decades-long, post–World War II drive toward unification, it is also recognizing—increasingly so—that it must also trade, compete, and be involved in Asia, America, Russia, the Middle East, Africa, and

Latin America. Pursuing regionalist and globalist agendas simultaneously involves delicate negotiations and compromises, the reconciliation of often contradictory goals, and hard choices that many in Europe are often unwilling to make. But that is precisely why the study of current European politics is so interesting and raises so many fascinating issues—issues of importance not just to Europeans but to Americans as well.

THE BOOK: A LOOK AHEAD

This introduction provides background and sets the context and contours of modern European politics. We have raised many questions here; now it is up to our contributing authors to answer them. For that reason, to facilitate comparison among countries and regions, and to help us better understand *comparatively* the politics of the region, we have asked all of our authors to follow the common outline suggested previously:

I. History, Background, and Political Culture
II. Socioeconomic Background, Class Structure, and Interest Groups
III. Political Parties and Elections
IV. Government, Bureaucracy, and Decision Making
V. Public Policies and Programs
VI. The New Globalism and Its Effects

We begin with Great Britain because, of all of the European countries, British traditions and institutions are closest to those of America; and pedagogically it is better to begin with a country that is close to what we already know rather than a complete unknown. We next move across the English Channel to a continental country, France, whose traditions and institutions, although democratic, have long been more divisive and tumultuous than those of Great Britain. Next, we consider Germany, the world's third most powerful economy (behind only the United States and Japan), a country recently reunified and certain to be a major factor in the twenty-first century; but a country whose history of authoritarianism, two world wars, and national arrogance combined with resentments still leaves many analysts uneasy about the future. The book next turns to Russia, a former Marxist-Leninist regime and former antagonist in the Cold War, which is now undergoing radical change but still leaving many uncertainties about the future.

The analysis next focuses on three regional areas historically on the periphery of Europe but now, in varying degrees, more closely integrated into the core. These areas are Northern Europe or Scandinavia, Southern or Mediterranean Europe, and Eastern Europe. From a comparative perspective, we will want to know why these areas remained on the periphery of Europe for a long time and the implications of that delayed integration for their future development. We will also want to know the internal politics of these regions and of the individual countries in them. Our coverage of these countries cannot possibly be as detailed as that of the larger countries, but we do want to convey the flavor of these distinct regions and of their separate political systems. So, in each of these chapters, we have asked our authors to provide for each of the main topics listed above a broad overview of the area as a whole, coupled with treatment of the individual countries. In that way we are able to see the larger picture but with enough details about individual countries that we can come to understand them as well.

The final chapter in our book deals with issues of European integration, including analyzing the history of integration, the main institutions of European integration, and current EU policies and controversies. As far as we know, this book is one of the few texts on European politics to not only integrate the themes of regionalism and globalization into the various country chapters but also to devote an entire special section to those themes. The reason, of course, as emphasized throughout this introduction, is that larger, regional EC/EU issues and decisions are now as important (often more so) as decisions taken at the level of the individual countries. To reflect this new reality, it is, therefore, imperative to look at the European community as a whole as well as at the individual countries within it.

This rich tapestry provides a picture of some of the world's leading, most exciting, most innovative countries, as well as the main social, political, economic, and regional and global currents that are coursing through them. We hope that some of the excitement that we feel for the subject area can be conveyed via this book to our students as well.

SUGGESTED READINGS

Ambrosius, Gerald, and William H. Hubbard, *A Social and Economic History of Twentieth Century Europe* (Cambridge, Harvard University Press, 1989).

Barzini, Luigi, *The Europeans* (New York, Penguin, 1983).

Berger, Suzanne (ed.), *Organizing Interests in Western Europe: Pluralism, Corporatism, and the Transformation of Politics* (New York, Cambridge University Press, 1981).

Brown, Eric, and John Dreijmanis (eds.), *Government Coalitions in Western Democracies* (New York, Longman, 1982).

Caplan, Richard, and John Feffer, *Europe's New Nationalisms: States and Minorities in Conflict* (New York, Oxford University Press, 1966).

Dahl, Robert A. (ed.), *Political Opposition in Western Democracies* (New Haven, Yale University Press, 1969).

Davies, Norman, *Europe: A History* (New York, Oxford University Press, 1996).

Dinan, Desmond, *Ever Closer Union: An Introduction to the European Community* (Boulder, Lynne Rienner, 1994).

Gallagher, Michael et al., *Representative Government in Modern Europe* (New York, McGraw Hill, 1995).

Hancock, W. Donald, *Politics in Western Europe* (Chatham, NJ, Chatham House, 1998).

Heisler, Martin, *Politics in Europe* (New York, McKay, 1974).

Inglehart, Ronald, *Culture Shifts in Advanced Industrial Society* (Princeton, Princeton University Press, 1990).

Kitschelt, Herbert, *The Transformation of European Social Democracy* (New York, Cambridge University Press, 1994).

Klausen, Jyette, and Louise A. Tilly, *European Integration in Social and Historical Perspective* (Lanham, MD, Rowman and Littlefield, 1997).

Kramer, Steven P., and Irene Kyriakopoulos, *Trouble in Paradise? Europe in the 21st Century* (Washington, DC National Defense University, Institute for National Strategic Studies, 1996).

Krause, Axel, *Inside the New Europe* (New York, Cornelia and Michael Bessie, 1991).

Laquer, Walter, *Europe in Our Time* (New York, Penguin, 1992).

Lewis, Flora, *Europe: A Tapestry of Nations* (New York, Simon and Schuster, 1987).

Lodge, Juliet, *Institutions and Policies of the European Community* (London, Frances Pinter, 1983).

McHale, Vincent, *Political Parties of Europe* (Westport, CT, Greenwood Publishers, 1983).

Miall, Hugh, *Shaping a New European Order* (New York, Council on Foreign Relations, 1994).

Moller, J. Ostrom, *The Future European Model* (Westport, CT, Praeger, 1995).

Padgett, Stephen, and William E. Patterson, *A History of Social Democracy in Post War Europe* (London, Longman, 1991).

Pinder, John, *European Community* (New York, Oxford University Press, 1991).

Roberts, Geoffrey K., and Patricia Hogwood, *European Politics Today* (Manchester, Eng., Manchester University Press, 1997).

Serfaty, Simon, *Memories of Europe's Future: Farewell to Yesteryear* (Washington, DC, Center for Strategic and International Studies, 1999).

Sharpe, L.J., *The Rise of Meso Government in Europe* (London, Sage, 1993).

Steiner, Jurg, *European Democracies* (New York, Longman, 1998).

Tiersky, Ronald (ed.), *Europe Today* (Lanham, MD, Rowman and Littlefield, 1999).

Treverton, Gregory F. (ed.), *The Shape of the New Europe* (New York, Council on Foreign Relations, 1992).

Urwin, D.W., and W.E. Paterson, *Politics in Western Europe Today* (London, Longman, 1990).

Wiarda, Howard J., *Corporatism and Comparative Politics: The Other Great "Ism"* (New York, M.E. Sharpe, 1997).

——— *Introduction to Comparative Politics* 2nd ed. (Houston, Harcourt Brace, 1999).

Wilson, Frank L., *The European Center—Right at the End of the Twentieth Century* (New York, St. Martin's, 1998).

2

ICELAND
Atlantic Ocean
SCOTLAND
Aberdeen
Atlantic Ocean
North Sea
Edinburgh
Glasgow
PENNINE CHAIN
NORTHERN IRELAND
Belfast
Irish Sea
Leeds
Liverpool
Manchester
Dublin
IRELAND
WALES
Birmingham
ENGLAND
THAMES
London
Cardiff
Bristol
English Channel
FRANC
SWEDEN
IREL
Copenhagen
PO
Berlin
ANY
Prague
CZECH RE
Vienna
FRANCE
AUSTRIA
Bern
LIECH.
SWITZERLAND

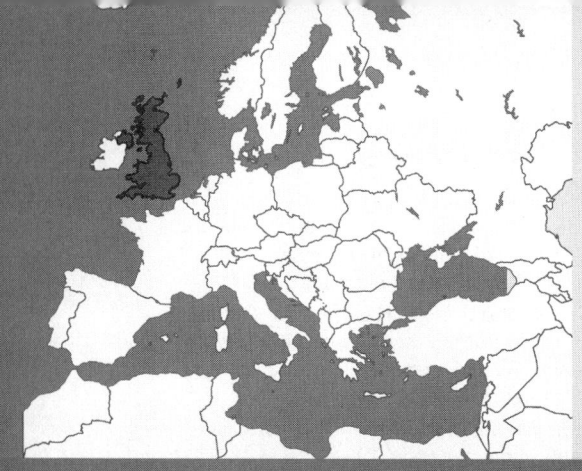

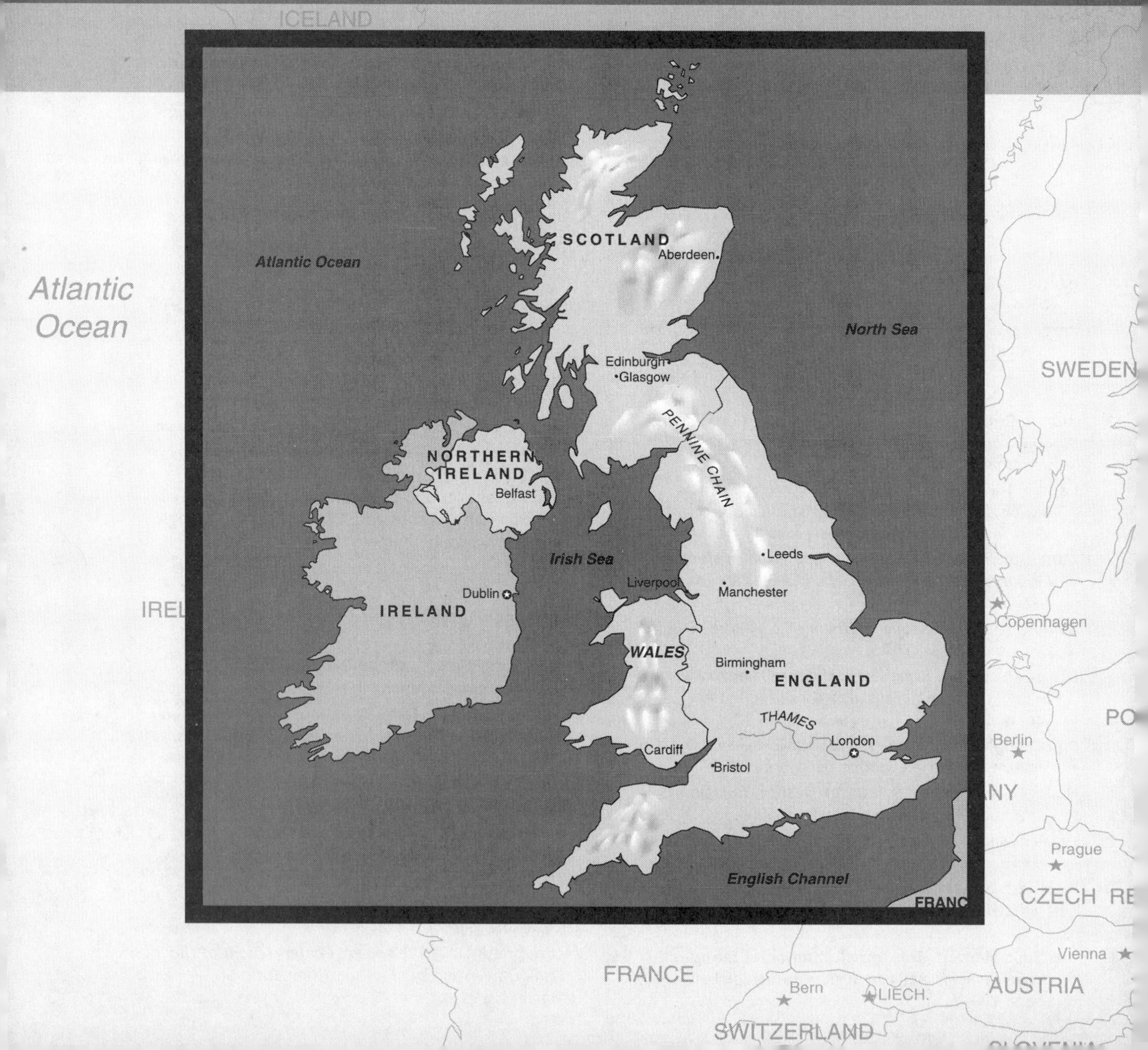

BRITAIN
Changing Yet Steadfast

John McCormick

COUNTRY PROFILE

Population:	59,000,000
Land Area:	245,000 sq. km.
Population per sq. km.:	244
Gross National Product:	$1,263.8 billion
Per Capita Income:	$21,400
Global Per Capita Income Rank:	22
Percent Urban:	89
Adult Literacy:	100% (claimed)
Life Expectancy	
Male:	75
Female:	80

INTRODUCTION

Britain is routinely used as the starting point for courses in West European politics in the United States, for several good reasons. First, it was the birthplace of the parliamentary system, and many of its political processes and institutions have inspired and been copied by other countries. For example, key features of the parliamentary system are reflected in the structures of government throughout Europe, including the process by which a bill becomes a law, the office of the prime minister, the role of the cabinet in government, and a belief in the rule of law.

Second, Britain was the birthplace of the industrial revolution, and although it is no longer the world's dominant economy, it has long had an influence on economic developments in the rest of the world. Early ideas about capitalism were influenced by the writings of Adam Smith and others; the development of the U.S. economy during the nineteenth century was helped by large infusions of British investment; and Britain has been particularly important as a focus for study since World War II because of its leading role in the development of state welfare, because of the problems it has faced in making adjustments to its post-imperial role in the world, and because of the market reforms made by the government of Margaret Thatcher (1979–1990). Those reforms have contributed to Britain's continuing role as a world leader in the extension of free-market principles.[1]

Third, the United States and Britain have a long history of exchanging political values and philosophies. This process began with the inspiration provided to American revolutionaries in the late eighteenth century by the writings and speeches of British political thinkers such as John Locke, and continued through to the alliance between Britain and the United States during World War II, the common positions taken on economic and foreign policy by Ronald Reagan and Margaret Thatcher, and the exchange of ideas between Bill Clinton and current British prime minister Tony Blair on what has become known as the "Third Way" in politics (see later in this chapter). Thus a study of the British political system offers us important insights into the underlying values and philosophies of government in the United States.

Fourth, although it is no longer the great military power that it once was, Britain still has the world's seventh largest economy and is both a key trading partner for the United States, a key point of access for U.S. policymakers wishing to influence European policy on a variety of issues, and a strong U.S. ally on many security matters. It is also a primary recipient of U.S. investment overseas and the biggest source of foreign direct investment in the United States, a fact that is surprising to many Americans, who usually assume that most foreign investment in this country comes from Japan or Germany.

Finally, strong cultural and social links exist between the United States and Britain: It is still the most familiar European country for Americans; the two countries not only share many common political and economic traditions and interests, but British culture also pervades the music that Americans listen to, the books they read, and the plays and movies they watch. The author George Bernard Shaw once quipped that the British and the Americans were two peoples divided by a common language, which says something both about what unites and what divides the two countries.

Despite Britain's familiarity, many Americans remain confused by its name. The United Kingdom of Great Britain and Northern Ireland (its official title) is actually four countries in one: Great Britain—comprising England, Scotland, and Wales—and Northern Ireland. England predominates because it conquered and assimilated the others and because it is home to more than four out of five Britons. Southeast England is the wealthiest and most influential part of the country and is dominated in turn by London, which is the political, financial, cultural, and communications center of Britain, and home to nearly one-fifth of the British population.

Many Americans can also be confused by the structure of the British political system. The British monarchy may provide valuable fodder for the tabloid press, but it also seems strangely undemocratic to those who are more familiar with a republic (a political system in which all government leaders are elected, directly or indirectly). The idea that the executive and the legislature should be fused is contrary to the American belief in the separation of powers, and it can seem that the parliamentary system allows too much power to be concentrated in too few hands; however, the system works—it is not perfect, but it has provided a model for most other democracies. All of the other countries covered in this book have based their governments mainly on the British parliamentary system.

Like all its neighbors, Britain is a small, crowded, and highly urbanized country. About the same size as Oregon, it has a population of fifty-eight million, giving it a population density of more than six hundred people per square mile (compared to less than seventy-five people per square mile in the United States). Britain has a gross national product (GNP) of just over one trillion dollars, more than 65 percent of which is generated by services. It is one of the world's largest producers of oil, natural gas, and coal, and exports a variety of manufactured goods, but it has relatively few other natural resources and must import raw materials such as cotton, wool, rubber, and tin, and about 10 percent of its food needs. Its economy in the late 1990s was one of the freest in the world and was growing faster than that of almost any other European country, but this latter-day boom came at the end of several painful decades of economic transition, a process that may not yet have ended.

In social terms, Britain lacks the kind of racial or religious variety that is so much a part of life in the United States, but it still has important class and regional divisions. About 96 percent of the population is white, and although racism remains a problem in some of the larger urban areas (notably London), ethnic minorities have become more successfully integrated in recent years. Social class was long the most defining characteristic of British society, with an obvious hierarchy in place by which most Britons placed themselves—or were placed—in the upper, middle, or working class. The class system still exists, but the expansion of the middle class has made it less obvious and more complex, and class-driven support for political parties has steadily decreased since World War II. The Blair government has made a particular point of promoting policies that are inclusive, contrasting with the economic and social divisiveness that often marked the policies of its predecessors.

In political terms, Britain is distinct from almost any other country in its record of evolutionary political development, driven by what has been described as a "genius for nonviolent progress."[2] There *has* been violence (including several serious race riots in recent years), and Britain's democratic record is far from spotless: questions are regularly raised about government secrecy, social inequalities, and an electoral system that handicaps smaller political parties, and British governments until recently were often criticized for human rights abuses in Northern Ireland. However, the ruling classes have made enough concessions at critical junctures over the centuries to avoid the kinds of political revolutions experienced by other European states. Even today, fundamental changes are coming to British politics, including new regional governments for Scotland, Wales, and Northern Ireland, an elected mayor for London, reforms to the electoral system and to the structure of the British Parliament, and constitutional changes that would ensure greater protection for human rights.

TABLE 2.1 Key Dates in British History

Date	Event
55 B.C.	Roman invasion
400–600	Germanic invasions
8th Century	Viking invasions begin
1066	Norman invasion
1215	Magna Carta signed
1265	Parliament founded
1534	Creation of the Church of England
1536	Union with Wales
1642–1649	Civil war leads to the deposition of the monarchy
1649–1660	Cromwell's republic
1660	Restoration of the monarchy
1688–1689	The Glorious Revolution confirms the ascendancy of Parliament
1707	Union with Scotland
1801	Legislative union with Ireland
1832	Great Reform Act
1914–1918	World War I
1918	Women over age thirty given the right to vote
1928	All women given the right to vote
1939–1945	World War II
1945	First Labour government elected
1948	Independence of India and Pakistan
1957–1968	Independence of most of Britain's African colonies
1968	Hostilities break out in Northern Ireland
1973	Britain joins the European Economic Community
1979	(May) Margaret Thatcher wins first of three elections
1982	War with Argentina over the Falklands/Malvinas
1990	(November) Thatcher resigns as leader of Conservative party and prime minister; replaced by John Major
1991	(January) British forces take part in U.S.-led attack on Iraq
1992	(April) Major leads Conservatives to fourth successive election victory
1994	Opening of Channel tunnel connecting Britain and France
1997	(May) Election of Tony Blair as prime minister ends nearly eighteen years of Conservative government; (August) Death of Diana, Princess of Wales, poses a challenge to the monarchy to reform
1998	(April) Peace agreement signed in Northern Ireland and approved by public referendum; (December) Britain joins U.S. in air attacks on Iraq
1999	(January) Creation of single European currency, the euro

BACKGROUND AND HISTORY

Few countries have a long history of evolutionary political development. Even "old world" Europe has many new political systems, such as Germany (1949), France (1958), and Spain (1975). With Britain, however, the roots of the political system are deep, and understanding the evolution of that system means briefly reviewing more than two thousand years of history.

The Romans and Their Legacy (55 B.C.–1066)

The native people of the British Isles were the Celts, ancestors of the Scots, Irish, and Welsh. When the Romans invaded in 55 B.C. and occupied what are now England and Wales, the Celts were pushed west and north, and England developed a social and political system very different from that of the rest of the British Isles—it had roads, carefully planned towns, and a thriving commercial system. The departure of the Romans at the beginning of the fifth century left behind a political vacuum into which moved several waves of invaders. By the mid-seventh century, Germanic tribes such as the Angles and the Saxons (from which come the names England and Anglo-Saxon) had colonized most of what is now England, all but destroying the remains of Roman culture.

A mission in A.D. 595 from the Pope in Rome brought Christianity to Britain, preceding a wave of Viking invasions in the eighth and ninth centuries. These invasions were followed in 1066 by the last successful invasion of Britain, by William, Duke of Normandy. This victory brought political stability and centralization to England, but the English and the Celts remained divided ethnically, culturally, and linguistically. Religious differences were added in 1534, when King Henry VIII dissolved England's ties with the Roman Catholic church and created the Church of England (the Episcopalians in the United States). The Scots today are mainly Catholic and Presbyterian, whereas the English are mainly Protestant. The broader British state took much longer to develop: The union with Wales was formalized in 1536, with Scotland in 1707, and with Ireland in 1801.

The End of Feudalism (1215–1689)

Until about eight hundred years ago, Britain—like all of Europe—was a feudal society. Sovereign power lay in the hands of the monarch, who ruled by divine right (he claimed to be answerable only to God) and governed the peasant majority through a land-owning aristocracy. The powers of monarchs and aristocrats began their long and sometimes violent decline in 1215 when King John signed the Magna Carta, a document that obliged him to agree that he should consult with his aristocrats before levying taxes, and that he could not arbitrarily arrest or seize property from his subjects.

A second step in the transfer of power was taken in 1265 with the convening of the first British parliament. Although it was unelected, met only sporadically, and was dominated by the aristocracy, monarchs came to rely on it for political support. The tensions between crown and Parliament continued, however, finally boiling over in 1642 with the outbreak of a civil war between monarchists and parliamentarians. This unrest led to the beheading in 1649 of King Charles I and the declaration of a brief republic (1649–1660) under the military dictatorship of Oliver Cromwell. When the despotic James II (1685–1688) tried to win back the divine right of monarchs, he was forced by Parliament to flee the country in the Glorious Revolution of 1688–1689, which provided the foundation for the publication in 1689 of a Bill of Rights. This document made clear the supremacy of Parliament over the monarch, required that the king's government be supported by a majority in Parliament, and made it illegal for the monarch to raise taxes or pass laws without the agreement of Parliament.

Economic Revolutions (Seventeenth–Nineteenth Centuries)

Beginning in the late 1600s, Britain underwent wide-ranging economic change, which in turn led to political and social change. New and more efficient processes for smelting iron and making steel were developed, the steam engine was invented, industry was mechanized, and business converted increasingly to large-scale enterprises. These advancements, in turn, brought about improvements in transport, which led to the growth of commerce and markets. The eighteenth century saw the expanding middle class demanding political reforms and a greater role in government.

Britain was now forged into the world's first and most powerful industrial state. By the mid-nineteenth century, it had become the "workshop of the world," producing two-thirds of the world's coal, half its steel, half its cotton goods, and virtually all of its machine tools. With monarchs showing little understanding of politics during the eighteenth century, it became common for the king's ministers (the cabinet) to meet without the king,[3] and for one of the ministers to act as a senior or "prime" minister. This arrangement was a limited form of democracy, though; Parliament was still dominated by aristocrats representing mainly rural areas, many of which had only a handful of voters, and in some of which a seat in Parliament could be bought from electors or a large landowner.

The new middle class of industrialists and entrepreneurs found this process unacceptable, and pressure for change led to the Great Reform Act of 1832. Although this law was perhaps less dramatic than its title suggests, it eliminated corrupt electoral districts, extended the vote to the wealthy and upper middle class, and further reduced aristocratic power. Additional reform acts in 1867 and 1884 further extended the vote, reduced royal powers, introduced secret voting, sparked the growth of mass-membership political parties, gave more power to the lower chamber of Parliament (the House of Commons), and created single-member parliamentary districts with roughly equal populations. The 1911 and 1949 Parliament Acts finally took most remaining significant political powers away from the aristocratic upper chamber of Parliament (the House of Lords), and women over the age of thirty were given the right to vote in 1919, and those over age eighteen in 1928.

The Imperial Era (Eighteenth Century–Early 1960s)

With its industry growing, Britain's priority was to find new markets and sources of raw materials and to build on its competitive advantage over its European rivals, particularly France. British explorers and entrepreneurs now traveled the world, staking claims to territory on every continent. Britain may have lost its thirteen American colonies in 1781, but it colonized Canada, Australia, New Zealand, parts of West Africa, most of southern and eastern Africa, many Caribbean and Pacific islands, the Asian subcontinent, and parts of southeast Asia. At its height during the late Victorian era, the British Empire included about one-quarter of the world's population.

The beginning of the end of the imperial era came with World War I, when the cream of a generation of young Britons died in one of the most brutal and mismanaged conflicts in the history of warfare. The United States and the U.S.S.R. began to emerge as economic and military powers, a transition that was finally confirmed by World War II. Britain entered the war in 1939 as the world's largest creditor nation, effectively fought alone against Nazi Germany for two years, and emerged in 1945 as one of the world's largest debtor nations. It may have been on the winning side, but its economy was devastated, its political influence was diminished, its export earnings and merchant shipping fleet were halved, and most of its colonies were agitating for independence.

Postwar Adjustment and the Welfare State (1945–1975)

Although Britain saw economic prosperity in the 1950s and 1960s, it slowly lost its preeminent position in the world. It continued to grow but found its influence relative to other countries—notably the United States, Japan, and even Germany—beginning to decline. Most notably, it began to dismantle its empire; India and Pakistan were given their independence in 1947, and over the next twenty years a steady program of decolonization continued. This process was the most obvious explanation for Britain's declining influence, but other reasons contributed as well: the cost of the war, the handicaps posed to industrial relations by deep class divisions, an educational system that was prejudiced against business as a career, low levels of mobility within the labor force, inadequate investments in industry, new plant, and research and development, and excessive government involvement in production and employment.[4]

The postwar period saw the completion of a welfare state and the shift to a managed economy. Pensions had been introduced in 1908 and national health and unemployment insurance in 1911,[5] but the welfare system was only completed after 1945, when voters wanting a new start swept a socialist Labour government into power. Labour created a national health service providing free care for everyone, and expanded welfare for the unemployed, the ill, and families with children. It also set out to keep unemployment low, and nationalized basic services such as railroads and the steel industry.

Succeeding Conservative governments agreed to follow roughly the same policies, and—whether the Conservatives or Labour were in power—British politics became driven by a consensus on the maintenance of welfare and of managing economic demand to sustain full employment. Nonetheless, the British economy continued its relative decline through the 1960s and 1970s, plagued by growing industrial unrest. In 1976, the Labour government of Harold Wilson was obliged to ask the International Monetary Fund for a loan to help offset a run on the pound and to help Britain service its debts. A new low was reached during the "winter of discontent" in 1978–1979 when public-sector workers went on strike across Britain, almost shutting the country down.

The Thatcher "Revolution"

Reflecting growing public concern about the state of the British economy, and about growing international competition, the Conservative party under the leadership of Margaret Thatcher was elected to office in 1979 and embarked on a program of wide-ranging change. Some political scientists deny that her policies amounted to a lasting revolution, or that they are even relevant to an understanding of Britain today; others take the opposite view. Wherever the truth lies, she unquestionably brought major changes both to economic policy and to the style of British government.

Thatcher was elected leader of the Conservative party in 1975, became prime minister with her first election victory in 1979, and won two more elections in 1983 and 1987 before losing the party leadership with an internal vote in November 1990. She claimed to reject the wisdom of consensus politics, argued that government was too involved in the economy, and felt that elected leaders were consulting with too many special interests (especially labor unions) before they made policy. Determined to follow her own brand of "conviction politics," Mrs. Thatcher launched an assault on socialism and labor unions and worked to create a new "enterprise culture" aimed at making British industry more competitive.

Her management style often brought her into conflict with her cabinet ministers, with her opponents being dubbed "wets" because they were too soft to administer the medicine she felt Britain needed. The most enduring element of her program was privatization, or the sale of state-owned services and industries to the private sector, a policy that has since been copied throughout Europe and as far afield as southeast Asia and Latin America. Whatever positive changes she brought to British economic culture, her Achilles heel was unemployment, which by the mid-1980s had reached a scale unseen since the 1930s.

The impact of Thatcherism on Britain is debatable. Her supporters argue that she instituted the changes needed to reverse Britain's economic decline by freeing up the marketplace, cutting the power of labor unions, reducing dependence on welfare, and promoting a stakeholder culture in which more Britons became involved in creating their own wealth and opportunities. To her detractors, she not only abused the powers of her office by taking an unusually forceful approach to governing, but she also failed to meet the needs of the underclass, allowed too many people to slip through the safety net of welfare, and widened the gap between the "haves" and the "have nots"; poverty and homelessness grew as a result of her tenure, as did the numbers of the *nouveaux riches,* and Britain became a less caring society.

Britain Today

With the relative decline in its economic and military power, Britain since World War II has shifted its focus from playing an independent global role to working more closely with its European neighbors. Many prominent British politicians—notably Winston Churchill—supported European cooperation as a means of avoiding future war, but Britain sat on the sidelines during the 1950s as Germany and France led the way.[6] It eventually joined the European Economic Community in 1973, its earlier applications vetoed by Charles de Gaulle of France. The refusal of British governments in the 1950s to involve themselves in the discussions that led to the design and launch of the Community heralded a tradition in which Britain has always been slightly out of step with its European partners, and thus has not always been able to influence the evolution of the Community to its advantage. Membership in what is now known as the European Union (EU) has brought economic integration for all of its members; EU law has superseded national law in many different areas; and growing intra-EU trade has encouraged Britain to build closer economic and political ties with its continental neighbors.

Recent years have seen great change both in the priorities and in the style of British government, and in the nature of society. This change is visible in the renewal of British cities, in the rise of a new entrepreneurial spirit that has transformed the attitudes of business and industry, and in the growth of the middle class

Recent years have seen a strengthening of the British economy, due in part to the rise of a new class of entrepreneurs prepared to take a more aggressive approach to the opportunities offered by the European Union.

and the consumer society. The average Briton is healthier, better educated, and better dressed than before, and a new spirit of liveliness and optimism is abroad, at least among the younger generations. Many people even remark (usually disparagingly, but regularly in a tone of bemusement) that Britain is being Americanized. Not only has its economy rediscovered the competitive culture that made it so strong in the nineteenth century, but many aspects of politics (notably election campaigns) have also taken on a more American character.

A new wave of changes has come as a result of the policies pursued since May 1997 by the Labour government of Tony Blair. Astonishing political analysts with the scale of its victory, the rejuvenated Labour party swept the internally

British prime minister Tony Blair has acted quickly to reform both his party and his country. After moving Labour to the political center, he introduced constitutional reforms that have given new powers to the regions, restructured Parliament, and reorganized the electoral system.

divided Conservative party out of office after eighteen years in power. Under Tony Blair, "New" Labour had abandoned many of its traditionally socialist ideas, adopted key elements of the Thatcher program, and moved closer to the center of the political spectrum. Blair has emphasized the importance of improving education, rebuilding the national healthcare system, and being tough on crime. As noted later in this chapter, however, his record in all three areas has been mixed.

Blair's government has been instrumental in bringing peace to the troubled province of Northern Ireland, where Protestant unionists who constitute a 60 percent majority want to continue to be part of the United Kingdom, whereas many Catholic nationalists want reunification with the Republic of Ireland. After nearly thirty years of strife, leading to more than thirty-five hundred deaths and much physical destruction, the two sides signed an agreement in March 1998 by which they agreed to allow the province to be governed by an elected assembly, while cross-border commissions addressed cooperation with Ireland. The primary unionist leader, David Trimble, and the main nationalist leader, John Hume, won the Nobel Peace Prize in 1998 for their efforts, but the peace remained tenuous, and a controversy over the decommissioning of terrorist weapons continued to boil as this book went to press.

Meanwhile, following referenda in 1997, regional assemblies for Scotland and Wales were established in 1999, providing the Scots and the Welsh with more control over local government issues. With public opinion in Scotland running in favor of greater self-determination and even complete independence, the establishment of these assemblies may prove to be a forerunner to fundamental change in the relationship among England, Scotland, and Wales. Whether this change will lead to the creation of a federal Britain or the breakup of Britain remains to be seen.

The Blair administration has also introduced changes to the structure of government. During 1998, a special commission was convened to look into the possibility of changing the electoral system, which as noted later in this chapter has not been entirely fair in terms of turning voter preferences into seats in

Parliament. Furthermore, the government began making major reforms to the House of Lords, the upper chamber of Parliament whose members are not elected. Another commission was created in early 1999 to look into the options regarding replacing the House of Lords with an elected chamber of some kind.

Unquestionably, as it enters the new millennium, Britain is undergoing significant political change, prompted by the wishes of a government that wants to see Britain compete more effectively on the global stage, to place more emphasis on a constructive relationship with its partners in the EU, to invest more heavily in the human capital of Britain, and to build a society that is less dependent on government. Borrowing from the emphasis placed by the Thatcher government on image (she was the first prime minister to employ an advertising agency to "sell" her party to the electorate), Blair has emphasized his opinion that Britain should be "repackaged" as a society that has deep roots in history and culture, but that is forward-looking and economically dynamic.

POLITICAL CULTURE

Tying down the political values of a society is always difficult, especially one with as long a history as Britain. Generally, though, most political scientists agree that the British are pragmatic, have faith in their political system (but not necessarily politicians), and are politically moderate, but that government is not sufficiently transparent, in the sense that the people do not have as much access as they might like to the workings of government.

Pragmatism

The British tend to keep their feet on the ground regarding their expectations of government and their aspirations for their own lives. They take a more empirical approach to problem solving than do the French or the Germans, who take a more abstract approach.[7] In other words, Britons tend to shy away from theory and to look at the practical reality of policies. In the United States, argues Vivien Hart, "the emphasis has been on what democracy is and should be, while Britain has been characterized by a more pragmatic and less urgent emphasis on what democracy is and can be."[8]

The two approaches bring out one of the basic differences between Americans and Britons: Americans tend to have an optimistic (some would say naive) view of the possibilities for democracy, and American political leaders often sprinkle their speeches with words such as "dream" and "vision," but Britons tend to be more down-to-earth and place more faith in what has been tried and tested. This is not to suggest that the British do not dream, but rather that they are less apt to overreach than are Americans or continental Europeans.

Among older Britons, realism has spilled over into pessimism, making many people gloomy about the changes they have seen. The media tend to perpetuate the problem through their morbid fascination with everything from lowered educational performance to worsening traffic problems, declining community spirit, and even the defeat of national soccer and cricket teams in international tournaments. While the older generation in the United States often talks about wanting to make life better for their children, the older generation in Britain tends to focus more on how life was simpler, better, and safer when they were younger. This perception flies in the face of reality, however, because all of the basic indicators—health care, education, economic wealth, individual freedoms, the state of the environment, and so on—suggest that life for most Britons has improved significantly in the last thirty years.

Faith in the Political System

Writing about the orientation of individuals toward political systems, Robert Dahl argues that favorable feelings indicate an "allegiant" orientation, neutral feelings reflect apathy and detachment, and unfavorable feelings reflect alienation.[9] Political alienation is often obvious in Italy and France and among disadvantaged Americans who feel cut off from government. Britain, by contrast, is marked by strong feelings of allegiance, reflected in the fact that most people still believe they can influence government.[10] These feelings are tied closely to the long history of political stability in Britain, where change has tended to be evolutionary and sequential, in contrast to the often revolutionary and violent change that has come to political systems in other European states.

Britons generally have a high degree of faith and trust in their political system, are more patriotic than their European neighbors, and are more trusting of their compatriots and of the citizens of other countries (except their traditional enemies or competitors, such as the French). Faith in the political system was long bound up in strong feelings of political and social deference, to the point where cynics occasionally described Britain as a Nanny State, or one in which the government acted like the archetypal Victorian nanny in arguing that it knew what was best for the people.

The British sense of allegiance is declining, however, because of a combination of changes in the class system, a growing respect for succeeding through effort and hard work rather than through privilege, a concern that the political system is not as responsive as it should be, and a declining respect for political leaders in the wake of several headline-making financial and political scandals in the late 1980s and early 1990s. Recent studies suggest that the British are now more willing to use unconventional forms of political participation than are the citizens of any other democracy: 56 percent are prepared to sign petitions, 35 percent to attend lawful demonstrations, 25 percent to join a boycott, 15 percent to join a wildcat strike, 13 percent to refuse to pay taxes, and 9 percent to block traffic.[11]

Social Liberalism

In contrast to many Americans, most Britons tend to take liberal positions on social and moral issues, and this view has an impact on public policy and expectations of government. For example, capital punishment was outlawed in 1965, homosexuality and abortion have been legal since 1967, British television has nothing like the degree of censorship found in the United States, and—perhaps most astonishing to Americans raised under the second amendment to the U.S. Constitution—all handguns were banned in Britain in 1998, partly because of a series of mass killings of the kind that are sadly all too common in the United States.

Part of the difference between Britain and the United States may be rooted in the relative role of religion in the two societies. About two-thirds of Britons still claim to believe in God, but, except in Northern Ireland, church attendance has steadily declined, to the point where only 13 percent of the population now attends church on Sunday, compared to 43 percent in the United States.[12] Social conservatism in the United States is often tied to religion and to the promotion of "traditional" family values. An attempt by prime minister John Major in 1993–1994 to focus on those same values in Britain won him little public sympathy or support; Britons exert considerable resistance to any attempts by government to influence the choices they make in their private lives.

A Closed Society

The British tend to be private people, hence the oft-quoted dictum that an Englishman's home is his castle. Perhaps because Britain is such a crowded country where a premium is placed on personal space, the British can often seem a little standoffish to Americans, who are used to striking up conversations with strangers at every opportunity.

This sense of privacy is reflected in the secrecy that often surrounds the functioning of government in Britain. Issues of national security are subject to secrecy in every democracy, but critics of closed government in Britain charge that state secrets are too narrowly defined in Britain, and that this secrecy has helped increase the power and reduce the accountability of the police, weakened the power of Parliament at the expense of central government, promoted the use of surveillance and reduced the right to personal privacy, and allowed the government to interfere with media freedom on issues such as Northern Ireland.

Such secrecy has become increasingly unacceptable, and there have been growing demands in recent years for greater freedom of information. Successive governments have promised more open government, and information has become more freely available, but the most significant changes may come if the Blair government follows through on its promise to introduce a Freedom of Information Act aimed at providing greater access by citizens to the government.

REPRESENTATION AND PARTICIPATION

As in most liberal democracies, regular political activity among Britons is low. Most people take some periodic, intensive interest in politics (usually in the lead-up to elections), but only about one in ten citizens has a sustained interest in politics. Voting and fundraising for parties are the most common forms of participation, but Britain also has a diverse and sophisticated interest group community, and a wide range of national and regional media that have an active influence on politics.

Social and Class Structure

Britain is predominantly Protestant, English-speaking, and white, but several important social divisions have an impact on the distribution and expression of political power.

Class   As with most societies that evolved out of feudalism and that still have an aristocracy, there is a class system in Britain, which is based less on wealth (as it is in the United States) than on social background and education. Britain has not experienced the kinds of revolutions, wars, or periods of mass immigration that have prompted social mobility in other European states, with the result that the vestiges of the class divisions created by feudalism and the industrial revolution still remain.[13] Although most will deny it, many Britons still classify each other (consciously or subconsciously) according to the kind of school they attended, their accents, their jobs, their social habits and lifestyles, the neighborhoods in which they live, and even the newspapers they read. About one-half of all Britons describe themselves as working class (skilled and unskilled manual workers) and about one-third as middle class (non-manual and managerial), and a strong correlation has traditionally existed between class and political activity. For example, the Labour party has long been seen as the champion of the working class, while the Conservative party has derived more support from the middle class.

Class identification has declined, however, as the working class has shrunk and the middle class has expanded, and as the proportion of Britons in managerial and professional occupations has grown and the number of manual workers has declined. These changes, in turn, have largely resulted from the decline of labor-intensive industries and the growth of the service sector. It is becoming increasingly difficult to make generalizations about class, and wealth and income differentials have narrowed.[14] Britain is also experiencing several phenomena with which Americans are familiar: the growth in the number of high-earning professionals and entrepreneurs, the persistence of poverty, and a growth in the income gap between the wealthy and the poor.

Region Despite the existence of a "United" Kingdom, regionalism is still alive and well in Britain. Each country has its own flag, its own culture, its own writers and artists, and its own national sports teams, and Welsh and Gaelic are still spoken by small minorities in Scotland, Wales, and Northern Ireland. Class and regional differences overlap, which is a result of the development of industry in the eighteenth and nineteenth centuries in Scotland, Wales, and the north of England. These regions saw the rise of the new industrial class of manual laborers and have since suffered the worst effects of industrial decline and economic adjustment.

Resentment against the national government in London is particularly strong in the poorer parts of Scotland and Wales, and regionalism has given rise to separatist movements, such as those championed by the Scottish National Party, which campaigns for Scottish independence. The relationship between parties and regions became particularly clear in the 1997 general election when the Conservatives lost all their parliamentary seats in Scotland, an event that gave added weight to the decision by the Labour government to create regional assemblies for Scotland and Wales in 1999.

Race This is much less of a political issue in Britain than in the United States or even Germany, but it is always present under the surface. Labor shortages in the 1950s encouraged British industry to recruit workers from the Caribbean and West Africa, and these new immigrants were joined in the late 1960s by Indians, Pakistanis, and Bangladeshis, many of whom were expelled from Uganda by the infamous Idi Amin. The growth of the non-white community led to an increase in racial tensions, and even to a warning by Conservative politician Enoch Powell in 1968 of the threats posed by immigration to the "British way of life," and the prospect of the streets running with "rivers of blood."

Many non-white immigrants initially had difficulty being integrated into British society and lived in inner-city areas, which—like those in the United States—were economically depressed. Tensions peaked during the 1980s with violent clashes between police and minorities in London and Manchester, but racism has since become a less critical issue as second- and third-generation immigrants are integrated more fully into society and the class system declines. Racial conflict has not gone away, however, as reflected in cases of racial harassment and several controversies in recent years involving the police and blacks in London, where 20 percent of the population is from an ethnic minority. Unlike several continental countries, such as Germany and France, however, right-wing racist movements in Britain are weak.

Elections and the Electoral System

The United States is a large country with several levels of government (national through local), each with their own elections. It also has a primary system, in which voters choose who will run on the ballot for the major political parties in the general election. Primaries promote democracy, but they also increase the number of elections and make elections longer and more expensive, especially at the congressional and presidential levels. All of these factors combined mean that the United States has more, longer, and more expensive elections than any other liberal democracy.

Britain is smaller than the United States, is a unitary state (meaning that all significant power is focused at the national level), and holds no primaries, so the election process is simpler, cheaper, and quicker. Parties choose who will run in their name, no party has more than one leader, and because those leaders are normally established public figures, they do

TABLE 2.2 Results of Recent General Elections in Britain

	1987		1992		1997	
	% Vote won	Seats won	% Vote won	Seats won	% Vote won	Seats won
Labour	30.8	229	34.4	271*	44.4	419*
Conservative	42.2	376*	41.9	336	31.4	165
Liberal Democrats**	22.6	22	17.8	20	17.2	46
Scottish Nationalists	1.3	3	1.6	3	2.0	6
Welsh Nationalists	0.4	3	0.7	4	0.5	4
Northern Irish parties	2.7	17	3.5	17	3.6	18
Official Unionist		9		9		10
Democratic Unionist		3		3		2
Popular Unionist		1		1		–
UK Unionist		–		–		1
Social Democratic and Labour Party		3		4		3
Sinn Fein		1		0		2
Others	0.4	0	0.8	0	0.9	1
TOTAL		650		651		659

*Includes Speaker of the House of Commons.
**SDP-Liberal Alliance in 1987.

not need the expensive and lengthy process of public familiarization demanded of candidates in U.S. elections. Whereas Americans elect five hundred thousand officeholders at many different levels, British voters are faced with just three elections.

The General Election This is the election by which members of the lower chamber of the Parliament—the House of Commons—are chosen, and it is run on the same lines as elections to the U.S. House of Representatives. The United Kingdom is divided into 659 constituencies (electoral districts) of roughly equal population size, each represented in the House of Commons by one Member of Parliament (MP). At least once every five years, all 659 seats must be contested in a general election, on a date chosen by the prime minister. Almost everyone over age eighteen can vote, and turnout is normally about 70 to 75 percent, which is considerably higher than the figures in the United States: 50 to 55 percent in presidential election years, and as low as 30 to 40 percent in non-presidential election years.

Why the differences in turnout? The most common excuse offered by American nonvoters is that they are not registered, but many are put off by the number and length of elections in this country and by the lack of party choice, whereas others believe they have little to gain from voting or are alienated by broken promises, the power of vested interests, and negative campaigns. Whether low voter turnout in the United States is a cause or an effect of declining faith in elected officials and negative campaigning is debatable.

Election campaigns in the United States can last several months, whereas British election campaigns normally last just three to four weeks, and people make a straight choice among the candidates from the different parties standing in their district. The choices are made easier by the fact that parties have more ideological consistency and that stronger party identification exists among voters, who tend to vote more for parties than for individuals. The differences in emphasis are visible on campaign posters and bumper stickers; in Britain, the name of the party dominates, whereas the name of the candidate dominates in the United States.

European Elections As a member of the EU, Britain has the right every five years to elect 87 British representatives to the 626-member European Parliament in Strasbourg, France. Candidates are fielded by the same parties that contest general elections. Direct elections to the European Parliament have been held only since 1979, the parliament has limited powers, and many British voters have mixed opinions on the EU, so turnout at European elections in Britain is the lowest in the EU: about 36 percent (but an all-time low of 24 percent in 1999). At the June 1999 elections, Labour won thirty of the British seats and the Conservatives won thirty-seven.

Local Government Elections Because Britain is a unitary state, and because local authorities have limited power, local elections tend to be overlooked by voters. Members are elected to district, county, city, and town councils on a fixed four-year cycle, but voters usually make their choices on the basis of national issues and the performance of the national government and vote along party lines. Local government elections are often used as a measure of the popularity of the national government; for example, John Major decided not to call a new general election in the summer of 1991 following a poor showing by his party in local government elections in May. He waited instead until 1992, and won. Unlike the United States, where city mayors are elected officials, British mayors—with the exception of the mayor of London—hold honorary positions with no political power. Voter turnout at the local level rarely exceeds 40 percent, but this is changing with elections to the new regional assemblies; turnout for the Scottish and Welsh Assembly elections in 1999 was 58 percent and 46 percent, respectively.

The British electoral system may be quick and cheap, but it is not always fair. Like the United States, Britain uses the winner-take-all system for general elections. Candidates for Parliament run in single-member districts and win on a simple plurality, meaning that the individual who wins the most votes wins the seat, whether or not he or she has a majority. At the national level, this system favors political parties that have concentrated blocks of support around the country and a relatively large number of safe seats (seats that their party is almost sure to win); however, this system works against the interests of parties that have more thinly spread nationwide support because they often lack the numbers needed in any one district to defeat opponents whose parties have strong local support. During 1998, the Blair government began investigating the possibility of reforming the electoral system, replacing the winner-take-all method with a form of proportional representation (PR) under which parties contesting elections would receive a number of seats in Parliament in proportion to their share of the vote. PR was used for elections to the European Parliament in 1999, and in combination with winner-take-all for Scottish and Welsh Assembly elections the same year.

Political Parties

American voters have relatively little party choice at elections, faced as they are with the moderately conservative Republicans, the moderately liberal Democrats, and smaller parties that rarely win seats. This country has traditionally disliked faction, which is why so many shades of opinion exist within the Republicans and Democrats, why the parties are so "flexible," and why many voters often split their tickets.

Parties in Britain (and in the rest of Western Europe) play a very different role in politics: There are many more of them, they cover a broader range of political ideologies, and they have stronger internal organization. Voters also have greater loyalty to parties, which they use to provide the reference points for their political opinions and for the choices they make at elections.

Although more than 150 parties contested the 1997 general election, and 10 won seats in Parliament, Britain since World War II has effectively been a two-party system dominated by Labour and the Conservatives, which between them usually take about 75 percent of the vote and about 90 percent of the seats in Parliament. Considerable policy fluctuation occurs within the two parties because—like U.S. parties—they are constantly maneuvering to win the same middle ground of the electorate while also trying to distinguish themselves from each other. This fluctuation makes it difficult always to find distinct ideologies or coherent sets of principles, and both major parties have significant factions within their ranks.

Labour The Labour party was founded in 1900, first came to prominence in the 1920s, but only won outright power for the first time in 1945. It immediately set about building a welfare state and a managed economy, nationalizing key industries, and creating a national health service, a social security system, and a subsidized education system. It lost power in 1951, but returned in 1964 and again in 1974 under the leadership of Harold Wilson. It went into opposition in 1979, losing four straight general elections and undergoing a severe crisis of confidence before finally regaining power in 1997 under the leadership of Tony Blair.

Labour's failures in the 1980s were ascribed to a combination of the political shrewdness of Conservative prime minister Margaret Thatcher, a string of "unelectable" party leaders, and the growing unpopularity of many of its more traditional left-wing socialist policies, including state ownership of key industries, support of labor unions, and redistributing wealth through taxation. The extent of its internal problems was emphasized in 1981 when a group of moderate Labourites broke away to form the Social Democratic Party (SDP). This group merged with the Liberal party in 1988 after having helped compel Labour to rethink and moderate its policies. The shift in Labour's philosophy was symbolized by its decision to replace its red flag symbol with a red rose, which sent a less militant and threatening message to voters.

Tony Blair (b.1953) was elected party leader in May 1994 and immediately made it clear that he was opposed to business as usual. He was not the typical Labour leader, coming from a strongly middle class background, raised on Christian Socialist principles, and reading law at Oxford University. Just forty-one years of age when he took over the helm of the party, he moved quickly to "modernize" the party and to distance it from its more radical ideas by adopting what he called a new "left-of-center agenda." One of his first priorities was to abandon the controversial Clause Four of the Labour Party constitution, which pledged "common ownership of the means of production, distribution and exchange"; in other words, Labour gave up its promise to undo privatization, one of the most successful of Margaret Thatcher's policies. Clause Four was abandoned in 1996, and Labour has since stood for more overtly free-market economic policies.

Like the Clinton administration, "New" Labour also adopted many other policies usually associated with the middle ground of politics, encroaching into traditionally conservative territory. For example, the Blair government has embraced the market economy, opposed traditional socialist ideas of taxing and spending, developed a closer relationship with business, reduced the influence of labor unions in the party, committed itself to developing a balanced budget, instituted a more pro-European policy (Labour was for many years hostile to the idea of European integration), and moved Labour toward a more pro-NATO and pro-U.S. stance in foreign policy. Blair has also counted improved education, reform of the national healthcare system, a tough position on crime, and constitutional reform among his priorities. Such policies are collectively part of what has become known as the "Third Way" in politics, a notion that has never been clearly defined but is taken to mean "capitalism with a conscience" or "market socialism." Several other European leaders—notably Gerhard Schroeder in Germany and Lionel Jospin in France—were also identified with this philosophy.

The Labour victory in May 1997 was astonishing in almost every sense. Labour was swept back into office with a 179-seat majority, defeating the Conservatives in many of their safe seats. At forty-four years old, Tony Blair became the third youngest prime minister in British history and the youngest since 1821. He was Britain's first truly post-imperial prime minister and the first born after World War II. The defeat of the Conservatives symbolized a widely felt need among Britons for change and a concern that Conservatives had paid too little attention to social problems. Blair quickly became the most popular prime minister since opinion polling began in the 1930s, and even as late as January 1999, Labour still had an approval rating of 55 percent compared to 29 percent for the deeply troubled Conservatives. A poll in *The Sunday Times* of London in February 1999 revealed that—nearly two years into his term in office—he was also considered the moral and spiritual leader of Britain, prompting the newspaper to quip that Blair could now apparently walk on water. By mid-2000, however, it was clear that the honeymoon was over; Blair was accused by his critics of an excessive centralization of control over the party, and his policies on Europe, the economy, and Northern Ireland had lost some of their luster.

The Conservatives The origins of the Conservatives (also known as the Tories) date back to the late seventeenth century. They have held power for thirty-six of the fifty-five years since the end of World War II, but despite the number of their postwar election victories, they have never won more than 42 to 44 percent of the national vote.

Similar to U.S. Republicans, the Conservatives are a pro-business, anti-regulation, moderate party, with many shades of opinion: the Tory wing emphasizes social discipline, authority, continuity, and morals, whereas the more moderate Whig tendency emphasizes economics, the creation of wealth, and efficient economic organization. Until 1975, when Margaret Thatcher became party leader, Conservative policies changed little, irrespective of the leader. Thatcher broke with tradition, and for more than a decade the party developed policies that reflected her values. She supported monetarist economic ideas of the kind favored by Ronald Reagan (such as controls on government spending, reducing the role of government in the marketplace, low taxation, and a free market), promoted private enterprise and private ownership, believed in a strong global role for Britain and close Anglo-American relations, and was hostile to many aspects of European integration.

Although the Conservatives fought the 1997 election against the background of a strong economy, they faced an electorate that was both ready for a change and tired of internal party squabbles. Prime Minister John Major was unable to pull the party together; it went into the election twenty percentage points behind Labour in opinion polls; and it sustained its worst election defeat since 1832. Conservative representation in the House of Commons was halved, the party lost all of its seats in Scotland and Wales, and even senior members of the cabinet (including several future contenders for the leadership of the party) lost their seats.

Debates have since raged concerning the reasons behind the defeat.[15] Britain at the time had rates of unemployment and inflation that were among the lowest in Europe (6 percent and 3 percent, respectively). It was also the party of Margaret Thatcher, whose policies of privatization and undermining the powers of labor unions had been popular and effective. The Conservatives had, however, become deeply divided (particularly over the issue of Europe), the party had been hurt by several financial scandals involving prominent backbenchers (in what became known as the "sleaze" factor), a lot of tactical voting occurred in the election (Labour and Liberal Democratic supporters voted for the other party in districts where one of them was in a strong position to challenge the incumbent Conservative[16]), and a new generation of young people who had known nothing but Conservative government was voting for the first time; 52 percent of people under twenty-five years old voted Labour, up from 35 percent in 1992. Many analysts also argued that the vote was ultimately less for Labour than against the Conservatives.

Following his defeat, John Major gracefully resigned as party leader and was replaced by William Hague (b. 1961), who has had the difficult task of pulling the Conservatives back together again and making them a true party of opposition. The task has been a hard one, however, given the substantial majority enjoyed by Labour and the popularity of Tony Blair and the Labour government. As this book went to press, the Conservatives were in a state of crisis,[17] and most commentators confidently expected Labour to win the next election (due by May 2002), but with a reduced majority.

Liberal Democrats A small moderate center party, the Liberal Democrats were created in 1988 when an SDP splinter group joined forces with the Liberal party, one of the oldest parties in Britain and for many years the major opposition to the Conservatives. For a while in the 1980s, an SDP-Liberal Alliance seemed poised to take over from Labour as the major opposition party. The Liberal Democrats contested their first general election in April 1992, winning nearly 18 percent of the vote and twenty seats. By 1993 there was talk (once again) of the Liberal Democrats being poised on the brink of a breakthrough. In the 1997 election they more than doubled their representation in Parliament, winning forty-six seats, the best result for a third party since the 1920s. Although the Liberal Democrat party is still very small, new attention is now being paid to it by political analysts, especially considering that its support and cooperation have been actively encouraged by the Blair government. The Liberal Democrats have been led since 1999 by Charles Kennedy (b. 1959).

Other Parties Other smaller parties in Britain include the Scottish Nationalists (who have yet to win back the support they enjoyed in the 1970s when the extent of Scotland's oil and natural gas resources was first discovered), the Welsh nationalist party Plaid Cymru, and at least six parties that are active only in Northern Ireland. Candidates for the larger parties must go through a rigorous selection procedure, but British law allows almost anyone to stand for Parliament under almost any guise, even from prison. The only formal requirement is the payment of a deposit of five hundred pounds (about eight hundred dollars), which is returned if the candidate wins more than 5 percent of the vote. Candidates who fail to cross the 5 percent barrier are described as having "lost their deposit," which is the most embarrassing possible result in an election.

Interest Groups

As with most modern liberal democracies, interest groups play a key political role in Britain. Most British groups are either sectional (existing mainly to represent and provide services to their members; for example, labor unions and professional organizations) or promotional (existing mainly to promote a particular cause). Literally thousands of interest groups operate in Britain, ranging from multi-million-member charities to groups with very limited objectives. As voters have become disillusioned with political parties in recent years, the memberships of interest groups have grown; more than one-half the adult population is now a member of at least one group, and many people belong to multiple groups.[18]

Interest group activity has increased significantly in recent decades as groups have become more professional and their methods have diversified. Where groups once focused their efforts on ministers and bureaucrats, they have worked increasingly to mobilize public opinion and have intensified their lobbying of Parliament (the term "to lobby" traces its roots to the way constituents would gather in the lobby of the Houses of Parliament to talk to their representatives). The EU has provided new channels for lobbying, notably giving groups access to the judicial review process through the European Court of Justice.

As in the United States, interest group activity in Britain occasionally builds to broader movements aimed at bringing political, economic, or social reform. Two particularly notable movements have transpired in Britain in recent years.

The Labor Movement Britain has about three hundred labor unions, the largest of which are affiliated to the Trades Union Congress (TUC) (roughly equivalent to the AFL-CIO). Unions were for a long time closely affiliated with the Labour party, having a 40 percent share in the electoral college that elected the leader of the Labour party and sponsoring about 40 percent of Labour candidates in general elections. The TUC also had arrangements with Labour governments where it agreed not to make large wage claims or to go on strike, in return for concessions. By the early 1970s, unions had so much power that a general strike was called, which ultimately obliged Edward Heath's Conservative government to call a general election, which it lost.

The failure of the Labour governments of Harold Wilson (1974–1976) and James Callaghan (1976–1979) to reach agreements with the unions on prices and wages led to another near-general strike in 1979. This event made Labour so unpopular that it lost the 1979 election, ushering in a Thatcher government bent on reducing union power. Laws were passed requiring union leaders to ballot their members before taking strike action, and unemployment reduced union membership from thirteen million to ten million in the 1980s.[19] In addition to a lengthy and divisive strike by coal miners in the mid-1980s (see the Policies and Policymaking section), print and journalists' unions also went on strike, but all three groups failed in meeting their goals. In recent years, unions have lost much of their support and many of their members, and their political influence has declined further as New Labour has weakened union influence on its policies.

Business Groups If the TUC represents workers, then employers are represented by the Confederation of British Industry (CBI). Financial institutions are politically important, mainly because of the influence of the financial district of the City of London (the City), which is the biggest market in the world for foreign exchange, gold, international insurance, and international commodities, and which has the world's third-largest stock market (after New York and Tokyo) when measured by value. Although City interests are kept separate from those of industry, and although no formal links exist between business and the Conservative party (such as those that once existed between unions and the Labour party), many senior managers in the City and at Britain's larger companies had significant influence within the Conservative party during the Major and Thatcher years. These people have not been ignored by the Blair government, which has made a point of cultivating contacts with business part of its philosophy of increasing productivity and promoting British economic influence in the EU.

The Media

As in most democracies, Britons tend to derive most of their information about politics from the mass media. They generally have a high level of political literacy and interest in national and international affairs, a situation that is sustained by one of the most active and well-respected mass media establishments in the world, catering to almost every taste and political persuasion. Unlike the United States, where most media tend to be local, Britain—like all European countries—has mainly national or regional media. These not only create an atmosphere in which people are interested less in local politics than in national or international politics, but the more serious sources also tend to provide much more sophisticated analysis of politics than is the case in the United States (with the exception of big city newspapers, key weekly or monthly journals, and public radio and television).

Until the late 1980s, British television viewers had access to just four terrestrial channels: two government-owned and commercial-free channels run by the British Broadcasting Corporation (BBC) and two independent commercial channels (ITV and Channel Four). (A new commercial channel—Channel 5—was created in 1993.) All stations are editorially independent, are required to give equal air time to the major political parties, and often become involved in political controversy. Users pay an annual license fee, which goes to supporting BBC TV and five national BBC radio channels. Despite being government-owned, the BBC has a reputation for being an impartial and dependable source of news both inside and outside Britain. Audience shares for the five channels have been greatly reduced in recent years with the spread of satellite television, offering access to domestic programming (put out mainly by Sky, Carlton, and Granada TV) and even to British versions of U.S. networks, such as Discovery, Nickelodeon, and the Disney Channel.

With the exception of major regional dailies (particularly those in Scotland), most newspapers are national morning papers, which between them are read by about 80 percent of the population. At least half a dozen serious papers of comment include *The Times, The Guardian,* and *The Independent,* and mass-circulation tabloids include *The Sun* (the biggest-selling newspaper in the world) and *The Daily Mirror.* The latter tend to be blatantly partisan and to present a simplified and exaggerated picture of politics; their popularity has also led to concerns that they allow their owners too much political influence. Particular criticism has been directed at Rupert Murdoch, whose News International Corporation owns Sky Television, three national daily newspapers, and two national Sunday newspapers. Murdoch is an Australian with U.S. citizenship whose papers tend to take strongly anti-EU and pro-Conservative editorial positions.

POLITICAL SYSTEM

The key to understanding the structure of the British political system is to appreciate that changes over the centuries have left many old institutions and traditions in place, while real political power has shifted to newer institutions. For example, the British monarch is head of state, and the prime minister (in theory) can act only in the name of the monarch. In fact, the monarch has only symbolic power, real executive power lies with the prime minister, and only Parliament has the right to pass, amend, or abolish laws (although it has lost some of those powers since 1973 to the EU).

In his classic commentary on the British political system—*The English Constitution,* published in 1867—constitutional scholar Walter Bagehot described British political institutions as being either "dignified" or "efficient."

The dignified elements, such as the monarchy and the House of Lords, are symbolic and decorative, "excite and preserve the reverence of the population," and have little political power. The efficient elements, such as the House of Commons, the cabinet, and the office of prime minister, are the parts with real political power, and with which Britain "works and rules."[20]

The Constitution

Americans have lived since 1790 with a written constitution in which the powers of government and the rights of the governed are outlined. Although most democracies have similar documents, constitutions do not by definition have to be written; they can also be abstract, consisting of laws and norms that have the same function as a single written document. Britain has taken the latter course because it has no written constitution in the sense that it has a single, codified document. Instead, it is governed on the basis of constitutional principles that come from five major sources.[21]

1. Common law, or the judgments handed down over time by British courts. Among the more significant are those dealing with freedom of expression and the sovereignty of Parliament (meaning that Parliament has the ultimate power and right to make or abolish any law it wishes).
2. Statute law, or Acts of Parliament that override common law and have the effect of constitutional law. Examples of statute law include Acts that have determined how elections must be held and that outline the relative powers of the two houses of Parliament.
3. European law. As a member of the EU, Britain is subject to laws adopted by the EU, which override British laws where the two conflict.
4. Traditions and conventions that do not have the force of law but that have been followed for so long that they are regarded as binding. For example, no laws say that the prime minister and cabinet should come out of the majority party in Parliament; it has simply become a tradition.
5. Commentaries written by constitutional authorities, such as Walter Bagehot, Albert Venn Dicey (author of *The Law of the Constitution,* published in 1885), and Vernon Bogdanor.

The U.S. Constitution consists of formal rules that spell out how government works, and the Supreme Court has the power to interpret and build on those rules. By contrast, and with typical British pragmatism, the rules of government in Britain are determined "on the basis of what has proved to work rather than on abstract first principles."[22] Although this approach allows the rules to be changed easily and flexibly, the system works only if general agreement exists on what government can and cannot do, and if elected officials "behave." Supporters argue that the absence of a codified constitution allows for greater flexibility, but concerns have been expressed in recent years that power is too centralized, that too much potential exists for the abuse of powers by a strong prime minister, that general elections produce skewed results, and that membership in the EU has changed the nature of government. The result has been growing support for a written constitution, which is now favored—according to opinion polls—by about 80 percent of Britons.

The absence of a single written document has combined with the importance of statute law to give the British government powers that would probably seem almost authoritarian to Americans. This became obvious in 1997–1999 when the Blair government made several key changes to the structure of government that probably would not be possible in the United States without constitutional amendments. These changes included the creation of regional assemblies in Northern

Ireland, Scotland, and Wales, and proposals to change the electoral system and to reform the House of Lords (see following section). The government has also discussed the introduction of a Bill of Rights that could be overridden by Parliament (this would grow out of the enactment into law of the European Convention on Human Rights, which Britain ratified in 1951). At the same time, the Blair government has begun to make greater use of the referendum as a means of putting major issues to a public vote; the creation of regional assemblies were put to referenda, and the government has promised to put the issue of joining the European single currency, the euro, to a vote after the next election.

Despite the flexibility of this arrangement, and although much of what the British constitution says is a matter of interpretation, the system has order and structure, based on five core principles: (1) Britain is a unitary state, (2) it is a constitutional monarchy, (3) Parliament is sovereign, (4) the rule of law is fundamental (everyone is equally subject to the same body of laws), and (5) Britain is a member of the EU.

The Monarchy

Except for a brief spell between 1649 and 1660 when a republic was proclaimed, Britain has been a monarchy since the tenth century. Kings and queens once had a virtual monopoly on political power, but they began giving it up with the Magna Carta, and the monarchy has moved from being an efficient institution to a dignified one. The British monarch is a ceremonial head of state and is expected to be no more than a neutral symbol of the history, the stability, the traditions, and the national identity of Britain. It is often said that the monarch reigns but does not rule. The present monarch—Queen Elizabeth II—is limited to the following so-called reserve powers:

- She has (wrote Bagehot) the right "to be consulted, the right to encourage, and the

Since succeeding to the throne in 1952, Queen Elizabeth II has seen considerable changes both in Britain's place in the world, and in the status of her own job. Pressures on the monarchy have been aimed at making it more relevant, modern, and accessible.

right to warn."[23] She meets with the prime minister at confidential weekly meetings and has access to secret government documents.

- She has the right to dissolve Parliament and call new elections, although in practice she does this only at the request of the prime minister.

- At the State Opening of Parliament, she gives an address in which she outlines the government's program; however, the address is written by the government, and the Queen simply reads it aloud. She must also give the Royal Assent to every piece of new legislation, but this is a formality; the last time a monarch vetoed a piece of legislation was in 1707, and the last time a ruler dismissed a government was in 1834.[24]

- The only time she might be able to make a political decision is if, after an election, no one party has an absolute majority. On the advice of the outgoing prime minister, she can then name the person she thinks is most likely in practical terms to be able to form a government. Queen Elizabeth has had to do this three times since she came to the throne in 1952.

- Above all, the Queen is "a visible symbol of unity."[25] As the symbol of supreme executive authority, she serves as a substitute for the state. The Queen is Commander-in-Chief, many public duties are carried out in her name, and British postage stamps, coins, and banknotes bear the Queen's image instead of the name of the country. As head of the Commonwealth (see the Policies and Policymaking section), the Queen also symbolizes Britain's relationship with its former colonies.

For centuries, the monarchy was imbued with an aura of mystery, and little was publicly known about its inner workings; in the words of Walter Bagehot, it was important not to "let in daylight upon magic." This mystery has changed in the last fifteen to twenty years as the private lives of Prince Charles (heir to the throne), Prince Andrew, and their ex-wives and girlfriends have become the focus of intense media coverage. Prince Charles has also caused controversy by being more willing than previous royal heirs to comment on public issues such as the state of British architecture, education, and the environment.

Although Queen Elizabeth—as an individual—is popular, opinion polls have revealed that public support for the monarchy has slipped since the mid-1980s from about 85 to 90 percent to about 70 to 75 percent. The death of Princess Diana, former wife of Prince Charles, in August 1997, sparked a fundamental reappraisal aimed at making the monarchy more relevant to public life in Britain. The once unthinkable—that a divorced heir to the throne could become king—has now been accepted, and attempts have been made to end the ban on the heir marrying a Catholic, to abandon the rule that a first-born daughter should be overtaken in the line of succession by a younger brother, and to expect the monarch to be the head of the Church of England. One of the great strengths of the British monarchy—and the major reason why it has lasted so long—is that it has been more adaptable than many of its continental European counterparts. The changes it now faces are just the latest in a long series of adjustments it has had to make to keep up with the times.

The Executive: Prime Minister and Cabinet

The monarch may be the head of state, but government in practice is headed by the prime minister, who provides policy leadership and oversees the implementation of the law through a cabinet of senior ministers; these are clear examples of efficient institutions. Unlike the situation in the United States, there is no clear separation of executive and legislative powers in Britain. By definition, the prime minister is the leader of the political party or coalition with the most seats in the House of Commons. Beyond that, the office of prime minister is defined mainly by conventions that have evolved over the past 250 years.

Although the prime minister is technically appointed by the monarch, the Queen in practice simply confirms the head of the party in the best position to form and lead a government. As long as prime ministers can keep the support of their party in Parliament, they have considerable power over deciding which laws will be passed and over running the country. In fact, within the scope of their jobs, prime ministers have much more power than presidents of the United States, whose decisions are constantly checked and balanced. Prime ministers are not autocrats, however, and their power is very much based on keeping the support of their party (see following section on the House of Commons).

The prime minister is the head of government and as such is responsible for setting the national political agenda, overseeing the military, appointing ambassadors, managing crises, leading his or her party, and representing Britain overseas; however, the core powers of the prime minister rest on two foundations:

1. The power to call elections to the House of Commons. These elections must be held at least once every five years, and prime ministers usually call them when the timing is best for their party. Alternatively (and rarely), they may have to call an election because they have lost a parliamentary vote or the support of their party.
2. The power of appointment. As well as being party leader, the prime minister decides on the size of the cabinet, calls and chairs cabinet meetings, alters the balance of government by appointing and removing members of the cabinet and all other senior government officials (about one hundred people in all), regularly reshuffles his or her cabinet (bringing in new members and either removing existing members or moving them to new posts), and can even reorganize government departments. About the only real limits on the prime minister's decisions in this respect are public opinion and political reality. By contrast, cabinet appointments and the reorganization of departments in the United States need Senate approval.

What kind of people become prime minister? Unlike U.S. presidents, several of whom in recent years have been state governors, British prime ministers are normally seasoned national politicians who have worked their way up through the ranks of their party and Parliament. They must be MPs, and they usually serve a lengthy apprenticeship before winning the leadership of their parties; John Major and Tony Blair moved up the hierarchy relatively quickly, serving as MPs for eleven years and fourteen years, respectively, before becoming prime ministers. Party leaders do not become prime ministers as a result of a national vote but because they happen to be the leader of the party that wins the most seats in the House of Commons. Like all other members of the House, they represent a particular district and must stand for reelection at the same time as all other MPs. Tony Blair represents the district of Sedgefield in northern England; if he were to lose his seat at an election, he could not be prime minister.

Just as the nature of the office of the presidency in the United States is affected by the personality of the incumbent, so too, different prime ministers bring different styles to the job.[26] Margaret Thatcher was notable for her forcefulness and for stretching the powers of the office almost to their limit. She was known to appoint weak ministers to the cabinet who could be easily controlled, and she reduced the number of cabinet meetings, publicly criticized some of her ministers, and fired twelve ministers in eleven years. By contrast, John Major made more use of his cabinet, emphasized collegiality and consensus, intervened less in the affairs of government departments, and allowed a greater variety of opinion in the cabinet.

Tony Blair has already developed a reputation for imposing strong discipline on his party, driven by his agenda of changing its ideological tilt. He has delegated discretion to strong ministers prepared to follow the government line, emphasized collegiality in the cabinet, and worked to identify himself in the public mind with popularist images, including his personal role in planning Britain's millennium celebrations, and his invitations

TABLE 2.3 Postwar Prime Ministers in Britain

Dates		Prime Minister	Governing Party
July	1945	Clement Attlee	Labour
February	1950	Clement Attlee	Labour
October	1951	Winston Churchill	Conservative
May	1955	Anthony Eden	Conservative
January	1957*	Harold Macmillan	Conservative
October	1959	Harold Macmillan	Conservative
October	1963*	Alec Douglas-Home	Conservative
October	1964	Harold Wilson	Labour
March	1966	Harold Wilson	Labour
June	1970	Edward Heath	Conservative
February	1974	Harold Wilson	Labour
October	1974	Harold Wilson	Labour
April	1976*	James Callaghan	Labour
May	1979	Margaret Thatcher	Conservative
June	1983	Margaret Thatcher	Conservative
June	1987	Margaret Thatcher	Conservative
November	1990*	John Major	Conservative
April	1992	John Major	Conservative
May	1997	Tony Blair	Labour

*In these years, leadership of the governing party changed—through health, resignation, or loss of political support—without a general election being held.

to 10 Downing Street—the London home of the prime minister—of celebrities involved in the arts.

The prime minister governs with the help of a cabinet, which, as in the United States, consists of all of the heads of senior government departments (such as the foreign secretary and the defense secretary), numbering about twenty to twenty-four in all. In the United States, cabinet members cannot be members of Congress, and cabinet experience is rarely a launchpad for a presidential bid. In Britain, by contrast, the cabinet is always appointed from within Parliament and is a critical testing ground for anyone with aspirations to becoming prime minister.

Whereas the U.S. cabinet is essentially a presidential advisory committee, the British cabinet is an important part of the policymaking structure of government: between them, the prime minister and cabinet constitute Her Majesty's Government. Key decisions may be made in smaller "inner cabinets," but the cabinet as a whole provides a base upon which to build those decisions. Prime ministers are technically no more than "first among equals" *(primus inter pares)*, but their powers of appointment mean that loyalty to the leader is an essential prerequisite for a cabinet position, and they have the authority to set the cabinet agenda. The cabinet has been described as the buckle that fastens the legislative and executive arms of the government and as the board of management of British government.[27]

The tenure of cabinet members is underpinned by the principle of collective responsibility. Once they have taken a policy decision, all cabinet members are expected to support it in public regardless of their personal feelings and to take equal and joint responsibility for the success or failure of the policy. If they cannot do this, then they must either resign or—more rarely—be fired. As noted previously, the manner in which cabinet decisions are taken depends on the management style of the prime minister. Margaret Thatcher led from the front, John Major was more consultative and collegial, and the Blair cabinet has so far followed the agenda set by the prime minister.[28] Prime ministers are not dictators, however, and cannot always rely on the unanimous support of the cabinet; even Thatcher regularly faced opposition from some of her more daring cabinet colleagues.

The Legislature: Parliament

The Houses of Parliament are situated in the district of Westminster in central London; hence, the British parliamentary system is called the Westminster model. This model dates back more than seven hundred years and has been adopted (wholly or in part) by virtually every other liberal democracy. The United States Congress copied the bicameral structure, the offices of Speaker of the House and party whips, the single-member district electoral system, and the basic legislative process—the introduction of a bill, assessment by special committees, floor debate, and final vote (repeated in both chambers).

Parliament is where laws are introduced, discussed, and either rejected or accepted, and where existing laws are amended or abolished. It may seem powerful, but because a prime minister with a good majority can normally count on the loyalty of party MPs, Parliament usually spends most of its time debating or confirming the program of the government and has much less power in relative terms than the U.S. Congress. The British Parliament has two chambers.

House of Lords The so-called upper house, the Lords recalls the days when Britain was ruled by aristocrats and is a prime example of a dignified institution. Until 1999, two-thirds of the members of the chamber were hereditary aristocrats; responding to growing calls for a reform of the Lords, and fulfilling an electoral pledge, the Blair administration removed the right of those with hereditary titles to sit in the Lords, which now consists of three groups of people:

1. The two archbishops and twenty-four bishops of the Church of England.
2. The twenty-one law lords, who are judges nominated to the House, and who function as the supreme court of appeal. They made headline news around the world in 1998 when they upheld the decision of the lower courts to detain the former Chilean dictator Augusto Pinochet during a visit to Britain. He was detained at the request of the Spanish government, which wanted to try him for crimes against Spanish citizens living in Chile. (He was later allowed to return to Chile.)
3. Life peers. These are mainly people who have been in public service and as a reward are given an honorary title for life by the Queen on the recommendation of the prime minister. All former prime ministers are automatically offered a peerage, so Margaret Thatcher now sits in the Lords as Lady Thatcher. Other people prominent in public life—such as actors, musicians, and entrepreneurs—may also be given a peerage. Many life peerages are political rewards, where favors are returned or where peerages are given to build party numbers in the Lords. Most peers are members of one of the major parties, but about one-third of them are "crossbench" peers or independents.

Because it is not elected, the Lords is unrepresentative and undemocratic, but it has little real power. About two to four of its members are usually appointed to the cabinet, it has its own special committees, and every parliamentary bill must go through the same stages in the Lords as it does in the Commons. The Lords can introduce, revise, or delay legislation, but it has little influence over laws on taxation and spending, and most of its decisions can be overruled by the Commons. The Lords does have its uses, though: it has more time to

The Houses of Parliament, on the banks of the Thames in the Westminster district of central London. Once at the heart of the British political system, it has seen its powers reduced in recent years as those of the European Union and Britain's regions have grown.

debate issues than the Commons, it can force concessions from the Commons, and because its members do not have to worry about reelection, they often debate controversial issues, such as the introduction of a Bill of Rights. The Lords is also a useful point of access for lobbyists and interest groups. A commission was appointed in 1999 to look into a new role and structure for the House of Lords.

House of Commons This is the more powerful chamber of Parliament and an example of an efficient institution. It consists of 659 MPs elected by direct universal vote from single-member districts. Debates are presided over by a Speaker, who is elected by the House from among its members, usually comes from the majority party, and is usually someone well respected and non-partisan. The last Speaker, Betty Boothroyd, was unusual in at least two respects: she was the first woman appointed to the job, and she came not from the governing Conservatives, but from the Labour party when it was still in opposition in 1992. Unlike the Speaker in the U.S. House of Representatives, who generally acts as the partisan leader of his party, the British Speaker is more of a chairperson and arbiter who keeps order and maintains the flow of business in the House (Fig. 2-1).

To encourage debate, the chamber of the House has been deliberately kept small, with benches rather than seats. The governing party sits on one side, with the prime minister and senior ministers on the front bench. MPs without government office, or with only junior office, sit behind the front bench and are known collectively as "backbenchers." The next biggest party in Parliament sits across from the governing party. Its leader sits directly opposite the prime minister, beside a shadow cabinet of opposition MPs responsible for keeping up with, and challenging, their counterparts on the government front bench. The leaders of the opposition and the shadow cabinet are fully recognized and salaried positions. If the opposition wins a majority in an election and becomes the government, the leader of the opposition would normally become prime minister, and the shadow cabinet would become the real cabinet. In other words, the shadow cabinet is a government in waiting.

Anyone who has seen the Commons in action wonders how it ever achieves anything. As *The Economist* once put it, MPs "snigger and smirk. They sneer and jeer. They murmur and yawn. They gossip salaciously in the bars. They honk and cackle when the Prime Minister or his opposite number is trying to talk. They are like unruly school-children, egged on by the frisson of a chance of being spanked by Madam Speaker but knowing they will usually get away with naughtiness." In fact, very little of the real work of Parliament actually takes place in the chamber of the Commons, where eloquence often predominates over substance. Like the chamber of the U.S. House of Representatives, it is normally quiet and sparsely attended, except during particularly controversial debates or Prime Minister's Question Time, a half-hour session that is held each week during which MPs can ask the prime minister for information on government policy. Most of the real work is done in the committees of Parliament, where specialists go over the details of bills and invite outside experts to give testimony.

At the same time, however, backbench support is critical to the power and influence of the two major parties. Party discipline is much tighter than in the U.S. Congress, where

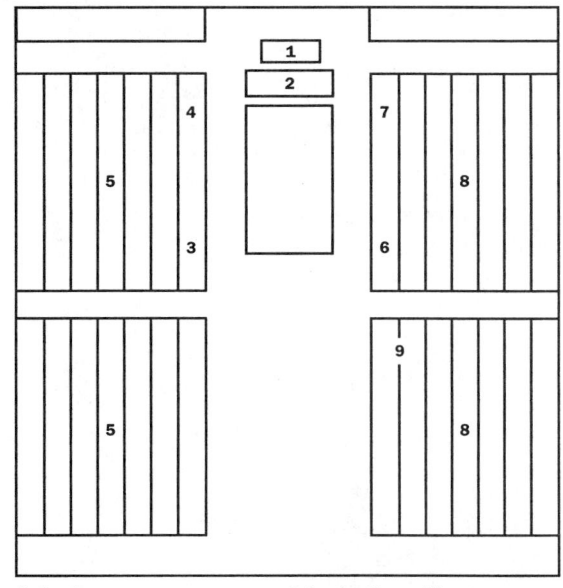

FIGURE 2.1 The House of Commons

Floor plan of the House of Commons.

1. Speaker
2. Clerks
3. Prime minister
4. Cabinet
5. Government party backbenchers
6. Leader of opposition
7. Shadow cabinet
8. Main opposition party backbenchers
9. MPs of other opposition parties

Democrats often vote with Republicans and vice versa. Party loyalty is the expected standard in the British system, but rumbles of discontent are normal, and party revolts have led to seven of the eleven Conservative leaders since 1900 being unseated by a vote within their own party. The last upset happened in November 1990, when Margaret Thatcher lost the annual contest for the leadership of her party. Many Conservative MPs felt she could not win another election, and she was replaced as party leader—and prime minister—by John Major. He sought his own mandate when he called a general election in 1992.

A breakdown of party cohesion—usually dubbed a "backbench rebellion" if the breakdown is big enough—is normally interpreted as a sign of weakness and can even lead to the fall of a government, the resignation of a prime

Queen Elizabeth—accompanied by her husband the Duke of Edinburgh—takes part in the ceremonies surrounding the annual State Opening of Parliament. Pomp and circumstance are a key part of government in Britain, helping emphasize the stability and continuity of the political system.

minister, or the calling of a new general election. One of the most important factors in John Major's failure to win the May 1997 general election was the public airing of deep divisions within his Conservative government over the EU.

The Judiciary

It is ironic that Britain—home to John Locke (1632–1704), the political theorist whose ideas about a social contract and the separation of powers are at the core of the U.S. Constitution—should have neither a written constitution nor a constitutional court (the former requires the latter). The U.S. Supreme Court has the power to interpret the constitution (judicial review), but no direct equivalent exists in Britain. Instead, judicial review is carried out in a complex system of courts topped by a Court of Appeal and the House of Lords, where law lords hear final appeals in five-person benches. Appointments to the higher courts are made either by the Lord Chancellor (who is a member of the cabinet) or by the prime minister after consultation with the Lord Chancellor; therefore, they are highly political.

The role of judicial review in the British system is changing with the growing powers of the European Court of Justice. One of the key institutions of the EU, the Luxembourg-based Court does not yet have a European constitution to interpret, but it does have a series of treaties and a growing body of European law, whose primacy over national law is established. The European Court is slowly developing the same kind of relationship with the British government as the U.S. Supreme Court has with its state governments, and acts as the final court of appeal on matters of European law.

Subnational Government

As a federal system, the United States has three levels of government: federal, state, and local. The U.S. Constitution sets out rules governing the relationship between federal and state government, giving each one distinct rights and responsibilities. Britain, by contrast, is a unitary state, where local government units have so little independent power that they can be reformed, restructured, or even abolished by the national government.

During the 1970s, the structure of local government was changed, but the reorganization was expensive and unpopular, and calls continued to be made for the creation of a workable new system, leading to more changes since 1994. Local government now takes place at two main levels:

1. Scotland, Wales, and Northern Ireland have their own elected regional assemblies. The 129-member Scottish Parliament has authority over a variety of local policy issues, such as education, and has limited tax-raising powers, whereas the 60-member Welsh Senedd has no tax-raising powers.
2. Scotland is divided into twenty-nine county councils, Wales has twenty-two county and country borough councils, and England has a complex patchwork of unitary and two-tier local authorities. They are responsible for issues such as education, transport, housing, highways, local services, refuse disposal, and the police.

Interestingly, London—which, with its surrounding suburbs, is home to about one-third of the British population—has lacked an elected city government since the 1980s, when it was administered by the Greater London Council. The Council was dominated by the Labour party and its leader Ken Livingstone (dubbed "Red Ken" by the tabloid media) and became a thorn in the flesh of the Thatcher government. Exemplifying the powers of national government over local bodies, Mrs. Thatcher abolished the Council in 1986. The Blair administration decided to restore the city government, and Ken Livingstone (who had been serving as an MP) was swept into office as the first directly elected mayor of London in May 2000.

POLICIES AND POLICYMAKING

As in most liberal democracies, public policies in Britain are made, implemented, and evaluated through a complex process involving many different actors. One study argues that the process involves an interplay among the public arena, Parliament, parties, the cabinet, the bureaucracy, and interest groups, and that it has traditionally been bound together by a tendency to bargain, compromise, and build consensus. The result is incremental rather than radical change.[29]

Britain is technically a constitutional monarchy, but because monarchs have lost all but their symbolic power, real control over decision making rests with the government (the prime minister and the cabinet), which works closely with senior bureaucrats and is accountable to Parliament, which alone has the power to make, amend, and abolish laws, at least in areas where authority has not been transferred to the EU. Because a solid government majority means that Parliament usually does little more than confirm most government decisions, its main value is that it provides a point of access for citizens and interest groups, and parliamentary debates and questions help keep the government accountable.

Bureaucrats play an important and often unseen role in government, helped as they are by several advantages that give them influence over government: (1) they hold long-term appointments, whereas turnover among ministers is high; (2) they have access to the papers of previous ministers, which new ministers do not; and (3) they are powerful traffic police, overseeing the flow of information from ministers to departments and vice versa. Civil servants are also often closely involved in the negotiations of new policies, laws, and regulations. A particularly notorious relationship of recent decades has been that between the Ministry of Agriculture and the National Farmers Union (NFU). The NFU is an interest group, but its links with the Ministry (including often daily meetings between senior members of the NFU and the Ministry) have made it a classic example of an "insider" group with close access to the corridors of power.

Despite the powers of bureaucrats and Parliament, the most important influence on policymaking in Britain is the interplay among public opinion, the media, and interest groups. Prime ministers constantly look at their standing in the polls and calculate the popularity of their decisions and the chances for their parties in the next election. U.S. presidents can shield themselves to some extent from public criticism by exploiting the aura surrounding their office and using checks and balances to spread the blame for failed policies and to claim credit for successful policies. By contrast, the unitary structure of British government means that the prime minister and cabinet are held more directly accountable, so much of what they can and cannot do is tied to their standing in the polls and to their relationship with their party.

Economic Policy

The keyword in British economic policy after World War II was "consensus": a tacit agreement between the Conservatives and Labour that, whichever was in power, they would work to maintain welfare, full employment, a mix of private and public ownership, and the traditional features of the constitution (for example, collective responsibility),[30] and would agree on policies through compromise involving discussions between government and interest groups, particularly labor unions. Although this approach seemed to help bring prosperity to Britain in the 1950s, a reversal of fortunes was apparent by the 1960s. Conservatives pointed the finger of blame at "creeping socialism," leading to a "British disease" consisting of three main features:

1. The growing costs of welfare, which demanded higher taxes and reduced the incentives to entrepreneurs to invest, or to workers to improve their productivity. At one time, the wealthiest Britons were subjected to a so-called supertax of 95 percent of their earnings, and many became tax-exiles as a result.
2. The excessive power of labor unions, which intimidated the government by calling frequent strikes and demanding higher wages for reduced working hours. By the 1970s, some of the best-known figures in national politics were union leaders.
3. A large public sector. The postwar Labour program of nationalization resulted in the government taking over large sectors of the economy, including airlines, railroads, and the coal, natural gas, iron, steel, and electricity supply industries. Critics argued that public ownership created inefficient monopolies, leading to reduced quality, a lack of competition, and inadequate investment and stagnation.

The left questioned the role of "creeping socialism." If welfare was to blame, they asked, then why did other countries with extensive welfare and high tax rates (such as France and Sweden) not have similar problems? Their explanations focused less on workers and more on management, who they blamed for failing to compete in the new global market and for failing to invest in new machinery and technology. As the dominant world power for so long, Britain had lost the will to compete, assuming that its products would sell themselves on their own merits. Allied to this complacency, the British class system ensured that entrepreneurial activity and the creation of "new" money was sneered at by many of those with "old" money, and that managers failed to communicate with their workers. Confrontation became more common than cooperation in relations between managers and workers, leading to bitterness, low productivity, and a sense of "Us versus Them."

Whatever the causes, by 1975 Britain had seen ten to fifteen years of relative economic decline. In that year, Margaret Thatcher became leader of the Conservative party. Accepting most of the standard conservative explanations of the British disease, she argued that major changes were needed if Britain's problems were to be addressed. After winning office in 1979, she pursued several key economic policies.

First, she set about reducing the power of labor unions, refusing to stand down in the face of strikes and union demands. The confrontation peaked in 1984–1985 when the National Union of Mineworkers (NUM) threatened to bring the country to a halt (and to bring down the Thatcher government) by stopping the supply of coal and the generation of electricity. Thatcher had anticipated the confrontation and had given the National Coal Board incentives to produce more coal, thereby building coal stocks. During the strike itself, a breakaway union kept producing coal, so Thatcher was in a position to ignore the demands of the NUM (which she described as "the enemy within."[31]) The strike collapsed, helping to bring an end to the era of strong labor unions.

Second, the Thatcher administration lowered taxes. The top rate of income tax was reduced from 83 percent to 40 percent, and the basic rate was fixed at 35 percent, the goal being to encourage small entrepreneurs and more private investment. Many new businesses were started, and although many failed, an average net increase of five hundred new firms every week took place in Britain in the early 1980s, peaking at nearly nine hundred per week in 1987. The number of self-employed people grew from 7 percent of the labor force to 11 percent, British overseas investment rose, and the number of private shareholders tripled between 1979 and 1989.[32]

Third, Thatcher began selling off publicly owned companies, so successfully that privatization became one of the foundations of Thatcherism. Between 1979 and 1989, 40 percent of previously state-owned industries were sold to the private sector, including British Aerospace (1981), Jaguar (1984), British Airways (1987), and Rolls Royce (1987). Profits and productivity improved in many of these companies, but whether as a result of privatization or of a general improvement in the management methods of British industry is unclear.[33] Among the most notable of the privatizations was the sale of public housing to its occupants, greatly expanding private home ownership and improving the quality of housing stock.

Finally, Thatcher encouraged competition. By reducing government subsidies, her administration tried to make basic services more competitive, efficient, and self-supporting. It tried, for example, to encourage universities to rely less on subsidies and to raise funds for themselves. Thatcher also tried to encourage the growth of private health in order to make public health more efficient.

Did Thatcherism succeed in addressing Britain's economic problems? The answer depends on whom you ask. Many people believe—as Thatcher warned—that the economic health of Britain would decline still further before it improved, and certainly some of the basic economic indicators supported this view. For example, unemployment more than doubled to 12 percent between 1979 and 1982, and inflation during the first fifteen months of the Thatcher era leaped from 8 percent to nearly 15 percent. (By early 2000, unemployment was back down to 5.8 percent, and inflation was 3 percent.)

However, the benefits of Thatcherite economic change were unequally distributed.

Areas that were poor remained relatively poor, the economic rift between the south and the industrial north persisted, and the number of homeless people on British city streets increased. Industrial productivity improved, but Thatcherite cuts in public spending led to a decrease in the quality of many public services, not least of them education and health. Much less was spent on education compared to other European countries, the high-school dropout rate grew, the quality of secondary education declined, and the reduction of university subsidies led to fewer places for students and faculty.

Overall, though, an aggregate improvement both in British economic health and in the attitudes of business toward customers has clearly taken place. From a time in the 1970s when Britain was widely known as the Sick Man of Europe, and Britons were obsessed with the economic decline of their country, the relative decline apparently has been halted, and by the mid-1990s Britain had the fastest-growing economy in the EU. Building and road construction have expanded, the number of private homeowners and shareholders has increased, and the number of luxury cars on the roads has increased. Along with lowered unemployment and a moderate inflation rate, Britain's gross domestic product (GDP) has grown substantially, and class distinctions have declined as the middle class has grown. Competition has helped improve the choices available to consumers and the quality of service provided by retailers.

Although Margaret Thatcher was loved by some and loathed by others, the policies of her government proved popular over the long-term, so much so that when Tony Blair became leader of the Labour party in 1993, he immediately set about "modernizing" the party and committing it to the maintenance of some of the more popular aspects of Thatcherism, most notably privatization. Indeed, many of the elements of the Labour manifesto as it went into the 1997 election sounded more conservative than socialist, including a balanced budget, greater independence for the Bank of England, efforts to reduce welfare dependency, promotion of the work ethic, close ties to business, and a rejection of special deals for labor unions. Simultaneously, however, the Blair government has emphasized the need to deal with the problems of the underclass and to pay greater attention to improving education and health care (see following section).

Although substantial changes have come to the priorities of domestic economic policy in the last twenty years, the biggest overall influence on that policy today is the EU, with which Britain now conducts about 60 percent of its trade (compared to about 11 to 12 percent with the United States and 2 percent with Japan). A substantial flow of foreign investment is entering into Britain, most coming from other EU states, but much also coming from the United States and southeast Asian corporations, which see Britain as a useful base from which to make inroads into the European market.

One of the most controversial issues facing the Blair government at the start of the new millennium is whether or not Britain should take part in the single European currency. This idea was first seriously mooted in 1979 and was taken a stage further in 1989 with the agreement of a three-stage plan that involved EU states controlling their interest rates, inflation rates, and budget deficits, and then entering a currency union in January 1999, eventually replacing their national currencies in July 2002 with a single European currency, the euro.

Several EU member states have hopes that the euro will compete with (or even replace) the U.S. dollar as the most influential unit of international exchange, but the idea of a single currency has proved controversial in Britain, which was not among the eleven countries that joined the euro in 1999. European integration has already meant a loss of national sovereignty, but such losses would pale by comparison to the kind of powers given up by a government that joined the European currency system. Public opinion in Britain is hostile to giving up the pound, but the Blair government has launched a program aimed at promoting greater awareness of the benefits of joining the euro, and has promised to put the idea to a national referendum following the next general election, which is due by May 2002 at the latest.

Social Policy

When asked to outline his priorities after winning office, Tony Blair often replied "education, education, and education." The quality of British education is generally very high, and British high school graduates are well prepared for college and university, but high-quality education is not available to all citizens. Britain also lags in the quality of its healthcare system; national health care has ensured that everyone has access to medical assistance, but there is a shortage of doctors and nurses, and patients requiring non-emergency surgery must often be put on waiting lists that may last several months.

One of the legacies of Thatcherism is that a new consensus has emerged in Britain that the attitude that the state must be responsible for providing a safety net should be abandoned, and a move should be made toward a new "stakeholder" ethic. The latter has been defined as the notion that although everyone should benefit from membership of society, they should do so only to the extent to which they have played by the rules of society.[34] The indications are that the Blair government is moving toward a substantial reduction in the reach of the welfare state. Plans are being made to encourage more people to join private healthcare schemes, to take responsibility for their own retirement needs rather than relying on state pensions, and to encourage private funding for education. Among other things, the government launched a "welfare to work" program that was aimed at encouraging the non-employed (such as mothers who choose to stay at home) to move back into the workplace as a means of reducing the welfare bill and tackling the social problems that sometimes come with workless households.

All of these principles and objectives aside, the immediate priority of the government, particularly according to its critics, is to focus more time and energy on improving the quality of public services. Polls in early 1999 suggested that conditions in the national health service were regarded as the dominant issue of concern by 49 percent of the electorate, and the quality of education by 39 percent of the electorate, and that 47 percent believed that the Blair administration had not kept its pre-election promises to address problems in these areas. In its first two years in office, the strategy of the administration was to blame such problems on its Conservative predecessors, but this tactic was becoming increasingly unviable, and expectations among voters were rising; however, trying to encourage a fundamental change in public attitudes toward the provision of basic services is likely to prove to be a tall order.

Foreign Policy

As the world's policeman and major imperial power of the eighteenth, nineteenth, and early twentieth centuries, Britain once traded with almost every part of the world, had its troops stationed in every continent, and had a navy that controlled the world's oceans. It is now only a middle-ranking economic and military power, but it is still a significant actor in world affairs: it has the world's seventh largest economy, it is one of the five countries with veto powers on the UN Security Council, it is a member of the Group of Seven industrialized countries, it is a nuclear power, and it still has a significant military. Its aspirations are much more modest than they once were, however, and it has narrowed its foreign policy interests to focus today on three main arenas: the EU, its relationship with NATO and the United States, and its role in the Commonwealth.

Britain and the European Union The EU traces its origins to the creation in 1952 of the European Coal and Steel Community, a limited attempt by six western European states to integrate their coal and steel industries (see Chapter 9). The underlying goal was to promote peace between long-time protagonists France and Germany, the argument being that if their economies became more closely tied, they would be less inclined to fight each other. The experiment was widened in 1958 with the creation of the European Economic Community, which was aimed at encouraging broader economic integration.

Britain watched these early moves from the sidelines, arguing that its interests lay outside Europe, but it found itself drawn increasingly to Europe during the 1960s as its empire was dismantled. It finally joined the EEC in 1973, and since then, membership has expanded to include every western European state except Norway, Switzerland, and Iceland. Several eastern European states have applied for membership, the informal requirements of which are that a country should be a European free-market democracy. The fifteen current members have a population of 373 million, and a GNP of nearly eight trillion dollars (compared to seven trillion dollars in the United States). Membership could eventually expand to another twenty-four countries.

European integration was initially focused on promoting free trade but has broadened and deepened significantly in the last decade. Few barriers to internal trade remain, EU citizens can live and work in any of the member states (and can even vote in local elections in some of them), intra-European investment and corporate takeovers have grown, internal transport networks are expanding, the European flag—a circle of twelve gold stars on a blue background—is an increasingly common sight throughout the EU, the member states have brought domestic laws into line with European law, and the EU has a growing network of administrative and lawmaking bodies, headquartered mainly in Brussels and Luxembourg.

Britons have always been reluctant Europeans. Their physical separation helped isolate them through the centuries from the political and economic turmoil of the continent, and many still think of Europe and Europeans as "foreign." Since joining the EU in 1973, however, they have had to rethink their attitudes toward their neighbors. Despite the doubters, membership in the EU is effectively irreversible, and Britain is working more closely with its EU partners. British economic dependence on the EU was forcefully illustrated in early 1996 by a crisis surrounding suspicions that a disease afflicting British cattle (bovine spongiform encephalopathy, or "mad cow disease") could be spread to humans. Britain's EU partners boycotted British meat and insisted on drastic remedial action, leading to a political standoff that was resolved only after intense negotiation. The stance of the Major government irritated many other EU governments, but it also showed how much influence Euro-skeptics had within the Conservative party and how their views were increasingly out of step with those of mainstream public opinion in Britain.

Some Britons remain hostile to the "federalist tendencies" of the EU, but increasing numbers (particularly professionals and those in their twenties and thirties) are now recognizing the benefits of membership. Ironically, Britain has one of the best records in the Union of changing national law to fit with EU law on issues as diverse as trade, agriculture, the environment, public health, transportation, and employment. Perhaps nothing better symbolized Britain's new ties to its neighbors than the completion in 1994—after many false starts—of a rail tunnel under the Channel between England and France. Despite its financial troubles, the tunnel is a key element in the high-speed rail network that is slowly linking all of the major cities and regions of the EU.

One area in which the EU has made only mixed progress has been the development of a common foreign policy. Backed by the vast size of the European market, which now accounts for 28 percent of global GNP, the fifteen member states have largely worked as one on global trade issues; however, they lack the political unity to work together on security and defense issues. Several member states (such as Finland and Ireland) are neutral, Germany is not allowed by international law to commit its troops outside the NATO area, and the two major military powers—Britain and France—often have different policy priorities. As noted in the following section, Britain is a supporter of the NATO alliance and U.S. leadership, but Germany and France tend toward a more independent European stance on security issues. It is difficult to see how the differences will be reconciled.

Britain and NATO Along with Canada, the United States, and most other West European countries, Britain has been committed since 1949 to the common defense policies of the North Atlantic Treaty Organization (NATO). NATO was founded to counterbalance the feared expansionist threats of the Soviet Union, and Britain subsequently relied heavily on U.S. missiles and personnel to back up its own defenses. With the cold war over, and the economic and military power of the EU increasing, western European states are more likely to take a line independent of the United States, leaving a question mark over NATO's future role and purpose.

France and Germany have already begun a limited experiment in the development of a European army; the Europeans are working more closely together in designing and building missiles and fighter aircraft; and economies of scale suggest that defense policies will be integrated and independent military ventures by the British or the French will become less common. Like France, Britain has an independent nuclear deterrent, but it is small compared to those of the United States and Russia. Its military is also a shadow of what it once was: its navy and air force are about the same size as those of France, but its army is only half as large.

Britain and the United States have long had a "special relationship," which the United States has often used as a conduit for its relations with the rest of western Europe. The relationship was closest during the Roosevelt-Churchill years, and again during the Reagan-Thatcher years, cooled somewhat during the first Clinton administration, but then warmed considerably with the election of Tony Blair. Although Britain joined most (but certainly not all) of its EU partners in the U.S.-led coalition against Iraq following its invasion of Kuwait in 1990, it was alone in providing political and military support for U.S. efforts to pressure Iraq into removing obstacles to UN arms inspectors during 1998, and Tony Blair proved the most hawkish of European leaders during the Kosovo crisis in 1999. The French in particular are wary of U.S. influence in European foreign and security policy, but Britain has long been an Atlanticist, promoting the idea of working with the United States and encouraging it to maintain a military presence in western Europe. How this approach will be affected by the EU's attempts to develop a common foreign and security policy remains to be seen.

Britain and the Commonwealth The third—and least important—of the arenas of British foreign policy is the Commonwealth. Once known as the British Commonwealth, this organization consists of fifty-one mostly former British colonies and dominions, including Canada, Australia, New Zealand, many Caribbean states, India, Nigeria, and most eastern and southern African countries (such as Kenya, Zambia, and South Africa). Together, they include about one-quarter of the world's population.

Less a political alliance than an economic and cultural alliance, the Commonwealth remains a significant commitment for Britain, not least because the Queen is head of the Commonwealth, and *de jure* head of state in several Commonwealth countries (including Canada, which is why the Queen's head appears on Canadian coins and banknotes). Similar to its relationship with NATO and the United States, however, Britain's commitments to the Commonwealth are likely to be reassessed as Britain's ties to the EU become stronger.

CONCLUSIONS

Britain is distinguished from almost every other country in the world by its long and evolutionary history of political development. The changes were often violent, but once a balance had been reached between Parliament and the monarchy in the seventeenth century, the foundations were set for a period of relative peace and prosperity that allowed Britain to build enduring political institutions, and to be the home of some of the world's most influential political and economic thinkers. Stability in turn provided the foundations for an industrial revolution and for the creation of a huge empire, both of which fundamentally altered the direction of Britain's political and economic development.

However, two world wars, the end of its empire, and the rise of the United States, Japan, and Germany as major economic powers combined to force Britain to undergo a process of significant political and economic change, which has not yet ended. It began by restructuring its economy, building a welfare system, and rethinking both its military role in the world and its attitude toward its European neighbors. Changes of that magnitude inevitably lead to introspection, but after a long period of pessimism, there are signs that Britain's economic readjustments have begun to develop some long-term stability.

In economic terms, the most significant change has come out of a redefinition of public and political attitudes toward the role of the state. The creation of a welfare system in the late 1940s, accompanied by a program of nationalization, promoted the view that the state should take care of its citizens "from cradle to grave." While this contributed to an improvement in the quality of life, it also created a dependent society, and one which dulled the spirit of enterprise. Just as the United States, Japan, and Germany began to enjoy sustained economic growth, Britain found its relative levels of wealth declining, and British industry lost its competitive edge.

Whether Margaret Thatcher was correct in her assessment of the problems that Britain faced by the mid-1970s, her response was to launch an attack on the welfare state and to reduce the role of government in economic management. The result was a reappraisal of the expectations placed on industry and the individual, and a promotion of the idea that neither could any longer always rely on the state for sustenance. The welfare state is still in place, but institutionalized dependency has been replaced by the "American" idea that individuals must take more responsibility for their own opportunities, and must be prepared to accept both the advantages and the disadvantages that come with that idea.

In terms of Britain's place in the world, the most significant changes in the last two generations have come out of the end of empire, and its belated and not-always-happy membership of the European Union. Britain has had to go through a process of redefining its global role, moving from a time when it was still a significant world power to one in which it has seen itself responding to events rather than driving the agenda to suit its own interests. Perhaps most galling, it has seen the initiatives in European politics being taken by two of its longest standing adversaries, the Germans and the French.

The EU has had its peaks and troughs, and Britain has often proved to be out of step with developments on the continent, but successive British governments have found themselves increasingly tying their economic, social and foreign policies into those of the EU. The big question now hanging over Britain is its attitude toward the single European currency. It was one of only three EU member states which opted not to join the euro in 1999 (the fourth nonparticipant, Greece, had not met the required terms for membership), but the Blair government was quick to emphasize that membership was not ruled out and that a referendum would be held after the next election with a view to possible membership in 2003.

Perhaps the most significant changes coming to Britain at the turn of the millennium are political and constitutional. Recent years have seen great changes in the balance of power between the major political parties, for example, with Labour moving more toward the center, the Liberal Democrats strengthening their hold on the middle left, and the Conservatives being compelled to redefine the nature of conservatism.

Meanwhile, the Blair administration has followed through on its electoral promises of fundamental change in the powers and roles of political institutions. The parliamentary system is often portrayed as enduring, and much is made of the long history of British political institutions and processes, but in fact they have undergone a steady process of evolution, and continue to do so today. The monarchy has been reforming itself in light of demands that it become more relevant; regional assemblies have been created for Scotland, Wales, and Northern Ireland; London now has its first-ever elected mayor; hereditary peers no longer sit in the House of Lords (and more changes in the structure of the chamber are on their way); proportional representation has been introduced into local and European elections (with the possibility that it may eventually be used in general elections); and there has been talk of significant improvements in the protection of individual rights.

Perhaps the most substantial effect of these changes has been a reduction in the powers of Parliament. From one direction, its law-making powers in a growing number of policy areas—from agriculture to the environment, development aid to poor countries, transportation and technology—have been steadily whittled away by the broadening responsibilities of the European Union. From another direction, its powers over many local government issues have been devolved to the new regional assemblies. It is no longer the legislative body that it once was, and whether the British people are better or worse off as a result remains to be seen.

Britain today is not what it was in the 1950s or even in the 1970s. A combination of external developments and the policies of reforming prime ministers has served to remold the role of Britain in the world, the structure of British government and politics, and the expectations of British citizens. Such changes are nothing new, and indeed the ability of the British to recognize the need for reform has perhaps been what has distinguished Britain from many of its continental neighbors, where the unmet pressures for change have often spilled over into violent revolution. The willingness by leaders and citizens to accept the need for change has helped ensure the endurance of British political institutions; the latest round of changes will hopefully help the country and its people prepare for the very different global environment of the twenty-first century.

INTERNET SITES

Houses of Parliament: http://www.parliament.uk/
Official home page for the House of Commons and the House of Lords, with links to many useful sources of information.

10 Downing Street: http://www.number-10.gov.uk/
Home page for the residence of the prime minister, with links to news, speeches and political data.

The British Monarchy: http://www.royal.gov.uk/
Official Web site of the monarchy, with information on its roles and responsibilities.

The Times: http://www.the-times.co.uk/
Web site for two of Britain's major newspapers: *The Times* and *The Sunday Times*.

BBC News: http://news.bbc.co.uk/
Home site of the British Broadcasting Corporation, an excellent source of domestic news about Britain and of world news.

FURTHER READING

Budge, Ian, Ivor Crewe, David McKay, and Ken Newton, *The New British Politics* (Harlow: Addison Wesley Longman, 1998).

Jones, Bill, and Dennis Kavanagh, *British Politics Today,* 6th ed. (Washington, DC: CQ Press, 1998).

Dunleavy, Patrick, Andrew Gamble, Ian Holliday, and Gillian Peele (eds.), *Developments in British Politics 6* (Basingstoke: Macmillan, 2000).

Kavanagh, Dennis, *British Politics: Continuities and Change,* 3rd ed. (Oxford: Oxford University Press, 1996).

BIBLIOGRAPHY

1. Budge, Ian, Ivor Crewe, David McKay, and Ken Newton, *The New British Politics* (Harlow: Addison Wesley Longman, 1998), p. 587.
2. Jacobs, E., and Robert Worcester, *We British* (London: Weidenfeld and Nicolson, 1990), pp. 138–139.
3. Richards, Peter, *Mackintosh's The Government and Politics of Britain* (London: Hutchinson, 1985), p. 14.
4. Jones, Bill, and Dennis Kavanagh, *British Politics Today,* 6th ed. (Washington, DC: CQ Press, 1998), pp. 179–185.
5. Norton, Philip, *The British Polity,* 3rd ed. (New York: Longman, 1994), p. 44.
6. McCormick, John, *The European Union: Politics and Policies,* 2nd ed. (Boulder, CO: Westview, 1999).
7. Norton, op. cit., pp. 28–29.
8. Hart, Vivien, *Distrust and Democracy* (Cambridge: Cambridge University Press, 1978), pp. 202–203.
9. Dahl, Robert (ed.), *Political Oppositions in Western Democracies* (New Haven, CT: Yale University Press, 1966), p. 353.
10. Almond, Gabriel A., and Sidney Verba (eds.), *The Civic Culture Revisited* (Newbury Park, CA: Sage Publications, 1989).
11. Wallace, M., and J. Jenkins, "The New Class, Postindustrialism and Neocorporatism: Three Images of Social Protest in the Western Democracies," in J. Jenkins and B. Klandermans (eds.), *The Politics of Social Protest* (London: University College London Press, 1995).
12. European Values Study, quoted in The Economist, *The World in 1992* (London: Economist Publications, 1991), p. 81.
13. Budge et al., op. cit., p. 37.
14. Jones and Kavanagh, op. cit., pp. 12–14.
15. For more discussion, see Sanders, op. cit.
16. Sanders, David, "Voting and the Electorate," *in* Patrick Dunleavy, Andrew Gamble, Ian Holliday, and Gillian Peele (eds.), *Developments in British Politics 5* (Basingstoke: Macmillan, 1997).
17. Dunleavy, Patrick, "Introduction: 'New Times' in British Politics," in ibid.
18. Kavanagh, Dennis, *British Politics: Continuities and Change,* 3rd ed. (Oxford: Oxford University Press, 1996), p. 183.
19. Ibid., p. 197.
20. Bagehot, Walter, *The English Constitution* (Ithaca, NY: Cornell University Press, 1963).
21. Kavanagh, op. cit., p. 48.
22. Norton, ibid., p. 57.
23. Bagehot, op. cit.
24. Norton, op. cit., p. 308.
25. Ibid.
26. Budge et al., op. cit., pp. 213–217.
27. Norton, op. cit.; Madgwick, Peter, *Introduction to British Politics* (London: Hutchinson, 1984), p. 46.
28. Jones and Kavanagh, op. cit., pp. 163–166.
29. Jordan, A.G., and J.J. Richardson, *British Politics and the Policy Process* (London: Allen and Unwin, 1987).
30. Barry, Norman, "Ideology," *in* Patrick Dunleavy, Andrew Gamble, and Gillian Peele, *Developments in British Politics 3* (New York: St. Martin's Press, 1990).
31. Young, Hugo, *One of Us* (London: Pan Books, 1990), p. 371.
32. Figures from Riddell, Peter, *The Thatcher Decade* (Oxford: Basil Blackwell, 1989), pp. 53, 72, 75, 118.
33. Ibid., pp. 93–94.
34. Finer, Catherine Jones, "Social Policy," *in* Dunleavy et al. (1997) op. cit.

3

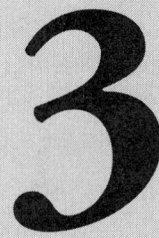

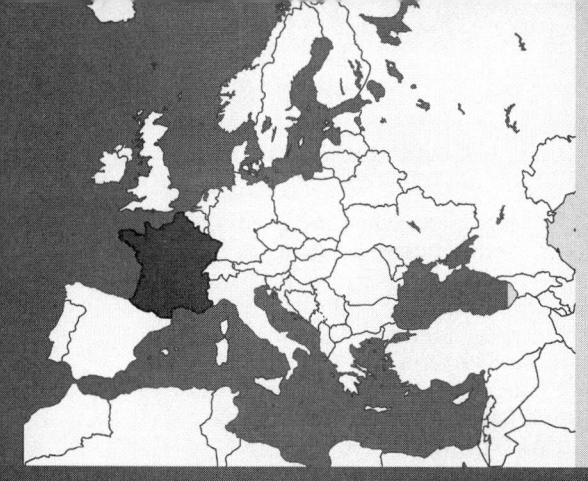

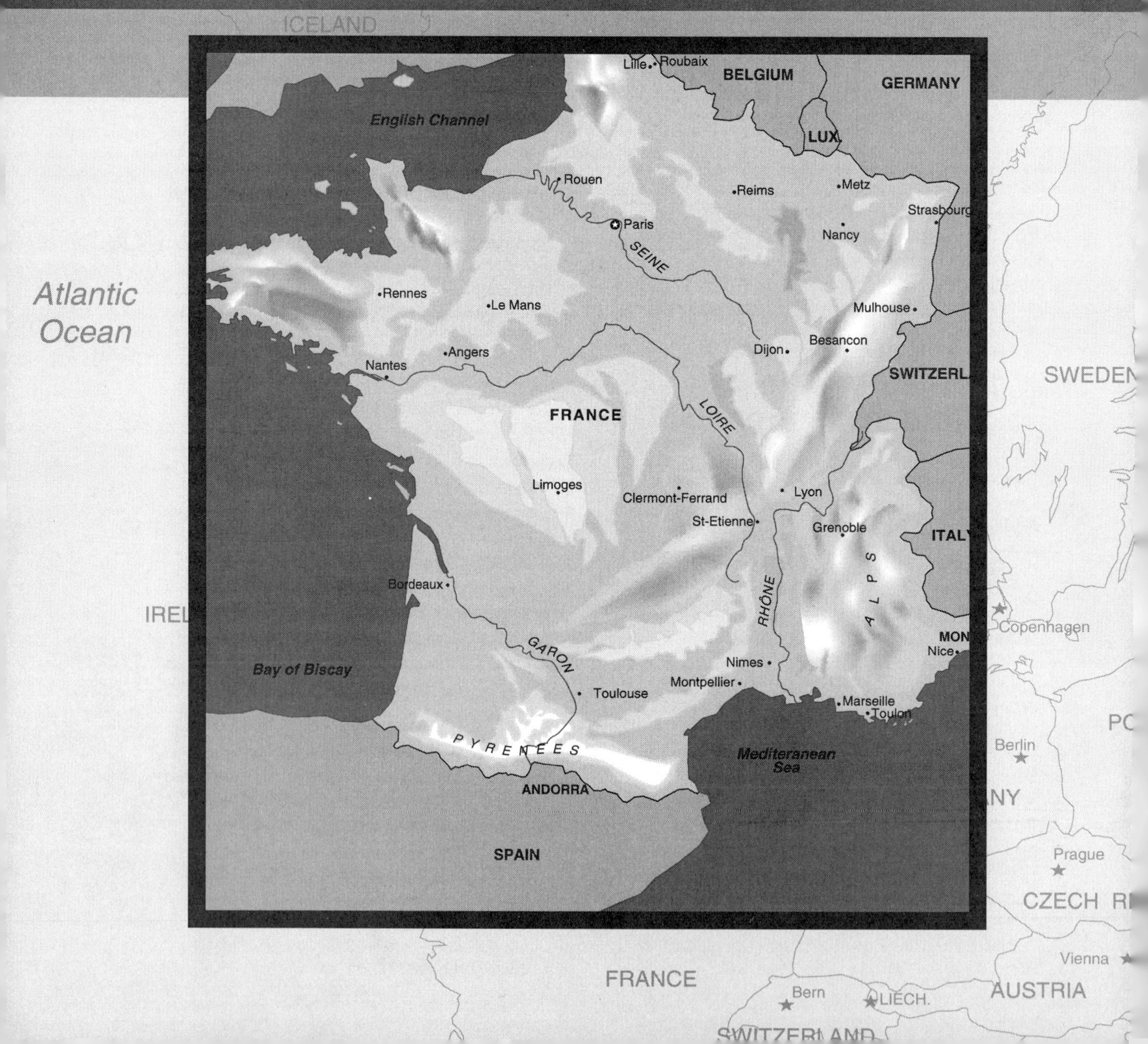

ICELAND
Atlantic Ocean
IREL
SWEDEN
Copenhagen
Berlin
PO
ANY
Prague
CZECH R
Vienna
AUSTRIA
FRANCE
Bern
LIECH.
SWITZERLAND
Lille
Roubaix
BELGIUM
GERMANY
LUX.
English Channel
Rouen
Reims
Metz
Strasbourg
Paris
Nancy
SEINE
Rennes
Le Mans
Mulhouse
Dijon
Besancon
Angers
Nantes
SWITZERL
FRANCE
LOIRE
Limoges
Clermont-Ferrand
Lyon
St-Etienne
Grenoble
ITAL
ALPS
Bordeaux
RHÔNE
MON
Nice
Bay of Biscay
GARON
Nimes
Montpellier
Toulouse
Marseille
Toulon
PYRENEES
Mediteranean Sea
ANDORRA
SPAIN

France at the Crossroads

An End to French Exceptionalism?

Amy G. Mazur and Andrew Appleton

COUNTRY PROFILE

Population:	59,000,000
Land Area:	552,000 sq. km.
Population per sq. km.:	107
Gross National Product:	$1,466 billion
Per Capita Income:	$24,940
Percent Urban:	78
Adult Literacy:	100% (claimed)
Life Expectancy	
Male:	74
Female:	82

INTRODUCTION

In 1986, two of the most talented national soccer teams ever assembled met in an enthralling quarter-final encounter in the World Cup in Mexico. At the time, the French team was at the height of its prowess, playing an attractive, open, passionate style of the game that wooed commentators and thrilled spectators. Led by their great midfield player, Michel Platini (who had turned the number ten shirt into *his* shirt), the French team dared to hope that they might prevail against the undisputed masters of flowing soccer, Brazil. Both teams were studded with players of legendary talent, and the match promised to be a true spectacle.

In the event, it turned into one of the most memorable games ever played. Although the match ended in a draw, the combination of talented players and open, attacking football kept the stadium crowd and more than two billion television viewers around the world biting their nails with the suspense. The outcome was finally decided by a penalty-shoot-out, and the almost unthinkable came to pass; France was on its way to a semi-final meeting against West Germany, and Brazil was on the way home. But the euphoria was short-lived; up against the powerful West Germans, with their disciplined and organized game (widely regarded as much less attractive than the French but nonetheless highly effective), France was unable to find its rhythm. The greatest French team ever, perhaps one of the great soccer teams of all time, would not win the World Cup.

What was remarkable about that team was that the players were almost all playing their professional careers in the French league at the time. Soccer, indeed sports in general, were not widely followed by the French, who traditionally preferred to spend their leisure time in social activities other than spectator sports. For outsiders, France was still the home of great food and wine, talented chefs, and knowledgeable waiters, a country whose role models were intellectuals and artists, where long lunches and café conversation were an indispensable part of the daily routine. For good soccer and the best professional leagues, one would have to go to neighboring Italy, England, West Germany, or even Spain. The only member of that French team who played abroad was Michel Platini, who had gone to further his career at the great Juventus club in Italy. Thus that French national side, a combination of the best French-born players, played a style of soccer that was its own, honed in the domestic league so maligned by outsiders, yet which was hardly known by the French public at large.

In 1998, the World Cup tournament was hosted by France. FIFA, soccer's governing international body, had taken a risk and chosen to stage the event in France, as part of a long-term strategy to increase the profile of the sport in countries where it had not always been in the limelight (the 1994 competition was held in the United States, and 2002 is due to take place in Japan and South Korea). The French government invested in a magnificent new stadium, the Stade de France, where the final match would be contested and a new champion enthroned. One of the architects of the French bid to host the World Cup was none other than the now-retired Michel Platini, who voiced his hopes that the French national team would be inspired by the home venue to do honor to the country.

Paris was a curious place to be, that June and July. On the one hand, World Cup fever was everywhere, on the boulevards and in the squares, the shops and the cafés; on the other hand, in the quarters of the city where foreigners and tourists are less common, the tournament could have been taking place on another continent. Where the Parisian public did seem to care, it was but to ask, "Have we (the French) lost yet?" Convinced that no French soccer team was capable of playing against favored countries such as Brazil, Germany, and Italy, the public contented itself with criticizing the decisions of the French team manager, Aimé Jacquet, and waiting for the inevitable defeat to happen.

Yet, it was Jacquet who had the last laugh. Result after result encouraged the French public to gradually abandon their skepticism and begin to embrace the fortunes of the national team. As France progressed from the group qualifying rounds into the elimination phase of the tournament, from quarter-final to semi-final and then on to the final, the support for the team began to reach a crescendo. The most remarkable thing was taking place off the field as much as on it; those who had traditionally been antipathetic to football began to develop a passion for the game centered around the performance of the national team. For example, prior to the World Cup the newspapers had been full of stories about soccer widows, women who would lose their husbands and partners to the television during the tournament. But the success of the national team prompted women to watch in record numbers, surprising all the social commentators. A broad national coalition emerged, linking intellectuals and workers, women and men, the young and the old, the middle and the working classes, and native-born and immigrant French into one moment of national joy, where none questioned another's allegiance to the country save for support of the football team. Even Jean-Marie Le Pen, the leader of the far right, who had tried to make the immigrant backgrounds of several of the players an issue, was forced to mute his criticisms in the face of the event.

On July 12, two days before the French national holiday that commemorates the storming of the Bastille during the Revolution of 1789, Jacquet's team stormed to a convincing 3-0 victory over Brazil. The man in the number ten shirt that day, Zinedine Zidane, popularly known as Zizu, became a new national hero as he scored two goals and earned a place alongside Michel Platini on the list of all-time great soccer players. The game itself had few echoes of that magnificent contest in 1986; despite the final score, it was a fairly dull affair that rarely produced the thrill and excitement of other matches. France had won the World Cup; but they won *despite* being French, playing un-French soccer, with a disciplined and physical style of play that had been mastered by its players who played in foreign leagues. All in all, it was rather odd.

In the meantime, the careful preparations for the event were nearly undone by the particularly French tradition of a transport strike. The French government believed that it had done everything possible to ensure that the World Cup would be a shining example to the rest of the globe of French organization and flair. Instead, the official carrier of the cup, Air France, was paralyzed on the eve of the tournament by a pilots' strike. Despite being much better paid and having better compensation packages than almost any other airline in the world, the pilots were demanding that Air France rescind many of the new measures it had proposed to meet the demands of global competition in the era of the deregulation of international airline competition. Many of the teams coming to play in France had to find alternative air transportation. The result was chaos. Even visitors who managed to find seats on other carriers arrived to find regional rail transport strikes around Paris and the south of the country that made getting to the match venues difficult. The socialist government of Lionel Jospin found itself embarrassed on the world stage by union-led work stoppages. How could this happen? It seemed very French indeed.

Beyond telling the story of how France pulled off, against all odds, not just hosting but winning the World Cup, this vignette sets the stage for the broader story currently unfolding in France, which is related in the rest of the chapter. This story is about a country, often criticized for its single-minded approach to running domestic and foreign affairs in a way that is out of step with its European neighbors, at the crossroads of changing what many foreign observers have seen as its peculiar ways. These changes were witnessed by the world during the 1998 World Cup and may indicate that French single-mindedness has given way to a new openness, made obligatory by the integration of Europe and globalization. Yet, as Francophiles and Francophobes alike have so often lamented in the past, "plus ca change, plus c'est la même chose"—the more things change, the more they stay the same. Given this philosophy, the question as to what these changes really mean is still up in the air.

Called exceptionalism by French specialists (and just plain French stubbornness by others), France has long had a history of doing things its own way. From French farmers who have used farm-related objects in a variety of creative ways to protest the EU Common Agricultural Policy (CAP)—cow dung on railroad tracks, cows in the streets of Paris, and, as recently as February 1999, wheat, flour, and chick peas flung at the Environmental Ministry staff—to the French Parliament refusing to take any responsibility in contributing to tensions in the Rwandan civil war; to the recent acquittal of several key ministers for responsibility in the contamination of public blood supplies with the AIDS virus in the 1980s, French exceptionalism has appeared to pervade society on all levels. But perhaps, as the story of the World Cup illustrates, this different French way of doing things may be beginning to break down.

Observers of France see this exceptionalism in terms of how the French have clung to the fundamental role of government in making people's lives better, whereas citizens and leaders in other countries have sought non-governmental avenues for helping people. After all, the French just elected a socialist majority to parliament. Espousing the big government ideas of much of the Parti Socialist (PS), Lionel Jospin (Prime Minister since 1997) is certainly no Tony Blair (the British Prime Minister), himself representative of the new brand of "social democracy lite" sweeping the rest of Europe. Whereas Blair has distanced his government from organized labor and cozied up to big business, much to the chagrin of the traditional Labour party voter, Jospin and the PS majority shocked the world of French business by adopting legislation that put into action a long-held demand of French organized labor—the 35-hour work week. The strong French belief in the state—"l'état"—is offset in a quite schizophrenic manner by the French tradition of making policy in the streets; countless pieces of legislation and ministerial decisions have been stymied by the common people collectively participating in (usually peaceful, although not always) protest rallies. Needless to say, since the Jospin government has been at the helm of the French state, French citizens have continued to take to the streets over a variety of policy issues.

The events swirling around the 1998 World Cup, therefore, illustrate well the double-edged nature of the ongoing changes; although some French traditions are being cast aside, others persist. On one hand, France's openness to global culture displayed in the World Cup is a signal of the changes. On the other hand, the strikes leading up to the tournament remind us that the French appear to be unwilling to abandon firmly entrenched patterns of political behavior.

Not only is it important to understand the nature of the French crossroads between change and continuity, but France also serves as a litmus test for the extent and reach of globalization, where the lines between national and global culture become quite blurred. Our hunch, before we dive into telling the story of continuity and change, is that France at the beginning of the twenty-first century is at such a crossroads largely because of growing European and global imperatives, where the old, single-minded, exceptional France is being transformed into something quite new that looks increasingly like other European countries. Of course these changes have to be *à la française* (the French way)—

slowly and not in all areas of social life—but we can see these changes at the end of the 1990s, particularly in the events surrounding the 1998 World Cup.

In this chapter, we tell the story of how, why, and in what areas the French are at the crossroads of change. To tell the story of how France is changing, it will be necessary to tell the story of how it stayed the same. At the end of this story, we may very well need to revise the tired phrase about France from "the more things change, the more they stay the same" to "the more things change, the more they are different." Whatever the new turn of phrase that may be applied to the France of the future, our aim is to present thoroughly the case for France being at a global crossroads.

THE BEST OF FRENCH HISTORY

> ... a people so unalterable in its primary instincts that it is recognizable in its portraits 2,000 or 3,000 years ago.
>
> Alexis de Tocqueville, *The Old Regime and the French Revolution,* 1831

This quote from Alexis de Tocqueville, a keen observer of eighteenth- and nineteenth-century society, about the historical continuity of French patterns, speaks volumes about the importance of French history for understanding contemporary France. Indeed, de Tocqueville goes on to show in his book how the state-centered political system that came out of the French Revolution of 1789–1793 was simply a continuation of what had begun under the Old Regime (the absolute monarchy, at its pinnacle under Louis XIV in the seventeenth century, which gave privileges to the aristocracy and clergy first and the middle class and common people last). Students of French politics and society follow de Tocqueville's lead in using the legacy of the past and his analysis of the centrality of the French state in the French political system to understand present-day France. His now 170-year-old book is still a must-read for students of French politics because it contains many masterful insights about the character of French history and political culture.

Not only has the past been an excellent predictor of France's present and future, but the French themselves are also in love with history of all kinds. Unlike the books found at the top of American bestseller lists, such as books on the battle between the sexes by Deborah Tannen, personal satire by Erma Bombeck, or self-help volumes by all and sundry, French bestseller lists are topped by historical analyses of France (as well as other countries and cultures). Although a deep appreciation of one's history can be good, many have argued that France has been burdened by its history, with past conflicts getting in the way of contemporary problem-solving. Indeed, Charles de Gaulle, founder of the Fifth Republic, head of the Free French exiled government during World War II, and President of the French Republic from 1958 to 1969, once said that the French are "weighed down by their history."

Given the French fascination with the past and the importance it plays in present-day lives, it is worth presenting a thumb-nail sketch of the development of the democracy in France or, as the French refer to democracy—*la République.* In our view, four conceptual themes need to be garnered from this abbreviated history of modern France; *l'état* (the state), *la nation* (the nation), *la France profonde* (the "real" France) and "the contentious French." Although other aspects of French history are still important today, many observers of France identify these four themes as the major facets of French exceptionalism (and all four themes can be seen at work in the 1998 World Cup). But before we see how the past plays into the present, let us take a look at the past. We now turn to a brief discussion of the most important events in the development of

TABLE 3.1 Political Development in Modern France

Regime Type	Approximate Dates
Absolute Monarchy/Old Regime	1643–1789
Revolution	1789–1792
First Republic/Directory	1792–1799
First Empire (Napoleon)	1799–1815
Absolute Monarchy I (Charles X—Bourbons)	1815–1830
Constitutional Monarchy (Louis-Philippe, Orleans)	1830–1848
Revolution	1848
Second Republic	1848–1851
Second Empire (Louis-Napoleon)	1851–1871
The Paris Commune	1871
The Third Republic	1871–1940
Fascist Vichy Regime in Southern France	1940–1944
Provisional Government	1944–1945
Fourth Republic	1946–1958
Fifth Republic	1958 to present
Elected Presidency	1963
Alternation of Left into Power	1981
Cohabitation I	1986–1988
Cohabitation with Right-Wing President and Left-Wing Prime Minister	1997–present

French democracy, a discussion of its geography, and an in-depth analysis of our four themes.

To understand anything about French political history, we must look at the political instability of France since 1789. Compared to most other Western democracies, France has had one of the most turbulent pasts. In terms of one measure of what political scientists call political development, meaning the development of a stable democratic political system or "regime," France has gone through different regimes a bit like college students go through pizzas. Since the eighteenth century, France has had five democratic regimes or republics, two periods of radical participatory democracy, two periods of absolute monarchy, one constitutional monarchy, two empires, a fascist dictatorship, and a provisional regime (Table 3.1). This list comes to a grand total of thirteen different regimes with five major regime types. For political science aficionados, France serves as one of the best laboratories in which to study democratic development.

We did not list France's regime instability as one of the conceptual themes that help us understand contemporary France because, simply put, it is a thing of the past. Both foreign and French experts of French politics agree that the Fifth Republic will be a lasting democratic regime that will have no more likelihood of falling to the dark forces of dictatorship than democracy in the United States or Great Britain. Two major turning points have occurred in what are called "the institutionalization" and "consolidation" of representative democracy under the Fifth Republic: first, the 1981 elections when the left-wing opposition Socialist Party won both the presidency (François Mitterrand) and the majority of seats in the National Assembly; and second, from 1986 to 1988, the cohabitation of a right-wing prime minister and parliament under Jacques Chirac and a left-wing president (Mitterrand). In both cases, situations where political leaders could have overstepped the bounds of the constitution were pulled off without any threat to the legitimacy of the Fifth Republic. After four different constitutions, the fifth one seems to be a keeper. We will return to the contours of this new and stable political landscape in our discussion of institutions that follows.

The idea of France, French national identity, and French culture is inextricably linked to the history of the French territory. For the most part, the borders of metropolitan France—the part of France located on the European continent—referred to as *l'hexagone,* date from well before the French revolution.[1] Geographically and culturally, France is at the crossroads of Europe; to say that it is a Southern European country would be to deny northern France's common identity with Northern Europe; the north and east of France are influenced by Belgium, Germany, and Switzerland. Yet the southeast borders on Italy, and in the southwest Spanish and Basque cultures are intermingled with what is French. As the two maps in Appendix A indicate, the shape of France in the seventeenth century has changed little in the ensuing four hundred years (Maps A.4 and A.5, p. 459).

A highly centralized political system[2] until the first decentralization laws in 1982, French attitudes, infrastructures, and politics are rooted in Paris. The ninety-six departments shown on the map were originally set up, as the leader of the Communist Party stated in a parliamentary debate in 1968, "to weld together the unity of the nation and to destroy provincial particularism" (Gourevitch, 14). Prior to 1982, the French national government held all formal taxing and spending power over the rest of France, (quaintly called "the provinces" by Parisians). The government-run transportation systems—highways, trains, and airways—all originated in Paris. In order to get from southeastern to southwestern France by train, one was obliged to go through Paris. Protesting farmers could merely select one major artery of the French highway system on which to deposit truckloads of cow dung in order to severely disrupt Parisian traffic patterns; they did not even have to go that close to Paris either! As an eighteenth-century French philosopher wrote, "It is Paris which shapes Frenchmen." As we will discuss in greater detail later, recent transfers of power to the regional level have taken away a certain degree of power in some policy domains, particularly social affairs. But this relatively recent transfer in no way cancels out the thousand-year legacy of the centralized French state and French culture.

The first two conceptual themes that run throughout French history and that still structure French political life today are the central role of the state or *l'état* in French political life and its inextricable links to the French nation. When we use the term state here, it does not mean a territorial unit, as in the state of Washington, but a more abstract notion that incorporates all of the different government structures that hold formal political power. When the French use the term *l'état,* they often mean governmental structures in Paris and the field offices that are attached to those offices at the departmental level, not the newer regional or more traditional local governments. When talking about the emergence of the French nation-state,[3] one of the oldest in

---

[1] Corsica was joined to France in the 1780s, Alsace-Lorraine was won over by the Germans in the Franco-Prussian War in 1871 and was given back to France in WWI. France also has several oversea departments and territories—DOM-TOMS—a leftover of France's colonial exploits.

[2] In general, government power is distributed in two ways between the national and subnational levels of government. In federal systems, like the United States, state-level and national governments share power together with local government being a lesser partner in the larger share of territorial power. In unitary systems, like France, power to make political decisions and the almighty control over the nation's purse-strings lies in the hands of government officials in the nation's capital rather than lower levels of government like the region or the department.

[3] A nation-state is a technical synonym for country. The concept of nation-state is associated with the development of European countries where state structures emerged alongside a strong feeling of national identity by a critical mass of people living within a given country's borders. In order for these new units of society to survive, governments had to gain the support of large numbers of people around the nation; hence developing national citizenship, patriotism, etc.

Western Europe, historians argue that the state came before the establishment of French national identity. That is, through the strong absolute monarchy, Paris-based state structures were put into place by the seventeenth century, including a centralized military, before the people who lived in France identified with being French.

It was not until the French Revolution (1789–1792), when the revolutionaries began to make the state accountable to the people—*le peuple*—particularly under the leadership of Robespierre, that French nation and state began to come together. Thus, from its beginnings, the French nation-state was connected to Paris's control over the provinces. The Jacobins (named for the Parisian street on which their headquarters were located), behind the leadership of Robespierre, took the monarchical notion of state and put it into its contemporary, democratic form. In fact, the name of these revolutionaries has been used to describe the way the democratic state relates to society—*jacobinisme*. In this particularly French approach to democracy, the state is seen as the prime guarantor of the republic, the general will of the French people—what one French philosopher of the eighteenth century, Jean-Jacques Rousseau called *le volonté général*, and, just as importantly, France's stature in the world—*grandeur*. This strong state ethos has developed in tandem with the instability of elected officials alongside the permanent presence of the bureaucracy and the bureaucrats who run government. This widely accepted active role of the French government is also called *dirigisme*, from the word *diriger* or to direct.

Napoleon, as general, appointed government head at the end of the Directorate, and self-appointed Emperor until 1814, greatly contributed to the development of a strong feeling of nationhood melded together by a centralized state. Indeed, his military exploits and the pride brought to the French were well known to future generations of illiterate peasants. This name recognition ultimately led to the election of Napoleon's nephew to the presidency forty years later under the Second Republic. Like his uncle, Louis-Napoleon capitalized on his popularity with and the patriotism of the French peasants to create an empire. These two episodes show how French national identity was linked to strong heroic leaders with a penchant for military campaigns and for creating their own empirical dynasties, as well as radical revolutionaries supporting social democracy. Indeed, the process by which "French peasants became Frenchmen" was arguably just as much attached to the successes of military dictatorship as with democratic revolution. No matter what the flavor of regime of the day, French national identity did not bubble up from the grassroots, as in the United States. Instead, it was placed in the French collective mind by powerful governmental leaders and elites. Thus, following de Tocqueville's emphasis on continuity in his analysis of the French Revolution, *l'état* was a key player in forming *la nation*, well before the French Revolution.

In the name of *jacobinisme, dirigisme,* and *grandeur,* the centralized state apparatus has taken a pivotal role in domestic affairs and in minimizing the role of nongovernmental organizations, movements, and interest groups. Thus, since the revolution, French elites have agreed that social change, democratization, and France's relations with the rest of the world should occur through an active and unified state. As the 1958 Fifth Republic constitution states, "France is a republic, indivisible, secular, democratic, and social."

In contrast to a seemingly homogenous national identity and a highly centralized Paris-based government, France actually has rich and diverse subcultures based at the regional and local levels, each with their own architectural styles, dialects and/or languages, customs, and food. In other words, the Jacobins were not successful in "destroying provincial particularisms." When the French talk about deep France—*la France profonde*—they are referring to the parts of France that have been far removed from Paris on a psychological as well as a geographical level. After all, France covers approximately the same landmass as Texas, so distances are relatively short by American standards. This difference in cultural perceptions of distance is well illustrated when French and Americans talk about car travel times. Whereas many Americans do not bat an eye at traveling three hundred miles for a short weekend jaunt, most French would only travel this same distance when going on their customary five-week summer vacation. Given that in France, like many other European countries, a great deal of cultural diversity is located in a relatively small geographical area, particularly when compared to the homogeneity of American culture and enormous distances, a road trip of three hundred miles from France will physically take you to a radically different cultural context and setting.

Despite efforts of the French state, through republican jacobinism and autocratic empires, to inculcate the French into French culture, regional cultures continue to exist; for example, the celtic-based breton culture in Brittany and the basque-influenced cultural traditions in the southwest of the country. Nonetheless, the centralized educational system that was developed to bring the republic to the countryside to "make peasants into Frenchmen"—French politicians until the 1960s still bragged that schoolchildren throughout the country were reading the same textbook at the same time on the same day—as well as more proactive campaigns to force people to be French, have made these subcultures subservient to French culture rather than making them composite parts of what is seen as French.

La France profonde also captures the highly rural and small-town side of France, in the present as well as the past. France continues to have the same number of towns or communes as it had more than one century ago—thirty-six thousand—the same number of towns as in all the rest of Western Europe combined. In 1987, 89 percent of these towns had fewer than twelve hundred inhabitants; one-tenth of 1 percent (35) of towns have populations larger than one hundred thousand people; only Paris has a population larger than one million (Erhmann and Schain, 31–33). Despite increased urbanization since World War II, a great deal of France outside of Paris is oriented toward the agricultural sector. Half of the land in France is devoted to agriculture, making up one-quarter of the land farmed by the twelve member states of the European Union in 1992. In 1987, official government statistics indicated that one million French were employed in agriculture—around 7 percent of the population—compared to around 2 percent in the United States. French farmers have resisted using large-scale industrial farming techniques. As a result, a high proportion of these farm employees own their own small-scale farms, although a significant proportion of French farms are large-scale. The importance and the vitality of small-scale French agriculture can be seen in the size of the dairy and produce sections of French supermarkets in both rural and urban France. You can find almost as many different brands of yogurt in French dairy aisles as you can find brands of breakfast cereal in American grocery stores.

These one million farmers and farm workers do business with a battalion of small shopkeepers and tradespeople. Small-town France with its bakeries, butchers, shoemakers, and close-knit communities, unlike small-town America, is still alive and well, albeit under some degree of threat. Although shopping malls increasingly dot the French horizon, rural France is still dominated by these small-town shops and services. Tourists flock to France to see these traditional and vital towns just as much as to see the Eiffel Tower and the Louvre Museum in Paris.

Throughout French history, rural France has been an important political force. Farmers, shopkeepers, and artisans have collectively been referred to as *les petits,* the small guys. Local political party officials and elected officials—*les notables*—have represented the interests of *les petits* as a political force against *les gros*—literally the big guys or fatcats. *Les gros* are associated with modernized urban France—in other words Parisian France—and include industrialists, managers, bankers, lawyers, doctors, and so forth.

To be sure, fewer and fewer people live off the land in *la France profonde.* Urban yuppies with children have increasingly been buying rural plots of land for their summer homes to spend their government-mandated five-week vacations. (Other Europeans have bought a great deal of the French countryside as well, with the Dutch and the Brits showing a strong force in southwestern rural France.) Rural France is increasingly under threat and is clearly at an important crossroads. In this light, *la France profonde* is not as powerful as it once was; however, rural France is still part and parcel of broader French cultural values and hence continues to serve as an important counterpoint to the centralized, Parisian-based French nation-state. Indeed, the stubbornness of the French farmers and their strangle-hold over French agricultural policy attests to the continuing importance of the *la France profonde.*

The fourth conceptual theme of the "contentious French" points to how the French are divided by a series of deeply held beliefs that cause at times quite cataclysmic conflicts centered around two poles of "us and them." These two-way conflicts have been expressed over the years in a variety of ways: killing the other side, not talking to the other side, not marrying the other side, not voting for the other side, not drinking with the other side, and the list goes on. Whatever its expression, the French are known for their long-held and heartfelt divisions. The deep emotional and sometimes violent expression of these divisions has at times been referred to as the *guerres franco-francaises*—the French cultural wars.

Indeed, these deep divisions that have emanated from pro-Republican left-wing tendencies and anti-Republican right-wing tendencies have led to the collapse and crisis of French democracy until the firm establishment of the Fifth Republic in the 1980s.

The notion of the contentious French, however, should not be seen in a strictly negative light. The French have a delight for public debate over political issues, which has sometimes fed into high levels of electoral participation and active civic participation in organizations, particularly among the current generation, quite the contrast to the political alienation of the United States's generation X. Regular commentaries in the French press marvel at the low levels of electoral participation in the United States. The quite healthy aspect of France's left-right division serves as a counterpoint to the more violent divisions of the past. Indeed, as many observers argue, as French democracy has developed, the dysfunctional aspects of the French cultural wars have given way to a more constructive and healthy approach to public debate and political participation that is so fundamental to stable democracies.

The fundamental left-right division has been around for more than two hundred years, often dating back to the French Revolution, showing yet again the near-magical touchstone nature of these three years of French history. One leading historian of the French Revolution, Francois Furet, announced at the revolution's bicentennial in 1989 that the conflicts that first erupted in the revolutionary period were only just resolved in the 1980s. In 1981, on the eve of his electoral defeat, then presidential candidate Valéry Giscard d'Estaing talked about the potential of these left-right divisions producing a France cut into two— "*une France coupée en deux.*" This set of divisions originally revolved around pro-democratic; *pour la République,* and anti-democratic forces, *contre la République.* The pro-democratic side represents what many

French identify as the "forces of change," whereas the anti-democratic side is the forces of order. Often difficult to pinpoint what these broad sides have meant—it sounds a bit like *Star Wars* à la francaise—each side encapsulates a certain set of principles on which French society and politics should be based.

The forces of change have typically been associated with the more "modern" elements of French society—urban professionals, students, and business as well as political positions that favor social equality, liberty, and government accountability to all classes in society. The forces of order are seen to be in touch with the more traditional sectors of French society—the Catholic church, the military, and *les petits*. Here social order is the most important value, even at the costs of equality and individual liberty. These long-established divisions still resound on the contemporary political scene.

Women as a group have been traditionally associated with the forces of order. It was not until a new generation of women became politically active through the women's movements of the 1970s that the image of French women as being part of the forces of order was replaced by a more diverse notion of cross-cutting interests among women. Indeed, one of the major reasons why French women were not given the right to vote until 1945 was because pro-Republican politicians feared that women were under the control of the Catholic church and other anti-Republican forces in society. In this view, women with the right to vote would vote for anti-Republican forces and hence against French democracy more generally. As Georges Clemenceau, a major French statesman and leader of the pro-democratic forces, articulated in 1907, "If the right to vote were given to women tomorrow, France would all of a sudden jump backwards into the middle ages" (Hause and Kenney, 16).

Another perennial dueling combo, which has receded now that the end of the French Revolution was officially declared in 1989 by Furet, is the clerical/anti-clerical division. This was a deeply bitter debate between those who felt that France should be Catholic and those who felt that France should be secular. Even though France is identified as a Catholic culture, it has much lower levels of regular churchgoers than, for instance, the comparatively religious United States. The separation between church and state in 1905 formally brought an end to the economic and political control of the Catholic church, but debates about the appropriate role of Catholicism vis à vis public life still raged on, even well into the contemporary period. In 1984, one million people swelled the streets of Paris to protest the withdrawal of state subsidies to private schools, the vast majority of which are Catholic. The government was forced to maintain the subsidies.

More recently, the clerical/anti-clerical and pro-Republic/anti-Republic divisions were used to frame the debate over whether female fundamentalist Muslim students should be allowed to wear the veil in public schools. Opponents of this practice supported an all-out ban on veils to protect "the indivisible and secular republic." The supporters of veil-wearing were depicted as enemies of the Republic because of their pursuit of orthodox religious practices in public schools. Thus, although these particular French cultural wars may no longer be at the forefront of French politics, they still remain important undercurrents to be dredged up in public debate and discussion.

A new set of us-and-them divisions has been intensifying since the early 1980s between the governors and the governed and between the haves and the have-nots—referred to as *la fracture sociale* or social fissure—particularly in the face of the new challenges of a global economy and Europeanization. The rising anxiety about the ability of politicians to govern has been expressed in most Western democracies, so the French are not exceptional in the recent rise in alienation. Moreover, the French have been known to periodically express a high degree of angst or malaise over the ability of their political system to govern fairly. More recently, increasing levels of malaise have been felt because of the political class of elected and appointed officials who dominate politics, particularly in the context of recent corruption scandals ranging from the involvement of public officials in the rigging of soccer matches—the mayor of Marseilles, Bernard Tapis, was indicted and put into prison for his part in the scandal—to nepotism in contracting. Edith Cresson, former prime minister and current European Union commissioner gave her dentist an EU grant to investigate AIDS, which he used to fund travel to his hometown. This incident was one of several highly public cases of misuse of EU funds that led the European Commission to resign in March 1999.

The particularly French tradition of *cumul des mandats,* literally accumulation of public offices, has served as a foundation for the social fracture and increasing malaise. Until 1986, no limit was placed on the number of public offices an individual could fill. Indeed, the accumulation of elected positions at the local, departmental, regional, and national levels contributed to creating a powerful ruling class in France that has been difficult to unseat. Typically, major national leaders are simultaneously members of the National Assembly, mayors of large towns, and heads of the departmental councils. Deputies do have to resign their seats when they are appointed to a cabinet position, but they can appoint anyone they choose, and so in reality retain control over their seats. After 1986, the accumulation of public office was limited to two per person.

The general feeling among an ever-increasing group of citizens is that the standard mix of politics is no longer working in the face of France's mounting economic and social problems. In the 1990s, public opinion polls have shown that the French perceive a widening gap between those who are economically well-off and those who are not. This social fissure has been exacerbated by the image of a political ruling class that is out of touch with the needs of the common citizen and by the government's apparent inability to deal with chronic unemployment. Whereas France's unemployment has been hovering around 13 to 14 percent of the workforce, the United States's has been dropping to record lows of 4 percent.

Discussions of revitalizing the political class with younger and more diverse members, including women, are put into the context of the French government's inability to deal with its economic woes. Currently only around 10.9 percent of the members of the National Assembly are women. Although this percentage is comparable to the United States, many other industrialized democracies have much higher numbers of women parliamentarians, with the Scandinavian countries coming much closer to sex parity. The French public has been voting less, casting more spoiled ballots—voting not to choose a candidate—and voting for outsider candidates and political parties. In the first round of the 1995 presidential elections, a record 37 percent of votes went to extreme left-wing or right-wing candidates. The winner, Jacques Chirac, from the established Gaullist party, received the lowest share of the popular vote of any Fifth Republic President—49.5 percent—with 6 percent of ballots being spoiled.

In France, unlike the United States where presidents have been elected with less than 30 percent of registered voters, winners have always received a clear majority. As we show later, many of the established political parties are confronted with the need for deep reform but seem incapable of doing it. Thus, this new cleavage is between what is perceived as an ossified ruling class based on old norms of jacobinism and elite politics and a more dynamic, diverse and multicultural society in search of something new. Put another way, the forces of change have become the forces of order, with the new forces of change coming from the grassroots of society. It is important to note that as much as this malaise has been on the rise, it in no way calls into question the political institutions of the Fifth Republic.

THE SOCIAL BASES OF POLITICS

Race and Immigration

For more than one century, France has been a country of immigration. Yet even prior to that, the geographic location of the country, standing as it does at the crossroads of Europe, meant that the culture and identity of the French emerged out of many different backgrounds. More so than most other European peoples, the French have had a constant preoccupation with what it means to belong to "The Nation"—in other words, what makes a French person French? What is the glue that binds the Flemish speaker in the north to the German speaker in Alsace, and the Breton speaker in the Brittany peninsula, to the Occitan (an old regional language) speaker in the south, or to the Corsican on the island from where Napoleon hailed? All of these people share the same flag, national anthem, and political institutions, yet the cheese, the wine, the songs, and the culture are very different in each of the regions.

All of this tells us very little about what it means to belong to the French nation, when such racial intermixing has been so fundamental in the forging of the social bases of the modern country. The irony is that in a country where the idea of national identity is taken so seriously, almost everything to do with the actual definition of that identity causes controversy and bitter division. The French are taught from an early age that it is important to belong to *la patrie* ("the fatherland"); it is just not quite so obvious what that means in a country of immigration. In a slightly earlier time, the great French leader, General de Gaulle, was said to have remarked that any country with 250 kinds of cheese is ungovernable. By this, he was suggesting, metaphorically, that the greatest challenge of governing France was to overcome local attachments and preferences and to forge a sense of unity among all citizens. Yet how should this be achieved?

Many nineteenth-century French historians flirted with racial theories of the foundations of the national character, citing the influence of the Gauls, the Romans, and the Franks. Ernest Renan, for example, argued that the catastrophic defeat of 1870–1871 at the hands of the Prussians was a consequence of the dilution of Frankish blood (supposedly more warlike) with that of the Gauls. Historians and philosophers such as Michelet, Taine, and Renan spilt much ink analyzing the formation of the French character in these or similar terms. Yet, the fact was that at the time of the French Revolution, and even one hundred years later, France was more remarkable for the diversity of its people than for the homogeneity of its national character.

In this optic, the French character had to be "invented" through the use of myths. As we pointed out previously, it was through the French state that these myths were promulgated, buttressed by a national education system and the enforcement of the national language. In his book *Peasants Into Frenchmen,* Eugene Weber recounts how children in Brittany were forced to stand in the corner of their schoolrooms for long periods, wearing dunce's hats, for the sin of using Breton (the old Celtic language of the region) rather than French. The myth of the revolution that placed the state in the hands of the people, the belief in the supremacy of French culture, the notion that France is the guardian of fundamental human rights and values, and so on, these are the components of the great national myth that is at the epicenter of the invented French character.

One of the great positivist thinkers of the late 1900s, Ernest Renan, in reply to the question

"What is the nation?" gave the somewhat puzzling answer, "It is a daily plebiscite." By this, Renan was suggesting that national identity is affective; it depends on the pride that individuals have in belonging to the group, the nation. To be French, therefore, one had to want to be French, to want to belong to (and possibly defend) the French nation. Prior to the modern era, the main thrust of public policy toward immigrants was what the French termed *assimilation*. This strategy is founded on the belief that the dominant French culture is manifestly superior to others, and that immigrants were to be assimilated into that culture. Given the superiority of that culture, should it not be obvious that immigrants would want to adopt that culture, even be grateful for the chance to adopt it?[4]

Yet in the post–World War II era, the traditional stress on assimilation began to break down, for two main reasons. On the one hand, the influx of immigrants during this period was from different countries than before; immigrants were not coming so much from Belgium, Poland, Central Europe, and Italy, but much more so from Spain, Portugal, and then Africa. The propulsion of decolonization and the pull of massive economic growth on mainland France drew many immigrants, especially beginning in the early 1960s, from former French colonies in Northern and sub-Saharan Africa. The culture shock for both groups—the French and the newly arrived immigrants—was tremendous. Many of the new immigrants were Islamic and/or black, which for reasons that will be explained briefly following was of particular concern to defenders of traditional French culture.

The second of the factors that has opened up the debate over assimilation is the attack on the myths of French national identity themselves. New historians began to challenge the prevailing view of the French Revolution as a great leap forward in human progress, preferring to see the revolutionaries as having unleashed a wave of dictatorial terror. So, too, they began to review the resistance against the Germans in World War II; the heroism of the period with the idea of an uncompromising struggle against foreign occupiers was tempered by the unearthing of mounds of evidence to show widespread collaboration and anti-semitism. Regionalist movements began to push for the recognition of their languages and culture, arguing that the creation of the national character had taken place through the eradication of their own cultures. The apparently inexorable globalization of culture—what Benjamin Barber ironically calls McDonaldism—seems to render French cultural specificity as nothing more than an outmoded curiosity in the contemporary world. In short, the foundational myths of the French character began to be portrayed as tarnished, irrelevant, or both.

Coupled with the poor living conditions and social precarity in which many immigrants found themselves, these factors have pushed many immigrant groups to take up a rival discourse, one of *intégration*. This concept rejects the notion that all immigrants shall become assimilated in French society through the shedding of their own culture and the adoption of the French way of life; rather, it suggests that French culture itself might be shaped and changed by the presence of so many diverse groups living on French soil, and that the French national character may be "pluralized." For defenders of the French state, the repository of French culture and identity, such a view is anathema; why would the French want to be anything else? From an American perspective, such a viewpoint might be considered racist, and indeed the xenophobic and racist

---

[4]During the days of their overseas empire, the French used to justify their colonial rule on the grounds of *la mission civilatrice* (the mission to civilize). Unlike the British, who were content to divide and conquer colonial populations through the use of the race card, the French set about trying to turn native populations into French. This was seen as an enlightened and liberal policy, given the superiority of French culture.

national front in France has picked up many of the same themes. But in France, such a view is not (by itself) considered racist at all, and many of the staunchest proponents of such a view are found on the political left. For example, when two schoolgirls tried to wear their traditional Islamic scarves to school, a Socialist government led the effort to ban them, based on the face that wearing clothing infused with religious symbolism challenged the power of the state to uphold secular principles through the public education system.

Today, the latest statistics show that more than 3.6 million immigrants live in France; about 1.5 million are from European countries, 1.4 million from North Africa (the Maghreb), 425,000 Southeast Asians, and 240,000 sub-Saharan Africans. France's overall population is fifty-nine million. Only about 70 percent of these people are strictly immigrants (i.e., having been born outside French soil); about 20 percent are children who have been born on French soil to foreign parents, and the remaining 10 percent are those born overseas but who have not yet attained their majority. To this can be added another 1.3 million people who have been naturalized as French citizens. Contrary to general misperceptions, the majority of immigrants are from European countries (about 60 percent). This proportion has fallen in contrast to previous decades, but nonetheless still challenges the person in the street's image of the average French immigrant.

Immigration to France showed a marked change in 1974. For the two decades before that (at least), the main reason to immigrate to France had been to find a paying job in the labor force. The difficulties in the wake of the oil shock of 1973–1974 meant that economic immigration began to dry up; immigration instead became more common as a means to reunite families that had been separated in earlier years. One consequence of this trend was the "feminization" of immigration as many women came to France to join husbands and families who had left their native countries in the 1960s. This feminization had important consequences for the visibility of immigrants in French society because it entailed a movement from single-person dwellings and government-run labor camps into family housing in urban areas as families were reunited. Over the last two decades, immigrants have moved up the socioeconomic ladder; for example, in 1975, 75 percent of immigrants from North Africa were unskilled laborers, whereas that proportion had fallen to less than 40 percent in 1990. Thus, the socioeconomic profile of the immigrant population is getting closer and closer to their nonimmigrant counterparts.

This phenomenon carries over into other areas as well. By 1990, only 18 percent of the immigrant population lived in housing lacking running water or electricity, compared to 57 percent in 1975; the nonimmigrant population in the same conditions was 10 percent (34 percent in 1975). This improvement is mostly explained by the movement of many immigrants into public housing, particularly those from North Africa and sub-Saharan Africa. The evidence also shows that, contrary to many misperceptions, immigrant children do just as well in school as their nonimmigrant peers; class differences are much better explanations than national origin of why some children do better in school than others. Although birth rates are higher among immigrant groups, they have been falling over the same period and are converging with those of the general population.

One of the main influences in the debate over race and immigration in modern France has been the fact that many of the immigrants from the Maghreb and sub-Saharan Africa are Islamic. The fiercely secular nature of French republicanism, bolstered by two centuries of debate over the relationship between church and state, leads many intellectuals and politicians—not to mention ordinary French citizens—to be instinctively distrustful of any

Members of an immigrant population fill a street in Paris. More than 3.6 million immigrants live in France; about 1.5 million are from European countries, 1.4 million from North Africa (the Maghreb), 425,000 Southeast Asians, and 240,000 sub-Saharan Africans.

religion that contains an explicit rejection of the secular. The specter of fundamentalist Islamic communities in France waging violent campaigns against the French state is one that has kept the government on edge in recent years; these fears were partially born out when an Algerian extremist network planted a series of bombs in the Paris train system in 1997. But a few facts are in order; only about 10 percent of the Islamic population in France belongs to fundamentalist sects (about the same proportion of devout Catholics), and opinion polls show that most immigrant populations are hostile to the fundamentalists. It does not appear that the Islamic community in France is anything like a secret "Fifth Column" of Islamic fundamentalism; nonetheless, many French citizens are distrustful of any of the otherwise innocuous rites (such as the ritual slaughter of animals, wearing headscarves, or daytime fasting at Ramadan) that they associate with a rather different kind of Islam.

Thus, the statistics seem to show that immigrants in France appear to be converging in many important ways with the general population; however, the media-created image of immigrants does not always display this melding; whether in movies or in television documentaries, the image of the young immigrant is one of a person caught between two worlds and fitting in neither, someone faced with social and economic exclusion; in short, a bleak vision of the plight of young *beurs* (children of those from North Africa). The reality is that there is some truth to this portrayal, but only for specific communities; those in poor suburbs of the large cities, where a noxious cocktail of economic deprivation, social exclusion, cultural marginalization, and boredom has sparked headline-grabbing incidents of protest and violence.

Yet, as many have remarked, France is no longer a culturally or socially monolithic nation; it is pluralist, with all the positives and negatives that arrangement entails. A visit to Barbès-Rochechouart and the Goutte d'Or in the north of Paris shows just how much immigration has become a part of the French social fabric; the market stalls are laden with exotic spices not previously seen in France, the vegetables on display are not always familiar to those reared in the French culinary tradition, and the pulses of African rhythms permeate the air. One could almost be in a major African city—Senegal or Dakar, perhaps—except for the street signs with their portentous names drawn from the pages of French history and standing as mute testimony to centuries of cultural invention.

Class

Class has been an important element in the dynamics of modern French history for at least two centuries. Objectively, class has been used to describe the important economic and social divisions running through the French population, and as a measure of inequality between these strata. Subjectively, class has played a key part in the definition of the seminal events of French history. From the role of the crowds from the Faubourg Saint-Antoine in the sacking of the Bastille to the Paris commune of 1871, from the revolution of 1848 to the communist resistance against the German occupiers in World War II, many of the important moments in the development of modern France have become imbued with deep class overtones.

One of the most telling (and poignant) things that a visitor to Paris can do is to walk through the famous cemetery of Père Lachaise. Many of the most famous figures in French historical, cultural, and artistic life are buried here, along with such prominent foreigners as Jim Morrison and Oscar Wilde. The northeast corner of the cemetery is lined by a wall made of cement and flintstones. Against this wall, in May 1871, the last of the *communards*—those who had seized control of Paris just seventy-two days before and declared it a free and independent commune—were summarily shot after a week of bloody resistance to the invading troops. Karl Marx glorified the Paris Commune of 1871 as the first genuine proletarian dictatorship, and the event took on added significance to those on the revolutionary left. The plot of land just opposite the "wall of the federals" became the official burial plot of the French Communist Party, and many of its leading intellectuals and sympathizers have been buried there over the years.

Yet not too far from Père Lachaise, in fact almost in view, the rather unique structure of the Church of Sacré Coeur sits atop the hill of Montmartre; a testament to the *guerre franco-francaise* between the forces of change and the forces of order. The white bulk of the church has come to symbolize and dominate the north of Paris in unmistakable fashion. The church was actually built as a monument to those who died in the Commune of 1871, the bloodiest event in modern French history, including the French Revolution of 1789–1794; however, Sacré Coeur was financed by a public subscription that was mainly underwritten by the conservative bourgeoisie, for whom it symbolizes pious atonement for the sins of the nation that had led it into civil war. The point is telling; no matter what the exact origins of the uprising of 1871, the Paris Commune came to stand as a class affair, and the monuments revered by class factions have endured through the years as a testament to the depth of class feelings in French society.

Of course, the Paris uprising of 1871 did not create the idea of class; in fact, many historians have questioned the degree to which the combatants were actually drawn from different class groups. It is possible that rather than being the harbinger of a new kind of politics (as Karl Marx suggested), the Commune of 1871 was actually the last in a long line of revolts between *les petits* and *les gros* that were alluded to previously. In many ways the organization of class into the political process in France has always been riven with ideological and tactical dissension, often making France look like less of a class-oriented country than other countries (Britain, for example). Yet in societal terms, class has played a central role in defining ideas about social station and social relationships.

Many sociologists have noted the impact of the advent of post-industrialism on traditional ideas about class that were formed in the heyday of industrial society. Much evidence suggests that in France class is becoming rather less important than it ever was in defining people's ideas about their place in society. One of these pieces of evidence is the degree to which French people feel that they belong to a social class. Since 1976, opinion polls show that the feeling of class attachment has been in fairly constant decline until the mid-1990s, when a small increase occurred. By 1994, as many as 38 percent of those polled responded that they did not consider themselves to be part of any social class, we can see that the idea of class is less important than it has been at other periods in French history.

Three out of five adults do think of themselves in class terms, though. In 1966, 21 percent of those polled thought of themselves as being middle class, while 39 percent identified themselves as working class. The same question posed in 1993 produced an entirely different response; 39 percent placed themselves within the middle class, while only 19 percent identified with the working class. What is interesting to note is that objectively industrial workers in the labor force have declined over the same period; in 1970, 39 percent of the labor force was industrial workers compared to 30 percent in 1988. So, in the 1960s, a close relationship existed between the number of people in traditional working-class jobs and the proportion of the population who thought of themselves as working class. By the 1990s, only about half of those in such jobs viewed themselves as part of the working classes.

What we can conclude from these numbers is that the big transformation of French society over the last thirty years has been the reduction of working-class consciousness. All over France, those who once would be likely to see themselves as being part of the *classes populaires* (the lower or working classes) now see themselves in other terms. This reduction in working-class consciousness has had some profound consequences for French politics, from the decline of trade unions and the erosion of the French Communist Party, to the emergence of new issues onto the political agenda that cut across traditional class lines (such as feminism, ecology, etc.). The recession of class can be seen on the streets of Paris, where the old working-class neighborhoods of the city such as La Bastille, Belleville, or La Villette have succumbed to renovation and gentrification. Small working-class cafés are disappearing, replaced with trendy restaurants and glitzy establishments aimed at a younger, more cosmopolitan clientele. The practice of an *express* (espresso coffee) and a *coup de rouge* (a small glass of red wine) on the way to work in the morning has given way to a leisurely *café crème* (coffee with milk) and a croissant.

Nonetheless, class antagonism still endures as an important symbol of the increasing gap between the haves and the have-nots. When the French government was looking for a site on which to build the new national stadium that would host the World Cup final, they chose a piece of land just outside the center of Paris in the working-class suburb of Saint-Denis. The communist mayor of the area protested at what he felt to be the insensitivity of the government in locating the project next to some of the most dilapidated housing in the Paris region; the plan became the focus of protest against the lack of government money for housing renovation and help to poorer quarters of French cities. When the French team played in the final against Brazil, local protesters tried to draw attention to the fact that most of the eighty thousand spectators in the stadium were those who had connections and could afford tickets for which outrageous prices were being charged, whereas the poor (among whom soccer passions run much higher) were excluded within their own neighborhood.

As class consciousness has receded, other forms of social attachment have become stronger. Some have argued that France is now, more than at any other time in French history, a "two-speed society," corresponding to the idea of the *fracture sociale* introduced previously. On the one hand, there are those who benefit from and thrive in the new global economy, those who have the education and skills to use technology and to work in a fast-changing environment. They are mobile, flexible, and can move easily from job to job.

On the other hand, there are those who lack such skills, and who find themselves increasingly subjected to the negative consequences of globalization, such as downsizing and the export of manufacturing. These people, lacking educational skills and technological competence, find themselves at the mercy of a labor market where good, skilled jobs are being lost in the manufacturing sector and where job growth is occurring in low-wage, no-skilled areas of the economy such as the service sector. This half of society is finding itself left behind as the technological revolution and globalization make their effects felt within France.

The idea of the "two-speed society" is not unique to France, yet it taps into the traditional French notion about *les petits* and *les gros*. Often in the past, these ideas have actually helped to divide the lower classes; today, the emergence of this new social fissure seems much closer to older conceptions of haves and have-nots. Once again, the political consequences are important; for example, opposition to European integration, as expressed in the referendum vote on the Maastricht Treaty in 1992 (in which the French electorate came very close to rejecting a treaty that was supposed to pave the way for a new round of European integration), may be best explained by the mobilization of the have-nots against a treaty that was supported by all the leading members of the French political elite.

Perhaps the most compelling sign of the transformation of the notion of class in French society is afforded by the wave of protest that swept France in December 1995. At the heart of the problem was the announcement of a government plan to reduce the social security deficit in France that had reached unmanageable proportions. The government was committed to reducing this deficit as a consequence of its preparation for the introduction of the single European currency, which necessitated that participant countries bring their budget deficits under control. Beginning with the national railroads (the SNCF) and the Paris metro system (the RATP), work stoppages and strikes gradually gripped the public sector in the country, supported by unions, social organization, and other groups. Eventually, the government was forced to back down to a large extent, but not before the existence of a massive wave of social discontent was revealed. Many sociologists and political scientists, trying to understand this latest round of social protest, saw it as an attempt to defend a French way of doing things and the French way of life against the twin thrusts of European integration and globalization.

Religion

France is constitutionally a secular country and has been so since the official separation of the church and state in 1905; however, the role of Catholicism in French society and French culture has been the subject of division and discord at least since the French Revolution, and the separation of 1905 did not put an end to the debate. The controversy over the wearing of headscarves by Muslims in school tells an important story about the place of religion in French society, albeit from a rather different perspective. The dramatic increase in the proportion of the French population who come from a religious background other than Catholicism attests to the broader changes in French society that have taken place over the second half of the twentieth century. This diversity also highlights the challenge to the long-held belief, among both secular Republicans and conservative Catholics, that a core set of values, fixed and immutable, defines France and French civilization. Of course, the core values identified by these two groups are radically different, yet they both see the influx of new religions and religious practices as being potentially destabilizing.

In terms of Catholicism, religious practice has declined significantly since the 1950s. At the beginning of that decade, nearly 90 percent of French children were baptized in the Catholic Church; by 1994, that number had dropped to 60 percent. More telling yet are the figures for church attendance; regular attendance has dropped from 25 percent in 1952 to just 10 percent in 1990. The phenomenon is even more striking if one looks at the difference between age groups; according to surveys, nearly 55 percent of those in the eighteen-to twenty-two-year-old age group have never practiced religion, compared with just 22 percent of the oldest group in society. By 1990, 35 percent of the French adult population declared that they do not believe in the existence of god, up from just 15 percent in 1972.

Over this period, the Catholic church has undergone a fundamental transformation as the number of regular churchgoers continues to decline. Prior to the 1960s, the Catholic church saw itself as the religious institution that could speak to and for the entire French population (perhaps excluding the million or so Protestants at the time). But in the last thirty years, it has come to see itself more as an institution that can administer to and advocate the interests of just the core group of Catholics who attend church on a regular basis. In the words of one observer, the church has become "an institution like any other." The numbers of those entering the priesthood has fallen, as has the demand for religious instruction; financially, the Catholic church has had to adjust its expenditures to meet the shortfall in contributions.

In doctrinal terms, the 1960s were also an important time for the church, particularly in the wake of Vatican II. The liberalization of theological doctrine was met with dismay by some, who actively resisted the modernization emanating from the Vatican. "Fundamentalist" Catholicism has been quite vigorous and visible within modern French religious life, and the conflicts between the mainstream church and its fundamentalist offshoots have been well publicized in the media. French Catholics have historically been quite conservative (there is a strong correlation, for example, between church attendance and right-wing voting), and at moments in French history this tendency has led to deep distrust on the part of secular Republicans of practicing Catholics. In recent years, links between fundamentalist Catholic groups and the nationalist extreme right—both rumored and proven—have reopened many of these old wounds.

One area where the presence of religion in French society has declined only minimally is in education. Private schools still enroll about 20 percent of all French children from kindergarten through secondary school, and most (although not all) of these schools are affiliated with the Catholic church. Education is one area where the separation of church and state is less than total; religious schools may receive a substantial part of their funding, primarily in the form of teachers' salaries, from the state, as long as they agree to teach a curriculum that is approved by the public authorities. The fact that children of non-practicing Catholics are attending religious schools to some degree demonstrates the success of the Catholic church in transforming itself into an independent institution in modern France. The depth of the reaction in the 1983–1984 demonstrations, which caught many observers by surprise, attests to the importance of the church in the realm of education.

Just as the distrust displayed toward Catholics has increased on the part of some of the French Republican elite, so too, suspicion exists about the growing number of Muslims in the country. Many of these perceptions about the extent and nature of Islamic practice are actually quite wrong, but it is difficult to ignore the fact that traditional Islamic views on the primacy of the *u'lama* (the religious community) over the political institutions of the state conflict with the French Republican hold on those same institutions. Although the main representatives of Islam in France, notably the head of the Paris Mosque, have been careful to be moderate and non-divisive in their public statements (for example, quickly condemning the bombings in France carried out by Algerian fundamentalists), some signs of a small but growing influence of fundamentalism exist in the poorer immigrant areas. The numbers may be small, but their existence has been used to exaggerate fears of a fundamentalist challenge to French secularism.

Perhaps the most pervasive manipulation of the alleged specter of Islamic fundamentalism has come from the extreme right, xenophobic Front National (FN) party of Jean-Marie Le Pen. The FN has made one of its core aims to "keep France French," which many people take to be an implicitly racist platform (although Le Pen always denies the charge). In the 1983 local elections in the town of Dreux, where the FN first made a significant electoral impact, the local party organizers carefully whipped up public sentiment against (mostly Islamic) immigrants by spreading stories and rumors about the supposed lifestyle of those immigrants; stories such as the pervasive ritual slaughter of sheep and goats in bathtubs in public housing, subversive activities against the French state, and so forth. Playing to the worst stereotypes of those unfamiliar with Islam, the FN was able to scare many voters into supporting its nationalist platform. Although Muslims compose such a small fraction of the French population, fears about militant Islam—generated mostly by events in other parts of the world—continue to enable the FN to exploit and manipulate certain elements of the public.

POLITICAL PARTIES AND INTERESTS

The State-Society Nexus in Politics

The traditional view of the organization of politics in France always suggested that the main channels through which the interests of citizens get organized into politics—interest groups and political parties—have been historically and comparatively weak. Although both groups have played a key role in the development of the political system and the attendant political culture of France, the organizational strength and stability of interest groups and political parties has not been high. In this view, France has had a lower level of general participation in trade unions and other interest groups than comparable Western democracies, and these groups have always been hampered by infighting among themselves (generally over ideology). Equally so, the traditional view of political parties in France is that they too are rather weak and have not really been able to respond to citizens' needs.

In recent years, however, this view has begun to change. The transformation of the institutions from the Fourth to the Fifth Republic, particularly with the addition of the directly elected presidency, has led to the consolidation of national political parties, with predictable and stable patterns of competition among them. The Fifth Republic has also seen a pluralization of society, with interest groups flourishing at the local level in a manner hitherto unfamiliar in France. Not just the number of interest groups has changed but also the role they play in making policy. Many observers have talked about the "corporatist" nature of certain sectors of French life, education and agriculture being the two most often cited. What this means is that successive governments have developed special relationships with certain interest groups, to whom they turn when advice and input is needed about specific policy proposals. In return, these interest groups make sure that their members are favorable to government action and do not engage in protest activities (such as strikes).

It is important to understand that for many years, the idea of interest groups or political parties was treated with a certain distrust in French political culture. For one, the French have long held a distrust of what we call intermediary institutions; that is, political organizations (such as interest groups and parties) that come between the citizenry and government. The distrust of intermediary institutions in the political process is found in the enlightenment thought of Jean-Jacques Rousseau. In elevating *"le volonté général"* to the summit of the political community, Rousseau explicitly rejected the notions of representative democracy and institutionalized interests that we are familiar with in countries like the United States. We might note that such thinking had as its root the experience of the French *ancien régime* with the corporate bodies that seemed bastions of privilege. Thus, Rousseau laid out a line of thought which explicitly rejected the presence of organized parties and interests at the core of the democratic process.

Rousseau's shadow was to loom large over the French Revolution, and his prescription for participatory democracy (the alternative to representative democracy) was to shape the regime as it lurched from absolutism to constitutional monarchy, from constitutional monarchy to republic, and finally the slide into terror and dictatorship. As foment rose in the latter half of the 1780s, the publication of the *Letters on the Character and Writings of Rousseau* by Madame de Staël caused a stir and was widely interpreted as a subversive act; on the heels of the dramatic events of 1789, a bust to the memory of Rousseau was erected in Paris in July of the following year. When Robespierre thundered to the National Convention in 1794 that "Our [the Jacobin] will is the General Will," it was the consecration of Rousseau's thought in the sphere of action. Consistent with this line, the Jacobins moved to outlaw any form of secondary association, arguing that the state alone acts as the guarantor of the interests of the citizenry.

The distrust of both parties and interest groups can be traced as a constant in French political life to the present day. When General de Gaulle found himself repudiated by the French public in the aftermath of the liberation, he blamed the defeat of his proposals for a new institutional framework on the obstruction of political parties and other organized interests. Upon his accession to power in 1958 after the virtual collapse of the Fourth Republic, he posed as one of his conditions the mandate to elaborate a new constitution that would diminish the role and influence of such interests. In subordinating parliament to the presidency, and then in moving to the direct election of the president by universal suffrage, the constitution of the Fifth Republic merely echoed the same themes of indivisible national sovereignty and direct democracy that seep from the wellspring of French political culture in the modern era.

Equally relevant here is the tendency of the French over the centuries to make public policy *dans la rue* (in the streets). The modern French political system, with its roots in the revolution and the triumph of popular action, has always been susceptible to the ever-present threat of mass protest. The graveyard of post-revolutionary French history is littered with examples of popular rebellion, successful and failed; the July revolution of 1830, the Three Glorious Days of 1848, the Commune of 1871, the aborted putsch of February 6, 1934, the Algerian insurrection of 1958, the student revolt of May 1968, and so on. The underlying theme of popular resistance to authority, however, is one that predates even the revolution and that must, therefore, be separated to some degree from the distrust of intermediary institutions discussed earlier. Resistance to royal absolutism was manifest well in advance of the tumultuous events of 1789, and the revolution was the logical end of a sequence of struggles between monarchy and populace. The unitary and indivisible image of the French political system, so deeply rooted in the political culture, amalgamates all political institutions—whether intermediary or not—with the prevailing structure of authority. Thus, in the context of popular rebellion against authority, no organization or institution can speak for the people; rather, all are tainted by their association with the system and thus subject to condemnation and disdain.

The distrust of political parties and interest groups as intermediaries in the political system is thus as old as the Republic. Yet this distrust was given new impetus upon de Gaulle's arrival to power in 1958. He is quoted as declaring that:

> In the history of France there have always been, in one form or another, feudal fiefdoms. Today . . . these fiefdoms are in the political parties, the trade unions, in certain sectors of business . . . of the press, the bureaucracy, etc. Those who represent this new feudalism never like a state that does its job and which, as a consequence, is able to dominate them.

Given this analysis of the entrenched power of parties and interest groups, de Gaulle's constitutional blueprint for the Fifth Republic provided for a strong executive that had the power to control the National Assembly. With a powerful president that (since 1962) has been directly elected, the executive has both the legitimacy and the privilege in this constitutional system to overcome what has been commonly interpreted in the French political lexicon as the deleterious effects of pluralism and interest group/party interactions. The institutions of the Fifth Republic act to shield the executive from the direct influence of such groups and to allow the state to control points of access available to these groups. In sum, the executive is conceptualized in terms of the executor of the will of the nation and the National Assembly as a subordinate forum for the expression of such divisive and narrow "feudal" interests.

Political Party System and Political Parties

Since the 1980s, five main political parties have regularly contested national elections. Two of these parties are on the political left: the Socialist Party (PS) and the French Communist Party (PCF). Two of them are on the political right: the liberal Union for French Democracy (UDF) and the more conservative Rally for the Republic (RPR). The last of them is the newer, extreme-right National Front (FN), which has managed to become a major electoral thorn in the side of the other parties. As we shall discuss briefly following, however, recent developments may signal a beginning of a decline for the FN because of internal disputes among its leaders.

The pattern of competition among these parties has been shaped by the particular kind of electoral system adopted under the Fifth Republic. That system is a two-round contest, in which the highest vote-getters in the first round of balloting go forward to a runoff in the second round (the requirement is to get at least 12.5 percent of the eligible votes). Before the FN upset the apple cart, the first ballot tended to act as a kind of primary in which the two candidates from the left-wing parties would battle for a place in the second round, and the same would be true on the right. Generally, the runoff would end up with one candidate from the left and one from the right opposing each other. The system was reinforced by mutual agreements between the parties; for example, the PS and the PCF would agree in advance that, even if both parties' candidates were actually eligible to stand in the second round, the one who had garnered fewer votes would voluntarily withdraw.

This comfortable pattern of competition was disrupted by the emergence of the extreme-right FN as a real electoral threat. Because the rules of the second ballot actually allow more than two competitors to go through to it, the FN found itself in the position of being able to run candidates in the second ballot. Although only a handful of FN candidates have actually succeeded in getting elected under this system, the presence of them in the second round has thrown the neat pattern of party competition that was beginning to be commonplace into confusion; furthermore, it has posed a major problem to the other political parties, particularly those on the right, who are constantly unsure of how to treat the FN. Although the other party leaders constantly reiterate their public opposition to making deals with such an extremist party, many people privately have argued that it is inevitable, and some have gone ahead and made such deals locally.

The FN was given a tremendous boost in 1986, when the PS government decided to change the electoral system to one based on proportional representation. At the time, President Mitterrand argued that proportional representation was a much fairer and less biased system; more cynical observers thought that it was a maneuver on the part of the government, faced with its own unpopularity in the opinion polls, to try and reduce the number of seats that the right might win in the new National Assembly. In the event, the main impact was to allow the FN to elect thirty-five members and to consolidate its foothold on the national political scene. The same election produced a narrow conservative/liberal coalition victory, and the new government promptly changed the system back to the two ballot one described earlier. Nonetheless, this moment, in addition to the extensive use of proportional representation in regional and local elections, allowed the FN to become an established fixture of the French party system.

The other aspect of the Fifth Republic that has forced change on the party system is the presidentialization of politics. Since the direct election of the president was approved by popular referendum in 1962, political parties have been forced to increasingly become vehicles for the presidential ambitions of their leaders. Not unlike the United States, where leading party figures jockey for position in the run-up to the next presidential election year, the French political elite have also embraced political parties as the route to achieving the highest office. It is no accident that many French observers are lamenting the "Americanization" of politics. Winning the presidency has gradually emerged as the priority for all of the mainstream parties, and it has forced them to adopt strategies that can help them to achieve this goal. This means choosing media-friendly candidates, trying to promote internal cohesion and avoiding rivalries that could lose votes, and making electoral alliances and deals with other political formations. Even for the parties such as the PCF and FN that currently have little realistic hope of winning a presidential election, their ability to control votes in potential deal-making is a vital part of their presence within the system.

The presidentialization of the French political system has also had another effect on political parties because it forces them to split their efforts between presidential politics and national, regional, and local electoral contests. This division produces often contradictory pressures on party organizations that often find themselves in confusion or conflict over competing goals. One of the more curious byproducts of this counterpressure is the tradition of dissidence, where a local party figure leaves the party (or is expelled), wins the election by running against the Parisian "party bosses," and then gets reintegrated back into the party with all forgiven! Although such episodes have their amusing, even comic side, they highlight the difficulties that French parties face in organizing in such a highly fragmented and diverse electoral market.

The evolution of the French party system over the life of the Fifth Republic can be divided simply into before and after 1981. Prior to that year, the left had not held power at the national level, but on May 10, 1981, Francois Mitterrand, the co-founder and leader of the modern PS, was elected to the presidency. National Assembly elections one month later returned a solid socialist majority, enabling the party to form the government. Until 1981, the president was always able to rely on a solid majority in parliament and could thus appoint a prime minister from the same party grouping; since Mitterrand's victory in 1981, each presidential term served has been marked by a period when the president and prime minister are from opposing party groupings (what the French call *cohabitation*). In short, the socialist victory at the polls in 1981 marked the maturation of the institutions of the Fifth Republic and of the party system; paradoxically, in hindsight, it has also led to the deepening of some of the problems that those more mature parties face.

The first decade of the Fifth Republic was characterized more than anything else by the decomposition of the old bickering party factions of the previous regime. The end of the 1960s was a period of great crisis for the left, particularly the socialists. The uprising of May 1968, which caught all of the parties, including the socialists and communists, by surprise, seemed to demonstrate the degree to which the aspirations of the working-class population were not being met by political parties. The next year, the Socialist Party candidate for president, Gaston Deferre, managed just over 5 percent of the vote in the presidential election, a complete humiliation. In this atmosphere, talks began among several socialist and leftist leaders about the creation of a new, broad-based Socialist Party; in 1969, the new PS was born, and in 1971 Mitterrand became its leader.

Mitterrand's strategy was based on (1) the creation of an alliance with the Communist Party to form a general opposition to the government, and (2) bringing other small leftist parties and groups into the PS. Both strategies were a tremendous success, and the victory of 1981 can be seen as a confirmation of Mitterrand's vision; however, the strategy also forced the Socialist Party to incorporate many different positions within its ranks, from the older generation of the now-defunct SFIO (the former Socialist Party) to the "autogestionnaire" (self-management) left of those such as Michel Rocard. With Mitterrand as leader and tactician, the PS was able to dominate the alliance passed with the communists (the so-called Union of the Left) and to prepare the victory of 1981. Unhindered by any question of relations with the Soviet Union (whereas the Communist Party remained dogged by the notion that it was a stooge of Moscow), and presenting itself as a modern, capable party of government, the PS won many converts from the moderate center with its new social democratic image.

In contrast, the PCF found itself unable to expand its base of support during the 1970s, despite the alliance with the PS. More than anything, the PCF was unable to soften and moderate its appeals to voters because of the commitment to democratic centralism—the organizational principle of the party since its founding in 1921 and one that reeked to many of authoritarianism. Unlike other European communist parties (most notably that of Italy), the PCF did not make much attempt to distance itself from communist orthodoxy, and it retained a distinctly pro-Soviet flavor. As the PCF began to be outdistanced by the PS in the quest for votes, leadership of the party became increasingly skeptical about the utility of the Union of the Left, and in 1977 it threatened to break with the PS unless the electoral alliance was renegotiated. This demand was really the critical moment in the development of modern French socialism; rather than accede to these demands, Mitterrand and the PS held firm and the Union of the Left came to an end. The immediate result was the loss of the 1978 parliamentary elections that many had thought that the left might win; however, it also marked the moment when the PS was able to demonstrate that it was the moderate, dynamic, independent, and modern force on the left capable of assuming power by itself. When the PS did win in 1981, it offered a token number of positions in the new government to the communists as a goodwill gesture[5] (perhaps more as a guarantee

---

[5]The gesture earned the disapproval of the Reagan Administration, which threatened to oppose giving a visa to one of the new Communist ministers who was scheduled to visit Washington.

against the future), but it was not under any obligation to do so.

The rejuvenation of the left in the 1970s and the growing strength of the PS was also the catalyst for changes on the ideological right. Until the mid-1970s, the conservative and Gaullist right had operated less as a party than as a movement bringing together anyone who sought office under the banner of "Gaullism." Precisely what Gaullism meant was not always well articulated. One of the strange aspects of the Gaullist movement was that the UNR was created in 1958 uniquely to support de Gaulle, with no other program or discernible ideology, yet de Gaulle himself shunned the movement! While General de Gaulle and his hand-picked successor, Georges Pompidou, were in the presidency, it did not matter so much; but when Pompidou died in 1974, the uncertainties began to matter much more. Without any obvious heir, but many pretenders, to the Gaullist mantle the movement failed to win the presidential election of 1974. Instead, the new president, Valéry Giscard d'Estaing, was a technocratic centrist who clearly harbored dreams of creating a center-right coalition that could act as a counterweight within the governmental majority to the presence of the Gaullists.

This outcome left the latter group embattled and facing seemingly inevitable decline; however, in 1976 the UDR (as it had become in the interim) was taken over by the young and ambitious Jacques Chirac. Chirac had been prime minister for the previous two years (having supported Giscard in the presidential election) but had been forced out because of the increasingly obvious conflicts between him and the president. Chirac wrestled control of the Gaullist party from the old "barons of Gaullism" and set about transforming it into a modern presidential party. In 1977, the name of the party was changed to the Rally for the Republic (RPR), and its program began to take on distinctly neo-liberal overtones. Although Chirac de-emphasized the Gaullist message over the next few years, the Gaullist heritage could be easily manipulated to draw in support from moderate right-wing elites and voters. Thus the RPR, much as the PS on the left, was faced with a set of internal tensions arising from the need to draw disparate ideological groups into one political organization.

Much in response to the creation of the RPR, President d'Estaing attempted to create a true party of the center-right that could compete with the RPR for voters in the first round of national elections; however, the nature of the center-right in France is such that close party cooperation is difficult at best; tensions between social Catholics on the one hand and moderate liberals on the other prevented the emergence of a truly unified political party. The outcome of Giscard's efforts was the Union for French Democracy (UDF), which acts as an umbrella organization to several small parties. The UDF was hastily cobbled together to contest the 1978 parliamentary elections; however, the primary intent of Giscard was to form a presidential vehicle that could counter Chirac's control of the RPR. The rivalry between Chirac and Giscard became increasingly intense between 1978 and 1981; in the presidential elections of that year, Chirac ran against Giscard in the first ballot. After he was eliminated (although receiving a respectable 18 percent of the vote), Chirac refused to endorse Giscard in the runoff against Mitterrand, leading many on the right to accuse him of betrayal after Mitterrand's victory.

The primary problem of the UDF was to overcome its weak organization and the internal feuds separating the composite political parties. The incentive for these parties to remain within the UDF is primarily generated by the aspirations of many of their leaders to get into national office (and for the most ambitious, to gain a foothold toward the presidency); but the ideological, programmatic, and historical differences among these parties are often too great to be contained within the umbrella formation. Recently, the UDF leadership decided to participate in discussions with the RPR about the formation of one umbrella party on the right that would engulf all of the constituent components of the UDF plus the RPR. The new formation was baptized The Alliance, and in theory will be the organization that will contest national elections in the name of the united right; however, participation in The Alliance has weakened the UDF. Liberal Democracy (DL), the largest of the parties within the UDF, announced that it could see no point in remaining within the UDF given the formation of The Alliance, and it withdrew. Whether the UDF continues to exist in any meaningful form, and whether The Alliance is able to meaningfully federate the right, are important questions that are as yet unanswered.

The arrival of the FN on the political stage in 1983 has altered the dynamics of political competition between parties and provoked a continuing crisis on the ideological right. The impetus for the dramatic breakthrough of the extreme right can be found in the economic crises of the 1970s and 1980s, the failure of the new left government to turn things around in 1981, the continual discord on the right, and the inability of the Communist Party to modernize its appeal to the working classes. The political landscape of the time, with rising discontent, mass unemployment, and the perception that France was being swamped by immigrants (as we have shown previously, a very inaccurate perception), created a situation that was ripe for exploitation by a skillful and unprincipled political party.

The FN was created in 1972 by Jean-Marie Le Pen but received little national attention until the local elections in 1983. The FN had been steadily recruiting at the local level through the late 1970s and early 1980s, but it lacked national media attention that would project it into the spotlight. The occasion was provided by the bickering and infighting in the right-wing parties in the town of Dreux, which enabled the FN to get enough votes to allow it to act as a power broker in the election. The question of whether the conservative right should accept an alliance with the racist and xenophobic FN was one that the Parisian elite could not ignore; equally so, the left was in search of an issue that could divide the right and turn attention away from its own problems of governing the country. Suddenly, the FN and its program of "France for the French" became the most visible topic of political debate and discussion, and the movement found itself with a national platform from which to disseminate its ideas.

Le Pen is an energetic and articulate speaker, whose oratorical skills command attention from even hostile observers. Although he has often been accused of racism and anti-semitism, and despite having been convicted by the courts both for having made injurious remarks about the nonexistence of gas chambers in Nazi Germany and more recently for assault on a rival candidate during an election campaign, Le Pen defends himself by portraying himself as the victim of a conspiracy to ignore the truth among the French political elite. Part populist, part demagogue, Le Pen has personalized the FN as his movement, the message of it being inseparable from his own presidential and leadership ambitions. The FN has largely become a populist party that speaks to those who are the most disgruntled within French society, often the poor and the unemployed. The simple prescription that it offers—take jobs away from immigrants and give them to "French" people—is one that appeals to those who are fed up with the seeming inability of the mainstream parties of either the left or the right to provide a solution to France's economic problems. Most recently, the issue of European integration has allowed the FN to extend its nationalist image and to attract right-wing voters who might be less susceptible to the racist elements of the party platform but who feel that the French national identity is becoming submerged in the new Europe.

French President Jacques Chirac. In the first round of the 1995 presidential election, a record 37 percent of votes went to extreme left-wing or right-wing candidates. The winner, Jacques Chirac, from the established Gaullist party, received the lowest share of the popular vote of any Fifth Republic President—49.5 percent.

The use of proportional representation in the parliamentary elections of 1986 cemented the position of the FN within the electoral geography of contemporary France. Although the party has never been able to repeat that feat after the reversion to the use of the two-ballot election system, it has continued to get between 12 and 15 percent of the vote in national elections and get candidates elected to regional and local councils. Although the party's national level of support makes it unlikely that it can win seats in the National Assembly, it does have regional strengths (particularly in the north and in the southeast) that enable it to challenge for primacy on the right. This popularity has given the FN enormous "blackmail" potential because it can decide to maintain its candidates in the second round of the election, splitting the vote of the right and generally permitting a left-wing candidate to be elected where otherwise this would not be possible. Indeed, it can be argued that the narrow victory of the left in 1997 was a consequence of the vote-splitting capacities of the FN.

The FN has also had to deal with the negative consequences of success. The movement has been divided since the earliest days between those who favored a more accommodating strategy with the classical right and those who argued for an extremist line with no compromise. Although the party was inevitably dependent on the personality of Le Pen, the strategic differences could be held in check because little room existed for maneuver outside of Le Pen's will. As the party began to develop a more and more autonomous organization, however, and to achieve repeated success at the local level, that has afforded more potential for those who wish to see the movement move beyond the "ghetto" of the extreme right. In late 1998, one of Le Pen's previously most trusted lieutenants, Bruno Mégret, announced that he intended to challenge Le Pen for leadership of the party. This decision set off a series of events that have torn the FN apart and led to the spectacle of two rival parts of the organization both claiming to be the true party. Most observers agree that Le Pen remains more popular among voters at large, whereas Mégret probably controls as much as two-thirds of the former party organization. Each of them headed a separate list in the European elections of June 1999; Le Pen's list managed 5.7 percent of the vote, and that of Mégret polled just 3.3 percent. The episode demonstrates the extent to which the competing pressures on French parties, born of the institutional configuration of the system discussed earlier, produce outcomes that place severe internal strains on parties from all sides of the ideological spectrum.

The late 1980s also witnessed the emergence of the Green movement as a potentially determinant electoral force. The first manifestation of the ecological movement in electoral politics occurred in 1974 with the candidacy of René Dumont in the presidential campaign (he scored just over 1 percent of the vote); not until 1989 did the Green movement make a significant breakthrough on the national electoral map. In that year, the Green party was able to field a record number of candidates in local elections; despite only getting a little under 1.5 percent of the national vote, this translated at the local level into more than thirteen hundred councilors elected. The extent of this success can be measured by the fact that the Greens had twice the number of councilors elected than the FN. Following that success, the Greens fielded a party list for the 1989 European Parliament elections and gained more than 10 percent of the national vote. This was enough to give the movement nine European Parliament seats out of the eighty-one allotted to France, and it placed the Greens ahead of the PCF in the national vote. Furthermore, the extent of the Green vote suggested that it was becoming a national force because it did relatively well in all areas of France.

The strategy pursued by the Green movement in France was one of "neither left nor right," symbolizing the aspiration to reject alliances of convenience with the major parties. Yet, from the heights of 1989, the Green movement in France has been split over the very same question. In 1988, the socialist government offered a place in the cabinet to Brice Lalonde, a leading environmental figure. The move was clearly intended to help the PS "capture" the green vote—with reason, for polls showed that in 1989 the majority of Green voters actually defected from the PS. But Lalonde's appointment proved hard to digest for the Green movement, and he subsequently launched his own pro-environment party, Generation Ecology (GE). Elections in 1993 and 1994 showed the degree to which the issues of alliances with the left in general and the PS in particular have eaten at the promising advance of the Green movement. Conflicts within and between the two main Green forces have reduced their appeal to many voters looking for an alternative to the seeming unending squabbles that characterize French party politics.

In the 1997 elections that brought the left to power, the Green movement accepted an electoral alliance with the PS, which did not run candidates against Green/GE candidates in selected constituencies. This enabled the Greens and GE to take a respectable 6.8 percent of the vote nationally, and to get seven members elected to the National Assembly. Those elected under the Green banner have joined a parliamentary group of thirty-four members called "Radical, Citizen, Green"; the group supports the socialist government but sits in a different party grouping in the National Assembly in order to mark what they see as the critical differences between them and the PS. The stated position of the group, however, identifies it as being "firmly on the left and committed to progressive ecology." This approach belies the attempt to portray the ecological movement as being neither left nor right, and perhaps signals the transformation of Green politics in France to a position in the party system more equivalent to the Greens in Germany, uneasy but natural coalition partners for social democratic governments.

Fundamentally, the problem that the Green movement faces is one of program. Many observers have pointed out that the ecological movement in France, although it has some core agreements such as the opposition to nuclear power, is divided in some rather contradictory ways. On the one hand, the movement grew out of the May 1968 libertarian culture, which emphasized opposition to industrialization and capitalism. Yet the more recent concerns of the Greens embrace solidarity with the unemployed, the Third World, the poor, and so on. The issue of European integration has been a particularly thorny one because it has highlighted the tensions between those who oppose it in the name of anti-capitalism and localism and those who embrace it under the rubric of progress and anti-statism. Particularly because the European Parliament has afforded the Greens with a platform from which to address environmental concerns, and because pollution is increasingly seen as a pan-European issue that knows no national borders, the attitude of the Green movement to European integration is highly ambiguous at best.

In summary, the party system in contemporary France has shown much more in common with other European democracies in recent years than ever before. Particularly notable is the ideological moderation of the major parties, especially on the left where the PCF has declined in strength and the PS has emerged as a pragmatic social democratic party in the European mold. French parties today offer relatively clear, moderate alternatives that allow voters to choose between them on positive rather than negative grounds. Opinion polls show that this belief reflects the ideological moderation of the electorate in general. This has permitted the regular alternation of parties in power, which had not happened previous to 1981. With no party having a hegemonic lock on the reigns of power and no moderate party condemned to permanent opposition, the French system has quietly begun to resemble a functioning and modern parliamentary democracy. Periods of power-sharing, or cohabitation (where the president and prime minister are from different parties or blocks) have shown that the system can function under these conditions and have also strengthened the role of Parliament (and thus parties) in the policy formation process (see following).

These signs of the modernization of French party competition must be tempered with the observation that not all is well. As modernization along these dimensions has occurred, voter apathy and disenchantment have also risen. Observers agree less about the existence of a trend, but in general abstention rates in French elections appear to be rising. Added to that, voters are more likely than in previous years to vote for parties other than the moderate, modern parties of government such as the PS and the RPR. The fact that voters have turned to extremist parties such as the FN or alternative parties such as the Greens signals a level of dissatisfaction with party politics that runs deep. These sentiments have not been helped by the scandals that have exposed the seamy world of party financing and that have put into question the organizing methods of the PS and the RPR. Opinion polls have shown that distrust of the political elite generally is on the rise, and that French voters are likely to express this dissatisfaction at election time in the form of protest voting of one kind or another. Internal disputes that run through all of the major parties have also clearly perpetuated the image that the parties are vehicles that elites use to get elected to government and that they are unable to address the concerns of the ordinary citizens.

Perhaps the biggest challenge to the party system is whether the ideological moderation that was noted earlier is actually the harbinger of ideological decomposition. It may be, as some have suggested, that the French electorate has become divided along lines other than those associated with classical ideologies and that make it difficult for any party to appeal to specific groups in society. As noted previously, the new fault lines in French society seem to separate those who benefit from

Europeanization and globalization from those who are being left behind, those who have reason to be optimistic about their future and to embrace these trends from those who are fearful of them. The two-speed society means that citizens expect different things from government; the "haves" look to the state to integrate and to open up French markets, to liberalize and to modernize, whereas the "have-nots" expect the state to protect them from these forces. The fault lines run right through the party system and pose the essential challenge to the continued evolution of French parties in the coming decades.

POLITICAL INSTITUTIONS AND PUBLIC POLICY FORMATION

An overview of the forms and functions of French political institutions, or state institutions in any country for that matter, could lead us into a black hole of detailed, dry discussions of legal procedure, executive process, and parliamentary practice. Indeed, students of European politics in the 1970s tried to develop a new way of studying politics that would shift the analysis from describing the various branches of government to explaining political activity on an individual level. The present generation of Europeanists has actually come back to analyzing the state, often following what has been called the new institutionalism where government institutions are seen as important players in the way public decisions get made and the overall development of democracy. This section combines the best of these different worlds of political science. On one hand it examines the form and function of the major institutions of government—the executive, the parliament, the judiciary, and the bureaucracy. On the other hand, it focuses on the nuts and bolts of these structures by questioning their roles in public policy formation. We also consider the territorial dimension of government by looking at whether the regions have become more involved in policy formation since the 1982 decentralization laws.

When we say public policy formation, we mean the start-to-finish process by which governments set their agenda, make public decisions, carry out those decisions and then evaluate the success of those decisions. Generally, policy formation process has three parts. First, preformulation, which includes (1) the definition of social conditions into social problems on which governments need to act; (2) the setting of the public and the government agenda as to which problems the government will address; and (3) the generation of potential policy ideas that may or may not be taken up by the government. The preformulation process is highly complex, often involving all three branches of governments as well as a myriad of nongovernmental group actors. The second phase—policy formulation—is where a government decision is taken, usually either by the chief executive or the legislature.

The third phase is the postformulation phase and includes implementation and evaluation. In implementation, policies are carried out and enforced by the bureaucracy, police, and/or courts. In the evaluation process, state and nonstate players decide either formally or informally to evaluate whether a given policy was successful or not. The evaluation of a policy often leads back to the beginning of the policy formation cycle. In many countries, depending on the legal system and culture, the judiciary goes beyond simple implementation and enforcement, often contributing to setting policy agendas and even changing the content of public policy. Judicial policymaking is particularly prevalent in the United States, where the judicial review of the Supreme Court can completely overturn legislation and executive orders and create new public policy outside of the legislative process.

Executive Legislative Relations: The Semi-Presidential System

Unlike other countries of Western Europe, which have parliamentary systems of executive-legislative relations, France has a semi-presidential system, which combines a presidential with parliamentary government. In presidential systems, like the United States, the chief executive is popularly elected and the legislature is elected separately from the president. Policy formation power is effectively shared between the institutionally divided executive and legislative branches of government, with the legislature having a real say in the outcome of legislation, called by experts a "transformative role." In parliamentary systems, policymaking power is fused between the legislature and the executive, with the cabinet and prime minister being selected through the election of the legislature, usually the lower house of parliament. In parliamentary systems, the chief executive plays the dominant role in policy formation, with the parliament playing more of an "arena" role where public affairs are debated.

France's system, designed to overcome the weaknesses of French parliamentary democracy under the Third and Fourth Republics, was intended to place a popularly elected president above what were seen by many as the "whims" of irresponsible political parties and hopelessly fragmented parliamentary majorities, while still preserving the collective responsibility of the cabinet government to parliament and, through the parliamentary elections, to the electorate. Unlike any other Western democracy, France has a two-headed (bicephalous) executive, with a president and a prime minister. The president is elected every seven years, and the lower house of parliament, the National Assembly,[6] every five years. The party composition of the cabinet or government is based on the distribution of seats in this lower house of parliament. France has an upper house, the Senate, which is elected by indirect suffrage and, as most upper houses in parliamentary systems, has very little influence in the content of legislation and relations with the cabinet.

The president has the power to appoint the prime minister and the cabinet, presides over the Council of ministers—all ministers with a major portfolio—and may dissolve the National Assembly. The framers of the Fifth Republic constitution also "armed" the president-dominated executive with an "arsenal of weapons" to reduce the power of parliament. For instance, article 44.3 allows the government to force parliament to adopt a bill in its entirety with only the amendments agreed to by the government, through what is called a blocked vote (*vote bloquée*). The parliamentary timetable was also restricted by the Fifth Republic constitution, allowing for only two three-month sessions.

In this system, as in all parliamentary systems, the government's agenda, as well as the legislative agenda, is set by the chief executive, through either the filter of the president's or prime minister's party. Indeed, more than 80 percent of all bills originate from the cabinet, and a good portion of these are not altered in the legislative formulation process. The power of the chief executive means the arena for preformulation as well as formulation is centered around the president's office, located at the Elysée palace, or the prime minister's office, at Matignon, and the top-level cabinet members' offices, not the parliament. The president and his staff control the decision agenda through a tentacled network of permanent and temporary interministerial and cabinet-level committees, councils, and study groups that the president names, presides over, or to which the president sends his representatives. In 1985, seven hundred employees staffed the Elysée, and its operating

---
[6]The words National Assembly and parliament are used interchangably.

The French National Assembly (or parliament). Members are seated left to right based on the ideological orientation of their party.

budget was eight times larger than the National Assembly's.

The policy formation power of the chief executive means that nongovernmental organizations that seek to influence public policy decisions in preformulation or formulation go to the chief executive rather than parliament. Moreover, unlike the way interest groups freely lobby members of Congress, groups must fit into the busy schedules of ministers or must wait for an invitation to express their opinions on pertinent policy decision. Interest group representatives are also included as permanent members of many of the interministerial committees that prepare legislation, another manifestation of corporatism. Thus, in general the chief executive committees are where pol-

icy problems, solutions, and proposals get hammered out. Parliamentary commissions on the same topics often tend to echo what went on in the cabinet committees. Indeed, many of the hard decisions of policy formulation take place before parliament even gets involved. Unlike the U.S. Congress, the French parliament has very little control over the budgetary process, which occurs behind closed doors in the cabinet. Budget politics in general are a low-profile policy issue that only make the back pages of the newspapers and are seldom the object of heated public debates so typical of the French political scene. As we discuss in the next section, policy implementation, evaluation, and oversight of the bureaucracy is also under the control of the

TABLE 3.2 The Dueling Dual Executive

President	P.M.	Outcome
1962–1968 de Gaulle (Gaullist)	Gaullist	Hyper-Presidential
1969–1973 Pompidou (Gaullist)	Gaullist	Hyper-Presidential
1974–1981 Giscard d'Estaing (Center-Right)	1974–1978 Gaullist	
	1978–1981 Center-Right	Tempered Presidential
1981–1986 Mitterrand (Socialist)	Socialist	Hyper-Presidential
1986–1988 Mitterrand (Socialist)	Gaullist	Cohabitation I
1988–1993 Mitterrand (Socialist)	Socialist	Tempered Presidential
1993–1995 Mitterrand (Socialist)	Gaullist	Cohabitation II
1995–1997 Chirac (Gaullist)	Gaullist	Hyper-Presidential
1997–present Chirac (Gaullist)	Socialist	Cohabitation III

Adapted from Table 2.1 in Keeler and Schain.

bicephalous chief executive. Parliament's "arena" role, therefore, means that it takes a backseat to the chief executive in all stages of the policy formation process.

Although it is clear that the bicephalous chief executive is in charge of policy formation in France, and the president is "armed" with formal constitutional powers, it is not always clear whether the president's office at the Elysée or the prime minister at Matignon calls the shots in the policy formation game. President de Gaulle's 1964 pronouncement that "The President is obviously alone in holding and delegating the authority of the state," has not always been the norm and is increasingly less so at the turn of the millennium. Whether the president and prime minister are like dueling partners or business partners all depends on the partisan line-up of the National Assembly and the presidency determined by the outcome of elections. Table 3.2 shows the three different scenarios for power sharing in the bicephalous chief executive: hyper-presidential, tempered presidential, and premier-presidential or cohabitation.

In the hyper-presidential mode, the president is of the same party as the majority party in parliament—a presidential majority—and so selects a prime minister from his or her party and a cabinet that reflects the parliamentary majority. With the presidential majority, the president has full reign over the legislative agenda and governmental affairs. The president acts as both head of state and head of government, with the premier acting as a "loyal lieutenant." The president's power is "tempered" when the majority in the National Assembly is not all from his own party. Under Presidents Giscard d'Estaing and Francois Mitterrand, the prime ministers were from a different party as the president, albeit from the same overall ideological affiliation. In these cases, the president must build coalitions of support through cabinet appointments and discussion with the National Assembly in order to get the presidential program adopted. In general, in a tempered presidential mode, the president is more concerned with foreign affairs and gives authority over the domestic policy agenda to the cabinet.

From 1986 to 1988, then from 1993 to 1995, and now since 1997, the power of the president was drastically reduced in the context of the election of a National Assembly with a majority from the opposite side of the ideological spectrum than the president. In this situation of cohabitation, the president must appoint a prime minister and cabinet from the opposing party and essentially give into the policy program of the government and presidential majority in parliament. Given that the parliamentary majority follows the lead of the prime minister, and the president's party in parliament is reduced to one of opposition, the president must take a backseat in defining the government program. In these situations, the president is obliged to become a near-figurehead in government affairs, emphasizing the ceremonial aspects of head of state. The prime minister takes on the full dual role of a single chief executive—head of state and head of government.

An active party leader and major framer of the socialist government policy agenda from 1981–1986, Francois Mitterrand, in his second term, under first a tempered presidential model and then cohabitation, was criticized in the French press for his distanced role in governmental affairs, likening his evolving role to that of a constitutional monarch more than a popularly elected president. Beginning in 1988, the satirical weekly newspaper, *le Canard Enchaîné,* regularly portrayed Mitterrand in its cartoons flying above France donning a royal crown. Since Mitterrand's two terms, the power of the president has never been the same, with the prime minister and cabinet taking an increasingly active role in policy formation, even in the context of a hyperpresidential situation.

The Bureaucracy and the Upper Civil Servants

Although the bureaucracy is technically under the control of the president and the prime minister's offices and is relied on to objectively implement public policy, upper civil servants working in the top managerial ranks of the French administration have a great deal of influence on all stages of policy formation. The power of the French *hautes fonctionnaires* emanates from their high level of training, *esprit de corps,* and government-guaranteed job opportunities in both the public and the private sector. High-level bureaucrats in most countries outside of the United States have a great deal of prestige, earn top salaries, and are generally seen to be important elites in society. The French model for training its administrative elite is often held up as an example for other countries. Through its state-run national administrative schools, like the prestigious Ecole Nationale d'Administration (ENA) and Ecole Polytéchnique (X), and its state-run system of professional placement agencies, called the Grands Corps—employment agencies for graduates of these leading-edge administrative schools or Grandes Ecoles—the French system produces generalist bureaucrats who can operate at high levels in any managerial situation. Indeed the Grandes Ecoles are seen as the Ivy League of France.

The Grands Corps also ensures that graduates are placed in good positions and are paid a good salary. Each functional grand corps essentially pays the salaries of its members no matter what they do, including running for public office. Many politicians who accumulate elected offices at different levels of government through the *cumul des mandats* have passed through the upper civil servant training system. Three of six Fifth Republic Presidents, for example, have been graduates of the Grandes Ecoles. Often, top bureaucrats are appointed to plum positions in business—up until recently nationalized industries—in the latter stages of their careers through a process called *pantouflage,* which literally means "putting on bedroom slippers." The idea here is that after a long career in public service, top bureaucrats are rewarded by being placed in cushy management positions in business where they end their careers in highly lucrative posts. Indeed, this process of training and placement produces an elite class of people, bonded together by old-school ties, who control top positions in government—appointed and elected—and business alike. The persistence of this elitism in public service has greatly contributed to the rising malaise about the government's ability to deal with the widening gap between the haves and have-nots, with the haves often being the very elites who appear to be so unresponsive to this fracture sociale.

Historically, in the context of frequent changes in regimes, these well-trained upper civil servants have maintained administrative continuity. Although upper civil servants are imbued with a strong sense of jacobin national duty to la République—ENA and the system of grand corps were put into place under the First Republic—many top-level civil servants have happily worked for democracy and dictatorship. Top bureaucrats who worked for the fascist regime of Vichy, for instance, continued to have successful careers under the Fourth and Fifth Republics. One official, Maurice Papon, as a departmental prefect played an important decisional role in rounding up French Jews to be sent to Nazi concentration camps. Not until Papon retired from an illustrious career as a bureaucrat and banker was he tried for his crimes against humanity. The lateness of his trial and the success of his career attest to the power and prestige of the upper civil service. Also, government records laws prevent any private individuals from examining classified government documents for forty years. (Indeed, the highly restrictive document laws were made ultimately to protect the state and public servants from too much public scrutiny that would potentially undermine the work of the state.) The Papon Affair only came to light in the context of the opening of these files. Thus, as an upper-level civil servant, Papon was immune and allowed to reap the full benefits of his position.

The corps of elite-trained bureaucrats are appointed to the staffs of the president, prime minister, and ministers, and less often to parliamentary members' staffs, which tend to be tiny and underfunded. They are also appointed for stints as departmental prefects in the provinces—an historically pivotal position for linking center to periphery—and as department heads within the functional divisions of each government ministry. For instance, the Bureau of Women's Rights had seven separate subdivisions: legal rights, violence, reproduction, external relations, research, education, and employment. Typically, upper-level civil servants spend two or three years working in a position and then shift to a different area of government to get more experience. The plum positions are running the president's staff, when a hyper-presidential model is in place, and the prime minister's staff, when cohabitation is in operation.

Somewhat like congressional staffers in the United States, members of ministerial and presidential staffs wield a great deal of power over what information their bosses get, who they see, and, most important, the type of policy proposals that come out of their offices. Politically appointed ministers rely heavily on the upper civil servants in their staffs. In many instances, particularly in left-wing governments, the ministers have received less education and are from lower classes than their staffs. As heads of central administration subdivisions and as departmental prefects, upper civil servants have a great deal of say in how policies get implemented as well as the process of state-initiated program evaluation.

Territorial Division of Power and Decentralization Since 1982

With France's legacy of centralized unitary government, a chief executive–dominated policy formation system, and a well-entrenched Paris-dominated elite, it is not surprising that decentralization of political power away from Paris has been greatly resisted. At the same time, the tradition of local power and culture had meant that there has always been an important counterbalance to national power. The influence of local government over many administrative functions, particularly over social delivery, is the norm in other unitary systems like Great Britain and Sweden, where the mid-level of government (e.g., counties and regions) has virtually no control over taxation, social service delivery, or legislation. Both formally and informally, French towns, depending on their size and the political activities of their mayors, have had a certain degree of independence from the Paris-based national government.

Despite the importance of local government autonomy, French public policy formation has been dominated by national government, with national legislation dictating the form of local-level policy. The popularly elected departmental councils up until the 1982 decentralization reforms were under the control of the administrative agents of the national government—the prefects. This particular type of unitary system was a dual system, with two administrative streams emanating from the national government—the prefects who were under the control of the Department of the Interior and the field services of each ministry. Indeed, under the direct control of the Ministry of the Interior, based in Paris, and usually staffed by a Paris-trained upper civil servant, the prefects were the major players who coordinated the relations between departmental councils, field services of the national administration, and oversaw the distribution of national funds to the city councils.

Despite several unsuccessful efforts to transfer power to the regions in the 1960s—for example, a 1969 referendum on setting up elected regional councils was defeated—the fourteen decentralization laws adopted from 1982 to 1986 have now successfully redirected policymaking power away from the prefects to twenty-two popularly elected regional councils and ninety-six departmental councils. The French territorial distribution of power still remains unitary. Unlike federal systems, the regions do not have their own constitutions or their own court systems. Regional council decisions do not supersede national legislation. In terms of policy formation, the sublevels of government are still basically involved with policy implementation, albeit with more political control over policy implementation than ever before.

The decentralization of power has largely taken place around who delivers and controls social services such as education, transportation, and health, with a large portion of the public funds for those services still coming from coffers at the national level. The major oversight instrument for public service delivery is the regional plan, which is elaborated by the regional councils and provides a policy roadmap for the economic development and coordination of public service delivery for each region. The regional councils oversee the affairs of the departments and the departments manage the affairs of the communes. Communes get 50 percent of their finance from bloc grants from the national, regional, and departmental levels and 50 percent from taxes. Regional councils are responsible for setting regional planning and constructing schools. Departmental councils are now responsible for the delivery of health and social services, construction of junior high schools, and the provision of school transportation. The various funding programs of the European Union that allocate funds to regional government have enhanced the power of the regions outside of the decentralization reforms. With the help of this EU funding, therefore, new regional policy networks have emerged around a new process of economic development that makes business and government more equal partners.

Some students of French policy formation, like Pierre Muller, see the emergence of the regions as a sign that the old style of state-centered policymaking is being significantly challenged from above by Europe and from below at the local level. Vivien Schmidt, an American student of decentralization, sees old patterns of French politics being transported to the regional levels with regions becoming "separate politico-administrative systems in their own right . . ." where the elected presidents of the councils ". . . have become new potentates in the periphery" (1990). Thus, French policy formation on a territorial axis has certainly become more complicated, but whether it has become more democratic remains to be seen. Indeed, the recent rise in alienation and malaise suggests that the new layers of bureaucracy have created more distance between the French and their governing institutions and perhaps even reduced the effectiveness of the government to deal with the problems posed by Europeanization and the global economy.

The Constitutional Council and the Code Law System

Another important recent change on the French institutional landscape has been the increased role of the Constitutional Council, France's highest court, in policy formation with regards to controlling the power of the two-headed executive and enhancing that of the parliamentary opposition. The jacobin tradition of limiting the power of the judiciary and making it subservient to the legislative and executive branches of government has made the judicial branch of government a weak partner in policy formation. Breaking from this tradition, the Constitutional Council has become an important independent actor in the national policy formation process through what Alec Stone has called the "judicialization" of the policy process. With seven members serving nine-year nonrenewable terms, the council can be called by the president, prime minister, the presidents of the two houses of parliament and, after the 1974 amendment to the constitution, by sixty deputies and sixty senators, to decide whether a piece of legislation conforms to the constitution. This decision occurs before the law is officially adopted—in technical terms, promulgated—and must be made within one month. Three members of council are chosen by the presidents of the Senate and the National Assembly, and three are picked by the president. All former presidents have a seat on the council as well, but none so far have actually been active.

Before the 1974 amendment, very few appeals were made—nine in fifteen years—and the rulings were in favor of the government. After the 1974 law, the council was called on to judge governmental legislation; many of these laws were rejected by the council. Increasingly after 1989, the government took into consideration past council decisions or jurisprudence in drafting legislation. Thus, not only were laws that were considered unconstitutional annulled, but the council had an indirect influence on policy formulation. Designed to strengthen the president's hand in executive-legislative relations in policy formulation, the Constitutional Council has actually been used by parliamentary opposition to block the implementation of a strong president's legislative agenda.

As much as the council has developed into an unplanned check on chief executive power, it does not have the checking power of the U.S. Supreme Court or even constitutional courts in other countries, like Germany, where individual court cases can be used as a test of constitutionality of a given law. Also, the highly political nature of the appointment process limits the accountability of the council. Nonetheless, its augmented role has forced the upper civil servants in the chief executive to draft legislation that conforms more to the constitution rather than to the elite politics of backroom decision making.

Beyond this unexpected development of the role of the Constitutional Council, the power of the courts more generally is very limited in the policymaking process. Unlike countries with common law legal systems where the lower courts play a significant role in policymaking through precedent setting and, in some countries, judicial review, jurisprudence in France does not lead to significant changes in policy content through judicial policymaking. As a result, individuals, interest groups, and trade unions in France do not use the courts as an avenue of direct social change to the same extent as do interest groups in countries where court decisions have the potential to become law.

For example, the courtroom has not been an important arena for enforcing civil rights. Even when the equal rights clauses in the preamble of the 1958 Constitution were legitimized by a 1971 Constitutional Council's decisions, groups did not come forward to file sex discrimination lawsuits based on the principle of equal rights between men and women stated in the preamble. In general, reflecting the dynamics of the Romano-Germanic legal system, citizenship and civil rights have been expanded through legislation, not through court battles. The jacobin informed legal culture has also underscored the absence of litigation-centered legal aid societies or watchdog groups that use the courts to ensure that civil rights are enforced. Likewise, the French legal tradition plays down the incentive of large settlements for court cases. Legislation sets the range of fines and prison sentences and states whether judges may award damages or not. The judge can extend limited damages only as long as the plaintiff requests them.

In the twenty-two equal employment cases taken to court from 1978 to 1986—and there were only this number during that time period—the highest settlement was $7,200. This is a far cry from some of the employment discrimination settlements in the United States, which can reach into the millions. Collective action suits, particularly in the area of employment discrimination in the workplace, are also rare. Thus, the courts in France neither have an important indirect role on the content of policy through judicial policymaking nor are they an important forum for the implementation of civil rights. Indeed, the classical jacobin hostility to the power of judges and courts continues to be an important factor in the weakness of judicial precedent in France. European Court of Justice (ECJ) decisions, which can supersede national jurisprudence and policy have had some impact on law in France, but not as much as in countries, like Great Britain, where common law traditions actually set precedent for policy. Still, interest groups increasingly look to ECJ jurisprudence to challenge French law.

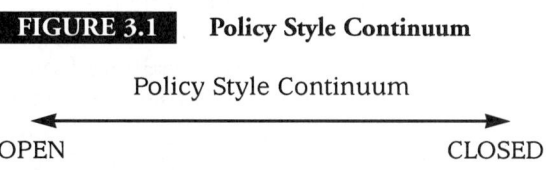

FIGURE 3.1 Policy Style Continuum

French Public Policy Formation in Action: Policy Styles and Women's Rights Legislation

Having looked at the different roles of the major political institutions in France, is it possible to talk about a single mode or style of policy formation that is typically French? Actually, there is not one single policy formation style. Although many people like to hold up France as the prototype for centralized, state-dominated decision making, when one takes a closer look, a broad range of policymaking styles can be found in France, particularly in the context of the recent changes in the power of the presidency, the shift of power to the regions, and the rise of the Constitutional Council as an important policymaking player. Indeed, as Frank Baumgartner has pointed out, there are actually many different modes of policy formation. These styles can be placed along a policy style continuum, shown in Figure 3.1, with one end being a closed style and the other an open style. We can place the policy formation dynamic on specific policies or even specific clusters of policies within a given functional area of government or policy sector along this continuum.

In the open policy formation style, preformulation and formulation is highly public—the issues are at the top of the government agenda, prevalent in the media, and the object of heavy-duty interest group action. Public dem-onstrations often involve red-faced ministers having to admit publicly that they made a mistake. In these cases, the legislation is reformulated or just dropped altogether. Parliament often has a more significant role, with cabinet staffs at a loss to control the policy-making game. The Constitutional Council gets involved in these issues that are placed at the open end of this policy style spectrum. In this open style, policies often do not make it beyond the formulation stage because they get removed from the legislative agenda by a ministry or are annulled by the Constitutional Council. Education and farming policies tend to be at this end of the spectrum.

On the closed end of the spectrum, the policy style involves fewer players, with very little public involvement and scrutiny. The major players in all stages of this closed policy style are the upper civil servants who work as staffers or division heads drafting the provision of legislation, implementing orders, and overseeing policy evaluation. The Constitutional Council and parliament take a back seat in this style, with the chief executive offices tending to call the shots. The major policy instruments tend to be executive orders and legislation that gets swept through parliament often with the *vote bloquée*. Examples of policies that get made in this fashion include industrial and energy policy. Whether a policy has an open or closed style depends on whether the policy was low or high on the governmental policy agenda.

We can see the closed policy style at work in the case of the 1983 equal employment law. Equal opportunity legislation in France has been focused primarily on sex discrimination and less on race discrimination. The 1983 law instituted new positive action programs at the firm level—what is called affirmative action in the United States. The new programs involved a complex process of studying men's and women's positions within each firm and developing state-sponsored programs that would bring women in line with men in the firm. This firm-level process was referred to as *égalité professionnelle*. This law also closed some loopholes in existing antidiscrimination law.

The notion of *égalité professionnelle* was introduced in the mid-1970s through a small study group on women's employment attached to the Ministry of Social Affairs. It was run by feminist-oriented bureaucrats, two of whom were upper civil servants. Feminist activists in the left-wing trade unions and feminist scholars communities had also supported this particular solution to persisting occupational segregation between men and women where women were consistently channeled into lower paying jobs as well as other indicators of a sex-segregated labor force.

An equal employment bill was put low on the center-right government's agenda in 1980, was removed by the 1981 elections, and was taken up again by the socialist government under a socialist presidential majority. Although the government study group by 1981 had been upgraded to a Ministry of Women's Rights with significant resources, the law received limited public attention and certain tacit government support. At the same time, very few feminist groups or women's movements were concerned with the adoption of an effective law. The new second-wave feminist movements that had been so active in the campaign to legalize abortions—as many as one million people demonstrated in the streets of Paris in the early 1970s for the legalization of abortion—had little interest in mobilizing for women's employment rights more generally. Indeed, the major advocate for this law was the Minister of Women's Rights, Yvette Roudy, and her supporters in the socialist ministry and one of the major trade unions. As a consequence, business and labor organizations were able to limit the law to symbolic reform, where no real concrete stipulations were included in the final law that was adopted.

It does not take a rocket scientist to see that implementation of a law in which very few people and groups believed is not going to be highly successful. Very few firms actually took advantage of the largely voluntary *égalité professionnelle* programs. Likewise, the new legal provisions were not used in the courtroom to pursue incidences of sex discrimination in the workplace. Even if the law was given more teeth, the dynamics of the French legal system discussed previously would have limited the legal impact of the 1983 law. In the cases of equal employment policy for women, the closed nature of the process produced a law that was highly symbolic and had very little lasting impact on women's rights or in creating an equal opportunity culture that would use the various legal and programmatic instruments designed to promote employment equality between the sexes.[7]

CURRENT TRENDS IN PUBLIC POLICY

It has become increasingly clear that the major challenges in contemporary France stem from the opening up of the French domestic market to global competition. In all areas of French economic life, from agriculture to aerospace, the same fundamental dilemmas underlie the French economy: to what degree can French business and French products compete in a global and European marketplace without the degree of state protection to which they have been traditionally accustomed. The processes of integration on the European level, and globalization on the world scale, have their own inevitable and unstoppable logic (at least for the foreseeable future), and no French government can keep France isolated from these trends. But the historical protections that the French state has afforded businesses in France from external competition, the cultural commitment to the use of state institutions as the means of promoting French business, and the extent and weight of the public sector, with all of the nationalized firms, means that the French have had a much greater way to go than other European countries in making the adjustment and much greater ingrained resistance to doing it.

The major crossroads really occurred, with hindsight, in 1981–1984. In the first months of its period in office, the PS (along with its PCF allies) attempted to introduce a very different set of policy imperatives than the previous presidential administration. Giscard d'Estaing was a moderate social reformer but something of an economic neo-liberal; along with his second Prime Minister, Raymond Barre, Giscard began to talk in terms of bringing French industry and business into global competition. The terms were not always well defined, and they often carried with them a hint of the classical notions of French superiority, but the move to a more globally competitive culture was definitely there. When the socialists came to power, they did so having spoken of a complete rupture with the past, and of an alternative to the trends in policymaking that were evident under Giscard. What this meant was elaborating a model of business and industry that would be a complete opposite to the neo-liberalism and deregulation that was taking place in the United States under Ronald Reagan and in Great Britain under Margaret Thatcher.

That alternative vision stressed the importance of the state and of government institutions in promoting French industry. Rather than seeing government as the problem, in the often repeated formula of Ronald Reagan, the French socialists thought that government would be essential to achieving economic reform. Rather than slashing public subsidies and privatizing noncompetitive state industries, as did Margaret Thatcher, the PS embarked on a program of nationalizing troubled

---

[7]For an in-depth analysis of the politics of the formation of equal employment policy in France, see Mazur (1995).

private firms and of making public money available to prop up ailing businesses. The whole approach was founded on the use of government institutions to protect and shield the French market from international forces; when the socialist's announced policies caused a run on the French franc, the government responded by placing severe export controls on currency. This reaction was symbolic of the underlying philosophy of the socialist program, and it symptomized the deep antagonisms between private investors and the new socialist government.

The imperatives of the international economy were too great for the socialist government to sustain, however. On the one hand, the French trade unions (that many people thought would be sympathetic to the new government) actually increased their demands for wage increases and better working conditions. Thus, unremitting pressures were made for more to be done in the way of public spending and state involvement in economic policymaking. On the other hand, the twin threats of capital flight and the withdrawal of investment made it difficult to steady the economic boat. By 1983–1984, the strains were becoming too great for the government to continue on the course it was following; Mitterrand decided to replace his Prime Minister, Pierre Mauroy, a favorite with the grassroots socialist organization, with Laurent Fabius, a technocrat and reformer. The new government abandoned its policy of Keynesian reflation and replaced it with a series of austerity measures designed to cut public spending and to reduce state protections for noncompetitive sectors of the economy (such as the steel industry).

From the introduction of austerity until the present time, successive governments of the center-right and the center-left have grappled with the problem of reducing public spending, decreasing the deficit, reforming the social security system, and trying to make France's nationalized industries globally competitive; that is, virtually the same problems facing the administrations in the United States and Great Britain. The center-right has pushed for privatization as a solution to the problems of noncompetitiveness, whereas the center-left has been more reluctant to sell off France's publicly owned firms; what is notable is that the latest center-left government, headed by Lionel Jospin, is quietly content to accept the privatization of certain corporations, a policy that they had vociferously criticized while in opposition. Unlike Great Britain, a consensus still unites both left and right around the public ownership of core activities such as rail transportation, electricity, and so on. Equally so, the commitment to certain "grand" activities such as aerospace remains strong. But even in these sectors, the French are experimenting with limited forms of privatization and competition.

The greatest single challenge facing the French government in the immediate future comes from the strict conditions that have been agreed upon as a condition for moving ahead with the single European currency (the euro). Today, prices are supposed to be marked in all French shops (as in other participating countries) in euros, and one can make purchases (in theory) in either French francs or euros. The euro has been introduced in stages, and once it is available as paper money, French francs, German deutschemarks, and other European currencies will be withdrawn and the European euro will become the only money available to consumers in these countries. The advantages of such a system, as anyone who has ever had to cross from one European country to another and change money will attest, are enormous, and the savings to European industry are potentially huge. But in order to run the system, a bank was needed, and the European Central Bank has been vested with control over the new currency.

For countries to enter the system, they needed to reduce their budget deficits and public sector borrowing. Although the details are tedious and sometimes impenetrable even to those familiar with the system, the bottom

An Airbus plane under construction in Toulouse, France. Cooperation has worked well in putting together the Airbus consortium, which is now the only real rival to Boeing.

line for every French government in recent years is that they have been forced to trim public expenditure, not only in the short term, but for the long haul as well. This taps into all sorts of sacred areas of French life, *les droits acquis* (rights that have been fought for over many years and that have often been won only after protracted struggle). Just as elsewhere in the developed world, the need to trim public expenditures comes at a time when social costs are rising. Not the least trivial problem is the aging of the population, which has and will place a severe strain on the capacity of the social security system. In other countries (for example Britain), the center-left government of Tony Blair continues to seek nongovernmental solutions to public problems, much in the same way that the Clinton administration has in the United States. But in France, as we have repeatedly pointed out, people look to and expect a solution from government. The institutions of the state are there to protect them and to nourish them. These feelings do not coexist well with the demands of European monetary integration that France faces.

Equally so, the opening up of European markets is a process that cannot be reversed. Although the French may have had a different idea in mind when they signed the Single Europe Act in the 1980s, it has proven to be a big exercise in neo-liberal deregulation, with only a few gestures to the French socialist vision of "social Europe." The French may have thought that they were exporting their model to the rest of the European Union in the mid-1980s, but the reality is that their markets have been opened up in a clinical fashion to increased external competition. Europe as a whole still retains certain trade practices and protections that look particularly irksome to a country such as the United States, but the French have found that their radius of action in the policy arena has been very much circumscribed by the further integration of Europe.

At this point, the process appears almost irreversible; successive events, particularly in the field of aerospace, have shown that the French must cooperate with European partners to ensure the survival of their most prestigious firms, such as Matra and Dassault. Cooperation has worked well in putting together the Airbus consortium, which is now the only real rival to Boeing; where the French refused (initially) to cooperate (such as in the production of military aircraft), their firms are in deep trouble.

FRANCE AT A GLOBAL CROSSROADS

So today, we see France at a major crossroads. Harking back to the World Cup, the changes were already in the air, and people had the sense that something profound was afoot. It was as if the French finally had a chance to look at themselves, free of political dogma, without social blinders, and to take stock of their place in the world as never before. Of course, the World Cup ended happily for the French, beating everyone else on the road to being crowned world champions for the first time, but there is more to France than football.

The French in 1998 came to see themselves more than ever before in terms of social and ethnic diversity. Although it is foolish to engage in endless arguments about which society is more tolerant, which is more racist, and so on, it is possible that France today is becoming more of a genuinely pluralist society in the manner that we are accustomed to elsewhere. Or, put another way, perhaps the old Republican discipline embedded in the notions of one indivisible nation that we have discussed previously is fading as the predominant modality of organizing the democratic forces in French society. Those forces, both on the moderate left and right, are increasingly accepting of the cultural plurality and vitality of modern France. Perhaps one tantalizing measure of this reform—certainly not pleasing to the palate of all French—is the manner in which cuisine is changing. Only recently, an article in the *New York Times* hailed the most talented new French chefs as those practicing "fusion" cooking; that is, blending styles from other countries and cultures with French cuisine. Such a thing would have been unthinkable at worst or avant garde at best just a few year ago, but now it is the rage.

The road to a more multicultural society, however, is not paved with gold. Indeed, the recent rise in social malaise and a general sense of increasing gaps between the haves and have-nots may be more a result of the seismic shifts going on in French society in this regard than any actual permanent ferment. In this scenario, the popular alienation from below will only be temporary and will be soon followed by a higher level of satisfaction with government performance as that government embraces the new grassroots movement toward cultural pluralism. In this vein, we see the current crossroads as an important turning point in the development of a more democratic society. By this, we mean that France's political institutions are becoming more open to inputs from a broad range of societal interests and more responsive to citizens' demands. Whether these demands will be sustainable in the era of globalization and integration is another matter.

As we have shown, France is at a crossroads not only in social and cultural terms, but in political terms as well. The Fifth Republic has successfully withstood the challenge of both time and some deep crises; it outlived its founder with whom it was almost directly equated, it outlived the election of a socialist president, and it has survived the emergence of an extreme right-wing party with an assiduous electorate. In short, the institutions appear to be solid.

But the changes that are afoot also imply once again a recasting of the party system that is far from complete. The PCF still has a way to go before it sheds entirely its Cold War, anti-capitalist persona, and it still has the capacity to scare those who do not really understand the French political system in its totality. The moderate right is still incapable of finding the grounds on which it can unify, although the latest attempt (The Alliance) has not been in operation sufficiently long to have been deemed to have failed as miserably as its predecessors. Although the extreme right seems to be engaged in a fratricidal struggle that may signal the end of its presence as an organized political party on the national political scene, one wonders about the one in seven voters who have cast their ballots for the party in recent elections. The governing center-left majority—*la gauche plurielle*—has yet to decide what kind of social democracy it really wishes to espouse; indeed, some might snidely suggest that it has yet to come to terms with what kind of social democracy is possible in this era of global and European constraint.

Undeniably, France has changed—sometimes slowly, sometimes fast—but it is also still French; the primacy of l'état is still there, both in the political culture and in daily life. Watching the lives of ordinary French people at the beginning of the twenty-first century, an observer cannot fail to be struck by the sheer presence of the French state, in big ways and small. From the state-run kindergarten to which parents take their children before work in the morning, to the rapid and efficient public transport used to get to the place of work, to the subsidized lunches, and so on, the state is still there, still looming over the French population. But still, the changes in the power of the regions, the Constitutional Court, and the presidency indicate that the French state is undergoing some fundamental retooling. In the final analysis, one cannot say that nothing has changed in this regard because it most surely has, but sometimes the changes are less obvious than the continuity.

FURTHER READING AND SOURCES

French Politics and Society. Academic journal on French Studies.
French Politics and Society Conference Group. Organized conference group of the American Political Science Association. Papers presented on two to three panels at APSA's annual meetings.

BIBLIOGRAPHY

Baumgartner, Frank R, "The Many Styles of Policymaking in France," in J.T.S. Keeler and M. Schain (eds.), *Chirac's Challenge* (New York: St. Martin's Press, 1996), pp. 85–103.

Daley, Tony (ed.), *The Mitterrand Era: Policy Alternatives and Political Mobilization in France* (London: MacMillan, 1996).

Erhmann, Henry W., and Martin A. Schain, *Politics in France* (New York: Harper Collins, 1993).

Gourevitch, Peter Alexis, *Paris and the Provinces* (London: George Allen & Unwin, 1980).

Hause, Steven C., and Anne R. Kenney, *Women's Suffrage and Social Politics in the French Third Republic* (Princeton: Princeton University Press, 1984).

Keeler, John T.S., and Martin Schain (eds.), *Chirac's Challenge: Liberalization, Europeanization, and Malaise in France* (New York: St. Martin's Press, 1996).

Mazur, Amy, *Gender Bias and the State: Symbolic Reform at Work in Fifth Republic France* (Pittsburgh: University of Pittsburgh Press, 1995).

Saffran, William, *The French Polity* (White Plains: Longman, 1995).

Schmidt, Vivien, *Democratizing France: The Political and Administrative History of Decentralization* (Cambridge: Cambridge University Press, 1990).

Stone, Alec, Constitutional Politics and Malaise in France, in J.T.S. Keeler and M. Schain (eds.), *Chirac's Challenge* (New York: St. Martin's Press, 1996), pp. 53–84.

Tiersky, Ronald, *France in the New Europe: Changing Yet Steadfast* (Belmont, CA: Wadsworth, 1997).

Tilly, Charles, *The Contentious French: Four Centuries of Popular Struggle* (Cambridge, MA and London, England: The Belknap Press of Harvard University Press, 1986).

Weber, Eugen, *Peasants into Frenchmen* (Palo Alto: Stanford University Press, 1976).

Wright, Gordon, *France in Modern Times* (New York: W.W. Norton, 1981).

4

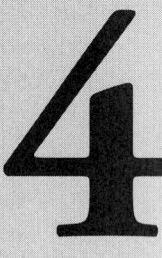

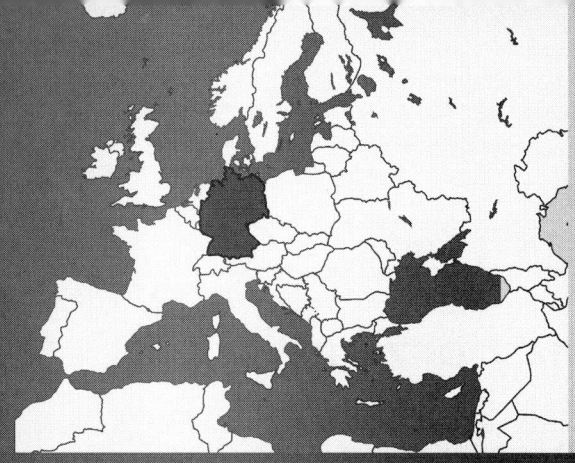

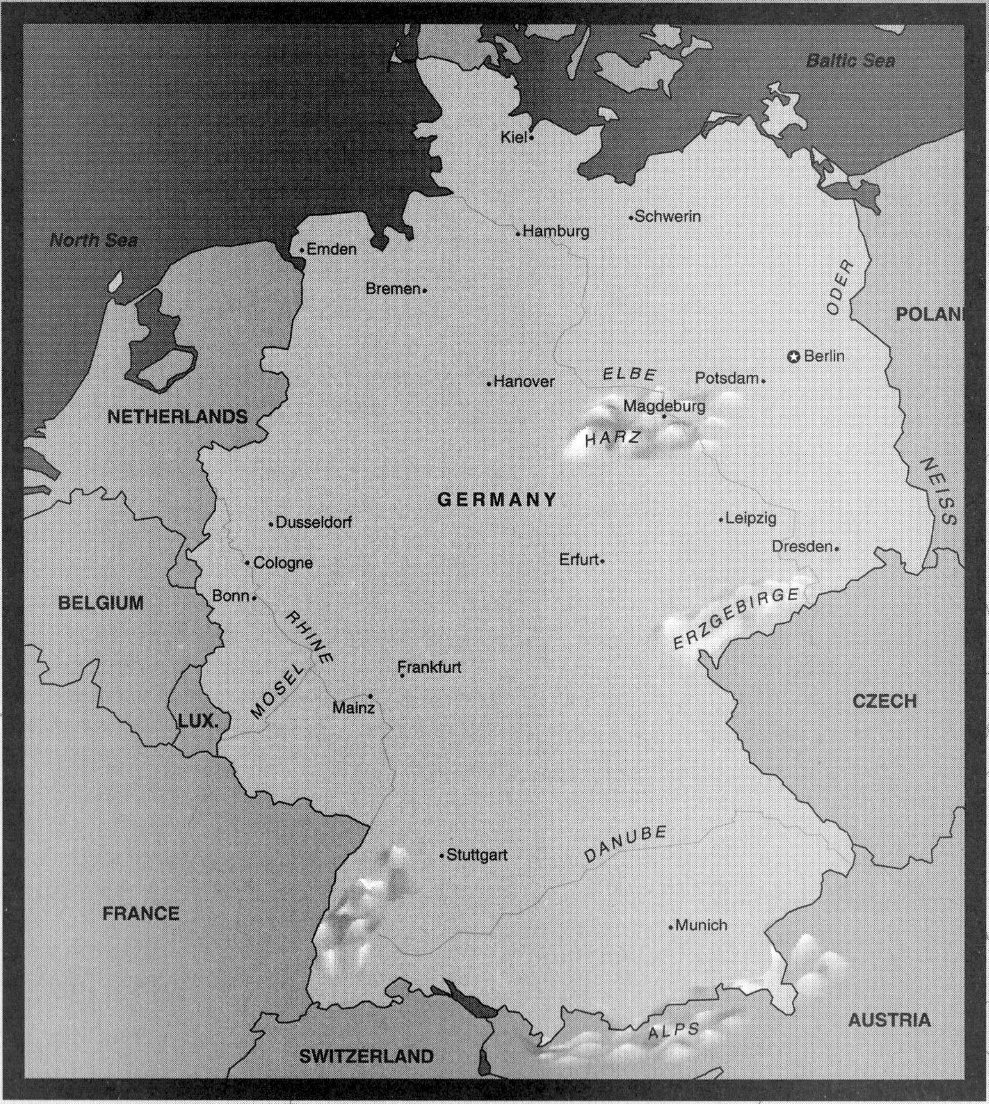

Baltic Sea
North Sea
Kiel
Schwerin
Hamburg
Emden
Bremen
ODER
POLAND
Berlin
Potsdam
ELBE
Hanover
Magdeburg
HARZ
NETHERLANDS
GERMANY
NEISS
Dusseldorf
Leipzig
Dresden
Cologne
Erfurt
BELGIUM
Bonn
ERZGEBIRGE
RHINE
MOSEL
Frankfurt
Mainz
LUX.
CZECH
DANUBE
Stuttgart
FRANCE
Munich
ALPS
AUSTRIA
SWITZERLAND

GERMANY

From Bonn Republic to Berlin Republic

Gerard Braunthal

COUNTRY PROFILE

Population:	82,000,000
Land Area:	357,000 sq. km.
Population per sq. km.:	235
Gross National Product:	$2,122.7 billion
Per Capita Income:	$25,850
Global Per Capita Income Rank:	13
Percent Urban:	87
Adult Literacy:	100% (claimed)
Life Expectancy	
Male:	74
Female:	80

INTRODUCTION

At the start of the twenty-first century, the Federal Republic of Germany is poised to become one of the top players in the international arena. It assumes this role from a new geographic setting, fraught with history and symbolism. In late 1998, a new Social Democratic and Greens coalition government took office; months later, it began to shift some of its operations from the sleepy provincial city of Bonn, the capital of the western Federal Republic (1949–1990), to the bustling cosmopolitan city of Berlin, the new capital of the unified Germany.

A brief glance back is necessary: in 1949, two rival capitalist and communist states were formed—the Federal Republic of Germany (FRG) and the German Democratic Republic (GDR). Four decades of cold war in Europe prevented unification, but with the end of the cold war in the late 1980s, the German problem could be resolved. On October 3, 1990, the GDR acceded to the FRG, thereby creating a unified Germany. Soon thereafter the new enlarged parliament, with deputies from western and eastern Germany, voted for Berlin as the new capital. In 1999, the government ministries, except for those remaining in Bonn, and the Bundestag (Lower House of Parliament) started to transfer their operations from Bonn to Berlin once new or reconverted buildings were ready for occupancy. The move, expected to last several years, was more than a geographic shift of public officials, civil servants, and their stacks of documents. It was also a symbolic move, providing evidence that the new government, led by Chancellor Gerhard Schröder, a Social Democrat, was determined to assert itself in international politics, befitting the Berlin Republic's importance on the European continent.

Such determination, not atypical for countries having the size, the large population, the technology, and the resources that characterize Germany, in turn worries other European countries that a powerful Germany may limit their national interests in the chess game of international politics. Germany's neighbors especially recall that this aggressive central European state was twice in a century responsible for the outbreak of catastrophic wars engulfing the continent (1914–1918) and the world (1939–1945). Before 1914 an imperial regime governed the country from its seat in Berlin; before 1939 the Nazis governed it from the same location.

In response to such national memories, German government officials, most of them born at the end of the Nazi period or soon thereafter, are eager to shed the burden of the country's history, which includes not only the wars of aggression but also the Nazi persecution of Jews, gypsies, and other minorities that led in most cases to their elimination in the Holocaust. The current government officials, staunch believers in the democratic system, insist that the Nazi past must not be forgotten but that it is time for Germany to shed its sense of collective guilt and instead to be considered as an equal partner in the community of nations.

Of course the Nazi past cannot be forgotten. The former concentration camps, haunting in their silence; the flood of documentaries and films, including *Schindler's List,* shown on German television; and the scores of books and articles on the infamous Hitler era serve as a constant reminder to the public that the Nazi regime, which most of the citizens at the time supported, was responsible for the horrors committed. A proposed major Holocaust memorial in Berlin serves as a further reminder of the dark past. It has been the subject of years of discussion as to whether there even should be another memorial (and if it was to be built what should be its design). In addition, the current German government has put pressure on the country's large business firms that operated in the 1930s and 1940s to compensate the east European slave laborers who worked for them at the time and on the German banks and insurance firms to make restitution payments to claimants.

Introduction

For the current generation of young Germans to come to grips with the past has been an ongoing task. In their search for national identity and normality, they have studied in school how Naziism arose during the Great Depression. Thus they flocked to an exhibition of the pictures of Leni Riefenstahl, Hitler's favorite filmmaker, to see what attracted most Germans, including older members of their families, to support the Hitler regime. They also flocked to meetings at which the American scholar Daniel Goldhagen, author of the controversial book *Hitler's Willing Executioners: Ordinary Germans and the Holocaust*, debated with German scholars his thesis that the German people's enduring pathological hatred of the Jews was characteristic of German history until the Nazi regime fell in 1945. Most of the scholars rejected his sweeping thesis.

But the fact that more than half a century has elapsed between the death of an estimated six million Jews in the Holocaust during World War II and the current scene in which right-wing skinheads and neo-Nazis terrorize dark-skinned foreigners at night worries German democrats. They accuse a small minority of right-wing youth of having learned nothing from the past. These socially alienated youth, who are often high school dropouts unable to get a job apprenticeship or a full-time job, bitterly resent the immigration of foreigners whom they see as rivals eager for jobs, good housing, and social welfare benefits. The right-wing youth have also staged mass demonstrations in numerous cities against a traveling historical exhibition showing the responsibility of many German soldiers for murdering an untold number of Jews, Slavs, and other groups during World War II.

Most Germans, young and old, know that the controversies over the German past and the current yearning for normality and a secure personal future will not end soon. For example, in October 1998, a famous writer, Martin Walser, on the occasion of receiving the country's top literary prize at the Frankfurt book fair, spoke up for a new normalcy and an end to making Auschwitz, the symbol of the Holocaust, "a routine threat, a tool of intimidation, a moral cudgel." He criticized the plans for the aforementioned Holocaust memorial in Berlin, which in one originally accepted design called for the construction of thousands of concrete pillars to be built close to the famous Brandenburg Gate. In a sharp response to Walser, Ignatz Bubis, the leader of Germany's small Jewish community, denounced Walser's remarks as "moral arson" (a remark that Bubis later withdrew) and deplored the "spreading intellectual nationalism" and the sinister quest for normalcy in Germany.[1]

The fiery debates about the past and the present reflect a tension among the German population that prevails in many contemporary states having experienced major historical upheavals. For Germany, the Hitler period remains at the core of the discussion about the past. Hitler's nationalist propaganda, his dream of creating a thousand-year Reich, and his claim that the German Aryan race is superior to all others were accepted by most Germans during his twelve years in power from 1933 to 1945. But foreign observers and a minority of Germans, some of whom engaged in a heroic and dangerous resistance against the regime, characterized such propaganda as demagogic. The trauma of the Hitler era has not evaporated entirely. Since the Nazi disaster, most German youth, except for the rightist gangs, reject nationalist symbols, which were at the heart of Nazi political culture. They are not eager to sing the German national anthem or to fly the German flag; many reject service in the armed forces and become conscientious objectors.

The past keeps intruding into the present in other ways. In 1999, a debate erupted in Germany over what name to give the Reichstag (Lower House of Parliament) building in Berlin, which had housed the parliaments from 1894,

---
[1] *The Economist,* February 6, 1999, p. 17.

The new Reichstag (Lower House of Parliment), relocated to Berlin.

the year it was built, to February 1933 when most of it was destroyed by fire.[2] During World War II, the Reichstag building suffered further heavy damage. It was not reconstructed until the 1990s as the new home of the Bundestag once it moved from Bonn to Berlin. The debate over keeping the building's name Reichstag centered on the term "Reich," which connotes empire, of which there were three—that of Charlemagne, Bismarck, and Hitler—in German history, as we shall see. Hitler's Reich especially tainted the word "Reichstag." A minority of Bundestag deputies preferred to retain the historic term "Reichstag," not because of any sympathy for Hitler, but because the building is a symbol of the country's history; however, the Bundestag Senior Council members decided on the convoluted term "Plenary Area, Reichstag Building." To add to the confusion, direction signs on nearby streets refer visitors to the "Bundestag."

The debate on the Reichstag name paralleled one on the shape of the eagle, the country's symbol, which adorns the reconstructed and now glass-domed (for more political transparency) plenary chamber. Hitler spoke at Nuremberg mass rallies in front of a fierce sharp-clawed Prussian eagle. From 1949 on, a pudgy eagle, known affectionately as "the fat hen," adorned the Bundestag chamber in Bonn. But critics asked in the media whether the eagle in the Berlin parliament building should not recover a touch of Prussian virility. Sir Norman Foster, the British architect, after having studied 235 eagles that have appeared in Prussian and German history, agreed with them; however, an official committee overseeing the reconstruction opted for the Bonn bird but in larger size. Debates about a parliament building's nomenclature and the shape of an eagle may sound ludicrous to foreign observers, but they touch on the nerves of a nation's political culture.

HISTORY, GEOGRAPHY, BACKGROUND, AND POLITICAL CULTURE

History

To understand the present and the immediate past, a brief look at German major historical developments must be made. German tribes inhabited Central Europe for centuries, but

---

[2]Most historians believe, but cannot prove, that a lone Dutch communist rather than the Nazis set the fire. The Nazis, afraid that a German Communist Party uprising was at hand, used the setting of the fire as an excuse to crush the party (Hans Mommsen, "The Political Effects of the Reichstag Fire," *in* Henry A. Turner, Jr., (ed.) *Nazism and the Third Reich* (New York: Quadrangle Books, 1972), pp. 109–149).

they did not unite to create a common state. It was not until A.D. 800 that Charlemagne founded the Holy Roman Empire, or First Reich. The Empire controlled a vast territory in Europe, but by the seventeenth century still lacked an effective centralized government. Weak German princes depended on French and British protection, whereas stronger princes wanted freedom to form their own states. For instance, the Wettins of Saxony, who were expanding to the east, became kings of Poland; the Welfs of Brunswick-Lüneburg became electors of Hanover and gained more influence when Elector George inherited Great Britain in 1714; and the Hohenzollerns of Brandenburg became kings of Prussia.

By 1740, Prussia and Austria became the leading rivals for dominance in Central Europe. The Hohenzollern family, which already possessed Brandenburg, acquired more unconnected territories in the west and Prussia in the east, which it had inherited as a Polish duchy in 1618 and converted into an independent kingdom in 1701. Soon all of its lands became known as the kingdom of Prussia. King Frederick William I of Prussia created in the territory a modern military state. His son, Frederick II the Great, who enjoyed French music and literature in his luxurious Sans Souci palace near Berlin, expanded Prussia after successfully conducting wars against Austria and Poland. He also reorganized the Prussian government and economy to better serve the army. Prussia became involved in the War of the Austrian Succession (1740–1748) and the Seven Years' War (1756–1763).

The French Revolution of 1789 sparked a desire among the numerous small German principalities and fiefdoms for national unification and liberal reforms. These aspirations were dashed during the early year of the nineteenth century when the armies of Napoleonic France repeatedly invaded the territories of Prussia and the other Germanic fiefdoms. In 1806, Napoleon reorganized the western German principalities into the Confederation of the Rhine. After Napoleon's defeat in Russia, Frederick William III of Prussia, joined by Russia and Austria, launched a war of liberation and defeated Napoleon at Leipzig in 1813 and at Paris in 1814.

Thereafter, the allied powers met at the Congress of Vienna from 1814 to 1815 to redraw the map of Europe. Prussia lost most of its Polish territory but gained much of Saxony and Swedish Pomerania, and more land in the Rhineland and Westphalia, which included the rich but undeveloped iron and coal deposits of the Ruhr and Saar. The Congress of Vienna dissolved the Holy Roman Empire of more than 240 duchies, principalities, and states, and on German territory created the German Confederation of thirty-nine states, under the domination of Austria. German rulers, who did not want to lose their individual sovereignty, suppressed the demand of German liberals for national unification and a democratic government. In 1830 and 1848, a wave of revolutions, sparked in Paris, swept the continent. During the 1848 revolutions, uprisings on German soil took place in Prussia, Bavaria, and the southwest, but the princes' military forces crushed them all; however, the princes, frightened by the uprisings, allowed delegates to meet at an assembly in Frankfurt. Yet, when the delegates drafted a liberal constitution for a united Germany to be governed by a hereditary emperor, an authoritarian King Frederick William IV, then governing Prussia, refused the offer.

In the 1860s, Prussia, under the leadership of King William I and his chief minister Otto von Bismarck, sought German unification. Their goal could not be realized without wars. In the Seven Weeks' War of 1866, the Prussian army defeated the Austrians; as a consequence, Prussia annexed Schleswig-Holstein, Hanover, and other states, and formed the North German Confederation in 1867. When the French declared war against Prussia in 1870, southern German states supported the Prussian armies that invaded France. In 1870, after a long siege of Paris, the French army surrendered. A triumphant Bismarck, who had convinced William I to accept the imperial crown, invited German princes to the famed Palace of Versailles near Paris for the coronation of the emperor (*Kaiser*). The peace treaty with France awarded Alsace and Lorraine to Germany. By then, Germany, under Prussian leadership, had become the most powerful continental European state.

The Second Reich (1871–1918) Emperor William I and Chancellor Bismarck, and their advisors drawn from the landed nobility (the Junkers), the bureaucracy, and the military, were chiefly responsible for creating a powerful Germany, made up of twenty-five component states. The governing authoritarian elites, centered in Prussia, had no desire to introduce a democratic system that might challenge their rule. Thus the Reichstag, with its elected deputies, had little influence on foreign or military policies, although some in domestic affairs, whereas the Bundesrat (the Upper House) was dominated by the Prussian-controlled central government, which appointed the princes as members.

The Industrial Revolution had its origin in the 1850s. It transformed Germany into Europe's most important manufacturing center and accelerated urbanization. In the 1880s, to ward off increasing dissatisfaction among the new blue-collar working class about their poor working conditions, housing, and health, Bismarck introduced a comprehensive health and accident insurance scheme, and disability and old-age pensions, which became a model for other countries. Any political gains that he may have made from this far-reaching scheme had already dissipated in the 1870s by his unsuccessful attempt, in the so-called cultural battle (*Kulturkampf*), to limit the power of the Catholic church. The Center Party, founded by Catholics, had become by 1878 the strongest party in the Reichstag. Although many workers joined this party, most cast their votes in the following decades for the German Social Democratic Party (SPD), founded as the Socialist Workers' Party of Germany in 1875, which demanded a democratic system and the right of workers to form trade unions. In 1878, Bismarck, worried about the growing socialist movement, convinced the Reichstag to pass an anti-socialist bill, which dissolved the new party's organization. The anti-socialist legislation remained in effect until 1890, but the legislation did not apply to the party's right to run candidates in elections; thus the Social Democrats had a large parliamentary group in the Reichstag. Facing a hostile emperor and chancellor, however, the SPD could not participate in any government or break the barrier preventing its leaders gaining posts in the administrative branch, the military, or the judiciary.

In foreign relations, Bismarck ensured that peace would prevail to give time for Germany to become a strong military power. He concluded a series of alliances to ensure the country's safety from aggression. To pacify the merchant class and to increase the country's prestige, he agreed that Germany should acquire colonies in Africa and the Pacific. To protect German agriculture and industry from cheap imports, he encouraged parliament to vote for high tariffs.

The Bismarck era came to an end in 1890 when the chancellor, worried about the growth of SPD, sought to abolish universal suffrage and make changes to the constitution that had been adopted in 1871. William I died in 1888 and was succeeded for one hundred days by an ailing Frederick III. Upon his death, William II assumed the reins of power. The new young emperor wanted to rule Germany in his own right, so he dismissed the autocratic Bismarck and appointed a succession of weak chancellors thereafter. Despite a change in policymakers, the military, and especially the navy, continued to expand its forces, supported by aggressive nationalist and anti-Semitic groups. Britain, France, and Russia, worried about this military expansion, formed an alliance against Germany. Although none of the European powers wanted a war, several crises precipitated its outbreak in 1914. World War I lasted four bitter years, with millions of casualties suffered on both sides. In 1918, Germany was in turmoil as sailors mutinied, workers staged strikes, and communist councils formed. Germany's powerful military machine and government collapsed; the top generals had to accept the Allied armistice terms. The emperor abdicated and fled the country. A Social Democratic leader proclaimed Germany a republic.

The Weimar Era In 1919, the new German government was forced to accept harsh peace terms imposed on it by the Versailles Treaty. The Allied powers demanded high reparations, the ceding of Alsace-Lorraine to France and West Prussia to Poland, the surrender of all colonial territories, a limitation in the size of the German army, and occupation of the Rhineland for fifteen years. The Allies insisted that the Germans had to accept full responsibility for their causing the war and had to pay a good share of its cost. The German government's acceptance of these harsh terms had disastrous consequences when Hitler, in the 1920s, accused its leaders of having betrayed the country and stabbing it in the back. His demagogic accusations did not fall on deaf ears among the populace, which was seeking a scapegoat for its economic difficulties.

In the meantime, in 1919, a constituent assembly adopted in the city of Weimar a democratic constitution, the first in the country's history and one of the most progressive in the world. The constitution set up a parliamentary system, guaranteed individual rights, and permitted national initiatives and referenda, but democracy had little chance to flourish. The fragile coalition governments had to cope with conservative civil servants and judges who were retained from the Empire era, and with communists on the left and Nazis on the right who favored nondemocratic systems. As a consequence, the president made increasing use of executive decrees, bypassing the weak chancellors, cabinet, and parliament. The Great Depression of 1929 had catastrophic consequences. Millions of workers, constituting more than one-third of the labor force, were unemployed, poverty stricken, and fearful of the future. In 1932, the Nazis became the strongest party in parliament, although they never received a majority of the vote. On January 30, 1933, President Paul von Hindenburg, counseled by ultraconservative leaders, appointed Adolf Hitler as chancellor, thereby dooming the fragile Weimar Republic.

The Third Reich Hitler, a former German army corporal who had served less than a year in prison following an aborted *putsch* (revolt) in 1923 to overthrow the Bavarian government, swiftly gained the support of most Germans as the new chancellor. He promised to give jobs to the workers and to restore the country's strength and honor. His ideology was a dangerous mixture of racist, anti-Semitic, and pseudosocialist ideas. To secure supreme power for himself, he called new elections for March 1933. He knew that by banning the communists and instituting a reign of terror against his democratic opponents, he would win. In the new Reichstag, the Nazis, the nationalist parties, and the Catholic Center passed the sweeping Enabling Act that allowed the new Nazi government to regulate all aspects of German life.

Hitler banned all political parties, except for the Nazi Party that he had created in the 1920s. He smashed the trade unions, forbade strikes, and put the unemployed in labor camps. He created a totalitarian system, in which his rule as Führer (leader) was uncontested. He consolidated the executive, legislative, judicial, and military authority in himself. When President Hindenburg died, Hitler also became head of state of the Third Reich, as he called the new system. In this system, the people were permanently mobilized through an intensive propaganda campaign and held down through a system of terror. Hitler permitted the short-lived SA (*Sturm Abteilung* or Brown Shirts), SS (*Schutzstaffel* or Black Shirts), and the Gestapo (secret police) to hunt down all alleged opponents and incarcerate them in concentration camps. The system of widespread police controls made opposition dangerous and futile. Jews became a special target. The Nuremberg Laws of September 1935 reduced them to second-class citizens and forbade them to marry non-Jews. On the night of November 8, 1938, known as *Kristallnacht* ("Night of the Broken Glass"), German officials used the assassination of a German diplomat in Paris by a Jew as a pretext to organize nationwide assaults against the oppressed minority and to set fire to synagogues and seize its properties. As restrictions against Jews multiplied, many emigrated to other countries.

In 1933, to move the economy forward, the Nazi leaders launched government-financed work creation programs, including major rearmament projects and construction of a network of *Autobahnen* (super-highways). By 1937, the country had reached full employment. Rearmament fit into Hitler's grand design in foreign policy. He claimed in the famous book *Mein Kampf* ("My Struggle"), written while imprisoned in 1923–1924 for the attempted *putsch* in Munich, that Germany had to become a world power by gaining living space in Eastern Europe and that it could not live under the Versailles Treaty's onerous burdens on Germany. Once he became chancellor in 1933, he gave up Germany's membership in the League of Nations and participation in a major disarmament conference. In March 1936, he moved troops illegally into the Rhineland, which had been demilitarized under the terms of the Versailles Treaty. The Western powers failed to protest or take any countermeasures. In March 1938, Hitler ordered German troops into Austria and proclaimed it to be part of the greater Reich. In their appeasement policy of Hitler, the British and French prime ministers at the Munich conference of September 1938 agreed to Hitler's annexation of the German-speaking Sudetenland of Czechoslovakia. In March 1939, German troops took over the rest of the country. On September 1, 1939, they invaded Poland. Britain and France realized only then that an expansionist Germany threatened their own survival, and they declared war on Germany. World War II had started.

Once German troops, in one *blitzkrieg* ("lightning war") after another, occupied most of continental Europe, Hitler's dream of a New European Order, in which he was backed militarily by Italy and Japan, seemed to come to fruition. He still had to contend with Britain, however, which beat back his air offensive, and with the Soviet Union, which, after having been invaded on June 22, 1941, rolled back his armies in the aftermath of the costly Battle of Stalingrad that ended in early 1943. During the years of German occupation in Europe, Hitler exploited the territories without mercy. The occupied states had to supply Germany with raw materials, food, and labor. By 1944, more than seven million foreign workers, including nearly two million prisoners of war, toiled in Germany.

In Eastern Europe, the Nazis subjected the Slavs, whom they considered to be racially inferior, to the most inhumane treatment, including mass killings. Similarly, throughout occupied Europe, the Nazis rounded up Jews and transported them to mass extermination camps, such as Auschwitz and Majdanek, located primarily in Eastern Europe. An estimated six million Jews perished in the camps, as well as large numbers of Roma and Sinti (gypsies), homosexuals, and other "enemies of the state."

After Japan bombarded Pearl Harbor in December 1941, the United States entered the war against the Axis powers, consisting of Germany, Italy, and Japan. Once American military forces were thrown into combat, the balance tipped increasingly toward the Allied side. In June 1944, Western forces invaded the

Hitler reviews his supporters at the Third German National Socialist Workers' Party Convention, Nuremburg, Germany, 1927.

continent at Normandy Beach in France; by then it was only a matter of time before Germany capitulated to its enemy forces in the West and East. On May 8, 1945, the costly and bloody war finally ended in Europe. Both sides suffered millions of casualties; the continent was devastated. Shortly before Germany's surrender, Hitler and Josef Goebbels, the propaganda minister, committed suicide, and most of the other top leaders were captured.

Occupation Germany's unconditional surrender ended Hitler's Third Reich. During the war, Allied leaders had already made plans for the postwar period. At the Yalta Conference in February 1945, U.S. President Franklin D. Roosevelt, British Prime Minister Winston Churchill, and Soviet General Secretary Josef Stalin met to discuss the future of Germany. They agreed that it would be divided into four zones of occupation. The British, American, and French would each govern a zone in western Germany, and the Soviets a zone in eastern Germany. Territories that the Nazis had seized between 1938 and 1941 were returned to the Austrian, Czechoslovakian, Yugoslavian, and French governments. The Soviet Union and Poland were to administer the former German territories, which included East Prussia and Silesia, lying to the east of the Oder and Neisse rivers. The former capital of Berlin, situated within the Soviet zone and having received a special status, was divided into four occupation sectors. An Allied Control Council, made up of the four military commanders heading each zone, was to make joint and unanimous decisions affecting all of Germany.

The Allied powers had agreed during their wartime conferences that Germany was to be de-Nazified, which meant that the Nazi system had to be eliminated, top Nazi and government leaders tried as war criminals, and lower-rank Nazi officials removed from their jobs and imprisoned or fined. At the major Nuremberg Trial, twelve of the top Nazi and government officials were condemned to death.

The Allies also agreed that Germany must be demilitarized to prevent it from waging future wars of aggression and must be democratized to prevent a recurrence of totalitarianism. The Western Allies initiated programs of political education and tried to revamp the educational system, the bureaucracy, and the judicial system, but, given the power of vested interests, met with only minimal success. The Russians imposed communism in their zone.

Although the wartime plans were enacted with varying degrees of success in the four zones, Allied commanders were faced with the immediate problem of coping with the aftermath of the wartime devastation, such as the destruction of 90 percent of houses in the cities, the standstill of industry, and the lack of enough food for the people. The problems were compounded by the influx of nine million Germans, who had been expelled from the eastern territories, and by the Allied policy to dismantle some German industry to meet Soviet demands for German reparations as compensation for offsetting the terrible havoc that the German armies had caused in the Soviet Union.

The hope by some observers that the four Allied commanders could develop a joint policy toward Germany was not met. The Soviets wanted to ensure that communism triumphed in their zone. They confiscated all large estates and nationalized all industries to prevent the landowning aristocracy and the industrialists from regaining political power. They forced the SPD to merge with the Communist Party in a new Socialist Unity Party (SED) and severely restricted the Christian Democrats and Liberal Democrats. They sent German communist leaders back from the Soviet Union to take up political posts. By 1948, the Soviets had laid the political and economic bases for a communist state.

The Western Allied powers sought to introduce democracy in their zones by encouraging anti-Nazis and non-Nazis to assume posts in local governments and, beginning in 1946, by allowing the major parties, including the Communist Party, to operate locally, and in 1947 in each Land (state). The Western Allies encouraged private enterprises rather than nationalized firms to form. They introduced only a few land reforms and broke up only a few major companies that had been heavily involved in the Nazi war machine. On January 1, 1947, Britain and the United States, to revive the lagging economy, merged their zones into Bizonia, an economic unit. The French, less enthusiastic about a revived strong Germany that might threaten it again, only joined Bizonia in 1949, although backing currency reform that strengthened the west German economy. The French gave the Saarland, with its rich coal mines, autonomous political status but merged it economically into France. In 1957, when a referendum showed the population wanted to be part of Germany again, France returned the territory to Germany.

As the Cold War between the Western Allies and the Soviets heated up in 1947, the Western Allies did not want to form a new united German state that might fall under Soviet domination. Thus, at a London conference in 1948, the United States, Britain, and France decided to create a semi-independent West German state. In response, the Russians, accusing the Allies of breaking the wartime accord to permit an all-German government to form in the postwar era, imposed a blockade on West Berlin from June 1948 until May 1949. The Western powers, to break the blockade, had to supply West Berlin by air.

In the meantime, West German representatives drafted a constitution, entitled Basic Law because of its provisional nature, for the new West German state. After Länder assemblies approved it on May 8, 1949, elections to the new West German Parliament were held in August. On September 21, the Western Allies terminated their military government in their zones, enabling the creation of the Federal Republic of Germany, with Bonn as its provisional capital.

The German Democratic Republic On October 7, Soviet authorities, in response to the Western Allied action, created the German Democratic Republic in their zone, with East Berlin as its capital. Two rival states were now operating on the territory of the former German Reich. The GDR was the smaller of the two states (and soon the poorer), had more than one-fourth of the population of West Germany, and had fewer urban concentrations. It was bounded by the Baltic Sea in the north, Czechoslovakia in the south, the Elbe river in the west, and the Oder-Neisse rivers in the east. The northern area of the GDR was primarily agricultural, whereas the southern area had some industries. As a result of Soviet reparations, the GDR industrial base was weakened considerably. The West German (and West European) economy received substantial assistance from the U.S.-financed Marshall Plan, but East Germany did not.

In the GDR, similar to other communist states with a one-party or one-party-dominant system, political power lay in the hands of the Socialist Unity Party (SED). Walter Ulbricht, its head, became the chief policymaker, holding more power than the president of the GDR, who was primarily the chief of state, or the prime minister, who headed the cabinet. Party cadres occupied all top positions in the national and Länder ministries, the army, and the economy. The politburo, the top SED organ, made the key decisions on domestic and foreign policies. To maintain a semblance of democracy, SED leaders allowed a few non-communist parties to exist but made sure that these parties had no significant powers.

Ulbricht survived national crises, such as the 1953 workers' uprising against the regime in Berlin, which was forcibly put down by Soviet troops when it spread to other areas. In its aftermath, Ulbricht made enough concessions to the workers to defuse their anger about economic hardships and the Soviet action. From 1958 on, Ulbricht, secure in his post, quickened the economy's collectivization. As in the Soviet Union, the state made central planning the chief instrument to ensure that the nationalized industries, small businesses, and agriculture carried out the government's five-year plans.

As a consequence of economic hardships and political repression, masses of dissatisfied people moved to West Germany through Berlin, the only opening in the closed frontier between the two states. In 1961, to keep the remaining population inside the GDR, Ulbricht ordered the building of the Wall between East and West Berlin. When a new economic crisis erupted in 1971, Erich Honecker took over Ulbricht's post as SED first secretary. The new chief replaced reformist SED leaders with loyal ideologues and ordered the conversion of more private businesses into state enterprises.

Honecker had to proceed cautiously, however, in making the GDR a model communist state. Even though the GDR was one of the most highly industrialized countries in the world and had the highest living standard of any communist-ruled state, the citizens were still dissatisfied with their material conditions, especially in comparison to West German citizens. To ease the dissatisfaction, Honecker liberalized social welfare support for low-income groups and citizens' rights to visit, or emigrate to, the FRG. Yet in 1976 he took a tough line again. He jailed or exiled to the FRG those intellectuals, artists, and others who demanded more civil rights for the people and increased the powers of the Ministry for State Security (Stasi), which kept all citizens under strict surveillance.

Unification Few Germans would have predicted that in 1989 the well-entrenched GDR authoritarian leaders would give up their power in a peaceful revolution of the people. When a reformist communist government in Hungary opened its frontier to Austria, a growing opposition emerged in the GDR. Thousands of GDR citizens headed for West Germany via Hungary and Austria. In the GDR, new civil rights groups and a newly formed Social Democratic Party organized to force the system's democratization, especially when Russian chief Mikhail Gorbachev told SED chiefs on October 7 that they would have to pay a high price if they did not make reforms. In Leipzig and other cities, thousands of dissatisfied citizens demonstrated weekly against the regime. On October 18, Honecker resigned, followed by the resignation of top SED and government leaders in the following weeks. On November 9, GDR officials opened the borders to West Berlin and West Germany. Millions of citizens poured into the FRG, most of whom had not been allowed to visit since 1961, for a peek at the well-stocked shops, a product of the capitalist system.

In the months that followed, a rapid democratization process took place in the GDR as new leaders and parties emerged. Following the legislative election in March 1990, the Christian Democratic Union (CDU), which had become the strongest party, formed a coalition cabinet with numerous old and new parties in East Berlin. But the new GDR government did not remain in power long because conservative and liberal party leaders in the FRG favored a swift unification of the two German states to provide stability and to meet the East German people's desires for more freedoms and a higher standard of living. Social Democratic and leftist party leaders, who wanted to preserve some of the GDR's social institutions, favored a slower process of unification but lost out. Therefore, on October 3, all East German institutions ended their independent existence as the GDR acceded to the FRG. The day marked the existence once again of a single German state.

Geography, Background, and Political Culture

The new united Germany borders the North Sea and the Baltic and has common frontiers with Denmark, The Netherlands, Belgium, Luxembourg, France, Switzerland, Austria, the Czech Republic, and Poland. Its size, about 357,000 square kilometers, is slightly smaller, in comparison, than Montana. Germany has a temperate climate, with wet winters and summers, and occasional high relative humidity. There are lowlands in the north, uplands in the center, and the Bavarian Alps in the south. Most of Germany's major rivers, such as the Rhine, Mosel, Neckar, and Ruhr, lie in the west. The Elbe river begins at the Czech border and flows to the North Sea; the Danube cuts across southern Germany before entering Austria. About 30 percent of Germany consists of woodland, situated mostly in the southern half of the country.

Germany's chief natural resources are iron ore, bituminous coal and lignite, potash, timber, uranium, copper, natural gas, salt, and nickel. The major agricultural crops consist of wheat, potatoes, sugar beets, and barley. The country's most important industries are engineering, automobile manufacturing, electronics, and chemicals, which account for much of its exports. Germany's principal trading partners are the EU member states, the United States, and Switzerland. Although Germany is the world's third-largest industrial nation (the United States and Japan outrank it) and is enjoying robust exports, the nation's prosperity has slowed down since 1990, partly because of the government's massive financial support (100 billion Deutsche Marks [DM] a year) to eastern Germany, which still lags behind the western part of the country. To ensure a strong currency, interest rates are high but inflation is low. Unemployment of more than four million (10 percent of the labor force) remains a major, seemingly intractable problem, which is not restricted to Germany.

The Federal Republic, as its name indicates, has a federal system, encompassing, since unification, sixteen constituent Länder, which have jurisdiction over education, cultural affairs, and religion. The national government has exclusive jurisdiction in foreign affairs, citizenship, immigration, customs, and currency. Both governing bodies have jurisdiction in civil and criminal law, and public relief. Relations between the national government and the states have not always been harmonious, especially when the national government has sought to increase its powers at their expense.

Unified Germany has a population of eighty-two million, of whom sixteen million live in the former GDR. Germany is thus the most populous nation in Europe. Western Germany is much more densely populated than eastern Germany. Nearly one-third of the population lives in cities of more than one hundred thousand people, but the great majority live in villages or small towns and cities. Non-Germans constitute about 8.5 percent of the population, including 2.4 percent who are Turkish. Among the many other ethnic groups are Italians, Greeks, Poles, and refugees from the former Yugoslavia. The population is 38 percent Protestant, of whom most live in the north of the country; 34 percent are Roman Catholic, of whom most live in the south; 1.7 percent are Moslem; and 26.3 percent are unaffiliated or other religions.

A diverse population can be expected to have diverse political values and norms, yet have certain commonalties that form the basis of a nation's political culture. The postwar West German governments sought to ensure that such values and norms fit into a commitment to the new democratic system. During the FRG's initial years, the commitment was minimal because the population was more concerned with the struggles of daily existence. Held responsible for an aggressive war and for the Holocaust, and feeling guilty for having supported a Nazi regime that brought disaster to themselves and others, some people only reluctantly identified themselves as being German. Allied officials and the German political elites built up a democratic political order, which the citizens accepted, but often with little enthusiasm. Thus, in 1949, about half of the respondents in a public opinion poll still concurred with the proposition that "National Socialism was a good idea, which was only badly carried out." By a two-to-one margin, they preferred a government that produced economic success and security rather than one that guaranteed political freedom.[3] In the early 1950s, only about one-fourth of respondents expressed any interest in political questions; few discussed politics with family or friends. Should a major economic crisis have broken out, perhaps a majority would not have backed a democratic government.

When political socialization took place in the schools and universities, and via the media, the citizens gradually developed a sense of pride in the country's democratic constitution and the political system, which often, but not always, responded to their needs. In numerous polls in the 1980s and 1990s, the citizens expressed solid support for the value and institutions of their parliamentary democratic system. Although they were satisfied with the system, more so than citizens of other West European countries, many criticized the politicians and the establishment parties.

Indeed, from 1968 on, the political culture in West Germany changed. Student, peace, ecology, and feminist movements, demanding more participatory democracy and more responsiveness on the part of the political elites, had varying degrees of success. This tilt toward greater liberalism was offset in the late 1980s and 1990s by the xenophobic intolerance toward foreigners or other ethnic or racial groups, including especially political asylum seekers, as well as by an increased nationalism toward others expressed by conservative and rightist groups. One 1998 poll indicated that about 13 percent of respondents had not shed their authoritarian and antiforeigner views.[4] Among these citizens are neo-Nazi youth,

---

[3] Max Kaase, "Bewusstseinslagen und Leitbilder in der Bundesrepublik Deutschland," in Werner Weidenfeld and Hartmut Zimmermann (eds.), *Deutschland-Handbuch: Eine doppelte Bilanz, 1949-1989* (Bundeszentale für politische Bildung, 1989), p. 205.

[4] Richard Stöss and Oskar Niedermayer, "Rechtsextremismus, politische Unzufriedenheit und das Wählerpotential rechtsextremer Parteien in der Bundesrepublik im Frühsommer 1998" (Arbeitspapiere des Otto-Stammer-Zentrums Nr. 1, Freie Universität Berlin, 1998), pp. 2-4, 15.

skinheads, and ultraconservative citizens. Their number is relatively small in comparison to the total population but might increase rapidly if a severe economic crisis were to erupt.

In this clash of values, the degree of freedoms that a democratic state allows its citizens is a measure of its commitment to democratic values. If the freedoms have been curtailed for dissidents and minorities, then the demarcation line between a democratic and an authoritarian state becomes less clear. On several occasions the government has curtailed the citizens' rights in the name of law and order. This has been true of political demonstrations staged to alter government policies, especially those dealing with the environment, nuclear energy, and nuclear arms. Violations of constitutional rights and human freedoms resulting from police overreaction and violent demonstrators have occurred. In addition, antiterrorist legislation has curtailed the citizens' freedoms, the state security services have been expanded, data banks have infringed on personal privacy, civil servants have been ousted for belonging to extremist parties while applicants for the civil service who have belonged to such parties have not been hired, and wiretapping has been extended. Despite these limitations on civil rights and freedoms, the government's record has been strong when compared to earlier periods of German history and when measured against the practices of many other Western democratic states.

SOCIAL AND ETHNIC GROUPS, CLASS STRUCTURE, INTEREST GROUPS, AND POLITICAL PARTIES

Social and Ethnic Groups

In recent decades, Germany, with a stratified social structure, has become increasingly heterogeneous in its population. An analysis of the family, the smallest social group, indicates that profound changes have taken place over the decades. Germany has one of the lowest birth rates in the world. More than half of the country's thirty million families have no children, and about half of the remaining families, or nearly one-fourth of the total, have only one child. Astonishingly, when compared to the size of families in the late nineteenth century, less than one family in four has two or more children. The cutback in the number of children has been caused by modern contraceptive techniques, the greater influx of women into the labor force, and economic difficulties of single-parent families.[5]

In the late 1990s, however, the number of newborns in western Germany rose modestly after having steadily declined since the 1950s. In eastern Germany, after unification, a precipitous drop in marriages and births occurred because of economic uncertainties, but by 1995 a reversal took place. Yet the modest birth increases in both parts of Germany have not offset a significant aging in the population, partly because of its greater longevity. According to specialists' projections, in the year 2040 the number of young people under twenty years of age will total only 15 percent (currently 22 percent) of the population, and those over sixty years of age will total 37 percent (currently 21 percent).[6]

After World War II, family life did not change appreciably, although the father became less authoritarian in relations with his wife and children. His traditional role of working outside the home and his wife being relegated to the home and taking care of the children changed gradually. Women, whether married, divorced, or a single parent, joined the labor force but were still expected to be the

---

[5]David P. Conradt, *The German Polity*. 6th ed. (White Plains, NY: Longman, 1996), p. 48.

[6]German Information Center, New York, *The Week in Germany*, February 20, 1998; Statistisches Bundesamt, *Mitteilung für die Presse*, October 8, 1998.

children's primary caretaker. As a result, women's participation in the labor force was at a lower ratio than some other comparable industrial states. Women married late or did not marry at all. Whatever marital status, discrimination against women continues in politics, the economy, and society. As in other countries, fewer women have made it to the top in politics and few women have the same income as men performing the same jobs.

The growth of strong social movements from the late 1960s to the 1980s paralleled the change in family relationships. Youth especially became concerned that the governments were doing little to safeguard the environment or to work for peace and justice. They formed environmental, antinuclear, and peace groups, often joined by social action groups of the churches. Their grassroots direct actions and demonstrations had a limited effect on government policies. Women, seeking greater gender equality, joined the feminist movement and raised the consciousness of the population to their problems. In the 1990s, these social movements have atrophied, partly because the political parties became more responsive to their demands and partly because many young people became disillusioned with politics and parties.

The diversity of social groups is mirrored in Germany's ethnic groups. A multiethnic society emerged in the FRG soon after its founding. The economic miracle of the 1950s produced a labor shortage, especially in the menial, low-paying jobs, such as street cleaning, refuse collection, and janitorial services, which few Germans were interested in filling. Thus the government and the employers actively recruited workers in the poorer European countries—Italy, Greece, Turkey, Portugal, and Spain—and the developing countries. By 1973 nearly 2.6 million foreign workers lived in the FRG; an economic recession that year and again in the early 1980s led to the exodus of many who had settled there. Since then the number of foreign workers has hovered around 1.9 million; however, if the number of family members who have joined the wage earners in Germany and the number of children born in Germany are added to this total, then the number of foreigners residing in the country tops seven million.

Foreigners are concentrated in the cities, where schools must cope with an influx of children who have difficulty adjusting to their new country of residence. Such a problem does not exist for children born in Germany of foreign parents. Yet often their parents are eager for them to maintain the customs and rituals of the parents' home country. This is especially true for the sizable group of Turks living in Berlin and other major cities. To add to the cultural adjustment problem is the difficulty many young foreigners have in finding suitable employment. As a result, social unrest is inevitable, which leads to occasional clashes with skinheads and neo-Nazi gangs who are ready to lash out at them.

Foreign youth are not the only ones who may be the butt of the right-wingers' attacks. One Turkish-born deputy in the European Parliament at Strasbourg, who is a German citizen, wrote in spring 1999 that he fears spending time in eastern Germany, where violence, including murder, against the comparatively few foreigners living there has been especially prevalent. According to him: "When the anti-foreigner gangs circle the houses, I too will not be able to hide my face and skin color behind the official pass of a German member of the European Parliament."[7] He decries the failure of the Germans to resolutely speak up against the continuing violence. As noted below, the question of foreigners, immigration, and citizenship has become a key issue in the country's domestic politics.

During the late 1980s and early 1990s, the government encouraged ethnic Germans whose ancestors had emigrated to Russia and Eastern

---

[7]*Die Tageszeitung*, March 31, 1999.

European states centuries ago to return home and immediately become German citizens. Abroad they had sought to maintain their German heritage, but in many cases they no longer spoke the language. Despite their new German citizenship, gained because national policy is to grant it by blood and not by place of birth, some of them were discriminated against for the same reasons that other ethnic groups suffered discrimination—they were outsiders competing for scarce affordable housing and jobs.

Class Structure

Germany's class structure is reflected in its occupational makeup. The largest groups are white-collar, technical, and service employees who constitute 47 percent of the workforce; industrial workers, who were at one time the largest group, constitute 36 percent; and the rest are small businesspersons, shopkeepers, independent professionals, and farmers. Gaps in income between the groups exist. Owners and directors of large enterprises had more than three times the income of workers, although obviously the wealthiest entrepreneurs exceeded that ratio by far. The gaps in income produce class antagonism, especially among the lowest income groups, the unemployed, and the underemployed who make up the underclass, constituting a minority of the labor force that has little prospect of gaining a position with a future. Although manual workers have a relatively high standard of living when compared to their counterparts in the Third World, nevertheless most of them will not be able to afford to buy an apartment or a house. The class antagonism that one could expect from continuing income differentials has been ameliorated by the existence of a strong social insurance scheme in the free-market economy. It ensures that all citizens have unemployment, old-age, health and disability insurance, and, for those who are eligible, child benefits, rent subsidies, and social assistance.

The educational system perpetuates class differences. Although all children receive a general education in primary and high schools, only a minority have the opportunity to attend a prestigious academic high school (*Gymnasium*), because of its stringent entrance requirements, and to attend a tuition-free university. Graduates of such schools are the ones who normally receive better jobs and better pay, except in periods of high unemployment, when their chances are almost as limited as youth who receive only a general education.

Interest Groups

Germany is not lacking in the number of groups, ranging from employer associations, trade unions, and churches to sports clubs and veterans associations, that represent the interests of its members. The necessity for economic groups to provide mutual assistance and to protect their members was recognized in Germany as early as the Middle Ages when merchant and craft guilds and the Hanseatic League were founded. They developed first as a company of traders with foreign lands and then blossomed into a mercantile association holding power in several German and foreign cities. These associations gradually declined in importance until German economic power revived as a result of the nineteenth-century Industrial Revolution. In 1876, the Central Association of German Industrialists, and in 1895, a rival League of Industrialists were formed to influence government policies. In 1919 the two associations buried the hatchet and founded the powerful National Association of German Industry, which was dominated by big business interests. During the Weimar era, the new association backed conservative cabinets and antidemocratic forces committed to preventing bolshevism and socialization of industry. Some industrialists supported Hitler financially; most collaborated with the Nazi government. As a consequence, a few were charged with war crimes at the Nuremberg trials held immediately after the war.

During the Federal Republic's founding years, the employer community formed several associations. The Federation of German Industry (*Bundesverband der Deutschen Industrie* [BDI]) speaks for big business and is politically powerful; the Federation of German Employers' Associations negotiates collective agreements with unions; and the Diet of German Industry and Commerce, a quasi-governmental organization, represents small businesses and artisans. It has a compulsory membership for its practitioners. Not surprisingly, the three associations have consistently provided greater support to the conservative political parties than to the moderate leftist parties.

The trade unions are a countervailing power to the employer associations. Before 1933, several rival union federations, each linked to a major political party, competed for the allegiance of workers and salaried employees. But after 1949, a single powerful German Federation of Labor (DGB), which currently comprises twelve separate unions with a total, but declining, membership of more than eight million, was organized. Unlike the Weimar unions, it is no longer linked directly to any party, but because most of its officials and members sympathize with the SPD, it expects to receive a more sympathetic treatment from an SPD-led rather than conservative government. The DGB in its initial years still had a neo-Marxist program, but it adopted a more moderate basic program in 1963. Since then, the DGB has supported a social market economy but has been a vigorous champion of the social welfare programs and the policy of codetermination, which provides for workers' representation on the boards of directors of industrial firms.

Three agricultural associations compose the Green Front organization, whose primary task is to convince national policymakers that the farmers' interests, necessitating price supports and direct subsidies for their crops, must be upheld. Such a position requires the government to back the costly European Union Common Agricultural Policy, which means high prices in a protected market. The German government has attempted to change the supranational policy but has met with stiff resistance from France and other EU countries whose farmers are even more insistent on high-level support.

In Germany, the numerous economic groups, to maximize their political effectiveness, put pressure on ministries to draft bills for legislative consideration that will not be inimical to their interests. The groups also seek direct representation in the local, state, and federal legislatures by requesting the parties to put the groups' officials on the party's electoral slates. Once elected, these legislators can represent their groups directly in the committee and plenary sessions dealing with issues of importance to them. As a consequence, less outside lobbying is necessary. In the German tradition of creating a social partnership (also known as democratic corporatism) one of the first steps of the new SPD-led government in 1998 was to create an Alliance for Jobs, at which representatives from business, the unions, and the government meet periodically to discuss matters of common concern, such as how to reduce unemployment.

The Protestant and Catholic churches also lobby government ministries and the legislature to enact policies that church members endorse. For instance, the Catholic church seeks more state support for its confessional schools, opposes an easing of abortion laws, wants stiffer divorce laws, and calls for greater controls over obscenity in the media. The liberal Protestant church has backed progressive legislation in domestic policies. In the former East Germany, the Protestant church was a refuge for dissident groups prior to the fall of the Wall in 1989.

Political Parties

The party system at the turn of the twenty-first century is merely the latest in a series of discontinuous ones since the empire era. From 1871 to 1918, parties played only a limited role in a nondemocratic system. During the brief Weimar era (1918–1933), the multiparty system, in which major democratic parties competed with numerous extremist, regional, and special interest parties, mirrored the deep schisms within the state. Unstable coalition cabinets had a short lifespan, contributing to the economic and social crises that peaked in the Great Depression. During the Hitler era (1933–1945), the monolithic Nazi party crushed all opposition. After World War II, new and restructured parties emerged in the four occupation zones. Thereafter, a dominant two-party system in the FRG confronted a dominant one-party system in the GDR. When the GDR collapsed in 1989–1990, its accession to the FRG led to both popular and grudging acceptance of the western party system.

A brief survey of the current parties indicates that the system is in a state of flux. Although the two major parties continue to dominate the parliament, the number of smaller parties gaining Bundestag seats has increased since the early 1980s. The Christian Democratic Union (CDU) and its Bavarian affiliate, the Christian Social Union (CSU), is one of the two major parties, having governed from 1949 to 1969 and from 1982 to 1998. The conservative CDU/CSU sees itself as a mass membership catchall party uniting Protestants and Catholics, most of whom belong to the small upper class, the larger middle class, the farmers, and the self-employed. Among the top party leaders, Chancellors Konrad Adenauer, in office from 1949 to 1963, and Helmut Kohl, in office from 1982 to 1998, stand out not only for their longevity as chancellors but also for their legislative accomplishments. They were staunch adherents of the social market economy, developed by Ludwig Erhard in 1948, before the FRG officially came into existence. They also emphasized law-and-order, taxation policies that favored the wealthy, limited social welfare budgets, and the nation's close alliance with the Western powers.

In late 1999, a prosecutorial investigation into one financial scandal affecting the CDU precipitated a host of revelations. Kohl and other top CDU leaders had no choice but to admit that in the 1980s and 1990s they had illegally raised for electoral campaigns sizable funds through secret bank accounts, bags of cash, and bought loyalty. These revelations shattered the party's image and standing in national politics. In January 2000 Kohl resigned as party chairman; three months later, the CDU chose Angela Merkel, the first woman and first east German to head a major German political party, as its new chairwoman.

The Social Democratic Party (SPD) was led in the postwar period (until his death in 1952) by Kurt Schumacher, the commanding head of the postwar social democratic movement whom the Nazis had imprisoned for years. During this period, the party advocated an economy based on planning rather than private profit and state ownership of the major means of production. After losing one national election after another, however, reformist party leaders at the 1959 Bad Godesberg SPD convention convinced delegates to accept a new program that basically supported the neocapitalist order. The leaders realized that neo-Marxist tenets repelled enough potential voters to prevent the party from scoring an electoral victory. Moreover, the leaders knew that their traditional voters, the industrial workers, were declining in numbers as salaried employees in the service sector grew in numbers. This change in the party's ideology eventually produced success. Willy Brandt, chancellor from 1969 to 1974, gained enough votes of salaried employees, civil servants, and students, while retaining those of the workers, to gain impressive victories in the 1969 and 1972 national election. His more conservative SPD successor, Helmut Schmidt, chancellor from 1974 to 1982, had more difficulty relating to the party members, most of whom are moderately leftist. Gerhard Schröder, the SPD chancellor who assumed office in 1998, had not expected to also become party chairman, but he accepted this post when his bitter rival Oskar Lafontaine resigned suddenly in early 1999 as minister of finance and party chairman. On ocacasion, Schröder has not found it easy to maintain support of the party's left wing.

In addition to the two major parties, three minor ones have had seats in the Bundestag in the 1990s. The Free Democratic Party (FDP) has espoused a liberal-conservative program since 1949 when it first gained seats in the Bundestag. As a party of the middle class and numerous employers, it has been committed to a free enterprise system, individual rights, and minimum state interference in the economy. From 1949 to 1998, it was the minor party in nearly all coalition cabinets, whether governed by the CDU/CSU or the SPD, in effect becoming a balancer of power. Such a role gave it undue influence in shaping policies, given its small voting clientele.

The Greens emerged in 1980 from the environmental movement of the late 1960s. The SPD viewed the new party, which ran candidates in municipal, Länder, and national elections, as a rival on its left flank, especially following the Greens' capture of Bundestag seats in the 1983 election. To reaffirm their antiestablishment position, the new deputies joyfully entered the Bundestag en masse, wearing jeans and sweaters, giving away flowers, and singing peace songs, thereby shocking the more staid deputies of other parties. In their manifesto, the Greens called, among numerous planks, for the dismantling of nuclear power plants, a conversion of the war industry to peaceful purposes, and laws banning discrimination against homosexuals. They assailed the stationing of U.S. nuclear weapons on German soil and requested the major powers to begin nuclear disarmament. The Greens' program attracted not only the support of young middle-class voters, many of them academics and students, but also civil servants and salaried employees.

The Party of Democratic Socialism (PDS), the successor of the Socialist Unity Party in the former GDR, gained Bundestag seats in the 1990, 1994, and 1998 national elections, and in numerous local councils and Länder parliaments. The PDS is in opposition in the Bundestag, but in two eastern Länder it shares in shaping state policies. In Saxony-Anhalt, it gave support to an SPD-Green coalition cabinet until 1998 and since then to an SPD minority government. In Mecklenburg-Pomerania, it is the minor party in the coalition cabinet with the SPD since the 1998 election, to the discomfort of some SPD national leaders who want to isolate it because of its communist past. The PDS remains strong in eastern Germany, especially in eastern Berlin, receiving votes not just from former communists but also from those who are dissatisfied with the economy. Its 1993 platform, containing an ideological mixture of communist, green, social democratic, feminist, and radical democratic elements, calls for society's fundamental transformation and a democratized economy, which would eventually lead to democratic socialism.

In the 1990s, three right-wing parties—the Republicans, the National Democratic Party, and the German People's Union—have run on racist and xenophobic platforms but have never received enough votes to be seated in the Bundestag. They have, however, won seats in some state legislatures and in the European Parliament, where their deputies, fortunately, have not been eloquent spokespersons for their dangerous antidemocratic platforms.

The rightists and other small parties have not been able to gain seats in the Bundestag because of the FRG's electoral system, which consists of a mixture of Weimar's proportional representation and the Anglo-Saxon single-member constituency. This unusual hybrid system was designed for the election of Bundestag deputies in order to reduce the number of splinter parties in parliament, which was a problem during Weimar. More specifically, the law stipulates that to gain Bundestag representation a party must either obtain a minimum of 5 percent of the national vote or win three seats in the districts. The provision has effectively shut out many minor parties. Each voter casts two votes,

Chancellor Gerhard Schröder addressing the Social Democratic Party Convention.

the first for his or her district candidate and the second—the more important one because it determines the composition of the Bundestag—for the party slate. In the district, the candidate who receives a plurality of votes wins the election. In the Länder, the number of seats allotted to each party is determined by the percentage of the total vote it receives under the complex system of proportional representation. A candidate may stand for election both in a district and on a party slate as added insurance of gaining a Bundestag seat. If a candidate is not placed high on the list, election is unlikely unless the party has received an unexpected avalanche of votes in the Land or has won a seat in the district.

The Basic Law grants parties a central role in the German system. They are supposed to help form the political will of the people, but they can be declared unconstitutional if the Constitutional Court rules that they intend to subvert the democratic basic order. The parties, having become more pragmatic and less ideological in recent decades, also provide political stability. Differences between them have narrowed, although intraparty schisms weaken their image. Their failure to solve serious economic and social problems had led to charges that they are not responsive to public needs, which in turn leads to a disillusionment with them and with politics in general.

POLITICAL INSTITUTIONS, LAW AND LEGAL SYSTEM, ROLE OF THE STATE, AND THE BUREAUCRACY

Political Institutions

The chief political institutions are the executive and the legislature. Within the executive branch, authority is divided between the chancellor, who is the chief policymaker, and the president, who is the ceremonial head of state.

The President In Weimar, the president had considerable executive power, which led him to appoint Hitler as Chancellor in 1933. To prevent a repetition of history, the Basic Law drafters limited the presidential powers to those held by the British monarch. As head of state, the president legally represents the Federal Republic to other states, accredits ambassadors, receives foreign diplomats, signs treaties and laws, and issues pardons, although a cabinet minister must countersign these actions.

The president swears in the chancellor and the cabinet ministers, and can dissolve the Bundestag, but only if a deadlock exists between it and the executive. Although the presidential powers are limited, the president is expected to become a conciliator in case of a major crisis. At other times, the president is supposed to remain nonpartisan and above politics, although since 1949 some holders of the post have been more outspoken on current issues than others. Recent CDU-nominated presidents, such as Richard von Weizsäcker and Roman Herzog, have enjoyed wide support among all strata of the population. Partisan divisions occur, however, during the nominating process of a new president because the candidates, one of whom is elected for five years with a two-term limit, are voted on by a special convention consisting of all Bundestag deputies and an equal number of members elected by Land parliaments. Each party represented in the Bundestag has the right to nominate a candidate for the post. In 1999, Johannes Rau, the SPD candidate and former minister-president of North Rhine-Westphalia, became president.

The Chancellor Months before a national election is scheduled, each of the two major parties will have selected a chancellor candidate to be the party's standard bearer during the campaign. Once the election results are in, the chancellor candidate of the party that wins at least a plurality of votes (a majority of more than 50 percent is rare in a multiparty system) forms a coalition cabinet with the party that is willing to share in governing the nation. The chancellor-elect proceeds to discuss with the coalition partner the outline of their government program and the makeup of the cabinet. Each coalition party seeks to have as many ministry posts as possible, but the major party obviously takes most posts, including many of the prestigious ones, such as finance and defense. Who occupies each post is the source of further discussions among top officials of both parties. As soon as an accord is reached between them on the program and the composition of the cabinet, which may take a few weeks, the president, as noted, swears in the chancellor, who must be approved by the Bundestag and the cabinet ministers.

The Basic Law stipulates that if the opposition party (or parties) in the Bundestag votes to oust a chancellor because of deep policy differences or other causes, it must first agree on a successor. This process, called a constructive vote of no confidence, was designed to stabilize the political system and to prevent the recurring changes in chancellors that took place during Weimar. At that time, the mutually hostile parties forced a chancellor to resign without agreeing on a replacement. In the FRG the chancellors can normally expect to remain in power as long as their party is numerically strong enough to keep forming coalition cabinets every four years; however, there have been instances in which chancellors resigned before the end of their four-year term of office, such as Brandt's resignation in 1974 when a spy scandal erupted for which he took responsibility or Schmidt's resignation in 1982 when the SPD and the FDP coalition partners could not reconcile their economic policy differences any longer.

The chancellor's political role can be compared to that of the British prime minister. A Basic Law provision stipulates that the chancellor shall determine and be responsible for general governmental policy guidelines. The chancellor must work closely with the cabinet ministers, who represent the ministries' interests. Serious policy differences must be settled either by interministerial conferences; the chancellery, which is responsible for coordination of bills and the cabinet agenda; or the cabinet. Should the policy differences remain serious, the chancellor may request a minister to resign or the minister may decide to resign, such as Lafontaine did in 1999. Major cabinet turnovers have been rare, although occasionally chancellors reshuffle their cabinets, shifting a minister from one post to another. In this game of musical chairs, some ministers are assigned to the more prestigious ones—foreign affairs, defense, finance, interior, and justice—whereas others have to be content with the less prestigious, nonpolitical, and technical ministries. A ministerial post is often the reward for loyal and outstanding party service or for having an expertise, such as in science or education, that is needed to head a ministry.

Parliament As in the United States, the German federal parliament consists of two houses: the Bundesrat represents the Länder and the Bundestag the people. The parliament, just like the U.S. Congress, debates domestic and foreign policy issues, mediates and integrates interest group claims, legislates, controls the budgets, and seeks to check the executive if necessary. Significant differences exist, however, between the American and German legislatures that can be traced to different historical and political circumstances and to the nature of the presidential and parliamentary systems.

In the Bundestag, whose members' term is four years, the centralized and disciplined parties play a role in the making of policy, which is initiated mostly in the executive branch and to a lesser extent in the legislative branch. The opposition party or parties serve as critics. Chancellor and ministers, who normally are also Bundestag members, have an opportunity to explain and defend their policies in party caucuses and in plenary sessions.

The Bundestag numbered 496 deputies up to German unification in 1990, and since then 656 deputies. The expanded membership reflects the number of the newly elected deputies from eastern Germany.[8] In 2002 the number of deputies will be reduced to 598 to make the legislative body more manageable. As a consequence, the country's electoral map will be redrawn to create 299 districts from the present 328. The number of women who are deputies in the Bundestag elected in 1998 totals 207 out of 656. This total does not correspond to the ratio of women to men in the voting population, which may be proof of the continuing discrimination against women in politics.

A Council of Elders, composed of members of all parties in the house, organizes its work, selects committee chairpersons, and sets agenda schedules. The Bundestag president, an official of the major governing party, is in charge of the plenary sessions. As in Congress, much of the legislative work is done in the numerous standing committees, which are formed by subject areas. Chairpersons are chosen on the basis of seniority, expertise, or power within the party. The governing parties receive a majority of such posts. Committee seats are distributed among the parties on a basis proportionate to their strength in the Bundestag. The committees do not have the veto power of their U.S. counterparts, but they review legislation introduced by the executive. The opposition parties have a further chance to challenge the executive, especially in budget matters, during plenary debates and question hours. Then the ministers or their state secretaries must provide information or defend their policy initiatives. As noted, the opposition can also attempt to topple the government through a constructive vote of no confidence.

---

[8]The number of Bundestag deputies varies slightly from one session to another because if a party wins more Bundestag seats in the voting for local candidates than it would be entitled to under strict proportional representation, it retains the extra seats under a system known as "overhang mandates."

The Bundesrat represents the interests of the Länder. Its approval is obligatory for federal legislation and administrative decrees affecting the Länder, which means that it has a suspensive veto power. If it vetoes a bill, the Bundestag has the power to override the veto by an equivalent majority. On other legislation, the Bundesrat may propose changes but has no veto power. As the Länder's legislative body, its sixty-nine members (forty-one before 1990) are appointed by and are members of the Länder cabinets, although top civil servants are deputized to sit in for the ministers in the committees where most discussions take place. In the plenary sessions, the three to six representatives of each Land (the number depends on the size of its population) must vote in a bloc on the basis of their cabinet's instructions. Occasionally, their votes reflect Land and regional rather than party interests, which means that the national governing coalition may not gain the support of all of its Bundesrat representatives.

From 1949 to 1991, the Christian Democrats won elections in a majority of the populous states, which gave them a Bundesrat majority, even when the SPD controlled the Bundestag from 1969 to 1982. The Christian Democrats, to gain more power during those years in Bundestag opposition, attempted in a suit before the Constitutional Court to make the Bundesrat coequal in power with the Bundestag in order to block the SPD-led government-sponsored legislation. The court, in a 1974 ruling against the CDU/CSU, said that the Bundestag had predominant legislative powers, despite the Bundesrat's suspensive veto power on bills directly affecting its interests. From 1991 to 1998, the SPD, the major opposition party in the Bundestag, had a majority in the Bundesrat. When it sought to delay or block legislation inimical to its goals, it was successful in some instances, such as fiscal bills. A few months after the SPD regained national power in late 1998, it and its coalition partner, the Greens, lost their Bundesrat majority because the Hesse Land election in February 1999 gave the CDU unexpected control of the Land government. Such Bundesrat changes can occur at times as a consequence of sixteen Länder elections held on different dates within one four-year Bundestag session.

Law and Legal System

The judiciary was an important branch of government during the Second Reich period (1871–1918) because of its close linkage to authoritarian state officials who determined political and economic affairs. The officials needed a set of conservative rules and norms to back up their powers. Thus, the courts supported the limitations on individual rights. During Weimar, the SPD-led governments failed to replace the conservative judges who had served in the imperial courts. As a consequence, the judges were lenient toward right-wing individuals and tough toward left-wing ones. During the Nazi era, judges became tools of the system and made decisions that were travesties of justice, such as the fateful rulings depriving Jews of their basic rights and eventually their lives.

The Basic Law drafters, knowing that the Nazis had obliterated all freedoms for individuals, symbolically listed the protection of rights in the first nineteen articles. Freedom of speech, assembly, and association are guaranteed, unless the democratic order is threatened. In that case, the Federal Constitutional Court must assent to its suspension. National, religious, racial, and sexual discrimination is prohibited. The Basic Law can be amended by a two-thirds vote of both houses of parliament, but the democratic constitutional order and the provisions relating to human dignity cannot be amended. These guarantees of rights and freedoms stem from the British, American, and French legal systems.

The German legal system, however, differs from the Anglo-Saxon legal tradition in which contending parties stand in adversarial relationships and the judge or court, remaining in theory a neutral arbiter, make their decisions in an ad hoc manner. In continental Europe, including Germany, laws, with their roots in Roman jurisprudence and the Napoleonic code, are codified, narrowing the judge's freedom of decision making. Judges are expected to back the state in safeguarding the implementation of laws designed to achieve major societal goals. Thus judges, especially those sitting in the Federal Constitutional Court, are closely linked to the political system. The Basic Law drafters, using the U.S. Supreme Court as a model, created a Federal Constitutional Court, a body that does not exist in most parliamentary systems and that did not exist previously in Germany. The court is obligated to guard citizens' rights and to rule on their individual constitutional complaints, to be the arbiter in federal-state conflicts, and to advise on the constitutionality of laws and decrees when parliament so requests it. The court's sixteen judges, who are divided into two chambers, have rendered important political decisions. In the 1950s, they banned the rightist Socialist Reich Party and the Communist Party for their hostility to the Basic Law. In the early 1970s, they upheld ministerial decrees not to take into the civil service or oust from it numerous, primarily leftist, teachers and other civil servants who, under the Radicals Decree of 1972, were charged with a lack of loyalty to the state. During the leftist terrorist wave of the late 1970s, they upheld the state agents' right to investigate alleged terrorist Red Army Faction supporters. The judges also rejected those laws liberalizing the right of women to have abortions if the laws violated an individual's right to life, which is guaranteed under the Basic Law.

Civil and criminal cases are handled by either local or district courts and on appeal by district and state appellate courts and the Federal High Court. This unitary system, which applies to all sixteen Länder, precludes an individual Land having its own jurisdiction; however, the Federal High Court handles not only civil and criminal cases on appeal but also disputes among the Länder. Specialized courts adjudicating administrative, social welfare, and labor disputes provide a venue for individual or group claims against state agencies. In the United States or Britain, such claims would be filed in regular courts or be settled out of court. German judges and legal scholars have discussed extensively whether the entire judicial system needs to be reformed and whether the civil and criminal codes need updating, but few changes have been made.

Role of the State and the Bureaucracy

The state has always played an important role in German history, often subsuming the rights of individual citizens to its own interests. During the nineteenth century, the Prussian state claimed to operate within the mantle of the *Rechtsstaat* (literally "rule of law state") based on the 1794 code and on Roman law. The code and the law were predicated on the theory that all governmental organs are governed by principles of justice and on the grant of private, civil, and political rights to individuals if these rights do not challenge state power. Because the rule of law was not yet the norm of the Prussian and German states, the legislatures challenged executive absolutism, but in vain. Unlike other Western states where individual rights were won at the expense of state power, in Germany they were linked to the state, except during the brief Weimar period. As noted, the Federal Republic's Basic Law limits the power of the state by guaranteeing individual rights; however, three articles (9, 18, and 21) in the Basic Law, known as "militant democracy," grant the government the power to deprive political parties, associations, and individuals of their freedoms and rights if they abuse them in order to destroy the free and democratic basic order. Thus individuals cannot give the "Heil Hitler" salute or create Nazi Internet sites. The

Constitutional Court has interpreted militant democracy to mean that citizens must actively defend the basic order. Civil libertarians have warned that legitimate criticism of the existing system could be curbed for partisan advantages, ostensibly to safeguard freedom and democracy. In that instance, militancy becomes intolerance.

The bureaucracy, also known in more neutral terms as the public service, has had a long tradition of serving the state, regardless of its authoritarian or democratic character. After 1945, the Western Allies sought to make the bureaucracy more democratic. This policy met with only moderate success against the entrenched interests and traditions of the held-over senior civil servants. The Western Allies weeded out from the public service the most active Nazi members who had been jailed as war criminals. Yet to provide for administrative expertise and continuity, they retained an estimated 90 percent of former civil servants in certain categories. Most judges, lawyers, police and security officers, teachers, and other civil servants remained in their posts after a token de-Nazification process. In May 1951, the CDU/CSU-led government promulgated a law allowing reinstatement of civil servants who had been dismissed or suspended after 1945 for Nazi activities. In the FRG's initial years, these conservative and apolitical civil servants only gradually became convinced democrats. As in earlier periods of German history, most of those in the higher civil service ranks have come from the upper and lower middle class, with few from the lower class.

The Western Allies attempted to eliminate the traditional tripartite distinction in the public service among civil servants, salaried employees, and manual workers, but failed because of strong pressure from civil service organizations to keep the status quo. From 1949 on, the West German government enacted numerous civil service laws, most of which set guidelines for Länder legislation and maintained the professional service traditions built up over the centuries. The Prussian civil service's nondemocratic rigid structures, which also included incorruptibility, efficiency, and impartiality, have hardly been altered, except for the public servant's loyalty to the democratic order. Numerous unsuccessful demands for reforms in the Länder suggest that the system could be improved.

The higher civil servants in the ministries, recruited primarily from law schools, must follow strict constitutional and legal norms. Once on the job, they may disagree with a political decision of their ministers, especially if such a decision tilts toward a social democratic or Green ideology. Usually, however, the career servants work competently and loyally for every administration regardless of its political coloration. The three-tiered public service is ranked according to four grades. For the higher service, applicants must have earned a university degree, completed a minimum of two years of training, and passed two state examinations. After a probationary period of six years, they receive permanent status, which provides them with a guaranteed lifelong security, a liberal pension scheme, and high social prestige. They can rise within a ministry to the top post of permanent state secretary, who is in charge of the bureaucracy. This post is more political than its counterpart in Britain because the German state secretary may be called on to answer questions in parliament. If a state secretary's partisan affiliation clashes with that of an incoming minister, he or she could be reassigned to another ministry or retired early.

In 1967, the government created the post of parliamentary state secretary. The holders of this post have not risen through the civil service hierarchy but are political appointees directly responsible to their minister. Their primary responsibility is to maintain contact with parliament. They, too, are empowered to answer questions directed to their ministry. For instance, the PDS deputies in the Bundestag have repeatedly asked interior ministry officials to provide information on what steps the ministry has taken to reduce the number of right-wing incidents of violence directed against foreigners. The purpose of such questions is to put the ministry on the defensive and to engender some action on its part; the questions also give public visibility to the party in its effort to convince the public that it seeks to promote the public interest.

Salaried employees and workers have a lower status and fewer privileges and rights than those accorded to civil servants. Thus, employees receive permanent status only after the age of forty and fifteen years of service. They cannot be promoted to the top nonpolitical ministerial posts. At the federal level, the percentage of employees and workers on the public payroll is higher than in the Länder because of the great number of personnel working for the federal railroads and postal service. The Länder and the local governments have a high percentage of civil servants because that status covers not only administrative staff in ministries, departments, or agencies but also teachers, health and social workers, police agents, television and radio staffs, trash collectors, municipal swimming instructors, and numerous other categories.

In the context of the "new" institutionalist approach, the German bureaucracy has adapted to the social and political protests that have become an integral part of the system. The civil servants, especially the younger ones, have become egalitarian and liberal and more responsive to changes in society. No longer can they and their ministers work in their ivory towers without responding to pressures from individuals, groups, and parties. Since the 1968 upheaval, when young people demanded more grassroots democracy, government officials and staff know that the political culture has changed and they better adjust to it.

PUBLIC POLICY, MAJOR DOMESTIC AND FOREIGN POLICY ISSUES, AND POLICYMAKING

Public Policy

The formulation of public policy is a dynamic and complex process in any political system. Normally, once the German cabinet agrees on the broad outlines of a policy, one ministry is charged with drafting a bill, which should reflect the cabinet's views. Civil servants, who are specialists in the field, prepare the first version of the bill, often after gaining advice from interest group officials. The draft is then circulated within the ministry and may be sent to other ministries for their review. If there are objections, which may come especially from the ministry of finance that is concerned about increased expenditures, top officials of the ministries hold strategy talks. Conflicts within one ministry may also occur if specialists differ on policy questions, thus necessitating compromise and repeated changes to the bill. In short, a protracted bargaining process takes place within a ministry or among ministries that determines the final wording of a bill before renewed cabinet approval.

During this stage, ministry officials seek to mobilize maximum support for a bill from party chiefs, interest group officials, and the general public. They need this support to enhance their own position vis-à-vis other ministries or parliament and to neutralize potential opposition from these constituencies at later stages of the legislative or administrative process. All ministries must work under the constraints of policy directives emanating not only from the chancellor and the cabinet but also from supranational organizations, such as the European Union. The chancellor's office plays a key role in trying to settle interministerial discords, acting as a clearinghouse for bills submitted by the ministries to the cabinet, and advising the top policymaker, the chancellor. If a bill is of great national interest, the chancellor can be expected to meet with the minister in charge of a bill, his own specialists, the deputies of the governing parties, and association officials.

Once the cabinet assents to the draft of a bill, parliament considers it. At that stage, ministry representatives become lobbyists. They unobtrusively contact deputies and attend committee meetings to provide expertise. Normally, the Bundestag acts as a ratifying organ for executive policy decisions because, under the principle of fusion of powers in a parliamentary system, the coalition cabinet has majority support in it. Thus the governing parties' deputies are expected to maintain party discipline and not vote against the position taken by their parliamentary group (*Fraktion*). Yet deputies of all parties, especially those subjected to pressure by association officials, attempt to make minor changes to bills in committees.

Many policymakers are involved in shaping a bill before it becomes law, thus making it difficult to measure their individual power. One SPD minister in Brandt's government wrote:

> The overwhelming number of bills submitted by me can be traced to me and my ministry's conceptions and preparatory work. In one or another case the suggestion to prepare a specific bill came from the coalition Fraktionen (party parliamentary groups), but was limited to their suggestion for a (ministerial) initiative. The way in which such initiatives were then considered and formulated was left up to me.

However, another minister wrote:

> The source of bills nearly always goes back to multiple impulses and demands, thus making a rare "monocausal" explanation. Parliamentary decisions, resolutions and electoral programs of parties, discussions among the public about long-range development trends or suddenly emerging problems, preparatory work in the ministries, the chancellor's decision about the government program, and, last but not least, the personal interest of a minister produce the most diverse combinations, which often make it impossible subsequently to sort out the decisive factors for the origin of a law.[9]

Once the policy is set in the executive and legislative branches, its implementation begins in the executive branch and may be challenged in the judicial branch. Thus the network of policymakers is wide, ranging from those located in the fulcrum of political power in the executive and the bureaucracy, to those in parliament, competing interest groups, and the Federal Constitutional Court. On domestic policy issues, interest groups and the public play a more active role than on foreign policy issues, but on all issues the political parties play a central role. In this constellation of forces shaping decisions, the role of the mass media must not be underestimated.

In summary, the host of social and ethnic groups, interest groups, and political parties put pressure on the chief decision makers in towns and cities, in the Länder, and in the national capital to produce legislation that benefits them. The decision makers in the executive and legislative branches may or may not be responsive to such pressures, but at times the pressures cancel each other out. Thus, at the national level, the dominant policymakers in the executive branch shape bills that their deputies in the Bundestag are expected to support. If the governing coalition has a Bundesrat majority, then passage of a bill is likely, but if it does not, then the opposition parties may veto a bill that needs Bundesrat approval or all parties may reach a compromise in the parliamentary joint conference

---

[9] Gerard Braunthal, "The Policy Function of the German Social Democratic Party," *Comparative Politics* 9, no. 2 (January 1977): 143.

committee, which consists of an equal number of deputies from both chambers.

Major Domestic and Foreign Policy Issues

The democratic political system in which policy decisions are made has the support of most citizens, but differences on specific policy issues arise continuously. On some issues, the major political parties hardly differ from one another; whereas on others they differ fundamentally. Among the domestic issues, some, detailed as follows, have become hotly debated and can be expected to be of continuing concern to policymakers in the years ahead.

Unification and Constitutional Issues During the 1990s, the German unification process was one of the key domestic issues facing every government. In 1990, Kohl sought a speedy unification of the two German states under article 23 of the Basic Law, which provides for the accession of German territories to the Federal Republic. He promised East German voters a "blooming landscape" that would bring capitalism's economic and social benefits at little cost. The SPD, the Greens, and East German dissidents favored instead a gradual unification process. They wanted to retain the GDR's positive accomplishments, such as full employment, low-cost housing, women's rights, an extensive day care system, and a network of local health centers. They insisted that unification could eventually be achieved under article 146 of the Basic Law, which would replace the Basic Law by a new constitution approved by the people. In this constitutional dispute, Kohl, having a majority of votes in the Bundestag, won.

The 1990 unification treaty stipulated, however, that the new parliament could deal with the question of modernizing or replacing the Basic Law, In May 1991, the Bundestag discussed this divisive issue. The governing CDU/CSU and FDP supported establishing a constitutional committee to modernize the Basic Law. The opposition SPD and Greens proposed a "constitutional council" that would draft a new constitution resting on the Basic Law. Such a constitution would include provisions guaranteeing all citizens the right to a job, adequate housing, gender equality, environmental protection, a ban on the export of arms, and a prohibition of atomic, biological, and chemical weapons for the armed forces. The two opposition parties called for a popular referendum to decide whether a new constitution should be adopted, but the CDU/CSU and FDP voted down their proposal, establishing instead a Joint Constitutional Commission, which rejected most of the SPD-Greens demands. The commission agreed to give the Länder greater control over legislative proposals, to increase the powers of the Bundesrat, and to strengthen gender equality, but little has been done to effect such modest changes.

Economic Issues The economic gap between the poor eastern and the wealthy western Germany has narrowed, but inequalities remain. Unemployment continues to hover around 20 percent of the east German labor force and 10 percent nationwide. Many businesses in eastern Germany have failed, and others have been taken over by west German or foreign companies, but with a major cut in the labor force. To fund costly investment and social welfare programs in the new Länder, the government has raised a yearly "solidarity" tax, which produces resentment among west Germans who are not eager to continue supporting the east Germans. In addition, a psychological divide has arisen between the "Wessies" (west Germans) who look down on their inferior "Ossies" (east Germans) compatriots. The Ossies in turn resent having been turned into a "banana" or "Deutsche Mark" republic, a mere appendage of the Federal Republic. They also are critical of west German leaders who have taken over most government and party posts in the new Länder and of west

The old Berlin Wall ran through this area. Today it is open, and the wall shown in the picture is only for symbolic and festive occasions.

German businesspeople who run the large eastern privatized firms.

When in 1993, Lafontaine, then the Saar's minister-president, proposed that in order to hold down national budget deficits, wages and pensions in the new Länder should be raised only gradually to western levels, an eastern SPD minister-president warned the top SPD chiefs that such a position would harm the party in the 1994 elections. He proved partly correct: if it had not been for disillusioned CDU and FDP voters, who were critical of Kohl's policies in eastern Germany and who switched their votes to the SPD, the party might have lost rather than won votes in eastern Germany. As it was, the SPD lost the 1994 national election, primarily because enough western German voters had more confidence in the ability of the CDU/CSU and FDP than the SPD to solve national economic problems.

The eastern Germans have espoused a political system based on democratic values and a genuine multiparty system based on the western German model, but, as noted, they have continued to resist becoming a dependent colony of the FRG, whose interests have been neglected. This disillusionment with government policies is not restricted to eastern Germans. In both parts of the country, a large underclass, consisting of the long-term unemployed, the homeless, the alcohol and drug users, and those working in a peripheral labor market of dead-end jobs, has arisen. Members of this underclass are marginalized in a consumer-oriented society and decry the parties' lack of concern about their plight. Many of the youth, disillusioned with politicians who are not addressing their concerns, drop out of society or join a rightist party or gang.

To counteract the economic and social problems, especially unemployment, the national governments have cut corporate taxes in order to encourage companies to invest more in the economy. The Schröder government may possibly lower the retirement age from sixty-five for men and sixty-two for women to sixty for everyone as a better way of opening up jobs for younger workers. Unions have proposed a reduction in overtime work to create more jobs, an expansion of flexible hour opportunities, and the granting of tax exemptions to minimum-wage earners in the service sector (the "McDonald's" jobs). The government, in a crash program in 1998–1999, also expanded the youth job apprenticeship program by funding one hundred thousand positions. The task is formidable because in late 1998 there were 428,000 unemployed youth, 460,000 young recipients of social assistance, and 150,000 youth who did not complete their school years or have an apprenticeship post.

The Schröder government also intends, in the coming years, to overhaul the tax system by cutting the highest and lowest income taxes. It will compensate for the loss in revenue by ending numerous tax breaks, including writeoffs for married couples, holders of large financial assets, and businesses. The funds from higher energy taxes will be used to lower the nonwage costs of social security payments made by employers and employees. These lower costs, it is hoped, will in turn make the price of German products more competitive on world markets, boost demand, and increase employment.

The German government's power to legislate in the domestic realm has been increasingly restricted by the EU, which has the competence, if accords can be reached by the member states, to issue yearly hundreds of regulations, directives, and laws that affect national agricultural, transportation, finance, environmental protection, consumer protection, health and safety at the workplace, and other sectors. Many of these policies are innovative rather than representing the least common denominator among the member states. Many EU directives need to be implemented by national laws. In some fields, such as social affairs, national decision makers, in Berlin and other capitals of member states, are the chief architects of policy. To coordinate supranational and national domestic policies, the German government has charged the ministry of economics, the chancellor's office, or individual ministries as the responsible agencies. The German Länder, which are affected by the EU's regional policies, share a regional observer in the German delegation to the EU.

Nuclear Power Each German government must make policy decisions among competing energy sources and in conservation and ecology. When oil shortages developed in the 1970s, the SPD-led government imposed conservation measures on the nation and planned to build up to forty nuclear power plants to supply 25 percent of the electricity by the mid-1980s. As energy consumption declined, however, it scaled down its ambitious plans to twenty-five new plants. Soon it faced opposition at the grassroots level from citizens' initiative groups who, in the aftermath of the Three Mile Island nuclear accident in Pennsylvania, urged a moratorium on any new plant construction. Chancellor Schmidt insisted that German nuclear plants were safe and that shutting them down would not solve the problem of waste disposal and would lead to an economic catastrophe. His party was deeply divided; many members quit it and joined the Greens, who were staunch opponents of nuclear power.

The Kohl government pursued a pronuclear policy, even after the Chernobyl disaster of 1986 and the continuing failure to find a safe nuclear waste disposal site in Germany. The government paid no heed to the demand from the SPD for a phaseout of all nuclear plants within a ten-year period and to the Greens' demand for the plants' immediate shutdown. After the 1998 election, the SPD and Greens policymakers had a chance to carry out their goals, but only if they could agree on a joint policy. During the negotiations to form a new government and agree on a legislative program, the Greens, yielding to the SPD, abandoned their goal of an immediate shutdown of all nuclear plants and the imposition of a steep ecological tax increase on energy. SPD leaders did not want to set a time limit on the closing of plants, but first mentioned a twenty-five-year limit. Then in 1999 they dropped that plan and said that the nineteen plants still in operation would close whenever the plants had outlived their forty-year life. The government held protracted talks with representatives of the nuclear power industry, the unions, and environmental groups that had been appointed to special commissions to deal with this explosive (so to speak) issue. In effect, the new SPD-Green government, by allowing plants to operate well into the twenty-first century hardly changed course from the Kohl government. According to a June 2000 accord, plants must close after thirty-two years in operation.

Foreign Workers, Political Asylum, and Citizenship Unlike the United States, Britain, or France, Germany has not seen itself as a land of immigration until recently. As a consequence, much discussion has centered on the related issues of foreign workers (known initially as "guest workers"), political asylum, and citizenship. Before the economic crisis of 1973, the government invited workers from poorer countries to work in the country's industries and service sector. But thereafter, faced by increasing unemployment, the government clamped down on the immigration of foreigners. The immigration did not stop entirely because citizens of European Union countries had the right to work in any EU member country, including Germany, and because illegal immigrants managed to be smuggled in.

During Kohl's administration, in the late 1980s and early 1990s, political asylum for foreigners became one of the most controversial domestic policy issues. It contributed to right-wing terrorism against foreigners. Partly to lessen right-wing actions and partly out of conviction, the Kohl government intended to amend the Basic Law's Article 16, which guarantees the right of asylum in Germany to foreigners faced by political, racial, or religious persecution in their home countries. The government had the public's support for an amendment as polls showed that most respondents criticized the misuse of the right to asylum of persons who came to Germany to escape poverty rather than political persecution in their home countries. But the government needed the SPD's legislative support to amend article 16 because a constitutional change requires a two-thirds vote in both houses of parliament. Kohl, weary of the discussions within a deeply split SPD, threatened to proclaim that Germany was in a "state of emergency" unless the SPD agreed to change article 16. The media and other parties reacted negatively to Kohl's threat because no such state of emergency existed and its proclamation would have bypassed the government's request for an amendment. Kohl, backing down under the increasing protest, did not proclaim a state of emergency.

Nonetheless, SPD leaders decided reluctantly that the party, which in the past had been a staunch supporter of article 16, had to change course and "swim with the tide" or else it might lose the 1994 election. For the party, which had a tradition of supporting the oppressed, such a radical switch in policy was painful. In May 1993, the major Bundestag parties agreed on appropriate legislation to amend article 16. Leftist critics charged, correctly at the time, that the parties had yielded to the political right, which in its vehement antiforeigner statements was increasingly setting the country's agenda.

Parenthetically, in 1999 the government's Office for the Protection of the Constitution warned the nation that the number of far-right supporters had increased by 11 percent in 1998 to 53,600, including 8,200 persons (7,600 in 1997) described as violent. Rightwing skinheads and other youth were especially active in eastern Germany, where half of all crimes against foreigners took place. The right-wing activists, to gain more support among youth, organized rock concerts at which skinhead bands played, and operated illegally two hundred homepages on the Internet filled with neo-Nazi hate propaganda.[10]

In 1998, the new Schröder cabinet decided that, despite expected resistance from rightist and conservative forces, the time was ripe to change the country's antiquated and restrictive naturalization laws. Its first plan was to give German citizenship automatically to children born in Germany if at least one of their parents also was born in Germany or had legally immigrated before the age of fourteen. Legal aliens could gain German citizenship after eight rather than fifteen years of residence, and minors after five years. The CDU/CSU launched a successful petition campaign opposing the government's citizenship proposal, collecting more than one million signatures nationwide in time to make an impact on the Hesse voters who provided the CDU and FDP with an unexpected electoral victory in February 1999. As a consequence, the SPD-Green state government was supplanted by a CDU-FDP coalition, which meant that in the Bundesrat the SPD lost its majority. For the Schröder government, this loss was a setback because controversial national SPD-Green bills can no longer be passed almost automatically. A footnote to the CDU/CSU petition drive: by May 1999 it had collected five million signatures, a signal that deep animosities toward foreigners continue to exist among a segment of the populace.

After the Hesse election, the SPD and the Greens weakened their original proposal and reached an accord with the liberal FDP, whose votes were needed in the Bundesrat to make the citizenship bill acceptable to it. The new version, enacted into law in 1999, stipulated that children born in Germany, who have at least one parent who has resided in Germany for eight years, will have dual citizenship until they reach the age of twenty-three. Then if they want to hold only a German passport they will have to renounce their original citizenship. This controversial citizenship issue is linked to the difficult task of integrating foreigners into a German society that is becoming increasingly multicultural but whose traditional governmental policy has been to restrict immigration.

Defense Policy The country's defense policy has aroused much passion in recent decades. In the 1950s, the West German conservative governments opted for rearmament, over the initial opposition of the SPD, which feared that a new German army might be seen by the country's neighbors, who could not forget Hitler's military attacks against them, as a new threat to their sovereignty. By 1958, however, a more reformist SPD switched position and supported the Bundeswehr (army), provided it was under strict civilian and parliamentary control. When the SPD was in power from 1969 to 1982, its pacifist left wing demanded, in vain, a reduction in the defense budget. Chancellor Schmidt pursued a pro-defense policy that did not differ from the earlier CDU/CSU policy. He encountered strong opposition within Germany to his plan for the United States and NATO to deploy intermediate-range nuclear missiles (Pershing II and cruise missiles)

---

[10]*New York Times,* March 26, 1999; *Süddeutsche Zeitung,* March 26, 1999.

in Western Europe, including the FRG. The deployment was designed to counter the buildup of Soviet SS-20 missiles aimed at Western Europe. Leftist critics, gaining strength within the party, called for arms control discussions with Moscow rather than a dangerous missile buildup. They feared that stationing more nuclear weapons in Western Europe would increase the risk of nuclear war. In 1982, Schmidt threatened to resign as chancellor if his party did not support him. Reluctantly it did, but soon thereafter he resigned when his coalition cabinet with the FDP broke apart over economic policies.

Once Kohl became chancellor in 1982, he continued Schmidt's defense policies. But in 1987, facing the combined pressure of a strong peace movement, the SPD, and the Greens, Kohl requested the U.S. government to remove the aging Pershing Ia missile launchers aimed at the Soviet Union from West German territory. The SPD's and FDP's critical position on defense, backed by popular opinion, made Kohl realize that he might lose the 1990 election unless he pressured the United States and Britain to agree to early talks with the Soviet Union on reducing the stock of short-range nuclear missiles and nuclear artillery weapons on German soil. He could not convince the Western Allies but won the 1990 election anyway.

Iraq's invasion of Kuwait in 1990 affected German defense policy. The Kohl government pledged eleven billion dollars to help defray the war's costs but did not send troops because a constitutional amendment would have been necessary to authorize German military deployment outside the NATO perimeter. The Basic Law's article 24, supplemented by the NATO treaty, forbids German military action unless it is part of a collective defense action falling within the NATO perimeter. Kohl's coalition partner, the FDP, as well as the SPD and the Greens, opposed such an amendment because the memory of World War II, when the *Wehrmacht* (army) occupied most of Europe, still played a role in West German defense strategies.

German unification in 1990 made the country's policymakers aware of their increasing international responsibilities. They wanted to erase the image of Germany being a strong economic power but unwilling to contribute its share to military actions. Kohl requested the Bundestag parties to pass a constitutional amendment allowing the government to participate in future military actions sanctioned by the United Nations, the European Union, or the Western European Union (a military pact). The SPD, whose votes were needed for an amendment, passed a resolution at its 1991 convention calling for German participation in UN peacekeeping forces, but only upon passage of a constitutional amendment and upon Bundestag authorization in each instance.

When the Constitutional Court ruled that no amendment was needed and when the parties agreed that Bundestag authorization for each military intervention was sufficient, the government intervened repeatedly in the conflicts in former Yugoslavia. In 1992 it sent ships and planes to help monitor the UN embargo against Serbia and Montenegro; in 1993 it authorized German personnel to serve in NATO's AWACS reconnaissance planes flying over Bosnia; and in 1999, when the Kosovo conflict erupted, its fighter jets, for the first time since World War II half a century earlier, were part of the NATO air contingents bombing military targets in Yugoslavia. The Yugoslavian Deputy Prime Minister Vuk Draskovic bitterly said: "We are not ready to make a distinction between the bombs of Adolf Hitler from 1941 and the bombs of NATO."[11] Germany also sent twenty-five hundred troops into Bosnia and four thousand into Macedonia as its contribution to international peacekeeping forces stationed there. Ironically, by the time the dangerous 1999 crisis had erupted, the formerly

---

[11] *New York Times,* March 26, 1999.

antiwar activist Joschka Fischer had become the German foreign minister who resolutely backed the NATO military action, although Schröder and he opposed sending German troops into a possible ground war, knowing that public opinion, especially in eastern Germany, was resolutely opposed to such an action. The 1999 Yugoslav war showed that in security issues, Germany can opt out of supranational efforts only with great difficulty. Indeed as a major continental power, its representatives in NATO and other security organizations can be expected to play a leading role.

The European Union and Other Foreign Policy Issues Germany has been a member of the United Nations and its agencies, and the European Union (EU) and other supranational bodies for decades. The Foreign Office is the chief coordinating agency for Germany's foreign policies with other states in the international arena. Germany's links to the United States, Britain, and France have been close but not always cordial. German-French cooperation, reinforced by periodic meetings of the two nations' leaders, has been one of the cornerstones of German foreign policy since 1949. Although differences have arisen on specific policies, Germany and France can be expected to maintain the fraternal relations that have characterized their policies since World War II, especially since they are the top trading partners and the dominant states in the EU.

Regardless of whether the CDU/CSU or the SPD is in power, the country has had close ties to the West. But during the late 1960s and the early 1970s, Willy Brandt, first as foreign minister and later as chancellor, began a rapprochement policy, known as *Ostpolitik* (Eastern policy), with the Soviet Union and Eastern European states. German firms have made major investments, supported by German government guarantees, in the former Soviet Union, Poland, the Czech Republic, and Hungary. Although the unstable economic situation in some of these countries has led to fewer new German investments than in earlier decades, a significant amount of trade still occurs between Germany and its Eastern partners.

From 1998 on, the Schröder government has continued the policies of his predecessors, but with a few modifications, especially in the European sphere. Schröder, unlike Kohl, warned the other fourteen EU member states that Germany could not expect to continue paying the highest sums yearly into EU coffers, much of which goes for agricultural subsidies, without a major review of EU finances. He said that an expansion of the EU to include Eastern European states would require lengthy diplomatic negotiations among EU member countries because of the high costs to the EU. The SPD-Green government also expected to coordinate its taxation and wage policies more closely with the other EU members in order to lower the EU's high total unemployment of seventeen million. To this effect, it put pressure on the European Central Bank, an independent agency, to cut interest rates as a spur to the economy. The German government expected to receive support for its pan-European efforts and for the conclusion of a European employment pact because thirteen of fifteen EU states in early 1999 were governed by left-centrist governments (only Spain and Ireland were not), which had the same objectives. These transnational efforts are expected to increase in coming years because the EU intends to develop common foreign and defense policies, which will be shaped by the most powerful states, including Germany. Whether such intentions of the EU to limit the national sovereignty of its member states will become a reality remains to be seen. In the meantime, the German government still makes key foreign policy decisions, but as in Kosovo in 1999, often in coordination with its partners.

In 1999, Foreign Minister Fischer announced that he would put more emphasis than his predecessor on human rights as a condition for improving relations with other countries, work more closely with nongovernmental international organizations, give greater support to the War Crimes Tribunal in the Hague, strengthen the Organization for Security and Cooperation in Europe, and uphold the United Nations. Despite such assertions, Fischer has been cautious not to alienate the United States, Russia, and other states with whom Germany has maintained close links in recent decades. Such links have been supported by all the parties in the Bundestag and by public opinion.

Development assistance to Third World states remains one of Germany's goals, but, similar to other industrial developed states, the assistance has been underfunded. As a consequence, serious poverty, underemployment, unemployment, and social problems remain prevalent in Third World states, which have been negatively affected or bypassed by the global economy.

CONCLUSION, PROSPECTS, PROBLEMS, AND FUTURE DIRECTIONS

A survey of Germany's history and its political institutions reveal sharp discontinuities and profound upheavals in the past but a greater stability since the end of World War II. The creation of two German states in 1949 divided the nation into two rival camps, one espousing the social market economy and the other the socialist planned economy.

The German Democratic Republic in the east evolved into a typical people's democracy or communist state, patterned on the model of the Soviet Union. The Socialist Unity Party held the reins of power, allowing the executive (the Council of State) administrative powers and granting the legislature (the People's Chamber) power to only ratify bills rather than to debate them. Although the state offered the citizens generous welfare benefits and full employment, their lack of individual freedoms was a source of constant dissatisfaction and contributed to the peaceful revolution of 1989 and the demise of the GDR in 1990.

The Federal Republic in the west had a parliamentary system typical of other European democratic states. The chancellor and the ministers were the chief policymakers in the domestic and international realms. Compared to some other parliamentary systems, such as that of Italy, which have frequent changes in cabinets but not necessarily among officeholders, most West German governments remained in office for four years, which corresponds to the Bundestag four-year cycle.

This pattern has continued in the Federal Republic since unification in 1990. Normally, the chancellor and the ministers in the coalition cabinets gain approval from parliament, if they control both houses, for their government program, which is formulated during coalition negotiations in the postelection phase. Even if they do not control the Bundesrat, those planks in their program, such as national defense, that need only Bundestag approval, are ensured passage; however, should the opposition holding a majority in the Bundesrat oppose a bill affecting the Länder, then it blocks a bill or forces a compromise.

The political parties, whose programs are not that far apart, have contributed to the system's stability, although new parties have emerged to challenge the major parties, the CDU/CSU and the SPD. Volatility in voting, which means that the voters are not as loyal to a party as they used to be, has caused the party system to become more fragmented and elections to be more unpredictable. A decades-long shift in class, religious, and other social characteristics means that the traditional constituencies on which the two major parties could depend for voter support are shrinking. The CDU/CSU, for instance, can no longer rely for victory on the decreasing number of devout Catholics or farmers; similarly, the SPD needs more than the loyal support of the decreasing number of unionized blue-collar workers. The two parties must rely instead on the support of a expanding new middle class, consisting of both public servants and salaried employees in the expanding service sector. This amorphous middle class lacks the religious and class identification of an earlier generation.

In the 1998 national election, for instance, Schröder sought in the SPD's election program to occupy the "New Middle" in the political spectrum in order to gain the support of this centrist clientele and to topple Kohl's well-entrenched CDU/CSU-FDP government. The SPD challenger, who was media conscious and media savvy, waged an American-style campaign in which personalities are more important than issues. Obviously, issues had to be addressed, but then in the style of the "Third Way" espoused by U.S. President Bill Clinton and British Prime Minister Tony Blair. This philosophy emphasizes technological innovation, especially in the communications field; competitive enterprise; and education rather than the leftist redistribution of wealth or the rightist unfettered laissez faire economy. Schröder's gamble paid off; he won the election.

The Schröder government, consisting of the moderately leftist SPD and the Greens, cannot expect automatic ratification for its government program from parliament because it lost its majority in the Bundesrat in early 1999; however, given the number of Länder elections in the interval between national elections, held at least every four years, the Schröder government may recover its majority in the Bundesrat in the coming years if it topples one of the few CDU-controlled Länder. Whether it succeeds or loses, the government, symbolically located in Berlin—a city that was in the storm center of the Cold War and that is located nearly midway between Paris and Moscow—has changed nuclear energy policy and liberalized the naturalization laws, and seeks to heal the psychological divide between western and eastern Germans.

In domestic politics, the government hopes to decrease the unacceptably high rate of national unemployment while maintaining the costly social welfare system. If it fails, social unrest will increase, especially in eastern Germany where popular resentment against being treated as a colony by national decision makers is already substantial. The dangerous activities of skinheads and neo-Nazi groups against foreigners is one manifestation of a continuing problem that defies an easy solution. The government in Bonn too often had failed to resolutely combat intolerance of minorities and foreigners. Worried about its international image and the loss of foreign investments in the country, it had taken resolute action against the perpetrators of violence only when an especially vicious attack against foreigners occurs, such as neo-Nazis setting fire in 1993 to an apartment building in Solingen (western Germany) that resulted in the deaths of five Turkish women and girls. The integration of foreigners into German society remains an ongoing problem, although numerous local efforts in schools and youth centers have been successful, candlelight protest demonstrations against rightist violence have taken place, and judges have dealt less leniently with rightists who have been found guilty of violating existing statutes.

In international politics, the Schröder government has shown an increased self-confidence and assertiveness in European fiscal and military policies. In fiscal policies, it seeks to regulate the international financial markets more closely. Whether such a regulation will be implemented and succeed remains to be seen. In the global economy, the multinational companies (including those owned by Germans) are powerful; whether the German and other EU governments can limit their activities is unpredictable. The German and other EU member states also have no power to change the policies of the independent European Central Bank and direct it, for instance, to reduce high interest rates that are designed to combat inflation. They want the bank to lower interest rates as a way to spur the economy and reduce unemployment. Similarly, the German government has tried to influence the country's independent Bundesbank to lower interest rates, but it has met with little success because the powerful bankers resist outside intervention.

An SPD-led government should include other items on the agenda of the new Berlin Republic if it remains true to its historical principles. Among them, and the sample is not inclusive, are greater gender equality; more direct democracy, including initiatives and referenda at the national level; increased environmental safeguards and data protection; recognition of nonmarried partnerships; and redistributive tax policies. Despite numerous political, economic, and social problems facing the republic, most of which transcend national borders, the democratic political institutions, civil liberties, civil society, and political culture—one-half century old in western Germany—have a firm base. Unless catastrophic economic developments occur, and they are not in sight, the democratic system in united Germany will continue to flourish.

SUGGESTED READINGS

Allen, Christopher, S., Germany, in Mark Kesselman, Joel Krieger, et al. (eds.), *European Politics in Transition*. 3d ed. (Boston: Houghton Mifflin, 1997).

Bracher, Karl Dietrich, *The German Dictatorship* (New York, Praeger, 1970).

Braunthal, Gerard, *The German Social Democrats Since 1969: A Party in Power and Opposition*. 2d ed. (Boulder, CO: Westview Press, 1994).

Conradt, David P., *The German Polity*. 6th ed. (White Plains, NY: Longman, 1996).

Conradt, David P., Gerald R. Kleinfeld, and Christian Soe (eds.), *Power Shift in Germany: The 1998 Election and the End of the Kohl Era* (New York: Berghahn, forthcoming 2000).

Craig, Gordon A., *The Germans* (New York: Putnam, 1982).

Dahrendorf, Ralf, *Society and Democracy in Germany* (Garden City, NY: Anchor, 1969).

Fuller, Linda. *Where Was the Working Class? Revolution in Eastern Germany* (Urbana, IL: University of Illinois Press, 1999).

Hampton, Mary, and Christian Soe (eds.), *Between Bonn and Berlin: German Politics Adrift?* (Lanham, MD: Rowman & Littlefield, 1999).

Katzenstein, Peter J., *Party and Politics in West Germany: The Growth of a Semisovereign State* (Philadelphia: Temple University Press, 1987).

Krisch, Henry, *The German Democratic Republic: The Search for Identity* (Boulder, CO: Westview Press, 1985).

Larres, Klaus (ed.), *Germany Since Unification: The Domestic and External Consequences* (New York: St. Martin's Press, 1998).

Maier, Charles S., *Dissolution: The Crisis of Communism and the End of East Germany* (Princeton, NJ: Princeton University Press, 1997).

Maier, Charles S., *The Unmasterable Past: History, Holocaust, and German National Identity* (Cambridge, MA: Harvard University Press, 1988).

Markovits, Andrei S., and Philip S. Gorski, *The German Left: Red, Green and Beyond* (New York: Oxford University Press, 1993).

Markovits, Andrei S., and Simon Reich, *The German Predicament: Memory and Power in the New Europe* (Ithaca, NY: Cornell University Press, 1997).

McFalls, Laurence, *Communism's Collapse, Democracy's Demise?* (New York: New York University Press, 1995).

Merkl, Peter H. (ed.), *The Federal Republic of Germany at 50: At the End of a Century of Turmoil* (New York: New York University Press, 1999).

Patton, David F., *Cold War Politics in Postwar Germany* (New York: St. Martin's Press, 1999).

Roberts, Geoffrey K., *Party Politics in the New Germany* (London: Cassell Academic, 1997).

Smith, Gordon, William E. Paterson, and Stephen Padgett (eds.), *Developments in German Politics 2* (Durham, NC: Duke University Press, 1996).

5

ICELAND
Atlantic Ocean
SWEDEN
Dublin
Copenhagen
GREAT BRITAIN
NETHERLANDS
The Hague
London
Berlin
GERMANY
Brussels
BELGIUM
LUX.
Luxembourg
Prague
Paris
CZECH
Vienna
FRANCE
Bern
LIECH.
AUSTRIA
SWITZERLAND

Norwegian Sea
Bering Sea
NORWAY
SWEDEN
FINLAND
Baltic Sea
St. Petersburg
Arkhangelsk
BEL.
MOSCOW
Nizhniy Novgorod
Kazan'
UKR.
Volgograd
Rostov
Astrakhan
Chelyabinsk
Ural Mts.
Ob
Irtysh
RUSSIA
Novosibirsk
Krasnoyarsk
Irkutsk
Lena
Verkhoyan Mts.
Yakutsk
Magadan
Sea of Okhotsk
Stanovol Mt
Amur
Khabarovsk
Vladivostok
Sea of Japan
CHINA
MONGOLIA
KAZAKHSTAN
AZERBAIJAN
UZBEKISTAN
TURKMENISTAN
KYRGYZSTAN

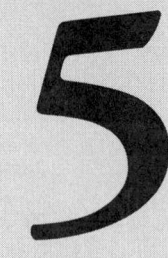

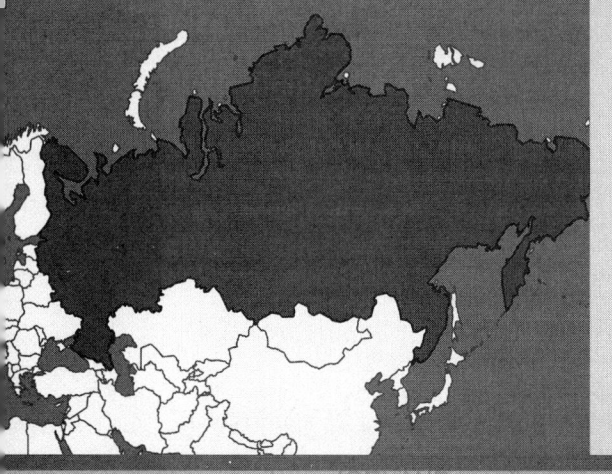

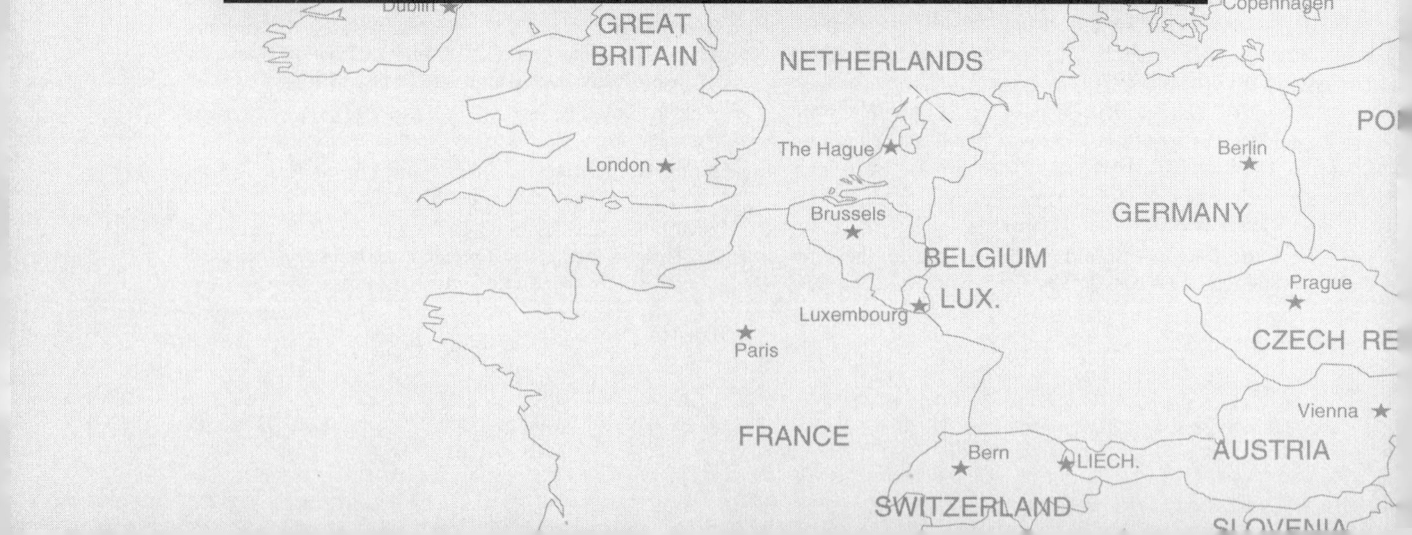

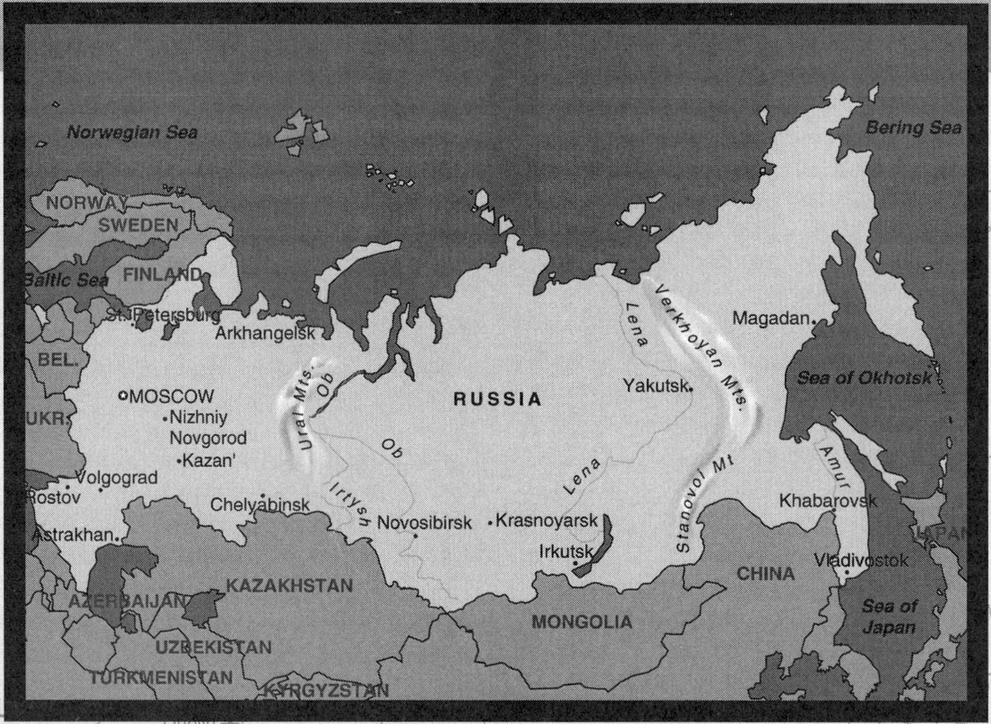

Russia

Joining the West, But Slowly

Steve D. Boilard

COUNTRY PROFILE

Population:	147,000,000
Land Area:	17,075,000 sq. km.
Population per sq. km.:	9
Gross National Product:	$337.9 billion
Per Capita Income:	$2,300
Global Per Capita Income Rank:	101
Percent Urban:	77
Adult Literacy:	99% (claimed)
Life Expectancy	
Male:	61
Female:	73

INTRODUCTION

Russia is a country undergoing an identity crisis. The collapse of the Soviet state in 1991, the discrediting of Marxist-Leninist ideology, the emergence of ethnonational conflict among Russia's citizens, the advent of religious pluralism, and the alarming rise in crime and corruption have thrown into turmoil whatever consensus about Russia's identity may have existed a decade ago. The eventual coalescence of a new Russian identity will severely test the forces of integration and globalization, and the stabilizing of a new Russian state will help define European politics in the twenty-first century.

As a geographical concept, Russia has existed for more than one thousand years. Its history has been epical, often tragic with periodic triumphs. By dint of its length and intensity, Russia's history is said to be deeply etched into the souls of its people. Even today, as Russia struggles to define itself in the post–Cold War world, many Russians harbor a somewhat fatalistic sense of their country's developmental trajectory, which has gained the momentum of a millennium. Still, the country, freed from the political straitjacket of the Soviet state, the misguided ideology of Marxism-Leninism, the geopolitical hostility of the Cold War, and the economic burden of its empires in Eurasia and Eastern Europe, has begun to stumble into a more promising direction.

Despite the economic and political collapse of the Soviet Union, Russia remains one of the most important players, at least potentially so, in European and world politics. It covers more territory than any other country in the world, outweighing the geographically largest European country—Germany—with more than forty-seven times the territory and almost twice the population. It possesses enormous reserves of oil, coal, natural gas, gold, and other valuable materials. Russia shares its 12,500-mile border with some strategically important countries, including China and North Korea, and has access to several major bodies of water, including the Pacific Ocean and the Caspian, Black, Baltic, and Barents seas. Russia has made tremendous contributions to science, space exploration, music, and literature. It also possesses the capacity, in the form of thermonuclear weapons, to destroy the world. Russia is an important country indeed.

As head of the post-Soviet Russian state throughout the 1990s, President Boris Yeltsin sought to guide his country back to Europe and the West more generally. The intentions of his successor, Vladimir Putin, were not immediately known when Yeltsin's resignation elevated Putin to acting president on December 31, 1999, although early clues suggested a more nationalistic and authoritarian approach. Moreover, a large segment of the population, including many of Russia's elected representatives, questioned Yeltsin's (and most Westerners') assumption that the failure of the Soviet Union must naturally trigger Russia's enlightened (or repentant) adoption of a Western liberal identity. Why Western? Why democratic? Is Russia even European, or distinctly Slavic, or Eurasian, or some shifting, crazy-quilt amalgam of all of these? Why indeed should this particular collection of territories and peoples constitute a unified state at all?

The sovereign state known as the Russian Federation that emerged from the rubble of the Soviet Union is the product of a variety of circumstances: its borders were defined by earlier administrative decisions by the Soviet authorities, its culture has been influenced by seven decades of communist indoctrination, and its demographics derive in large part from massive relocation programs ordered by Soviet dictator Josef Stalin.

At the same time, Russia is subject to external forces that pervade the post-bipolar, rapidly integrating world and to internal conflicts and divisions. No particular outcome is assured, but Russia's political, economic, and military development in the early twenty-first century will certainly help to define the boundaries and security of Europe as a whole.

HISTORY, GEOGRAPHY, BACKGROUND, AND POLITICAL CULTURE

Although foreigners historically have labeled Russia "inscrutable" and an "enigma," valuable insight into contemporary Russian politics and society can be gleaned from a review of its history and geographical and cultural background.

Establishing the Russian State

From prehistoric times, the Slavic peoples occupying the area of what is now European Russia were subject to successive waves of invasion. These early Eastern Slavs came under the control of Scandinavian Vikings (Varangians) in the ninth century. After successive conquests, the Varangians established a capital at Kiev (the capital of modern Ukraine). The result was Kievan Rus—a united Russian state. Subsequent rulers expanded the borders of Rus, adopted a written language based on the Cyrillic alphabet, and established the Russian Orthodox church. By the eleventh century, the state had developed a distinct identity and boasted considerable commercial, cultural, and religious importance.

After its zenith in the eleventh century, Kievan Rus steadily declined, falling victim to a combination of internecine battles, disrupted trade, and periodic raids by marauding armies. In the thirteenth century, Kievan Rus fell to the Mongols ("Tatars" in Russian parlance). Kiev was destroyed, and Moscow steadily grew in importance. For two centuries the Mongols maintained domination over the Russians and exacted annual tribute. Although the Mongols generally allowed Russians to continue their day-to-day lives, the "Mongol Yoke" was economically and politically oppressive. When Russians periodically rose up against the Mongols, they encountered savage counterforce and retribution.

The Russians, led by Ivan III ("the Great"), eventually overthrew their Mongol oppressors, terminating the Mongol Conquest in 1480. Ivan III also seized control of the cities of Tver and Novgorod, consolidating Muscovite Russia. With Constantinople's fall to the Turks in 1453, Moscow assumed itself to be the "Third Rome," strengthening the concept of Russia as a united Christian empire. Ivan III adopted the title "Tsar" (a Russian variation on "Caesar"), and Russia's Tsarist era began.

The powers of the tsar were consolidated and increased under Ivan III's grandson, Ivan IV ("the Terrible"). But with Ivan IV's death in 1584, Russia's ruling circle became plagued with conspiratorial regents, foreign intrigue, and a series of false pretenders to the throne. The "Time of Troubles" had descended upon Russia, and embattled rivals called on foreign powers, including Sweden and Poland, to intervene. This condition of domestic turmoil and foreign occupation continued until 1613. With the Poles driven from Moscow the year before, the Russian Assembly (*Zemsky Sobor*) elevated Mikhail Romanov to tsar and made the title hereditary. The House of Romanov would rule Russia for the next three centuries, until the revolution of 1917.

Imperial Russia

Russia became a European power of significance and took on a more Western identity under Tsar Peter I ("the Great"), the Romanov who ruled the country from 1689 to 1725. Peter's Russia, continually at war, secured several impressive victories over other powers. Peter developed Russia's navy and more effectively organized its army, and he reoriented the country's focus to the West.

Peter traveled extensively in Europe, and he was eager to transplant large features of its culture to Russia. His interest in the West was perhaps best symbolized by his moving Russia's capital city from Moscow to St. Petersburg (on the shore of the Baltic Sea) in 1712. Peter's appreciation for the West also manifested itself in "Westernizing" policies, whereby arts and sciences, court customs, and even Russia's penchant for long beards were modified to conform with Western trends. Peter developed a reputation as a modernizer and social reformer, which contrasted sharply with many of his predecessors (and not a few of his successors).

A successor who did share Peter's affinity for Western ways was Catherine II ("the Great"), who ruled Russia from 1762 until her death in 1796. Formerly a German princess, Catherine considered herself a great ruler and a philosopher of the Enlightenment era. Despite her familiarity with liberal ideas, however, Catherine did little to attenuate the autocratic nature of the Russian court. She is often described as an "enlightened despot" by Russian and Western historians alike. In fact, Catherine's despotism and her distrust of and ambivalence toward the peasantry was symptomatic of the Russian monarchy. The imperial edifice sat atop an oppressed, sometimes restive, population.

Russia's international position under the tsars swung between strength and weakness. Russia emerged as a Great Power in the eighteenth century, and at one point in the early nineteenth century it and France were the two major powers on the Continent. Napoleon's invasion of Russia and occupation of Moscow, followed by Tsar Alexander I's pursuit of Napoleon's retreating army and subsequent occupation of Paris, are illustrative of the shifting balance of power. Russia participated as one of the four Great Powers at the Congress of Vienna in 1815, but its fortunes continued to shift with the dynastic and imperial wars so characteristic of nineteenth-century Europe's international relations and diplomacy.

Domestically, a pattern of alternating reform and repression had taken root in Russia. With the Russian population displaying ever-greater restiveness and engaging in occasional uprisings, the tsar, Alexander II, finally removed a significant cause of popular unrest by abolishing serfdom in 1861—the year before Abraham Lincoln's Emancipation Proclamation. By this time, however, even the freeing of the serfs could not appease radical groups opposed to the regime. Intellectuals, nationalists, populists, and revolutionaries advocated a variety of visions for their country. A pronounced cleavage divided the regime's opponents between "Slavophiles," who advocated an ethnically distinct Slavic state grounded in Orthodoxy, and "Westernizers" who sought to resurrect and expand Russia's European identity and politics, which had begun under Peter I. The discontinuity of the two visions was nevertheless papered over as the radicals found common cause in their disdain for the current regime. The government unwittingly helped to unite its opponents through the imposition of widespread censorship, the practice of religious and political persecution, and its involvement in unpopular (and sometimes disastrous) foreign wars. This division between Slavophiles and Westernizers still exists in Russian politics today.

Public unrest was exacerbated with the onset of Russia's Industrial Revolution in the last decades of the nineteenth century. Exploitive and unsafe working conditions, food shortages, and urban overcrowding composed a new category of grievances beyond the now familiar authoritarianism of the regime. By the time the final tsar, Nicholas II, assumed power in 1894, living conditions in the cities were so intolerable that the burgeoning urban population became a fertile recruiting ground for the growing reformist and revolutionary groups. This "proletariat," as the Marxist revolutionaries called it, assumed a pivotal role in the revolutionary events that were to transpire. It was in the proletariat's interest that a growing revolutionary group, the Social Democratic Labor Party, putatively would fight.

The Russian Revolution

Founded in 1903, the Social Democrats increasingly became divided over the issue of how to proceed along the revolutionary path. The Menshevik (minority) group sought to develop a broad-based party acting according to the ideal of workers' democracy. For them, the revolution itself remained an eventuality beyond the immediate future, requiring first the full development of capitalism. The Bolshevik (majority) group, headed by V. I. Lenin, preferred to create an elite party that would guide the revolution without the direct participation of the workers. For the Bolsheviks (and Lenin in particular), the workers could not rise above their "trade union consciousness" and required an intellectual "vanguard"—the Bolsheviks—to act on their behalf. The Bolsheviks believed that the capitalist stage of development could be bypassed, and they sought an immediate transition to socialism.

On "Bloody Sunday" in 1905, the slaughter of more than one hundred unarmed protestors by guards at the tsar's Winter Palace knocked out one of the regime's few remaining props: the popular belief that governmental underlings and renegades, rather than the tsar himself, were responsible for the people's privations. In the following months, demonstrations, riots, and assassinations would collectively constitute the 1905 Revolution, and by October, Nicholas conceded to establish the trappings of a constitutional monarchy. Within one year, however, the tsar had reneged on most of his promised reforms. General public dissatisfaction with the regime continued, and increasingly radical revolutionary groups continued to agitate against the government.

Then, in 1914, Russia was drawn into war against Germany in defense of its Slavic ally, Serbia. The resultant First World War created conditions for a successful coup de grace against the tsarist regime. Simultaneously weakening the country and galvanizing public opposition, the war cut the tsar's power base, including his own armies, from under him. In March 1917, Nicholas abdicated the throne in favor of his brother, Michael. Refusing that poisoned chalice, Michael turned sovereign power over to a "provisional government." Fatally, the new government refused to remove Russia from the war—perhaps the most important and immediate demand of the disaffected population. Meanwhile, Lenin's Bolsheviks, who were not part of the provisional government, established a power base in the Petrograd (nee St. Petersburg) Soviet, as the local revolutionary council was known. With the promise of "land, bread, and peace," the Bolsheviks gained popular support. Emboldened by the government's disarray as well as their own successes, the Bolsheviks overthrew the provisional government on November 17, 1917.

Although Lenin was successful at toppling the old regime, three more years passed before the Bolsheviks (now calling themselves communists) consolidated power. During that time a civil war raged, pitting the communists against the "White" armies—a motley combination of monarchists, Mensheviks, and other groups. To gain the necessary *peredyshka* (breathing space) to contend with these domestic opponents, Lenin's new regime signed an armistice with Germany at Brest-Litovsk in 1918. The terms for Russia were harsh. The Russians transferred gold and other wealth to Berlin, and the transfer of western territory to Germany forced a moving of Russia's capital to Moscow. But Lenin presumed that the protagonists of the "imperialists' war" would ultimately destroy one another, so he considered it expedient to make short-term deals with and concessions to the imperialists in Berlin. True to this Machiavellian logic, Lenin would abrogate the Brest-Litovsk treaty after Germany was defeated several months later.

Far from freeing Russia from battles with foreign armies, however, the Brest-Litovsk treaty prompted tsarist Russia's allies, including the United States, Britain, Japan, and others to enter Russian territory with the declared intention of reestablishing an eastern front against Germany. Not at all enamored with the new regime in Russia, the Western forces gave succor to the White armies—a fact that in later years was not neglected in Moscow-approved accounts of Soviet history. After Germany's defeat, the Allied forces were largely withdrawn, and the communists went on to secure their victory over the Whites. In the process, the communists proceeded to establish Soviet Socialist Republics in neighboring Armenia, Azerbaijan, Belorussia, Georgia, and the Ukraine. Communist Russia initially maintained that these new republics should be considered independent countries, but by the end of 1922 they had all been absorbed in the new Union of Soviet Socialist Republics. The U.S.S.R. was born.

The Soviet Union

Lenin maintained that the Russian Revolution was fought in the interests of all the world's workers, not just the Russian proletariat. The Soviet Union was thus established as a repository of the world's revolutionary flame, to be reignited at such a time as would be warranted by international developments. The revolutionary goal of fundamentally transforming world civilization could be achieved, according to Lenin's logic, only by securing the shorter term, but essential, objective of the Soviet Union's security and viability. Once this goal was accomplished, Moscow could lead the way to the world communist (or socialist) revolution.

Thus the Soviet Union emerged as a country whose leadership was at once conservative (in its desire to stabilize its rule) and revolutionary (in its declared goal of eventually fomenting world revolution). The established governments of the world were therefore not inclined to extend friendly relations with a country that sought their ultimate demise, and the U.S.S.R. spent its first years in diplomatic isolation.

After Lenin's death in 1924, Josef Stalin had contrived a successful path to supreme power using a combination of political manipulation and ideological contortion. During the time of Stalin's rule, the Soviet Union pursued a range of effective, often harsh modernization and militarization policies. The country's production, investment, and development were dictated by "five-year plans," a testament to the communists' hubris in harnessing the economy but nevertheless brutally effective. The progress achieved by the interwar Soviet Union is remarkable by a variety of standards: industrialization, mechanization, and urbanization; the building of infrastructure, the creation of a world-class army, the establishment of a complex bureaucracy; progress in science and technology; and increases in literacy and life expectancy. All this, while consolidating and centralizing power in a totalitarian fashion over a population that could never be considered wholly, or even largely, accepting of the communist regime.

This last feat reflects the core of what would come to be known as Stalinism: the domination of the population, even of most of the government bureaucrats, by a pervasive system of ideological indoctrination, omnipresent surveillance, and political punishment (including exile, imprisonment, and execution). The Second World War's demands on Soviet manpower required the mitigation of the worst of these excesses, and Stalin's death in 1953 paved the way for Khrushchev's "de-Stalinization." Yet the core of the Soviet political system continued to rest on the political neutralization and physical restriction of the hapless population.

The Cold War and Superpowerdom

When the Soviet Union, along with the United States, emerged from the Second World War victorious in 1945, the Soviets had seized or reclaimed most of the territory between Stalingrad and Berlin. The borders of the Soviet Union itself had been pushed to the Baltic Sea and into eastern Poland and Romania, and the Red Army occupied most of Eastern Europe. British and American forces, now with the assistance of liberated France, occupied the continent's western territory. The ideological antipathy and politicomilitary suspicion between the Soviet Union and the West—only submerged, never eliminated during the wartime alliance—returned with a vengeance. Geopolitical disagreements became strategic conflicts, and the war-ravaged continent was divided between the nascent "superpowers" that resided at its eastern and western flanks.

For the next four decades, the Cold War ensued, whose fundamental logic of bipolar competition would largely direct the Soviet Union's development until its demise in 1991. As a superpower, Moscow enjoyed an expanded sphere of influence that reached beyond Europe to southeast Asia, Africa, and even Latin America. Its nuclear arsenal earned Moscow negotiating leverage with Washington, eventually blossoming into a period of "detente" in the late 1960s and 1970s.

Having secured a measure of international prestige and strategic stability with the West, the post-Stalin leadership permitted Soviet domestic policies to thaw somewhat. The Soviet Union progressively adopted the societal and political trappings of other industrialized states. But at the same time social discipline, industrial strength, economic health, and other vital signs began to decline at an alarming rate. More worrisome still, the U.S.S.R.'s client states in Eastern Europe were experiencing an ominous level of popular protests and dissent.

Gorbachev's Reforms

By the beginning of the 1980s, the declining cohesion of Moscow's empire was witnessed by the rise of the solidarity movement in Poland and the civil war in Soviet-backed Afghanistan. At the same time, Soviet society was displaying signs of social, economic, and environmental decline through such indicators as decreasing life expectancy and diminishing agricultural yields. Brezhnev's own ill health and advanced age prevented his making any substantial course corrections, and the Soviet system was still on the path of decline when he succumbed to a heart attack in 1982. Brezhnev's next two successors died shortly after assuming office and effected few meaningful reforms.

Such was the setting when Mikhail Gorbachev took the post of general secretary in 1985. Healthy and only fifty-four years old, Gorbachev was from a younger generation of Soviet leaders. He immediately acknowledged that all was not well with the U.S.S.R., and before long he was calling for radical reforms. During his seven years in power, Gorbachev undertook the most far-reaching reforms in Soviet history. He did not initially conceive them as such; he developed his reform program gradually and improvisationally. For all his commitment to reform, Gorbachev remained a socialist to the end.

Beginning with a policy of *glasnost* ("openness") to renew public faith in the country and encourage greater social discipline, Gorbachev soon recognized that fuller, more structural changes were needed. He began to introduce significant, although limited, market reforms. He moved to partially separate the functions of the party and the state. He established a new legislature, which was filled through secret, multicandidate elections in 1989. Gorbachev's reforms were not an effort to transform the Soviet Union into a true republic, however. Instead, he allowed the people limited (though frequently real) choice in selecting their leaders. Yet even this limited transfer of power to the people was enough to undermine the supreme authority of the party, which was the central support of the Soviet regime. The new legislature soon amended the constitution to

"Big Mac" in Moscow. After the fall of communism in 1991, foreign investment began to come in.

permit opposition parties to form. In a free market of competing ideologies, the party's days were numbered.

Meanwhile, the East European peoples interpreted Gorbachev's domestic reforms as a tacit endorsement of democratization movements in their own countries. Protests and demonstrations became more fervent, and by the fall of 1989 virtually all of the East European countries had overthrown their communist governments. These successful revolutions in turn provided powerful inspiration for the nationalist forces within the U.S.S.R. By allowing the countries of Eastern Europe to break away from the Soviet sphere of influence, Gorbachev lent credibility to the growing belief that Moscow was unwilling to use military force against its own secessionists.

In reality, the Soviet leadership was sharply divided over the question of how to respond to domestic demands for popular sovereignty and national self-determination. Gorbachev encountered increasingly hostile opposition from other party elites who thought his reform agenda foolishly defeatist. These conservatives insisted that the Soviet Union could be preserved only be maintaining one-party rule and a unified state. Then, in August 1991, with Gorbachev on the verge of signing a treaty with the country's fifteen constituent republics that granted them unprecedented political and economic autonomy, a small group of conservative party and military leaders staged a coup attempt. Gorbachev was placed under house arrest, and the coup leaders created an eight-man committee to rule in his place.

For all its drama, the coup collapsed after three days. A variety of factors contributed to its failure. Most important, the coup leaders failed to detain Boris Yeltsin, the popular elected leader of the Russian Soviet Federated Socialist Republic (RSFSR) and vociferous critic of the conservatives. Yeltsin proclaimed his own control of the RFSFR and called for general strikes and public resistance. Yeltsin also called on the military not to obey the "usurpers." Most military units heeded this call, and the coup fizzled.

The Demise of the Soviet Union

The coup attempt was the climax of the Soviet Union's demise, and the denouement was over in just four more months. The reformist image of the party nurtured by Gorbachev was now destroyed by the coup attempt, and even Gorbachev was ultimately forced to renounce his party membership. In practical terms, the coup attempt catapulted to completion the disaggregation of the union. Republics that only days earlier were prepared to voluntarily sign a treaty proclaiming their ultimate allegiance to Moscow in exchange for greater latitude under that tutelage now balked at such a stingy offer. Now was the time to break free of the Soviets' deadly embrace. Before the end of the year, all of the Soviet republics, including even Russia, were reconstituted as sovereign states.

The breakup of the Soviet Union was occasioned by two revolutions. National revolutions, fought on behalf of the republics' titular nationalities, caused the Soviet Union to divide along its internal provincial boundaries. This caused Gorbachev's Moscow, as the seat of the Soviet government, to quickly fade into irrelevancy. At the same time, a democratic revolution destroyed the Soviet state itself.

Yeltsin's Moscow, as the capital of the Russian republic, took on a new importance and relevance. It symbolized Russian national self-determination, as well as anticommunism and popular sovereignty. Underlying these revolutions was a current of consumer dissatisfaction. Bolstered by less sanitized economic and social data made available by glasnost, the long-time dissatisfaction with the quality and variety of consumer goods, the condition and reliability of transportation, the allocation of living space, and other aspects of living standards was channeled into the campaigns for national self-determination and popular sovereignty.

The formal dissolution of the USSR was marked by a resignation speech by Gorbachev on Christmas Day, 1991, and on the next day, a formal legislative action by the Soviet parliament. The Soviet Union had succumbed to both aspects of revolution—territorial secession and political rejection. But the 15 new countries that stood in its place now faced the tasks of recreating territorial and political states, and of satisfying their populations' expectations for improvement of living standards.

The Reemergence of Russia

In some ways the post-Soviet Russian state that emerged from the ruins of the USSR resembled its pre-Soviet ancestor. Russia's pre-revolutionary borders once again generally demarcated the boundaries of Moscow's dominion. Pre-revolutionary place names, such as St. Petersburg and Yekaterinburg, were resurrected. The pre-revolutionary flag replaced the Soviet-era hammer and sickle. The communists were once again an opposition party, and everywhere monuments to Lenin and his comrades were being torn down.

But the Russian Federation is not a restoration of pre-revolutionary Russia. Russia's government, economy, and people have changed dramatically. What exists today as Russia is a new, unique entity. None of the earlier conceptions of Russia contained this particular amalgam of ethnic and national groups (in large measure the result of Stalin's deportation policies). None was democratic in any meaningful sense of the term. And just as important, the international environment in which Russia now finds itself has itself undergone monumental changes. Russia today is as new as it is old.

Democratization and Political Culture

The post-Soviet Russian Federation was born as something less than a functioning democracy. Yeltsin was ruling the country by emergency powers granted by the Russian parliament after the August 1991 coup attempt. The country's bureaucracy and economic institutions were largely under the control of Soviet-era apparatchiks. Serving as the country's constitution was the heavily amended version of the RSFSR's 1978 constitution. And only the most rudimentary forms of political parties and interest groups struggled to aggregate and articulate the people's post-Soviet interests. Although state sovereignty was secured, achieving the goal of popular sovereignty was only beginning, and the objective of improved living conditions, by some measures, was losing ground.

Although the Soviet Union's seven years under Gorbachev largely validated the thesis of the Soviet state's irredeemability (it could not be reformed, only destroyed), it undermined the conception of Russians as a passive people. But given the preconceptions developed during the Soviet period, it is not surprising that most Western governments and universities, as well as Gorbachev himself, did not ever really understand the enormous power of the newly liberated citizenry until after the entire Soviet edifice had collapsed. The Soviet Union was not conquered by the West as a culmination of the Cold War, although its collapse was hastened by pressures from the United States and elsewhere. Instead, it was torn apart mainly by its own people, infused with a sense of self-determination and liberated by a regime that had lost the ability, or the stomach, to continue oppressing them.

Immediately after gaining independence, Russia's post-Soviet leadership took pains to distance itself from the old regime. The banishment of the Communist Party, Yeltsin's public commitment to democracy and capitalism, and the country's close cooperation—even friendship—with its erstwhile adversaries in the West all forced a rapid and thorough reevaluation of Russia's essence. It was as though the crude and heavy blanket of Soviet communism had been pulled back to reveal a relatively sane society and leadership. Perhaps Russia could be a "normal" country after all.

But did this new view simply substitute one oversimplification of Russia for another? Soviet totalitarianism had collapsed, but Russian democracy had not yet fully materialized. In its first decade after independence, Russia disappointed the new optimists. Yeltsin's unconstitutional dissolution of the parliament in 1993 raised questions about the principle of rule of law in Russia. The forced resignations of a pro-Western foreign minister and pro-market economic advisers in 1995 undermined the government's commitment to reform. The Duma's symbolic efforts to restore the old Soviet Union in 1996 suggested imperialist ambitions. The protracted economic crisis in the late 1990s weakened the state and exacerbated crime, corruption, and poverty. More important, the Russian people began to show an attraction to the ghosts of the past: through substantial electoral support for communists and nationalists, through violent hostility toward successful entrepreneurs, and through renewed cynicism about government and politics. It was thought the hard lessons learned throughout seventy-five years of Sovietism (and centuries of tsarism) were forgotten with the passage of a few months and years. Perhaps the Russian people really were "beyond democracy."

The case of Russia raises interesting questions not just about the Russians but also about democracy itself. Is it simply a matter of setting into place the proper institutions, laws, and leaders? Or does it require a particular mindset on the part of the people? Can it be imposed from without, or does it need to arise from within? The record in other countries is mixed, and so it is in Russia. Certainly, the Bolsheviks were able to suddenly, even brutally, impose on the Russians a new political system. But was the Soviet experiment essentially a foreign (or "universal") system, discovered by Marx and imported by Lenin? Or was it simply another variant of the unique, crypto-authoritarian Russian culture?

Certainly, Russians in the 1990s used their political freedom to elect illiberal persons and parties; however, there is a contradiction in the pessimists' claim that Russia's parliamentary elections in 1993 and 1995 strengthened the antidemocratic hue of the Russian government. Russian democracy is not measured by the proportion of self-professed "democrats" in the legislature. More to the point is how the legislators are selected and whether they have adequate power to carry out their mandate. So the fact that Russians freely chose "communists" or "nationalists" or even "monarchists" is less important in measuring Russia's possession of democracy than the fact that they made their choice freely. Democracy affords voters the ability to make unwise choices—an opportunity occasionally seized with gusto even by Americans. Moreover, results from the December 1999 parliamentary elections suggested waning support for extremist parties.

Yet identifying the presence of electoral democracy in Russia is not to say that Russia has attained "Western" liberal democracy. Democracy encompasses more than procedures. It is based on something more organic, more elemental. And that ingredient springs from the society and political culture rather than from the government.

Russia's democratic institutions are still being established, but even if clear and consistent electoral laws were in place; even if the convoluted electoral system could produce a parliament precisely reflecting the people's will; even if that parliament had clearly defined, adequate powers to act on the people's expressed preferences—even if, in other words, a perfect constitution could be imposed on Russia—Russian democracy would still require one vital element: a supportive political culture.

A country's political culture is the set of basic values, beliefs, attitudes, and assumptions the people hold about their political system and political life in general. It derives from any number of sources, just as nonpolitical culture does. History and geography play major roles in the shaping of political culture and thus militate against any sudden change in its composition. But political culture does evolve with economic, political, societal, and other forms of development.

This view puts the thesis about Russia's congenital absolutism in perspective. If the concept of political culture has significance, then Russians may find it difficult, perhaps even impossible, to make an expeditious transition to democracy. As a society, Russians have learned to be skeptical about their ability to genuinely influence government policy. This skepticism should come as no surprise. Russia's experience with Soviet rule taught them not to place blind faith in the bare institutions of democratic governance. Constitutions, legislatures, elections, the bureaucracy, the media, the schools, the courts—all were subordinate to the party, and thus could not be relied on to protect, let alone serve, the interests of the people. Soviet ideology claimed that the Communist Party of the Soviet Union was inherently endued with the people's interests, although the party putatively had an omniscient, "enlightened" understanding of those interests as befits a vanguard party.

Of course, a healthy skepticism about political elites might serve the citizens of a democracy well. But the experience with Soviet rule and an understanding of tsarist history might place Russian attitudes beyond skepticism into the realm of cynicism and potentially even nihilism. For Russia to successfully effect a transition to liberal democracy, its political culture will have to evolve to include a greater sense of efficacy and a willingness to participate. Only then will Russia truly be able to join the West and become part of the post–Cold War incarnation of Europe.

SOCIAL AND ETHNIC GROUPS, CLASS STRUCTURE, INTEREST GROUPS, AND POLITICAL PARTIES

Russia's population is spread across a vast and varied land and includes numerous ethnic and national minority groups. In addition, notwithstanding the Soviets' claims to have abolished classes, modern Russian society is divided by the vestiges of insidious class stratification, partly modified by the new opportunities and pitfalls created by the new economic system. Some of these social cleavages may change, and others may be politically accommodated as Russia attempts to stabilize its political, economic, and social systems.

Ethnic and National Groups

The centripetal forces that helped dissolve the Soviet Bloc and the Soviet Union itself continue to play out in the former Soviet republics. No issue cuts more directly to the essence of Russia as a state and as a nation. As a state, the Russian Federation requires political cohesion. As a people, Russians require a national identity. Both exigencies are complicated by the presence of ethnonational minorities with a desire for self-determination. How the government approaches these issues is determining the face of Russia at the opening of the new millennium.

Russia's ethnic and racial groups are the legacy of tsarist and Soviet annexations and internal policies. The tsars assembled their empire with sporadic annexations of contiguous lands—a process that was constitutionally distinct from the other European powers' acquisition of overseas colonies. Unlike other multinational European empires, namely the Austro-Hungarian, the Russian empire maintained authoritarian control over its disparate peoples: Lithuanians, Crimean Tatars, Ural Cossacks, and numerous others. Yet despite St. Petersburg's periodic attempts at Russification, the Russian state even in the nineteenth century was limited in its power to co-opt the national identity of its non-Russian subjects.

The Bolsheviks approached the Russian empire's multinational character with a new ideological perspective when they wrested control from the monarchy in 1917. Marxist doctrine saw national groups as a manifestation of bourgeois manipulation. But once the new regime's power had stabilized, the party maintained an ambiguous, even schizophrenic policy toward its disparate nationalities, summed up in the phrase "national in form, socialist in content."

In order to discourage nationalist tensions and conflicts within the U.S.S.R., the Soviet regime accorded formal autonomy to various recognized national and ethnic groups. In the longer term, the regime sought to create a "new Soviet man"—a non-national (or perhaps transnational) "Soviet" identity. The U.S.S.R.'s citizens were to become the vanguard of a new type of society, unburdened by the disunity of national, class, and religious cleavages. In many respects, however, the regime's understanding of "Soviet" bore a canny resemblance to Russianism.

Neither the attempts to placate national groups through limited self-government nor the attempts to assimilate them into a greater Soviet identity were ultimately successful. These strategies, coupled with varying doses of oppression and propaganda, did manage generally to contain the "nationalities problem" for most of the twentieth century. But as we have seen, lingering ethnonationalist pressures eventually boiled over in the Gorbachev era and contributed to the demise of the U.S.S.R. The nationalists effectively cut along the dotted lines that were the Soviet Union's internal provincial borders.

All the more troubling, therefore, that the map of the post-Soviet Russian Federation is crisscrossed with a spiderweb of dotted lines (see Figure 5.1). Of course, the presence of administrative divisions is not necessarily fatal; many of the eighty-nine territorial divisions contain overwhelmingly Russian populations and serve as mere administrative districts. Still, twenty-one of these regions (putatively autonomous "republics") contain substantial non-Russian populations, and a few, such as Chechnya, claim independence from Moscow. With almost one in five Russian citizens claiming non-Russian ethnic background, post-Soviet Russia must contend with the complicated

Social and Ethnic Groups, Class Structure, Interest Groups, and Political Parties 189

FIGURE 5.1 Map of Administrative Divisions of the Russian Federation

ethnonational legacy of the tsars and the Soviets. Ethnic Germans, Ukrainians, Tatars, and Chuvashes, for example, predominate in certain enclaves as a result of historic settlement patterns and Stalin's deportation policies. Similarly, although 71 percent of Russia's population identifies itself as Russian Orthodox, many regions are populated by persons of other faiths. Islam, for example, is the predominant religion in the Caucasus, and Muslims collectively constitute about 6 percent of the country's population.

The relationship between the federal and republican governments (center-periphery relations, in political scientists' parlance) was reconstituted through the Federation Treaty between Moscow and the regions, signed in March 1992, and again with the Yeltsin Constitution of December 1993. Although the referendum enacting the constitution failed in seventeen of the eighty-nine regions, all eighty-nine regions are considered bound by its provisions. The constitution makes no provision for secession—a right that had been afforded by the Federation Treaty. Still, the division of power between Moscow and the regions remained fluid at the time of the constitution's adoption.

Even after the adoption of the Yeltsin Constitution in December 1993, continued efforts were undertaken to finesse the nationalities issue. For example, Moscow signed bilateral "power-sharing" treaties with many republics and regions that provide for their unique circumstances and histories; however, two outright wars between the federal government and the rebellious republic of Chechnya in the mid-1990s and at the turn of the millennium proved an enormous setback to Moscow's efforts to gain the trust and cooperation of the regions. The wars against Chechnya eerily resembled (in motivation, but not intensity) Soviet Moscow's military attacks on the secessionist Soviet republic of Lithuania in 1991. The first Chechen war proved enormously unpopular with ethnic Russians and non-Russian minorities alike, and it showcased the military's ineptness and inability to effectively constrain poorly armed guerrillas within Russia's borders. The second war, however, coming at a time of greater disillusionment and frustration among Russians, enjoyed greater public support (at least initially) and helped enrich the political fortunes of Vladimir Putin, who managed it as prime minister. The spread of Chechen-inspired terrorism, including a bomb attack in Moscow in the summer of 2000, threatened to erode that public support.

Today, a decade after the collapse of the Soviet Union, the Russian Federation has failed to arrest the nationalistic forces that were partly responsible for Russia's independence in the first place. Russia's quasi-federal nature has placated some groups, but for others it has merely provided a basis for confrontational autonomy claims and independence drives.

Although the level of center-periphery conflict in Chechnya is unique within Russia, ethnonational disputes plague other regions of the country as well. For example, conflict among the national groups within the Caucasus republic of North Ossetia has prompted military intervention by Moscow. Further, resentment by the dozen "donor regions" (i.e., those, such as Tatarstan, Sverdlovsk, and St. Petersburg that contribute more to the federal budget than they receive in return) may encourage new independence drives, especially if the economy worsens and the federal government continues to be perceived as inept and corrupt.

The fundamental problem is that Russia is a multinational state without a tradition of civil societal relations. Under tsars and Soviets alike, it was held together only by totalitarian power. The same forces that in the long term might be expected to create a civil society—increased communication, efficient transportation, and integrated trade—in the short run are creating conflict. No simple answer to this puzzle is forthcoming. The political and demographic sins of the country's tsarist and Soviet past haunt modern Russia. Preserving the country's territorial integrity while dismantling the Communist Party's centralized structures makes for a difficult prescription because the tasks that compose it work at cross purposes, at least in the short term.

The last part of Russia's ethnonational puzzle concerns Russian national identity. Twenty-five million ethnic Russians live beyond the country's borders. The alleged mistreatment of Russian minorities abroad has provided a potent issue for Russian nationalists who decry Gorbachev's poor stewardship of the Soviet Union and Yeltsin's purported "selling out" to the West. By a similar logic, Russian nationalists argue that Russian minorities in "ethnic" republics on Russian territory require special protection. Those conservative nationalists who had opposed the breakup of the Soviet Union can hardly be expected now to take lightly any territorial concessions by Moscow to Russia's ethnic regions. Caught between ethnonational minorities demanding protections (often in the form of greater autonomy) and Russian nationalists insisting on greater state cohesion, the government's options are not enviable.

Perhaps the most effective vaccines against Russia's ethnonational unrest are economic prosperity and political stability, both of which are in precious short supply. Ultranationalism feeds on discontent and wounded pride. Liberal pluralism can take root only where a reasonable expectation exists that one's individual needs can be satisfied under the aegis of

Boris Yeltsin shakes hands with his successor, Vladimir Putin.

existing governmental and societal institutions. When this confidence is finally achieved, ultranationalism's appeal will be largely neutralized.

In the final analysis, center-periphery relations may prove to be the most critical issue for the Russian Federation's long-term development. The politics of center-periphery relations is not so much a geographical matter (as the term implies), as it is a matter of governmental hierarchy and relative autonomy. While the parliament and president in Moscow debate such matters as the pace of economic reform, appropriate responses to crime, and the country's relations with the West, power quietly slips from Moscow to the regions.

A certain irony infuses Russia's ethnonational situation, as it does so many facets of life in the former Soviet Union. Russian nationalism played an important role in the breakup of the Soviet Union, and Yeltsin tapped into it as a key component of his power base. Yet Russian nationalism has been a fickle ally, eventually being co-opted by Vladimir Zhirinovsky and far-right opponents of Yeltsin's reformist policies. It remains an open question whether democratic pluralism can take root in such an environment, and how President Putin will respond to nationalist sentiment.

Development of Parties and Interest Groups

The efforts to develop political democracy in Russia build on a past of frustration and disappointment. The country's absolutist tendencies are evident throughout its history. Until the last few years before the 1917 Revolution, the tsarist monarchy forewent even the symbolic pretenses of democracy. In contrast, the Soviet Union undertook great efforts to hide its authoritarian nature, relying heavily on periodic elections to justify the regime's authority. That the elections offered no real choice and that one party—the Communist Party of the

Soviet Union (CPSU)—possessed a monopoly of power provided only two of many reasons that invalidated Moscow's claim that the country was therefore democratic. So long as one-party rule remained the sine qua non of Soviet rule, honest evaluators could dismiss the mechanical trappings of democracy, such as elections, as so much window dressing. Then came Gorbachev's reforms and the subsequent collapse of the Soviet Union.

Real electoral choice is the heart of genuine democracy, and well-defined, responsible parties are especially well suited for facilitating that choice. The success of Russia's transition from authoritarianism to liberal democracy, if it occurs, will depend in no small measure on the creation of viable, distinct parties and the conducting of periodic, fair elections.

The Soviet political system was often described as a "one-party" system. Yet the CPSU was never a political party in the Western sense of the term. The 1977 Constitution called the CPSU "the nucleus of [the Soviet] system," and post-Soviet Russian critics have labeled it a quasi-state organization. Its contrast with the democratic ideal of a political party is stark. The CPSU did not so much aggregate group interests as it sought to indoctrinate Soviet subjects. Rather than putting up candidates to acquire governmental power, the party was practically indistinguishable from the government. It did not offer alternatives to governmental programs; it dictated those programs. The party sought above all to mobilize, co-opt, and control the 10 percent of the population that joined its ranks often in search of the concomitant privileges that a party state afforded.

After three-quarters of a century under such a system, Russians can be forgiven some hesitation in warming to the practice of multiparty democracy. Thus the sardonic reply to Gorbachev's unprecedented introduction of multiparty elections in 1989: "Isn't one party bad enough?" Like the founders of the United States two centuries earlier, the leaders of post-Soviet Russia initially eschewed political parties as distasteful, divisive, and even antidemocratic entities. Throughout his tenure as Russia's president, Boris Yeltsin would not formally associate himself with any political group. He conceived of the presidency as properly above the squalid business of party politics—a sentiment earlier held by such notable figures as George Washington and France's Charles de Gaulle. Although the virtue of the Russian presidency has nevertheless suffered without the connivance of party affiliation, the development of parties in Russia has clearly been a chaotic affair that has enmeshed many of its perpetrators.

Once the CPSU's monopoly was broken in 1990, thousands of new groups sprang up to fill the void. Yet few if any of these groups could immediately be considered parties. They were too small and amorphous, and they lacked any clear role in the political system. They were given to factionalism, and many were geographically isolated. In Gorbachev's final year, the Soviet Union was transformed from a one-party system not to a multiparty state, but to a no-party state.

Even after the collapse of the Soviet Union and the establishment of the Russian Federation as a sovereign country, Russia's political landscape was fractious and anomic. For the first several years of Russia's independence, nascent party organizations were short-lived—dividing, combining, dissolving altogether, and reemerging with new ideological foundations. Their development and behavior more closely resembled narrowly defined interest groups than political parties.

Not only were Russia's political groupings being narrowly segmented along functional or interest lines, but they also tended to be defined along regional lines. The vast geographic and cultural differences among Russia's disparate peoples provide fertile ground for regional parties, which in turn may threaten the viability of the Russian Federation as a cohesive political entity.

The post-Soviet government scrambled to adopt regulations, registration procedures, and electoral laws to structure the emerging multi-party system. (Even then, a law on presidential elections was not adopted until 2000.) A fluctuating number of factions and blocs developed within the Congress of People's Deputies. One year after the collapse of the Soviet Union, about two dozen parties were formally registered in the Russian Federation. A much larger number of political organizations—by some counts more than one thousand—did not formally register, but in one way or another had surfaced as countrywide political groups. By the end of 1992, Russia had more political organizations than seats in its legislature.

The first post-Soviet Russian elections, in December 1993, forced some discipline on the chaotic and amorphous congeries of party groups. By the time of the September 1993 deadline, 140 national groups had registered. Only thirty-five of these groups managed to submit the requisite number of signatures to participate in the elections. Consolidation and invalidation reduced voters' choices still further, with thirteen "electoral associations" ultimately appearing on the ballot. Of these, only eight managed to obtain the 5 percent of the vote required to gain Duma seats allocated through proportional representation (PR). These were Russia's Choice, the Liberal Democratic Party, the Communist Party of the Russian Federation, the Agrarian party, Yabloko, Women of Russia, Russian Unity and Accord, and the Democratic Party of Russia (see Table 5.1).

Russia's party system was finally beginning to coalesce. As the first Russia-wide elections to be held since the demise of the Soviet Union, the 1993 parliamentary elections infused the victorious parties with a certain legitimacy and credibility that were previously unknown in Russia. The performance of these parties in the newly constituted parliament helped establish a legislative record by which they could be distinguished. The procedural requirements imposed by the new constitution nudged the parties to take up the arcane democratic arts of compromise and coalition building.

Not that everyone was pleased with the election results. Almost one quarter of the popular vote went to Vladimir Zhirinovsky's ultranationalist Liberal Democratic Party. Another 12 percent went to the communists. But what is most important about Russia's founding election was not so much the distribution of political power that resulted, but the establishment of the principle of popular sovereignty. The general population, the state bureaucrats, and the various parliamentary contestants all accepted the electoral outcome.

The next parliamentary elections, which incorporated new registration procedures, occurred two years later. About eight thousand candidates and forty-three parties were registered. But despite the political and geographical fragmentation evident in post-Soviet Russia's first years, electoral politics now seemed to be solidifying around a handful of viable parties. Indeed, more than half the deputies elected in 1995 had served in the first Duma, and all but four of the forty-three parties vying for "party list" seats failed to secure the five percent of the vote required to be awarded seats (Table 5.1).

This time the Communist Party of the Russian Federation (CPRF) received the largest number of votes cast. In the words of the British magazine *The Economist,* "Nobody could sensibly accuse Russians, of all people, of voting for communists in ignorance of the possible consequences." Or could they? The meaning of labels such as communism, reformism, and conservatism had been contorted and twisted during the campaign, throughout the perestroika era, and indeed throughout the Soviet era. Yet the high proportion of votes going to the communists suggested, at the very least, that a substantial segment of the Russian population desired to balance the presidential "party of power" with opposition forces.

Russia closed out the turbulent and often tragic twentieth century with its third election

TABLE 5.1 1995 Duma Election Results, by Party

Party	PR Seats	District Seats	Total Seats
Communist Party of the Russian Federation (CPRF)	99	58	157
Our Home Is Russia	50	5	55
Liberal Democratic Party of Russia	50	1	51
Yabloko	31	14	45
Agrarian Party of Russia	0	20	20
Power to the People	0	9	9
Russia's Democratic Choice	0	9	9
Congress of Russian Communities	0	5	5
Forward, Russia	0	3	3
Ivan Rybkin Bloc	0	3	3
Women of Russia	0	3	3
Gurov–Vladimir Lysenko–Pamfilova	0	2	2
Communists–Working Russia–For the Soviet Union	0	1	1
Govorukhin Bloc	0	1	1
Trade Unions and Industrialists of Russia–Labor Union	0	1	1
Other Unions and Blocs	0	8	8
Independent (no party affiliation)	0	78	78

Source: Open Media Resource Institute.

to the Duma. On December 19, 1999, Russians finally appeared to give the government a working majority in the Duma. Although the CPRF still received the largest number of seats, its percentage of Duma seats had dropped by one-third (see Table 5.2). The number of parties appearing on the ballot had dropped from forty-three (in 1995) to twenty-six, and four-fifths of the party votes cast went to the six parties that cleared the 5 percent threshold (compared with only one-half in 1995). Clearly, the consolidation of Russia's political landscape was continuing, although this landscape had by no means stabilized.

The Russian Duma was now dominated by fewer than a half-dozen parties, but what could be said about the ideologies they represented? Evaluating the general political philosophies of Russia's political parties presents frustrating conceptual difficulties. Post-Soviet Russia lacks a meaningful left-right political spectrum. The West's Cold War–era practice of defining "communism" as the left endpoint of an ideological spectrum offers little assistance in post-Soviet Russia. If "conservative" and "orthodox" are characteristics of the right side of the ideological spectrum, where should one place the revolutionary communists of contemporary Russia who long for a return to the old (Soviet) order? Should "reformists" be placed leftward on the familiar Western continuum (with progressives) or rightward (with laissez-faire capitalists)? Other issues on which Russia's emergent parties can be distinguished do not lend themselves to the traditional left-right spectrum. Nationalism and imperialism are two critical issues coloring Russian politics at the dawn of the third millennium, but they are not easily placed on the familiar left-right continuum. The task becomes even more difficult with the unusual combinations of values that are amalgamated within some party platforms.

This is not simply a methodological problem. It illustrates the amorphous nature of contemporary Russian politics. In the first months of the 1996–1999 Duma, coalitions were built between "reformers" and communists against

TABLE 5.2   1999 Duma Elections

Political Parties	PR Seats	District Seats	Total
Communist Party of the Russian Federation (CPRF)	67	47	114
Unity	64	9	73
Fatherland-All Russia (OVR)	37	29	66
Union of Right Forces (SPS)	24	5	29
Zhirinovsky's Bloc	17		17
Yabloko	16	5	21
Our Home Is Russia		8	8
Movement in Support of the Army		2	2
Russian All People Unity		2	2
Spiritual Legacy		1	1
General Andrei Nikolaev, academician Svyatoslav Fedorov Bloc		1	1
Congress of the Russian Societies and Yurii Boldyrev Movement		1	1
Party of Pensioners		1	1
Russian Socialist Party		1	1
Independent Candidates		113	113
Total	225	225	450

nationalists. Similar coalitions among ideologically strange bedfellows were created to run in the 1999 Duma elections. Such alliances resulted more from political expediency than from any harmony of fundamental values. The subordination of ideology to short-term tactical gains becomes especially clear when one recalls that the communists and nationalists were frequently allied against the democrats in the 1993–1995 Duma. In other words, the coalition building in modern Russian politics resembles the forging of alliances in nineteenth-century Europe's balance of power system. In both systems, ideology matters less than political survival.

A significant portion of Russia's political landscape consists of congeries of parties in the amorphous category known as the "swamp." The swamp is largely defined by what it is not: it is not "extremist" in the way that the parties identified by hues (communist Reds, ultranationalist Browns, environmentalist Greens) seem to be. Within the swamp, and to some extent even at the extremes, Russian politics is characterized not so much as a competition of ideologies as a clash of personalities.

Nonetheless, three loosely defined groups (not parties) have emerged from the morass of post-Soviet Russian politics to have particular influence in defining the political debate. These three groups are the new communists, the reformists, and the conservative nationalists. It bears emphasizing that these categories are fluid and amorphous and not mutually exclusive.

The New Communists   Although Yeltsin initially banned or severely restricted the Communist Party and affiliated parties in the Russian Federation, many of these restrictions soon were scaled back by the Russian Constitutional Court. In addition, social and economic dislocations caused by Yeltsin's liberalization policies spawned popular frustration that helped create a backlash against the reformists. More than one dozen new Russian communist groups quickly sprang up to capitalize on these conditions. The Communist Party of the Russian Federation (CPRF), established in February 1993, most effectively claimed the legacy of the old CPSU. Gennady Zyuganov, a former mathematics teacher who had served in the CPSU's propaganda department, was elected as the CPRF's chairman.

With about one-half million members, the CPRF is by far the largest party in the Russian Federation. It also has the largest share of seats in the Duma (114 of 450 in March 2000 runoff elections), and Zyuganov came in a close second to Yeltsin in the 1996 presidential election. The CPRF is among the best organized of the parties, drawing on an organizational structure that never entirely dissolved with the demise of the CPSU. The party is especially strong in the industrial cities, among older Russians, and among Russia's "new poor." Veterans and apparatchiki from the Soviet period also are well represented.

The CPRF is no radical, neo-Bolshevik organization. Rather, it is neoconservative in the sense that it decries the changes recently undergone by the once-great Russian/Soviet state; however, the CPRF's communist lineage is anathema to most younger Russians, and the party's aging base will inevitably shrink with the passage of years.

For much of the 1990s, several other communist-aligned groups existed, although they fragmented in the lead-up to the 1999 parliamentary elections. One of these parties was the Russian Communist Workers' Party (RCWP). Led by Viktor Tyulkin, the RCWP dismissed the CPRF as an insincere pretender to the esteemed mantle of communism. By the 1999 parliamentary elections, however, this bloc fragmented into several obscure parties, including "Communists, Workers of Russia for the Soviet Union" and "Stalin's Bloc for the U.S.S.R." These niche groups collectively garnered only a few percentage points of the vote. These other radical factions of communists regularly engage in protests against the government and celebrations of the revolution, but they have had little impact on large policy questions.

Closely related to the communists is the Agrarian Party, founded in early 1993 by Mikhail Lapshin. The party embraced in particular the first element of the old Bolshevik slogan of "land, bread, and peace." The idea of land reform traditionally resonated with the Russian population, which remains overwhelmingly rural. Compared to the RCWP, the Agrarian Party was somewhat moderate and regularly engaged in tactical coalitions with other, even reformist parties. Indeed, Lapshin defected to a new group, Fatherland-All Russia, formed by former Prime Minister Yevgeny Primakov in 1999. The demise of the agrarians was another blow to the communists.

Reformist Parties The hardest category to define is that of the reformists. Most post-Soviet Russian politicians claim to support *some* conception of reform—to do otherwise is to accept the status quo, which is enormously unpopular. But the reformist category is generally understood to comprise those parties committed to market economics and democratic pluralism. Two of the four parties that surmounted the 5 percent threshold in the 1995 Duma elections could be considered reformist by this definition.

Although the reformists share a general political and economic philosophy, political unity has largely eluded them. Indeed, about ten of the forty-three parties on the 1995 ballot could be considered reformist, and by dividing the reformist vote among themselves, only two parties cleared the 5 percent threshold for PR representation. Several smaller reformist parties are represented in the Duma (with representatives elected to single-member districts), but seldom do all vote together on legislation or appointment confirmations. The divisions within the reformist ranks may reveal a primary flaw of their political approach: Their commitment to liberty and pluralism may be manifesting itself as an unwillingness to compromise individual beliefs. In addition, the general cause of reform is so vague as to allow quite varied interpretations and prescriptions.

Russia's closest equivalent to a "government" party is the Unity bloc. The bloc was formed in 1999, replacing the previous "government" party, Our Home Is Russia (known by its Russian acronym, NDR). While NDR secured fifty-five seats in the 1995 Duma elections, Unity garnered seventy-three in 2000. (NDR, still tied to former Prime Minister Viktor Chernomyrdin, earned only eight seats in 2000.)

As a pragmatic grouping of groups and individuals supporting the Russian government and the status quo, Unity does not have a well-defined ideology, but it is expected to generally promote a continuation of Yeltsin's broad strategies for privatization and democratization.

Other reformist parties tend to challenge the government party as too wedded to the status quo. One of these, Yabloko, has enjoyed a measure of popular support and a presence in the Duma, but has repeatedly rebuffed overtures to join the government's blocs (first NDR, and then Unity). Yabloko is one of the six parties to win seats through PR in 1999, and was one of the four parties with PR seats in 1995. Its presence has diminished from forty-five to twenty-one seats between those two elections, partly because of the defection of one of its founding members.

Another reformist party with PR seats in 1999 is the Union of Rights Forces, known by its Russian acronym SPS. Led by former Prime Minister Sergei Kirienko, SPS has twenty-nine seats in the Duma. It is perhaps more committed to economic privatization than Yabloko, and it strongly endorses greater personal freedoms. Its ideology is evident in a series of referendum questions that it proposed to place before the voters:

1. Are you for broadening the legal and political guarantees of protection of Russian citizens' private property (including apartments, homes, plots of land, accounts in banks and other credit organizations) from infringements by others, including the state?
2. Do you agree that State Duma deputies and members of the Federation Council of the Federal Assembly of the Russian Federation who have committed criminal acts should bear criminal responsibility, just as other Russian citizens do?
3. Do you favor having only contract soldiers take part in military actions in local conflicts?
4. Are you for amendments to the Russian Constitution that would limit the right of the president of Russia to dismiss the government of Russia?

Conservative/Nationalist Parties The conservatives and nationalists generally promote a stronger state and a restoration of Russian greatness. For this they are occasionally associated with the communists, but conservatives and nationalists usually do not share the communists' ideological beliefs. Neither are the conservative/nationalist parties necessarily averse to some of the reformists' economic objectives, although conservatives and nationalists usually reject the liberal pluralism often associated with reform. Mostly conservative/nationalist parties are committed to the nation of Russia over the individuals that constitute it.

Best known within the conservative/nationalist group is the Liberal Democratic party (LDP). The appealing name was established when Vladimir Bogachev and Lev Ubozhko founded the rather innocuous Liberal Democratic Party of Russia in the summer of 1989. The party, committed to market capitalism and the rule of law, became the first party to be registered in the Soviet Union. But the party soon came under the extremist sway of Vladimir Zhirinovsky, who reestablished the party as the Liberal Democratic Party of the U.S.S.R. in March 1990. Zhirinovsky ran for the presidency against Yeltsin (and others) in 1991 and came in third with more than six million votes. He was associated with the other conservative/nationalist organizations Nashi ("Ours") and Pamyat ("Memory") before rising to prominence within the LDP. As a leader of the LDP, Zhirinovsky supported the August 1991 coup against Gorbachev. The LDP was reregistered as a Russian political party in 1992. The following year Zhirinovsky led the party to a surprising victory in parliamentary elections, garnering the largest number of proportional representation seats in the Duma (59, with almost one-quarter of the popular vote). In 1995, the LDP received somewhat less support, with 11 percent of the PR vote, but this was the second best showing of all the parties running. In 1999, the Central Electoral Commission banned the LDP from the ballot because of violations of registration laws; however, Zhirinovsky managed to head a hastily created substitute called "Zhirinovsky's Bloc," which secured seventeen seats.

Under Zhirinovsky, the LDP established itself as a well-known and potentially powerful force in Russian politics. Zhirinovsky's political rhetoric is an odd amalgam of ethnic chauvinism, sexism, and anti-Westernism. Aside from a general advocacy of Russian imperialism and a desire to generate controversy, Zhirinovsky's stand on particular issues is difficult to predict. The LDP has frequently been a vociferous critic of Yeltsin's foreign policies. Yet the party has also sided with the president and reformist parties on several issues, particularly when it promised a quid pro quo or could be portrayed as a "pro-Russian" stance. For example, the LDP was virtually the sole major supporter of Yeltsin's war in Chechnya.

In many ways, the LDP remains a protest party. With the controversial, iconoclastic Zhirinovsky as its leader, the party receives considerable press coverage and is well-known in Russia and abroad. Although the party has enjoyed substantial popular support in Duma elections, Zhirinovsky fared poorly in the 1996 and 1999 presidential elections, with less than 6 percent and less than 3 percent of the vote, respectively. Evidently, many Russians who cast protest votes in the parliament are unwilling to extend this practice to the politically more powerful presidency.

Other parties have competed for the nationalist vote, although few have matched the LDP's level of electoral success. The Congress of Russian Communities (KRO) was a nationalistic party of minor significance until it was co-opted by Yuri Skokov and the popular former General Aleksandr Lebed in anticipation of the 1995 Duma elections. The party failed to meet the 5 percent threshold for PR seats, however, and Lebed and Skokov split over ideological and political disagreements. Lebed went to run for president in 1996, placing third. Since his departure, the KRO was co-opted by Yuri Boldyrev, who left the Yabloko party he had co-founded. The KRO failed to meet the 5 percent PR threshold and secured only one district seat in the 1999 Duma elections. Lebed, however, went on to be elected governor of Siberia's Krasnoyarsk region in June 1998, and was seen as a potential candidate for the 2000 presidential election.

Another party vying for the nationalist vote in 1999 was Fatherland—All Russia. It garnered the third-largest number of votes (sixty-six). Headed by former Prime Minister Yevgeny Primakov, the party is not overtly chauvinistic; however, its campaign stressed dissatisfaction with the current government, emphasizing "broken promises," "betrayal," and mismanagement that has put the country "on the brink of catastrophe." It promised to restore Russia's strength and place in the world. These themes appeared to find some resonance with Russia's acting president, Vladimir Putin, who was elevated less than two weeks after the parliamentary elections.

Russia has several fringe conservative/nationalist parties, including neo-Nazi and anti-Semitic movements. These parties have generally been prevented from appearing on the ballot, however, and in any event have only a tiny popular following.

Many parties and other political groups in contemporary Russian politics are not easily placed in the three aforementioned categories. Most of these are relatively small and without much influence. In addition, Russia's parties are not the only groups carrying out political

Vladimir Putin, succeeding to the presidency of Russia, came out of a background in Russia's KGB (the secret intelligence service) and promised to bring strong, authoritative rule back to Russia.

functions. Political activity in Russia is channeled through clans, ethnic associations, and myriad other groupings. More than party structures, interpersonal relationships matter in post-Soviet Russian politics. More generally, Russia's party system is still relatively undeveloped, Russia's voters are relatively disengaged, Russia's parliament lacks discipline and power, and the Russian state itself remains somewhat weak. It remained to be seen whether this would change in the post-Yeltsin era that began January 1, 2000.

POLITICAL INSTITUTIONS, LAW AND LEGAL SYSTEM, ROLE OF THE STATE, AND BUREAUCRACY

An all-new Russian constitution, adopted in December 1993, formally establishes and confers authority to Russia's political institutions, bureaucracy, and legal system; however, implementing the ideal expressed by the constitution is hindered by the presence of structures, ideas, and individuals remaining from the Soviet period. No constitution's expressed ideals can ever be perfectly translated into reality, of course; but the gulf between theory and reality is so great for Russia's political system that analysts at the dawn of the twenty-first century harbored serious doubts about the country's prospects for ever joining the rest of Europe as a Western-style democracy.

The new constitution came about under less than auspicious circumstances. During its first two years as an independent state, Russia retained a heavily amended version of its Soviet-era constitution. Some of these amendments sought to eradicate Marxist-Leninist principles, but others resulted from the parliament's desire to reduce Yeltsin's power. For his

Red Square, Moscow, Russia.

part, Yeltsin conducted several efforts to create a new constitution from scratch. A constitutional crisis mounted until the fall of 1993, when Yeltsin issued a decree suspending parliament, establishing a new legislative body, and calling for new elections in December. The parliamentary leadership responded by declaring that Yeltsin had forfeited the presidency and by swearing in the vice president, Aleksandr Rutskoi, as Yeltsin's replacement. With Yeltsin and Rutskoi both claiming to be the real president, Yeltsin ultimately called in Russian troops to storm the parliament building. After a brief battle, the remaining parliament members surrendered. Now, with his major governmental rivals suspended, in prison, or dead (more than one hundred people died in the October "events," as they came to be known), Yeltsin made a final push to establish a new constitutional order. A new draft constitution, tailor-made to suit Yeltsin's vision for his country and his rule, was put before the voters at the same time as the already scheduled parliamentary elections in December 1993. The constitution was approved with 58 percent of the votes cast.

Unlike the U.S. Constitution, the constitution of the Russian Federation is detailed and specific, comprising 137 separate articles. A mix of old (Soviet) principles and specifically anti-Soviet ones, the Yeltsin constitution specifies a separation of state power into three branches, ensures "ideological pluralism" by proscribing any state-sponsored ideology, and maintains a separation of church and state. Forty-eight articles grouped as "Human and Civil Rights and Freedoms" provide a liberal and expansive, even majestic, expression of human rights. The listing of affronts to human rights that are proscribed by this chapter serves as a catalog of the various abuses practiced by the Soviet state: diminution of human dignity, prolonged detention without judicial action, invasion of privacy, forced renunciation of opinions, censorship, and many others.

More prosaically, the constitution describes the specific powers and responsibilities of the major offices and institutions of the Russian Federation, as follows.

The Presidency

The Yeltsin constitution designates the president as the head of state. Like the president of France, however, the Russian president possesses powers far beyond the ceremonial role that "head of state" implies. In this sense, Russia has an executive presidency. The Russian president appoints the prime minister (with the parliament's consent), appoints governmental ministers (after vetting by the prime minister), and nominates justices (for approval by the parliament). He also may call referenda and grant pardons.

The constitution also grants to the president the power to issue decrees and directives, which are legally binding throughout the country so long as they do not contradict the constitution or federal laws. Although this power is potentially enormous, it is limited by the willingness of the federal and local bureaucracies to implement the decrees. Yeltsin felt some frustration in this regard, and in June 1996 he resorted to the peculiar device of decreeing that all decrees must be faithfully executed. This effort failed to appreciably bolster the effectiveness of the decrees, however.

Although his power over the bureaucracy is severely limited, the president wields considerable power over the federal parliament and cabinet. If his choice for prime minister is rejected three times by the lower house (Duma), then he has the power to dissolve the Duma and call new elections. If the Duma passes a vote of no confidence in the government, then the president may either dissolve the Duma or dismiss the government; however, the Duma may not be dissolved when it has initiated impeachment charges against the president. The president may introduce martial law and declare a state of emergency, but while either of these processes is in effect the president may not dissolve the Duma. A new (or, one supposes, renewed) government must be appointed only when a new president takes office.

The president also wields formal power over the regions of the federation. The constitution permits him to use "reconciliatory procedures" to settle differences between the federal and regional authorities. He also may suspend acts of the regional executives if he finds that they contradict the federal constitution or federal law, until "the appropriate court" decides the question. As noted previously, he may declare states of emergency and martial law in particular regions.

No provision exists in the Yeltsin constitution for a vice president. Perhaps the memory of vice presidential betrayals (by Gorbachev's vice president during the August 1991 coup, and by Yeltsin's during the October 1993 "events") were still too fresh. In the event of a president's incapacitation, presidential powers pass to the prime minister. (This occurred for twenty-three hours on November 5–6, 1996, while Yeltsin underwent cardiac bypass surgery.) If a president dies, is permanently incapacitated, or resigns (as Yeltsin did on December 31, 1999), new presidential elections must be held within three months. The acting president may not dissolve the Duma, call a referendum, or propose constitutional amendments.

The president takes the lead in conducting Russia's relations with other countries. The president is commander-in-chief of the armed forces and is generally responsible for conducting the country's foreign policy. He appoints ambassadors and other diplomats. The constitution affords him the power to approve the country's military doctrine, although numerous informal and formal structures are involved in the drafting of military and foreign policy. The president conducts international negotiations and signs international treaties (which require ratification by parliament) and recognizes foreign diplomats.

In the making and directing of policy, the president is assisted by the "power ministries" (defense, foreign affairs, interior, and security). Unlike the other ministers, who report to the prime minister, the power ministers report directly to the president. In addition, the president is advised by a network of formal and informal consultative groups.

Overall, the distinction between the president and the "government" (i.e., the prime minister and his cabinet) is vague, given the president's influence over the makeup and actions of those offices. Yet when it suited him to do so, Yeltsin blamed social and economic problems on the actions of "incompetent ministers." As will be discussed following, continuous cabinet reshuffling would handicap the state's ability to effectuate long-term policies.

Elections

The president of the Russian Federation may serve two four-year terms. The presidency is open to all Russian citizens at least thirty-five years of age who have resided in the country for at least ten years. The president is elected by a direct vote of the citizenry through a two-round process. An initial election selects the two top candidates, who then compete in a runoff election. Voters are afforded the option of choosing "none of the above" in Russian elections. The winner of the two-person race must receive more votes than this "protest" vote. Failing this, new elections must be called within three months.

Post-Soviet Russia's first presidential campaign was held in June 1996—five years after Yeltsin became president of the RSFSR. Of the seventy-eight presidential candidates who registered, eleven met all of the requirements to participate in the election. The candidacies that attracted the most attention were those of Yeltsin (as the incumbent), the LDP's Vladimir Zhirinovsky (as the most controversial), and the CPRF's Gennady Zyuganov (with the greatest support of potential voters in the spring of 1996).

The most tragic character in the presidential elections was Mikhail Gorbachev. He announced his candidacy on March 21, claiming that the need for his return was obvious. Still hailed abroad as a heroic figure, but seen at home as the person who presided over the collapse of the Soviet Union, Gorbachev was truly a prophet without honor in his own country. Opposed by conservatives and communists (for destroying the Soviet Union) and reformists (for never renouncing socialism), Gorbachev's popularity ratings never rose above 1 or 2 percent in preelection polls.

The 1996 presidential elections were simultaneously a referendum on Yeltsin's leadership (including his handling of the war in Chechnya), a test of the democrats' ability to unite behind a single candidate, and a gauge of the communists' resurgent strength. Yeltsin was shameless in his election-season populism, making reckless promises about new affluence and governmental accountability. Although few people accepted these promises at face value, Yeltsin's firm verbal commitment to political and economic reform played well with the country's new elites. Yeltsin, with the support of the major media outlets, cast Zyuganov's platform as a return to the stagnation and oppression of the Soviet period under Stalin and Leonid Brezhnev. For his part, Zyuganov portrayed Yeltsin's leadership as misguided and inept, facilitating the decline of Russian prestige and the increase of crime and inequality.

Zyuganov's initial commanding lead waned as the election date approached. It became clear that Russian voters were less concerned about ideology than about their personal living conditions. Many voters said that their decision on whether to support Yeltsin hinged on their assessment of whether he could ensure that salaries and pensions would be paid on time and whether he could restore their lost savings. In the first round, Russians cast the plurality of their vote (35 percent) for Yeltsin. Zyuganov came in second with 32 percent. Immediately afterward, Yeltsin appointed the third votegetter (Aleksandr Lebed) to head the Russian Security Council, and Lebed returned the favor with an endorsement for Yeltsin in the runoff election. Yeltsin made several other personnel changes, presumably devised to bolster his reformist credentials.

In the final days of the runoff campaign Yeltsin's health became a major issue. He abruptly canceled campaign appearances and did not show up at a scheduled public appearance on voting day to cast his ballot. Yeltsin had had a history of heart problems, and his time in power had been marked by periodic mysterious absences. Nevertheless, Yeltsin won the second round handily, with 53.7 percent of the vote to Zyuganov's 40.4 percent.

Yeltsin's reelection ensured a precious measure of continuity in the morass of post-Soviet Russian politics. Yet it also postponed for another four years a scheduled opportunity to infuse the presidency with a more vibrant, effective leader. Yeltsin's second term ended six months early, however, when he unexpectedly resigned on New Year's Eve, 1999. Power passed to the Prime Minister, Vladimir Putin, in the country's first constitutional transfer of executive power.

Putin became elected president in his own right on March 26, 2000. Receiving almost 53 percent of the vote, Putin gained the majority necessary to avoid a runoff election. His nearest competitor was CPRF chairman Zyuganov, who earned about 29 percent of the vote. Although the usual charges of media bias and even instances of voting fraud were made by Putin's opponents, Putin's margin of victory was so large that he almost certainly earned the support of a large plurality of the voters. Perennial democratic opposition candidate Grigory Yavlinsky captured less than 6 percent of the vote, and Vladimr Zhirinovsky earned only about 2.5 percent.

The Government

Although the president's decision-making powers are enormous, the constitution formally places executive power in the government. "Government" is defined in the European sense, meaning the prime minister (formally called the chairman of the government), deputy prime ministers, and federal ministers. Collectively, the federal ministers compose the cabinet. In its capacity as the executive branch, the government is charged with carrying out the laws and policies of the Russian Federation. The government also submits a federal budget to the Duma and oversees the implementation of the final budget.

The prime minister is nominated by the president and confirmed by the Duma. If the Duma rejects a nominee, then the president must make a new nomination (the same candidate may be renominated) within one week. If the Duma rejects three consecutive nominations, then the president makes a fourth nomination and dissolves the Duma. One might expect this provision to militate against the Duma's hasty rejection of nominees. After the Duma is dissolved, new parliamentary elections are called.

Once confirmed, the new prime minister proposes a list of nominees for deputy prime ministers and a cabinet. The president may accept or reject those nominees. Government ministers may not simultaneously hold legislative seats. The number of ministers within the cabinet has varied, generally in the low twenties, as Yeltsin and his prime ministers reconfigured responsibilities to fit the political needs of the moment.

The Duma's powers over the government are complex and heavily checked by the president. A simple majority of deputies may pass a vote of no confidence in the government. The president may either accept the Duma's vote, in which case he announces the government's dissolution, or he may reject the vote of no confidence. If the Duma's vote is rejected, the

Duma may pass a second vote of no confidence within three months of the first. In this case, the president must either announce the government's resignation or dissolve the Duma. Once again, self-interested deputies might be hesitant to push the president to the wall. This principle was illustrated in 1994, when the Duma passed a vote of no confidence in the government. After its first vote of no confidence was rejected by Yeltsin, the Duma was unable to muster a majority to pass a second, more destabilizing vote of no confidence.

Yeltsin's prime ministers were generally political moderates, particularly, Viktor Chernomyrdin, who was prime minister from December 1992 until March 1998. (Chernomyrdin later became Russia's special envoy to Yugoslavia.) Although none of his prime ministers' governments were dissolved by a vote of no confidence, Yeltsin replaced prime ministers either to neutralize rivals or to achieve other political aims. For example, he replaced Chernomyrdin when his popularity with the Duma and his overall influence appeared to reach a high point. Then, five months later, Yeltsin fired Chernomyrdin's successor, Sergei Kiriyenko, in response to Russia's August 1998 financial collapse.

The new prime minister, former intelligence chief Yevgeny Primakov, enjoyed growing power at the expense of Yeltsin until May 1999, when Yeltsin replaced him with Interior Minister Sergei Stepashin. This move was occasioned by the Duma's imminent, although ultimately unsuccessful, efforts to impeach Yeltsin for "instigating" the collapse of the Soviet Union in 1991 and other "crimes." Although many Duma leaders initially vowed to vote against Stepashin, whom they regarded as a reformer and Yeltsin loyalist, the threat of parliamentary dissolution again compelled the Duma to confirm him.

Three months later, Yeltsin removed Stepashin. He was replaced with Vladimir Putin, a former KGB officer who most recently headed Russia's Federal Security Service and its Security Council. Several months later, Putin became the acting president when Yeltsin resigned.

The Legislature

Like most democratic governments (and some nondemocratic ones), Russia's legislature takes the form of a bicameral parliament. This Federal Assembly, as it is known, is charged with the usual representation and lawmaking tasks, as well as with providing certain checks on the other branches of government. It is, however, significantly less powerful than the Gorbachev-era Congress of People's Deputies, which it replaced.

The upper house of the Federal Assembly is the Federation Council, and in several ways it resembles the U.S. Senate. Like the Senate, the Federation Council is constituted on the basis of equal geographical representation. Each of Russia's 89 regions sends two representatives to the Federation Council, for a total of 178 members. And, like the Senate, the Federation Council ratifies treaties (along with the Duma) and possesses the power to impeach the president. The Federation Council holds powers relating to the Russian Federation's justice system, including approving and dismissing the prosecutor-general, and approving or rejecting the president's nominees for justices on Russia's three high courts. In addition, the Federation Council approves internal border revisions, approves presidential decrees of martial law, and "decides the possibility" of deployment of the military abroad.

Members of the Federation Council elect a chairman and a deputy chairman, who preside over its sessions. Legislative work is conducted in various policy committees. Sessions are supposed to be open to the public, except as stipulated by the Federation Council's code of procedure.

Half of the Federation Council (one of each region's two seats) is composed of regional governors. As regional executives, these governors have tended to be more loyal to the federal executive (that is, the president) than to members of the lower house. The other half of the Federation Council is made up of regional legislative leaders. The two representatives from each region are not "elected" to the Federation Council; rather, they automatically become deputies of the Federation Council by virtue of their regional offices. As a result, these regional leaders split their time between their regional and federal positions, making the Federation Council a part-time body.

The Federation Council is more ideologically moderate and less politically controversial than the Duma. The proportion of communists in the upper half is considerably lower than that of the lower house, and only twenty-eight of the 178 deputies can be considered "oppositionists."

Similar to many parliamentary systems, Russia's lower house, the State Duma, is the more powerful of the two chambers. Because its 450 deputies are directly elected as representatives to the federal parliament, the Duma enjoys a stronger mandate than the Federation Council. The Duma is the more important and more powerful chamber in making legislation because it initiates all legislation and can override a rejection of a bill by the Federation Council. The constitution also provides for the censure of the government by the Duma. The term of office for Duma deputies is four years. The Duma elects a speaker to preside over the body.

The constitution reserves for the Duma various powers: approving the president's nominee for prime minister, deciding votes of confidence, appointing and removing the chairman of the Central Bank, appointing and removing the officer for human rights, initiating articles of impeachment against the president, and issuing declarations of amnesty. The Duma used this last power shortly after it convened in 1994, granting amnesty to the leaders of the 1991 attempted coup against Gorbachev and the 1993 "October events" against Yeltsin.

In 1999, the Duma's communist leadership attempted to impeach Yeltsin, but votes on all five of the indictments failed.

As a result of the December 1999 Duma elections, the balance of power in the lower house shifted further away from the extremes (communist-nationalists and reformists) and toward more pragmatic, moderate parties such as Unity and the Union of Right Forces. Such parties have the benefit of well-connected and powerful benefactors (such as former Prime Minister Sergei Kirienko and Moscow Mayor Yuri Luzhkov). But they may also lack the originality or zealotry that may be necessary to effect a complete transition away from Sovietism. Critical for determining how the Duma elections would affect Russia's development was (1) how the party fractions solidified, and (2) whether acting-President Putin would be elected in his own right at presidential elections scheduled for March. He was. If the executive and legislative branches were both controlled by the same political party or group, then the leadership could be spared the obstructionism that tended to characterize the Duma's relations with Yeltsin.

Lawmaking

The making of federal laws involves checks and balances between the two houses of parliament and the president. It should be emphasized that, although the legislative process is specified in the Russian constitution, the de facto process is somewhat different. The system is understood to be quite corrupt and subject to various political pressures. Extraconstitutional actors such as the business leaders and criminal gangs can wield enormous influence, as might be expected in a nascent democracy. Nevertheless, the formal process of introducing and enacting legislation generally follows the process described hereafter.

All bills are introduced in the Duma, although legislative proposals may be initiated by members of either house, as well as by the president, the government, the three central courts, and the regional legislatures. The Duma deliberates on bills in committee (there were about two dozen committees in early 2000), after which they are submitted to the entire body for approval or rejection. Within five days after a bill is adopted by the full Duma (usually by a majority vote), it is passed on to the Federation Council for consideration. The Federation Council need not consider a bill at all, unless it concerns the federal budgetary and fiscal matters, international treaties, Russian borders, or matters of war and peace. The Federation Council has fourteen days to approve the legislation (again by majority vote) or to reject it. If it does not act within that time, then the legislation is considered approved. If the Federation Council rejects a bill, it is returned to the Duma for repeat consideration. A two-thirds vote of approval by the Duma overrides rejection by the Federation Council.

Once a bill has passed out of the Federal Assembly, either with bicameral acceptance or with a two-thirds vote of the Duma, the legislation is forwarded to the president. If he signs it within fourteen days, it becomes law and is made public. If the president rejects the bill, it is returned for repeat consideration by the two legislative chambers. A two-thirds vote of approval by both chambers overrides the president's veto. In 1996, the Constitutional Court upheld an additional method for the president to block legislation: he may return to the Federal Assembly a law which he finds to be legally flawed or improperly passed. In effect, the president can exercise judicial review.

The adoption of federal constitutional laws requires a three-quarters majority of the Federation Council and a two-thirds majority of the Duma before going to the president for approval.

Legal System

The institutional structures created by the constitution and the body of laws passed by the legislature amount to little without a concomitant commitment to the principle of rule of law. The significance of a law-governed state is not simply that it has working laws, but that in the final analysis laws, and not politics, personality, or naked power, regulate the actions of society and the government. The Soviet Union, like tsarist Russia before it, observed no such principle. The regime was not bound in any meaningful way by an enforceable constitution, and laws affected the general population in an arbitrary and capricious fashion. In short, law in the Soviet Union was subordinate to the regime.

The Yeltsin leadership set itself upon the task of reforming the legal system with the same ambition, and perhaps the same lack of preparation, as it did reforming the economic and political systems. Few legal procedures and institutions were left untouched by the reform program. Some of the reforms simply applied international norms to the Russian legal system; for example, a requirement that all laws be published was instituted. Others filled large voids that the Soviet legal system had never had reason to address—consumer protection requirements and laws protecting intellectual property, for example. But the most important reforms concerned limitations on state power.

One of the most important bulwarks of a law-governed state is an independent high court with jurisdiction over constitutional issues. Through the 1993 constitution, Yeltsin sought to recast the Russian Constitutional Court as such a body. The Russian constitution grants to the Constitutional Court the power of judicial review: to determine whether laws and governmental actions conform to the constitution. The court also decides questions of competence between the central governmental bodies and is charged with resolving disputes between the central and regional governments. On paper the Constitutional Court indeed appears to be an important guardian of the constitution. The court did not become operational, however, until February 1995, when the Duma finally confirmed all nineteen of its justices and the court elected its chairman. That chairman, Vladimir Tumanov, was involved in the writing of the 1993 constitution and, therefore, was perhaps ideally suited for the job. Tumanov reached mandatory retirement age (seventy) in 1997, and was replaced by Marat Baglai.

A Constitutional Court is only as powerful as the rest of the government allows it to be. Many people wondered how much judicial independence would be tolerated by President Yeltsin, who had suspended the last Constitutional Court after it ruled unconstitutional his dissolution of the Supreme Soviet in the fall of 1993. The powers of the Justice Ministry and the prosecutor general would also be critical.

The Yeltsin Constitution establishes two additional high courts: The Supreme Court of the Russian Federation is the highest court of appeal for civil, administrative, and criminal law. In matters of impeachment, the Supreme Court must verify the Duma's findings of presidential criminality, and the Constitutional Court must verify that the proper impeachment procedures are followed. The Supreme Arbitration Court of the Russian Federation is the highest court of appeal for cases concerning economic matters. The Russian judiciary system includes a network of courts of arbitration, which settles economic disputes; however, it is widely understood that the rich and politically influential are able to either bypass or manipulate this system, at least at the lower levels.

To help isolate the courts from political pressure, judges in Russia are immune from criminal prosecution. This provision is difficult and important given the party's co-optation of the courts in the Soviet period and the incidents of bribery and other forms of corruption in the post-Soviet court system. In 1995 alone, some fifty-four judges were removed from the bench for misconduct. Such removal is carried out by boards of judicial peers and is considered to be distinct from criminal prosecution.

In 1991, the Soviet KGB was replaced by two major Russian organizations. The Ministry of Security became Russia's primary domestic investigatory and law-enforcement body. A separate Foreign Intelligence Service (SVR) was created to carry out foreign security operations. On paper the division of operations was akin to the United States's functional distinction between the FBI and the CIA.

Several days after the December 1993 parliamentary elections, Yeltsin dissolved the Ministry of Security and replaced it with the Federal Security Service (FSB). It was understood that Yeltsin was motivated by the Ministry of Security's insufficient opposition against parliamentary Speaker Ruslan Khasbulatov's forces during the October "events." Since that time, the FSB has operated as a fairly nonpoliticized (by historical Russian standards) law-enforcement body.

The Russian Federation also has an Interior Ministry that is concerned with domestic order and security. Overall, the various responsibilities that were held by the KGB have been assumed not only by these organizations (FSB, SVR, and the Interior Ministry), but also by the Procuracy, the Economics Ministry, the Justice Ministry, and other agencies. As the country's largest city and a major venue for crime, Moscow has created its own Moscow Regional Agency for Combating Organized Crime, which is modeled after the U.S. Federal Bureau of Investigation.

Notwithstanding Russia's reconstituted legal and judicial system, various forms of crime unquestionably have increased dramatically in post-Soviet Russia. Worsening crime statistics dogged Yeltsin since Russian independence. This is reflected in personal crimes such as homicides and assaults, vice crimes such as prostitution and drug abuse, and property crimes such as burglary and theft. Law enforcement in post-Soviet Russia is clearly ineffective. The militia (as the Russian police are called) is generally underpaid and poorly equipped. Corruption is rampant. Lacking proper training, resources, and numbers, the militia in many parts of the country is an unreliable law-enforcement institution. Even more than in countries without a history of "communalism," theft of personal and state property in Russia has become commonplace. Some sources estimate that the lion's share of the former public patrimony (factories, machinery, typewriters, computers, office furniture, etc.) has been stolen in one way or another. The courts are so overworked that the swift administration of justice is impossible. Even when court decisions are obtained, more than half of them are not implemented.

More broadly, the phenomenon of increasing crime is the continuation of a trend that began with Gorbachev's glasnost and perestroika, which granted freedoms to a society that lacked a strong sense of civic values. But the Russian public has been unwilling to simply shrug off increasing crime as the price of independence. Neither can much solace be drawn from the frequently overlooked fact that crime and corruption existed in the Soviet period. Indeed, a 1999 study by the Russian Ministry of Education found that the demise of the Soviet Union has brought with it the disintegration of a social infrastructure, including camps and programs for children and youth, which helped to deter crime. The report found that Russian society now harbors a large number of unsupervised youth who are turning to crime, alcoholism, and other social pathologies.

Crime is an ugly and constant reality in Russia, made more visible by the relatively free press and the campaign speeches of opposition political groups. The causes are varied, including the exacerbation of the moral vacuum initially fostered by the Soviets and the absence of a supportive political culture, but there are also more tangible causes. Easy access to weapons is especially problematic. After seizing power, the Bolsheviks somewhat understandably banned the personal possession of most guns. In Yeltsin's Russia the ban was revoked, and the legal possession of guns has proliferated (although numerous restrictions remain). Their illegal possession has posed an ever greater problem. Hundreds of thousands of automatic weapons are stolen or illegally sold from government armories. Russian Army soldiers, who after the collapse of the Soviet Union had endured chronically low morale and poor living conditions, commonly sell their rifles or barter them for other goods. Any number of other types of military hardware, including even artillery pieces, are available on the black market.

Another structural contributor to Russian crime is its post-communist economy. Russia's economic system has been freed of centralized state control, but a functioning market capable of imposing discipline on economic transactions has developed only slowly. Until the establishment of widely accepted rules, price reference points, consumer protections, and other fundamental elements of a functioning economy, the market is speculative and parasitic, rather than productive and disciplining. Such an environment breeds corruption, exploitation, and crime.

The criminal opportunities afforded by the transitional economy and corrupt and inefficient law enforcement create ideal conditions for organized crime. Russians commonly refer to the criminal gangs that plague them as the Mafiya because of the similarity to the entrenched criminal syndicates based in Italy. In fact, the major Italian Mafia families have established a presence in Russia.

To make matters worse, Russia suffers from widespread official corruption. Military officers, members of parliament, members of the government, and various law-enforcement officials have been caught in corruption scandals.

Official corruption extends to the regional and local levels. Local officials commonly require bribes for the provision of basic services. Widespread corruption within law-enforcement agencies has dealt a serious blow to the public trust that is needed to undergird a law-governed state. Just as business owners find themselves having to pay "protection" money to racketeers, criminal gangs routinely budget funds to bribe law-enforcement personnel. Official corruption on such a scale discourages investment and hinders Russia's economic development.

Perhaps the most frightening aspect of Russian crime concerns the country's nuclear stockpiles. Russia inherited most of the Soviet Union's nuclear weapons and many of its nuclear production facilities and reactors. Security at the facilities is dangerously lax. Small quantities of nuclear material have simply disappeared. Recordkeeping is so bad that precise figures are impossible to obtain. Particularly worrisome is the involvement of organized crime.

As Thomas Hobbes wrote in the seventeenth century, governments are created for the maintenance of "peace and common defense." The other tasks that have been adopted by governments—redistributing wealth, maintaining an infrastructure, providing education, regulating cable television—are subordinate to the basic necessity of establishing order.

It is unclear whether Yeltsin's victory over Zyuganov in the 1996 presidential election reflected popular acceptance of Yeltsin campaign's argument that communist-imposed order was worse than no order at all. Alternatively, Yeltsin's victory might have reflected the population's belief that increased material benefits were more likely under Yeltsin's leadership. In either event, it seemed certain that the majority of voters rejected Zyuganov's argument that only the communists could reimpose a measure of order in Russia. This conclusion was bolstered by the outcome of parliamentary elections in 1999, as well as the 2000 presidential election.

Role of the State

The emergence of an independent Russia from the wreckage of the Soviet Union hastened the process of redefining Russia as a political entity. Although questions of Russia's national identity and geopolitical role might be debated without resolution for years to come, the establishment of Russia as a sovereign state required the immediate creation or co-option of governmental structures.

President Boris Yeltsin and his lieutenants redefined Russia's basis as a political entity: declaring first its autonomy and then its full independence from Soviet Moscow, and banning all political parties from state organizations and enterprises. Yeltsin bolstered Russia' political independence in symbolic ways as well, such as by adopting the pre-Revolution Russian flag and renaming the country the Russian Federation (*Rossiiskaya Federatsiya*). None of this is to say, of course, that Russia was recreated as a *tabula rasa,* (clean slate) with its peoples and culture cleansed of all traces of Soviet contamination. The disintegration of the U.S.S.R. did not and could not return the peoples that had lived within it to a Hobbesian state of nature. Instead, the new Russian Federation (as well as the other successors to the U.S.S.R.) co-opted many of the institutions, laws, and physical and economic infrastructure that were part of the Soviet state. What made the Russian Federation unique—what clearly distinguished it from the Soviet state—was the source of its political legitimacy and the basis of its political authority.

In order for these political constraints on the state to be fully meaningful, a functioning civil society must arise to take over roles previously maintained by the state. As discussed previously, such a civil society has been slow in developing. In the Soviet period, putatively "civic" groups such as unions, trade associations, and even sports clubs and religious groups were controlled by the state, often through the Communist Party. Although some autonomous groups are emerging in modern Russia, they have been poorly organized and somewhat incohesive. In addition, the Russian government has taken some ominous steps to require registration of Russia's approximately ten thousand "non-governmental organizations." Many reformists worry that this could be the first step in bringing Russia's fledgling civil society under the control of the state.

At the same time, Russia is experiencing a "crisis of the state." The collapse and repudiation of the communist-led Soviet state left Russian leaders with precious little foundation on which to found a new state. Although it is internationally recognized as a sovereign entity, the Russian state has had difficulty consolidating its authority over its citizens. With about half of Russian citizens refusing to pay taxes, the state cannot collect enough revenue to fund its operations. The state is politically unstable, with various groups and regions threatening to secede and with major constitutional conflicts festering within the government. Extra-constitutional activity by business tycoons, criminal syndicates, military officers, and religious leaders challenge the authority of the state. It will take time, wise policies, and a good measure of luck before the Russian state emerges from its crisis.

PUBLIC POLICY, MAJOR DOMESTIC AND FOREIGN POLICY ISSUES, AND POLICYMAKING

Russia's policymaking apparatus is still developing. Courts are still interpreting basic provisions of the constitution, the legislative and executive branches are still clarifying their respective roles, and the responsiveness to public opinion is still evolving. Despite this, Russia's leaders are faced with critical domestic and foreign policy concerns, including the collapse of the Russian stock market and the imminent expansion of NATO into the former Soviet Union, which demand immediate action. In addition, the Russian public expects action on numerous issues, particularly living standards and crime, as a measure of the government's worthiness. The result has been a necessarily tentative, improvisational approach to public policy.

Under Yeltsin the Russian state undertook the monumental effort of rebuilding Russian society. Little by way of instructive experience was offered by the Gorbachev years, which focused primarily on economic reform and which pursued societal reform only to the extent that it contributed to stabilizing the state. By contrast, the reformers who found themselves at the levers of post-Soviet Russian power sought more fully to "normalize" society. This was a tall order indeed. But in retrospect the administration made measurable, if incremental progress. At the time of his elevation to acting president, Putin seemed determined to continue that progress, albeit with a somewhat greater weighting for national strength and respect. He also seemed to enjoy some advantages over Yeltsin in carrying out his agenda, in the form of a honeymoon period as post-Soviet Russia's first "new" president. At forty-seven-years old, Putin has relative youth and health to afford him a vigor unknown to Yeltsin in his later years.

By far the majority of salient domestic policy issues relate to the economy. Wage arrears, shrinking pensions, ruble devaluations, stock issues and crashes, shortages of goods, bank failures, tax collections, and rent increases constitute some of the major issues of concern to the Russian people centered on economics. Officially, Russia has committed itself to turning over most economic allocation questions to the market. Article 8 of the constitution states that, "A unified economic space, the free movement of commodities, services and finances, and support for competition and freedom of economic activity shall be guaranteed in the Russian Federation." Yet, as with so much of the constitution, there is no clear indication how this guarantee is to be realized.

In the first months after achieving independence, Russia's economic policy followed a relatively aggressive liberalization plan under the leadership of Anatoly Chubais. Adopting what some have called a form of "shock therapy," the Russian leadership freed virtually all prices in January 1992. Next, many of the state-owned industries were privatized through a program that distributed certificates for all citizens to purchase shares of those industries. In addition, many privately owned small businesses sprang up to offer popular goods and services. In March 1996, a new civil code came into force to address land purchases, sales, donations, leases, loan credits, and contracts.

Despite some initial successes, the liberalization plan did not fulfill the high expectations that were set for it. (Yeltsin had promised that a market-based, productive economy would emerge within about six months.) Instead, consumer purchasing power plummeted, unemployment reached the double digits, wages and pensions went unpaid for months at a time, the ruble was repeatedly devalued, many transactions turned to barter, and organized crime infiltrated businesses. Russia became, in a word, broke, and had to rely on the World Bank, the International Monetary Fund, and foreign aid to bail it out. As Yeltsin stated in his resignation speech on December 31, 1999,

> I did all I could. I want to ask you for forgiveness because many of our hopes have not come true, because what we thought would be easy turned out to be painfully difficult. I ask you to forgive me for not fulfilling some hopes of those people who believed that we would be able to jump from the gray, stagnating totalitarian past into a bright, rich and civilized future in one go.
>
> I myself believed in this. But it could not be done in one fell swoop. In some respects, I was too naive. Some of the problems were too complex. We struggled on through mistakes and failures.

The Russian experience has been at variance with other former communist countries, such as those in Eastern Europe, that have successfully implemented shock therapy. In part, Russia's failure is the result of its longer, more entrenched experience with communism; in part it is because of the government's failure to follow through on reforms. The Parliament blocked Yeltsin's proposals for land reform and governmental austerity, and Yeltsin continually reshuffled his ministers and advisers to achieve short-term political goals. With further gridlock following the August 1998 collapse of the Russian stock market, many observers put off any hope of an effective policy response to Russia's prolonged economic crisis until after new parliamentary and presidential elections. Now that those elections have taken place, there is hope that the Russian government can finally move forward.

The new Russian leadership also faces major challenges in the form of declining social conditions. As noted earlier, crime, poverty, prostitution, homelessness, and various other social ills have emerged as serious threats to Russian society. Russia's housing infrastructure, which was inadequate even during the Soviet period, has further deteriorated. The educational system is in disarray, with outdated, communist-influenced textbooks, cramped facilities, virtually no technical equipment, and inadequate teachers' salaries. The welfare system, which was a defining characteristic of the communist state, has collapsed because of a combination of intentional reductions and unplanned escalating demand. Russia has tried to respond to these twin crises of exploding social problems and disintegrating infrastructure with a raft of policies, decrees, and laws; however, the ideological fragmentation of the legislature has prevented any cohesive program, and the political fragmentation of the government and the dearth of resources stymied the implementation of even piecemeal responses. Eventual success at bringing Russia's social problems under control will require that the state consolidate and stabilize its authority. To a large extent, however, the Russian state's authority currently appears to depend on its ability to mitigate these social ills.

Homelessness, health problems, alcoholism, and lowered life expectancy have become endemic in postcommunist Russia.

Foreign Policy

The primary global issue of the 1990s became the crafting, or at least the stabilization, of post–Cold War, post-Soviet international relations. These two elements (the passing of the Cold War and of the Soviet Union) are difficult to separate: the Cold War presupposed a strong and antagonistic Soviet Union. Yet the converse is even more relevant because the Soviet Union required the Cold War for its survival. Without the division of Europe into two hostile military and ideological blocs, and without the apocalyptic stakes of mutual assured destruction, the Soviet Union could retain neither its claim as a superpower nor indeed its justification as an authoritarian, one-party state. The Soviet Union's ultimate inability to ride out, let alone win, the Cold War would have tremendous implications for the development of Russian foreign policy in the post-Soviet era. Russia is now a greatly reduced power, with only a fraction of its former geopolitical weight. Nevertheless, the foreign policy of Yeltsin's Russia, like that of Stalin's Soviet Union, has far-reaching consequences for Europe and beyond.

The diplomacy of Yeltsin's Russia in the 1990s, operating from a position of weakness, generally sought to normalize the international relationships that were either exacerbated by the Cold War or thrown into turmoil by the collapse of the bipolar order. The list of accomplishments is impressive: In 1992, Moscow and Washington signed the START II treaty, which committed both countries to deep reductions in their strategic nuclear arsenals. This treaty was finally ratified by the Duma in April 2000, after which work began in earnest to develop a START III treaty for still further nuclear reductions. In addition, Yeltsin pursued Russian membership in various international organizations that once were associated with the West: the General Agreement on Tariffs and Trade (GATT; later the World Trade Organization), the Council of Europe, the Group of Seven (which, to Yeltsin's delight, added Russia as an associate member in 1997), the Organization for Economic Cooperation and Development (OECD), and even NATO's "Partnership for Peace." In these and other ways, Russia, under Yeltsin's leadership, gradually moved into the international mainstream, albeit no longer acting as the superpower it was before.

Yeltsin, however, encountered mounting domestic opposition to his foreign policy. As the president of an emerging democratic state, Yeltsin had to consider the wishes and demands of the Parliament, the Constitutional Court, and the voters. This balancing act forced him into tactical retreats, such as the firing of controversial foreign and defense ministers, and the adopting of more nationalistic rhetoric. As *The Economist* observed, Yeltsin's "greatest contribution was not as a builder, but as a destroyer of the discredited but still-potent communist edifice."

Immediately upon assuming the post of acting president, Vladimir Putin made statements about the need to strengthen Russia's place in the world. He also signed a new Russian security doctrine that seemed to emphasize Russia's need to defend its interests, even with nuclear weapons. Although it was unclear how much of this policy was directed at his domestic audience, Western diplomats expected that their countries' relations with Russia would cool, at least initially, under the new president.

Institutions

The Foreign Ministry naturally holds a significant claim for foreign policymaking responsibilities, but the exigencies of domestic politics has brought challenges in the form of other institutional factors. The Parliament (first the Supreme Soviet, and later the Duma) increasingly has challenged the Foreign Ministry's policies and actions, generally opposing what was perceived to be the Yeltsin leadership's obsequiousness toward the West. In addition, the quintessentially Soviet KGB has been broken into two parts, with one responsible for intelligence gathering and the other dealing with domestic security. Specific intelligence and security functions have remained a matter of interdepartmental and constitutional disputes.

An independent Russian military and a Defense Ministry were created in May 1992, marking the end of Moscow's hope that the defense of the former Soviet republics could be coordinated through the Commonwealth of Independent States (CIS). But some Russian military leaders soon found themselves at odds with the Kremlin, and a series of intrigues, scandals, and reorganizations kept the military leadership in flux. Meanwhile, the morale, funding, and equipping of military troops continued to decline, resulting in a highly unreliable defensive force.

In addition to the numerous legislative committees, government ministries, and presidential councils associated with foreign policy, various nongovernmental and quasi-governmental foreign policy think tanks also have emerged, including the high-profile Council for Foreign and Defense Policy. Several of these councils have directly opposed the government's foreign policy agendas.

Although Moscow's official foreign policy pronouncements in the early and mid-1990s cast Russia as a global power, with legitimate interests across Europe, the Middle East, China, and Africa, as the decade wore on it became clear that Russia's foreign policy interests were focused much closer to home. By the late 1990s, Russian foreign policy came to focus primarily in the "near abroad" (that is, the territory of the other fourteen former Soviet republics).

Most of the countries of the former Soviet Union (including Russia but excluding the three Baltic states) compose the Commonwealth of Independent States (CIS). The CIS was created in December 1991 at the same time as the Soviet Union was dissolving, yet the CIS is not a successor to the U.S.S.R. In essence, it is a framework for coordinating economic, diplomatic, and security relations among its members. Some subgroups (such as the Slavic states, the Central Asian states, and others) have developed better-integrated associations within the CIS. It is unlikely, however, that the CIS will ever approach the level of integration experienced by the European Union. NAFTA might be a more realistic model.

Moscow's policies in the near abroad have sought to maintain a politically friendly, stable ring of countries on Russia's periphery; to preserve and enhance Moscow's trade access; and to protect the rights of ethnic Russians living abroad. To a large extent Russia has been successful in achieving these ends; however, Russia's policy in the near abroad has raised complaints that Russia is in essence trying to reestablish the Soviet Union. Although some Russian parties and politicians have in fact stated this objective, it is unlikely that Moscow could ever exert and maintain control over the near abroad. In the post–Cold War era, there is no longer a fixed boundary (or Iron Curtain) marking Moscow's sphere of influence. Any blatant violation of a country's sovereignty by Moscow, even in the near abroad, would be unlikely to be tolerated by the rest of Europe. The shift of the European balance of power toward an expanded NATO ensures this protection, and NATO's actions in the Balkans demonstrates this guarantee.

Russia still can be expected to exert influence in the near abroad, devoting its diplomatic energies, using aggressive economic and trade actions, and even engaging in espionage and making subtle military threats. But Russian foreign policy, as with its peacekeeping missions in Bosnia and Kosovo, will need to remain within the boundaries of the "new world order" if Russia is to have any hope of rejoining the West.

CONCLUSIONS, PROSPECTS, PROBLEMS, AND FUTURE DIRECTIONS

Russia is one of the world's most resilient countries. More than a millennium has passed since the founding of Kievan Rus in the ninth century. Since that time, Russia's history has been marked by disruptive and sometimes cataclysmic epochs. It suffered under the Mongol yoke for two centuries; it was ruled by the House of Romanov for three hundred years; it expanded its frontiers through continual imperial conquest; it was overrun by the armies of Napoleon and Hitler, and it repulsed both at enormous cost; it was stifled by the totalitarian control of the communists for most of the twentieth century. Given such a history, Russia's first decade as an independent post-Soviet state can hardly be viewed as definitive.

Instead, post-Soviet efforts to change the course of Russian history—to transfer sovereignty to the people and to free the market, and ultimately to reunite with the West—have encountered monumental roadblocks. The person best positioned to effect those changes—Vladimir Putin—may be faced with new opportunities. The Duma, once dominated by opposition groups, seems to be aligned with the presidency. (From the time of his assuming the acting presidency on December 31, 1999, to the time of his inauguration in May 2000, Putin simultaneously retained his post as prime minister.)

Despite the continuation of stubborn economic and societal problems, there is still cause for hope that in its more recent incarnation, Russia may succeed in finally bringing to its people a measure of liberty, security, and prosperity. Unlike all of its predecessors, the Russian Federation places ultimate political power in the hands of the people. This change has not merely been a formality. The expression of the people's will via election has been heeded by all political contenders, which is no small feat for an infant democracy. This achievement, more than any of the myriad other changes Russia has undergone during the final decade of the twentieth century, has the potential for radically altering the course of Russia's development. The making of public policy now is limited by the tolerance of public opinion. Whereas the Communist Party of the Soviet Union claimed that its policies were by definition in the interest of the people, the actions of today's Russian leaders must meet the standard of public acceptance. Whereas the Soviet Union's leadership was assembled through the *nomenklatura* system, the Russian Federation's leadership is chosen through the marketplace of political ideas (and, as in the West, misleading campaign advertising).

A watershed in Russia's democratic development continued with the presidential election in the summer of 1996, which was important at three levels. Most important, it marked a further institutionalization of democratic mechanisms. The losers in both rounds of voting accepted the electorate's verdict, and the ultimate winner—Yeltsin—seemed to understand the nature of his mandate.

Secondly, the elections expressed the people's unwillingness to succumb to the communists' appeals for a reinstitutionalization of Soviet values. Of course, the voters' rejection of Zyuganov was distinct from a wholehearted endorsement of Yeltsin's policies, as illustrated by the first round of voting, in which Yeltsin garnered barely one of every three votes. Only with the second round's starker choice of Yeltsin or Zyuganov did the electorate consolidate around Yeltsin.

Third, the presidential election provided continuity in the form of Yeltsin's (and centrist Viktor Chernomyrdin's) leadership. What this leadership lacked in comparison to the democratic ideal was at least partly compensated for by the virtue of leadership stability in tumultuous times.

There comes a point, however, that the benefits of leadership stability are outweighed by the liabilities of political torpor or rigidity. Such a point arguably was reached under Gorbachev, and may have been passed during Yeltsin's tenure. The passing of the Russian leadership to Putin opens new opportunities, as well as new perils, as Russia—a country that witnessed the turning of the first millennium—now embarks on its third millennium.

Will Russia join the West? Eventually, logic would compel it to do so. Russia's history, values, and culture are in many ways grounded in Europe. Other former Soviet bloc countries in Eastern Europe have enjoyed economic and political benefits from rejoining the West. Western countries and international organizations offer financial support as a reward for Western-style reforms. Russian security against Islamic extremism and Chinese aggression at its southern borders would benefit from a Western connection. And countries following Western economic and political models enjoy greater political stability and wealth than others.

Unfortunately, peoples and governments generally have a poor track record for doing what is logical and what is in their own interests. Additional missteps may still be in store for Russia. Yet in the words of Israeli politician Abba Eban, "History teaches us that men and nations behave wisely once they have exhausted all other alternatives." In Russia's case, most of the worst alternatives have already been exhausted.

SUGGESTED READINGS

Allensworth, Wayne, *The Russian Question: Nationalism, Modernization, and Post-Communist Russia*. Lanham, MD: Rowman and Littlefield, 1998.

Aron, Leon R., *Yeltsin: A Revolutionary Life*. London: HarperCollins, 2000.

Boilard, Steve D., *Reinterpreting Russia: An Annotated Bibliography of Books on Russia, the Soviet Union, and the Russian Federation, 1991–1996*. Lanham, MD: Scarecrow Press, 1997.

Boilard, Steve D., *Russia at the Twenty-First Century: Politics and Social Change in the Post-Soviet Era*. Fort Worth: Harcourt Brace, 1998.

Braginskii, Sergei, *Incentives and Institutions: The Transition to a Market Economy in Russia*. Princeton, NJ: Princeton University Press, 2000.

Cox, Michael (ed.), *Rethinking the Soviet Collapse: Sovietology, the Death of Communism and the New Russia*. New York: Pinter, 1998.

Field, Mark G. and Judyth L. Twigg (eds.), *Russia's Torn Safety Nets: Health and Social Welfare During the Transition*. New York: St. Martin's Press, 2000.

Gaidar, Egor. *Days of Defeat and Victory* (tr. by Jane Ann Miller). Seattle: University of Washington Press, 1999.

Hancock, M. Donald and John Logue (eds.), *Transitions to Capitalism and Democracy in Russia and Central Europe: Achievements, Problems, Prospects*. Westport, CT: Praeger, 2000.

Husband, William B. (ed.), *The Human Tradition in Modern Russia*. Wilmington, DE: SR Books, 2000.

Nagy, Proska, *The Meltdown of the Russian State: The Deformation and Collapse of the State in Russia*. Cheltenham: Edward Elgar, 2000.

Nichols, Thomas M., *The Russian Presidency: Society and Politics in the Second Russian Republic*. New York: St. Martin's Press, 1999.

Nicholson, Martin, *Towards a Russia of the Regions*. New York: Oxford University Press, 1999.

Riasanovsky, Nicholas V., *A History of Russia,* 6th ed. New York: Oxford University Press, 2000.

Robinson, Neil (ed.), *Institutions and Political Change in Russia.* New York: St. Martin's Press, 2000.

Shaw, Denis J. B., *Russia in the Modern World: A New Geography.* Oxford: Blackwell, 1999.

Shleifer, Andrei, *Without a Map: Political Tactics and Economic Reform in Russia.* Cambridge, MA: MIT Press, 2000.

Silverman, Bertram, *New Rich, New Poor, New Russia: Winners and Losers on the Russian Road to Capitalism.* Armonk, NY: M.E. Sharpe, 2000.

Treadgold, Donald W., *Twentieth Century Russia,* 9th ed. Boulder, CO: Westview Press, 2000.

Ulrich, Marybeth Peterson, *Democratizing Communist Militaries: The Cases of the Czech and Russian Armed Forces.* Ann Arbor: University of Michigan Press, 1999.

Weigle, Marcia A., *Russia's Liberal Project: State-Society Relations in the Transition from Communism.* University Park, PA: Pennsylvania State University Press, 2000.

Woodruff, David, *Money Unmade: Barter and the Fate of Russian Capitalism.* Ithaca, NY: Cornell University Press, 1999.

Yeltsin, Boris, *The Struggle for Russia.* New York: Times Books, 1995.

6

ICELAND
Norwegian Sea
Hammerfest
Alta
Kirkenes
Harstad
Narvik
Kiruna
Rovaniemi
Lulea
Skelleftea
Umea
Ostersund
Vaasa
FINLAND
SWEDEN
Gulf of Bothnia
Tampere
NORWAY
Bergen
Gavle
Helsinki
Oslo
Uppsala
Stockholm
ESTONIA
Goteborg
Russia
LATVIA
North Sea
DENMARK
Baltic Sea
Copenhagen
Vejle
LITHUANIA
Russia
BELARUS
Germany
Poland

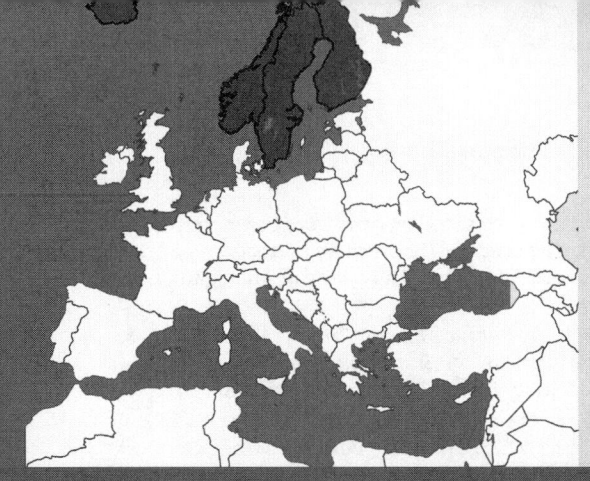

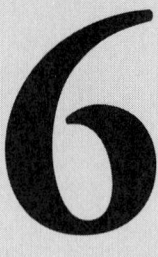

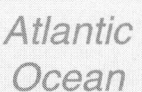

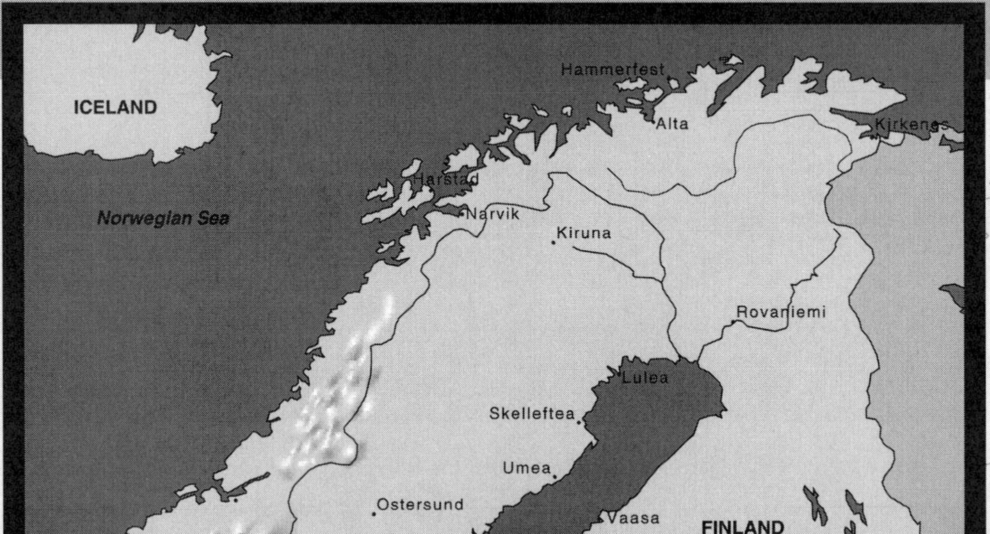

The Nordic Countries

David Gress

COUNTRY PROFILES

Denmark
Population:	5,330,000
Land Area:	43,000 sq. km.
Population per sq. km.:	125
Gross National Product:	$176.4 billion
Per Capita Income:	$33,260
Global Per Capita Income Rank:	6
Percent Urban:	86
Adult Literacy:	100% (claimed)
Life Expectancy	Male: 73
	Female: 78

Finland
Population:	5,171,000
Land Area:	338,000 sq. km.
Population per sq. km.:	17
Gross National Product:	$124.3 billion
Per Capita Income:	$24,110
Global Per Capita Income Rank:	19
Percent Urban:	64
Adult Literacy:	100% (claimed)
Life Expectancy	Male: 73
	Female: 81

Iceland
Population:	274,000
Land Area:	103,000 sq. km.
Population per sq. km.:	3
Gross National Product:	$7.7 billion
Per Capita Income:	$28,010
Global Per Capita Income Rank:	11
Percent Urban:	85
Adult Literacy:	100% (claimed)
Life Expectancy	Male: 76
	Female: 82

Norway
Population:	4,018,000
Land Area:	324,000 sq. km.
Population per sq. km.:	14
Gross National Product:	$152.1 billion
Per Capita Income:	$34,330
Global Per Capita Income Rank:	4
Percent Urban:	74
Adult Literacy:	100% (claimed)
Life Expectancy	Male: 76
	Female: 81

Sweden
Population:	8,861,000
Land Area:	450,000 sq. km.
Population per sq. km.:	22
Gross National Product:	$226.9 billion
Per Capita Income:	$25,620
Global Per Capita Income Rank:	14
Percent Urban:	83
Adult Literacy:	100% (claimed)
Life Expectancy	Male: 77
	Female: 82

Those who believe Nordic "mediocrity" is a fruit of the welfare state are certainly wrong. Rather than mediocrity, we might say that there is a passion for equality. But this attitude was present long before the welfare state began. It is a substantial part of our cultural heritage; it is in our blood. The welfare state did not create this passion for equality, but rather is itself an economic, social, cultural, and organizational expression of efforts to promote it.

Bent Rold Andersen

The ancient right of the Swedish people to tax itself is to be exercised by the *Riksdag* (parliament) alone.

Constitution of Sweden, 1809

You may think it's the middle class
You may think it's the big investors
You may think it's the experts
You may think it's the CEOs

But it's the people that builds the country . . .

Ulf Lundell[1]

NORDIC TEMPERAMENTS, NORDIC VALUES

In the early 1980s, *Daedalus,* the journal of the American Academy of Arts and Sciences, published two consecutive issues on the societies and cultures of the five Nordic nations—Denmark, Finland, Iceland, Norway, and Sweden. The two issues were entitled, respectively, *The Nordic Enigma* and *Nordic Voices*. The issues signaled a friendly, if puzzled, interest in the doings of these twenty-odd million, seemingly ordinary and easily comprehensible folk who inhabited the northern margins of Europe, who mostly spoke similar languages, who were accommodating and peace-loving in international relations, indeed to a fault, who lived under long-established and stable systems of democratic government, and who shared one apparently dominating obsession: a passion for social and economic equality, reflected in that most Nordic and perhaps most deceptive of all institutions, the universal welfare state or, as Nordics prefer to call it, the welfare society.

At about the same time, an exhibition of Nordic art visited the United States. It focused on the painters of the period 1880–1920, such as the Norwegian Edvard Munch, the Swedes Anders Zorn and Eugene (the "painting prince"), the Finn Akseli Gallen-Kallela, and the Danes P. F. Krøyer, Michael Ancher, and others of the Skagen school, named after the windswept and rain-lashed fishing village at the northern tip of the Jutland peninsula where these artists found their favorite subjects. What these artists had in common, apart from the time they lived in, was a fascination with how light and the relations among shapes and human figures affected or created atmosphere and with using light and color to evoke sharp and often poignant moods of cheer or regret, exuberance or sadness, joy or fear. Although they were contemporary with the more famous Impressionists of France and used some of the same devices—heavy brushstrokes, limpid outlines, a focus on water, foliage, and reflected objects—these Nordic artists also had other purposes, which had to do with the world they lived in. This was a world of cooler, softer, more slanting light and, the exhibition implied, of emotions and relationships shaped by that softer light: relationships less openly expressed, emotions more likely to live

---

[1] Bent Rold Andersen (b. 1924) was minister of social affairs in Denmark and a prominent defender of the egalitarian principles of social democratic redistribution and social policy. Ulf Lundell (b. 1949) is a Swedish writer, musician, and performer who, in a very Nordic mode, blends some of the qualities, romanticism, and political sensibilities of such American artists as the later Bob Dylan, Bruce Springsteen, and John Mellencamp. The quotes: Andersen 1984, 111; the Swedish constitution (*regeringsform,* RF) of 1809 quoted in Halvarson et al. 1999, 2; Lundell lyrics, in my translation, from the track "Folket bygger landet" ("The people builds the country") on the significantly titled double CD *På andra sidan drömmarna* ("On the far side of the dreams"), EMI 7243 475196 2 (1996). Quoted by permission.

in long silences and steady gazes than in the eruptions and excitements of more southerly temperaments.

The title of this exhibition, *Northern Lights,* was therefore evocative, if not terribly original. It referred not only to the night-time phenomenon of the *aurora borealis,* the shimmering red-blue curtains or circles in the sky caused by ionizing radiation and visible at high latitudes in times of intense sunspot activity, but also to the low-hanging sun and long, long twilights of the Nordic summer and the brief, dark days and seemingly endless nights of the Nordic winter. Even at the southernmost extremity of the Nordic region, at just below 55 degrees of latitude (the same as the southernmost tip of the Alaska panhandle), the sun is up for nineteen hours at the summer solstice, but for only six at the winter solstice. In the 120-mile-wide slice of land on each side of the 60th degree of northern latitude, the slice occupied by the three northern capitals of Oslo, Stockholm, and Helsinki, and which is home to more people than any other similar belt of territory in the region, the sun rises at 2:30 a.m. at midsummer and sets at 11:00 p.m., whereas it barely creeps above the horizon for four and a half hours on December 22, the shortest day.[2] The quality of the Northern light shifts as one proceeds northward. In Denmark, the so-called light nights from early May to early August are, when clear, backlit from below the northern horizon by the sun, but they are still nights: you need your headlights to drive. In central Sweden, the midsummer night is blue-gray and you can easily read a newspaper by the much stronger indirect light of the barely hidden sun. And in the northern parts of Norway, Sweden, and Finland, midnight at midsummer is like an early morning or late evening: the sun is up and it is daytime, though the shadows are long.

Are the long days of summer and the long nights of winter merely functions of latitude or do they correlate with a type of personality and a way of hiding or expressing feelings characteristic of the North, or even with the kind of society and culture to be found there? Are Nordic people truly, in the main, cautious, phlegmatic, prone to bury rather than express or share emotions, and full of poignant, unexpressed longings? Ask them, and they will point to as many differences as similarities among the five nations, or among groups within them, but they will also assert that there is something they all share, something deeper than the passion for social equality and on which that passion draws. The purpose of this chapter is to provide an introduction, through a survey of the history, the politics, the societies, and the cultures of the Nordic region, to these differences and similarities, and to the place of these nations in contemporary Europe and the contemporary world.

A few words of caution are in order. Americans, especially older Americans, may remember the caricature of the slow, silent, and not very bright Scandinavian—a Swede, usually, as most Nordic immigrants to the United States were Swedes—as a stereotype along with the dumb Pole, the excitable Italian, and the talkative Irishman. Of course this was an ethnic stereotype, and ethnic stereotypes are no longer considered politically correct, but at the same time they do not come out of nowhere. It is no accident that the stereotypical Swede was slow and silent, whereas the stereotypical Irishman was mercurial and loquacious—the very opposite, in fact. The stereotype becomes prejudice when the slow, silent Swede is taken to be stupid, but there is no doubt that restraint, introversion, modesty, silent endurance, and a stoical, defeatist, or simply underhanded tendency to brood rather than talk were, for centuries, recognized as prevalent traits, whether desirable or not, of many Nordic people—so prevalent, in fact, that they gave rise not only to an ethnic stereotype in America but to

---

[2]The times given are for Stockholm, located at 19° eastern longitude, and ignoring summer or daylight time.

innumerable stories, works of art, and jokes in the Nordic countries themselves.

The following are just two examples. The first is from the thirteenth-century Icelandic story or historical novel known as *Njal's Saga*, considered by many to be the supreme example of the most uniquely Nordic form of literature. *Njal's Saga* is one of several fictionalized accounts of the lives, passions, and fates of people in Iceland in the decades before and after the Icelanders adopted Christianity by a democratic vote in their folk-assembly, the Althing, in A.D. 1000. Composed some two to three centuries after the events and people they portray, the sagas are primarily stories of passion and character, of how people, weak, strong, greedy, or noble, discover desire—for sex, power, or riches—and how their strengths and weaknesses shape or corrupt their desires in clashes with others.

A recurrent theme of the sagas is how actions, whether justified or not, in the remote past can have fatal effects in the present. This theme is often coupled with another, that of brooding over wrongs and delayed revenge. Our example is that of the woman Hallgerd who, when young, marries the farmer Gunnar of Hlidarend. When she was a girl, Hallgerd's uncle said of her that she had "a thief's eyes." As Gunnar's wife, she soon proves wilful and unruly, provoking murders and intrigues. On one occasion Gunnar punishes her for stealing by slapping her face. She promises him that he will regret that blow.

The man Hallgerd stole from refuses to accept Gunnar's offer of redress and a feud develops, in the course of which Gunnar is attacked and kills several men.[3] The Icelanders had no king or state authority and were constantly threatened by violence escalating into family feuds. In order to cut short these effects in Gunnar's case, the Althing sentences him to exile. If he does not leave Iceland for three years, he will be an outlaw and can be killed with impunity. Gunnar prepares to leave, but on the way to the sea his horse stumbles on a hillside opposite his farm. Looking back at his home in the distance he is so taken with its beauty that he decides to stay. Soon, his enemies discover that he is home and gather for an attack. Gunnar's reputation as one of the strongest and bravest men of Iceland is such that if they do not kill him while he is an outlaw, they fear that he will come after them instead. They attack his house, at first without success, but eventually their numbers tell. Gunnar is wounded and at one point his bowstring breaks. He asks Hallgerd for two locks of her hair for a new bowstring. Here is the moment she has been waiting for for twenty years. She refuses him her hair, reminding him of the slap he gave her when he caught her stealing.[4] Gunnar's mother, standing by, who never liked Hallgerd, tells her that her reputation will suffer for what she has done. Hallgerd is unrepentant, and eventually Gunnar is killed.

The other example is the film *Cries and Whispers* by Ingmar Bergman, the best-known Nordic filmmaker of the twentieth century. The film, which won U.S. Motion Picture Academy and other awards when it was released in 1972, is set in a large country house sometime around 1900. The house is inhabited by three sisters, one of whom, Agnes, is dying of cancer, while the two others, Maria and Karin, struggle to understand how the three of them grew so distant. A servant, Anna, is the only one in the

---

[3] Just before he is assaulted, Gunnar has a prophetic dream. The tone-poem known in English as "The Dream of Gunnar" by the Danish composer Carl Nielsen (1865–1931) is not so much an evocation of this episode as a lyrical evocation of the remote Northern atmosphere of the sagas. Its Danish title is merely "A Saga-Dream." It is recorded, for instance, on Carl Nielsen, *Orchestral Music*, the Danish National Radio Symphony Orchestra conducted by Gennady Rozhdestvensky (Chandos CD CHAN 9287, 1994). *Njal's Saga* has been translated into English several times; the best translation is that of Magnus Magnusson and Hermann Pálsson in the Penguin Classics (London 1960, frequently reprinted).

[4] The idea of using hair for a bowstring is highly unrealistic, which is a characteristic of *Njal's Saga*. Its combat scenes in particular are grotesque and detract somewhat from the emotional realism of the story. Listen for example to this from chapter 30: "Gunnar saw the spear coming, whirled round faster than the eye could follow, caught the spear in flight with his left hand and hurled it back at Karl's ship. The man who was in its way fell dead."

house who is emotionally able to comfort Agnes as she dies. The entire house is bathed in red tones, which adds to the stifling atmosphere of the film. Conversations are brief and often vacuous; the force of the story and the nature of the relationships are conveyed largely through what is not said or partly said. Karin, the eldest, is dominant but also frustrated, as flashbacks with her deceased or disappeared husband, a self-satisfied oaf, show. Maria is more emotional and seemingly open to passion, but in fact is deceptive and sneaky, unable to convert her desires to vital energy; her passion confines itself to a furtive affair with the doctor who is attending Agnes.

Reading the sagas or watching a film such as *Cries and Whispers* powerfully confirms the stereotype of the Nordic personality as repressed and unable to express itself except by rare and extreme behavior. These two examples also add the critical point that silent endurance is not necessarily healthy: it can be a perversion arising from or leading to dishonesty and corruption. Both the themes of brooding silence and delayed revenge, as well as the idea that silence of this kind can be a curse, are commonplaces of Nordic self-understanding and self-criticism and, as the examples show, of Nordic art.

While stereotypes are not mere invention, they are also not universally true. That of the silent Scandinavian, whether dignified or, as Bergman would have it, neurotically or even psychotically repressed, is more often applied to Swedes, Norwegians, and Icelanders than to Finns or Danes. In the late nineteenth century, a Danish children's book about the nations of Europe allegedly said of the Finns that they "go for their knives at the least provocation."[5] The Danes are often described as the Irish of the North: easy-going, undisciplined, and fond of alcohol. These characterizations, too, have some value, but only if they are not taken too seriously. Finns do not consider themselves especially excitable or prone to knife-fights, and in fact are the only Nordic nation that has its own special word for tough, silent struggling against nature, enemies, or, in modern times, economic crises: *sisu*. As for the Danes, long-term immigrants have found them less easy-going than initial impressions suggest. On the other hand, some evidence for Danish lack of discipline may be found in the odd fact that Danes suffer accidents at work at twice the rate of Swedes. The difference cannot be attributed to alcohol, since drinking on the job has become almost as unacceptable in Denmark as elsewhere in the Protestant or post-Protestant West. The difference in accident rates was startlingly illustrated in the late 1990s when Danes and Swedes together built the first bridge between the two countries, across the shallow eight-mile sound between Copenhagen and Malmö. The job was the same, work conditions and qualifications identical, and yet the Danish rate of accidents was still higher.[6] Some suggested that the Danes have more accidents because they are less inclined to obey rules, including safety rules. If true, this would mean that the Danish accident rate is part of the cost of a more libertarian and individualistic attitude toward life. Yet if the Danes are more libertarian, why is it that it was in Sweden that the rules prohibiting shops from staying open in the evenings and on weekends were abolished in 1972, whereas the Danes in 2001 were still, with minor exceptions, prevented by law from shopping on Saturday afternoons and Sundays?

---

[5] A clumsy rendering of the untranslatably pithy *finnerne har let til kniven*, literally, "the Finns go easily for their knives." The saying is a joke in today's Denmark and may be nothing more than a modern urban legend.

[6] Danes also have approximately 20 percent more car accidents measured in terms of miles driven than the Swedes. Here, alcohol may play a part, as may the fact that most Danes drive less and so get less practice than most Swedes, which in turn is because cars, due to taxes, are more than twice as expensive in Denmark than in Sweden and so more of a luxury item. However, differences in accident rates among societies are not abstract facts but reflect deep sociocultural patterns. The French demographer Emmanuel Todd made a stab at some correlations in this area in the 1980s, but this research was not followed up. Why, for example, do the English, who have some of the densest and fastest traffic in the world, have the world's lowest per capita risk of traffic fatalities?

Bergman set his story of the three sisters in 1900. That time, which was also the time of the artists exhibited in *Northern Lights,* was, as Sigmund Freud was arguing in Vienna, a time of repressed sexuality and repressed feelings in general throughout the West, not just in Scandinavia, though the Nordics may have brought their own legacy of gloom and brooding sadness to the Victorian norms of bourgeois respectability. It was also a time of extraordinary literary, social, and artistic efflorescence, as documented not only in painting, but in literature, music, and poetry, in the works of writers such as August Strindberg, Henrik Ibsen, and Henrik Pontoppidan and composers such as Jean Sibelius, Carl Nielsen, and Vilhelm Stenhammar. It was a creative time in politics as well; in all the nations, this was the age when the modern political parties emerged and when elite and mass movements laid the foundations and gave initial shape and value to what later became the Nordic model or the Nordic welfare society. It was, finally, a time when Nordic cultural and political figures were in frequent contact with each other and when writers, scholars, and composers across the five nations visited each other and drew on each other's inspiration. They also drew on the common inspiration of the Nordic past, as expressed in the Icelandic sagas and the legacy of the time when all the North shared a common language and culture; it was, therefore, quite typical that Carl Nielsen should compose a tone-poem called "The Dream of Gunnar" and have it instantly understood what he was trying to evoke. The past in question was the time of late pagan and early Christian Scandinavia, the centuries around A.D. 1000 often, and inaccurately, referred to as the Viking Age.[7] One measure of this interest in the Nordic past was that names of saga characters such as Egil, Gunnar, Helga, or Sigrid became popular with parents in the decades around 1900.[8] In earlier centuries, the only Nordic names in common use were names of Christian saints or of kings, such as Olaf, Knud, Erik, or Sven.

What these nineteenth- and early twentieth-century writers, teachers, artists, and thinkers looked for in the deep past was the origins of what they themselves felt to be characteristically Nordic: not just silence, modesty, and endurance, but a tradition of equal respect for all, the idea that all members of society were in some sense equals and that pride and courage were not a function of rank or fortune, and a tradition of respect for women and of seeing strong women as the foundation of the family and of society. They looked in two places: the pagan or early Christian past of the Viking Age and the time of the sagas, and the later Christian or more precisely Lutheran traditions of parish-based local solidarity and self-help.[9] Lutheranism emphasized literacy and solidarity within the local parish, both of which were important features of the kind of social contract in which those who can do so care for those who through no fault of their own are too poor or weak to care for themselves. Arising from both these legacies, the reimagining of the authentically Nordic spirit was, as I have indicated, one of the wellsprings of the modern passion for equality that sustained a great deal of Nordic social, economic, educational, and cultural policy in the century that followed.

Yet this North, that of 1900, was a poor North, a North where those who made the works of art we have mentioned were few. It

---

[7] Inaccurately because most people in Scandinavia a thousand years ago were not vikings, which is a word meaning "pirate, adventurer," but farmers. Yet the age, roughly from 800–1200 and ending about the time the sagas were written in Iceland as a sort of memory of the past, had a distinct identity, and calling it the Viking Age is somewhat more pithy and exciting than calling it the age of agricultural development, of rising kingship, or of exploration and settlement.

[8] Saga-names remained popular until the 1960s, when I attended school in Denmark with Gunnars and Helgas. After that they fell almost completely out of use again.

[9] For the Lutheran roots of the welfare society see Knudsen 2000.

was a society, or a range of societies, largely poor, with little of the legacy of great houses or rich dynasties of princes and patrons that had done so much to shape the civilization of Britain, France, or the United States. Below a narrow elite of royalty, civil servants, and rich landowners or businessmen lived the more than 80 percent who were artisans, schoolteachers, other low-level functionaries, fishermen, farmers, or landless laborers. But this poverty, when contrasted to the greater concentrations of wealth in private hands in other countries, only tended to confirm the notion that Nordic societies were traditionally more egalitarian. If most are poor and the few who are not are mostly favored servants of the state, a kind of equality does indeed exist. One way of interpreting Nordic social and economic policy in the twentieth century—which some will consider rather positive and generous—is to say that it aimed at broadening equality while raising prosperity. Economic growth, which was the result of hard work and good luck, made it possible for these policies to succeed remarkably well, though not without the unintended effects and occasional perversions that are the inevitable concomitant of all human endeavor.

Times, however, have indeed changed. A Swedish woman, born in 1891 and not atypical, had thirteen siblings. The children had to borrow one another's shoes to go to school, so that only some of them attended school on any given day. The local board of poor relief offered help. Yet their father turned down offers of shoes or clothing. "Give my regards and say thank you," he always said, "there will be others who need it more." Here, in a nutshell, is a real-life example of the old, patient, self-denying Nordic personality at its most (needlessly?) heroic. Here, also, is one of the most enduring principles of that personality: to reject charity which is not the fruit of one's own work.

In a similar vein, until the 1950s two girls, Save (blonde, healthy, and happy) and Waste (brunette, thin, and unhappy), were familiar characters to Swedish schoolchildren, since they appeared in little stories popularized in schoolbooks that inculcated the message that saving was virtuous and wasting damaging to one's own joy and that of others. This, again, was a poor society with no margins. Being completely self-sufficient and spending no money at all, ever, was an often-achieved goal of rural Swedes. And yet around them, by mid-century, another world was evolving, one with different standards, expectations, and behavior. This new world created and was in turn shaped by the dominating trait of the late twentieth century in Scandinavia: the hugely expanded presence of the state, of government, of political decisions and political control of society and economy. By the end of the twentieth century, the welfare state or welfare society was highly developed, massive, a commanding presence in daily life. Deep down, its purpose may still have been to maintain equality while promoting prosperity, but along the line the clarity of original vision became blurred. From the 1960s on, politicians, civil servants, and academic experts increasingly saw the purpose of government as promoting equality of condition by directing people's lives in preferred directions, or, in the Swedish formulation, *att lägga livet till rätta*, "arranging life in the right way" so that individual behavior would promote collective goals. And who determined those goals? The elite, the politicians, the experts, and the civil servants. The growth of government had many reasons and justifications, chief among them the promotion of equality and a better society. But who defined *better*? That, too, changed, from the early egalitarian and progressive politicians and radical intellectuals of the early part of the century to the more complex spectrum of politicians, experts, academics, pressure groups, and special interests of the later years.

What, in all this change, happened to the strong, silent, modest, and long-suffering Scandinavian? The Swedish writer Kerstin

Ekman, author of a cycle of novels set in early twentieth century rural Sweden that focused on the clash between native goodness and the inflexible rules of a harsh Protestant moralism in a society of want, commented in 2000 that if the Nordics were once silent and self-sacrificing, they had since become loud and self-centered. "We were once the quiet ones, internalizing problems and difficulties. Now, we talk more than anybody about our problems. We have lost the power of reflection."[10] Indeed—and this leads to my final introductory vignette—contemporary Scandinavia, especially Denmark and Sweden, may strike foreigners, not least Americans, as exceptionally, often tastelessly uninhibited in speech, language, and customs. America, to be sure, has its share of exhibitionism and bad taste—witness the *Jerry Springer Show,* a huge favorite with Nordic audiences—but I doubt that the American public will soon be watching a government-sponsored prime-time TV spot like this one:

> An elegant young woman is cleaning up her dresser. She rummages through drawers, tossing various items aside. At the back of one drawer she finds a sex toy, a vibrator. She takes it out, looks at it, switches it on—nothing happens. Its batteries are dead. She swears rudely (the censorious beep is unknown in Scandinavia), leaves her apartment and is about to toss the vibrator down the garbage chute. At that moment the opposite door opens and an old lady sticks her head out. Embarrassed, the young woman puts the vibrator in her coat pocket. We next see her strolling along one of the artificial lakes in the center of Copenhagen with her dog. As soon as she thinks herself unobserved, she takes the vibrator from her pocket and tosses it into the lake. She then sits down at a cafe to order a cup of coffee. Camera pans to the lake, where her dog is retrieving the object. The dog rushes up to his mistress, wagging his tail and presenting her with the vibrator.[11]

That is the end of the spot, which was produced by the Danish Environmental Agency to send the message: don't discard used electrical appliances, but return them to authorized collection points.

BASIC ISSUES AND PATTERNS

This chapter interweaves discussion by issues with discussion of historical development and social change in order to paint a portrait of the political culture, social and economic characteristics, and international position and context of the Nordic nation-states which, in alphabetical order, are Denmark, Finland, Iceland, Norway, and Sweden. We begin at the core of what observers rightly consider the essence of what distinguishes the Nordic societies from the rest of the advanced industrial world, namely the particular Nordic configuration of values and social policy, encapsulated in two phrases, the "Nordic model" and the "welfare state" or "welfare society." Some people, including many Scandinavians, consider the Nordic welfare state as more than a mechanism for achieving social equality or taking care of the weak; to them, it is an expression of cultural identity, as stated by the former Danish minister of social services in the epigraph at the head of the chapter. It is therefore right that we begin and end with it and with its politico-cultural context, the so-called Nordic model of policymaking, which is also more than a matter of politics but rather expresses deeply rooted customs and manners.

---

[10]Interview in *Weekendavisen* (Copenhagen), October 6–12, 2000.

[11]Cruder examples abound. In the summer of 2000 the Danish Pharmaceutical Association launched a billboard campaign on how to combat various forms of fungus. It showed a large mushroom with accompanying, grossly explicit text about what other kinds of fungus—on feet, in the genital region—people might want to worry about. Again, Americans are also explicit, not least about their health or sex problems, but not, I think, at this public level and in this sort of official or semi-official context.

This section asks whether it makes sense to study the Nordic countries as a whole and raises and illustrates the question of internal similarities and differences among the countries. The next is an overview of the Nordic model, followed by sections on geography and history, the formation of the modern political and social systems, the rise and development of the welfare state, political culture, and the creation of the contemporary social, economic, cultural, and political landscape of the Nordic countries with particular emphasis on the period since around 1970. These are followed by an account of foreign and security policy, including the policies and politics of foreign aid, and concludes by asking what the future of the Nordic model and of the Nordic societies in general may be in the changed international and domestic political, cultural, and economic environment.

The chapter includes an argument about what is characteristic about Nordic societies and about their contemporary shape and direction. As you have seen, my basic answer to the first question is that what is characteristic is a particular notion of equality manifested in the political preferences and social policies of the twentieth century, and that these preferences and policies were themselves rooted in ideas and debates that took shape in the nineteenth century and which harked back to values of the Viking Age and the sagas. As for the character of contemporary Scandinavia, I advance two claims. One is that the influences shaping the political and social profile of the Nordic societies at the beginning of the twenty-first century became manifest during what one observer calls "the long 1970s," the period from around 1966 to around 1983, a time of profound ideological and cultural change which was only indirectly provoked by political and economic conditions, but all the more by the results of the vast social changes of the preceding generation.[12] The long 1970s produced, in interaction with international economic, political, and ideological conditions, the politics and value structures of contemporary Scandinavia, as exemplified by state feminism, environmentalism, and the transfer and subsidy state. What happened in those years also, and in ways hardly apparent at the time, prefigured the manner in which the Nordic countries would adapt to the large-scale changes in the international economic and political system of the later 1980s and 1990s; chief among them the end of the Cold War and the process of European political and economic integration.

The second claim is that all European societies and nation-states began to undergo, more or less willingly, processes of sometimes drastic adaptation to changed economic and political conditions, both domestically and internationally, in the last years of the twentieth century. These adaptations struck the Nordic societies more deeply and for a longer time, due to their particular mix of economic and political structures, values, and policies. It can be argued that the Nordic process of adaptation to the changing international environment was both longer and in some ways harder than that of, say, Britain or Germany.

The first section has already introduced, without explaining, various names for the region we are discussing. Here is some explanation. Since the early nineteenth century, Nordics themselves have preferred to speak of their region as *Norden,* the North, by which they mean the territory and peoples of the five nation-states. In the English-speaking world, the name *Scandinavia* used to be the most common designation; however, this suffers, from the Nordic point of view, from being primarily a geographical term referring to the Scandinavian Peninsula, which consists of the present-day territories of Sweden and Norway. Using Scandinavia to mean *Norden* thus risks excluding the Danes, Finns, and Icelanders, who do not live on the Scandinavian Peninsula. In this chapter, I will occasionally, for the

---

[12]Arvidsson 1999.

sake of variation, use Scandinavia as the equivalent of "Nordic region," "Nordic countries," or simply "the North," with the N capitalized to distinguish that name from the geographical direction.

A basic issue is whether the Nordic societies are similar enough to form the subject of a single chapter in a work such as this. Seen from within, the Nordic countries seem different, and it is true, as many point out, that most Nordic people who are not professionally or politically involved with common Nordic organizations, policies, or initiatives, do not spend much time thinking of themselves as part of a Nordic entity and that the influences that reach them from abroad come rather from the United States or the rest of Europe than from Nordic neighbors. Nevertheless, fundamental features of the history and politics of Nordic societies can reasonably be understood and explained as aspects of a single, if somewhat unwieldy and flexible entity, and reasons for this are given in the section on geopolitics and historical background below. As far as possible, joint features are emphasized and when examples of issues and developments are provided from one country, they are usually of a kind where similar examples could be chosen from the others. It is important not to overstate the similarities, and differences are noted wherever appropriate. We are dealing with five nation-states whose citizens consider their own countries no less independent or autonomous than those of France or Germany, but who nevertheless have more in common than do the British and the French, or the Germans and the Italians.

Were this chapter written twenty years ago, we would stress the differences and emphasize that the talk of a common Nordic identity was largely just that—talk to be deployed at the meetings of groups professionally involved with that airy concept, such as the Nordic Council. True, as we have seen, Nordic intellectuals swore by the idea of common Nordic values from the mid-nineteenth century on, but by the 1980s this often passionate commitment to a Nordic identity had degenerated to a mix of sentiment and official verbiage. Its chief practical expression was the rule that passports need not be shown when traveling within the Nordic region. Against this somewhat thin structure of common identity, solid facts could be adduced: the fact that Denmark, Norway, and Iceland were members of NATO, whereas Sweden and Finland were neutral; that Denmark was in the European Community (which later became the European Union or EU), while the others were not, or that despite the much-vaunted similarity of the Danish, Norwegian, and Swedish languages ordinary people found it increasingly difficult to understand each other, especially since the obligatory teaching of the other Nordic languages deteriorated in each of the three countries.

By 2000, this picture had changed. Only Iceland and Norway were now outside the EU, while the fall of the Soviet Union had transformed the problems of common security and reduced the significance of the unaligned posture of Sweden and Finland. Although all five nations, and the minority populations in them, were facing the same waves of globalization, American-inspired mass culture, and European integration, and one might therefore expect any common identity to be further eroded, signs of interest in regional character and in the particular qualities of regional culture, customs, and institutions had revived. The differences remained, and mutual understanding was no easier, since the educational authorities still had not seen fit to raise the standards for learning the languages of Sweden and Norway in Denmark and vice versa. But in a number of spheres, from the pan-Nordic expansion of the middle-class consumer taste exemplified by the IKEA furniture chain—which first spread from Sweden to Copenhagen in the 1960s—to the cross-fertilization and borrowing of popular culture, including rock music, among the countries, a subsoil of rich variation on certain basic and common themes survived and seemed likely to persist. From the vantage point of 2000, similarities or, better, a range of common values remained vital, although this range was quite a wide one. One needed only to look at the innumerable technical and bureaucratic incompatibilities exposed by the Copenhagen-Malmö bridge which, when it opened in 2000, was supposed to make it easier not just to travel and shop between Denmark and Sweden but to live in one country and work in the other, a half hour away by car or train. It was a symbol of these incompatibilities that Swedish trains stopped on green and moved on red whereas Danish trains did the opposite.

In general, the more you look at current policies, values, and social structures, the more striking the differences and the subtler the similarities that remain. We will encounter many examples of both differences and similarities in the following sections; here are just a few as preliminary illustrations. The first is about family policy. Norway permits voluntary joint taxation of the incomes of a husband and wife. If the spouses choose this option, the level at which the top rate of income tax applies is higher than for a single taxpayer. Norway also, uniquely in the region, grants parents a cash subsidy for child care that is not dependent on the parents' using government-approved day care; if they do use day care, the costs are tax deductible. Such policies show that the Norwegian government defends the nuclear family by making it easier for parents to bear the costs of rearing children in a high-tax, egalitarian society. By contrast, Denmark and Sweden have not allowed joint taxation since around 1970 and do not allow any deductions for child-rearing costs. Instead, they subsidize the cost of government-approved day care.

The gradient of differences is not uniform among the countries. If you look at the system of government and administration, at the way policy is developed, and at the relative power of central vs. regional and local government, Denmark and Sweden display substantial differences, a reflection of their historical legacies. But in other areas, notably the content of social policies, attitudes toward family and religion, and education, Denmark and Sweden fall toward the same end of the range of variations, with Finland, Iceland, and Norway at some distance toward the other end. The Danish and Swedish languages are also more closely related than either is to Norwegian, much less Icelandic. The Norwegians and the Finns display more conservative values, which are reflected in policy, whereas Danes and Swedes appear to be both more collectivist, willing to surrender power to government, and more individualistic, a seeming paradox to which we shall return. Danish-Swedish similarities vis-à-vis Norway in these fields were not obvious, though perhaps latently present, in the first few decades after World War II. In any case, they were then overshadowed by the joint Danish and Norwegian experience of German occupation and by joint feelings of mingled resentment of and inferiority to Sweden, seen—rightly—as richer, more powerful, and more ambitious.

But Denmark and Sweden are not the same either, even in values and social policies. In Denmark, to take a rather different example, prostitutes advertise on the Internet, whereas in Sweden and Norway prostitution is illegal, and customers risk arrest and having their names published. In the fall of 2000, a Danish prostitute successfully claimed a tax deduction for the business expense of having her breasts enlarged. This was challenged by the minister of taxation—yes, the Nordic countries each have such a creature—and the matter went to court. Such examples seem to confirm Denmark's reputation, stemming from the 1950s and 1960s, for sexual liberation and liberality in general. But is Denmark really more liberal? I already mentioned that in Denmark shops may not stay open more than a certain number of hours a week, which means that most shops close at 5:30 p.m. In Sweden all restrictions on opening hours were abolished in

1972. That was a liberal policy in the classic or European sense of a policy favoring free enterprise and consumer choice. Behind its often collectivist facade, Sweden in the 1990s developed a dynamic and international business culture that was the envy of Denmark and Norway. One is tempted, by analogy to American political usage, to say that Danes are often liberal in the American sense, that is, tolerant of what used to be called deviant or immoral behavior, but at the same time trusting in government to ensure desired social outcomes, whereas the Swedes, who also trust in government, nevertheless have a more commercially liberal and dynamic outlook when it comes to business innovation, modernization, and economic growth.

Works on Nordic society and politics face two traps. One is to overdo similarities by speaking insistently of the North or Scandinavia and not alluding to national cases. The other is to overdo the national distinctions, to qualify every statement by noting what country or countries of the five it applies to, or laboriously to explain everything by reference to all five countries. This chapter adopts a middle course. It focuses on major trends and developments, which are also those where common features and responses are most apparent or the variations most obvious. It gives concrete examples of policies, attitudes, and behavior without always explaining how far these apply beyond the particular country where they were found. It also tends to speak more of Denmark and Sweden than of Finland, Iceland, and Norway, not because the latter three are less important, but simply for reasons of space, convenience, and the patience of the reader, and because Denmark, and even more so Sweden, are the leading cases of the Nordic model and the welfare state. In return, the particular features of Finland, Iceland, and Norway—and the question whether these particular features should modify the general picture of a Nordic model of economics, politics, and policymaking—are limited, mostly, to the sections on historical background and the political systems.

Any description of a society and its functioning must be in terms of some theory of why the society works as it does. Whereas this account is intended as an explanatory and interpretive survey, it can be useful to show on one or two occasions how social scientific theories can be relevant and indeed necessary to understand social realities, and how those realities look different, depending on what theory one adopts. The main example chosen here is the welfare state itself, which as we have noted is fundamental in any account of Nordic society. We will see how what theory one adopts to account for Nordic social policy influences how one understands its history, mode of operation, and prospects for the future.

THE NORDIC MODEL

Standard accounts of the Nordic model of the welfare society often locate its beginning in the economic crisis years of the early 1930s. There is some truth to this, but in accordance with the argument that the Nordic model grew out of traditional values and out of the effort of earlier thinkers to revitalize those values one should view the model as evolving over a century and passing important thresholds in three eras of innovation and politico-cultural activity. The early 1930s was one such era, but so were the 1890s and the long 1970s. For two decades since the early 1980s, the model appeared to be in a phase of consolidation, with many policy initiatives but few genuinely new ideas. Observers at century's end wondered how long it would survive without needing another phase of innovation and reform. European integration, globalization, and the opening and expansion of global markets for capital and goods were among the external factors that indicated a need for reform and modernization of the Nordic transfer and subsidy states. Among internal factors were the demographic projections that indicated that, to survive, the welfare societies needed more taxpayers and in particular more highly skilled taxpayers to add value to the economy from which the revenues to fund social services and transfers must come. At the same time, many Nordic taxpayers, responding to economic incentives, were working less and taking earlier retirement than ever before, a trend that, if continued, would indeed imperil the state's ability to deliver on its promises.

Contradictory strains and pressures in the model's external environment thus contrasted with the model's apparent stagnation. Though the 1980s and 1990s were not a time of great policy innovation, they were years of intense debate on the direction and future of the Nordic model. One observer commented in 1984 that "the Nordic dilemma is the tension between equity and liberty: how to stimulate and ensure pluralism within a frozen structure of institutions."[13] This observer, sympathetic to the Nordic welfare society, was making a sharper criticism than he knew, for one of the problems of these years was precisely that liberty was not at a premium. Instead, leading politicians such as the Swedish prime minister Olof Palme (1929–1986, prime minister from 1969) spoke of "equality and equity," not liberty, as the goals of policy and of "realizing freedom not against the collective, but through and within the collective."[14] Palme's use of the word "collective" to mean "one's fellow-citizens, one's society" was, perhaps unintentionally, chilling. For it was the same word used by the totalitarian communist regimes then still in power in Eastern Europe to describe the anonymous groups that everywhere, at work and outside work, represented the ubiquitous power and will of the state to crush dissent and enforce conformity of belief and behavior. It also expressed Palme's passionate belief that individual liberty in itself was of no value and might be dangerous, because it permitted the strong to dominate the weak.

Until now the terms *welfare state, welfare society,* and *Nordic model* have been used interchangeably to describe what gives politics and society in the Nordic region their distinctive flavor and identity. One crude measure of that distinctive flavor is that the number of people employed by all levels of government in Denmark, Norway, and Sweden is more than 30 percent of the workforce in these countries, whereas the average for the rest of the European Union is 16.5 percent, barely half the Nordic level. Another is that the value of all taxes, direct and indirect, in Denmark, Norway, and Sweden, amounts to half or slightly more of the gross domestic product or GDP. A third is that the total value of public expenditure, including salaries to government employees, public investment, and transfers and subsidies, in those three countries is in the range of 55 to 60 percent of GDP, with the figures for the rest of the OECD (Organization for Economic Cooperation and Development) area being about twenty percentage points lower both for the value of taxes and the amount of public expenditure.[15] These are countries, in other words, where government or the public sector is a dominant, if not the dominant, factor in the economy as well as in society and in the world-view and mentality of the citizens.

These figures are one measure of the status of the Nordic welfare society at the year 2000. Clearly, we are dealing with something quite different from what Americans mean when they speak of welfare. To most Americans, welfare is something they never encounter, a system of emergency assistance to marginal people, most of whom are not part of the normally functioning economy, and whose numbers in any case shrank in the 1990s boom. Economists and sociologists have a broader definition. The word welfare literally means that which makes people fare well, that is, live

---

[13]Dahl 1984, 107.

[14]Arvidsson 1999, 41.

[15]OECD 2000, 42, SAF 2000, 51, 53.

out their full potential. Hence, welfare to economists and sociologists consists of all the tools and policies that give people the best chances to live out their full potential. Ultimately, welfare in this sense cannot be distinguished from the social, political, and economic system of a society as a whole. All societies provide welfare; they differ in how they do it and how well they succeed.[16]

To understand the politics and culture of the North, it is necessary to forget the narrow definition of welfare as "emergency benefits" and to understand that, to Nordics, welfare is a word with strong positive connotations and one that describes not something unusual or reserved for emergencies, but something that everyone encounters at all stages of life. Welfare in the colloquial American sense does have a Nordic equivalent, and that is the emergency assistance available to people who have no other source of income, such as a regular job, a pension, or regular unemployment benefits. But this assistance is only a minute and not very important part of that vast and complex structure known as the Nordic welfare state or welfare society.

In Nordic parlance, the phrases welfare state and welfare society refer to much the same thing, but with a difference of emphasis. The welfare state is the structure of government, agencies, and institutions that collect taxes and deliver services. When people refer to the welfare society, it implies that this structure, with its dominant public sector, its heavy tax burden, and its government-funded provision of education, health care, and the special subsidies available to many different categories of people and activity, is not generally perceived as a cost or a burden, but as an asset, something worth maintaining and cherishing. A welfare society is something to which all contribute and from which all benefit, a form of collectivized solidarity. The underlying assumption, which only few openly doubt, is that this welfare society is indeed what its name promises, that is, a system of nationwide, universal care that supports everyone's quality of life while simultaneously promoting social and economic equality of condition. Because this assumption remains strong, promises to cut taxes have little appeal in Nordic countries, even though those countries have the highest tax burdens in the world. This is because if taxes are cut, the level of public services must also be cut, and since everyone uses or relies on these services, a threat to cut them is perceived as a threat to everyone's well-being.

The idea of a Nordic model in the fuller sense involves more than the welfare state. It includes the social, economic, and political environment, practices, and traditions that made the welfare state possible and desirable to large majorities, in part by ensuring or appearing to ensure both increasing prosperity and substantial redistribution of wealth. In this sense, the economic and institutional aspects of the Nordic model of welfare state comprise the following characteristics and expectations, which are enumerated here in summary form to give background for the subsequent discussion. The points will be covered again in their historical and political context later in the chapter.

- Labor market cooperation in the shape of "a set of agreements to limit conflict between capital and labor." This definition neatly places the model in its historical context, namely the time when the words capital and labor had easily definable sociological senses[17]

- Full employment; this has been an overriding goal for various ideological and fiscal reasons since World War II, though it did not originally include married women: the fiscal reason is that the welfare state

---

[16]The classic account of welfare in this broader, sociological sense is Wilensky 1975.

[17]Weaver 1987, 292–293.

requires the highest possible number of contributors, that is taxpayers; the ideological reason is that work provides dignity and identity
- Consensus and compromise in political decisions
- The "strong society," a notion implying that people flourish when their social environment is strong; but it is important for understanding Nordic values that society is here understood as something to be nourished and directed by government acting on the basis of popular consensus
- Universalist social service provision
- Centralized organization of society
- Corporatism, the idea that major economic and political decisions are made in negotiations among government, the trade unions, which include over 80 percent of the workforce, and perhaps, but hardly always, business
- Women's full right to paid employment; again, as in the case of the full employment goal, there were both fiscal and ideological reasons for this demand, which from the 1960s was emphatically expanded to include married women: women need to work to provide taxes; women should not be dependent on a male breadwinner; each worker is held responsible for him or herself[18]

Some elements of what this model means in practice can be seen from the following list of characteristics of the model at the end of the twentieth century:

- More state intervention and government responsibility than in other advanced societies
- The largest single share of the workforce is employed in the social and educational sectors
- The largest share of public sector employees is also found in these sectors
- For historical reasons, Nordics view government and its role as more legitimate than other Europeans and especially Anglo-Saxons
- Social rights—to education, health care, pensions, subsidies, transfers—are based on citizenship or residence and not on participation in the labor market
- Welfare systems are not class based or means-tested; they include the rich as well
- These systems are generous and redistributive
- Benefits and services provided in kind play a greater role than cash transfers; that is, people are not given money to spend on services as they want; the services are provided whether people use them or not

An interesting twist to the definition of the Nordic model is provided by the Swedish political scientist Leif Lewin, for whom the essence of the model is a style of policymaking. He sees it emerging, in its Swedish version, in stages from the 1866 reform of government, which marked an important move in the direction of popular representation, to 1917, when the principle was established that governments should be drawn from the groups representing a majority of the voters. In his account of Swedish political development, these decisive political changes reflected a politics of compromise in which all preferences were honored and everyone got something.[19] The welfare state, on this view, is simply one, if perhaps the most significant, result of policies deliberately arrived at by methods of compromise and consensus-seeking.

The Nordic model is thus both a tradition of politics and a set of policies and practices emerging from that tradition. As indicated above, these were all based on an underlying

---

[18] Petterson 1994, 32–33.

[19] Bosworth & Rivlin 1987, 318–321, and Lewin 1988.

preference for equality as a national political and social goal. The Nordic model also implies something that is no longer, in the twenty-first century, as self-evident as it once was, and that is national homogeneity. If you have an economy where government takes more than half your income in return for promising to take care of major life obligations such as educating your children, protecting your health, and taking care of your aged relatives, and if the right to these benefits depends on residence and citizenship, then the entire society is part of an implied social contract in which everyone gives to everyone else via the public sector. Such a universalist system becomes part of your national identity. If citizens sense that nonmembers of society are exploiting the system or that it is under threat from other systems better able to satisfy their members, its legitimacy may begin to dwindle, and that is precisely what some observers argue will occur in the twenty-first century.

The legitimacy of the Nordic model as a welfare state and as a way of doing politics and organizing society rests on other unspoken assumptions, such as the steady growth in public spending and hence in public power and public employment. Doubts about the system's long-term viability began the moment that the rising curve of public spending hit its limit in the 1980s, a point to which we shall return.

GEOGRAPHY, PEOPLES, LANGUAGES, AND HISTORICAL LEGACIES

The Nordic countries are the most northerly independent states in the world. The smallest in size and most southerly of them, Denmark, reaches just below the 55th degree of latitude; the North Cape of Norway, the top of mainland Scandinavia, is well above the Arctic Circle at about 71 degrees. By coincidence, Alaska fills about the same gap, with the southernmost tip of the panhandle on the same latitude as southern Denmark, and Barrow on the north coast at that of the North Cape. In addition to Denmark and mainland Scandinavia, which includes, from west to east, Norway, Sweden, and Finland, the region includes the thinly inhabited volcanic island of Iceland, located some four hours by plane to the northwest of central Scandinavia. These five independent states have one obvious trait in common, and that is that their national flags share the same pattern, a horizontal Latin cross on a field of a single color. In Iceland and Norway, the cross is double, one inside the other. The pattern originated in Denmark, whose flag, a white cross on red known as the *Dannebrog* or "colored cloth of the Danes," came down from heaven, according to legend, on June 15, 1219.[20] This took place in Estonia, which the Danish king Waldemar II conquered. Turning from legend to history, sources describe a Danish cross banner in the thirteenth century. When Sweden became independent of Denmark in the sixteenth century, the Swedes adopted the same style of flag, but with a yellow cross on blue instead of white on red. The Norwegians, when they in turn became independent of Denmark in 1814, put a blue cross to symbolize liberty inside the white cross of the *Dannebrog* for their flag. The Finns later chose blue on white, to symbolize the lakes and snow of their northern land, and the Icelanders, last of the five to achieve sovereignty from Denmark in 1944 chose a red cross within a white on a blue field.

The Nordic region also includes the former Danish colony and now self-governing territory of Greenland, the largest island in

---

[20]The white cross on red was a crusading symbol of the period and also became the flag of the Sovereign Military Order of Malta (the Knights of Malta, established during the First Crusade at the end of the eleventh century, and today a Catholic lay order that runs hospitals and other charitable services). Waldemar's expedition to Estonia was a military crusade to conquer and convert the pagan Ests.

the world, consisting of 95 percent ice and with some 55,000 people clinging to a few settlements, mostly on the western coastal edge of the ice. Geologically, Greenland is part of the North American continental plate and its capital, Nuuk (formerly Godthåb), is closer to New York than to Copenhagen. Greenland stretches from the 60th to the 84th degree of latitude. It has its own flag, which is deliberately not cast in the cross and field pattern of the *Dannebrog* but uses the same colors, red and white, to symbolize a sun rising over the horizon.

The Nordic region includes a few other special territories. In the North Atlantic between Iceland and Norway we find another Danish dependency, the autonomous Faeroe Islands, home to some 40,000 people who raise sheep, fish, harvest eiderdown, occasionally—to the fury of environmentalist ideologues—hunt killer whales, and speak their own Nordic language, closer to Icelandic than to Danish. Also in the North Atlantic, but much further north, are some Norwegian islands: the volcano of Jan Mayen and the archipelago of Svalbard, some six hundred miles northwest of the north coast of Norway, formerly valuable for its mineral deposits but today largely reserved to Arctic tourists and explorers. In the Baltic, between Sweden and Finland, are the self-governing Åland islands, an archipelago of 25,000 Swedish-speakers under Finnish overlordship. Finally, the Nordic countries are home to various minority populations who do not enjoy political autonomy. The two most important such groups—not counting the largely non-European and nonwhite refugees and immigrants that have come since the 1960s—are the Germans of south Jutland and the 50,000 Lapps or Sami of northern Norway, Sweden, and Finland, the region informally known as Lapland.[21]

Not counting the Atlantic elements of the region, the most westerly point of the central Scandinavian countries is in Norway at just short of 5 degrees of eastern longitude. The easternmost point is a place on the present-day Finnish-Russian border, but Norway reaches almost as far east, for that huge and elongated land continues across the top of both Sweden and Finland to abut the Kola Peninsula of Russia at about 31 degrees of eastern longitude. Why Norway goes so far north and east is the result of history, as is so much else.

Although the Nordic countries fill the same tier of latitude as Alaska, they enjoy a milder climate. Crops will grow to near the Arctic Circle, which is unimaginable in Alaska, and although agriculture ceased being essential to the Nordic economies in the 1960s, being able to grow food was, in earlier centuries, a precondition of permanent human settlement and later of national independence. The milder climate is due to the Gulf Stream which flows off the west coast of Norway which consequently has some of the wettest as well as mildest weather in the region. Further east the Gulf Stream has a less dramatic effect, and winters can be cold and long in northern Sweden and Finland. Even so, the Baltic Sea and its continuations, the shallow Gulfs of Bothnia and of Finland, bring Gulf Stream water into the heart of eastern Scandinavia and attenuate what would otherwise be a harsh continental climate. The effect can be dramatic: just east of the Baltic it is not unusual to have snow in early May, whereas it is rare indeed only 100 miles east across the water in southern Sweden and Denmark.

Denmark, the smallest of the countries, is flat, densely populated, and consists, within its

---

[21]Sami is the name preferred by the people themselves. The name Lapp comes from a Finnish word meaning "those who live to the side." The name Lapp became current in Finnish, Swedish, and Russian, whereas Norwegians in older times referred to the Lapps as Finns, as in *Finmark*, the Norwegian name for northernmost Norway, meaning the region of the Lapps—not of the Finns. This variation may have very old origins. The Greek explorer Pytheas, who may have visited the area about 300 B.C., spoke of a people he called *fennoi* or Finns and which were almost certainly Lapps whom he met in what is now Norway. Perhaps that is what they then called themselves, or were called by their Indo-European speaking neighbors.

Copenhagen, Denmark.

present-day borders, of the Jutland peninsula and a number of islands, the most important of which is Zealand where the capital, Copenhagen, is located. The capital region is home to a third of the entire population of 5.3 million. The other countries are all much bigger and more thinly populated. Sweden, the largest both in size and population, stretches a thousand miles from south to north. Two thirds of its territory is forest and today the 8.8 million inhabitants live mostly in the clearings, valleys, coastal areas, and lowlands with the greatest concentrations around Stockholm in the east, Gothenburg in the west, and the formerly Danish city of Malmö in the south. Norway is almost as large as Sweden but dramatically more mountainous, with only parts of the coastline and the shores of the major inlets or fjords suitable for habitation. The main ridges of the Scandinavian mountains, which belong geologically to the same era as the Appalachians in North America or the Highlands of Scotland, run through Norway, making internal travel difficult until modern times, when Norwegian engineers became the world's most skilled tunnelers. The population of 4.2 million is heavily concentrated in the Oslo Fjord region and the extreme south-east of present-day Norway where the land is less rugged, with secondary concentrations on the long west coast. Finland is named *Suomi* in Finnish, which means the land of a thousand lakes; in fact, present-day Finland has about thirty thousand lakes and even more islands. With few mountains, much of the land is easily accessible by road or boat, but inland from the Baltic the climate worsens and sources of income are few. Therefore the 5.1 million people live mostly within 50 miles of the southern and south-western coasts. Iceland, finally, is geologically the youngest, being a volcanic island that emerged from the Mid-Atlantic Ridge about a million years ago. Although four times the size of Denmark it has only a fraction of the population, about 270,000. Iceland is thus a nation the size of a smallish European or American city. It is also the youngest nation, since Icelanders have the highest fertility rate among the Nordics and tend to procreate somewhat earlier. Iceland displays several other unusual sociological features (discussed later).

You may have noticed that "present-day" is stressed when mentioning the dimensions or location of countries. This is because the contemporary configuration of five independent states in their current borders only dates from 1944, when Iceland achieved full sovereignty and Finland lost the eastern part of its ancient province of Karelia to the Soviet Union for good. Nor is it clear that the age of changes is over: Denmark granted Greenland home rule within the "realm of Denmark" in 1979, while at century's end some Faeroese were agitating for complete independence. Although the native populations have been around for thousands of years, the states in which they live and the borders between those states have changed drastically.

Continuous human settlement in the region dates from the later phases of the last Ice Age, a time about ten thousand years ago when central Scandinavia was still under ice and the sea levels much lower than today. Few traces remain of these earliest hunter-gatherers because they lived near the shoreline which is now under water, for example in the North Sea which did not exist then. For millennia, scattered paleolithic tribes, probably not more than a few thousand people in all, lived from time to time at various spots along the coastline, which withdrew as the ice melted and the sea level rose. For a time about five to six thousand years ago the shoreline of northern Denmark was higher and the climate substantially warmer than today throughout southern Scandinavia and comparable to that of the coastal Pacific Northwest today.[22] The disappearing ice-sheet over northern Scandinavia left another legacy. As the weight of ice disappeared, the land-surface of northern Finland and Sweden began to rise and is still rising rapidly at about one centimeter (0.4 inches) a year or more than three feet every century. This is making the Gulf of Bothnia shallower and narrower as the waters are being tipped gradually into the southern Baltic.

Ancestors of the current native populations of Denmark, Norway, Sweden, and Finland probably filtered into the region from the south some three to four thousand years ago. Older scholarship assumed that when burial habits and material culture changed, so did the people and their language. In the later third millennium B.C., a new type of pottery, the so-called Corded Ware, spread, along with the custom of single rather than group graves, across much of central and northern Europe. It was tempting to assume that these new styles meant new people, that these new people dominated and replaced the previous inhabitants, and to identify the new settlers with Indo-Europeans who, in the Nordic region, would become the North Germanic speakers of later ages. More recent scholarship is less sure that new styles of pottery or burial mean that a group of newcomers speaking a new language physically moved in and displaced the earlier inhabitants, transforming both the ethnic composition and the language of the region. Nor are the links between changes in material culture, changes in population, and language change as clear as they once seemed. Nevertheless, some sort of major cultural change spread to most of Scandinavia around 2000 B.C., and it was probably around this time that most people of the Nordic region became speakers of an Indo-European language, whether by peaceful

---

[22]This puts the claims of an alleged global warming into perspective. Average temperatures even in historic times have undergone greater changes than predicted by those who believe in man-made global warming. As for the warm phase of the paleolithic, the so-called Litorina period, the average temperature in July was then four degrees centigrade above today, which would have made Denmark about as warm as Seattle and snow in winter a rare event.

adoption, physical displacement, or—more probably—a combination.

One reason that modern archaeologists doubt that a wave of Indo-Europeans using Corded Ware pottery moved like a front through Scandinavia bringing an entirely new population to the region is that Corded Ware culture spread to southern and western Finland, but Indo-European speech did not. Ethnically, as measured by blood type frequencies and other genetic markers, Finns and Swedes are indistinguishable. Culturally, both populations show a gradient, which can be traced far back in the archaeological record, from a southern, agrarian, European social type as found in Denmark to a northern and eastern, nomadic and hunting pattern of life related to that of the early populations of northern Russia and Siberia.[23] But if Swedes and Finns for millennia have had much the same sociogeographic profile, the languages of the historic peoples of the two countries are utterly distinct. Finnish constitutes with Samic or Lapp and Estonian a branch of the Uralic language family which also includes, as very remote relatives, Hungarian and some languages of northern Siberia. Swedish, by contrast, which is also the native language of about ten percent of Finns, belongs with Danish to the East Nordic subgroup of North Germanic languages; the West Nordic subgroup comprises Norwegian, Faeroese, and Icelandic.

Danish and Swedish are close siblings; indeed the dialects of southern Sweden, especially of the Skåne region, which used to be part of Denmark, have as much in common with east Danish dialects as with those of central Sweden. Danish and Swedish are closer to each other than full-fledged Scots is to standard English. The main difference is that Danish at some point between the fifteenth and seventeenth centuries adopted a stress accent, whereas Swedish, like Norwegian and Icelandic, retained the original Nordic system of pitch accents, which gives those languages a lilting, musical sound. Another difference that has accelerated in the past century is that Danes tend to pronounce distinctly only the stressed syllable of every word, with the others being swallowed in a drawn-out mumble. Recordings of educated speakers of standard Danish who were born in the nineteenth century show that this change or, as many would have it, deterioration is of recent date. In Swedish, Norwegian, and Icelandic all syllables, whatever their pitch, are clearly enunciated. This makes it generally easier for a Dane to understand a Swede or Norwegian than vice versa.

Faeroese and Icelandic cannot be understood by other Nordic speakers. Norwegian or, more correctly, the Norwegian languages, are, although West Nordic, comprehensible to Danes and Swedes. The reason for this is that Norway, which was one of the three original kingdoms of the North, fell under Danish domination in the fourteenth century. Thereafter the language of administration and instruction and, after the Reformation, of religion, was Danish, which at that time was more similar to its Nordic sister languages than today. Norwegian ceased to be written and survived only in the form of rural dialects, primarily in the west of the country. When Norway regained its sovereignty from Denmark in 1814, Danish was the language of Norway, though spoken with the local intonation. Some Norwegians, led by the schoolteacher Ivar Aasen and influenced by the contemporary Romantic idea that the language of a nation manifests its true and mystical identity, determined to resurrect the old Norwegian language. By 1850, they had recreated a Norwegian language on the basis of the surviving dialects of the west country. This resurrected Norwegian, known as *landsmål,* "language of the country," and later as *nynorsk* or New Norwegian, became the language of instruction and communication in much of western Norway, while the eastern part with the capital of Oslo and about three

---

[23]Carpelan in Norrback et al. 1993–99, 1:178–180.

quarters of the population continued to speak and write in a local form of Danish called *riksmål,* "language of the realm" or *bokmål,* "book-speech." Both this Norwegian Danish and the resurrected New Norwegian came in various types. The most extreme variant of New Norwegian was deeply obscure to *bokmål* speakers, but even it was not as alien as Icelandic, because the dialects used to create New Norwegian were themselves influenced by Danish and because they had dropped the archaic inflections and conjugations retained in Icelandic. Thus it was possible for politicians from the late nineteenth century by a series of reforms to Norwegianize *bokmål* by changing the Danish endings and grammar, and to promote, in the west of the country, a milder version of New Norwegian comprehensible to others. So, although Norway in the year 2000 still had two major variants of its language, they were not as far apart as they were in 1850.

History as distinct from prehistory begins when it is possible, however crudely, to reconstruct the story of events on the basis of written sources of one kind or another. In this sense history began late in Scandinavia, since it is not until the tenth century that we can begin to tell a consecutive, coherent tale. But the oldest written document from the North is some six centuries older. It is, or was, the golden drinking-horn found by a farm-girl in the earth near Gallehus in southern Jutland in 1635. Almost a century later, another, smaller golden horn was found nearby. They no longer exist. In 1802 they were stolen from the royal art collection and melted down.

No one knows how the horns came to be where they were found. Both were covered with figures, and the larger horn also carried a runic inscription which read "I, Lægæst of Holt [or son of Holt], made the horn."[24] The language was Primitive Germanic, so archaic in form that it was not yet recognizably Nordic. Indeed, the Gallehus inscription is the oldest evidence of any Germanic language. Many have found it symbolic that the first word in the oldest piece of writing in the North is the word "I"—a harbinger of the proud individualism of the Nordic peoples?

Our records for early Nordic history are a mixture of legend and memories of actual people and events. The most detailed early chronicle, the *Deeds of the Danes* written in convoluted Latin by Saxo Grammaticus in the twelfth century, contained many stories, legends, and poems that, if Saxo had not preserved them in his Latin translations, would have been lost. When we can compare Saxo to other evidence we can speak of history, and this does not begin to be the case until the middle of the Viking Age in the tenth century. At that time the process by which the three national kingdoms of Denmark, Norway, and Sweden crystallized out of the power-struggles of local chieftains and princes was almost complete.

In Norway, these struggles provoked the departure of some thousands of people who did not want to live under a king; starting in the late ninth century, they sailed with their ponies and other gear in open boats almost a thousand miles due west across some of the roughest water in the world, the North Atlantic, and settled Iceland, which had formerly been visited only by the occasional Irish hermit. Iceland therefore is "the only European society whose origins are known."[25] In Iceland, these antimonarchists established a unique society. As the literary critic and Anglo-Saxon scholar Tom Shippey noted, "it was a country that ought to have been a Utopia. It had no foreign policy, no defence forces, no king, no lords, no peasants, no dispossessed aborigines, no battles (till late on), no dangerous animals,

---

[24]For language buffs, the original read *ek hlewagastir holtijar horna tawido.* The *-ijar* ending of *holt-* is a genitive either of descent or of place. *horna* is accusative singular of horn. *tawido,* first person singular of the past tense, is the remote ancestor of the English word *did* in the sense of "make."

[25]Tomasson 1980, 4.

and no very clear taxes. What, given this blank slate, could possibly go wrong? Why is their literature all about killing each other?"[26] Of course the Icelandic sagas are not all about killing each other, but they are about passion, wealth, and social and sexual status.

Iceland was thus Nordic, but with differences lasting to the present. Since we will not be speaking much about Iceland in later sections, I will mention them here. For one thing, as already mentioned, the Icelanders are few. They know each other better than the inhabitants of a smallish city of the same size in America, for unlike any real-life American city, Iceland has accepted little non-Nordic immigration. The U.S. personnel at the air base of Keflavik, established during World War II, are not encouraged to mingle much with the locals. Icelanders treasure their national characteristics, which include strong traditions of singing and tale-telling. Although the national religion in Iceland, as in the rest of the Nordic region, is Lutheran Protestantism, Icelanders retain many customs and beliefs from the pagan past, for example the belief that everyone has a guardian spirit, a *fylgja,* or that it is bad luck to mention a child's name until it is christened. With few exceptions, they have no regular surnames but use patronymics, as did other Nordics until the seventeenth-eighteenth century: Sveinn's son Einar is Einar Sveinsson, and Einar's son Björn is in turn Björn Einarsson, whereas his daughter Gudrun is Gudrun Einarsdottir. And all of them—Sveinn, Einar, Björn, and Gudrun—are listed under their Christian names in the telephone book. First you find the Gudruns and then run down the list to the Gudrun Einarsdottirs, who will be numerous but not that numerous, until you find the one you want through the address.

Another difference is that the Icelanders were the only Nordic nation with a fertility rate greater than replacement until they, too, dropped below it in the later 1990s. All the others have not been replacing themselves since the 1970s, though the Norwegians have come closest. Iceland still has the region's highest fertility rate as well as the youngest median age. The Nordic model of welfare society is also somewhat different in Iceland. Benefits and pensions are funded to a greater degree through actuarially sound insurance systems and not through general taxation as in the rest of the region. Icelanders also depart from the general Nordic or European pattern of behavior in that they show no desire to shorten their working lives. Everywhere else in Europe the average age of retirement fell in the last decades of the twentieth century and was effectively about 60 years in Scandinavia by 2000; an unsustainable age, given that the workforce would soon begin to shrink as the effects of declining fertility began to make themselves felt in the small cohorts of young people. In Iceland, however, where they had more babies, they also worked longer. The average age of retirement in Iceland in 2000 was just short of 70 years, an absolute world record. Icelanders start working early, too. All schoolchildren from 14 and up are given easy summer jobs, mostly in the open air, by the local authorities. The common element in all these distinctive traits is that Icelanders consider their country, its culture and economy as a joint family asset for which everyone is, in a serious way, responsible and which you can rely on others to protect as you do yourself. So you work hard, put in more value than you take out, and have at least two children early so that life, and Iceland, can continue.[27]

By around 1000 the new Nordic kings and many of their people were Christian. Having established monarchies, the kings began competing with each other to see who was the

---

[26] Quoted on the back of Byock 1988.

[27] On the Icelandic version of the Nordic model, see Olafsson 1999. The same scholar is publishing, in 2001, an English translation of his book *The Icelandic Way* which explains the subject in more detail. A lively book on modern Icelandic life and society, but with little on politics or the welfare state as such, is Lacy 1999.

strongest and where the frontiers between the kingdoms would run. In a sense this chapter did not end until 1905, when Norway left the union with Sweden. Until the mid-seventeenth century, Denmark was the strongest, most populous, and richest of the three. In the early eleventh century, Danish kings, notably Canute the Great, ruled England, the most prosperous part of Norway, and large parts of Sweden.[28] Norway, as we saw, lost its independence in the later fourteenth century to Denmark and was reduced to the status of a mere province in 1536. All three kingdoms looked different than they do today. Denmark included what is now southern Sweden, Norway included large parts of what is now western Sweden, and Sweden included Finland, which, unlike Norway, was never an independent state before 1918. Finland was the eastern part of Sweden. Many of the people spoke the strange Finnish language but that did not make them less Swedish. Unlike the Norwegians, the Finns had no early history of statehood to look back to. Sweden conquered Finland starting with the so-called "First Crusade" of 1155 and culminating in the peace with Novgorod (Russia) in 1323. From then until the end of the Great Northern War (1700–1721), Finland included the Karelian Isthmus and the coastal town of Viborg (Viipuri in Finnish), the "key to Finland."

From 1397–1523 Danish kings ruled in all three kingdoms in the Union of Kalmar, though the Swedes were often in rebellion. Scholars trace the strengthening of a distinctive Swedish national identity based on anti-Danish self-assertion to the first of these rebellions in 1435. For three centuries after Sweden regained independence in 1523, it was "an axiom of Swedish policy that Denmark was the unsleeping enemy."[29] The fact that these two peoples easily understood one another's language was no bar to this mutual hatred, which was greater among Swedes than among Danes. This hatred, whether reasonable or not, of the Dane or "the Jute", as the Swedes often called him, recognizing the Jutes as the toughest of Danes, was not merely diplomatic or military. More atavistic images survived. As late as the nineteenth century, peasants in Småland in southern Sweden believed that Danes were not human, but werewolves.[30]

In the 1520s and 1530s, the Protestant Reformation, the most profound transformation of the Nordic societies after Christianization five centuries earlier and before the social and economic revolutions four centuries later, swept through the North. In both kingdoms, popular mass movements claiming to demystify Christianity and restore the pure teaching of the Gospels joined with royal power and aristocratic greed in dismantling the established church, abolishing the sacramental ministry and the Latin rites, and confiscating church lands and wealth. Although the mass of the people probably resented the Catholic church somewhat less than Nordic schoolchildren were once taught they did, the Reformation clearly rode on strong waves of popular demand. The high point was reached in Denmark in 1536, when the leading Lutheran reformer, Hans Tavsen, stepped in to protect his enemies, the bishops, assembled for a diet of estates in Copenhagen, from an enraged lynch mob of burgers. Within days the old hierarchy was abolished in Denmark, and state officers, called superintendents, installed as regional overseers of the new parish-based national Lutheran church. In Sweden, the bishops were retained but stripped of their property and status. In both kingdoms, the church leaders were henceforth to be mere administrators, not landowners or spiritual leaders within an

---

[28]Canute or Knut Sveinsson Danakonung (998–1035), as he was known to his Norse-speaking subjects, is buried in his English capital of Winchester.

[29]Roberts 1979, 7.

[30]Ibid., 68.

international organization owing allegiance to anyone other than the king.

It is hard to overrate the long-term significance of the Reformation in Scandinavia. The national Lutheran churches became, in the eyes of the vast majority, expressions both of true Christianity and of national identity. Even when Christianity ceased to have daily meaning for most Nordics, as happened during the twentieth century, people retained a sense that their *folkekirke,* the church of the people, was part of themselves and a keystone of the nation. More than four fifths were still baptized and buried in church at the end of the twentieth century and over 90 percent were members of the national churches. As suggested earlier, the post-Reformation social order based on the parish and emphasizing social discipline, literacy, and mutual protection within the parish was one of the roots of the Nordic model and the welfare state.

By the mid-seventeenth century Sweden gained the upper hand in the competition with Denmark thanks to its superior fiscal and administrative system, a creation of the first king of independent Sweden, the savvy and ruthless Gustavus I (ruled 1523–1560). This system was unique in Europe for its streamlined and goal-directed ability to wring taxes and soldiers out of the people with a minimum of waste and inefficiency. Sweden had the advantage of being able to construct a system of government from scratch and also the paradoxical advantage of being too poor to rely, as did other European states, on mercenaries and on bribes to win diplomatic victories. Much of the relentlessly rational character of this early modern Swedish state survives in the Swedish edition of the welfare state, chiefly in the notion that government knows best and in the same government's conscious and determined will to shape the people in the people's interests, which it is the job of government to determine.

Thanks to its superior efficiency as well as to the export revenues earned by its iron and copper mines, Sweden briefly became a European great power and was one of the three main signatories to the peace of Westphalia that put an end to the destructive Thirty Years' War in 1648 and established the ground rules of international relations that largely still apply today. Shortly after, the Swedes carried out the most brilliant strike in Nordic military history when, in late 1657, they invaded Denmark from the south and then, in the ice winter that followed, crossed the frozen straits to Copenhagen and shocked the Danish king into ceding the eastern third of his country, which became the south Swedish region of Skåne, today home to a fourth of Sweden's people. These Swedish victories confirmed Swedes in their belief that the Swedes were the most heroic, the oldest, and the noblest of all the nations of the world, a claim first made at the Church Council of Basel in 1434 by a Swedish bishop, Ragnvald of Växjö.[31]

Military greatness was not to last. By 1721, Sweden was exhausted, starving, and defeated by a coalition of enemies. Although they kept their Danish and Norwegian provinces, the Swedes had to give big chunks of Finland to Russia, and in 1809 the rest of Finland followed after a short war in which the Swedish commanders, despite exceptions of conspicuous skill and heroism, made almost every error in the book, a far cry from the dash and skill of a century earlier. Fortunately for Sweden, its new crown prince, the French count Bernadotte, was able to switch sides in the then-raging Napoleonic wars so that Sweden joined the winning coalition and extorted Norway from Denmark in 1814. The Norwegians quickly anticipated this by declaring independence and giving themselves a free constitution first. Bernadotte, who was now the king of Sweden, promised to respect this constitution, and for ninety years Sweden and Norway were a genuine joint monarchy, with Norway having its own parliament and administrative system, unlike earlier when it was subject to Denmark.

---

[31] Ibid., 70–72.

Later in the nineteenth century, Denmark suffered a further and final loss of territory when the creator of united Germany, the Prussian chancellor Otto von Bismarck, took advantage of some exceptionally incompetent Danish politicians who virtually invited the Prussians to attack although those same politicians had done nothing to strengthen Denmark's defenses. The war was over the south Danish or north German provinces of Schleswig and Holstein. These had for centuries been governed jointly from Copenhagen, but as German-speaking provinces and not as part of the Danish kingdom. In the mid-nineteenth century, Danish nationalists wanted to draw a new border to include those inhabitants of Schleswig who considered themselves Danes and excluding all the rest, who wanted to be part of a larger German entity. Unfortunately this attempt violated the ancient agreement that the provinces be united forever, and Bismarck was therefore legally justified in opposing the Danish attempt to separate them. The resulting war of 1864 was quickly won by Prussia, which then took both provinces in full, including the Danish minority in the north. It was not until 1920, after a referendum imposed by the allied victors over Germany in World War I, that the districts of Schleswig with Danish majorities came to Denmark—they did not return to Denmark, for they had never legally or administratively been part of it.

FOUNDATIONS OF MODERN SCANDINAVIA

In both Sweden and Denmark, the experience of defeat in 1809 and 1864 produced a revulsion from war and a new attitude: to win within what was lost without. The Swedish poet Esaias Tegnér (1782–1846) wanted to "regain Finland within Sweden" by encouraging national pride and teaching about the national past. In Denmark, the Italian-born engineer Enrico Dalgas launched a more physically demanding enterprise: he formed an association to put the great moors of western Jutland under cultivation. As a result, these unusual, sombre landscapes virtually disappeared into forest and farmland, though the Danes at the time did not consider it a bad bargain. They were too hungry to be environmentalists.

Population grew rapidly in the nineteenth century. Sweden without Finland had 2.4 million inhabitants in 1810, 4.2 million in 1870, and 5.5 million in 1910, after which the rate of increase slowed as the birth rate fell. Cities throughout Scandinavia were few. Stockholm had 66,000 people in 1810, Copenhagen 140,000. In 1900 Stockholm reached 301,000, Copenhagen about 500,000. Mortality remained high in the cities throughout the century, due to bad water. The rate was twice that of rural areas and worse than that of Dickensian London.

Swedes provided the largest Nordic share of emigrants, most of them to the United States. Rural overpopulation and famine in the nineteenth century promoted emigration. One million Swedes, a quarter of the population, left between 1830 and 1923, with the high point in the 1880s. Tegnér attributed the rapid rise in population in his time to "peace, vaccine, and potatoes." He was right. Obligatory smallpox vaccination was introduced in Sweden in 1815, while the potato, known since the sixteenth century, reached its full potential as a basic and nourishing diet in the nineteenth century.

How could the Swedish state measure its population accurately and successfully impose a program of universal vaccination? The answers to such questions bring us near the heart of what makes the Nordic model tick. The welfare state, to say it again, may have been created in the twentieth century, but it made sense because it used and developed the discipline, the allegiance, the respect for government, and the desire to see in government a tool of rational progress that had been ingrained in Swedes for centuries. The Swedes, and to a less degree the other Nordics, have also been lucky in that government has been able to recruit a long line of committed public servants, devoted to the idea of beneficent government and to using government power to "arrange life well," in the contemporary phrase. This tradition, too, has deep roots, as does the will to create and use the tools necessary for beneficent state action. Such action requires knowledge, and Swedish administrators in the Age of Liberty (1719–1772) were among the first in the world to develop and apply statistics, then known as "political arithmetic," to measure and evaluate population and resources in order to plan prosperity—a truly original idea in Europe of the time.

Here is a revealing vignette. The Swedish government carried out the first accurate census in world history in 1756 and was alarmed by the results. The government needed to know the numbers in order to plan how best to use the human resources of the country and to make sure of an adequate supply of future soldiers. The census revealed high infant mortality, which was hardly surprising in Europe at the time, but no one had ever seen the numbers before. Being rational as well as relentlessly consistent, the Swedish government deduced that since infant mortality, by depriving the country of future workers and soldiers, was an obstacle to growth and prosperity, it had to be reduced. In the eighteenth century, before modern knowledge of germs and infection, there was no way to bring down mortality by medical means, which were unknown. Instead, the government did something archetypally Swedish, which only made sense in a society as disciplined and goal-directed as Sweden, and that was to issue, in 1764, a *Manual for Christian Couples on the Care of Children*. Copies of this document were distributed to all the religious leaders of Sweden with an order that couples intending to marry, or couples in which the wife was pregnant, be given it and examined in its contents by the religious leader. The remarkable fact is that this manual, even though it knew nothing of germs or the danger of infection, significantly reduced infant mortality over the next decades. Another remarkable fact is that the government could issue such a document fully expecting that the religious leaders would distribute it and that future parents would read and obey it.

Does that mean that most Swedes could read? Yes; Swedish literacy was by far the highest in the world at 90 percent by 1810. Even the poorest homes usually had a Bible, a hymn-book, a few prayer books and of course, in young households, the manual on child care. Already in the Church Act of 1686, the Swedish state encouraged parents to teach children to read with the minister's help. The minister was also required by this act to visit all households in his parish once a year—why? To make sure they were living a godly life, but also as a form of early social work, to see if the parents were living responsibly and to check on children's welfare. The intrusive competent state has a long ancestry in Sweden.

Sweden fought no war after the very small one of 1814. Norway fought Germany in the spring of 1940. Denmark went to war twice more in the nineteenth century and was occupied by Germany in 1940. Finland had a much bloodier history: the civil war of 1918 and the wars with the Soviet Union in 1939–1940 and 1941–1944 cost the country over 100,000 dead, almost all young men, and as many wounded, as well as much territory. Apart from these episodes, development has been largely peaceful, but not entirely so. The social discipline of Swedes may be striking, but farther back in history we see another tradition, of occasional violent rebellion to demand redress of grievances. Somewhere deep down, Swedes sensed that if a strong government was going to mobilize and mold them for the common good, they also had the right to demand that government be just and fair. Periodical uprisings against the strong state are a theme of older Swedish history. Gustavus I, the first king of independent Sweden, founded the strong state but not all Swedes accepted it, and he faced three violent rebellions, which he put down with great brutality.

As late as 1743, a delegation of the notoriously independent and stubborn men of the forest region of Dalarna northwest of Stockholm went to the capital to protest the severe inflation caused by the war that the dominant party of government had launched, unsuccessfully, against Russia to regain the parts of Finland ceded in 1721. This protest march became violent when the government refused to grant the demands. The resulting outbreak, known by the grimly humorous name of *stora daldansen,* "the big dance of the Dale-men," resulted in 140 dead in Stockholm. In 1811, peasants throughout Sweden protested the crown prince's mobilization plans against Denmark. About a thousand peasants and land-laborers in Skåne marched on the army headquarters at Klågerup Castle armed with guns, axes, and pitchforks. The army killed about 30 and wounded many.

After conquering Finland, Russia granted it autonomy in 1809, which meant that Finland retained the government and administration of Sweden as defined by the Swedish constitutional document known as the "form of government" of 1772, which was that of an absolute monarchy with all power emanating from the king or his representative, that is to say, after the Russian conquest, the Russian governor-general. During the nineteenth century, Finns developed a national identity in opposition to both Sweden and Russia. For the first time, Finnish intellectuals posited a Finnish nation that was not simply an eastern province of Sweden, now under Russia. Not surprisingly, these thinkers seized on the Finnish language, so different from both Swedish and Russian, as the unmistakable sign that the Finns were a nation to themselves, although it would not have occurred to anyone

before 1809 to think that. An early high point of Finnish linguistic and cultural nationalism was the *Kalevala,* the work of the poet Elias Lönnrot. Just like Ivar Aasen in Norway, he looked for the true and uncorrupted spirit of a formerly dependent people. Like Aasen when he went to rural west Norway to find the remnants of what he considered the authentic language of Norway, so Lönnrot went to the most remote, traditional region of Finland—Karelia—to find the national spirit of Finland by recording the folktales, songs, and legends of the people, which he then refashioned and published as a complete legendarium of ancient Finnish mythology.[32]

The Russians supported these advocates of Finnish as a symbol of nationhood, the so-called Fennomans, because their nationalism tended to reduce the social and political role of those Finns who spoke Swedish (the Swecomans), a group that included peasants and craftsmen along the west coast as well as the old bureaucratic elite. It was in the Russian interest that there should be a Finnish nation because such a nation would not want to return to being part of Sweden, since a nation should not be subject to another, according to nineteenth-century nationalist theory. By the 1860s, Finland was no longer Sweden but, in the view of most leading Finns, ought not to become Russia either; it was something else, namely Finnish; a Finnish nation had been born.[33]

Around the mid-nineteenth century, a movement known as Scandinavism affected

---

[32]Not all nationalists were Fennomans. At mid-century, the Swecoman J. L. Runeberg (1804–1877) published *The Stories of Ensign Stål,* a cycle of poems based on events of the war of 1808–1809, in which Sweden lost Finland but also, Runeberg implied, the war that, despite defeat, consolidated a Finnish as opposed to a merely eastern Swedish identity. The opening poem of the cycle became the Finnish national anthem. Its theme is "our country is poor, remote, and defeated, but for us it is a land of gold, it is our land." Because they were originally written in Swedish, the unforgettably vivid, moving, funny, and poignant *Stories of Ensign Stål* soon became national favorites in Sweden as well.

[33]Singleton 1989, 75.

students, writers, and thinkers in Denmark, Norway, and Sweden. Scandinavism crystallized politically in Swedish and Norwegian support for Danish nationalist opposition to the German Schleswig-Holsteiners' self-determination. The movement lost credibility when the king of Sweden-Norway first promised, then was forced by his cabinet to renege on the promise, to support Denmark in the Second Schleswig War of 1864. The movement argued that despite all the wars of the past, the three Nordic nations had a common heritage and a common spirit and should work for ever-closer cooperation and even full union such as was temporarily achieved in the fifteenth century, but with the difference that a new union should be of three equals, not one dominated by a single country, as the earlier union was by Denmark. Its focus on common Nordic values was picked up by those philosophers and advocates mentioned earlier in the chapter who, in the years around 1900, tried to distil a Nordic spirit or a Nordic tradition from re-imagined memories of the pagan or Christian past and whose work looked forward to the Nordic model and the welfare state. Scandinavism also had certain practical effects in the shorter term. It was thanks to the Scandinavist idea of frequent and closer political cooperation that Nordic governments in the later nineteenth century instituted regular economic cooperation and meetings of economic and financial policymakers and analysts. They even formed a short-lived postal and currency union, which had the enduring result that the currency unit of all three countries is the crown, or *krone/krona*. Another, probably more significant policy result of Scandinavist ideas was that the Nordic governments in the same period produced a uniform commercial code, meaning that the rules of buying, selling, and otherwise doing business became virtually identical in the three countries.

Tegnér's idea of compensating for external defeat by enlightening the people was also one aim of N. F. S. Grundtvig (1783–1872), a Danish minister, poet, and educator who is held by many to have forged the essential values of modern Danish society. He is appealed to in the twenty-first century by progressives and conservatives, proponents and critics of the welfare state, and defenders and enemies of the national church. The reason for this broad appeal is that he was, throughout his long life, both productive and versatile, writing sermons, hymns, and innumerable articles on issues of the day. He also sat for a time in the first constitutional assembly. If one were to point to one underlying theme of Grundtvig's life, one could call him a Christian nationalist. He wanted both to rejuvenate the Danish national Lutheran church and to reform Danish society by a program of mass education in history, literature, and the Nordic spirit. As an enthusiastic Scandinavist he believed that the Nordic nations, above all Denmark, represented a uniquely valuable set of traditions and instincts that he wanted to study, preserve, and pass on through his popular lectures and by promoting the so-called folk high school movement. The folk high schools were adult colleges initially intended to serve the uneducated or little-educated young of the countryside. They were invited to spend a year or two at these colleges, not to obtain a degree or an academic qualification, but to learn, in free and informal settings, about their history, literature, and traditions. Some folk high schools had particular emphases, such as athletics, crafts, or music, but all maintained a basic, broad program of general subjects and were not supposed to specialize. The heyday of the folk high schools—which were copied in Sweden, Norway, and elsewhere in Europe—was around 1900. By the 1990s, they had become parking places for the long-term unemployed, because the government paid the fees for them and thus indirectly subsidized the schools, and because few others had the time or resources to take a year or two out of their working lives to weave baskets or hear stories about the Vikings. When the government reduced its subsidy and youth unemployment simultaneously dropped in Denmark, the number of applicants collapsed and many folk high schools had to close.

Grundtvig's most popular saying, a favorite quote of proponents of the Nordic model, was that "we shall have advanced far in well-being when few have too much and fewer too little." The quote is from one of his songs and hardly worth the profound attention it gets, but its popularity in later days suggests that Grundtvig struck a chord when he identified well-being—his actual word means wealth or prosperity—with an egalitarian distribution of resources with few rich people and even fewer poor people. Taking quotes such as this, social democrats and progressives in the twentieth century turned Grundtvig into a prophet of the egalitarian welfare society, implying that this society reflected deeply rooted Danish values. This may be true. On the other hand, such advocates of Grundtvig as the archetypal Dane ignored what to Grundtvig was most essential, namely Christian faith and building a national community around this faith. Even more than a nationalist, Grundtvig was a Christian and sometimes a mystic, cherishing a vision of the sacramental unity of the people before the altar. One wonders what he would think of the enthusiasm of those who claim him for their own opinions while despising or ignoring the religion he represented.

Since Finland, like Iceland, does not appear as often as the three central Nordic nations in this chapter, this historical section is the place to mention some remarkable Finnish "firsts" in political development. Between 1907 and 1917, Finland obtained the world's first unicameral legislature, became the first country in Europe with universal adult suffrage, that is, where women as well as men could vote, and had the world's first prime minister from a social democratic party.

These firsts occurred in a country that, until 1809, was a province of Sweden and from 1809–1917 of Russia. This may not be as surprising as it seems. There is a rule in historical sociology that poorer, dependent regions, further from the centers of government and culture, in short what is known as the periphery, sometimes can be more creative, industrious, imaginative, or efficient than the center, that is to say, the more prosperous, organized, and powerful regions. Sweden showed this by defeating Denmark in the economic and military competition of the seventeenth century. Elites in peripheral regions have greater incentives to think boldly and to organize the resources at their command, whether moral or physical, as efficiently as possible, especially if they convince themselves that competing and doing one's best is worthwhile, that it will gain them something—independence, prosperity, self-respect, or national vigor. Sometimes, of course, peripheral elites give up beforehand and become disgruntled and resentful, full of self-pity and blaming others for their problems. That happened in Denmark after 1864, when Denmark was the periphery in relation to Germany. The Finns, whether thanks to their *sisu* (endurance, morale, stubborn strength) or to Russian tolerance of their activities, or simply because of the boost of energy they got from the exhilaration of shaping and formulating a new national identity, did not give up.

Economic progress helped them. After some severe famines, the last such in Scandinavia, in the 1860s and 1870s, the Finnish economy developed in growing independence of Russia, thanks largely to the influence of the Finnish Diet of four estates, which operated, when called, as established by the Swedish form of government of 1719, which had not been wholly superseded by the absolutist constitution of 1772. In 1863, the Russians allowed the Diet to assemble, for the first time since 1809, with the philosopher and Fennoman J. V. Snellman (1806–1881) as a leading figure. He took a particular interest in steady economic development, returning the Finnish currency, the *markka,* to a silver, later a gold standard, and granting the Bank of Finland autonomy in managing the money supply and fiscal policy.

From 1890–1905, the tsarist Russian government abandoned its earlier policy of promoting Finnish national identity, a policy generally popular in Finland, especially with the Fennomans, and which had gained Russia great respect, and tried to increase the Russification of Finland. This reactionary and great-Russian policy did not succeed, except in provoking and irritating all Finns and driving the pro-Russian Fennomans and the anti-Russian and pro-Swedish Swecomans together. The Russification policy collapsed in the wake of the first Russian revolution of 1905 when the tsarist government was forced to grant Russia itself a modest form of democratic representation. In Finland, which already had experienced a representative assembly—the diet of 1863, suppressed in 1890—the Russians in 1905 restored and extended autonomy. By the November Manifesto of 1905, the Russians promised the Finns the first two "firsts" in the political sphere, which at once put that nation ahead of its Scandinavian sisters. One was a 200-member unicameral diet, the *Eduskunta* or *Riksdag*. The second was that this legislature was to be elected by universal adult suffrage. So Finland became in 1907 the first nation in Europe—Australia being the first in the world—where women had the right to vote. Denmark followed in 1915, Sweden in 1917, Norway in 1913. The third first followed in 1917 when, in the process of winning complete independence from Russia, the parliament chose Oskari Tokoi, a social democrat, as prime minister, the first of many social democratic heads of government in Scandinavia.

Finnish independence was a consequence of the Russian Revolution of 1917. At that time, the political landscape in Finland was still dominated by the rivalry of Fennomans and Swecomans. In both camps were found farmers, artisans, and civil servants. In the years before and after independence, the majority Fennomans divided into two groups. One was known as the Old Finns, or compliants, in favor of collaboration with Russians. This group became the National Coalition Party, the closest analogy in Finland to a conservative party, though with the significant difference that these Finnish conservatives inherited the Old Finn interest in accommodating Russia. The NCP continued this policy even when Russia became the communist Soviet Union, which, to say the least, made the NCP unlike any other conservative party in Europe. The other branch of the Fennoman nationalists were the Young Finns or constitutionalists, which became the dominant element of the liberal or free enterprise party, which disappeared from parliament in 1983.

The social democrats of Finland were not initially a party dominated by urban workers, of whom there were few in Finland, but rather one of landless laborers and poor farmers. Of these there were many, which helps to explain the extraordinary fact that the Finnish social democratic party was the largest even in the first free election of 1907 and won an absolute majority of the seats in the *Eduskunta* in 1916. Ever since, the Social Democrats (SSP, for *Suomen Sosiaalidemokrattinen Puolue*) have, with brief exceptions, been the largest party in Finland. The fourth traditional Finnish party, the Center Party, grew out of the Agrarian Union, which as its name suggests originally represented the farming interest. By midcentury, the Center Party had become a broad coalition of nonsocialist domestic interests. In relations with the Soviet Union, the CP, like the NCP, favored bending to Soviet wishes for Finnish foreign policy and discouraging debate or criticism of the Soviet Union in Finland itself—the so-called policy of Finlandization. The greatest exponent of this policy was the long-time CP leader Urho Kekkonen, who was president of Finland from 1956–1981.

PARTIES AND CONSTITUTIONS

With the November Manifesto, Finland moved from autocracy to constitutional government in a matter of weeks. For different reasons, the passage was rapid in Denmark as well, which was an absolute, hereditary monarchy in February 1848 and a constitutional monarchy with popular sovereignty a month later. In February, power came from the king, in March, it came from the people to the king who exercised it on the people's behalf. In Sweden, the passage was slower. Unlike Denmark, where the chief nobles governed until 1660 and the king as absolute monarch after that, Sweden retained its medieval system of making policy through assemblies, or diets, of four estates, the clergy, the tax-exempt nobility, the burgers, and the peasants. Uniquely in Europe, the fourth estate, the peasantry, did not disappear or sink into serfdom. Although several Swedish kings tried to introduce absolutism on the continental or Danish model, they never succeeded for long. Sooner or later, they were forced to turn to the estates to raise taxes and get their policies approved. Of course, the diets of estates were weighted in favor of the nobility, and the king's wishes always commanded respect and deference, but the mere fact that burgers and peasants attended made the inherited Swedish constitution more democratic than that of any other early modern European state. In the eighteenth century, after the adventurist and costly foreign policy of Europe's last warrior-king, Charles XII, Sweden enjoyed a 50-year interlude known as the Age of Liberty, in which the four-estate diet successfully claimed the right to appoint and approve the king's councillors, that is, the top policymakers. It also approved taxes and passed laws, which was clearly a form of parliamentary government. In 1766, the Swedish diet enacted the first freedom of speech guarantee enacted and abolished censorship—21 years before the American Bill of Rights—although both these liberal measures were abolished by Gustavus III in 1772, the last Swedish king to impose absolutism.

This regime ended when Sweden lost the war with Russia in 1809. Following the defeat, the estates enacted and compelled the king to sign a new constitution. This document brought the king back under the rule of law by giving the executive power to the king and his council and the legislative power to the king and the Diet. Both king and diet could propose laws that the other party could veto, with one vital exception, namely money bills. Only the diet, not the king alone, could impose taxes on the people: "The ancient right of the Swedish people to tax itself is to be exercised by the Diet alone." Notice that these founding fathers saw taxation as a right, that is, something valuable, and not as a duty. The language is an interesting anticipation of the thinking behind the Nordic model: that the people cherish the chance to contribute, through giving part of their resources to government, to the common welfare.

The 1809 constitution remained in force with major modifications until 1974. When written, its main purpose was to avoid both the weak government of the Age of Liberty and absolutism. The result was a system of government in which the king and his councillors, drawn largely from the nobility, continued to get most of what they wanted but avoided antagonizing the non-noble members of the Diet. This collaborative, aristocratic constitutionalism slowly eroded until a directly elected Diet and universal suffrage were achieved. The first stage was passed in 1866, when the king approved a modified form of direct election to the Diet. The big winners in this deal were the fourth estate, the farmers, who were guaranteed protective tariffs and a disproportionate weight in the assembly. The next half-century was what has been called a regime of notables, that is, of well-meaning but conservative administrators and civil servants. These were men who did not fully understand the most significant force affecting all of Scandinavia, the industrial revolution, which arrived in the North about a century later than in England. Industry, which at the time in Sweden meant mines, smelting, machines, and machine tools, needed free trade, which was not won until further struggle in the early twentieth century. Finally, in 1921, full direct representation was achieved and the twentieth-century party system took final shape.

This system, in Sweden as elsewhere in the North, emerged from the constitutional struggles of the nineteenth century, which reflected underlying social and class conflicts. In the early part of that century, the legacy or threat of absolutism polarized the political elite into two main groups, a conservative group favoring a strong monarchy and only very gradual change, and a liberal group favoring popular sovereignty and control of the executive by an elected national assembly—not, as yet, elected by universal suffrage, but by elections favoring the votes of the educated middle class, the main liberal constituency.

By the early twentieth century, the industrial revolution had finally taken hold in Scandinavia and was producing new cleavages and constituencies, chief among them the industrial workers, who did not fit the earlier categories, and the businessmen, who wanted a social order favoring the creation of wealth and its protection, but who also wanted free trade and therefore opposed the old conservatives who consisted of large landowners and civil servants who favored protectionism. The Russian Revolution in 1917 provoked a split in the working-class parties between the majority Social Democrats who believed that democracy itself would lead to a more socialist order of society, and the minority communists who despised democracy as an obstacle on the road to revolution.

A striking feature of the Nordic political landscape as it took shape in the early twentieth century was the fragmentation of the nonsocialist element. Instead of joining forces, the nonsocialist parties continued to remain deeply divided on a range of issues, of which free trade vs. protectionism was, for long, the most important. Furthermore, in Scandinavia cultural and educational modernization preceded industrialization rather than coming after it, as was the case in the major European nation-states. This process of cultural modernization meant that issues such as education and the role of the church became highly important to political figures and helped to crystallize divisions and allegiances within what later became the nonsocialist parties.

Accordingly, by the 1920s, a standard pattern had emerged of five political parties in the Scandinavian countries, representing five major coalitions of interests. From the left, these were, in the first half of the century, the communists, the Social Democrats, the urban middle-class liberals, the farmers, and the conservatives. By the second half of the century the spectrum was changing. By the 1940s, farming was no longer the single largest occupation, and, increasingly in the postwar years, defending agricultural interests was no longer enough to carry a major political party, so the liberal-agrarian parties re-emphasized their liberal positions on free enterprise and individual rights. In the Nordic area, where government had become the dominant element of society and economy, liberals felt that rights and individual liberty needed protection against government, not, as American liberals would have it, by means of government. Thus the former agrarian parties tried to reposition themselves as defenders of classical liberalism.

This succeeded in Denmark, where the liberals (*Venstre,* a word meaning "Left" and harking back to the nineteenth century when liberals were the left wing, as opposed to the conservative right wing) replaced the Conservative Party as the largest nonsocialist grouping in the 1970s. It did not work in Norway and Sweden, where the agrarian and liberal parties remained relatively small, and the largest coalition of business and free-market interests continued to reside primarily within the conservative parties (*Høyre,* the Right, in Norway, and, since 1932, *Moderata Samlingspartiet* or the Moderate Coalition Party in Sweden). In Sweden, the former farmers' party, *Centerpartiet* (C, the Center Party) was further bedeviled, since the 1970s, by splits on environmental and educational policy. Sweden was the only Nordic country that used nuclear energy for part of its power supply, a policy strongly supported in the 1960s and 1970s by the Social Democrats (*Socialdemokratiska Arbetarepartiet* or SAP) and Conservatives on the grounds that domestically produced nuclear energy promoted growth and employment and saved money that would otherwise be spent on foreign oil and coal. The Center Party was deeply divided on this as on education, where many nonsocialist voters considered that neither the Center party nor the liberals, *Folkpartiet* (Fp, the People's Party) were staunch enough in opposing what they saw as social democratic and anticapitalist indoctrination in schools. As a consequence of the cleavages on energy and education, neither the Center nor the People's Party came close to rivaling the Conservatives as a credible party of free-market ideas. Instead, the Environment Party emerged in the 1990s to capitalize on the antinuclear and green vote, and the Christian Democrats (CD) to gain votes from those who thought the Center and People's Party were not fighting the culture war vigorously enough. By the late 1990s the CD was the second largest nonsocialist party and was threatening to push the Center below the 4 percent minimum necessary for parliamentary representation.

Venstre's success in mobilizing the nonsocialist vote in Denmark since the 1970s was limited. The Danish party system is the most prone to fragmentation and schism of any in Scandinavia. Partly this can be explained by the low barrier to entry into parliament, which makes it potentially more rewarding to form splinter parties. But why do so many choose to pursue these rewards rather than working in larger parties, given that a new and often single-issue party, even if it manages to enter parliament, can never hope to outgrow the major parties? The answer must have something to do with the Danish lack of discipline and of the relentless consistency with which Swedes, whether left or right, pursue their goals. In any event, from the late 1960s on the Danish voters provided a spectacle of upheavals in the party system, first by massive shifts among the five parties already represented and then, from 1973, by throwing new parties into the *Folketing,* most dramatically in that same year when the brand-new Progress Party (*Fremskridtspartiet*), founded and led by an eccentric tax-dodging lawyer, Mogens Glistrup (b. 1924), briefly became the second-largest party with 16 percent of the vote. Glistrup's success on a platform of abolishing most taxes and most government might seem to contradict what was mentioned earlier about tax-cutting having no appeal in Nordic societies. Glistrup modifies but does not invalidate that observation. For one thing, he never exceeded his initial success of 16 percent. For another, the only effect Glistrup's party and its successors had in Danish politics over the next thirty years was to unite all the other parties, left and right, in hostile opposition to his radical views. Even *Venstre,* whose spokesmen might otherwise have been more ambitious in their critique of the ever-expanding state, became indistinguishable in its high-tax, high-spending policies from the Social Democrats out of sheer fear of being tarred with Glistrup's brush.

Another set of changes took place among the left parties. Starting in the late 1950s, new cleavages began to replace the split in the labor movement and its political parties caused by the Russian Revolution. Many people wanted a leftist, socialist party with political credibility, one more radical than the Social Democrats, which such people regarded as soft sellouts to capitalism, but also one more electable than the communists who were forever tainted by their subservience to the Soviet Union which was still perceived by many as threatening the West with conquest and oppression. In the search for such new leftist parties with electoral appeal, voters supported a handful of alternative, radical, but noncommunist parties, most successfully in Denmark thanks to the low barrier to entry into parliament. When the Soviet Union dissolved in 1991, the communists were finally relieved of their allegiance. In Denmark, the party dissolved itself and its leaders migrated to other leftist groupings, some of which could be described as continuations of local communism by other names. In Sweden, where the 4-percent barrier to entry discouraged fragmentation, the communists had for long been engaged in re-designing their public posture as precisely the kind of more radical, but not totalitarian, leftist party desired by those who thought the Social Democrats were too soft on employers, business, and the rich. After 1991, this redesign of the Swedish communist party as merely the Left Party reached its culmination.

The cleavages opened by issues such as free trade, education, and religion, as well as issues of social and welfare policy, provided for a large number of cross-party deals and allegiances. The old liberals had divided into a centrist party with more socially progressive views, with others, who considered liberalism mainly an economic doctrine of free trade and free enterprise, joining and shaping a modernized conservative party. Despite these cleavages, and despite the fundamental tension between the social democratic or socialist parties of wage-earners and the business and employer interests served by one or more of the nonsocialist parties, elections in Scandinavia have rarely been purely ideological battles. One exception was the so-called Cossack election of 1928 in Sweden, when *Högern,* the Right or conservative party, accused the Social Democrats of wanting to introduce a Bolshevik takeover of private property if they won.

The five-party system lasted longest in Sweden, where fragmentation and new parties were discouraged because no party that did not receive four percent of the national vote obtained representation. It was not until the 1980s that two new parties, an environmentalist party and a Christian party, were able to mobilize enough support to enter the Diet. In Denmark, the required number of votes was lower, and the five-party system never as solid. The last time the Danish national assembly or *Folketing* had only five parties was in 1973.

Nordic constitutional traditions and doctrines differ from those of America. In the United States, the division of powers is taken seriously and often leads to gridlock between the branches of government. Also in the United States, government and policy must ultimately conform to the rules of a document, the U.S. Constitution, which differs from other laws in that it describes the rules by which other laws may be made and executed, and in that it cannot be repealed nor easily changed or amended. The Constitution is not at the disposal of the legislature (Congress) alone, but is to be obeyed, applied, and interpreted equally by all three branches, with the courts playing a leading role in interpretation.

The Nordic countries do not accept such a thorough division of powers, at least not since governments began abiding by the doctrine of parliamentarism, the idea that the prime minister and his cabinet must enjoy the confidence of a majority of the delegates to parliament. If the government loses a vote in parliament or the opposition parties pass a motion of no confidence, parliamentarism demands that the government resign. This principle was honored in Norway from 1884, in Denmark from 1901, and in Sweden from 1917.

In the 1980s an interesting situation arose in Denmark when the conservative-led minority government accepted defeat on a number of motions requiring the government to oppose NATO security policy. Denmark was a NATO member and the government was in favor of NATO's policy, which involved deploying theater nuclear missiles in Europe to deter Soviet attack. The defeats in parliament therefore meant that the government go against its own preferred policy and carry out the alternative security policy of the opposition parties. Parliamentarism demanded that the government take the consequences of being outvoted

City Hall, Copenhagen, Denmark.

and resign. But the government did no such thing. Some observers considered that this behavior undermined parliamentarism by leaving it up to the government of the day to decide whether any particular defeat was serious enough to warrant its resignation. It is also true, however, that if the opposition parties, led by the Social Democrats, had truly wanted the government to resign, they needed only to introduce a motion of no confidence. They did not do so because they knew that such a motion would fail, since the tiny center or Radical Liberal Party, which was antidefense but sympathetic to the conservative-led government's economic and fiscal reforms, would not support it.

Parliamentarism expresses the fundamental Nordic constitutional doctrine which is similar to what the British call parliamentary sovereignty or, in the Danish phrase, the idea that "nobody is above and nobody next to parliament." That is to say, the parliament, as the representative assembly of the people, from whom all power comes, is absolutely sovereign. Parliament can delegate some of its power to ministers, but, as parliamentarism requires, a government only holds this power as long as it enjoys the confidence of the parliament as a whole.

Nordic constitutions do not have the exalted status of the U.S. Constitution. A Nordic written constitution consists of one or more "basic laws" (*grundlov, grundlag*), which explain how governments are constituted, parliaments assembled, and laws enacted. In their current versions, they also include guarantees of civil rights in varying detail, least in the Danish and most in the Swedish case. They vary in length and in the provisions for amendment. The Danish basic law, most recently revised in 1953, is the shortest; the others have all been revised frequently and in 1974 and 2000 Sweden and Finland received entirely new *grundlagar*. The Danish basic law is the most cumbersome to revise and its 1953 formulations, many of them similar to those of the first edition of 1849, have become remote from contemporary political and institutional reality, and by the end of the century many considered that time was ripe for a thorough expansion and revision. However, since few could agree on what those revisions should be—some wanted provisions guaranteeing the right to work, others more elaborate definitions of civil rights, others protection of refugees or of the environment—and since constitutional reform was not a salient issue in Danish political debate, a revision was not likely. The Danish basic law appears to mandate the division of powers by stating that the executive power lies with the king and his ministers, the legislative power with the king and the parliament, and the judicial power with the courts. However, these words are misleading. For one thing, the monarch's powers are purely formal. The Danish and Norwegian basic laws state that the king appoints the ministers of government, determines each minister's duties, and governs the country through them. What these words mean today is that the party leaders in parliament decide whom they want as prime minister, that the monarch will appoint that person, and that the new prime minister will then tell the king what other ministers he wants appointed. No one can be appointed prime minister and form a government unless that person enjoys the support of parliament, which is the ultimate sovereign.

Nor should American readers be confused by the provision that the courts are independent. It is true that judges cannot be removed from office, but Nordic courts do not have the constitutional right and duty of U.S. courts to determine whether a law or an act of government is constitutional. Nordic courts will defer to parliamentary authority and will not challenge legislation on constitutional grounds. In Nordic doctrine, only parliament can correct parliament. It is thus not true to say that powers are divided in Nordic government; rather, powers are concentrated, because the executive is subject to the legislature and no one outside parliament can challenge its acts on constitutional grounds.[34] This concentration of power is greatest in Denmark, whereas it is modified in the other countries in various ways. In none of the countries, however, is the supreme authority of parliament seriously challenged.

The Danish basic law is the most difficult to amend, as any amendment requires the approval of two successive parliaments, followed by a referendum in which 40 percent of the eligible voters must approve the new version. There is thus no point in introducing amendments of single clauses, as the procedure is the same for amending a single clause as for amending the whole document. The Norwegian, Swedish, and Finnish basic laws require only the approval of two successive parliaments and have all been frequently amended.[35] All basic laws include guarantees of civil rights, rules for choosing government ministers, electing parliament, passing laws, and provisions for government in conditions of emergency. In Denmark, Norway, and Finland, these provisions and others are found in a single law; Sweden has, for historic reasons, three basic laws, of which the *regeringsform* (RF) of 1974 with later revisions is the most important. It contains almost everything

---

[34]In 1919, the Danish government expropriated large parts of the big estates in order to provide land for landless peasants. The former owners sued on the ground that the expropriations violated the Basic Law's guarantee that those expropriated were entitled to full compensation, which they had not been given. They lost, as the Danish Supreme Court found that it had no standing to criticize an act of parliament on constitutional grounds. In 1998, a group of Danish citizens brought a complaint against the prime minister for violating the Basic Law by surrendering sovereignty to the European Union without popular consent. Again, the plaintiffs lost, but this time the Supreme Court did, very tentatively, begin to engage in real constitutional discussion of an act of the parliament. These and similar cases in other Nordic countries have led some to argue that the old doctrine of parliamentarism may be crumbling and a genuine constitutional jurisprudence may be on its way.

[35]The Finnish law permits amendment by two-thirds majority vote of one parliament if five sixths of those present want it.

included in the other countries' basic laws except for the rules on succession to the monarchy and those on freedom of speech, which were traditionally given in separate instruments in Sweden, ever since the first freedom of speech ordinance of 1766 and the ordinance of succession of 1810. The current ordinances date from 1975.

The Swedish RF of 1974 is a longer document than the Norwegian or Danish basic laws, in that it goes into more detail about the tasks and duties of parliament and government and the mechanics of their operation and spells out certain rights at greater length, referring in each case to other laws and provisions where these matters are regulated. One important change from the earlier RF was that the upper chamber of parliament was abolished and the number of delegates in the new unicameral *Riksdag* increased to 350. Sweden also in 1974 abolished the last residual rights of the monarchy, so that the king no longer appoints government ministers, presides at meetings of the council of ministers, or signs bills into law; these powers, purely formal in any case, now belong to the speaker of the parliament.

Norway has certain rules not found in the other countries. One is that the Norwegian parliament, like the U.S. Congress, is elected for a fixed term of four years and cannot be dissolved at other times. If the government loses a vote of confidence, a new government must be formed based on the existing distribution of power among the parties. In the other countries, the prime minister's right to dissolve parliament and call elections at any time is an important political tool. Another provision peculiar to Norway is that ministers of government cannot be at the same time members of parliament, nor can senior employees of government departments. This, again, is reminiscent of U.S. practice. In Denmark, the idea that parliament has all the power is so ingrained that if a minister is appointed who is not a member of parliament, a safe seat will be found for that minister at the next general election. Both these Norwegian rules modify strict parliamentarism, the first by discouraging votes of no confidence and the second by distinguishing the government from parliament more sharply than in the other countries. The Norwegian basic law is, with its revisions, the oldest surviving constitution in Europe. It dates from 1814 and, by tradition, changes to the basic law are written in a slightly modified version of the now-obsolete Danish used in Norway at that time.

Unlike Denmark, Norway, and Sweden, Finland is a republic. The first independent constitution codified parliamentarism by making the government dependent on parliament's support. In addition to the formal powers retained by the king in other Nordic countries, the new head of state, the president, was given the power to conduct foreign policy. When a cautious and consistent foreign policy of appeasing the Soviet Union was deemed essential after World War II, the president's powers grew. It seemed clear to everyone that foreign policy was of paramount importance and that it would do no good to subject the delicate relations with the Soviets to the shifting political climate of parliament. The president's growing authority based on the people's trust in him as the person able to deal with the Soviets also increased his authority in domestic affairs; the line between the two, formalized in the 1919 constitution, was often referred to as "a line drawn in water." During the long incumbency of Urho Kekkoken from 1956–1981 Finland came close to a semi-presidential system reminiscent of France, where the president ran foreign policy and constituted a pole of political power and influence distinct from and independent of parliament and the ministerial government.

After Kekkonen's death this changed. The president's foreign policy prerogative apart, parliamentarism grew stronger in Finland as the formerly fragmented party landscape consolidated into a pattern of three dominant

TABLE 6.1 Political Parties in the Nordic Countries

	Denmark	Finland	Iceland	Norway	Sweden
Name of parliament	Folketing	Eduskunta/Riksdag	Althing	Storting	Riksdag
Total number of seats	179	200	63	165	349
Date of last election	March 1998	March 1999	May 1999	September 1997	September 1998
Turnout (%)	86.8	65.3	84.1	78.0	81.4
Social Democrats	**Socialdemokratiet** 36.0 63 +1	**Social Democrats** (Suomen Sosiaali- demokraattinen Puolue) 22.9 51		**Arbeiderpartiet** 35.0 65	**SAP** (Socialdemokratiska Arbetarepartiet) 36.4 131
Socialists and former communists	Socialist People's Party (Socialistisk Folkeparti) 7.5 13 Unity List (Enhedslisten) 2.7 5	Left Alliance (Vasemmistoliitto) 10.9 20	Left-Green Alliance (Vinstrihreyfing) 9.1 6	Socialist Left Party (Sosialistisk Venstreparti) 6.0 9	Left Party (Vänsterpartiet) 12.0 43
Greens		Greens (Vihreä Liitto) 5.1 11			Environmentalists (Miljöpartiet) 4.5 16
Centrists	**Radical Liberals** (Radikale Venstre) 3.9 7 Center Democrats (Centrum- demokraterne) 4.3 8	Center (Suomen Keskusta) 22.4 47	Alliance (Samfylkingin) 26.8 17	Center (Senterpartiet) 7.9 11	Center (Centerpartiet) 5.1 18
Christian parties	Christian People's Party (Kristeligt Folkeparti) 2.5 4	Christian Union of Finland (Suomen Kristillinen Liitto) 4.2 10		Christian People's Party (Kristeligt Folkeparti) 13.7 25	Christian Democrats (Kristdemokraterna) 11.8 42

	Denmark	Finland	Iceland	Norway	Sweden
Liberals	Venstre 24.0 42 +1		Progressive Party (Framsóknarflokkurin) 18.4 12; Liberal Party (Frjáslyndi flokkurin) 4.2 2	Venstre 4.5 6	People's Party (Folkpartiet) 4.7 17
Conservatives	Conservative People's Party (Konservative Folkeparti) 8.9 15 +1	Alliance (Kansallinen Kokoomus) 21.0 46	Independence Party (Sjálfstædhisflokkurin) 40.7 26	Right (Høyre) 14.3 23	Moderates (Moderaterna) 22.9 82
Libertarian	Freedom 2000 (Frihed 2000) 2.4 4			Progress Party (Fremskrittspartiet) 15.3 25	
Nationalist	Danish People's Party (Dansk Folkeparti) 7.4 13	True Finns (Perussuomalaiset) 1.0 1			
Others		Swedish Party (Svenska Folkpartiet) 5.1 12; Reform Group (Remonttiryhmä) 1.1 1		Nonpolitical 0.4 1	
Head of state	Margrethe II (since 1972)	Tarja Halonen (SSP), president since 2000	Ólafur Ragnar Grímsson (Socialist), president since 1996	Harald V (since 1991)	Carl XVI Gustaf (since 1973)

The figures given are, first, number of seats, and second, share of votes cast. The number of votes does not total 100 because some votes were cast for parties that did not gain representation. Parties in government at time of writing are emphasized. The parties are grouped by approximate location on the political spectrum. Parties in government at time of writing are emphasized, followed by radical socialists, greens, and ex-communists—often found in the same party—then centrists, liberals, conservatives, nationalists, and a few small groups with no particular political position. The figure "+1" after certain Danish parties indicates a member elected on the Faeroes or in Greenland.

The presidents of Finland and Iceland and the monarchs of Denmark, Norway, and Sweden are listed. However, the monarchs are heads of state only in the formal sense. The actual head of state in those countries is the head of the government.

parties, the Social Democrats, the Center, and the National Coalition or conservative party. Reform in the Soviet Union reduced the implied threat to Finland if it abandoned its subservience to Soviet international politics, and this relaxed the domestic atmosphere as well. There was no longer as strong a felt need for a presidency independent of the parliament and government. As a sign of these changes, the rules for electing the president were changed in 1994 so that the president would henceforth be chosen by popular rather than indirect vote.

In 2000, an entirely new basic law was enacted, superseding four earlier basic laws and tying the presidency closely to the parliamentary system of government. No longer was the president to constitute the other pole of a dyarchy but he or she, like the government, would be subject to parliament's goodwill. Parliamentarism was written into the new Finnish *grundlag* or *perustuslaki* more emphatically than in any other Nordic basic law. Other innovations included a catalogue of basic rights including such newly fashionable rights as the right to social care and the environment's right to be protected against pollution and exploitation. The key changes, though, were undoubtedly the detailed provisions strengthening parliament's position vis-à-vis the government and the government's vis-à-vis the president. From now on, the power to choose and control the government would lie with parliament alone and not, as before, with parliament or the president depending on the balance of power between them.

A constitution is more than a text, it is also a system of government and a way of life, and the reality of a country's constitution can differ considerably from what can be read in the written document. The Nordic basic laws circumscribe and formalize the powers and limitations of government. That is all well and good. In reality, government has many ways to expand its power. For example, the reader of a Nordic basic law might conclude that laws need the approval of parliament and the king's signature at a meeting of the council of state. That is formally true. However, many more regulations and orders affecting people's daily lives are passed as decrees or proclamations which do not require the formal apparatus of legislation but have the force of law. In a similar vein, the basic laws all mandate personal security from government intrusion. Again, well and good; the police cannot tap your phone or enter your living quarters without a search warrant, and if government wants your property, it must pay you for it. What the basic law will not tell you is that Nordic governments have, by decree or bureaucratic practice, opened up innumerable ways in which officials can legally enter your home or tell you what you can or cannot do with your property. A Danish lawyer in 2000 enumerated 162 different government agencies entitled to enter your home at any time with no warrant of any kind to see if you are complying with regulations, ranging from building inspectors to water safety inspectors and, of course, tax collectors. If someone sent by any one of those 162 different agencies rang your doorbell even at four in the morning, you would have to let him in or go to jail. That the police were almost the single agency not empowered to enter your home without a warrant was small comfort to those many people who, by 2000, felt that Nordic governments, however benevolent, had become quite big enough and that it was time to make the constitutional reality fit the text once again.

Governments act on citizens in many ways hardly imagined or captured by the authors of those documents. That is one reason that the Nordic basic laws or written constitutions do not reflect political reality. Another is that parliamentarism, which is written into the Finnish and Swedish basic laws and strongly implied by their Norwegian and Danish counterparts, does not mean that government policies are freely arrived at in open debate. Parliamentarism survives in the sense that governments serve at the pleasure of a majority in parliament. But in complex societies, especially ones where government spends well over half the national income and employs a quarter of the workforce, decisions about government cannot easily be made in true and open deliberation of all members of parliament. Instead, laws and decrees are prepared by expert groups and the top politicians in government and submitted to parliament for decision.

This process of decision making can be relied on because of a vital corollary of the parliamentary principle, one unknown in a presidential system with checks and balances such as that of the United States. This corollary is party discipline. In the loose American party system, where the executive is distinct from Congress, delegates do not always vote with their party. Thus deal-making—*you support me on this, I'll support you on that*—is characteristic of politics in the United States. In Scandinavia, by contrast, parties know that gaining, keeping, or opposing government power requires them to hold together in parliament. Their policy platforms tend to be specific and centrally determined. Individual delegates are not expected or encouraged to have their own opinions or to make private deals with other parties, indeed doing so would be suicidal, because one's chances of joining or influencing government depend in part on how good a party loyalist one is.

Another factor that contributes to party discipline is the larger number of parties. (Table 6.1 lists the parties represented in parliament at the most recent election at the time of writing, as well as other basic political information). As we have seen, the standard Nordic party landscape as it functioned through most of the twentieth century had five main parties, two on the left, one in the center leaning to either side depending on circumstances, and two on the right. With that number of parties in play, discipline was even more important to prevent shifts of allegiance that could overthrow governments, as happened on a few notable occasions.

In the Nordic countries, delegates to parliament are not elected, as in Britain or the United States, in single member constituencies, but rather by proportional representation from lists established by the party leaders. This feature further adds to party discipline and hierarchy, because the delegates owe their position not just to the voters but to the party apparatus that put their names on the lists for election. The argument for proportional representation is that it gives the parties representation in parliament as precisely as possible according to their total share of the vote. Even smaller parties that could never hope to win a single constituency outright can thus be represented, as long as they gain a certain share of the overall vote—as we have seen, the needed share is 2 percent in Denmark and 4 percent in Sweden. A result such as that of Britain in 1997, in which Tony Blair and his New Labour party won 418 of 659 seats with 43 percent of the vote against 165 for the Tories with 30 percent, whereas in 1992 the Tories' 48 percent only got them 336 seats, is impossible with proportional representation.

FROM "THE PEOPLE'S HOME" TO THE "STRONG SOCIETY"

In 1928, the Swedish social democratic leader Per Albin Hansson (1885–1946) used the word *folkhem*, "people's home," to describe the social and economic goals of the labor movement and its party, the Social Democrats. The people's home was a society where everyone cared for one another without the barriers that divided "citizens into privileged and disadvantaged, rulers and dependents, rich and poor, propertied and impoverished, exploited and exploiters."[36] Hansson had coined a

---

[36]Quoted in Stig Hadenius et al., eds., *Sveriges historia* (Stockholm: Bonnier 1996), 378.

powerful image that resonated for decades in Swedish political culture. As late as 1985, in social and economic conditions vastly different from those of 1928, Hansson's second successor as social democratic party leader and prime minister, Olof Palme, still quoted Hansson's sentimental words at every campaign meeting.

The people's home symbolized two guiding beliefs of Nordic social democracy, egalitarianism and solidarity. Both were to be achieved through government action, considered more rational than and superior to the unfettered market in providing for the common good. Government action to provide for major life tasks such as education, health care, care of the old, and pensions became the foundation of Nordic society and influenced people's values, behavior, and expectations in many ways. That is why the Nordic model is not simply a set of policies or a large state sector, but a culture and a way of life. In later years, the idea that government, rather than civil society or the market, must provide the solidarity and comfort of the people's home was expressed in another Swedish social democratic phrase, the "strong society." This was society as buttressed and permeated in all its corners by the state and its agents; society seen as incapable, weak, and vulnerable if deprived of encompassing, maternal government action.

Denmark was the first country to introduce a universal and tax-financed benefit in the first law on old age pensions (1891), which gave everyone aged 60 or older the right to a public pension regardless of whether they had been in the workforce or paid any premiums. At that time life expectancy was about 50, so few people took up the pension. The law nevertheless established fundamental principles of what later became the Nordic model of social security, education, and health provision, namely that the benefits were universal, available to everyone within the specified group, and that they were financed from general government revenues and not from earmarked premiums.

Later, as the welfare society developed from the 1930s on, two further principles emerged.

One was egalitarianism: the purpose of the welfare state was not just to help the needy, but to work in tandem with other policies to equalize post-tax incomes and ultimately living conditions in general. The daily standard of living of the high earner and the low earner should not be too different. How that policy goal harmonized with another goal, to maximize economic growth, was seemingly not a problem for decades. The extent to which it became a problem by the year 2000 is something we will look at later.

The other principle of the developed Nordic model was individualism, that is, the principle that individuals, not families or households, paid tax and received benefits. This principle was not fully introduced until the 1970s, when the Nordic countries, with the partial exception of Norway, abolished joint taxation of married couples. Yet this individualism, introduced in part to liberate women from dependence on a male breadwinner, coexisted with a far-reaching collectivism. In order to finance universal, tax-financed health, education, care of the aged, and pensions, Nordic governments needed to take well over half of GDP. How compatible such a dominant state was with individual liberty was another question that was not raised within the consensus culture until late in the century, and then mainly by economists.[37]

The development of Nordic societies in the twentieth century falls into two great eras. The first was the era of the people's home, of full employment, rising productivity, and rising mass prosperity from the 1930s to the 1970s. In this period, and especially in the three postwar decades, the Nordic model produced both economic growth and an expanding public sector.

---

[37]Especially by the Swedish economist Assar Lindbeck, formerly a social democrat, who in the 1970s began asking how far the advanced Swedish model and its sociocultural effects was compatible with liberty, initiative, and entrerpreneurship. Lundberg 1985, 28–30, and Lindbeck 1997.

The different countries moved in different rhythms; thus, the 1930s—the Depression decade in America—were, in Sweden, a decade of full employment and rising prosperity, whereas Denmark, Norway, and Finland suffered high unemployment and tough times, particularly for farmers. The 1950s, which in Germany and America, for example, were high-growth years, were, in Denmark and Norway, an era of slower growth and dammed-up expectations which exploded in the high growth 1960s.

The second era began, as far as the economy is concerned, in the 1970s, but its social and political roots were in the 1960s. It was an era of greater contradictions and confusions in politics, economic, and culture than the preceding. Some trends from the earlier era continued and accelerated, others changed direction. Therefore, depending on what perspective one adopts—economic, social, political, or cultural—the second era had a different duration and a different end. In some respects it had not ended by 2000, in others it was possible to see the lineaments of a third era of the Nordic model.

Our perspective combines the four dimensions of economy, society, politics, and culture by understanding the interplay between them. On this combined perspective, one name for the second era might be "the era of the half-empty glass." As prosperity was finally becoming near-universal in the 1960s, at least as judged by all previous history, and leading figures such as the long-serving Swedish minister of finance, Gunnar Sträng, declared that the welfare state was built, a new generation of complainers appeared who saw crisis everywhere. Beginning in the mid-1960s, political and academic elites discovered new problems, even as Scandinavians were richer and more equal than ever before. According to them, Sweden and other Nordic societies were, despite the growing prosperity and equality, characterized by too much inequality, too much capitalism, too much bad and hard work, and too much environmental destruction. The latter point of complaint is worth noting, since many people think that environmentalism and environmentalist policies are a feature of the 1990s and 2000s. The Swedes were early on that bandwagon with a range of highly alarmist tracts in the later 1960s. In the light of 1990s and 2000s mentalities, the focus on the inhuman pressure of work and the fear of the future in terms of natural environmental degradation and depletion of nature and natural resources are striking.

Why did the government sector in the Nordic countries become so large, growing from around 30 percent of GDP in 1960 to well over half by the 1980s? Its defenders, which include most Nordic people, will say that government grew first in response to the Depression, when large numbers of people were destitute, and later because the public wanted security and equality, deemed to be among the chief and valued effects of the welfare society. Yet people in other countries also wanted to alleviate the effects of economic crisis and improve public services but did not build states that dominated society and economy as much as the Nordic states did. The Nordic welfare states are not the only way to provide benefits, even though many Nordics consider them superior to other ways, such as the American pattern of providing education, health care, and other benefits largely outside government, or the insurance-based benefit systems of Continental Europe.

So the question remains. Scholars have advanced three explanations that are not mutually exclusive and all contain some part of the truth. They are listed here in summary fashion:

- The power resources theory, which holds that the welfare states are the natural result of social democratic parties, representing the nonrich, wage-earning majority, taking over government and carrying out redistributive and egalitarian policies designed to modify market outcomes

- The rational choice or constitutional theory, which states that systems of proportional representation encourage rational political actors to form long-lasting majority governing coalitions to redistribute resources, grant benefits to their own voters, and thereby secure their own hold on power
- The cultural theory, which I have partly subscribed to above, and which attributes the welfare states to long-standing cultural and social patterns in the North; Nordics have always liked equality and solidarity, and used government to promote them as soon as it became possible

Note that the first two are saying the same thing; namely, that the Nordic welfare states appeared because the dominant political force, the social democrats, wanted them and by controlling government had the means to create them. The difference is that the first theory, favored by political scientists, assumes that the social democratic leaders were acting altruistically to promote the interests of ordinary wage-earners who, in their belief, were unable to achieve their basic life tasks under market conditions. The second theory, favored by economists, assumes that politicians, like other people, act in their rational self-interest. Politicians want power and use it to benefit those who vote for them. Representing the wage-earning majority, social democratic politicians wanted to redistribute and equalize the market outcomes, which, by definition, gave the greatest rewards to the minority. The point of the second theory is that the political systems of the Nordic countries favored long-standing coalitions able to take resources from the minority and redistribute them to the majority.

The first theory congratulates the social democrats on a job well done and assumes that without the welfare states wage-earners and poorer people in the North would be worse off than they are with them. The second theory is agnostic on whether redistribution and egalitarianism in fact helped wage-earners or whether rising prosperity for the majority would have come about in any case. The first theory assumes that the social democratic welfare states do not seriously hamper individual initiative, that any disincentive to entrepreneurship at the top is richly outweighed by the additional resources provided to the less well off. The second theory is, again, agnostic, though some of its economist proponents clearly think that the Nordic welfare states at century's end were hindering the effective use of resources and redistributing too much to the wrong recipients.[38]

The second theory comes closer than the first to explaining why the Nordic welfare states took such an unusual trajectory. But it does not and perhaps cannot tell us why Nordics established political systems that—if the theory holds—were so well suited to a politics of state expansion and collective provision of benefits. Here the third, the cultural theory may come in handy, though it should not be overdone. Each society has its own historical legacies, and not all are effective in the present.

All theories agree, and the evidence shows, that the Nordic societies today are profoundly shaped by the dominant political force of the twentieth century, the organized labor movement with its two branches: the social democratic party (called the Labor party in Norway) and the confederation of manual and craft workers' unions, known in Denmark, Norway, and Sweden as the LO (*Landsorganisationen,* the countrywide organization). From the beginning these two forces, one in parliament and government, and the other in society at large, were committed to raising the living standards of the worst paid and of all wage-earners through economic and fiscal policies

---

[38]The power resources theory in Korpi 1987; the cultural theory in Knudsen 1999; and the rational choice or constitutional theory in Moberg 1999. Among the concerned economists we may list Lindbeck 1997 and Olson 1995, but for a necessary corrective to Olson see Moberg 2000.

and through collective bargaining with employers. But the Scandinavian labor movements began as more than just organizations of factory workers. When they began in the late nineteenth century, there were few factory workers, and many of their members were craft apprentices or landless farmworkers. These people had other concerns than pay, and one of them was alcohol. In all the Nordic countries but most of all in Sweden, the temperance movement, which began in the mid-nineteenth century as an outgrowth of religious revivalism in the early years of the century, became a crucial element of the social democratic coalition of interests. Since Swedish alcohol policy in particular deviates from the European norm, it provides an interesting sidelight on Nordic society.

Alcohol policy in the North illustrates both variations within the region and how some governments consider it their right and duty to discourage behavior considered socially harmful. In the old days, Swedish homeowners, that is, farmers, were allowed to distill their own spirits. Homeowners paid a tax for distilling whether they distilled or not and so they had an incentive to do so. Consumption in mid-nineteenth century was about six gallons of pure alcohol per capita per annum, three times today's level, and it was concentrated not on beer, which was weak, or wine, which was unknown outside the richest circles, but on *akvavit,* which at the time was a 94-proof liquor similar to vodka and with the same social effects as vodka in today's Russia. All four Nordic countries—Iceland was still subject to Denmark—changed policy around 1920. Denmark increased the tax twenty-fold within twelve months, cutting consumption by putting frequent use of *akvavit* beyond the means of poor people. In Denmark, the teetotal movement was not strong and most people thought that if you could reduce *akvavit* consumption and persuade people to drink more beer, that would be enough. In Sweden, the teetotalers were far stronger: the entire leadership of the social democratic party was nondrinking, which marked a contrast to the Danish leader at the time, Thorvald Stauning, who was known to enjoy an occasional "damp evening," as the Danish phrase has it.

In Sweden, feelings ran so high that the social democratic government called an advisory referendum in 1922 in which total prohibition was narrowly defeated by 51 percent of those voting, although only half bothered to vote. The Swedish artist Albert Engström contributed to the narrow victory with a famous poster. The culture clash was patent: on the one hand those who saw alcohol as a scourge of the poor and the weak, on the other those who saw it as part of a civilized life and, in particular, a necessary component of Swedish folk rituals, such as the annual crayfish dinner.

Instead of prohibition, Swedes got control. Alcoholic beverages were sold only in state stores and, until the 1950s, purchases were rationed, with a male head of household receiving the maximum allowance and single women usually none. From 1965 to 1977, beer was permitted to be sold in ordinary stores, but the government stopped the experiment when sales got too high. Since then, all alcoholic drink can again only be purchased in state stores, and citizens are encouraged to keep an eye out for excessive drinkers. No public agency in Sweden is allowed to spend money on alcohol, and private businesses are discouraged from doing so and are required to maintain a nondrinking policy at work.

In the late 1990s, the EU doomed the Swedish import regulations that prohibited travelers from other EU countries from bringing in whatever alcoholic beverages they wanted. Most likely, the state store system, also found in Norway and Finland, is also doomed, and the Swedish government will need to find other ways to restrict consumption. The policy has seemingly been successful; in Denmark, where the rules are lax, people drink about twice as much, although since Swedes are also more likely to have illegal stills, the actual figures may be less far apart.

In hindsight, the 1930s stand as the decisive decade in the formation of contemporary Nordic society. There may be some nostalgia in this, because from the vantage point of 2000 the immediately formative years were the 1970s, as we shall see. There is also truth to it, however, because the sociocultural, economic, and political upheavals of the long 1970s were themselves rooted in what was created in the 1930s.

As you will recall, the power resources theory says that the Nordic model was largely the creation of social democrats, who came into power throughout the North in the 1920s and consolidated that hold in the 1930s. A variant of this theory says that the welfare states and the Nordic model were less a creation of social democrats than a product of farmers' conflict with the urban middle class.[39] It was the farmers who wanted universalist, tax-financed provision of pensions and benefits, because many of them were too poor to afford premiums. This agrarian interest deflected Sweden and Denmark from following the Continental insurance method of social provision. In Sweden, this variant argues, the further development of the universalist welfare state was due more to middle class interests in the state taking over basic life tasks rather than to genuine egalitarianism. Most people did not so much want equality as *trygghet* (security) and within the framework of homogeneous Nordic nations they imposed this demand on each other, and it worked for most of a century.[40] The idea was still viable in 2000, though cracks were showing. Yet surprisingly few cracks, given that international comparisons showed that collectivized health, education, child care, and care of the aged in Nordic countries were not of notably higher quality than in other countries with smaller government sectors and a larger role for the market, private charities, and families.[41]

The argument that farmers' interests were critical partly holds for Denmark, the most dramatic case of social policy change in the 1930s. Denmark was worse hit than Sweden by the collapse of international trade and the international deflation that reduced Danish export earnings, which at the time were still mainly derived from agricultural exports to Britain. In late 1932, unemployment reached the appalling figure of 44 percent. In early 1933, the Social Democratic and Radical Liberal government formed the so-called *Kanslergade* agreement, named for the street where Stauning, the prime minister, lived, with the Agrarian (liberal) party. As part of the agreement, the parliament passed four social policy reform acts, which improved health insurance for the poor, imposed obligatory accident cover for employees, improved unemployment benefits, and, the most important, a law on public benefits to the poor that took care of those not entitled to regular unemployment or sickness benefit and abolished the older rule that those who received poor relief temporarily lost certain civil rights such as the right to vote. When the king had signed the bills into law in May 1933, the minister for social policy, K. K. Steincke, said:

> Show us one country in this world that offers the sick, the old, children, the unemployed, and the needy in general social legislation at the level of the social reform just enacted. I

---

[39]Baldwin 1990.

[40]Abrahamson 1999, 38, quotes a Norwegian sociologist who writes that "the link between general equality attitudes and the support for welfare measures has grown weaker and weaker" and that *"equality is not the central value in the welfare state . . . security is"* (emphasis in original). But if the security is illusory, that is, if the high taxes do not in fact provide guaranteed top quality, and people start realizing this, then what?

[41]Measuring quality of results in these key areas of the welfare state is notoriously difficult. The OECD is attempting to compare health results in forthcoming studies. For education the main clearinghouse for comparative studies is the International Association for the Evaluation of Educational Achievement, located in the Netherlands.

do not in any way exaggerate the significance of the social reform, but I also want to warn the more exuberant extremists on both flanks against underestimating it, because those who have brought it into port also know what it means in many ways for orderly development in a time of crisis and as assistance to the needy in this common people's society of ours.[42]

The social reform had great symbolic importance, but it did not for many years notably increase public spending. In the 1930s, the single biggest increase in Danish government spending was not the increased subsidies to local authorities for emergency assistance or other help to the unemployed, the uninsured old, or the poor, but a program of low-interest loans to the many farmers whose farms were worth less than the mortgages on them. This loan program of 1936 cost the taxpayer about four times as much per year as Steincke's four acts of 1933. Arguably, therefore, the biggest beneficiaries of the 1930s welfare programs in Denmark and Sweden were the farmers. They were needy; but arguably not more so than the urban poor, whether unemployed, underemployed, or old. However, the agrarian interest was powerful: in the 1930s, and indeed until the late 1950s, agriculture provided the majority of Danish exports by value. Keeping the farmers in business was as important if not more so than maintaining social peace in the towns, even for a social democratic government.

The Swedish road to the welfare state was more deliberate. Since the late nineteenth century, Swedish economists had contributed substantially to international scholarship on the functioning of a modern economy. By the 1920s and 1930s, a group of younger economists close to the Social Democratic party began formulating proposals for far-reaching state management of the economy to assure both redistribution and growth, but without the Marxist demand for putting an end to private property. These younger economists, such as Gunnar Myrdal (1898–1987), believed that it was more useful, as he put it, to socialize consumption than to socialize production. If government policy could equalize resources among citizens while maintaining a productive private sector, this would, in their view, be the best of all possible worlds. This design, which was often called the Swedish model, operated with astonishing success from the 1930s to the 1970s.[43]

One plank of this Swedish model was that the government's fiscal and tax policies should aim at maintaining demand. In this sense it anticipated the principles of Keynesian economics, named after the British economist John Maynard Keynes (1885–1946), who argued in the 1920s and 1930s that severe recessions could be mitigated if the government would maintain demand by running deficits in crisis years. In 1928, eight years before Keynes published his most influential work, *The General Theory of Employment, Interest and Money*, the Swedish economist and social democrat Ernst Wigforss (1881–1977) wrote that in times of depression it was the "friendly spendthrift" who hired people by spending loosely who was socially useful, whereas the saver was stopping recovery. If business refused to use people's savings to hire, the state should give people work at market wages, since this would add demand and buying power to the economy which would have a multiplier effect. He continued:

> The fact is that if I want to make work for a hundred people it is not necessary for me to employ all hundred of them. The world fortunately works so that if I can get work for an unemployed tailor, he can buy new shoes and in that way an unemployed cobbler gets work. The crisis is characterized by behavior

---

[42] Quoted in Kaarsted 1991, 100–101.

[43] Lundberg 1985.

which constitutes what is called a vicious circle and which means that first a few lose income which means that those people who are used to supplying their needs also cannot sell their goods and then become unemployed. One can say that crisis feeds on itself once it starts. It is a well known fact, but it works the same way once recovery starts.[44]

These homely images reflected a Sweden of farmers, craftsmen, and industrial workers, and in that society adding demand worked. It was different in the Scandinavia of the 1970s and after, when most people worked in the service sector and many in the public sector, and government consumed two thirds or more of the national product. In such an economy, unemployment turned out to be less amenable to fiscal policy that added to aggregate demand. Teachers, doctors, academics, and social workers did not offer goods for sale that could be bought in greater quantities if the public's buying power grew. The old remedies for unemployment and fiscal imbalances did not take, or not adequately so. Other means had to be found.

Wigforss advocated economic planning, a gradual growth of central management of money and the use of capital. He warned that the social democrats were caught between two traditions, revolutionary Marxism, which advocated outright socialization, and liberalism which saw business and the market as sacrosanct. He proposed a new strategy which discarded Marxist fatalism, the idea that revolution was inevitable, and thereby solved another Marxist dilemma by abandoning it, namely the question whether revolution was far in the future or close. Instead, the social democrats should solve the crisis by economic planning, pumping demand into the economy and asserting control over the major functions rather than the ownership of business and capital assets. This ideology of planning later became known as functional socialism. It did not matter who owned the shares as long as the business adapted to the overall policies of the social democratic party. The new ideology retained the socialist idea of freedom. That idea meant using government power to shape the economy so that the broad masses were freed from need and suffering, which were still held to be necessary consequences of private property and capitalism.

As in Denmark, the international crisis of the early 1930s led to an agreement among the social democrats and liberals in 1933, the so-called "cow trade," whereby the social democratic prime minister Per Albin Hansson split the conservative front by cutting a deal with the agrarian party. In return for abandoning free trade and accepting protection of the farmers, Hansson got the agrarians to support his program of subsidized employment at market wages, which rapidly increased demand and led to a period of almost full employment for the rest of the 1930s. According to the Swedish political scientist Leif Lewin, Hansson acted strategically to obtain a best possible outcome: the alternative that, while not being anyone's first preference, was nevertheless that which a majority could support. A pure majority decision would have delayed action on unemployment.

With the "cow trade," Sweden was well launched on its particular path of social peace, sustained growth, equality, and solidarity, one that soon achieved near-mythical status among international admirers. The best known of these admirers was the American journalist Marquis Childs, who in 1936 published an enthusiastic and sentimental book on Sweden entitled *Sweden: The Middle Way,* in which he wrote of "a people who cultivated their garden, their rocky, remote, lonely garden, with patience, with courage, and with an extraordinary degree of intelligence."[45] Certainly the "cow trade" and other measures of the 1930s

---

[44] Quoted in Lewin 1984, 172.

[45] Quoted in *Daedalus* 113:1, *The Nordic Enigma,* v.

brought social stability and growing satisfaction, but Childs's rosy picture rather reflected what policy intellectuals such as Gunnar Myrdal and Ernst Wigforss wanted than reality.

One effect of the 1930s reforms was that central government grew relative to local government, both fiscally and politically. Under the older rules, local authorities determined need and the level of public support. The new rules increased uniformity, provided central government subsidies to municipalities, and began the process of transferring resources from richer to poorer municipalities. This meant that central government revenues had to grow, so what is known in the Nordic countries as "state tax"—as distinct from county and *kommune* or local tax, and church tax—grew. In Denmark, the poorer half of the population paid little or no state tax until the 1930s, and in Sweden it remained true at the century's end that state tax was only owed on incomes at or above the median, which in 2000 was about 250,000 *kronor* or $30,000 at purchasing power parity.

A second plank of the Swedish model was industrial peace. In December 1938, representatives of the LO (the confederation of trade unions) and of the employers' organizations met near Stockholm and concluded what became known as the Saltsjöbaden agreement. This entailed that wages would be set by collective bargaining, usually every other year, among union and employer representatives and that strikes would be forbidden while the collective agreements were in force. The wage scales agreed by each union and for each industry would be binding on all, including nonmembers, although there were not many of these. One of the striking features of Nordic societies was that union membership remained high, even when it was dropping in other countries. In 2000, close to 90 percent of the workforce was, as the Nordic phrase has it, "organized," and it remained true then as in the 1930s that collective bargaining determined compensation for the vast majority of occupations, including those of graduates and many professionals, whether they were members or not.

In Denmark, the union confederation and the employers had reached a similar agreement as early as 1899. This so-called General Agreement, many times amended, has been called the basic law of the labor market. It gives the employer the right to "direct and allocate work" in return for the relevant union's right to represent employees and negotiate on their behalf. The General Agreement in Denmark and the Saltsjöbaden agreement in Sweden enjoyed a peculiar status; they were not laws, and in both countries the negotiating parties explicitly stated that government should not seek to regulate the labor market or industrial relations by law. Yet collective agreements on wages and working conditions had the force of law. An employer could not pay according to performance or offer individual employment contracts; what went into the contracts, whether in the public or private sector, was centrally decided and, until the 1980s, allowed only minor local variations. During the twentieth century, as public employment grew, new unions for white-collar and government employees grew up outside the LO umbrella, but these, too, were part of the quasi-legal structure of the Nordic labor market.

The third plank of the Swedish model was the so-called solidaristic wage policy first formulated in the 1930s and more effectively by another social democratic economist, Gösta Rehn, in the late 1940s.[46] This phrase meant three things. First, that the same type of work should receive the same compensation without regard to profitability or productivity in individual firms or regions. Second, that the government should support union efforts to raise the pay of the worst off more rapidly than that of the better off and should seek through fiscal policy to minimize inequality in

---

[46]Lundberg 1985, 18.

net disposable income. Third, that the government should squeeze business profits by, for example, imposing heavy payroll taxes, forcing the least profitable firms out of business, but should also by selective subsidies help the employees of these firms to find work in more profitable industries. The solidaristic wage policy was thus also an industrial policy. In Alice Rivlin's neutral words, "Compressing the wage scale by raising the lower end was expected to drive firms with low productivity out of business and shift industrial structure toward capital-intensive, high-productivity industries."[47] This policy went with and was smoothed by the Saltsjöbaden model of industrial relations. For several decades it produced growing equality of net income, but the trend turned in the 1980s. Wages in the mid-1980s were the most unevenly-distributed component of income in Sweden.[48] During the 1990s, inequalities in net disposable income grew in Finland, Norway, and Sweden, as in most other Western countries, though not in Denmark.

The economist and former social democrat Assar Lindbeck described the Swedish model as a society dominated by large institutions, public as well as private, linked by formal or informal structures and, as a consequence, a fiscal and economic policy mix that favored insiders, the already successful, that is, well-established big business which was able to adapt to and benefit from the system of rules built up by the welfare state. The deal was that, in accordance with the functional socialism of Wigforss and Myrdal, Swedish big business would earn revenue; the state would control its use, not, for example, allowing individual businessmen to earn significantly more than the average; in general the state would promote business so that business could finance social expansion. In practice, "all unions should take more or less the same wage from employers, even if that led to difficulties for the less profitable firms and even if not everything possible was actually taken from the more profitable firms."[49] One consequence of this was that a few capitalists accumulated large fortunes in an overall atmosphere of increasing equality. The downside was that it became difficult for new entrants to survive. For example, with the exception of the Rausing companies, whose fortunes began with a valuable patent on the design of milk cartons, no successful big manufacturing businesses such as L million Ericsson, Electrolux, Volvo, or Asea were founded in the four decades after 1950.

In 1944, Gunnar Myrdal wrote a program for the postwar strategy of the labor movement. It assumed that the end of World War II would lead to worldwide economic crisis as pent-up consumer demand exploded and government expenditure fell. The strategy envisaged a far-reaching socialization of the economy. In the event, the crisis failed to appear, but one metaphor from Myrdal's program survived: the metaphor of the "harvest time" of socialism that would come when the labor movement and its political arm, the social democratic party, had seized the high ground of political and economic control of society and was able to direct it for the benefit of all.

Twelve years later, the Swedish prime minister Tage Erlander (1901–1985) launched the notion of the "strong society" in a parliamentary debate.[50] The strong society was the idea that the social democratic policies of redistribution and collective provision of education, health care, and pensions made society strong and able to take up new challenges. In another speech that same year, 1956, Erlander—who led the government without interruption for 23 years, a world record in a democratic country—suggested that the welfare state was more or less complete. The work was mostly done, the

---

[47]Bosworth & Rivlin 1987, 5.
[48]Flanagan 1987, 151.
[49]Leif Lewin, ibid. 320.
[50]Arvidsson 1999, 27.

harvest time was at hand. He had no idea what the harvesters would be like.

FROM FAITH TO FEAR

In the election campaign of 1960, the Danish social democrats urged voters to "make good times better." Optimism was in the air and in the figures. All across the North, the years around 1960 marked an extraordinary and, as it turned out, short-lived amalgam of psychological well-being, high growth rates, low or zero inflation, full employment, and rapidly rising real incomes. Well could the social democratic governing parties congratulate themselves on jobs well done, proclaim the welfare state more or less complete, and look to new horizons.

Viggo Kampmann (1910–1976), the Danish prime minister who took his party into the 1960 election, agreed with Erlander, who stated in 1956 that the welfare state was fully evolved. In an election speech, Kampmann noted that the welfare state was in place and that people were getting better off. His next words were a blend of old social democratic principles and newer faith in political management, a faith that, unknown to Kampmann, presaged conflict and trouble ahead. "We will not," Kampmann said, "let individuals reap the fruits of prosperity. We will take the wealth and use it for common purposes. We will build universities and seats of learning."[51] Social democracy in Scandinavia had always stood for expropriating profits for collective use. Now, the basic goals of the universalist welfare state having been met, and the economy regulated onto a path of growth, the next stage was at hand.

Kampmann's social democratic Danish government passed a number of laws collectively known as the lesser social reform (the big one was the one of 1933). The most significant of these was the law on public provision of welfare of 1961 which abolished the older three-tier system of special assistance, municipal assistance, and poor relief. In the future, people with no other source of income or support received a standard welfare payment known as cash benefit (*kontanthjælp*). The general thrust of these reforms, which can be paralleled in Sweden and Norway, was to change the direction of social policy from emergency intervention to promoting general welfare as defined in Nordic culture, that is to say, in the direction of more equality of living conditions and of providing unearned resources to the poorest or weakest members of society, without regard to merit.

Kampmann and Erlander were both egalitarians and optimists. Unfortunately matters turned out to be less simple than the technocrats of 1960 thought. By turning to new fields, the social democratic leaders seemed to imply that there was more work to be done, that a social democratic utopia was still to be built. Younger social democrats and people further left, who sensed that their kind of politics and belief were on the upswing, interpreted these promises and beliefs differently. They did not see a completed welfare state, but a society still ridden with inequality and oppression and which would remain so as long as the basic sin, private property, was not abolished. What the technocrats saw as an infinite, continuing progress toward more social and economic equality was to a younger generation a signal for a revolutionary new beginning.

In 1968, a leading representative of the older ruling elite, the Swedish finance minister Gunnar Sträng (1906–1992, minister from 1955 to 1976), could state with a mixture of pride and complacency that the welfare state was more or less complete.[52] This at the very time that powerful coalitions of younger politicians,

---

[51] Quoted in Kirby 1993, 390.

[52] Arvidsson 1999, 41.

Christmas markets in Stockholm, Sweden.

academics, and administrators were discovering new reasons to say that everything was far from well, and that the Nordic countries were flawed, incomplete, unjust societies requiring further drastic and radical change.

Starting in the mid-1960s, when the economies were growing faster than ever before or since and real disposable income rising by 8 to 10 percent a year, a change came over politics and society in the North. Where the older generation saw achievement and looked to an ever better and more secure future, a new generation of politicians, intellectuals, and journalists saw fear, polarization, exploitation, insecurity, and risk. This is called the "glass half empty" syndrome. All the problems supposedly solved by the Nordic welfare society returned with a number of new twists. A new society was needed, the elite worriers successfully argued, not one like Soviet Russia, but one in which alienation was abolished not just at work, but in the family, in personal relations, in the inner corners of the psyche. This was a recipe for permanent discontent, which also provided countless reasons for more public spending.

In the 1970s the Finnish sociologist Erik Allardt surveyed Nordic social values and found that pluralities of 40 to 70 percent, lowest in Norway and highest in Finland, believed that some people made too much money. "These respondents, remember, enjoy the most equal distribution by far in all of Western Europe and are ruled by some of the most 'democratic' governments on earth. Still, they seem to be dissatisfied and want even more equality."[53] The glass, once again, was not half full, but half empty.

---

[53]Cited in Dahl 1984, 94–95.

The key figure of the new era was Olof Palme (1929–1986), Erlander's successor as prime minister. Palme devoted much of his life to winning friends among pro-Soviet Third World countries such as Cuba and to presenting Sweden as a "moral great power," a voice for peace and an end to imperialism on the global stage. This posturing came to a sudden end after Palme himself was shot to death in Stockholm in February 1986, a crime that was never solved. In his lifetime, he was a new kind of politician. His supporters found him charismatic, eloquent, a true friend of the oppressed. His enemies, who were many, called him manipulative, emotional, foul-mouthed, and paranoid. He was given to outbursts against American politicians and conservatives at home. The conservative party leader, Gösta Bohman, was a "devil." The British conservative leader and prime minister Margaret Thatcher was "not quite a fascist." His language about communist dictators was, by contrast, moderate and sympathetic. In 1984, Palme publicly hoped that the U.S. president Ronald Reagan would lose the election because Reagan was endangering world peace. Within Sweden, Palme played a more substantial role as a charismatic and confrontational leader of the new coalition of radical socialist politicians, civil servants, and intellectuals who believed that the Swedish model as it was built up since the 1930s was only the stepping stone for the genuine transition to socialism.

Palme sensed his direction early. As long ago as 1955, he wrote an influential article with the economist Assar Lindbeck, who later disavowed his co-author's policies as prime minister, arguing that resources and programs for social change could be aimed at marginal groups who had not enjoyed the fruits of growth and rising prosperity—invalids, the mentally ill, unwed mothers, students. The last group was an odd one to include, since students in the 1950s were a small category, perhaps 5 percent of the relevant age cohorts, and destined for high status. But Palme, at least, could spot a category of future allies and knew that the student population was expanding, as it did sixfold between 1950 and 1970. He also, like Viggo Kampmann in Denmark, advocated more money for research and development, which was granted.

One way that the new groups justified their more radical egalitarianism and socialism was by pointing, as Palme did in 1955, to those groups who had not shared in the economic success of the Swedish model with its combination of full employment and growing public spending. The key document was a 1965 Swedish government report on low-income groups. Its findings were used to argue for a radicalization of the solidaristic wage policy, for further taxes on the rich, and for a greater government role in the economy. For the first time since the 1940s, some social democrats began to speak of nationalization, which had formerly been a nonissue in Sweden, where the government allowed big business to survive as long as it got to redistribute profits and direct investments. A prominent younger social democrat advocated, for example, nationalizing "those industries that try to satisfy artificially constructed demand such as the cosmetic industry." Another argued that "we must try by shaping opinion to persuade those with higher pay to abstain from higher standards of living."[54] Another demand spurred by the low income report was equal pay for equal time worked with no distinction of quality or competence. Common to these social democratic statements of around 1970 was the idea that money was power and having assets gave you power over others, which was bad. Therefore government should expropriate what it deemed to be excess profits or pay and redistribute the proceeds to the less fortunate.

Sweden became, in the eyes of politicians, bureaucrats, and ideologues, a country of capitalist oppression, and the state began accelerating the desire for "another society." The new

---

[54]Arvidsson 288–289.

rhetoric affected even solid pillars of the old consensus. Rudolf Meidner, an economist with LO who had been one of the authors of the 1940s Swedish model, in 1975 proposed that the government should establish investment funds owned and administered by the unions which would buy up private businesses. Criticizing excess profits, Meidner wrote that "we won't allow them [the capitalists] to buy themselves off."[55] The capitalists were no longer partners, but suspicious characters who had to be reined in.

In 1970 another document of great symbolic importance appeared, one that became a bestseller throughout Scandinavia and was read by all those who saw the Nordic societies as bastions of capitalist oppression and inequality. This was the book *Report from a Mopping-Pail*, written by Maja Ekelöf, a single mother of three who worked as a cleaning lady. She described a life of drudgery, low pay, and little dignity. Her portrait was true, but was exploited beyond its merits to defend a radical socialism. For one thing, Ekelöf's *Report* was more a portrait of the 1950s than of the time when it was read and used as an ideological bludgeon. Nor did many of Ekelöf's readers notice that one of the book's themes is how her three children, despite their deprived background, worked hard in school and made successes of themselves. With the social democratic–inspired educational reforms of the 1970s, excelling in school was discouraged as elitist.

In 1971, soon after Palme had taken over the social democratic government, the British journalist Roland Huntford—who later wrote best-selling books about the Antarctic explorers Amundsen, Scott, and Shackleton—published a book about Sweden based on several years' residence with the deliberately shocking title *The New Totalitarians*. In it, Huntford characterized Swedes as willing victims of their own oppression by a domineering state. The Swedes, Huntford said, were conditioned by centuries of subservience to accept that the state and its agents, the bureaucracy, knew best. That was why they willingly went along with coercive rules on alcohol consumption, with high taxes, and with an educational policy that penalized independent schools. What was missing in Sweden, Huntford believed, was a liberal middle class in the British or Continental European sense, a social segment of people with independent means who could form a base of social power and cultural influence to balance the state. Without such an alternative base of power and opinion, Sweden had become, in his view, frighteningly conformist and excessively egalitarian. Few Swedes took Huntford seriously at the time, although his basic point, that Sweden had a large public sector and a government that believed strongly in shaping citizens' behavior in approved directions, was hardly controversial. It was not until the late 1970s that a small antistatist group of Swedish intellectuals, financially assisted by the Swedish Employers' Federation, began questioning the legitimacy of the strong state and the socialist tendency to make the state coextensive with society. By the 1990s, even though the state had not shrunk or shed much of its power, the political culture of Sweden had become more open to liberal ideas.[56]

Economically, the long 1970s began as boom years and ended as years of stagflation, the combination of low growth and high inflation that bedeviled most of the Western world from 1974–1981. Sweden avoided one component of this unfortunate era, namely high unemployment. By a combination of active labor market policies and subsidies, the Swedes

---

[55]Niklasson 1997, 57.

[56]The group in question is the Timbro group which by 2000 had become a respected interlocutor in public debate after years of being vilified by the dominant prosocialist intellectuals. Their website is http://www.timbro.se. Personal note: since 1980, I have found Timbro's materials invaluable as alternative sources of inspiration, indignation, and insight on Sweden.

TABLE 6.2 Social Expenditure, 1995, as a Percentage of GDP in Selected Countries (Does Not Include Spending on Education, Child Care, or Elder Care)

	Denmark	Finland	Germany	Norway	Sweden	UK	USA
1. Gross public social expenditure	32.2	31.9	27.1	27.6	33.0	22.4	15.8
2. Pension spending	7.7	9.1	10.9	6.2	9.0	7.3	6.3
3. Unemployment	4.6	4.0	1.4	1.1	2.3	0.9	0.3
4. Disability spending	2.3	4.0	1.4	2.7	2.4	2.8	1.0
5. Sickness benefits	0.7	0.5	0.5	1.2	1.2	0.2	0.2
6. Public expenditure on health	5.3	5.7	8.1	6.6	5.9	5.7	6.3
7. Other (1)	11.7	8.6	4.7	9.8	12.3	5.5	1.5
8. Public cash benefits	21.4	22.9	17.3	15.6	21.4	15.4	8.7
9. Public social services and health	10.8	9.1	9.8	12.0	11.6	7.0	7.1
10. Net voluntary private social expenditure	0.5	0.7	0.8		1.4	3.6	7.8
11. Gross total social expenditure	33.6	33.2	29.6	28.5	35.5	27.0	24.1
12. Direct taxes and social contributions paid on cash benefits	6.1	5.1	1.2	2.7	5.2	0.4	0.3
13. Indirect taxes	8.0	5.5	4.1	6.9	5.8	3.7	0.9
14. Net public social expenditure	23.6	25.1	25.0	21.0	25.4	22.3	17.5
15. Net total social expenditure	**24.4**	**25.7**	**27.7**	**25.7**	**26.0**	**24.5**	**24.5**

Source: OECD, *Social Expenditure Database*, Paris.

(1) Includes public spending grouped across the following social policy areas: services for the elderly and disabled; family cash benefits; family services; active labour market policies; and other contingencies such as cash benefits to those on low income.

The table shows that the net amount (line 15) is closely similar in all countries, which given that the United States has the highest per capita GDP also makes the U.S. the most generous social spender. The explanation for this apparent riddle, given that Nordic welfare states are considered more generous, is twofold. Line 10 reveals that Americans devote 7.8 percent of GDP to private social expenditure. The biggest item here is health insurance, which is not provided by government as in Scandinavia. The second reason can be read in lines 12 through 13, which reveal that Nordics, especially Danes, pay high taxes on their social benefits—the rather astonishing figure of 8 percent of GDP taken in indirect taxes on benefits mainly reflects the 25 percent VAT that applies to all purchases, including food—whereas benefits are hardly taxed at all in Britain and the United States.

succeeded in keeping unemployment under 4 percent until 1991. In all Nordic countries, the long 1970s were years of rapid expansion of public employment, which grew by 6 percent a year every year in the 1970s in Sweden; private sector employment, by contrast, grew hardly at all from 1970–2000. By 2000, the public sector employed over 30 percent of the workforce in Denmark, Norway, and Sweden; Finland stood a little lower at 25 percent.[57]

Many of the new public employees were women; in Denmark, the proportion of married women working jumped from 42 to 66 percent in the 1970s.[58] That figure reflects the most important social trend of the long 1970s, which was the integration of women into the workforce. This trend changed the face of the Nordic welfare societies. As married women and mothers began working in large numbers, they posed demands for day care and for paid maternal leave. Both were granted, as women's work was now seen as a condition of full citizenship in the welfare state and as a decisive and desirable step away from the old male-breadwinner family. Women should be autonomous citizens in the welfare state, that is, doing paid work and paying taxes. By the 1990s, Nordic women could take from one to two years of paid maternity leave and could rely on government to provide day care places so they could return to work. The decisive policies encouraging full employment of women and enabling them to combine work and motherhood justify speaking of a "state feminism" as one of the most significant

---

[57]OECD 2000, 42.

[58]Skrede 1999, 180.

features of the late twentieth-century Nordic welfare state.

The Nordic countries had not formerly been high-tax countries. Starting in the late 1960s, they began to diverge from the North Atlantic norm, culminating in the late 1990s in the position that Denmark, Norway, and Sweden had the world's highest tax burden. By then they occupied a distinct niche in the OECD spectrum, characterized by large public sectors—30 percent of the workforce vs. 15 percent in the United States—and by tax-financed public provision of pensions, aid to the unemployed, health care, child care, and education. If one included voluntary or privately financed benefits, such as health care in the United States, which was not as a rule provided by government, the total social expenditure was remarkably similar across countries. (See Table 6.2, which provides some figures to show comparison of social expenditures in various countries.) The difference was that the Nordics used taxes to pay for services and that most services were provided outside the market.

CRISIS OR TRANSFORMATION OF THE NORDIC MODEL

In the world of politics and policymaking, the long 1970s marked a change from an ethic of responsibility to an ethic of conviction. Instead of appealing to broad interests, politicians were rewarded for demonstrating their commitment to causes and single issues. The media insisted on striking sound bites that the same media could later use to hit the politicians with if they deviated from their promises. This generated a hectic atmosphere of nervous posturing which was characteristic of Nordic and of all Western politics by the end of the century. The Swedish political scientist Leif Lewin, writing in 1984, noted other changes. Authority and deference were things of the past. Strategic thinking and acting in politics became suspicious. Lewin called for a revival of respect for politics as a calling, in the words of the German sociologist Max Weber (1864–1920) and for greater attention to the strategic element of political decisions.

By the time of the second oil shock of 1979 and the recession that followed some observers were starting to note that the selfsame institutions and practices that had encouraged and enabled growth and spreading prosperity as well as increased life-chances for many were becoming obstacles to renewal and forces of reaction rather than forces of growth. The near-total unionization of the workforce, the politicization of management and decisions in all parts of the economy and society, and the government monopoly of services were products of the era of high capitalism in the North, the era of confrontation between owners and workers, and the era of great inequalities of status and resources. Those days were over; by 1980, only about 1 percent of the value produced in Nordic societies went to those who owned the means of production, that is, the much-maligned capitalists. The rhetoric of the labor organizations nevertheless continued to sound as though little had changed since the 1930s; indeed, that things had, if anything, gotten worse—the glass half empty syndrome again—so that the ordinary people needed the organizations and their political allies more than ever in order to overcome, surpass, or replace capitalism.

Despite the vehemently anticapitalist rhetoric and ideology of large parts of the political, media, and academic elite, Sweden and the North generally remained throughout the long 1970s and after a region of many equal folk and a few extremely rich ones. Since the late nineteenth century, the Swedish economy had been characterized by a heavy concentration of mining and manufacturing in the hands of a small group of people, the fifteen families, of which the most famous were the Wallenbergs, one of whose number, the diplomat Raoul Wallenberg, was murdered in the Soviet Union after having helped to free thousands of Hungarian Jews from Nazi persecution during World War II.[59] The Swedish model of political economy favored these existing concentrations which had formed a comfortable symbiosis with the redistributive state, as long as the state permitted them to expand. Rudolf Meidner's proposal to establish wage-earner funds and to use them to socialize ownership of major businesses was a break with this symbiosis. Capitalism was immoral, proponents argued, because it led to unequal resources, and functional socialism—making outcomes equal while leaving ownership of big business intact—did not go far enough in abolishing immorality and inequality. In 1983, Palme's government sought to pass the relevant legislation but was stopped by intense public opposition, including the largest demonstrations ever seen in Sweden. A modified and watered-down proposal was enacted instead which was overtaken in the 1990s when the Swedish economy, after another crisis, entered a new period of rapid growth based on information technology.

Major strikes by white-collar and graduate employees in Sweden in 1980 and a tax reform in 1981 that slightly lowered the 90 percent marginal tax rate were signs of discontent. From 1976-1982, the Swedish government was, for the first time since 1932, not led by social democrats, but so unused were the so-called bourgeois parties to power that they did little to change course. Instead, they subsidized dying industries such as shipbuilding, a policy dropped when Palme came back into power in 1982.

In Denmark and Sweden the early 1980s were an era of economic reorientation. Both countries, after years of devaluations to defend exports and discourage imports, turned to a fixed exchange rate policy and to anti-inflationary monetary and fiscal policy. Sweden had the better starting position for change. Until the late 1970s, Sweden had always balanced its government budget, so it had no net public debt, and enjoyed regular surpluses on its current account and therefore had no foreign debt either. In Denmark, public debt had been brought down in the early 1970s only to rise rapidly when the government responded to the 1974-1975 OPEC-induced recession by allowing inflation to rip and expanding public services. The foreign debt position was worse, for Denmark had run deficits on the current account every year since 1963, and was to continue doing so until 1989. For much of the period 1975-1994, the Danish economy was out of synch with those of the other rich countries.[60] In the late 1970s, most of the rich world enjoyed a fragile recovery from the first oil shock; Denmark entered a period of stagflation—high unemployment coupled with high inflation—earlier and deeper than others. In the early 1980s, the Danish economy was, in the words of the minister of finance, "at the edge of the abyss," or, by some measures, part way into the abyss—an abyss of hyperinflation and out-of-control deficits on both current account and the government budget. When the rest of the industrial world hit recession in 1982-1983, Denmark was already starting to recover after interest rates on government bonds peaked at 22 percent.

---

[59] Wallenberg was Swedish consul in Budapest in the last months of World War II, in which capacity he issued thousands of emergency Swedish passports to enable Hungarian Jews to escape arrest by the Germans. In February 1945 he turned himself in to the advancing Soviet forces. Why he, a diplomat with immunity, did this, and why he never returned, remained mysterious. Documents that came to light after the fall of the Soviet Union give some answers. Wallenberg had contacts with Moscow which he hoped to use to help the surviving Jews of Europe, so when he gave himself up to the Soviets in Hungary, he was intending to be taken to Moscow to pursue his diplomatic work on behalf of the Jews. He was also providing information to the American Office of Strategic Services, the forerunner of the CIA. This was known to the Soviets, who tried to persuade him to become a double agent. Had he agreed, he would have been sent back to Sweden in triumph and would have become a prized Soviet asset. He refused, and since he was now useless to the Soviets, Stalin had him killed in early 1947.

[60] Nannestad 1999b.

The problems of the developed Nordic model were assessed by Assar Lindbeck after he left the Social Democratic party. In writings of the 1980s and 1990s, he suggested that high marginal tax rates depressed labor supply and hindered productivity growth. High taxes encouraged people to seek subsidies for all manner of activities, which induced what he termed a "learned helplessness." Furthermore, the tax system encouraged tactical thinking to evade taxes and seek subsidies and imposed a "high tax on honesty." Beating the system became a game in which the gains did not necessarily go to the most productive and prosperity was due less to productive effort than to luck and ability to play the system for subsidies and exemptions. "It could be argued that from the point of view of rewarding productive contributions it is largely the wrong type of people that become rich in Sweden."[61]

High marginal taxes, including indirect taxes such as value added tax (VAT) of 25 percent on all goods and services induce tax-avoiding behavior. To hire a plumber at the full rate including VAT, say $40 an hour, a Nordic taxpayer must earn $120 before tax, but, since VAT and taxes are owed on the $40, the plumber himself only sees about $10, a ratio of 12:1 between what the customer needs to make and the plumber's net pay. If the same customer pays the plumber half his usual rate off the books, the plumber gets twice as much, namely $20. The customer still needs to earn three times the amount, but that is now $60 and the ratio of customer's required gross income to plumber's take-home pay drops to 3:1. Examples such as this illustrate why the gray economy grew since the 1970s, but few knew by how much. Even the father of the Swedish model, Gunnar Myrdal, wrote in his old age that the Swedes had become a "nation of cheaters." By some estimates, probably exaggerated, 25 percent of resources were employed in the gray economy by the 1990s.

In a high tax environment, moreover, people will prefer activities that are cost free or can be carried out outside the normal economy. For example, they will prefer more leisure to more pay, because in their leisure time they can do their own household repairs and maybe carry out a little barter or gray-market business. In both Denmark and Sweden, the union federations in 2000 were demanding a sixth week of paid vacation rather than higher pay, most of which would be taken in taxes. The demand reinforced a trend in the Nordic countries toward shorter working hours; in 2000, the typical Nordic wage-earner worked about 1700 hours per year vs. almost 2000 hours for an American worker. Indeed, the total number of hours worked in Denmark fell by 8 percent between 1960 and 2000 throughout the workforce. The government warned that the trend toward fewer hours worked was unsustainable and would be more unsustainable in the future when the workforce would start to shrink and when the number of old age pensioners would grow relative to those of working age. Moreover, in all Nordic countries except Iceland, the average age of retirement continued to fall. By 2000, less than half of those aged 60 to 65 were in regular paid employment.

These trends were hardly surprising since the tax rates discouraged initiative and marginal effort. Another effect of the system, noted by Lindbeck already in the early 1980s, was that as wage-earners did more work for themselves, such as repairs and construction work, for which they were not trained, they brought their children to be cared for by government employees. Impersonal activities such as construction and maintenance were done privately and personal activities such as child care were collectivized. Highly trained professionals, such as doctors, did their own housing improvements rather than spending more hours seeing patients, because the extra money earned was less after tax than the money saved by not hiring experts to do the

---

[61] Comments in Bosworth & Rivlin 1987, 244–245.

housing work. But a doctor is not most effectively employed pouring concrete, so that the system, by discouraging the highly trained from doing more of what they are trained for, misallocates resources on a large scale. Efforts to correct such distortions, for example by allowing homeowners to deduct the cost of improvements from their taxable income, or by making it cheaper to employ construction workers and other specialists, stranded on government opposition to lowering taxes or union opposition to varying wage rates.

A third feature of the Nordic model at century's end was that as government expenditure rose since the 1960s, the increases went not so much to funding core services such as health care, basic education, and care of the old, whose share of the budget remained fairly constant. The bulk of the increases consisted of spending on new categories, ranging from transfers to proliferating categories of people deemed in need of help to new types of training and re-education. Primary schools could not afford to replace twenty-year-old textbooks while at the same time governments found the money to conduct expensive television campaigns against drinking, smoking, throwing away electrical appliances, and walking your dog without a leash. Spending on causes favored by influential constituencies in the political parties and the civil service grew, while crowding out private savings and private initiative.

Although the tax burden in Denmark, Norway, and Sweden was the highest in the world, the systems were not identical. The biggest sources of revenue in Denmark were the income tax collected by local, county, and central government, and the VAT. In addition, Denmark was characterized by many special taxes on consumer goods, ranging from chocolate and playing cards to household appliances and, most severely, cars, which carried a 180-percent registration duty.[62] These were in addition to the VAT that was added to the total cost and was thus in many cases a tax on a tax. In Sweden, by contrast, in 2000 only 5 percent of tax revenues came from personal income tax. Social contributions and payroll taxes provided about 30 percent.

Denmark had nonsocialist governments from 1982 to 1993, but the welfare state continued to expand, as it did under conservative Margaret Thatcher in the United Kingdom. This record casts doubt on the power resources model as an account of how and why the Nordic welfare states have become as large as they have. As we have seen, the model has been the preferred explanation of political scientists, especially those sympathetic to the welfare state, and has been supported and purveyed by the social democratic parties and the labor movements generally—that is, the explanation that says we got welfare states because we, the social democrats and workers, fought for them, extracted resources from the capitalists, and built them. Accordingly the welfare states were the creation of social democracy; a theory that in 2000 was still the official ideology and bedrock belief of social democratic politicians and many intellectuals.

The model further claimed that the welfare state was part of the distributional struggle in capitalist societies between the working class and the employers and owners of capital. The welfare state became possible when the workers could accumulate enough voting power to redistribute wealth and provide public services by political means. The Polish-born political scientist Adam Przeworski has spoken

---

[62]The ferocious Danish 180 percent new car tax had a paradoxical effect. In order to sell cars in Denmark, manufacturers gave Danish dealers special discounts, so that the pre-tax price of cars in Denmark was the lowest in the EU. Since the registration tax was not owed if the car was exported, and since movement of goods was free within the EU, other Europeans would come to Denmark to buy their cars and take them home, thus undercutting their own local dealers. But if, conversely, a Dane brought a car back from another EU country it became liable to the 180 percent tax before it could be driven in Denmark. Danes said that when they bought a car they paid for three: one for themselves and two for the minister of taxation. The result of the high car tax was that Danes had the oldest and smallest cars in the EU. In Denmark, minivans, mobile homes, and SUV's were for the very rich only.

of wage-earners' political power as "paper stones," the paper being the ballots by which the social democratic parties took power and carried out their agenda. Another European political scientist with a Marxist background, the Dane Gøsta Esping-Andersen, also stresses class alliances such as the Swedish "cow trade" of the 1930s and the simultaneous Danish agreement on social reform, which, as we saw, helped farmers as much as they helped factory workers.[63]

Even at century's end, "the bottom line remains that the welfare state is seen as an opportunity for the working class to limit the influence of the market on the distribution of wealth in society."[64] Accordingly, the model predicted that when nonsocialist parties opposed to the superinclusive expansive welfare state took power they would reduce the size of government, because (1) politics mattered and (2) policy was determined by the class and social affiliation and interests of those in power. But nothing of the sort happened when nonsocialists were in charge in Denmark in 1982–1993, in Sweden in 1976–1982 and 1991–1994, or in Norway under Høyre in the 1980s or the Agrarian Party in 1997–1999. The model fails, at least when applied to the period during and after the long 1970s.

A better explanation for the post-1970s is that of public choice theory or of what the American political scientist Paul Pierson calls the "new politics of the welfare state," in which the welfare state and its managers have changed the terms of policymaking by creating politico-economic conditions favorable to their own survival.[65] In short, the welfare state and its managers coopt everyone, including those considered inveterate opponents by the power resources model, that is, business and property owners. They coopt by giving everyone the chance or promise of benefits in return for high taxes and by convincing them that these benefits are and will be available in sufficient amounts and quality. A new social contract is set up. One can call this vote-buying or support-buying; it is the key to policy blockages and policy conflicts in many countries.

Even though public spending was not cut in the 1980s and 1990s in Denmark or Sweden, both countries underwent dramatic economic change, although at ten years' interval. After years of stagflation and growing deficits, the Danish government reversed decades of policy by tying the currency to the European Monetary System (EMS) in 1982. The turn to fixed exchange rates was also a turn to a noninflationary fiscal policy, which was the only policy sustainable under fixed exchange rates. It took some years to squeeze inflationary expectations out of the system and out of people's behavior. The current account deficits continued and foreign debt rose rapidly. In 1986, the government introduced a harsh package of measures to increase the cost of debt and encourage saving. Over the next six years, the current account deficit disappeared and government budgets came into balance, at the cost of high unemployment and a near-cessation of productive investment. The current account deficit needed to be tackled because every year that it continued it needed

---

[63]Przeworski and Sprague 1986, Esping-Andersen 1985.

[64]Green-Pedersen 1999, 245.

[65]Green-Pedersen 1999 quoting Pierson 1996. To an observer outside the ivory tower the idea that the nonsocialist parties were able or willing seriously to reduce the size of government or public spending after taking power in Denmark in 1982 was most implausible; in other words, to such an observer, the power resources theory was, at best, a theory applicable to a long-gone historical epoch. It was simply not on anyone's cards to reduce taxes or the size of government, no matter what one's preferences. For several reasons. Nordics, and Danes in particular, make policy by consensus, and decisions passed by small majorities are rare indeed. Second, even the nonsocialists had by the 1980s accepted the idea that a universalist welfare state was popularly demanded and politically necessary, even if perhaps economically harmful. Third, the nonsocialist majority in Denmark was not a large one. The nonsocialists were determined to rescue the economy and public finances from social democratic misrule, as they saw it, but to do so they needed confidence and peace and would not risk the conflicts that any serious attempt to reorient the Danish economy would have entailed.

to be financed by foreign borrowing. As foreign debt grew, so did the cost of servicing it, adding to the amounts that needed to be financed. In fact the cost of foreign debt service was the most serious item in the current account; net of that cost, the Danish current account would have been positive already in 1981. It was a major triumph that by the early 1990s the current account became positive, as did government budgets, thanks to a strict fiscal policy that raised taxes to cover rising costs. Public employment continued to grow, swallowing most of the increase in the workforce.

The turnaround in Sweden, which had not had Denmark's problems of foreign debt and deficits to deal with before the 1990s, was even more dramatic. The crisis hit in 1990–1991, when real interest rates throughout Europe jumped several percentage points. The 1980s boom had produced large fortunes from real estate investment; many of these were reinvested outside Sweden at the top of the market, which was possible for the first time because the government in the 1980s had liberalized the rules governing capital flows and foreign investment. When recession hit Europe in 1991, Sweden was unusually vulnerable thanks to these investments. Real estate values quickly fell in Sweden as well and, by 1992, the country was in its deepest slump since the early 1930s. From 1990 to 1994 domestic demand plummeted; for example, in 1993 fewer cars were sold in Sweden than in a typical year of the 1950s, and unemployment rose from less than 3 percent to more than 13 percent of the workforce, marking the end of six decades of full employment. Public debt more than doubled in 1990–1994 as government declined to raise taxes and borrowed instead to finance the growing demand for benefits. Until 1992 the government sought to maintain the Swedish *krona*'s parity within the EMS but had to give up when the Bank of Sweden's short-term marginal interest rate reached 1,000 percent. Once Sweden abandoned the fixed parity the currency promptly sank about 25 percent in value against the EMS currencies, the largest devaluation in Swedish economic history. The most spectacular aspect of the crisis was a series of bank failures which saddled the taxpayer with over 100 billion *kronor* (about $13 billion) in bad debts, an outcome similar to the savings and loan debacle in the United States.

The 1990s recession in Sweden came after a decade and a half of low growth rates, a symptom that the type of production on which postwar growth had been based—heavy industry, mass manufacturing—was losing steam as generator of wealth and employment. But Sweden in the 1990s, as Denmark ten years earlier, had its own problems. All of the industrialized world faced the transition from the second to the third industrial revolution, but Sweden entered the phase of accelerated change with imbalances that had not been corrected while the going was good. The main obstacle to adaptation was an expanding public sector of not very productive caring professions. The solidaristic wage policy fueled wage inflation in a climate of low growth, full-employment policy, and service sector expansion. In the 1980s, politicians and union leaders still acted as though manufacturing was generating the growth to pay for increased wages for all. The old Swedish model assumed high growth to make solidaristic wage policies and constantly increasing real earnings possible.

One of the pillars of the Swedish version of the Nordic model collapsed in the early 1990s. This was the tradition of making policy in administrative agencies whose boards consisted of representatives of organized interests such as LO and the SAF or employers' federation, a tradition known in the political science literature as corporatism. In Sweden, unlike the other Nordic countries, government ministers are not responsible for the administration of their departments. Rather, the administrative units are considered autonomous within the overall political control of the government as a collective unit. Such a sharp distinction between the political sphere of government, based on parliamentarism, and the administration of the state is unusual. It also means that the top levels of administration become particularly significant as the places where general government policy is translated into practice. Given that the Swedish state, through its agencies, handles two thirds or more of the national income, the people who control those levels have great power over the daily lives and economic well-being of their fellow-citizens.

The reason for putting the major agencies under joint control of organized interests was that these interests should reach consensus on common goals so that policy would be consistent. Throughout the 1980s, the government was undermining the independence of the agencies, of which the Revenue Service and the Labor Market Agency were the most important, and in 1991 SAF and other employers' organizations took the consequence of this by withdrawing their members from the governing boards of all the central administrative agencies which made up the heart of the corporatist network of policymaking. In response, union representatives had to leave the boards as well. Since then, the administrative agencies that form the core of the Swedish governing system have operated without representatives from the organized interests in the labor market. Economic, fiscal, and labor market policies, now made almost entirely by top civil servants, have become more controversial and one of the essentials of the Swedish model, the solidaristic wage policy, has lost much of its legitimacy.

In Norway the welfare state and Norwegian version of the Nordic model with its state control of investment and regional subsidies survived thanks to oil. In the mid-1980s, as in the other Nordic countries, financial deregulation stimulated a consumer boom which ended quickly in Norway because the price of oil fell sharply in 1986, which affected government spending directly. In the 1990s, Norway enjoyed a run of good years padded by oil revenues and avoided excessive consumer booms. Oil wealth masked imbalances in the mainland economy; for example, the OECD believed that if you counted people in employment schemes or those given disability pensions on slender grounds, real unemployment in Norway in the later 1990s was about 11 percent. But as long as the oil flowed, Norway could easily afford such costs.[66]

ECONOMY AND SOCIETY AT THE TURN OF THE CENTURY

Danes, Finns, and Norwegians have traditionally both admired and resented Swedes. Sweden was bigger and richer, it had bigger industries and a more streamlined and efficient welfare state. Sweden's crisis of the early 1990s, when the Swedish currency became worth less than the Danish or Norwegian *krone,* caused some ill-concealed glee. By the end of the decade, although Sweden had not yet seriously tackled the unbalanced incentives and the deep-seated political culture of collectivism, the old attitudes could again be justified. Swedish growth rates around 2000 were the highest in the region, with manufacturing output growing at 10 to 11 percent a year. Sweden in 2000 ranked second after Britain as recipient of U.S. direct investment in Europe, and the country was at the European forefront of information technology-based investment and production. Business orders grew by 26 percent in 1999–2000 and real GDP grew over 5 percent in 2000. The government was even planning a long-term gradual lowering of marginal tax rates to encourage employment and saving by firms and individuals. A government report of 1993 pointing out that Sweden had slipped from second to seventeenth place in the international

---

[66]On changes in social policy to reflect changing international conditions in the first half of the 1990s see Stephens 1996.

standard of living stakes came as a salutary shock to Swedish elite opinion. With their customary goal-oriented consistency, Swedes began tackling their problems and by 2000 had made substantial headway.

Although the Swedish social democrats, back in power since 1994, kept up the language of the middle way and of social democracy as the common citizen's guarantee against the forces of the market, Sweden was adapting to global market conditions, albeit with its inherited profile of policy traditions and with its version of the Nordic model largely intact. One important measure of this adaptation was the reform of the public pension system that took effect in 2000. As before, the bulk of public pension payments were straight transfers from wage-earners to pensioners, funded by a 16 percent tax on income up to about $35,000. But as a new departure, each wage-earner would in future be able to allocate another 2.5 percent of gross income to an individual retirement account investing in Swedish or foreign securities at various levels of risk.

Over time, a growing share of pension payments would come from these accounts.[67] Over three fourths of wage-earners availed themselves of this option and analysts noted a preference for international and higher risk stocks even among Swedes from traditionally social democratic regions. Few shared the egalitarian guilt of one young lady deeply imbued with the ideology of the long 1970s, who stated: "I feel fear at the choice of pension investments. And guilt. Not because I might make the wrong choice of mutual fund, but because of the harm my choice will cause. No one can convince me that the stock market is anything but a market that favors the few and turns the majority into losers. The libertarian belief in the invisible hand that makes things better for everyone in a free market is to me pure superstition."[68] Another measure of adaptation was the spread of the Internet. By 2000, 50 percent of Norwegian households had Internet access, with the figure for Sweden being 44 percent, for Finland 38 percent, and for Denmark 35 percent. Finns had the highest density of mobile telephones anywhere, with 90 percent of 15- to 39-year-olds using them regularly.[69]

Political culture in Scandinavia remains consensus-oriented. Social democratic ideas, such as that the market is a danger that needs to be restrained by political power, continue to dominate public discussion. This is hardly to be wondered at in societies where everyone expects to benefit from politically controlled and defined public services. Of course, not everyone benefits equally. Economic analysis shows that the greatest beneficiaries of the welfare state are women, partly because the child and elder care sectors and the schools, which are the largest consumers of resources, overwhelmingly employ women rather than men, and because women, who live longer, also draw more pensions. Men, on the other hand, are net contributors and tend over their lifetime to pay in substantially more than they receive.[70]

The party system changed dramatically in Denmark in the 1970s and then settled into a variant of its traditional pattern of five larger

---

[67]Among other changes, the transfer portion of the total future pension in a given year would henceforth depend on how much the government received in contributions. Hitherto, the state pension had been a guaranteed fraction of earned income and the amount of tax allocated to pensions was set accordingly. By dropping this guarantee the government began tackling the problem of the increasing number of pensioners relative to wage-earners. Also, in the old system one stopped accruing pension rights at 65; this limit was now abolished. Third, in the old system only income above a certain level gave pension rights; the new system had no lower limit, thus including summer and part-time work from age 16 and up. For persons near retirement age in 2000 transitional rules applied.

[68]*Svenska Dagbladet,* October 26, 2000.

[69]*Economist,* June 24, 2000.

[70]Jensen and Raffelhüschen 1999, for Denmark. Also OECD 2000.

and several smaller parties. In Sweden, Christian Democratic and environmentalist parties were taking votes from the two center parties and threatened one of them with extinction. Beyond that, observers pointed out that Swedish parties in 2000 had lost a third of their members since 1991, a dramatic drop. If the trend, which was constant, continued, the parties would have no members by 2012. That would not stop them from functioning since they had been state-supported since 1965 and so were not dependent on member subscriptions. Likewise, in Denmark only about five percent of voters were members of a party in 2000, although the decline in membership appeared to have slowed in that country. But in all Nordic countries the question was whether parties in the future would consist entirely of politicians and policymakers; there would be no ordinary members. Parties without members could still formulate policy, thanks to the media and new forms of influence—think tanks, experts, interest groups—but policy would be more erratic and shifting and power would further move to the bureaucracy, the professional administrators, and away from parliaments. Experts and pressure groups would govern, blending paternalism and single-issue populism.[71]

Voter turnout in elections was traditionally high (88 to 90 percent) in Nordic countries, but declined slightly in the 1990s. This was a rational reaction to two things: shrinking differences among parties and loss of voter influence on policy, which was formed by compromise among parties or determined in Brussels, by the EU Commission and other European agencies. Participation in elections for the European Parliament was much lower, about 50 to 60 percent, showing that voters believed that their influence was derisory at the European level. In a society where people's economic behavior is shaped and hedged by political decisions, the parties remain important, but voters encounter parties in the media—television, the Internet, newspapers—not as members. Since the media do not represent any opinion but their own, their power creates a problem: party politics and public policy are increasingly driven by what politicians think people want. And how do they know? From what their experts and the media tell them.

Because politicians and experts rely on the media to tell them what people think, they tend to overrate their power. Likewise many academics, who deal in words, overrate the power of the media and of public education in general, which also deal in words and images. An example will illustrate this. One of the most talked-about issues at the turn of the century in the Nordic countries was immigration. In Denmark and Sweden, where the number of non-Nordic immigrants was highest, 6 and 10 percent respectively of the population were not of north or west European origin, being mostly Muslim and coming from the Middle East, Africa, and, more recently, the Balkans. The bulk of these immigrants had arrived under rules permitting family reunion which were interpreted generously. For example, a Turk born in Denmark and who had never lived in Turkey would marry, by family arrangement, a woman whom he had never met from his parents' native Turkish village; she, and in some cases her relatives, would then obtain the right to move to Denmark and receive the same benefits as other residents. These non-Western immigrants differed from earlier immigrants in three ways: they tended to live in their own neighborhoods, often dreary public housing; they had a higher unemployment rate and so used more benefits than the average; and their young people displayed twice the average crime rate. The latter fact was dramatized by a rash of much-publicized rapes of underage Danish girls by boys of Middle Eastern origin in Denmark in 1999–2000.

Reactions to these phenomena varied sharply. On the one hand the academic and

---

[71]Petersson et al. 2000.

media elite advocated multiculturalism and urged native Nordics to enjoy the new social and cultural pluralism brought by these non-Nordic and non-Christian groups. On the other, many ordinary folk resented what they saw as hordes of lazy, arrogant thugs who refused to assimilate, whose conservative, orthodox Islamic religion was incompatible with Nordic Christian culture, and who exploited a welfare society built by the hard-earned tax *kroner* of native residents. The elite blamed the immigrants' problems of crime and unemployment on discrimination by Nordic employers and citizens; others blamed the immigrants' own behavior. In particular, the elite blamed what they saw as rising chauvinism and racism on certain media; according to this analysis, the Danish People's Party and other anti-immigrant phenomena were largely created and fed by deliberate propaganda. Remedies for discrimination as manifested in immigrants' unemployment and crime rates were, in the elite view, more government regulation to encourage businesses to hire immigrants and more multiculturalist teaching in schools.

In an exhaustive study of attitudes to immigration the political scientist Peter Nannestad cast doubt on this interpretation. He found that people's views on immigrants rested on rational calculation. In times of higher unemployment, immigrants were resented because people saw them as competing if not for jobs, then at least for benefits. At other times, people's negative views reflected perceptions, for example of the higher crime rate among younger second-generation immigrants. In other words, the media did not create opinion, but followed it, and the anti-immigrant newspapers and journalists were not manipulators but exploiters of pre-existing attitudes.[72]

By the 1990s the wave of renewed change beginning in the long 1970s, which required expanding the state and political power, had waned, but the momentum of the new, second and third generation welfare state, was powerful. Warning voices were now pointing out that the Nordic societies had slipped in the prosperity league. If one purpose of the Nordic model was to combine prosperity with equality of both opportunity and, largely, of condition, that purpose was perhaps no longer being served. So, one question for the coming century was whether the Nordic model still served the common interest, and, if not, what revisions or changes should be made to secure an acceptable future for the people of Scandinavia, "those equal folk," as the Norwegian journalist Hans Dahl called them in 1984.

Whatever the future of the political system or of the infighting over control of the vast government sectors, one thing had become clear even to radical socialists by 2000, and that was that future prosperity was ultimately to be derived from one place only: successful businesses able to provide a maximum of value added to the economy and thereby, through its skilled and well-paid employees, the tax base for the future welfare state. Most people also saw the information and communication technologies as the area that could best provide such businesses. In this context it may be worth mentioning that one of the all-time success stories in the North in the 1990s was that of the Finnish company Nokia.[73] It began in 1865 as a lumber mill and during the

---

[72]Nannestad 1999a. In the same vein, economists argued that the reason for higher unemployment among immigrants was not discrimination by employers but the rigid labor market and minimum wage rules that made it excessively difficult to hire immigrants at wages reflecting their productivity. The benefit system, furthermore, provided little incentive for immigrants to learn Danish or Swedish and to seek whatever jobs they could find. The data are clear: immigrants to the U.S. find employment at three times the rate of immigrants to Scandinavia. The difference is that the U.S. labor market is open and benefits modest. Also, the U.S. encourages immigrants with skills useful to the economy. The Nordic welfare states with their rigid labor markets provide few incentives for skilled immigrants but rather encourage a passive welfare existence, in the American sense of that word. Ironically, the Danish government in 2000 launched an initiative called the "spacious labor market" aimed at getting everyone into work. This was policy by propaganda and re-education, where what was needed was fewer rules; but then, policy was made by paternalistic experts with a bias toward education and regulation, and not by economists.

[73]*Economist,* October 14, 2000.

Cold War produced toilet paper and rubber boots, not least for the Soviet Union. The collapse of the Soviet Union hit the Finnish economy hard, and the recession was worse than that of Sweden in the 1990s. The economy shrank by more than 10 percent in 1991–1992, and unemployment reached 17 percent of the workforce. The reason was not just that the Soviet market for Finnish construction, ships, and machines disappeared. Other reasons were similar to those that affected Sweden: deregulated financial markets leading at first to a consumer boom and rapid inflation of real estate and other asset prices and then to deflation when international inflation fell and real interest rates turned positive. By the late 1990s the Finns had largely recovered from the high unemployment and low growth of the first post-Soviet years, with GDP growth around 5 percent in 1999–2000, and the Finnish economy was showing signs instead of overheating. As in the other Nordic countries, housing costs in and near the main cities were rising faster than the general level of inflation or living standards.

Nokia weathered the crisis of the early 1990s by reinventing itself as a producer of mobile telephone equipment, although it had been producing televisions and radio telephones since the 1960s. Since then, Nokia has been nothing but a mobile telephone company and as such hugely successful, accounting for a quarter of Finland's exports and nearly 4 percent of its GDP. Most shareholders were American and they wondered if Nokia could survive the challenge of combining the Internet and the mobile telephone. By analogy, Finland's remarkable success in coming out of the severe post-Soviet recession was at risk because of the aging population, low retirement with less than half of the 55- to 65-year-old age group working, and a rigid labor market. As in Sweden and Denmark, collective bargaining governed all employment contracts, not just those of union members, who comprised more than 80 percent of the workforce. The International Monetary Fund suggested in summer 2000 that Finland should cut taxes a little and introduce measures to increase the supply of labor. "If not tackled promptly, these problems could undermine the prospects for robust longer-run economic growth."[74] Identical observations were made of the Danish, Norwegian, and Swedish economies.

All the Nordic countries were near the top of the international prosperity tables. Denmark ranked second in the EU after Luxembourg in 2000 at about $25,000 of per capita income at purchasing power parity rates; Sweden 8th at $21,600, Finland 10th at $21,160. For comparison, Germany stood at $22,710, the UK at $21,570 and the United States led the league at $32,710. However, the high Nordic figures need to be taken in context. The Nordics, especially the Danes, may not be as rich as the bare figures suggest. The most obvious reason is that Nordics pay twice as much to the government in taxes as Americans do and half as much again as non-Nordic Europeans. But there is more. In Germany, Britain, and America, much childcare and care of the old is still done by family and thus does not figure in the economy. In Nordic countries, the government hires people to carry out such care. The high per capita GDP figure thus does not reflect only prosperity—though most Danes clearly are not poor—but also the fact that a larger proportion of the population is required to produce Denmark's $25,000 per capita than Germany's $22,710. Danes look rich on paper because the workforce is relatively larger; it is larger in part because the government has collectivized former family functions; the people who carry out these functions are paid from tax revenues, which must therefore be high. In all Nordic countries in 2000, more than two thirds of the adult population were either public employees or lived on transfer payments of one kind or another. It was probably no coincidence that levels of

---

[74]Quoted in *The Scandinavian Economies 30*, 8 (July 2000), 17.

public support for the welfare state were at about the same level, about 70 percent in favor with only 30 percent of respondents desiring a lower level of public spending, lower taxes, and fewer benefits.[75]

Governments in the late 1990s found new sources of revenue in the so-called green taxes, levied on activities that yielded CO_2 or the so-called greenhouse gas emissions, such as burning coal in power plants or driving cars. The official Danish line was that green taxes were intended to reduce the use of the so-called nonrenewable resources such as coal and to reduce CO_2 emissions, held responsible by leading politicians and many experts for helping to cause a warming of global temperatures expected in the twenty-first century. Like the other Nordic countries, Denmark had signed the Kyoto Protocol promising to reduce its CO_2 emissions by as much as 20 percent by 2010. Most people believed the environmental scare stories and therefore supported these taxes, but whatever the scientific merits of the case, the taxes soon became yet another source of government revenue which, because it was politically popular, could be increased at a time when even social democrats hesitated to increase the income tax which, for an average taxpayer with partly tax deductible mortgage interest, stood at near 50 percent.

CULTURE, EDUCATION, RELIGION, VALUES

During the long 1970s literature and the arts in all Nordic countries became intensely politicized. This also happened elsewhere in the West as part of the revolutionary wave that began in Germany, France, and the United States in the mid-1960s stimulated by opposition to the Vietnam War and to what adherents called U.S. imperialism in general. The difference in Scandinavia was that the revolutionary ideology met little opposition; it was warmly embraced by many establishment figures such as the Swedish prime minister Olof Palme. The result was that Marxists, radicals, and self-styled anti-imperialist revolutionaries of all kinds easily took over the leading media, the institutions of culture, and higher education. That is not to say that most professors or students were revolutionaries, merely that the revolutionaries controlled the debate and set the terms of argument.

Towards the end of this period a new phase began, which coexisted with the politicized culture for the rest of the century. This was an inward turn toward confessional literature, a form of self-dramatization in which authors revealed all about themselves in barely fictionalized accounts of their passions, addictions, sexual exploits, or sexual suffering. This wave culminated in books such as *The Highest Caste,* a novel set in India and Stockholm and consisting of the dramatized diary of a year in the life of a woman writer who goes to India for some vague reasons and, on returning to Sweden notes, in the intervals of drug addiction and unrequited passion, the antics and behavior of friends and associates who gather at a particular bar in central Stockholm. What made *The Highest Caste* a minor sensation when it appeared in 1997 was that the author, Carina Rydberg, used the real names of her characters, including that of the man she was in love with.

One of the few Nordic intellectuals who resisted the revolutionary politicization of the long 1970s was the Swedish writer Sven Delblanc. One of his later works, *Moria land,* is a story of deception set in an imaginary Sweden partly occupied by the Soviet Union and partly controlled by a pro-Soviet party of appeasers, who are imagined to be people of a similar stripe to the middle-class intellectuals of Delblanc's own time who accepted the anti-American and revolutionary ideology. In an essay written in the 1980s, Delblanc explained that he was opposed not so much to the

---
[75]Andersen et al. 1999.

ideology as to the moralizing puritanism that, in his opinion, lay behind it and to which he himself was not immune:

> Deep in my Swedish folk-soul the voice of conscience tells me that good and enjoyable things are sinful, unless they are commanded by God, the state, or the national health. Whatever is good must be legitimated by some form of fictitious "utility."[76]

In the 1990s, many of the earlier revolutionaries had made their peace with the system and constituted the new elite. However, unlike their predecessors they faced no ideological challenge. The fronts had changed. Where the arguments in the long 1970s were over the right path to revolution and over the finer points of Marxist doctrine, in the 1990s and 2000s they were rather about national identity, immigration, and multiculturalism.

Some of the fiercest debates of the 1970s and after concerned education. In all Nordic countries, as elsewhere in the West, the school system changed in the 1960s from being selective and stratified to being uniform and egalitarian. Most people left school proper after seven or nine years, typically going on to some form of practical training. With the reforms of the 1960s, nine or ten years of schooling became obligatory. In the old system, only about ten percent of a cohort went on to the *gymnasium,* which was only for those aiming at higher education. As higher education expanded to include almost half of each cohort, the twelve-year school ending in three years of *gymnasium* also became the rule rather than the exception. The curricula also changed dramatically. The older *gymnasium* offered a choice of a mathematics- or a language-based curriculum, both going into some depth. The post-1960s *gymnasium* offered a greater mix of choices but at a much lower level of intensity and demand. By 2000, the *gymnasier* were in many respects like American high schools, that is, for the many, not the elite,

and standards, in the opinion of many teachers, had declined. Danish maths teachers complained, for example, that pupils in the first year of *gymnasium* could no longer handle fractions and simple algebra; matters formerly taught in sixth and seventh grade.

Changes in curricula and school organization reflected changes in the beliefs of teachers and educational experts, as well as politicians.[77] Progressive ideologues of the 1960s had taken the Greek philosopher Plato's view that "the child is even more the property of the state than of the parents."[78] The family was a nest of indoctrination and inequality. Mothers were too ignorant to raise children and only succeeded in inculcating bourgeois values. Mothers treated children as private property; if private property were abolished and socialism introduced, the family as the cell of bourgeois society would be destroyed, and with it "things that socialist society must combat or restrain," such as owning and consuming things, living in detached houses, and personal success. The gray uniformity and poverty of communism were often the ideal of such intellectuals, who hoped that collectivizing everyday life would "free mothers for production" and "get rid of the idea of private ownership within the family especially concerning children."[79]

Educational reforms of the long 1970s, still in place in 2000, downplayed skills and emphasized socialization. A leading Danish social democratic politician, who as minister of education promoted the egalitarian school system, was famous, or notorious, for believing that "what everyone can't learn no one should be allowed to learn."[80] In Sweden, an

---

[76]Delblanc 1986, 137.

[77]Enkvist 2000 is a critical history of changing educational ideas and practice in Sweden from the long 1970s on.

[78]Quoted in N. G. L. Hammond, *A History of Greece 479–323 B.C.,* 2nd ed. (Oxford University Press 1967), 588.

[79]The writer Göran Palm quoted in Arvidsson 1999, 108–109.

[80]The original source for this has proved difficult to track down; the politician in question, Ritt Bjerregaard, first seems to have said it at a conference in 1972.

official report on grading stated that "the hitherto prevailing role of grading as the main criterion of selection for further education and working life means that work in school risks being focused on communicating knowledge and skills."[81] That was elitist and unacceptable. Therefore grades must be abolished or reduced in significance.

Discipline became largely optional after teachers stopped being figures of authority, to be addressed by their last names and in the polite form of address, and adopted the character of older playmates rather than sources of knowledge. Danish schools, especially in the cities, were the most anarchic; Swedish schools, despite informal modes of address, retained more of the old habits. The teaching profession itself changed as the so-called 1968 generation, the generation of those at university or in teacher training during the radical phase of the late 1960s, took it over. Social science and history textbooks and instruction in the long 1970s and after often reflected a second-hand, crude Marxism and anti-Americanism. Throughout the North, but especially in Denmark, pupils fled the tough subjects of maths and physics in favor of the softer options of literature and social studies. By 2000 employer organizations were warning of a future shortage of engineers and computer specialists and of a threat to living standards and economic growth if the young could not be persuaded to tackle the difficult subjects.

In writing about religion in Scandinavia one is sometimes reminded of the section on snakes in an old book about Ireland. It was a very short section, which read in its entirety: "Snakes. There are no snakes to be met with in the entire island." Likewise one has at times been almost able to say about religion in the North: "Religion. There are no religious people to be met with in these countries." Throughout the region, average church attendance is about 5 percent. Less than half the population believes in God or the afterlife. These impressions can, however, be misleading. First, though attendance and official religious activity is low-key, all Nordic countries except Sweden have Lutheran Protestantism as their official religion. Sweden disestablished its episcopal Lutheran church in 2000, but this merely made the church an independent organization receiving public support. The main effect of the change was that church affairs were no longer decided in parliament.

In some parts of the area, notably western Norway and Denmark, religious revivalism and religious influence on society and culture is far from negligible. The nineteenth-century Danish poet and mystic Grundtvig was an intellectual ancestor of the ideology of the Nordic model and the egalitarian welfare society. One might also mention that the single most important Christian philosopher of the modern West, Søren Kierkegaard (1813–1855), was Danish. Kierkegaard was no prophet of the welfare state. His concern was the individual and the irreducible singularity of Christian faith which, he held, could only be that of an individual and never a collective idea.

Third, multiculturalism has brought non-Christian religious elements into Nordic societies. Somewhere between 1 and 1.5 million residents of the Nordic area are non-European, most of them Muslim, and most of them concentrated in Danish and Swedish cities. Their presence has provoked a rise both in multiculturalist and antimulticulturalist feeling among native Nordics, including the idea that the inherited official religions are part of the national identity. Fourth, Lutheranism, at least in its modern guise, has never been a church-going faith, counting allegiance by the number of warm bodies in church on Sunday.

Fifth, however secularized Scandinavia may seem, the region is profoundly, pervasively colored by its Christian and particularly its Lutheran heritage. As we have seen, some scholars trace the Nordic version of the welfare society to Lutheran roots. Martin Luther

---

[81] Östergren 1988, 81.

(1483–1546) taught, following Saint Augustine (354–430), that earthly society had a spiritual and a political or social dimension. The public authorities governed the latter, but by abolishing the hierarchical, supranational Catholic church the Lutheran authorities also took over the administration of spiritual needs. The Catholic church had maintained hospitals and other forms of charity because doing good for others was considered pleasing to God and thus beneficial for the eternal destiny of those who did good. Lutheranism cut that link. Organized charity outside the towns collapsed, then revived at the parish level. The parishes, the local congregations, became the cells of Lutheran society. This promoted a form of local democracy and gave the parishes the responsibility of collecting taxes and dispensing charity. As late as the 1960s it was still the chairman of the parish council who, in Denmark, determined who would receive what Americans call welfare, that is, benefits in case of need. Local self-government and a society pervaded by Lutheran norms of discipline and work laid the social and cultural foundations of the modern welfare state. Nordic social democracy may be less a local variant of international Marxism than the modern form of Lutheran social activism.[82]

In all of the nineteenth century in Sweden there were less than 15,000 divorces; Sweden had that many a year by the 1990s. Denmark and Sweden have the Western world's highest illegitimacy rates. Over two thirds of first children are born to unmarried couples; in most cases the couple will marry, often when the second or third child arrives. Illegitimacy carries no stigma; indeed marrying before the first child is now unusual.[83] The concept of illegitimacy has disappeared from national statistics since the mid-1980s. These figures have exploded since 1960, but there are precedents. In the late eighteenth century half of children born in Stockholm were illegitimate, and in the nineteenth century a custom known as the Stockholm marriage developed, similar to the "paperless cohabitation" of today. The reason was that unmarried women under the laws of the time had adult rights whereas married women had no right to their own income whether from assets or from work.

In the 1960s a group of Swedish intellectuals launched a debate on morality and fidelity. The writer Lars Gyllensten proposed infidelity as an ethical ideal and argued that if realized as a social norm it would make people nicer.[84] A doctor, Gunnar Biörck, responded as a spokesman for "silent opinion," blaming artists and intellectuals for proposing models of behavior that led to increased alcoholism, drug addiction, venereal disease, and crime. Biörck was a spokesman for conservative principles of hierarchy, order, and obedience, which progressive liberalism undermined. These conservative principles, Biörck found, were best preserved in the Soviet Union, which was "today a bulwark for the defense of centuries of European tradition."[85] This may seem a bizarre statement, given that the communist-ruled Soviet Union was hostile to European tradition, but it was characteristically Swedish, blending a conservative variant of neutralism with right-

---

[82] Knudsen 1997; Hettne et al. 1999, 223–235.

[83] A study by the Danish Institute of Social Research in 2000 found that most people in their 20s lived as unmarried couples. Marriage was rare, but more common when a second or third child arrived later. A researcher described unmarried cohabiting as a "marriage trap." The study uncovered an interesting social distinction. The better educated and better off the couple, the higher the chance of marriage. Couples lower on the social ladder tended to remain unmarried and to break up at a higher rate.

[84] Gyllensten later explained that he had been misunderstood; he decided to advocate infidelity as a statement of protest against orthodoxies of any kind, religious and political as well as sexual. Gyllensten 1979, 180–181.

[85] Quoted Arvidsson 1999, 104. In the small Nordic countries where the leading participants in public debate are few and know each other, their arguments in the prestige media often focus on one topic at a time. These debates occasionally touch on, reveal, or come to symbolize moments of political or cultural change. They are then labeled and, as "the X debate," retroactively come to be seen as important turning points. Other examples, in addition to "the infidelity debate" in Sweden in 1965–66, are "the blasphemy debate" in Norway of 1958, when the writer Arnulf Øverland attacked leading clergymen in public, or, in a different area, "the planned economy debate" in Sweden in 1948, when, as explained in the section on the Nordic economies, virtually all opinion-shapers formed up for or against the government's proposal to introduce economic planning.

Norwegian prime minister Gro Harlem Brundtland. Over 40 percent of the ministers in a typical Nordic government are women.

wing anti-Americanism and an inherited respect for Sweden's ancient neighbor, trading partner, and sometime enemy Russia, whose hierarchical and despotic culture people like Biörck saw preserved under communism.

Starting with Denmark in 1989, the Nordic countries gave same-sex couples the right to register their partnerships and receive the same legal rights as married couples, except the right of adoption. Such measures reflected the sexual liberation and the hostility to old moralities of the long 1970s, but also longstanding cultural attitudes that, in the North, were never as strict as in Catholic Europe or the United States. In the 1950s, an era generally assumed to be conservative and nuclear-family-oriented, a Danish woman doctor, Kirsten Auken, published a survey of sexual behavior documenting that barely one out of a hundred married women had not had pre-marital sex, a substantially lower figure than the contemporaneous Kinsey Report found in the United States. The liberated Nordics are an old tradition. On the other hand, until the late 1960s only about 10 percent of children were born out of wedlock; by the 1990s, this figure was over half in Scandinavia; lowest in Norway, highest in Sweden and Denmark. The number of divorces began to rise rapidly from 1968 and the same year the birth rate went below replacement for the first time in Denmark.

Something had decidedly changed in social values when even younger members of the Norwegian and Swedish royal families, often considered as guardians of tradition, lived with sexual partners without benefit of marriage. In 2000, the crown prince of Norway, Haakon, announced his engagement to a woman with whom he had been living for some time. This was not in itself astonishing. What took some people aback, even in 2000, was that the woman was a single mother and that the father of her child had been convicted of drug-dealing. But the outcry was limited. Most people applauded Haakon's behavior because it proved that royals were no different from anyone else.

The most profound social changes in Scandinavia in the later twentieth century stemmed from the rise in female employment. From 1970 to 1990 the number of women of working age who were unpaid homemakers fell by half in Sweden, and most of the 300,000 jobs created in those two decades were public sector jobs in day care, elder care, and education, fields that overwhelmingly employed women. Thus women now cared for other people's children and aged parents for pay whereas they used to care for their own for free. Affirmative action policies arrived in the 1980s and 1990s, yet, until the late 1990s, few women held top business jobs and occupational segregation in Scandinavia was greater than in the United States. One of the reasons for this was the sheer size of the caring sector, which, with education and health care included, employed about 15 percent of the entire workforce and almost a third of employed women. Prominent women in Scandinavia tended to be politicians or leading administrators in the public sector, such as Gro Harlem Brundtland, prime minister of Norway in the 1980s and early 1990s, or Tarja Halonen, president of Finland since 2000. By the later 1990s, about 40 percent of the ministers in a typical Nordic government were women, but less than 10 percent of the board members of major corporations.

In 1982 an LO economist, Anna Hedborg, who with Rudolf Meidner wrote the first proposal for wage-earner funds, defined part-time work, desired by many women, as tax evasion. "If you go to part time you are withholding from society the value of your work. You use society's time for private purposes: baking bread, painting your windows, making jam, or whatever."[86] Such a statement reflected the idea of the strong society gone overboard to where the state was the society and the state owned its subjects and their production. Curiously, although she was an economist, Hedborg ignored the fact that the tax burden encouraged people to cut down on paid work and do their own repairs.

Nordic, and especially, Swedish social policy since the long 1970s has sought to undermine the economic and social role of the family because families are not identical, so they give children different opportunities, which is undesirable from an egalitarian point of view. All Nordic governments put considerable effort into equalizing conditions not just among different social groups but between men and women. This reflects the principles of state feminism mentioned earlier: that the government considers paid employment a basic condition of citizenship and will therefore promote full female employment by providing day care and paid maternity leave and will treat women and men equally as individual taxpayers and benefit recipients. In the early 1970s, Nordic governments, with the partial exception of Norway, abolished joint taxation of couples' incomes which encouraged married women to work by reducing their marginal tax. This measure and other policies reflecting the state feminism of the late-model Nordic welfare state have vastly improved many women's economic situation, although one reason that married or cohabiting women work is that the high taxes and egalitarian income distribution mean that a couple needs two incomes to survive. Critics point out that state feminist policies have erased the family as a social and economic unit, since each adult member is encouraged to be economically self-sufficient and this self-sufficiency spills over into social and psychological roles as well.[87] Nordic tax codes, unlike that of the United States, do not recognize the notion of a

---

[86] Quoted Östergren 1988, 231.

[87] Popenoe 1988, which is partly about Sweden, is a sensitive and sociologically profound analysis of what happens when governments decide to ignore the family as a social unit.

dependent, so there are no tax advantages to being a parent. Instead, the state provides a modest grant to parents of children up to the age of 18, which in 2000 was about $1200 a year in Denmark. Single parents—who are almost always mothers—receive special benefits.

Each country has an equality commission charged with monitoring compliance with the goal of equality. Yet feminists are not content, partly because, as we have seen, women tend to be employed in the caring sector and by government, that is to say in lower-level, non-managerial jobs paying less well than traditionally male jobs in manufacturing or top jobs in new industries such as information technology. From the 1990s on, therefore, the policy agenda for sexual equality has shifted toward encouraging more private employers to give women good jobs and to promoting more women to management ranks in the public sector. Some progress has occurred, but what some of the feminists do not always take into account is that many women prefer the lower paid government jobs in teaching and in day and elder care because they are undemanding.

We close this section with a paradox. One rallying-cry of the long 1970s was the right to be different and to resist conforming to capitalist society. As we have also seen, individualism was also a feature of social reforms of the period, in the sense that the state stopped recognizing the family as the cell of society and instead took taxes from and gave benefits to individuals. The result was a highly collectivized economy, with government consuming well over half the national income, coexisting with an individualistic and antifamilist political and social ethos. At the same time, governments, especially in Sweden, expanded their already long list of things that they felt they had to do to make people better. This often led to paternalism. For example, a leading representative of the Swedish Broadcasting Corporation, the state-financed radio and television channel which until the 1980s had a monopoly of broadcasting in Sweden, as its sister organizations had elsewhere in Scandinavia, refuted the idea that the public should have the right to choose what programs to watch with the following argument: "The argument from freedom of choice is confusing. Freedom of choice entails of course that people choose not to watch informative programming. People become less aware. It is wrong to give people what they want."[88] It is wrong to give people what they want. If one wants to understand the Nordic societies and their tensions, it is worth meditating on that statement and what it means.

FOREIGN AND SECURITY POLICY

The Nordic foreign policy traditions reflect the varying national and geopolitical legacies. Sweden has remained unaligned and neutral since 1814 and relied on a modest but determined deterrent force and its remote geographical position to avoid entanglement in the world wars and the Cold War. Denmark and Norway were occupied by Germany from 1940 to 1945. In both countries politicians and people learned the lesson that weak unaligned states are at the mercy of ruthless neighbors and so joined NATO in 1949 to avoid a repetition of 1940. In 1973, Denmark was the first Nordic country to join what was then the European Economic Community and which became the European Union in 1992.[89] In 1994, Sweden and Finland followed. Norway twice voted no in referenda to joining, but conformed to all necessary EU regulations in order to maintain free trade with EU countries. In 2000, Denmark voted against joining the common European currency, which Finland was joining. Sweden remained undecided.

Nordic governments and publics consider their region an area of peace, and sometimes give the impression that they think the region

---

[88]Quoted Arvidsson 1999, 170.

[89]Greenland, granted home rule in 1979, and the Faeroes, which are seeking independence, remain outside the EU though part of the "realm of Denmark."

Swedish prime minister Goran Persson.

is peaceful because its inhabitants are morally superior to others. The Swedish social democratic prime minister since 1996, Göran Persson, wanted Sweden to be seen as an "ethical superpower." But the region was not always peaceful. Before 1814, Denmark and Sweden were often at war, especially between 1523 and 1720. Denmark was the leading power until the 1640s, when Sweden's age of greatness began. Interestingly, today's reputations—the Swedes tough and determined, the Danes disorganized and casual—have a long history. A Swedish spy reported on Danish military preparations against Sweden in 1657 that "they were so disorderly that it made one's stomach ache to see it."[90]

By contrast, when the king of Sweden asked the tough peasants of the Dalarna region for soldiers to fight the Danes in that same war, he got more than he expected. The rule was that the king could ask for one man in twenty. On this occasion the Dale-men offered one in seven, and those of Närke offered to send every man able to bear arms. Fear and hatred of the Dane, long after Denmark had ceased being a serious threat to Swedish independence, was deep-rooted in Sweden and meant that the kings could always command enthusiastic and determined support for wars against the hereditary enemy, whereas many Swedes saw less reason for fighting Russians, Poles, or Germans. The Danes, by contrast, seem to have been less eager to fight Swedes; moreover, the Danish kings tended to use mercenaries where the Swedish rulers used national troops and evolved a sophisticated system of recruitment and training for them. As late as 1788 an unpopular king, Gustavus III, was saved from a possible coup when Denmark declared war on Sweden. However much they may have disliked the king, the Swedish people would always rally when threatened by their cousins to the west.

Kings of Sweden fought, uniquely in Europe, sword in hand at the head of their armies. Four generations of them, from Gustavus Adolphus (ruled 1611–1632) to Charles XII (ruled 1697–1718) displayed great personal courage as well as brilliant gifts of strategy and leadership. Gustavus and Charles both fell in battle in the space of less than a century, a record unmatched in any other country in the post-medieval period. The memory of military glory may be unfashionable and, with the decline in historical knowledge, forgotten. Still, as the historian Michael Roberts suggested, "the experience of greatness does in some undefined way mark Sweden off from its Scandinavian neighbours."[91] Some whiff of having once been "the land of honor and heroes" remains in Sweden as an undercurrent of

---

[90]Quoted in Ulf Sundberg, *Sveriges Krig 1521–1814* (Stockholm: Hjalmarson & Högberg 1998), 230.

[91]Roberts 1979, 156.

determination, commitment, and stubborn refusal to give up that is not found in quite the same form or measure in the other countries, with the partial exception of Finland which was part of Sweden during the age of greatness (1630–1718) and contributed more than its share of warriors to the enterprise. Few nowadays take pride in or understand what martial valor can mean to a society and a people; the modern emphasis is rather on the futility of war and what even successful wars cost those who must fight them, suffer the loss of fathers, husbands, and sons, and pay the bills. Historians have estimated that Charles XII's eighteen years of war cost Sweden about 200,000 men, the equivalent of twelve cohorts of twenty-year olds put together. Economically minded people have also pointed out that wars are enormous exercises in pure capital destruction and can therefore, except in self-defense, hardly be rational enterprises to anyone who wants to maximize general prosperity and well-being.

Most Swedes would agree with this universal modern belief, but the undercurrent remains and was movingly stated by the novelist and popular historian Frans G. Bengtsson in his life of Charles XII. In 1707 the king led his victorious army eastward out of central Europe, the scene of many Swedish victories for over seventy years; his goal was Russia and czar Peter, and the result was defeat and the end of Sweden as a great power. Bengtsson contemplates the ranks of *karoliner,* "soldiers of Charles," in their dark blue uniforms and speaks for them to the lands they are leaving:

> Farewell, Europe, now we go. This is the last of us, in these costumes, in our old style, for now we march toward what will be for us the fall of the gods . . . Farewell, Europe, and thank you for what has been. If we have sometimes been hard to digest, it is over now, and if in future we Swedes should appear on battlefields here, it will happen decently and mildly, with briefcases, in order to make solemn speeches, but never again with pike and musket.
>
> For beyond the fall of the gods we shall live on as the centuries roll, but only as shadows. Cleansed, humanitarian, and understanding shadows no doubt, maybe even sometimes happy shadows, as though we were dicing on a tablet of gold on the plains of Ida in the realm of better gods, but shadows nevertheless. We shall still beget some creation or other worth noticing, some greatness for the world to contemplate. In the study of flowers, in flights of mystical vision, in the trills of blonde Nordic nightingales and other suchlike matters we shall still produce wonderful things, but all such will seem a little thin and insubstantial beside the old. "The sword has the best task and must perform it"—was that perhaps, when all is said and done, true for us as well, as a people, and not just for him whom we followed?[92]

---

[92]Bengtsson 1935, 1:342–343. The language of this wonderful biography by a master stylist is drenched in reminiscences of Scandinavia's legendary past. So, in this passage, we find allusions to the fall of the gods, the *ragnarok* of pagan myth, and to the golden gameboard found as a relic of the old gods by the human survivors of *ragnarok* on the plain of Ida, where formerly stood Valhalla. The "study of flowers" refers to Carl Linnaeus (1707–1778), the most famous of all Swedish scientists, who founded modern botany and invented the system of naming natural organisms still in use today. The "flights of mystical vision" are those of Emmanuel Swedenborg (1688–1772), a scientist, economist, and inventor, who underwent a mystical revelation in 1743 and founded a new religion based on the idea that human life continues after death in a vast spiritual world of many dimensions, which he described in detail. The Swedenborgian church survives to this day; most of its members are American. The "blonde Nordic nightingale" was Jenny Lind (1820–1887), one of the first operatic superstars. Three examples of Swedish fame and originality which served science, mysticism, and art. But Bengtsson's patronizing tone is unjustified, at least as applied to Linnaeus. As Michael Roberts writes, "Without the characteristic spirit, and the no less characteristic endurance, of the men of the Age of Greatness, the brilliance of the scientific achievements of the Age of Liberty would scarcely have been possible" (Roberts 1979, 153). As Linnaeus built on such earlier and universalist savants as Olof Rudbeck, so the historians of the eighteenth and nineteenth centuries built on the indefatigable documentations of seventeenth-century predecessors. For American readers, Bengtsson's dramatic and high-spirited recreation of the Viking Age, *The Long Ships,* is highly recommended, but avoid the silly motion picture adaptation starring Kirk Douglas and Robert Widmark.

The Prussian victory in the war of 1864 taught Danes the false lesson that Denmark could not resist German aggression. A truer lesson would have been that a foolish government that does not prepare for war and then unnecessarily provokes a strong and well-prepared opponent risks disaster. The false lesson traumatized Danes into thinking that their territory was indefensible and produced a defeatist, neutralist, and resentful spirit among politicians and intellectuals. In the 1930s, Nazi Germany seemed a bigger threat than Bismarck's Prussia, yet the Danish government refused to improve defenses. In his New Year's speech for 1940, the social democratic prime minister, Stauning, declared: "Due to the character of the country we cannot create a defense establishment such as other countries can, even if we had wanted to, and these circumstances, added to the disinclination to go to war which has grown up in the population, have led Denmark to a position that makes any notion of an effective combat capability impossible."[93] Stauning and his government clearly would neither have understood nor agreed with John Stuart Mill when he said: "War is an ugly thing, but not the ugliest of things: the decayed and degraded state of moral and patriotic feeling which thinks nothing *worth* a war, is worse . . . A man who has nothing which he is willing to fight for, nothing which he cares about more than he does about his own personal safety, is a miserable creature who has no chance of being free."[94] How different was the Swedish attitude, expressed by Per Albin Hansson in August 1939: "Our readiness is good." Sweden was in fact little better prepared than Denmark, but was not defeatist.

Nor did the Danes in 1940 understand the practical objection to the policy of instant surrender raised by some in the opposition parties, namely that if Germany chose to attack Denmark, it would be part of a general offensive in the West. Germany would not be able to devote huge armies to conquering Denmark, and would be under pressure to complete the conquest in a short time. All Denmark had to do was to establish a credible defense force sufficient to deter such an attack by a relatively small number of troops. In the event, Germany occupied Denmark on April 9, 1940, with 38,000 troops, a small number and less than even the small Danish army of the time—if it had been fully deployed, armed, and under alert. In the event, the army was neither deployed, nor properly armed, nor under alert. The government had deprived itself even of the small means it had left itself after the cutbacks and drawdowns of the 1920s and 1930s, means that, if used to the full, might have deterred or defeated the forces that the Germans were able to bring to bear, given that they were at the same time planning their offensive against France.

Norway had also followed a neutralist policy in the 1930s and was equally unprepared for the German assault on April 9. However, a quick-witted Norwegian officer commanding a battery in the long Oslo Fjord managed to sink one of the German battleships ferrying troops to Oslo, giving the king and government a few precious hours to escape the capital. Thanks to the country's size and terrain, Norwegian troops maintained resistance for some weeks, assisted in the far north by a British expeditionary force. By June 1940 the Germans were in complete control, but the government had escaped to London, and Norway remained at war with Germany. The occupation regime in Norway was therefore harsher than in Denmark, where both Germans and the Danish government, which remained in place, pursued a mutually agreeable policy of cooperation for over three years.

In August 1943, the Danish government resigned over German demands that the

---

[93]Quoted in Kaarsted 1991, 185.

[94]"The Contest in America" (1862), in *Collected Works*, vol. 21, *Essays on Equality, Law and Education* (University of Toronto Press 1984), 141–142.

A street scene in Oslo, Norway.

Danish authorities take stronger measures against saboteurs, including the death penalty. In October of that year, the Nazi government in Berlin attempted to round up and deport the Danish Jews, but, forewarned by a sympathetic German diplomat, Danish resistance groups were able to save nearly all of their Jewish compatriots and send them to neutral Sweden for the remainder of the war. This episode justly earned Denmark some much-needed credibility among the Allies. Another such episode was that the Danish minister to the United States, Henrik Kauffmann (1888–1963), had refused to obey orders of the collaborationist government in Copenhagen after April 9, 1940. Instead, he unilaterally declared himself to be the representative of the true Danish national interest. In 1941, Kauffmann signed a treaty with the U.S. government permitting the Americans to build bases in Greenland. The Danish government dismissed him from his post, but he ignored that and continued to be recognized in Washington, D.C., as a legitimate ambassador. Thanks in large part to Kauffmann's initiative, the United States decided to recognize Denmark as a co-belligerent along with Norway so that both Nordic countries could become charter members of the United Nations in 1945.

After liberation, the Danish government retroactively approved Kauffmann's actions and renewed the Greenland Treaty in 1951, after Denmark had joined NATO. Unknown to the Danish public, the Danish government, under this treaty, permitted the United States to deploy nuclear weapons at Thule Air Base in northern Greenland, thus violating the official Danish and Norwegian policy of not permitting nuclear-armed forces on their territories in peacetime, and from 1957–1968 the United States flew regular nuclear-armed bomber missions from Thule, which formed a crucial part of the advanced U.S. deterrent in the years when bombers were the primary U.S. retaliatory force against Soviet attack. When this secret deal came to light in 1995 after having been long known only to top politicians, historians argued that the American rights in Greenland formed part of an implicit security bargain with Denmark in return for which the United States and NATO would accept low Danish defense spending in general.[95]

The story of wartime Denmark as a country of latent opposition to Germany which erupted into open sabotage and resistance after 1943 took some knocks in the 1990s when revisionist historians began looking at what some of them called "the hidden history of Denmark." In both Denmark and Norway, the Nazis in 1941 recruited volunteers to fight alongside the German Army on the eastern front, against the Soviet Union. Since the Norwegian government was in exile and fighting Germany, no Norwegian volunteer could be in doubt that he was committing treason and would be punished if Germany lost the war. In Denmark, where the government remained in place, the 9,000 or so volunteers had reason to believe that the government approved their action. Volunteers from the Danish Army were given official leave and promised reinstatement in rank and pension rights after the war. The volunteers suffered heavy losses; over 4,500 Danes fell or were taken prisoner on the eastern front, about three times the number of people who fell in the resistance.[96] After liberation, the government stated that the volunteers should have realized that the promises were given under duress. In the liberation summer of 1945, Denmark passed retroactive laws penalizing close collaboration with the Germans. Volunteering for military service carried an automatic four year prison sentence and loss of all pension rights.

Finland lost close to 100,000 men in war with the Soviet Union in 1939–1940 and 1941–1944 or 2 percent of the population, which would correspond to the United States having lost 2.8 million in World War II. This experience gave Finland quite a different history from its Nordic neighbors, but a history well concealed from outsiders by the official picture of peaceful and harmonious coexistence with the Soviet Union after 1944. In 2000, a Finnish film, *The Ambush,* appeared; one of the few noteworthy public representations of the war, it is the story of a bicycle platoon sent on a scouting mission through eastern Karelia in the summer of 1941. Its commander believes that his fiancée has been murdered by Soviet partisans, but is obliged to lead his force far beyond the Soviet lines and back again.

When Finland signed the second armistice with the Soviet Union in 1944, it surrendered the same territory as in 1940 and agreed to pay heavy reparations, but escaped occupation. In 1948, the Soviet Union imposed a treaty of "friendship, cooperation, and mutual assistance" requiring Finland to help the Soviet Union in any conflict with Germany or a country allied with Germany, which in practice meant NATO. For over forty years, Finnish governments followed this line. The most notable exponent of the idea of harmonious relations with the Soviet Union was the long-time president Urho Kekkonen, who after the fall of the Soviet Union was shown to have had intimate ties to the Soviet secret police. But even before that became known, Kekkoken had long stultified Finnish political culture by establishing a pro-Soviet type of neutralism as being in Finland's national interest and defining that

---

[95] Danish Institute of International Affairs, *Greenland in the Cold War* (Copenhagen: DUPI 1998).

[96] Their first commander, C. P. Kryssing, rose to general in the SS and was recognized by German military colleagues as one of the best artillerymen in the war. He was also one of the very few who dared to defy the almighty head of the SS, Heinrich Himmler. When the SS broke its promises and disbanded the Danish volunteer unit, dispersing its members to other formations, Kryssing officially protested. He was overruled, but his courage astonished the Germans.

interest as friendship with the Soviet Union. In 1962, he said, "Whoever is for Kekkonen is for friendship with the Soviet Union and whoever is against Kekkonen is against friendship with the Soviet Union."[97] The implication was that friendship with the Soviet Union was a good and necessary thing and that he, Kekkonen, guaranteed it.

Critics defined this anticipatory subordination to Soviet interests as "Finlandization," an ambiguous notion. Some saw it as clever survival, others as "egregious subservience."[98] The critical point was that Kekkonen pretended and came to believe, anticommunist though he had once been, that it was necessary and virtuous to serve Soviet interests in the wider world, for example by acting as a proxy for Soviet "peace" initiatives directed against the democracies, sending back refugees from the Soviet Union, not permitting criticism of the Soviet Union in the media, or ruining the careers of promising people within Finland who were no less patriotic than he but who feared the effects of aligning Finland with Soviet foreign policy.

The Soviet Union took control of Finnish foreign and security policy in 1948, and in the same year communists seized power in Czechoslovakia, while Soviet forces in Germany tried to force the Western Allies out of Berlin. Many Europeans and Americans feared that the Soviet Union, like Nazi Germany, was out to conquer Europe. In Scandinavia, Danes and Norwegians feared a new April 9, that is, a new surprise attack by a totalitarian enemy. In response to the Soviet moves, the Western nations began the discussions that led to the Atlantic Alliance in 1949. The Nordics were offered the chance to join. Norway was prepared at once, fearing Soviet moves in the far north and realizing that Norwegian security could only be guaranteed by the stronger Western powers. The Danish government, still tainted with the neutralism of the 1930s, hoped for a purely Nordic defensive alliance that would be less provocative to the Soviets than joining a United States-led Western alliance. A Nordic alliance required Sweden to lead it and to be the main supplier of arms and military forces, but this was beyond Swedish capabilities, so the Swedes asked if a prospective Nordic alliance could buy arms in the United States. The Americans replied that the United States had no arms to spare for non-allies; a Nordic alliance would have to be self-supporting. Sweden then informed Norway and Denmark that they could not undertake a mutual security pact, after which the Danes gave up their efforts and both Denmark and Norway joined NATO as founding members in 1949.

Soon after joining NATO, Danes and Norwegians stated that they would not accept nuclear weapons or permanently stationed foreign troops in ordinary times of peace. This policy was partly to reassure domestic neutralists and partly to maintain what became known as the Nordic balance. This notion, first mooted in 1721 when Russia defeated Sweden in the Great Northern War, meant in essence that Nordic security policies should aim at national independence but without provoking the Soviet Union. In Nordic eyes, the Nordic balance after 1949 meant that the Soviets would not annex Finland so long as Sweden remained neutral and Denmark and Norway refused foreign troops. Well-meaning Nordic politicians and analysts regarded it as a real balance, one that reassured the Soviet Union that the area would not become highly militarized and allowed Norway and Denmark, though NATO members, to have good-neighborly relations with Moscow. The Soviets did not respect any such implicit bargain. To them, the Nordic balance was a useful idea because it weakened NATO's northern flank and allowed them to pursue their long-term strategy, which was not to maintain the balance of power but to shift it in their favor by making Sweden subservient

---

[97] Quoted in Singleton 1989, 141.

[98] Kirby 1993, 426.

and persuading Denmark and Norway to leave NATO and enter the Soviet security orbit. In the 1980s, this strategy came close to success.

Since the 1960s, the Nordic governments have given generously of their taxpayers' money to poor countries, especially in sub-Saharan Africa and parts of Asia. In the later 1960s, the Swedish economist Gunnar Myrdal, whom we have already met as the author of the postwar program of the Swedish labor movement, wrote a three-volume study of Asia in which he proposed that poor countries could achieve both growth and greater equality if they rejected capitalist economics.[99] For thirty years, foreign aid policy in the Nordic countries was administered by people hostile to free markets and who sincerely believed, first, that poverty in the Third World was due to Western exploitation, and, second, that rich Westerners should feel guilty about their wealth and should redistribute it to poor countries. These people entered an alliance with like-minded ruling elites in poor countries such as Tanzania, which under the socialist president Julius Nyerere became the single largest recipient of Danish aid, or Mozambique, which under the socialist regime that followed decolonization became the largest recipient of Swedish aid after India. These regimes, supported by elite socialists in Scandinavia and elsewhere, believed that one could achieve growth by protecting local industries and minimizing imports. In Scandinavia, the foreign aid bureaucracy became one of the strongholds of anticapitalism and anti-Americanism. Its leaders saw themselves as soldiers in the revolutionary struggle against capitalism worldwide and took pride in refusing to apply normal economic success criteria to their aid programs or to their favored recipient countries. The criteria for giving aid were not that the aid should promote growth but that it should alleviate the worst poverty and—especially in the Swedish case—support a country's nonaligned, that is to say, socialist and anti-Western, position. The latter criterion explains why much Swedish aid went to places like Cuba, Nicaragua under the Sandinistas, and North Vietnam.

Alleviating the worst poverty is not possible in the longer term unless the country in question adopts economic policies that promote growth. Until the late 1990s, Nordic foreign aid included no demands that the recipient countries pursue growth policies. Substituting locally protected industries for imports does not produce growth but only more poverty. The urban elites in places like Tanzania destroyed their own agricultures while producing nothing of value in their protected industries. To such elites, generous Nordic aid was a tool that enabled them to pursue their harmful policies longer than would otherwise have been the case. And the aid was generous. By the 1990s, Sweden and Denmark were giving 1 percent of GDP in annual aid as originally suggested by the socialist and protectionist government of India in 1960. In 2000 that was about $1.4 billion for Denmark and $2 billion for Sweden. The combined Nordic aid budgets were over twice the aid budget of the World Bank and consisted entirely of gifts, whereas the World Bank granted most of its aid in the form of loans. Nowhere else in the developed world are larger amounts handed out with less control than by DANIDA and SIDA, the Danish and Swedish development agencies. Attempts to evaluate whether the development assistance so generously provided by politicians at taxpayers' expense actually promoted development—that is, better living conditions and growth—in poor countries came late and reluctantly. The foreign aid establishments included hardly any trained development economists, that is, people qualified to estimate how to achieve growth in a poor country or to assess the effect of foreign aid on growth in such a country. By contrast, the World Bank employed 2,000 development economists.[100]

---

[99] Gunnar Myrdal, *Asian Drama: An Inquiry into the Poverty of Nations.* A Twentieth-Century Fund Study (New York: Pantheon 1968).

[100] Paldam 1997, 18, 22, 205.

Many of the politicians and activists who demanded and got rapid and permanent increases in development aid from the Nordic governments were themselves opposed to economic growth if that meant markets and free enterprise. In providing large amounts of foreign aid to preferred regimes in the Third World these politicians and activists were gratifying their own need to demonstrate altruism, as they conceived it, with taxpayers' money. Instead of favoring growth, they favored collectivism and socialism. Some argued that development aid was also a security policy because it won goodwill in poor countries, which were a majority in the UN, and because it was a form of insurance or payoff against poor countries simply marching north and taking what they wanted by force.

In the 1990s, analysts in both Denmark and Sweden concluded that the bulk of development aid had little positive and some negative effect on growth in recipient countries and that the prime criterion, to alleviate poverty, had not been met in many cases. Where it had been met, it was because the country in question had already decided to abandon the import substitution strategy and to pursue more market-oriented policies of growth involving the time-tested principles of open markets, low taxation, the rule of law, and trying to minimize corruption and graft.

The rise of foreign aid bureaucracies in the Nordic countries was part of the anticapitalist and anti-American political culture of the long 1970s. Few symbolized this culture better than Olof Palme and his increasingly anti-American and pro-Soviet bias. A critical moment occurred in February 1968, when Palme, who was then minister of education, joined a demonstration in Stockholm against the American war in Vietnam sponsored by various communist groups and an umbrella organization chaired by Gunnar Myrdal. As prime minister from 1969, Palme pursued this line which led to a freeze in Swedish-American relations. Another revealing incident began the following year, when the new American ambassador, a black college president named Jerome Holland, arrived in Sweden. When Holland drove to the royal palace to present his credentials in April 1970, enraged anti-American demonstrators shouted "nigger" at him, in a delicious reversal of bigotry: these were self-styled anti-imperialist and progressive demonstrators, but Holland was an American, so no insult was bad enough for him. When Palme visited America later that spring he claimed to have been upset by being denounced as a racist and when he returned to Sweden he wrote the American ambassador a pompous note to complain. In Palme's eyes the attacks on him were serious; calling the American ambassador a nigger was not serious because, as Palme later said, "of course nothing more serious happened."[101]

Around this time Palme began propagating the idea that the United States and the Soviet Union were equally nefarious threats to peace and equally responsible for oppression in the world. In the 1975 program of the Social Democratic Party, this notion of the moral equivalence of the superpowers became official doctrine. Because the Swedish political elite was not familiar with United States or NATO policies or the reasons for them, the doctrine of moral equivalence became, in practice, a doctrine that criticized America morning, noon, and night but regarded Soviet claims and positions with sympathy. The superpowers may have been morally equivalent, but the Soviets got the benefit of the doubt in almost every case. This became especially ludicrous in the 1980s. In September 1981, a Soviet submarine on a spying mission in Swedish waters outside the naval base of Karlskrona—built by Charles XI in 1680 to combat the Danish threat—went aground on a skerry. The submarine was of a type designated as Whisky-class in NATO, so the episode became known as "whisky on the rocks." It soon became clear that Soviet submarines were routinely patrolling Swedish waters, but

---

[101]Östergren 1984, 180.

the Swedish government refused to recognize this fact because it would disturb its cherished ideology, first, by casting doubt on the Soviet Union's peaceful intentions, and second, by focusing attention on Swedish territorial security. This was embarrassing because Palme and the Swedish elite were not interested in talking about defending Sweden, but rather about American imperialism, the Third World, global inequality, and helping socialist regimes in Africa, Asia, and Latin America. For the rest of the 1980s, Swedish official foreign policy went through contortions to ignore the Soviet threat and to denigrate U.S. and NATO security policies as harmful to peace. When the Soviet Union under Mikhail Gorbachev decided to throw in the towel and abandon the policy of confrontation with the West, the Swedish line was wholly discredited, and Palme's ideology had, in the views of independent analysts, done lasting harm to Sweden's standing among the Western democratic nations.[102] Swedish foreign policy, another commentator said, passed, in Palme's day, through three stages: neutralist, activist, and pathetic.[103]

Palme's unsolved murder in 1986 marked the symbolic end of the Palme era of a self-aggrandizing Sweden strutting across the stage of the United Nations claiming to have a particular moral standing because of its unaligned status. In 1990, with the Soviet threat to Scandinavia apparently receding, Sweden suddenly discovered that it could join the European Community (since 1992 the European Union) without compromising its neutrality, and did so in 1994, along with Finland, where foreign policy thinking, though officially more pro-Soviet, had never been as naive as in Sweden. It also turned out in the 1990s that Sweden had not been as neutralist as its official posture suggested. Throughout the Cold War, Sweden bought military supplies from and exchanged intelligence information with NATO countries, including the United States. Military experts were never in doubt that the only threat to Sweden came from the Soviet Union, just as the major threat to Sweden since 1700 had been Russia. But for decades they could not speak out in public.

The end of the Cold War was a great relief to all the Nordics. The Norwegians remained concerned that the Russian Confederation, the successor to the Soviet Union, retained strong military concentrations on the Kola Peninsula, just across the Norwegian border, and the fact that Norway again rejected EU membership in 1994 to some extent left Norway exposed to a continuing Russian threat. This was made worse when NATO rearranged its military organization in the 1990s, moving its Northern Command from Norway to Britain and moving Denmark from the Northern to the Central Command. Denmark was the greatest beneficiary of the end of the Cold War. The security threat to the country largely disappeared, allowing Denmark to play an active role in democratizing the newly independent Baltic states and in supplying forces for various UN and NATO interventions, notably in Bosnia. At Sarajevo in 1994 Danish troops went into combat for the first time since 1864, when an armored battalion shelled Bosnian Serb positions around the city to enforce the free passage of supplies to the besieged city.

Attitudes to Europe and international issues at century's end are less politicized than during the unhappy days of the Cold War, when security policy was often hostage to domestic rivalries and illusions about the peaceful intentions of the Soviet Union and about the imperialistic nature of America flourished among the elites. The Nordic populations are part of the global communications revolution, and if many are concerned that globalization threatens comfortable domestic arrangements, including the Nordic model of the welfare society, others see scope for harmonizing a modernized form of the Nordic model with whatever challenges

---

[102]On several occasions in the 1980s, the Swedish government clumsily tried to prevent some of these experts—who were not its employees—from publishing their critical assessments of Swedish policy. See Ries 1989 and Dörfer 1992, 152.

[103]Cited by Östergren 1984, 312.

European integration or global markets may present. The Nordic countries, from Iceland to Finland and from the North Cape of Norway to the Danish-German border, will continue to reflect their long-term history and their more recent and various experiences and will continue to provide an original set of tones in the European concert of cultures and nations.

Art, literature, and humor tell more about a people and a culture than textbooks. This survey of the Nordic societies, their history, contemporary political, economic, and social characteristics, and the outlook for their future has provided basic evidence and perspectives for the greater familiarity which can be found in further study and in encounters with the literary and artistic products of Nordic culture. A few glimpses have already been offered, in the belief that it is through such glimpses, based on a firm basis of historical facts, that understanding of other societies grows.

In that same vein, we end with an image. It is taken from the verse of Östen Sjöstrand, a Swedish poet of the later twentieth century who was not particularly interested in things that concerned many of his fellow-writers and poets intensely, such as politics and ideology, but rather in faith, love, and the mysteries and promises of physics and cosmology. The image can be read as a striking and subtly optimistic portrait of the Nordic personality at its best: youthful, earnest, striving to please yet self-assertive, and—what is perhaps less often found in today's more prosperous than in yesterday's poor and hungry world—grateful for the gift of everyday life:

> And through straight, new corridors
> You rush
> Your chest aching with the need to be competent,
> The need to compete,
> With the desire for and the right
>   To a life of your own:
> To the ability
> Without false coin
> And false dependence,
> To choose for yourself distance and closeness,
> Soil to grow from, rock to spring from, and
>   a beginning: o love! . . .
>   And every day,
>   Our everyday,
>   Is a wonder.[104]

ACKNOWLEDGMENTS

The author would like to thank the editor, Howard Wiarda, for patience and exhortation and the following for providing me with material and suggestions: Peter Abrahamson and Tim Knudsen, University of Copenhagen; Denis Bouget, University of Nantes; Erik Moberg, Lövestad, Sweden; Peter Nannestad, Aarhus University; Stefán Ólafsson, University of Iceland; Olof Petersson, Center for Business and Policy Studies, Stockholm; Mauricio Rojas, Center för Välfärd efter Välfärdsstaten, Stockholm; Diane Sainsbury, University of Stockholm; Kari Skrede, Statistics Norway, Oslo; and Jan Trost, University of Uppsala. Particular thanks to Hilary Barnes, formerly of Copenhagen and now of Tours, France, and for over thirty years the *Financial Times* and *Economist* correspondent in Scandinavia, for continuing to send me his invaluable newsletter *The Scandinavian Economies*.

If I were to name all those from whom I have, since the 1970s, learned about the welfare state, Nordic political culture, Nordic history, and Nordic security, the list would be overlong, so I won't try to establish it. Few outside Scandinavia study Nordic history, economics, politics, or culture full-time, and I am not one of them. All the more reason to thank all those who have taught me and to beg excuse for misunderstandings, exaggerations, and other errors.

---

[104]Sjöstrand 1981, 240–241, from the collection *Strömöverföring* (1977); my translation.

BIBLIOGRAPHY

Abrahamson, Peter 1999. "The Scandinavian Model of Welfare." In Bouget & Palier

Allardt, Erik, et al. 1981, eds. *Nordic Democracy.* Copenhagen: The Danish Institute.

Almond, Gabriel 1956. "Comparative Political Systems." *Journal of Politics* 18: 391-409.

Andersen, Bent Rold 1984. "Rationality and Irrationality of the Welfare State." *Daedalus* 113:1, *The Nordic Enigma,* 109-139.

Andersen, Jørgen Goul, Per Arnt Pettersen, Stefan Svalfors, and Hannu Uusitalo. "The Legitimacy of the Nordic Welfare States: Trends, Variations and Cleavages." In Kautto et al. 1999.

Arvidsson, Claes 1999. *Ett annat land – Sverige och det långa 70-talet.* Stockholm: Timbro.

Auerbach, Alan J.; Laurence J. Kotlikoff; and Willi Leibfritz 1999, eds. *Generational Accounting around the World.* University of Chicago Press.

Baldwin, Peter 1990. *The Politics of Social Solidarity: Class Bases of the European Welfare State 1875-1975.* Cambridge University Press.

Blom-Hansen, Jens 1998. "Macroeconomic Control of Local Governments in Scandinavia: The Formative Years." *SPS* 21: 129-160.

Bosworth, Barry P., and Alice M. Rivlin 1987, eds. *The Swedish Economy.* Washington, D.C.: Brookings Institution.

Bouget, Denis, and Palier, Bruno 1999, eds. *Comparing Social Welfare Systems in Nordic Europe and France.* Nantes: Maison des Sciences de l'Homme Ange-Guépin.

Byock, Jesse L. 1988. *Medieval Iceland: Society, Sagas, and Power.* Berkeley: University of California Press.

Dahl, Hans A. 1984. "Those Equal Folk." *Daedalus* 113:1, *The Nordic Enigma,* 93-107.

Delblanc, Sven 1986. *Fågelfrö.* Stockholm: Bonniers.

Dörfer, Ingemar 1992. *Nollpunkten: Sverige i det andra kalla kriget.* Stockholm: Timbro.

id. 1996. *Sverige är inte neutralt längre.* Stockholm: Timbro.

Einhorn, Eric; and Logue, John 1989. *Modern Welfare States: Politics and Policies in Social Democratic Scandinavia.* New York: Praeger.

Enkvist, Inger 2000. *Feltänkt – en kritisk granskning av idébakgrunden till svensk utbildningspolitik.* Stockholm: SNS.

Esping-Andersen, Gøsta 1990. *Three Worlds of Welfare Capitalism.* Princeton University Press.

id. 1996, ed. *Welfare States in Transition: National Adaptations in Global Economies.* London: SAGE Publications.

id. 1999. *Social Foundations of Postindustrial Economies.* Oxford University Press.

Finnemann, Niels Ole 1985. *I Broderskabets Aan— den socialdemokratiske arbejderbevægelses idéhistorie 1871-1977.* Copenhagen: Gyldendal.

Flanagan, Robert J. "Efficiency and Equality in Swedish Labor Markets." In Bosworth & Rivlin 1987.

Freeman, Richard B.; Robert Topel; and Birgitta Swedenborg 1997, eds. *The Welfare State in Transition: Reforming the Swedish Model.* University of Chicago Press.

Green-Pedersen, Christoffer 1999. "The Danish Welfare State under Bourgeois Reign: The Dilemma of Popular Entrenchment and Economic Constraints." *SPS* 22: 243-260.

Hagemann, Robert P., and Christoph John. "Generational Accounts in Sweden." In Auerbach et al. 1999.

Halvarson, Arne; Kjell Lundmark, and Ulf Staberg 1999. *Sveriges statsskick.* 11th ed. Stockholm: Almquist & Wiksell.

Heckscher, Gunnar 1984. *The Welfare State and Beyond: Success and Problems in Scandinavia.* University of Minnesota Press.

Hettne, Björn; Sverker Sörlin; and Uffe Østergaard 1999. *Den globala nationalismen : nationalstatens historia och framtid.* Stockholm: SNS.

Jensen, Svend E. H. and Bernd Raffelhüschen. "Public Debt, Welfare Reforms, and Intergenerational Distribution of Tax Burdens in Denmark." In Auerbach et al. 1999.

Kautto, Mikko, et al. 1999, eds. *Nordic Social Policy: Changing Welfare States.* London: Routledge.

Kirby, David 1995. *The Baltic World 1772-1993: Europe's Northern Periphery in an Age of Change.* London: Longman.

Knudsen, Tim 2000. "Tilblivelsen af den universalistiske velfærdsstat." In id., ed., *Protestantismen og den nordiske velfærdsstat.* Aarhus University Press.

Korpi, Walter 1983. *The Democratic Class Struggle.* London: Routledge.

Lacy, Terry G. 1999. *Ring of Seasons: Iceland, Its Culture and History.* Ann Arbor: University of Michigan Press.

Lewin, Leif 1988. *Ideology and Strategy: A Century of Swedish Politics.* Cambridge University Press.

Lijphart, Arend 1998. "Consensus and Consensus Democracy: Cultural, Structural, Functional, and Rational-Choice Explanations." *SPS* 21:99-108.

id. 1999. *Patterns of Democracy: Government Forms and Performance in Thirty-Six Countries.* New Haven, Ct.: Yale University Press.

Lindbeck, Assar 1975. *Swedish Economic Policy.* London: Macmillan.

id. 1997. *The Swedish Experiment.* Stockholm: SNS.

id.; Per Molander; Torsten Persson; Olof Petersson; Agnar Sandmo; Birgitta Swedenborg, and Niels Thygesen 1994. *Turning Sweden around.* MIT Press. Translation of *Nya villkor för ekonomi och politik.* SOU 1993: 16. Stockholm: Allmänna förlaget.

Lindbom, Anders 1998. "Institutional Legacies and the Role of Citizens in the Scandinavian Welfare State." *SPS* 21: 109–128.

Lundberg, Erik 1985. "The Rise and Fall of the Swedish Model." *Journal of Economic Literature* 33: 1–36.

Moberg, Erik 1999. "The Expanding Public Sector: a Threat to Democracy?" In *The Limits of Government: On Policy Competence and Economic Growth.* Gunnar Eliasson & Nils Karlson, eds. New Brunswick, N.J.: Transaction Publishers.

id. 2000. "The Swedish Model: A Comment on Mancur Olson's Analysis." In *A Not-so-Dismal Science: A Broader View of Economies and Societies.* Mancur Olson & Satu Kähkönen, eds. Oxford University Press.

Nannestad, Peter 1999 a. *Solidaritetens pris: Danske holdninger til flygtninge og indvandrere 1987–1993.* Aarhus University Press.

id. 1999 b. "Keeping the Bumblebee Flying: Economic Policy in the Welfare State of Denmark, 1973–1994." Unpublished manuscript.

Nannestad, Peter, and Martin Paldam 1996. *Government's Free Lunch? A Study of Danish Mass-Level Reactions to Possible Income Tax Cuts.* Aarhus: Aarhus University Press.

Niklasson, Lars; Ingemar Ståhl, and Kurt Wickman 1997. *Ännu mera planekonomi? Marknadsekonomisk årsbok 1997.* Stockholm: Timbro.

OECD 2000. *Economic Surveys: Denmark,* June 2000. Paris: OECD.

Ólafsson, Stéfan 1999. "The Icelandic Model: Social Security and Welfare in Comparative Perspective." In Bouget & Palier.

Olson, Mancur 1995. "The Devolution of the Nordic and Teutonic Economies." *American Economic Review* 85: 22–27.

id. 1996. "The Varieties of Eurosclerosis: The Rise and Decline of Nations since 1982." In Nicholas Crafts and Gianni Toniolo, eds., *Economic Growth in Europe since 1945.* New York: Cambridge University Press.

Paldam, Martin 1991. "The Development of the Rich Welfare State of Denmark." In Magnus Blomström & Patricio Meller, eds., *Diverging Paths: Comparing a Century of Scandinavian and Latin American Development.* Washington, DC: Inter-American Development Bank.

id. 1997. *Dansk ulandshjælp. Altruismens politiske økonomi.* Aarhus University Press.

Petersson, Olof 1994a. *The Government and Politics of the Nordic Countries.* Stockholm: Fritzes.

id. 1994b. *Swedish Government and Politics.* Stockholm: Fritzes.

Pierson, Paul 1996. "The New Politics of the Welfare State." *World Politics* 48:143–179.

Popenoe, David 1988. *Disturbing the Nest: Family Change and Decline in Modern Societies.* New York: Aldine de Gruyter.

Przeworski, Adam, and John Sprague 1986. *Paper Stones: A History of Electoral Socialism.* University of Chicago Press.

Roberts, Michael 1979. *The Swedish Imperial Experience 1560–1718.* Cambridge University Press.

SAF 2000. *Facts about the Swedish Economy 2000.* Stockholm: SAF (Svenska Arbetsgivareföreningen), http://www.saf.se/ekonomi/fase2000/FASE.PDF

Sainsbury, Diane 1999. "The Nordic Countries." In ead., ed., *Gender and Welfare State Regimes.* Oxford University Press.

Singleton, Fred 1989. *Finland: A Short History.* Cambridge University Press.

Sjöstrand, Östen 1981. *Dikter.* Stockholm: Bonniers.

Skrede, Kari 1999. "Shaping Gender Equality—The Role of the State." In Bouget & Palier.

Steigum, Erling, Jr., and Carl Gjersen. "Generational Accounting and Depletable Natural Resources: The Case of Norway." In Auerbach et al. 1999.

Stephens, John D. "The Scandinavian Welfare States: Achievements, Crisis, and Prospects." In Esping-Andersen 1996.

Tomasson, Richard F. 1980. *Iceland: The First New Society.* Minneapolis: University of Minnesota Press.

Weaver, R. Kent 1987. "Political Foundations of Swedish Economic Policy." In Bosworth & Rivlin.

Wilensky, Harold L. 1975. *The Welfare State and Equality: Structural and Ideological Roots of Public Expenditures.* University of California Press.

Östergren, Bertil 1984. *Vem är Olof Palme?* Stockholm: Timbro.

id. 1988. *Den falska enigheten.* Stockholm: Timbro.

7

NORWAY
North Atlantic Ocean
SWEDEN
ESTONIA
LATVIA
LITHUANIA
IRELAND
DENMARK
U. K.
POLAND
BELARUS
NETHERLANDS
GERMANY
BELGIUM
LUX.
CZECH REP.
SLOVAKIA
FRANCE
AUSTRIA
HUNGARY
SWITZERLAND
ROMANIA
Bay of Biscay
SLOVENIA
CROATIA
Milan
Venice
Genoa
La Coruna
Bilbao
BOSNIA
Porto
Valladolid
ANDORRA
Florence
SERBIA
BULGARIA
Coimbra
Salamanca
ITALY
Adriatic Sea
MONTENEGRO
PORTUGAL
Madrid
Barcelona
Rome
MACEDONIA
Xanthi
Lisbon
SPAIN
Valencia
Naples
Bari
ALBANIA
Kalamaria
Palma
SARDINA
Aegean Sea
Cordoba
BALEARIC ISLANDS
Tyrrhenian Sea
GREECE
Sevilla
Agrinion
Khalkis
Malaga
Palermo
Patrai
SICILY
Athens
Catania
Ionian Sea
Khania
CRETE
MOROCCO
Mediterranean Sea
TUNISIA
ALGERIA
LIBYA

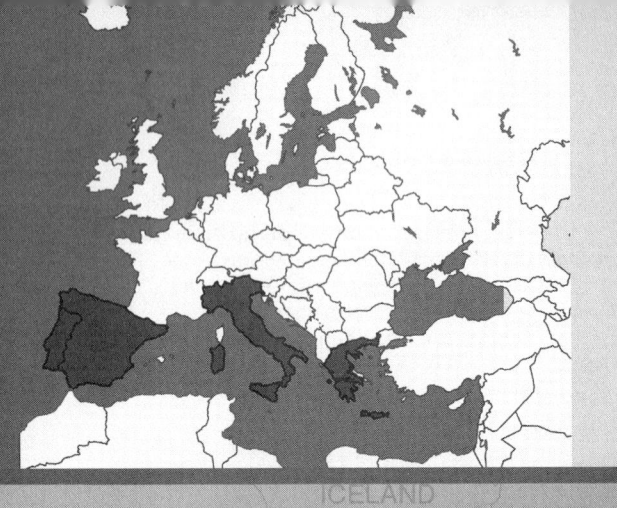

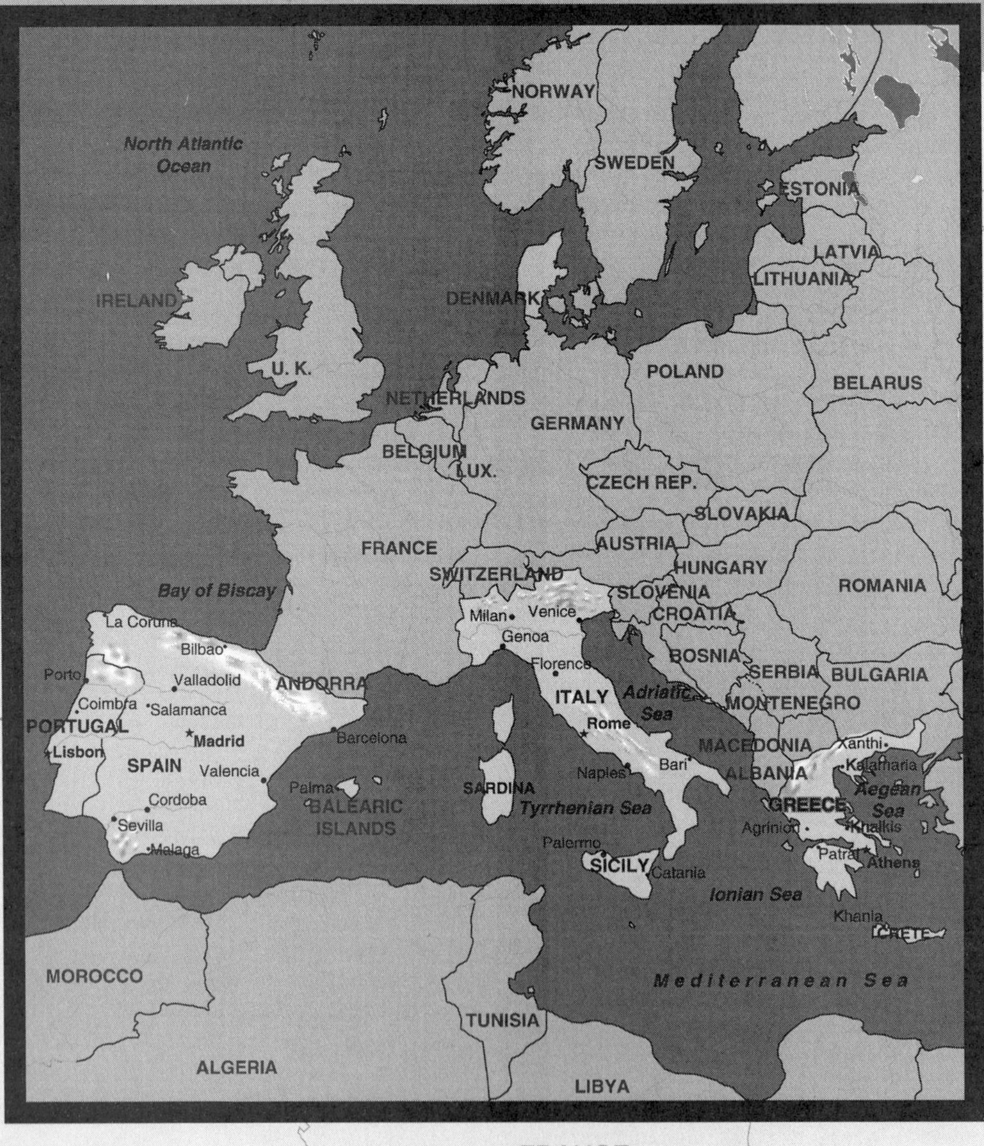

Southern or Mediterranean Europe:
Politics and the Political System of Greece, Italy, Portugal, and Spain

Howard J. Wiarda

COUNTRY PROFILES

Greece
Population:	11,000,000
Land Area:	132,000 sq. km.
Population per sq. km.:	82
Gross National Product:	$122.9 billion
Per Capita Income:	$11,650
Global Per Capita Income Rank:	47
Percent Urban:	60
Adult Literacy:	97% (claimed)
Life Expectancy	Male: 75
	Female: 81

Italy
Population:	58,000,000
Land Area:	301,000 sq. km.
Population per sq. km.:	196
Gross National Product:	$1,166.2 billion
Per Capita Income:	$20,250
Global Per Capita Income Rank:	25
Percent Urban:	67
Adult Literacy:	98% (claimed)
Life Expectancy	Male: 75
	Female: 82

Portugal
Population:	10,000,000
Land Area:	92,000 sq. km.
Population per sq. km.:	109
Gross National Product:	$106.4 billion
Per Capita Income:	$10,690
Global Per Capita Income Rank:	51
Percent Urban:	37
Adult Literacy:	98% (claimed)
Life Expectancy	Male: 65
	Female: 73

Spain
Population:	39,000,000
Land Area:	506,000 sq. km.
Population per sq. km.:	79
Gross National Product:	$553.7 billion
Per Capita Income:	$14,080
Global Per Capita Income Rank:	39
Percent Urban:	77
Adult Literacy:	97% (claimed)
Life Expectancy	Male: 75
	Female: 82

INTRODUCTION: THE IMPORTANCE OF SOUTHERN EUROPE

For a long time, Southern or "Mediterranean" Europe had lagged in terms of economic, social, and political development, behind both the core areas of Europe (Britain, France, Germany, and the Benelux countries) and the Northern or Scandinavian countries. But now Southern Europe has become very much alive, dynamic, and on-the-go. With dynamic, growing economies and democratic political systems, the nations of Southern Europe (Greece, Italy, Portugal, and Spain) have taken their place among the leading countries of Europe.[1] From positions of economic backwardness and political authoritarianism only a few short decades ago, all four of these nations have now joined the ranks of what the World Bank calls "advanced industrial nations"; all four have undertaken successful transitions to democracy.

It is often viewed as a mystery why Southern Europe lagged behind for so long. After all, Greece and Italy two thousand years ago were the cradles of Western civilization, and in the sixteenth century Spain and Portugal were the leading colonial nations and ranked among the strongest powers in Europe. But following their years of glory, all four of these nations went into centuries-long periods of decline. It has taken a long time for them to recover.

Greece, Italy, Portugal, and Spain lacked both the economic resources and industry of the core European countries, *and* their strong political institutions; but why did Southern Europe also come to lag behind Scandinavia, another peripheral European area? After all, in the mid-nineteenth century the Scandinavian countries were at the same underdeveloped level as Southern Europe: poor, rural, unindustrialized, undemocratic. But then Scandinavia forged ahead, industrialized, became democratic, and emerged as among, it not *the,* most developed, most modern countries in Europe. Meanwhile, for another hundred years, Southern Europe continued to falter. Why?

The answers are complex and are explained in greater detail in the main body of this chapter. Some of the reasons include the facts that Southern European social structure was more rigid and class-ridden than that of Scandinavia, that the inequitable landholding system of Southern Europe held back development, that traditional religious beliefs and ideology postponed and retarded development, that there was no national consensus on the direction these countries should take, that their rural economies were backward and their industrialization late, that political conflict and upheaval prevented stable economic growth, that political institutions and infrastructure were weak, and that neither entrepreneurial spirit and a capitalist growth ethic *nor* a commitment to democratic ideas were strongly present. All of these deep-seated problems had to be overcome before Southern Europe could enter a period of rapid growth. But now that growth has occurred, and Southern Europe in recent decades has come alive with energy, spirit, new wealth, and dynamism.

We speak of "Southern Europe" as if it were a single unified region, and in some characteristics indeed it is. All of the countries border on the Mediterranean, except Portugal, which also faces south but toward the Atlantic. All of the countries, despite mountainous areas where snow falls, are baked by the warm Mediterranean sun. None of them have large areas (like the American Midwest or the North European plains) of rich, fertile, level ground suitable to mechanized agriculture; instead, much of their surface areas are stony, and rugged, making it difficult to earn a living from

---

[1] For some purposes, France may also be considered a Southern European country, but France is a mixed case in this regard, stretching from south to north, with characteristics of both areas. Similarly with Turkey and the former Yugoslavia: both border on the Mediterranean, but they deserve separate and independent treatment, and for purposes of this chapter are not considered "Southern European."

farming, let alone to produce a surplus. Hence, the traditional crops of the Southern European countries: grapes, olives, and cork.

It remains controversial as to whether Southern Europe also has a common sociological and political-cultural heritage and, if so, whether that still applies today. For instance, much of Southern Europe long had a two-class social structure whose rigidities impeded development; but now much of the area—just like the rest of Europe—is becoming middle class and thereby changing its politics as well. For a long time, it was also said that traditional religious beliefs (Eastern Orthodoxy in Greece, Roman Catholicism in Italy, Portugal, and Spain) not only impeded development but also lent a particular (organic, hierarchical, corporatist) character to Southern European development when it did begin. However, now Southern Europe is becoming urban, better educated, and secular just like the rest of Europe, and the social, value, and political systems are changing as well. Similarly, it was long argued that Southern Europe was anti-capitalist, patronage-dominated, and lacked a strong work ethic or sense of trust in one's neighbors; but now Southern Europe has developed a creative entrepreneurial class that is as dynamic and forward-looking as any in the world. So the old generalizations and stereotypes don't hold up anymore; some scholars are now arguing that the advanced Italian economy is really closer to Sweden's than to its historic Mediterranean neighbors.

As implied in that last comment, the differences among the Southern European countries at this stage may be as great as their historic similarities. Greece is, as noted, Eastern Orthodox in its religion, whereas Italy, Portugal, and Spain are predominantly Roman Catholic; although there are similarities in these religions and in the political regimes (often authoritarian) they legitimated, there are also great differences, plus none of these countries is very religious anymore. In economics, all the countries of Southern Europe lagged behind their core European and Scandinavian counterparts in the early twentieth century; but in the period between World Wars I and II, Italy took off economically, and in the post–World War II period, as a founding member of the EEC, developed economically and socially, surpassing Great Britain in gross national product, and emerging as one of the biggest and most prosperous countries in the world. Similarly sociologically: at one point Italy was, like the rest of Southern Europe, a traditional, two-class, risk-avoiding society in which only family and close friends could be trusted; but now Italy is multi-class, much more socially mobile, and cosmopolitan in outlook, like Central or Northern Europe. Meanwhile, Greece, Portugal, and Spain fell behind economically and sociologically until the 1950s, when they initiated new policies and began to catch up, and until the 1970s politically when these three countries also experienced democratic breakthroughs. By almost any measure, therefore, Italy is the most developed Southern European country, but Greece, Portugal, and Spain have also made both economic and political breakthroughs and may, therefore, be coming to resemble Italy once again. The question is whether the political cultures and political sociologies of these countries are still similar and whether, as a group, they are still distinguishable from other countries in Europe.

Although Italy as a whole is prosperous and in the top rank of countries economically, the south of Italy, the *Mezzogiorno,* is still poor and closer to its Mediterranean neighbors. Greece, Portugal, and Spain (like Ireland) are still only at about two-thirds to three-quarters of the general Western European standard of living. So Southern Europe, although now forging ahead, still has a ways to go to catch up to the core countries. But as compared with Eastern Europe, Southern Europe is way ahead economically, sociologically, and maybe politically as well. Although Southern Europe is at roughly 70 to 80 percent of the European average economically, Eastern Europe and

Russia are way behind at only about 10 percent of the European average. Herein lies a good basis for thinking comparatively and placing the countries of Europe in separate categories: wealthy countries in the European core and Scandinavia, countries at 70 to 80 percent of the European average in the south, and still very poor countries (at the level of many developing nations) to the east.

Meanwhile, there are other interesting reasons to study Southern or Mediterranean Europe. First, with the end of the Cold War, the U.S. and NATO strategic focus has shifted south. During the early Cold War, the main U.S. and NATO preoccupation was a Soviet attack through Central Europe; later, the focus shifted to the Mediterranean: the Middle East conflict and its spillover effects, Cyprus and the Greece-Turkey conflict, instability in the Balkans and especially the former Yugoslavia, and other issues. As a result, U.S. and NATO security planning also shifted toward the Mediterranean area. Some NATO military functions were transferred from Brussels to Napoli in Italy; the U.S. Mediterranean fleet was beefed up; and Southern European issues came to have a higher priority in U.S. strategic thinking.

It is also across the Mediterranean that Europe confronts the Third World: North Africa, the Middle East, and sub-Saharan Africa. And the problems associated with that part of the world specifically and the Third World in general: Islamic fundamentalism, terrorism, drugs, poverty, transmittable disease, pollution, and immigration. For this reason, many Europeans began to view the Mediterranean in the same way that residents of the American Southwest view the Rio Grande: as a source of both potential possibilities *and* of problems. Across the Mediterranean and across the Rio Grande are two of the places in the world where the First World and the Third World come face to face and where the problems in the one tend to become problems in the other. As a result, the nations of Europe, especially Southern Europe, began to reach across the Mediterranean for the first time, to devise cooperative programs on pollution, immigration, and other hot issues, and to try to find common ground with their neighbors in North Africa. Just as the United States is now reaching across the Rio Grande for the first time, recognizing that unless we do something, Mexican and Central American problems will start to become our problems through unchecked immigration, and devising common cooperative, multinational policies, so Europe is starting to reach across the Mediterranean because many of their front-burner issues are kindled there.

The nations of Southern Europe and their delayed development are, first of all, interesting in their own right as individual countries. Second, they are interesting because of the comparisons that can be drawn among them, both the similarities as well as the differences. Third, Southern Europe is interesting as a bloc, as a group of nations with often common and/or parallel development experiences, quite different from those of Scandinavia and Eastern Europe, and now facing a common set of problems, across the Mediterranean and elsewhere. Fourth, the nations of Southern Europe are well worth studying because, after decades and even centuries of backwardness and authoritarianism, their economic takeoffs and political transitions to democracy in the 1970s are now being touted as models for Latin America, Russia, and Eastern Europe to follow. Whether Russia and Eastern Europe can or will follow the Southern European model—and what, precisely, that model consists of—is a subject to which we return in this chapter and in Chapter 8.

HISTORY, GEOGRAPHY, BACKGROUND, AND POLITICAL CULTURE

Southern European history goes back a long ways, some twenty-five hundred years, to the founding of Western civilization in Greece and

Rome. If one includes the prehistoric cave paintings at Altamira in northern Spain and at Lascaux, Montignac in France, it is clear that European history stretches back many more thousands of years.

At the time that ancient Greece and then Rome were in their heyday, the Mediterranean Sea was the main center of trade and civilized life, and the countries located on its littoral were leaders in art, philosophy, science, government, and military organization. But with the fall of Rome in A.D. 476, the ancient world and much of its culture and society collapsed; society, economics, and politics during much of the subsequent Middle or "Dark" Ages reverted to a more primitive form. Although society and civilization in the *western* part of the former Roman empire largely disintegrated and went into a decline during this period, in the east, in Byzantium (including Greece), the Empire, the Orthodox Christian church, and their culture and political structure continued to survive for another thousand years, albeit in attenuated form, with its center in Constantinople (now Istanbul), until it finally fell to the Turks in 1453. Greece's history is thus more commingled with the Near East than the other Southern European countries.

It took Western Europe a long time—about one thousand years—to recover from the devastation and disintegration brought on by Rome's collapse. When that recovery did begin, it was now concentrated in the north or central "core" of Europe, and no longer in the south. A key turning point was the crowning of the French king Charlemagne by the pope in the year 800, which definitively linked the papacy and Christendom to the north of Europe rather than to the eastern church at Byzantium. True, Italy had the Renaissance; Greece flourished off and on as part of the Eastern empire; and Spain and Portugal roared as colonial powers during the sixteenth century. But the great revolutions of early modern times, the major events that made the beginning of the *modern* world—the Protestant Reformation, the Industrial Revolution, the movement toward limited, representative government, the Enlightenment, and the development of modern, experimental science—all occurred in Northern Europe, not in the south. Hence, the north of Europe—the low countries (Holland, Belgium), England, France, Germany, and eventually Scandinavia—was destined to forge ahead into the modern world, whereas the south lagged behind. Greece's domination by the Turks and Italy's divisive regions controlled in various parts by Austria, France, and Spain further retarded progress.

Part of the problem of Southern Europe's comparative underdevelopment was geographical. First, all four countries—Greece, Italy, Portugal, and Spain—tend to be stony, harsh, dry, arid, and generally nonfertile—not amenable to the large-scale growing of wheat and grains as in the northern area of Europe. Second and related, because of the chopped-up, rocky terrain, none of these countries has navigable river systems capable—as in France or the U.S.—of knitting these societies together internally. A third factor is that the mountains and distinct geographic regions tended to divide these countries into what Spaniards call "patrias chicas," where loyalty went to the "small country" of the traditional home village rather than to the modernizing nation-state. A fourth geographic factor was natural resources: none of these countries has petroleum, iron ore, aluminum, or other of the essential resources necessary for modernization and industrialization. Hence, whereas nature has been kind to Southern Europe in terms of sun, moderate temperatures, and gorgeous blue skies, it has been less kind in terms of rainfall, fertile land, and resources.

Not only did the south fall behind, but it also remained locked in a quasi-feudal, semi-medieval, and largely traditional sociopolitical mode that continued to hold back its development. In all of the Southern European societies, the landholding system remained backward and semi-feudal, preventing modernization and perpetuating a two-class social structure that was similarly feudal and medieval. Politics was

A cobblestone street in Peloponnese, Greece.

dominated by ideas and institutions of royal absolutism, authoritarianism, and top-down rule that prevented the flowering of democracy. Science was slow to develop, and intellectual life was closed, formalistic, and based on rote memorization. Traditional religious beliefs (Catholicism in Italy, Portugal, and Spain; Eastern Orthodoxy in Greece) held back progress, discouraged or snuffed out pluralism, maintained unity between church and state, and prevented Southern Europe from modernizing at a pace equal to that of Northern Europe.

The growing backwardness of Southern Europe as compared with the dynamism of Northern or "core" Europe gave rise to one of the main interpretations of European (and other) politics that is still often used today: core-periphery relations. By the seventeenth century, if not earlier, the center of European political and economic life had shifted away from the south or Mediterranean Europe and toward the north: Holland, Belgium, England, France, and Germany. This shift was important, significant, and curious because in the fifteenth century the Italian city-states (Venice, Genoa, Naples, etc.) had led Europe in trade, banking, commerce, and capitalism; in the sixteenth century, with their vast colonies in Asia and Latin America, Spain and Portugal had been Europe's most dynamic and powerful countries.

But the separate Italian city-states were never (until much later in the nineteenth century) able to consolidate as a single nation-state, and thus over time were unable to compete with bigger, unified Spain, France, England, Austria, and Germany. Italy in the nineteenth century was thus dismissed as "only a geographic expression" and not considered a serious country. Meanwhile, Spain and Portugal, although rich in colonies and precious metals, were unable to use their colonial wealth to develop native industries and infrastructure. Instead, the gold, silver, and precious commodities of Asia and Latin

America flowed *through* the colonial powers of Spain and Portugal but without benefiting them in any permanent way, and on to England and Holland where they helped stimulate the Industrial Revolution. Meanwhile, Spain and Portugal remained poor and backward, squandered their power and colonial resources in an unsuccessful, century-long effort to maintain Catholic orthodoxy in Europe in the face of the Protestant Reformation, and by the end of the sixteenth century were already reduced to second-rate power status in Europe.

Spain, Portugal, Greece, and Italy—the Mediterranean countries—were no longer the leaders in Europe. Rather, that distinction had passed to the North in the seventeenth century and thereafter. Southern Europe remained locked in feudalism, backwardness, and the Middle Ages, whereas the northern countries assumed the leadership in Western modernization; however—and this concept is at the heart of the core-periphery interpretation—not only did the south lag behind, but it was also exploited and victimized by the north, which, according to the theory, drained the south's resources and used them for its own advancement while keeping the south poor. That other large, peripheral area of Europe, Eastern Europe, was often viewed, or viewed itself, in the same light, as an area of exploitation, conquest, and victimization by the core. In other words, the wealth of the Northern European countries was at least in part based on the poverty and exploitation of the south and east of Europe.

A note of caution is appropriate here because these themes are controversial. For one thing, Northern or Core Europe's success was also based strongly on its own economic, entrepreneurial, and policy accomplishments, and only in part on its exploitation of other areas of Europe. Second, one needs to distinguish between countries, for while Spain, Portugal, and Greece clearly lagged and were exploited, Italy—or at least its northern provinces—continued to do quite well and was better integrated into the core area. Indeed, that theme emerges several times in this chapter: that Italy is a generally more prosperous and successful country than its Southern European neighbors.

Although backwardness and underdevelopment constitute the main picture of Southern Europe during the seventeenth and eighteenth centuries, some further distinctions need to be drawn that make the portrayal more complex. First, already at this early date, we can see the differences not only between Italy and its neighbors but also between a more prosperous Northern Italy and the poor, more traditional south. Similarly in Spain: the provinces of Catalonia and the Basque country (both, like Northern Italy, closer to the more prosperous areas of Europe) forged ahead while the rest of Spain remained poor and illiterate. In Greece, Turkish control for so many centuries (1453–1821) held back Greek development until independence was finally achieved in 1821; and even then Greece remained torn and divided. In all four countries the main cities and the capitals were more prosperous, enlightened, and middle class in the eighteenth century, whereas the countryside remained poor and traditional.

Similarly in terms of time periods: in all four countries a split in the national psyche began to develop in the eighteenth century and carrying over to the nineteenth between those who were traditional and backward-looking and those who were more progressive, rationalist, reformist, and European-looking. This split often had a geographic and sociological basis as well: the cities modern and the countryside traditional; the modern or modernizing sector including the middle class, commercial elements, and educated persons, and the traditional elements including the landholding class, rural elements, and religious institutions. This split would not only divide Southern Europe in terms of its domestic politics, but it also persisted in modified form through the nineteenth century, producing many conflicts and civil wars that further retarded development, and on into the twentieth where it was overlain with class conflict and vast political differences. These political divisions in turn further held back Southern Europe's economic development.

The French Revolution of 1789 was a major turning point, and not just in France. In Southern Europe it precipitated an even deeper divide in society than had existed in the earlier centuries and led to a pattern of on-again, off-again civil conflict between liberals and conservatives that tore society apart. In Greece these conflicts were complicated even more by the struggles for independence from the Turks in the early nineteenth century, and in Italy by the *resorgimento* or movement for national unity. Liberals and revolutionaries, in addition to fighting for independence and unity, sought to change Southern European society in its fundamentals: to abolish special privileges for the elites, to disestablish the official religion, to abolish the guild system and the foundation of traditional corporatism, to introduce individualism and to elevate individual rights over group rights and community solidarity, to do away with or limit the monarchy, and to bring in the classic, nineteenth-century freedoms (of press, assembly, religion, etc.). Liberals wanted Southern Europe to be more like its northern neighbors and, ideally, to immediately catch up to the level of development that it took Northern Europe hundreds of years to accomplish.

Some reactionaries sought to restore the status quo ante, to return to the orderly, traditional, quasi-feudal society that existed before 1789. More thoughtful conservatives recognized the impossibility of turning the clock back but nevertheless feared excessive individualism in countries not prepared for that; the cutting of all the ancient ties of group solidarity and community, the loss of religious or moral values, and a too-fast rush toward modernity and liberalism in societies that at that time lacked the organizational and institutional base to support it. They feared too-rapid change would not produce freedom and moderate democracy but rather chaos and anarchy. The differences between liberals and conservatives in Southern Europe were so great that they produced repeated conflict and civil wars throughout the nineteenth century.

These fights often focused on the monarchy as *the* symbol of the nation. Liberals wanted to check the monarchy, to have its absolutism limited by a constitution, to fashion a system of government like the British with a *constitutional* monarchy and an elected parliament. Conservatives, in contrast, sought to preserve the integrity of the monarchy and the strength and centrality of the state, fearing anything less than that in a context of nations with deep divisions and weak, grassroots associational life would produce national disintegration. Both sides in this debate were at least partially correct, but in the meantime the constant fighting between the two sides produced frequent polarization, conflict, and a lack of progress. Caught up in these repeated crises, Southern Europe continued to fall ever further behind its northern neighbors.

Following the French Revolution, liberals and republicans in the early nineteenth century made a bid for power. But they were soon turned back by the conservative forces who, in the face of renewed liberal challenges, often turned into full reactionaries. In the 1830s, 1840s, 1850s, 1860s, and 1870s—obviously varying from country to country—the liberals tried repeatedly to assert their agenda, only to have it repeatedly frustrated by conservatives. Recall from the introduction to this book that in the core of Europe this period of the early- and mid-nineteenth century was one of industrialization and accelerated economic growth; but in the south of Europe, torn by political and social conflict, industrialization and economic growth were perpetually postponed. Meanwhile, finally, during the 1860s, Italy, which had long been divided into feuding city-states whose rivalries added another retarding element to Italian development, was unified under Giuseppe Garibaldi into a single nation-state. Greece also achieved a limited, conditional monarchy in the 1860s.

By the last third of the nineteenth century and including the first decade of the twentieth, *all* of the countries of Southern Europe had calmed down somewhat and stabilized. All came to accept one or another form of limited, constitutional government. All accepted some, usually limited, liberties and freedoms. They remained monarchies, but the monarchy was no longer absolute, and checks and balances, as well as many basic civil and political rights, were introduced. Some of the hottest and most divisive issues—church-state relations, centralism versus local autonomy, and monarchy versus republicanism—were smoothed over and compromised, even if not finally resolved. In this context of greater political stability, investment felt more secure, industrialization could begin, national infrastructure (roads, railroads, port facilities, telephone and telegraph, etc.) was developed, and the economies of the area finally began to take off.

Because industrialization came so late to Southern Europe, and the workers were so poor, the trade unionism that was spawned tended to be considerably more radical than in the north of Europe. The early Greek, Italian, Portuguese, and Spanish trade unions were heavily influenced by anarchist, communist, anarcho-syndicalist, and socialist ideas. They believed in direct political action—strikes, marches on the centers of power, violence, and assassination—over calm, collective bargaining. For example, when the king of Spain married in 1903, the anarchists threw bombs at the wedding party—not an auspicious start for the marriage! Governments of the area often responded to the radicals by refusing to enact any social reforms for the workers and calling out the police and army to beat up striking workers. The "labor problem" was exacerbated by the immense social and class differences between workers and employers or landowners in Southern Europe, which made it almost impossible for the two groups to sit down around a common bargaining table and work things out. So while the general picture is one of increased stability and economic growth in the decades leading up to World War I, beneath the surface increased class conflict added one more layer of problems to countries already deeply divided by other issues. There were circulations in power among the elites (*transformismo* in Italy, *rotativismo* in Portugal) but little genuine democratization.

The decades just before World War I constituted what historian Barbara Tuchman called "the proud tower" of traditional European society. Nowhere was that more true than in Southern Europe. There, especially, class lines were still rigidly drawn; the elites monopolized social, economic, and political power; and the masses were expected to accept their lower-class station in life as God-given. Southern Europe remained a rigidly hierarchical society, with the class lines sharply defined, and little social mobility. Politics and social life still mainly revolved around the small village, family and clan ties, and patron-client relations. Few of the democratizing or leveling reforms that were already being introduced in the core countries had as yet been introduced in the south.

World War I and its social and political effects had a profound, often devastating impact on Southern Europe. In the midst of the war, the Russian Revolution occurred, which was then followed by social and economic upheaval in Germany and other countries. These events had major repercussions throughout Southern Europe. The numbers of strikes and bombings increased and the level of violence escalated. Economic upheaval, recessions, and eventually full-scale depression occurred during the 1930s. Class and social conflict increased. Radical groups of both left and right became even more radical and violent; many of them formed their own armed militias. Meanwhile, there were increased popular pressures from below, rumblings of military movements and threatened coups, hardened attitudes on the part of traditional elites, and strong right-wing as well as left-wing movements. Vast political changes were also underway: Portugal abolished the monarchy and declared a republic in 1910; Italy had its last liberal prime minister in 1921; Spain had a dictatorship in the 1920s and declared a republic in 1931; whereas in Greece a new Liberal Party was elected in 1910 that faced repeated attacks from all sides.

Developments on the left almost immediately produced a reaction on the right, and vice versa. In terms of "grand systems," the right-wing reactions at this stage produced no longer a return to absolute monarchy but now to corporatism. In 1922, Benito Mussolini staged his march on Rome, seized power, snuffed out nascent republicanism, and turned Italy into a fascist regime: a combination of personalism, authoritarianism, populism, and corporatism. In Portugal, the First Republic lasted longer (1910–1926), only to be replaced in that year by a military regime and then the corporatist-authoritarian dictatorship of Antonio Salazar (1928–1974). In Spain, the monarchy sought to perpetuate itself by allying with a military dictatorship (1923–1929), gave way to a republic (1931–1936), which triggered full-scale civil war (1936–1939), and led to a similarly authoritarian-corporatist regime under General Francisco Franco (1939–1975). In Greece, a reformist monarchy had come to power in the 1860s accompanied by expansionist economic policies throughout the rest of the nineteenth century, followed by the liberal regime of Eleuthérios Venizelos in the early twentieth century. But Greece was deeply divided politically in the period after World War I, defeated by Turkey in 1921, and devastated by depression in the 1930s; in 1936, the liberal regime was replaced by the corporatist dictatorship of General Ionnis Metaxas.

These corporatist regimes varied from country to country, but they also had many similarities: All were authoritarian. All sought to reestablish "social peace" after the earlier strikes and upheavals. All provided for a strong state that would both maintain order and help promote economic development. All were based at least ostensibly on Catholic or Christian (Orthodox in the Greek case) ideas of organic social unity and national harmony. All sought to organize society along functional or group lines as compared with the earlier system of individual or geographic representation. So within the legislature, advisory councils, as well as government regulatory and policymaking agencies, for instance, business, labor, fisheries, religious bodies, and other corporate units, were all represented *by group* rather than on the basis of one-person, one-vote. All of these regimes also used police-state tactics to keep their peoples in line: repression, jailings, torture, censorship, secret police, and the like. Over time, particularly as they faced economic and political crises in the 1930s and then war in the 1940s, all of them largely abandoned their earlier religious bases and corporatist representational principles in favor of full-fledged dictatorship that snuffed out all opposition. Of the four countries, Italy was the most successful at stimulating economic growth during this period, even though democracy had been extinguished.

During World War II and for the first three decades afterward, the histories of these countries diverged sharply. Italy had allied itself with Nazi Germany in the war, suffered devastating defeat, saw the Mussolini regime collapse and disintegrate, and witnessed terrible destruction in the war. Defeat may have been a blessing in disguise, however, because after the war Italy rebuilt, joined NATO and the EEC, became a full-fledged democracy, and saw its economy take off and prosper to become one of the largest and wealthiest economies in the world. In contrast, Spain and Portugal stayed neutral in the war, suffered privation but not wartime destruction or defeat, and emerged from the war without either upheaval or collapse. But that situation also enabled their long-time dictators to hang onto power, postponed needed economic reforms until the 1950s and 1960s, and prevented democracy—until the Salazar regime was overthrown in 1974 and Franco died in 1975. Greece, like Italy, was the scene of intense fighting during the war, involving not just Allied (U.S., British) versus Axis (Germany, Italy) forces but also a domestic civil war: socialists and communists versus conservatives, monarchists, and anticommunists. Even after the civil war was settled in 1949, Greece continued to be torn between republican, monarchist, communist, military, and democratic forces.

Only after the mid-1970s did Southern Europe begin to reacquire its unity and cohesion. Recall that Italy, but not the other countries, had been both prospering and democratic since the end of World War II. In 1969, the ailing Salazar was replaced by the younger Marcello Caetano, but the old Salazar regime, now more liberal and open than before, lived on. In 1974, however, it was overthrown by a military revolt that went radically to the left for the next year before settling in a moderate democratic direction. That same year the colonels who had been governing Greece for the previous seven years were overthrown, paving the way for democracy. In Spain, Franco died in 1975, which similarly enabled that country to flower into a democracy. The restoration of democracy in the mid-1970s in these three countries not only restored political freedom but also made them eligible to join the European Economic Community, which Greece did in 1981, and Spain and Portugal followed in 1986. Greece and Portugal had long been members of NATO, but when Spain eventually ratified by popular vote in 1986 its earlier (1981) decision to join, the circle of Southern European membership was now complete. Thus the two great "clubs" of Europe, NATO and the EC, had become not just exclusive but also democratic.

Greece, Portugal, and Spain are newer democracies than is Italy, so in the following pages we will examine if their democratic institutions (civic culture, interest groups, political parties, government institutions, and public policy) are still weaker as well. Similarly in the economic sphere: Italy has the strongest economy in Southern Europe, whereas Greece, Portugal, and Spain are only between 70 and 80 percent of the more prosperous European economic average. These economic differences may also help us to understand both the relative stability of political institutions and democracy in these countries and the differences among them in their ability to carry out effective public policies for the benefit of their peoples.

Political Culture

Political culture refers to the values, beliefs, ideas, and orientations that citizens have about their political system, and the sociocultural institutions that shape those values. Political cultures can be *parochial* (backward, traditional, uninvolved, nonparticipatory), *subject* (aroused but suppressed by authoritarianism or totalitarianism), or *civic* (participatory, tolerant, democratic).

Historically, political culture in the four Southern European countries has been mainly "parochial" and "subject": only recently has it become "civic." It is also deeply divided. The roots of these splits, as we have seen, go back at least to the eighteenth century, perhaps earlier. At that time, a basic division developed in the political culture between those who remained conservative, traditional, deeply religious, backward-looking and feudal or medieval in outlook, and those (a minority current) who were liberal, progressive, secular, forward-looking, and more modern. These splits, then and in the future, tore Greece, Italy, Portugal, and Spain apart and prevented the growth of unity, democracy and development. In Greece, recall that these splits were complicated by hatred of the occupying Turks, and in Italy by continued regional divisions and foreign occupations.

Recall that the divisions in the political culture of these countries also had a geographic and a socioeconomic base. The dominant conservative, traditional political culture was strongly entrenched in the nobility, the church, the army, the landholding class, and among peasants, and was particularly strong in the rural, traditional, often illiterate countryside. The liberal, modern political culture was found among intellectuals, students, and commercial interests, and was concentrated in the large cities, especially the capital city. In addition, regional differences often existed: the north of Italy was progressive and modern whereas the south remained traditional.

The disputes between the traditional Greece, Italy, Portugal, and Spain, and the modern, between conservatives and liberals, between religious elements and the more secular, simmered for decades, even centuries. In the seventeenth and eighteenth centuries, these religious, educational, and intellectual debates were mainly confined to handfuls of people. They were sometimes accompanied by important policy debates as well, for example over reform of the school curriculum, the relations of church and state, styles of dress and behavior, and freedom of trade and commerce. Until the French Revolution in 1789, these debates were usually kept within peaceful bounds and did not degenerate into major violence or civil conflict.

After 1789, however, these debates over political culture and, hence, over the future direction of the country, deepened, became more polarized, and sometimes provoked civil war. More people were mobilized and became involved, and the political and economic stakes involved (political power, access to government favors, and commercial possibilities) were higher. Greece was torn by religious and political as well as anti-Turkish conflict; Spain was divided by a succession of liberal-conservative civil wars; Portugal was similarly conflictual; and feuding among Italy's still-not-unified city-states was rife.

In the last third of the nineteenth century, the political situation in Southern Europe began to stabilize somewhat. To end the seemingly perpetual conflicts of the earlier part of the century, a compromise was reached: the monarchy would continue in power, but it would be limited by a constitution, checks and balances, and a parliament and/or constitutionally mandated prime minister.

After being long delayed and retarded, however, this period of the late nineteenth century was also the period when large-scale industrialization came to Southern Europe. Because of late industrialization and because Southern European workers were often exceedingly poor, the worker movements spawned there by industrialization were often more radical than those in Northern Europe. Their ranks included socialists, communists, anarchists, and anarcho-syndicalists (who wanted to abolish all government and have power concentrated directly in the hands of the workers' organizations, or "syndicates"). Many of these groups believed in revolutionary violence, assassination, direct action, and the general strike as means of advancing their interests, not collective bargaining. So, in addition to the other conflicts already tearing Greece, Italy, Portugal, and Spain apart, a new, class-based, and ideological conflict was added to the simmering cauldron.

These political and ideological conflicts persisted into the first decades of the twentieth century, through World War I, and beyond. They were accelerated and deepened by the Russian Revolution in 1917 and by the economic and social crises in many countries that followed the war. In Portugal, a democratic republic had replaced the monarchy in 1910, but it was chaotic, riven by violence and conflict, and was overthrown by a military dictatorship in 1926 that brought long-time authoritarian Antonio Salazar to power. In Italy, republicanism and liberalism were discredited in World

War I and afterward and were replaced in 1922 by the fascist regime of Benito Mussolini. In Spain, a similarly wobbly monarchy turned to a military dictatorship for support (1923-1929), but in 1931 a republic was declared, its chaotic existence was followed by a civil war (1936–1939), which resulted in the victory of General Francisco Franco and his authoritarian regime (1939–1975). Greece was also unstable during this period, and from 1936 to 1941 turned to the authoritarian corporatist regime of Ioannis Metaxas.

All of these regimes sought to end the conflict that had plagued them for so long over political culture, national values, and the future directions of their countries. They did so, initially, by trying to combine various features of their countries' background into an organic, unified whole. For example, they sought to eliminate class conflict by combining business and labor into a unified corporatist arrangement; they sought to reconcile religious and anti-religious sentiment in a modernized, updated church-state agreement; and they sought to overcome decades and even centuries of backwardness by initiating state-led industrialization. But to achieve these goals and to deal with the opposition trade unions and political parties that objected to the changes being made, they used increasingly authoritarian, even totalitarian, methods of control and dictatorship. Increasingly, these regimes dealt with an inchoate political culture, the conflict of ideologies, and rising societal pluralism by snuffing out those groups and ideas opposed to themselves. They sought to solve the problem of a deeply divided political culture by imposing the ideas and values (order, discipline, authority, rank, place, religion, top-down rule—no bumper stickers advocating "Question Authority" here!) of one sector of society on the nation as a whole. And to do that required full-scale dictatorship or fascism.

After World War II, all of these regimes were discredited and ostracized, and eventually fell. Mussolini was assassinated in 1944; Italy was defeated in the war, fascism collapsed, and in 1946 a new democracy was proclaimed. In Portugal, Salazar suffered a stroke in 1968, was replaced by his long-time protege Marcelo Caetano, who was then overthrown in a military coup in 1974 that, after a year and more of instability, led to democracy. The similarly authoritarian Greek colonels who had been in power since 1967 were overthrown only three months after Caetano's ouster, leading to renewed democracy there. In Spain, Franco died in 1975, ushering in a peaceful transition to democracy that became a model for other countries.

Thus, by the mid-1970s, all of the countries of Southern Europe had reestablished, or established for the first time, democracy. Moreover, their political cultures had also become more democratic. Nevertheless, in all four countries this transition was still incomplete; not all groups had been reconciled to democracy; and anti-democratic and traditional ideas still dominated in certain quarters. But, of course, these attitudes changed over time and varied from country to country.

Greece Greece has become a democracy, but it is still a deeply divided democracy. Its political culture is often fragmented into such intensely contending factions that it is difficult to forge a consensus among them. The effective formulation and implementation of public policy are also difficult in this context.

The basic split in Greek political culture is between the left and the right. This split is accompanied by strong anti-Turkish attitudes (because of the earlier Ottoman occupation of Greece as well as Turkish atrocities since then), by intense pride in the accomplishments of ancient Greece, and by concern for the Greek ethnic communities (the Greek diaspora) in all of its surrounding countries.

In political party terms, the left is represented by the Panhellenic Socialist Party (PASOK) and the right by the New Democracy

(ND), but the party labels obscure a far deeper split in Greek society between what is often called the "family of change" and the "family of order." The family of change is progressive, forward-looking, even revolutionary: the heir to the eighteenth-century liberals and Enlightenment nationalists. The family of order tends to stand for stability, the status quo, and conservatism; it is the heir of eighteenth-century traditionalism. This split in Greece obviously predates the present political parties and goes back hundreds of years, at least to the eighteenth century, and represents a fundamental split in Greek political culture.

This basic split reflects not just attitudes and opinions but has a social base as well—as it did in earlier times. As society changes, of course, so do the values, and the relative balances between them, of the political culture. The "family of change" mainly has an urban base. It now consists of trade union members, intellectuals, university-educated young persons, and the progressive middle class, as well as some radical peasant elements. The "family of order" has a rural base, consisting of peasants, big and small landowners, and more religious persons, but it also has support in urban areas among businesspeople and the more conservative middle class.

Within these two major "families" are further subdivisions. The family of change includes communists, socialists, and liberal democrats. The family of order includes monarchists, religious elements, and neoliberal businessmen. Not only do the two "families" have fierce rivalries, but within the two families the feuds and backbiting may also be intense.

Even deeper than this partisan/ideological split in Greece is a more fundamental variety of divides because Greece is also split among rival families, clans, and "tribes." Some of these splits go back for generations and are often based on ancient social slights, clean versus dirty business deals, bad marriages, and bad family relations. The clans and families are often linked by elaborately complex connections, and lower class elements are often linked to these leading families by ties of patronage and clientelism. Indeed, beneath the political/ideological level in virtually all areas of modern Greek life—parties, government institutions, public policy, and who benefits from it—loom these elaborate patronage relations.

Meanwhile, a growing element in Greece does not want to be a part of either of the historic feuding "families," or of the traditional patronage networks. This growing middle class is increasingly affluent and European in its thinking, is tired of all the intensive feuding and the instability that often goes with it, and prefers a nice, stable, middle-of-the-road political system. We will have to wait and see if this group becomes dominant in the future, especially as Greece integrates more closely into Europe.

Italy Italy has similarly been a deeply divided society. Many of these splits persist to this day; however, Italy has by now become so prosperous that some of the earlier class, family, and regional/ideological divisions are becoming less pronounced.

Italy, like Greece, is the product of an ancient civilization, yet it was unified as a nation-state only in the 1860s. Because of these divisions and its lateness in becoming a nation, Italy was often denigrated by other nations, slights that Italians felt strongly. Even after unification, however, regionalism in Italy remained strong; and, as in the rest of Southern Europe, families, clans, and tribes served as the basis of social and political life. The conflict between the spiritual and the temporal also remained strong in Italy—perhaps even stronger than in the rest of Southern Europe because the Vatican was located there and its role and status added another divisive issue to an already deeply divided country.

Like Greece, Italy has its "family of change" and its "family of order." Once again, these splits are reflected in the political party systems; the family of change has been represented mainly by first the Socialist Party, and then the Italian Communist Party (PCI), and the family of order by the Christian Democrats.

These two "families" have long histories, and they represent distinct and virtually incompatible political cultures and ways of life. If one were born into a communist family, one grew up as a communist, went to communist bars and grocery stores, cheered for a communist soccer team, joined a communist union, most likely married into another communist family, worked in a communist-dominated job place, and departed this world through a communist funeral parlor. In contrast, if one were born into a Christian-Democratic family, one would go to Catholic schools, join Catholic youth groups, marry another Christian Democrat, join the Christian Democratic Party, go to Christian Democrat bars and grocery stores, exit life with the church's blessing, and so on. In other words, both of these "families" were closed, exclusive, and implied lifetime commitments; they involved wholly different ways of life that were all but incompatible. These deep divisions were reflected in Italian political culture and the national political system as well.

In Italy, these historic political-cultural differences were reinforced and made more complicated by the regional split between north and south. Nowhere else in Southern Europe is the regional divide so sharp as in Italy. The north is far more affluent, more oriented toward Europe and modernity, and less patient with these historic political differences. Moreover, the north has a far denser web of "associability"—all of those neighborhood, community, and other groups that occupy the space between the individual and the government—which is conducive to pluralism and democracy. In contrast, the south is not only still poorer but far more traditional in its attitudes as well, more inclined to support the old values (including the historic cultural divide described previously) with fewer community groups and trust in neighbors that they bring, and oriented more toward patronage and spoils (family connections and who you know) than the modern and more efficient north.

Meanwhile, Italy and its political culture along with it continues to change. For one thing, much of Italy has become so affluent, almost on a par with Northern Europe, that many of the old values—and the historic feuds that went with them—are declining. For another, Italy is far less religious and far less Catholic than it used to be, so the old religious divides and prohibitions (against abortion, divorce, and family planning) are fading. Third, the end of the Cold War means not only a change in the party system but also in the character and makeup of the two families (less rigid, less ideological, and no longer representing wholly different and incompatible ways of life) that undergird them. A fourth change involves Italy's entry into the European Union: Italy's economy is so strong that it became a charter member of the EU and, with that, met the requirement that it put aside some of its historic internal differences and conform more closely to EU standards.

Portugal Portuguese political culture has long been conservative, traditional, and devoutly Catholic. For a long time, Portugal was known as the most conservative and Catholic country in Europe. But at least since the eighteenth century, there was also a liberal, rationalist, progressive, and European-oriented current in Portuguese political culture derived from the Enlightenment. Long a minority view, in the nineteenth century this liberal current burned brighter in the form of growing republican sentiment, checks on royal authority, growing (but still limited) liberal reforms, and eventually the establishment of a republic in 1910. But the republic was unstable, chaotic, and was opposed by conservative forces who conspired to overthrow it in 1926.

When Salazar came to power in 1928, he sought to turn the clock back, to restore the traditional, Catholic, conservative society of the past. To do so, he used dictatorial methods—not the full-fledged fascism of Mussolini but nevertheless authoritarian—to suppress and snuff out the liberal, radical, and socialist elements. To tourists, Portugal looked like a quaint, whitewashed, throwback to medievalism, but beneath the surface the other, liberal Portugal continued to exist. In 1974, this "other Portugal" exploded in revolution.

Portugal went through a period of instability in the mid- to late 1970s. At one point it appeared that the more radical elements would seize power and do to conservative Portugal what the conservatives under Salazar had done to them: snuff them out. But over time the moderate and conservative elements recovered.

Today, Portugal is a functioning democracy. Public opinion surveys show overwhelming support—80 to 85 percent—for democracy. Moreover, sentiment in favor of extreme solutions, from either the right or the left, is declining. It is inconceivable that either of the options that still seemed possible only twenty-five years ago—fascism or communism—would garner wide support.

Nevertheless, there are still disturbing elements in Portuguese political culture. Some groups have not yet or fully reconciled themselves to democracy, and the traditions of elitism and top-down rule by a small cabal are still strong. In addition, when the Portuguese are asked, what is the best government you have had in the past thirty years, a stunningly large percentage still say "Salazar." That does not mean that Portuguese democracy is in danger, only that many Portuguese still favor the authority, discipline, and law-and-order of the old regime.

Spain Spanish political culture has become thoroughly democratic in the period since Franco died in 1975. Perhaps nowhere else was the desire to join Europe, not just in the economic sense but politically, culturally, and psychologically as well, so strong. Having been cut off ("Europe stops at the Pyrenees") and isolated from Europe for so long, Spain in the 1960s and beyond was eager to embrace Europe in its progressive, enlightened, democratic, culturally advanced form. To Spaniards, "Europe" was not just a geographic location but an abstract ideal as well.

Like Portugal, only more, Spain experienced a split in its cultural soul in the eighteenth century between its more conservative, traditional, and Catholic elements and its modern, progressive, European-oriented ones. In the nineteenth century, this split intensified, producing the series of civil wars known as the Carlist Wars, after one of the claimants to the throne. The culmination of these conflicts was the bloody, vicious, take-no-prisoners Spanish Civil War of 1936–1939.

Following his victory in the civil war, Generalissimo Francisco Franco, like Salazar in Portugal, sought to restore the traditional, Catholic, conservative Spain. School textbooks, the controlled media, and Franco's authoritarian regime all emphasized the traditional values of honor, obedience, order, discipline, and historic Catholicism. Meanwhile, the liberal or radical "other Spain" was forced underground or into exile, or was jailed or eliminated.

But in the 1960s and afterward, under the influence of a more literate and educated Spanish population, greater affluence and accelerated social change, and the cultural impact of foreign influences and millions of tourists, Spanish political culture began to change. It demanded greater freedom, openness, and democracy. The prior economic, societal, and cultural changes made the political transition easier.

Today Spain is a full-fledged democracy and its political culture reflects that transition. Democracy is supported overwhelmingly by 80 to 85 percent of the population; almost no one wants to revert to some other kind of system. Although Spain, like Portugal, still has strong elements of elitism, social hierarchy, and inequality, in the political sphere it is thoroughly democratic; along with Italy, it is the most democratic of the Southern European countries. There are degrees of democracy, pockets of anti-democratic sentiment, and significant regional differences, but unlike Portugal there is little nostalgia for the earlier authoritarian regime and very little sentiment in favor of a communist dictatorship. Spain has become thoroughly democratic and, as in the rest of Southern Europe, the great *systems* debates of the past—between tradition and modernity, authoritarianism and democracy, socialism and capitalism—are largely over. In all four countries, a modern and democratic, social and political system and a modern, mixed economy are now thoroughly established and a part of the political culture.

SOCIOECONOMIC BACKGROUND, CLASS STRUCTURE, AND INTEREST GROUPS

Greece, Italy, Portugal, and Spain have, in the past, been among the poorer countries in Europe. They have often been referred to as marginal, on the periphery, and underdeveloped. Economically, these four countries have lagged behind the more prosperous countries of Northern Europe. In addition, using sociological measures, they have tended to be more illiterate, less urban, with greater health problems, and lower life expectancy. Prior to World War I and even up to World War II, they were commonly referred to as feudal or semifeudal. Italy was a partial exception, ranking ahead of its Southern European neighbors on most measures, but still behind those countries in the northern core. Similarly, Greece and Spain ranked behind Italy but ahead of Portugal which, along with Albania, was always listed, depressingly, as the poorest country in Europe.

All of these social and economic traits, which characterized Southern Europe as less developed, also carried political implications. There was a two-class social structure, which in politics translated into a nondemocratic system of elites and masses. The elites dominated, whereas the poor, usually illiterate, mass of the population was excluded from political participation. The political system was patronal or patrimonialist, organized on a patron-client basis in which patronage was doled out by those in power in return for loyalty and service on the part of their *clientela;* in this kind of political environment, modern political parties, interest groups, government institutions, and effective public policies had little chance to grow. In the absence of a strong middle class, in addition, there was little political stability, frequent conflicts and civil strife, frequent military interventions in politics, and the absence of a strong civil society—groups and associations serving as stable intermediaries between the individual and the state. These conditions of strife, and instability, in turn, served to further prevent economic growth and societal modernization.

These conditions of poverty and traditionalism and the economic and political vicious circles that go with them are characteristic of what we would today call the developing nations or "Third World." Until the 1950s, Greece, Portugal, and Spain *did* have such low literacy, low per capita income, and low living standards that they were classified with the developing nations rather than the already developed ones. Italy had made a partial break with its poverty-ridden past somewhat earlier, but even in the 1950s it had, particularly in the south, such extensive poverty that it was still closer to the Third World of developing nations than to the First World of modern, industrial nations. One can understand a great deal about Southern European politics if one understands the low level of social and economic development of these countries even extending into the post–World War II period.

But now, much of this has changed, even while some of the earlier features remain. Italy has emerged as having one of the most dynamic economies in the world, sixth in gross national product, and with living standards and life expectancy approximating those of the Northern European countries. Spain and Portugal have also moved out of the ranks of developing countries into the category of modern industrial nations, with Spain having a per capita income about 80 percent of the Western European average and Portugal at about 70 percent—still not up to their Northern European neighbors' level but a marked improvement over their underdeveloped past. Because of past political volatility, Greece in 1995 was still listed with the moderate-income countries, although at the highest level in that category; but by 1997 Greece had also made it over the hump into the high-income level.

Since the 1950s, in other words, all or most of Southern Europe has broken the back of underdevelopment and poverty and made it into the ranks of developed modern nations. This transition is a stupendous achievement in a relatively short time; indeed, much of Southern Europe over the past four decades has experienced miracle economic and social growth rates second in the world only to those of Japan and East Asia. These are no longer poor, backward, underdeveloped countries but rather modern, dynamic ones. They still have *pockets* of poverty, illiteracy, and underdevelopment, as do other modern nations, and some are still poorer than others; but none of them any longer has the society-wide *culture* of poverty and backwardness that they had in the past.

Of course, just as poverty and semi-feudalism shaped their politics and traditional ways of doing things in the past, so now their rising wealth and modernity call forth a new form of politics in the present. This chapter explores how rising affluence, accelerated social change, and overall modernization in Southern Europe have fundamentally changed the region's political system as well. We begin with some further information on socioeconomic conditions, then discuss changing class and social structure, and finally show how these changes affect the interest group structure and changing political power relations in Greece, Italy, Portugal, and Spain.

Socioeconomic Background

Up through the mid-1950s, much of Southern Europe remained desperately poor. During the years of World War II, there had been mass privation, impoverishment, and even starvation in Southern Europe, and the depressed conditions continued for a decade or more after the war. But then prosperity kicked in, first in Italy, followed later by growing affluence in Spain, Greece, and Portugal. The rising wealth was fueled by the general peace and prosperity of the times, the European Common Market which tended to lift all boats, and increased trade and investment, including prominently from the United States. During this period, Southern Europe went from being part of the poor Third World to being among the affluent of the First World. In the process of these quite remarkable transformations, the social structure of Southern Europe also underwent profound changes, which in turn transformed the political system as well.

From being generally poor, rural, peripheral, and underdeveloped at the end of World War II, all of the countries of Southern Europe have in the past fifty years shot up in the rankings of the world's nations to a position now where *all* are judged by the World Bank to be "high-income countries"—the Bank's highest category. Italy was the first to make that rank, followed by Spain, then Portugal, and most recently Greece. The Southern European countries are now ranked with the world's richest nations.

With a gross national product (GNP, 1997 figures) of $1.155 trillion per year, Italy is the sixth-largest economy in the world. Spain has a GNP of $570 billion per year and is the tenth-largest economy in the world. Greece and Portugal are much smaller countries and,

TABLE 7.1	Basic Indicators of Southern European Social and Economic Life*								
				(1998)					
Country	GNP (in billions)	Rank	GNP/capita	Illiteracy	Child Malnutrition	Mortality rate per thousand	Life Expectancy Men	Women	% urban
Italy	$1,155.4	6	$20,120.00	0	0	7.0	75.0	81.0	67
Spain	$ 570.1	10	$14,510.00	0	0	6.0	73.0	81.0	77
Greece	$ 126.2	31	$12,010.00	0	0	9.0	75.0	87.0	60
Portugal	$ 103.9	33	$10,450.00	0	0	8.0	72.0	79.0	37

* *Source:* World Bank, *World Development Report,* 1998–99 (New York, Oxford University Press, 1999).

therefore, have considerably smaller GNPs. Greece's GNP is $126 billion per year and ranks thirty-first in the world. Portugal's GNP is $104 billion per year, which makes it thirty-third in the world.

On a per-person or per capita basis, however, all of the countries rank near the top or in the "high-income" bracket. Italy again tops the list with an average yearly income of $20,120 per person. Spain is second at $14,510; Greece is third at $12,010; and Portugal, fourth at $10,450. Thus, while all the Southern European countries are at high-income levels, Italy's per capital income remains twice that of Portugal and almost twice as high as Greece's. Spain is in between.

If we look at social or quality-of-life indicators, we again see high ratings for all four countries, but with considerable disparities among them. Once more, Italy leads the group in virtually all categories. Italy is listed as having virtually no illiteracy, no child malnutrition, an under-five mortality rate of seven per thousand, and life expectancy at birth of seventy-five for males and eighty-one for females—among the highest in the world. Italy is 67 percent urban. Spain is listed as having no illiteracy, no child malnutrition, an under-five mortality rate of six per thousand, and life expectancy of seventy-three for males and eighty-one for females. Spain is 77 percent urban. Greece also indicates no illiteracy, no child malnutrition, an under-five mortality rate of nine per thousand, and life expectancy of seventy-five for men and eighty-one for women. Greece is 60 percent urban. In Portugal, there is officially no adult illiteracy, no child malnutrition, an under-five mortality rate of eight per thousand, and life expectancy of seventy-two for males and seventy-nine for females. Portugal is the most rural of the four countries at 63 percent.

Two things are striking about these figures. First, how high the rankings are for all four Southern European countries. Second, how improved all the figures are over the situation fifty years ago. Some of the figures are probably exaggerated, but there is no doubt of the remarkable changes for the better. These figures are summarized in Table 7.1.

Classes and Social Structure

For a long time—far longer than in Northern Europe—Southern Europe had what might be called a feudal or semi-feudal social structure. That means it was basically two-class: elite and mass, lords and peasants, upper and lower. Of course, in all the countries some people always fell in between, who constituted what is often referred to as the "old" or "traditional" middle class. The traditional middle class consisted of soldiers, artisans, and craftsmen, small merchants and shopkeepers, and some government bureaucrats. But these groups were small in numbers and did not constitute a coherent, unified *middle class* as in the north of Europe. Rather, in the south they were weak and divided. So the fundamental two-class system persisted in Southern Europe through World War I and, more so in poorer Greece, Portugal, and Spain than in Italy, even through World War II and beyond.

The persistence of this fundamental two-class system into the mid-twentieth century also carried far-reaching political implications. It meant that the mass of the population, the great majority of people, was excluded from participation far longer than in other countries. It also meant that democracy was later in arriving in Southern Europe than in the countries of the north.

The power structure of the Southern European countries similarly reflected this underlying two-class social structure. These societies were not genuinely pluralist or democratic. Instead, they were dominated by a handful of elites, military officers, clerics, landowners, high government officials, and the nobility or those tied into the royal family. It was often said that politics during this period rested on a triumvirate of power: church, army, and nobility. Usually, the same upper-class families dominated all three of these institutions, and the government as well. Frequent rivalries and conflicts erupted between or among the elites, in which the peasants and lower classes were used as "cannon fodder" for the competing elite groups, but no real democracy existed. This system was intra-elite politics without the mass of the population participating except as pawns of the several factions.

In Northern Europe, the "proud tower" of this traditional two-class social structure crumbled in the decades preceding World War I, or in the war itself, or even earlier in some countries. But in Southern Europe—with Italy again the main exception—the traditional power structure and its non-democratic character persisted until at least the mid-twentieth century.

Society and the class structure in Southern Europe were not entirely unchanging, but the elites managed by various means to hang onto their power for a long time despite the changes. For example, in the last third of the nineteenth century, the Southern European countries began to develop a business-entrepreneurial class to go along with its landed classes, but the new business elites were usually absorbed into the older landed and noble class and did not develop as a separate, pluralist group. Concurrently and into the twentieth century, a new and modern middle class developed. Its demands for greater participation in the political process helped stimulate the founding of the Portuguese Republic in 1910, the Italian Republic in 1921, the Spanish Republic in 1931, and Greek liberalism in the early part of the century. But the middle classes of Southern Europe were also deeply divided politically and ideologically, could not consolidate their hold on power, and their divisions precipitated conflict and civil war, the overthrow of republican regimes, and the dictatorships of Mussolini, Salazar, Franco, and Metaxas and, later, the Greek colonels. These dictatorships, in turn, sought to turn back the clock, to hold back and control social change, and to prevent the natural social processes leading to pluralism and democracy from happening.

Similarly, with the trade union movement and peasant groups: By the 1920s and 1930s, all of the countries of Southern Europe had significant trade union movements that could no longer be ignored or dealt with simply by sending the police or army to beat them up. The strategy now became to co-opt the compliant unions, create official, corporativist unions that would help control and manage the labor movement, and suppress the radical and intransigent unions. By these means the elites were able over time to bend to change, absorb some new social groups, while retaining their own power intact. As Southern Europe developed, therefore, it did not necessarily become more pluralist and democratic; instead, the old structure of power continued, modified by change but not destroyed by it.

The process was by no means as peaceful and antiseptic as we have described it. Greece seemed to teeter precipitously on the verge of civil war almost constantly from the 1920s to the 1970s. Italy overthrew the monarchy in 1921 and then had one year of republican government before Mussolini's fascist dictatorship came to power with its strict state controls over both labor and capital—and virtually everyone and everything else. Portugal had a military coup in 1926, a series of labor/left revolts in the 1930s against Salazar's dictatorship and his tight controls on the working class, and finally a social explosion in the mid-1970s. Spain is perhaps the paradigm case of the conflict society produced by the effort to co-opt new interest groups, on the one hand, and their desire to remain independent, on the other: the dictatorship of Primo de Rivera in the 1920s, the fall of the monarchy in 1931, a particularly chaotic and violent republic from 1931 to 1936, a full-scale civil war from 1936 to 1939, followed by the long Franco dictatorship from 1939 to 1975.

The rules of the Southern European political "game" during this period, roughly from the 1910s to the 1970s (Italy changed its system of politics earlier than the others) were as follows:

1. A new and rising social group (business, labor, the middle class) had to demonstrate through numbers and political influence a certain level of power capability: the capacity to challenge or threaten the prevailing system. Until it reached that threshold, the group could be, and often was, suppressed.
2. Once a group reached that threshold of power and capability, it could be co-opted into the system, have its right ("juridical personality") to bargain in the political process recognized, and receive certain benefits (jobs, patronage, social programs) from the system.
3. By being co-opted in this way, however, a group was forced to give up its right to challenge the system, to pursue a revolutionary strategy, or to seek to destroy other, already established groups.
4. Those new or aspiring groups, mainly communists, socialists, and other radicals, who refused to make this political bargain, who refused co-optation and insisted on maintaining their independence, and who continued to follow a revolutionary strategy, received no recognition from the state, were denied legitimacy, and were frequently brutalized.

The co-optive political strategy thus invited new groups to join the system but usually under state or elite auspices. Those that refused the carrot of co-optation received the stick of repression. Meanwhile, the co-optive strategy itself had as its implication the persistence of an elitist, top-down, basically two-class system instead of genuine pluralism and democracy. The co-optive, statist strategy used to absorb and thus control these rising social groups was called "corporatism," which stood as an alternative to liberal-pluralism, on the one hand, and Marxism or Marxism-Leninism, on the other. Moreover, one can see why the stark, either-or choices posed by this strategy would often lead to bloodshed, civil strife, dictatorship, and/or civil war.

The corporatist co-optation strategy and the corporatist-authoritarian regimes (Franco in Spain, Metaxas in Greece, Mussolini in Italy, and Salazar in Portugal) that accompanied it in Southern Europe turned back the tide of liberalism, pluralism, and social democracy that had been gradually rising in the north or core of Europe. Remember that Southern Europe already lagged behind Northern Europe in terms of industrialization, economic growth, and social modernization. Now with the advent of corporatism, roughly from the 1920s to the 1970s, it came to lag even further behind socially and especially politically. One additional result is that Southern Europe during this period never developed the networks of civil society groups, the genuinely competitive and pluralist interest-group structure, that the other European countries had. So here is one more reason for Southern Europe's falling behind the rest of Europe and the absence of democracy in the region, in Italy until after World War II and in Greece, Portugal, and Spain until the mid-1970s.

Southern Europe's social and political development, in terms of the evolution of new groups, genuine social pluralism, and an infrastructure of competitive interest groups, is therefore not a continuous, evolutionary, progressive one. Instead it was (1) late in developing in the first place, and then (2) postponed and retarded by approximately fifty years of upheaval, civil strife, top-down or statist corporatism, and often bloody dictatorship. Hence, only in the past thirty years (fifty in the case of Italy) has a genuinely pluralist society and competitive interest-group system begun to develop. The very newness of the pluralism that exists and the weakness, still, of the interest groups help account for the fact that Southern European democracy is more precarious than we would like it to be.

Greece Greece does not have a well-organized or effective system of interest groups that combine individual demands into coherent pressure groups or that serve as a basis for pluralism in the country. Instead, the Greek system tends to be based more on patronage and patron-client relations, and the main instruments of patronage are the political parties, not the interest groups. In this system, joining a political party and establishing direct personal contacts with party officials, rather than working through interest groups, is considered the best way to get ahead.

Unlike other advanced industrial countries, Greece has only a handful of usually quite fragile interest groups. The few interest groups that do exist tend to confine their demands to economic issues, and in the intervals between the often intensive wage negotiations, the interest groups go into dormancy. This situation is a result of the long Ottoman (Turkish) occupation of Greece, of delayed development and industrialization, and of long rule by a Greek oligarchy that used patronage politics rather than interest groups. In the modern era, the role that pressure groups play in other countries was largely absorbed by Greece's political parties. The party system, not the interest groups, is the broker that aggregates interests, brings issues to the public, and serves as the transmission belt between the citizen and the state. In addition, it should be remembered that Greece, like Portugal, is a small country where everyone who counts knows everyone else who counts, and their family histories and backgrounds. In this context, large-scale interest groups may not be necessary; to get what you want, you call up your friend, cousin, or patron-godfather in the government party, or ministry, and, Voila!, it happens.

The General Confederation of Greek Workers (GSEE) is the largest labor organization in the country, but the trade unions are often hemmed in by government-imposed legal restrictions (a product of corporatism) on the one hand, and by their often compromising close relations with political parties on the other. Organized labor is divided among socialist, communist, and more conservative factions and depends on the state or its political party connections to get its agenda fulfilled. These divisions weaken labor, and its dependence on government or party favors weakens it still more.

Public distrust of trade unions in Greece is matched only by distrust of business. Private industry in Greece is represented by the Association of Greek Industrialists (SEV), but most private business firms, like their labor counterparts, rely on patronage and political contacts to get what they want from the government, not on interest-group lobbying. With the end of military rule in 1974, with Greece joining the common market in 1981, and with increased prosperity, business is held in higher repute than it was before.

Rather like Catholicism in Italy, Portugal, and Spain, Orthodox Christianity in Greece is bound up with the culture, society, and national identity. For this reason, separation of church and state is an alien concept in Greece, as it is in the other Southern European countries. For a long time, the Orthodox church isolated Greece from the Reformation, the Enlightenment, and modernity; today, the church is struggling to remain relevant in an increasingly secular society. The Orthodox church, however, continues to receive subsidies from the government and remains influential politically. Nevertheless, religion is less important than it once was, and recent governments have sought to achieve somewhat greater separation between church and state.

Another important influence—more than a "mere" interest group—is the military. The military is part of the backbone of the state, in the past almost a fourth branch of government. The armed forces play this powerful role, including seizing power from 1967–1974, because civilian institutions are so weak, the political parties are so divided, and the government is often so inept. When that happens, the military may feel obliged to step into power, but the armed forces are divided like the rest of Greek society, and each civilian political faction has its reflection within the military.

Other important influences include the students who, as Greece has settled down and become more prosperous, are declining in power; women, who are rising in influence; and government bureaucrats who are influential because they staff the large Greek state apparatus.

Greece is the least institutionalized of the Southern European countries. Patronage, clientelism, and personalism have long dominated, not competitive interest-group lobbying. Greece has a system of limited, often regulated pluralism, not the full-blown, unregulated pluralism of the United States or Great Britain. Although European (mainly) in wealth, culture, and formal political system, the limited number of interest groups and the strength of the church, army, and oligarchy suggest resemblances to some Latin American countries.

Italy Italians are often said to view government officials with suspicion or indifference; at the same time, they want the state to take responsibility for their welfare. The practice of politics varies throughout the country: in the more traditional south and the islands (Sardinia, Sicily), politics is still often dominated by patron-client relations; but in the north and more urban areas, while patronage still operates, more functional and class-based interest groups have grown up.

At the national level, such major private companies as Fiat (the auto maker) are so powerful that they communicate directly with the government and political parties without the need of joining other interest groups. Many of the country's state-owned corporations are also influential in lobbying the government in support of their interests. Some powerful individuals, families, and clans similarly have direct access to the government without interest-group intermediaries.

Among organized interests, the most powerful are the business groups: the Italian Confederation of Small and Medium Industry and the General Confederation of Italian Industry—Cofindustria. Cofindustria had especially strong ties to the long-ruling Christian Democratic Party; it also had largely taken over or established a clientelistic relationship with the Ministry of Industry.

The major labor groups in Italy were founded by the political parties and maintain close ties to the parties. Hence, there are communist, Christian-Democratic, and socialist, as well as other neutral unions. Because they are so deeply divided on political grounds, the Italian labor movement has long been weak; however, in the late 1960s and 1970s, organized labor became more militant and demanding.

German driver Michael Schumacher, FIAT managing director Paolo Cantarella, Brazilian driver Rubens Barrichello, Ferrari's president Luca di Montezemolo, Italian test driver Luca Badoer, FIAT honorary president Gianni Agnelli, and Ferrari's general manager Jean Todt attend the unveiling of the new "Ferrari F1 2000" F1 car, at the Ferrari headquarters in Maranello, northern Italy.

It threatened to close down industry and the state if its demands were not met, and it achieved some of its demands as Italy became more prosperous. Like organized business, organized labor has largely taken over and hived off for itself whole sections of government ministries, principally the labor and social welfare ministries.

The Roman Catholic church has been an integral part of Italian society and politics for hundreds of years. Many church-associated groups—for men, women, and youth—also operate like interest groups. But while nominally Catholic, few Italians regularly attend mass anymore or associate with the church. Hence the church as a political institution has lost power and stays out of day-to-day politics; nor could it prevent Italy from adopting liberal abortion, divorce, and family planning laws.

Agricultural interests in Italy have weakened as the country has become more urban and industrial. Professional associations have gained in strength as the country has become better educated. Other important interests include women and students, with each of the parties having a section designated for these groups. The interest groups often have a clientelistic relationship with the parties as well as with state agencies.

Italy has a complex interest-group system that often varies according to region. It is both pluralistic and based on elaborate networks of patron-client relations simultaneously. It has elements of both liberalism (free associability) and corporatism (co-opted, quasi-official groups) also tied into the political parties. It is, as with many aspects of Italian politics, confusing, often chaotic, and yet functional.

Portugal Portugal was an elite-dominated (church, aristocracy, army) society through the nineteenth century and beyond—some would say through the revolution and upheavals of the mid-1970s. But for much of the twentieth century, corresponding to the periods of military rule and the Salazar dictatorship, that elite dominance was maintained by suppressing the working class and keeping the emerging middle class apathetic.

Only since the mid-1970s has Portugal begun to emerge as a genuinely pluralist—and hence democratic—society. Although Portugal's population is still one of the most Catholic in Europe, the church as an institution has considerably less political power than it once had. The aristocracy has also declined in power, having lost much of its wealth and political influence in the 1970s upheavals. The third leg of this traditional triumvirate of power, the army, has returned to the barracks, been reduced in size and budget, and is generally subordinate to civilian authority.

Meanwhile, other, newer interest groups have risen in influence. The trade union movement threw off the shackles of authoritarian control in the 1974 revolution and has emerged as a major political force, but its power has often been diluted by internal rivalries between socialist and communist unions. The main labor organizations are the General Union of Workers (GT) associated with the Socialist party, and the General Confederation of Portuguese Workers—National Intersindical (CGTP-IN) closely tied to the communists. Peasant groups also rose up in the mid-1970s, but they have since become less activist. Student and street groups were also active as protesters in the 1970s.

As Portugal has settled down politically following the 1974 revolution, joined Europe, and become more prosperous, a new interest-group power balance has emerged in the country. The middle class and all of its myriad groups and associations—the state bureaucracy, doctors' associations, lawyers' associations, university groups, etc.—is emerging as the dominant class in the country. At the same time, the business class, which is seen as essential if the country is to remain prosperous, has emerged as the most influential group and is able to influence government policy on a variety of issues. Its argument, that without the jobs and prosperity that business creates, the entire national economy and, with it, the political system, will falter, is powerful; even recent socialist governments in Portugal have recognized the influence of such essential groups as the banks, commercial establishments, industrialists, and importer-exporters.

Portugal is more socially pluralist now than ever before in its history, which has provided a more solid base for democracy. But Portugal does not have the incredible interest-group hurly burly of American interest-group lobbying; its system is still one of more limited pluralism.

Spain Spain's interest-group trajectory and current situation often run parallel to Portugal's except that Spain is a far larger country, considerably more developed, and therefore with a more complex interest-group situation.

As in Portugal, Spain's nineteenth-century social configuration rested on a triumvirate of power: the Catholic church, the army, and the oligarchy or nobility. This system, in the context of a continuing monarchy reinforced over time by military repression and eventually dictatorship, lasted until 1931. All other groups—organized labor, peasants, and the emerging middle class—were repressed or had their rights limited.

When the monarchy fell and a republic was proclaimed (1931–1936), Spain experienced an explosion of political participation and pluralism. All of the previously suppressed groups organized and went out into the streets. Many of them were armed and used violence and assassination against their foes; the traditional groups also armed and, with their private militias, were at least equally violent. Many people saw this as pluralism run amuck; Spain's most famous philosopher, José Ortega y Gassett, wrote a book at this time calling Spain an "invertebrated" [polarized, fragmented, disintegrated] society. In 1936, Franco, the army, and the more traditional groups launched a civil war to restore order and discipline to a society they saw sinking into anarchic chaos.

Franco's rule (1939–1975) was much like Salazar's in Portugal but more violent, particularly in its early years. He suppressed the radical peasant and labor groups and all those who had fought against him in the civil war, while creating a structure of official, state-controlled, or corporatist groups to replace them. He depoliticized the population and, for a long time until the 1960s, kept the middle class apathetic. His base of power was the traditional triumvirate of army, church, and oligarchy. But as Spain became more prosperous in the 1960s and 1970s, the business, commercial, banking, and industrial sectors became more influential.

After Franco died in 1975, Spain, like Portugal, experienced another explosion of political participation and effusive pluralism. The previously suppressed labor and peasant groups reemerged from underground or from exile. But they were, once again, deeply divided between their communist and socialist factions. The Workers Commissions (CCOO) were closely associated with the Spanish Communist Party (PCE), whereas the General Union of Workers (UGT) was tied into the Socialist Party (PSOE). At the same time, a *host* of new middle-class, professional, community, and neighborhood groups also emerged. But this time the process and the interest-group struggle were not so anarchic and chaotic as in the 1930s because virtually everyone in Spain had that earlier, bloody experience in mind and did not want to repeat the events that led to national breakdown and civil war.

As in Portugal, only more so, Spanish business boomed during this period. With the new prosperity, the joining of Europe, and the absolute necessity politically of continuing a policy of job creation and wealth, the business groups—especially the umbrella Spanish Confederation of Employers Organization (CEOE)—emerged as the dominant groups in the country, more powerful than the church, the army, or organized labor. As elsewhere in Southern Europe and in Europe more generally, that meant that industrialists, bankers, investors, commercial elements, importer-exporters, and owners of large firms had more power than anyone. Spain had emerged as a pluralist society, but its pluralism was increasingly weighted in favor of big business.

Spain is such a large and complex country that we must also take into account regional variations. In this respect, Spain is more like Italy and less like Greece or Portugal. Greece and Portugal are essentially one-city countries with power and influence concentrated in their capitals, but Italy and Spain have multiple large cities in their distinct regions with often quite different social and interest-group systems. Spain has thus a *national* interest-group system centered in Madrid, but it also has differing regional and local interest-group structures in its major provinces and regional capitals: Catalonia (Barcelona), the Basque Country, Valencia, Seville, Galicia, and so on. To fully understand Spain, the interest-group power structure in each of these regional centers must be taken into account; equally important is how these regionally based interest groups are tied into the larger national interest-group system.

Spain, like Greece, Italy, and Portugal, has emerged since World War II and especially the mid-1970s as a much more pluralist and democratic country. The social pluralism that emerged earlier undergirds the pluralism that exists in the political realm and makes it quite unlikely that any of these countries would revert to authoritarian dictatorship. At the same time, the changing balance of power within this pluralism is also significant as the middle class and big business increasingly become the dominant groups.

POLITICAL PARTIES AND ELECTIONS

Most of Southern Europe has not had a very long or happy experience with political parties. The political party system of Italy dates only from the end of World War II and of Greece, Portugal, and Spain only from the mid-1970s.

Not only has Southern European party history been short, but it has also been generally unhappy. For one thing, political parties in Southern Europe have often been viewed in the same way that George Washington saw "factions": as divisive agencies that tear the country apart and are more interested in their own ends (power, spoils, patronage) than in the good of the nation as a whole. For another, the historic political parties in these countries have often been agents of the elites, concerned mainly with maintaining or enhancing the elites' own wealth and power, and devoid of ideology, real programs, or interest in popular participation. Then, under the Greek dictatorships, Mussolini, Salazar, and Franco, the old political parties were destroyed and replaced by one-party states that were agents of control, not democracy. The result of this long and sad political party history, as well as the current negative views toward political parties, is that throughout Southern Europe parties are among the least respected of political institutions, with their public approval ratings generally in the low 15 to 25 percent range.

The origins of political parties in Southern Europe date back to that same eighteenth-century split in the "soul" of these countries that we talked about earlier in the discussion of political culture. The split was between conservative, religious, and traditionalist elements, and more liberal, enlightened, and progressive elements. There were no political parties per se but only factions vying for influence within the *ancien regime*. The nucleus of later political parties was nevertheless formed.

Following the French Revolution and throughout the nineteenth century, these factions and the political parties that followed in Southern Europe became more polarized as well as somewhat better organized. Recall, however, that unlike the United States, the Southern European countries in the nineteenth century were still governed by monarchies; they were not republics or democracies. Nevertheless, the factions that had begun to emerge in the eighteenth century now began to develop into political parties operating within and under the monarchy. In Spain, this took the form of Carlists (after one faction of the royal family) versus liberals, in Portugal it was monarchists versus republicans, in Greece liberals versus conservatives and monarchists. Italy also had such factions, but it lagged behind in developing national political parties because the country was not unified as a nation until the 1860s.

The parties that existed during this period were almost exclusively elite parties. They had little in the way of programs, ideology, or mass following. Often, they consisted simply of rival groups of nobles jockeying for power and influence before the royal court. If the parties reached out into the country-at-large, they consisted simply of rival elite families trying to curry favor with the government or seeking to gain jobs, contracts, or special privileges from it. The coin of politics was patronage, still in an almost quasi-feudal relationships: loyalty and support in return for jobs and favors. Because these were still monarchies, there was no democracy or elections; if one elite faction needed to mobilize broader support in one of the innumerable civil wars and constant maneuverings of this period, it would round up its peasants, friends, relatives, and allied clans to do battle with another elite faction. This was not democracy or even political parties as we know them; nevertheless, the seeds were planted.

Toward the end of the nineteenth century and carrying over, depending on the country, into the first two or three decades of the twentieth, more ideological and mass-based political parties began to organize. These included socialist, communist, anarchist, and anarcho-syndicalist parties. Often employing violence or violent tactics against the ruling elites and monarchies, nevertheless these more radical parties remained small in numbers. More important were the democratic, republican, and liberal parties that urged the establishment of a republic and the abolition of the monarchy. That step came in Portugal in 1910, in Italy in 1921, and in Spain in 1931. Greece had been moving toward a system of limited constitutional monarchy since the mid-nineteenth century; it had a liberal regime early in the twentieth century; nevertheless, relations between the monarchy and the civilian government were frequently testy, and eventually the monarchy was abolished in 1974.

The establishment of republics early in the twentieth century did not stop the infighting, however; if anything, it intensified it. Now the radical parties came out from the underground and, fueled by the industrialization and urbanization of this period, expanded their mass base among the working class. The emerging middle class also organized for political action. And conservatives and monarchists, in the new republican circumstances, also formed political parties. There was great turmoil and conflict among all of these parties; many of them organized their own armed militias; violence spread; and the threat, if not the actuality, of civil war loomed.

Faced with the rise and organization of the lower classes, feeling threatened by the spectre of Marxism and bolshevism, and in the context of the economic and political breakdown of the 1920s and 1930s, the more traditional elements reacted. These included the church, the army, and the elite groups: the same groups that had formed the conservative coalitions of the nineteenth and even eighteenth centuries. They sought to turn the clock back, to restore the *status quo ante,* and to resurrect the monarchy and a more conservative political order. Other, shrewder political leaders (Metaxas in Greece, Mussolini in Italy, Salazar in Portugal, and Franco in Spain) sought to capitalize on this conservative backlash while accommodating at least somewhat to the rising social forces. Thus, they sought in their regimes to repress, illegalize, and snuff out the most radical and revolutionary movements, parties, and labor organizations, even while incorporating the more moderate groups but under state control and through state-run trade unions and other groups. At the same time, opportunistically, they also moved against the monarchists and other radical-right movements. In the meantime, they used dictatorship and repression against all groups as a way of cementing their own personal controls. Out of this combination of strategies was born the Southern European version of corporatism or fascism—less bloody, less warlike, more Catholic, less racial and ethnic persecution, less totalitarian than its Nazi counterpart: authoritarianism rather than totalitarianism.

Once in power, all of these corporatist or fascistic (Mussolini was the one who coined the term) regimes also had a major effect on the emerging party systems. Arguing that the factionalism and constant infighting among the parties were destroying the country, these leaders abolished *all* political parties: those of the right as well as those of the left. In these respects they were continuing in a long tradition of anti-party, anti-faction sentiment in Southern Europe. In their place, they created one-party states: official appendages of the dictatorships serving as patronage instruments to help maintain them in power.

Because there was no democracy and no contested elections under these fascist or corporatist-authoritarian regimes, the official parties took on other functions. They served as additional instruments of control, alongside the police, the censorship, and other agencies of dictatorship. They functioned to rally the regime's supporters and to exclude all others from participation. They also served as giant patronage agencies, doling out funds, jobs, government contracts, toys for children, sewing machines for widows, and so on, in return for political support from all of these recipients. In addition, anyone who wanted to get a government job, or virtually any other kind of job, had to be a member of the official party. So, the official party in these countries was really a giant political machine to serve the goals of the dictatorship and to keep the people under control. They were not instruments of democracy or popular participation.

As these regimes began to wind down in their last years, some of the groups and parties that had previously been suppressed began to resurface. For example, although communist, socialist, and other opposition groups had often been brutally suppressed by these regimes, they did not necessarily completely disappear but went into exile or underground. Now, sensing the end of the dictatorship, these groups began to reemerge and prepare the ground for their increased political activity once the authoritarian of fascist regime was gone. Other groups, who were prohibited from organizing as independent political parties, nevertheless organized "study groups" or "research centers"—ways to get around the prohibition on opposition political activities. These developments occurred when the regimes in power were old, tired, or in collapse and unable or unwilling to continue suppressing them. Thus, many of the political parties that would emerge in the new democratic era already had a nucleus of organization, even while the old dictatorships were uttering their last gasps. These parties would now emerge as the party systems that continue to play a strong democratic role today.

Greece

Greek political parties have traditionally been based on patronage, clientelism, and personal or family connections as distinct from programs or ideology. They have tended to be small parties, with little mass appeal, catering to narrow segments of the population, and with little national organization. In a highly personalistic and family-oriented society such as Greece, a personal patronage connection to someone in power was more important than either interest-group lobbying or political party campaigning. Now this traditional system has all begun to change, although even with the emergence of modern political parties, patronage mechanisms continue to operate.

The best organized party in Greece is the Panhellenic Socialist Movement (PASOK). It was founded in 1974 by the flamboyant, former Berkeley economics professor, Andreas Papandreou, and is the heir of earlier Greek left-wing parties. PASOK is a socialist party, often militantly so at least in its rhetoric, and has a strong electoral base in the trade unions, among students and intellectuals, and among urban elements. PASOK began as an attempt to create a modern socialist party devoid of personalism and clientelism, but under Papandreou it too succumbed to those traits. The party enjoyed a meteoric rise in popularity and won the 1981 election with an overwhelming electoral mandate, capitalizing also on the widespread desire for change then present. But in office, Papandreou ran a chaotic administration and, although moderated over time, his radical Marxism, strident anti-Americanism, and opposition to Greece's membership in the EC (it had joined in 1981, just before PASOK came to power) antagonized many people both inside Greece and internationally. Papandreou managed to win a second election in 1985 but by a smaller margin and then, as scandal plagued his administration, lost successive elections in 1989 and 1990; however, in 1993 a more moderate PASOK made an electoral comeback.

Papandreou was eventually replaced by younger leadership.

The other major party in modern Greece is New Democracy (ND). ND is more conservative, really center-right, and attracts votes from the middle class, businessmen, and rural elements. For a long time, ND was headed by Konstantinas Karamanlis, the old warhorse of the party and a skilled politician who had dominated Greek politics in the 1950s and early 1960s; that is, before the military government eliminated *all* political parties. After the military's ouster, ND won parliamentary majorities in 1974 and 1977, then lost the next two elections to PASOK, then came back to power in the early 1990s only to lose once more to PASOK in 1993.

Other parties in Greece include Political Spring (PA), a personalist party; *Synapismos,* a left-wing splinter group; and the Communist Party of Greece (KKE), which enjoyed considerable support in the 1940s as the backbone of the anti-Nazi resistance but has since declined in popularity and split into rival factions. During the 1990s, some thirty other parties existed on and off in Greece, most of them small and personalistic.

By the late 1990s, the two largest Greek parties, PASOK and New Democracy, had become more mass-based and issues-oriented, although the patronage aspects were still strongly present. Greece, along with the rest of Southern Europe, had moved toward a two-party system and toward the model of other West European political systems. These changes were aided by other, larger social forces that were fundamentally altering the Greek landscape as they had altered the other countries in the area: massive urbanization, higher levels of education, widespread industrialization, broad social change, greater affluence, and overall Europeanization.

Italy

Since World War II, Italy has had two major parties (Christian Democrats—DC, and the Italian Communist Party—PCI), several minor parties (Republican, Liberal, Radical, Proletarian, and Social Movement-National Right or fascist), and one party, the Italian Socialist Party (PSI), that is intermediary between major and minor. It is in essence a two-and-a-half-party system—like the United States with the Reform Party running.

The party system is fluid, unstable, and always changing. Patronage and having a connection are at least as important as programs or ideology. Neither the parties nor the party system is held in high esteem by the voters. At the same time, Italians often identify closely with their parties as with a family: one is born a "little communist or Christian Democrat," marries into the same "family," joins a communist or Christian-Democrat union, shops in communist or Christian Democrat stores, and dies in that same larger "family." Corruption, bribing, and payoffs are rampant within the system. The parties have an incestuous relationship with the state and with the interest group, serving as agencies of access to government jobs, contracts, and special favors. The parties are torn by rival factions, baronies, and regional differences.

For almost all of the post–World War II period, the Christian Democrats have been the party in power and the communists the party of opposition. That arrangement means the DC has had the main opportunity for access to graft, government jobs, and spoils. What often appears to be instability in Italian government and DC leadership is really the several barons and factions of the party taking their turn at power and at the "great public watering trough": government jobs and corruption. The DC is vaguely "Christian" in origins and orientation, but it lacks a clear program or ideology and was mainly oriented toward power and patronage. The only clear aspect of its program was to keep the communists out of power, which it did successfully for half a century.

The PCI seemed to be consigned to the role of a permanent opposition. After all, Italy is a Western country, a NATO member, and a charter member of the EC; it would not do during the Cold War to have communists in power in a major Western country. Although in opposition at the national level, the communists controlled many of Italy's regional governments, *all* of its important city governments (Rome, Milan, Turin, Naples, Venice, Bologna, and Florence), and numerous patronage agencies within the state apparatus. The PCI was founded as a Moscow-oriented communist party, but it later developed a more moderate, democratic, and pluralist orientation ("Euro-communism"), gained in electoral popularity, and sought to enter government by obliging the Christian Democrats to share power with it.

The Socialist Party or PSI was founded more than one hundred years ago but has been constantly torn by divisions and ideological schisms. The basic split was between those who favored a revolutionary path to socialism (and thus an alliance with the PCI) and those who favored an evolutionary or parliamentary path (and thus an alliance with the DC). The parliamentary faction became dominant, favoring NATO membership and close Italian ties with the U.S. This split and evolution would also occur in the Spanish Socialist Party (PSOE).

The minor parties in Italy remained just that, although their electoral influence ebbed and flowed. At times their power might be enhanced by an alliance with the DC to help give that party a majority in Italy's parliamentary system.

Recently, the Italian political party system—always highly factional, patronage-based, and disorganized—has turned topsy-turvy. Because of a series of corruption charges, the long-dominant Christian Democrats have imploded, self-destructed, and been voted out of power. With the collapse of the Soviet Union and the discrediting of Marxism-Leninism, the PCI also disintegrated and was reorganized as the Democratic Party of the Left. Meanwhile, a new right-of-center party, the *Forza Italia* (Italian Force), headed by media executive Silvio Berlusconi, was organized and, for a time, thanks to the discrediting of the major parties, enjoyed a meteoric rise in popularity with the flamboyant Berlusconi briefly becoming prime minister. But as Berlusconi was discredited and faced criminal prosecution, and with the Christian Democrats in complete disarray, a revived left-wing alliance headed by former communists won the following election and managed to patch together a coalition government.

But this coalition consists of no fewer than ten parties and two outside "partners." Plus, the former communist who headed the coalition, Massimo D'Alema, had to face the problem that the old PCI itself has split, with the right-wing communists (now called Left Democrats) supporting his government and the more militant old-line communists divided over whether to support him or not. If that sounds confusing, consider that today Italy's four biggest parties are the divided communists (former and actual), the former fascist party (National Alliance) now reviving over the issue of North African immigration, a one-man party (Berlusconi's) with no national organization, and a northern separatist party. It does not augur well for political parties or government stability in Italy. But then, it never has; or maybe that is not what's important in Italy. Read on.

Portugal

The present-day Portuguese political party system emerged only after the 1974 overthrow of the long-lasting Salazar-Caetano dictatorship. Some of these parties emerged from the clandestine underground; some came back from exile; others developed out of the "study groups" that were really disguised political parties emerging in the last few years of the old regime. Within a year, by 1975, a new but full-fledged party system was already in place.

The main Portuguese political parties, proceeding from left to right, are as follows:

Portuguese Communist Party (PCP) The PCP is an old-time communist party formed in the Stalinist mold. It was long headed by Moscow-oriented Alvaro Cunhal and is now run by younger leaders who are trying to guide it in more moderate directions. The PCP is strong among trade union groups, around Lisbon, and among peasants in Portugal's impoverished south. In 1975, the party made a bid to take power through a communist putsch but failed. Its electoral strength was declined from 18–19 percent in the mid-1970s to less than 10 percent today.

Portuguese Socialist Party (PSP) The PSP has emerged as the largest party on the moderate left. Long headed by exiled politician Mario Soares, who upon his return to Portugal became prime minister and later president, the PSP has moderated its view away from Marxism to a social-democratic position. The socialists won the first parliamentary election in 1975 and formed the first post-Salazar democratic government, then headed a coalition government in the late 1970s and early 1980s, and came back to power in 1995 under a new leader Antonio Guterres. The party's voting support fluctuates between 40–45 percent when it is victorious and 30–35 percent when it is down.

Social Democratic Party (PSD) The PSD began in the mid-1970s as a liberal-democratic party and has gravitated to become the country's main center-right party. Like the socialists (and as its mirror image), the PSD gets about 40–45 percent in good times and 30–35 percent in bad. It was in opposition to the socialists in the mid-1970s, in coalition in the late 1970s, and as the single governing party under Prime Minister Anibal Cavaco Silva from the mid-1980s to the mid-1990s.

Social Democratic Center (CDS)/Popular Party (PP) The CDS is a more conservative Christian-Democratic party. It is not a radical-right party, however, and is frequently looked on by the other main parties as a potential coalition partner. Because the Portuguese electorate has again become more conservative since the upheavals of the mid-1970s, the CDS was expected to be the chief beneficiary of the rightward trend; but in fact the PSD has profited most from this trend. With its electoral support declining, the CDS morphed into the neoliberal Popular Party (PP).

In addition, Portugal has other small leftist groups as well as a monarchist party that have some support but not enough to meet the requirement (5 percent of the vote) of a political party.

Although Portugal is a multiparty system, two of the parties have become larger and there may be tendency toward a stable, centrist, multiparty system. At the same time, the extreme elements on both the left and right have been isolated and have become smaller. With the PSP and PSD now having alternated in power through a series of regular democratic elections, Portugal may have achieved the democratic political system that was impeded for so long.

Spain

The Spanish political party system is parallel in many respects to the Portuguese party system, but with many particularities of its own. The historical background is similar; the lineup of the parties in the Spanish multiparty system is parallel; and, like Portugal, Spain has emerged as a stable democratic system.

Today's Spanish political party system dates to 1975 when the old dictator Francisco Franco died, although at least some of the parties dated back to the Spanish Republic of the 1930s or earlier. Some of these new parties (communists and socialists) emerged from the underground; some came back from exile; some emerged from informal study groups; and still others developed out of factions in the Franco regime. By 1977 when the first post-Franco elections were held, a new, full-fledged party system was already in place.

The chief Spanish political parties, once again going from left to right, are as follows:

Spanish Communist Party (PCE) The PCE is far less Stalinist than the Portuguese PCP. Instead, the PCE follows what has been called the Euro-communist route: more democratic and less Leninist. The Spanish PCE is particularly strong in the trade unions, and in the 1970s had considerable support from young people. But in recent elections the PCE has dropped to about 7–8 percent of the electorate and is limited to being a potential coalition partner rather than having any hope of achieving power by itself.

Spanish Socialist Workers Party (PSOE) The PSOE is the Spanish socialist party. Like the PCE, it has a long history going back to the 1930s and earlier, of underground activities during the Franco era, and of democratic advocacy since Franco died. The PSOE is strong in the trade unions, in the cities, and among young people. Under the leadership of Felipe González, it has gradually shed its earlier Marxist language, and on the basis of being a moderate, center-left party, won the elections of 1982, 1986, 1989, and 1993. It can garner more than 40 percent of the vote. But over time the party in power proved corrupt, lost popular support, and was voted out of office in 1996.

Popular Party (PP) The PP arose out of the remnants of the old Franco regime, but it has evolved as a modern, democratic, center-right party. Its membership and voters consist of bureaucratic elements, Christian-democrats, some former monarchists, business elements, and a large part of the middle class. Under José Maria Aznar, the party modernized itself, and on that basis narrowly defeated the PSOE in the 1996 election with 38 percent of the vote. In office, the PP pursued a moderate, partially neoliberal, and above all pragmatic program; its accomplishments recognized, the PP won again in 2000 with 44 percent of the vote and a majority in the parliament.

Like Portugal, Spain also has small extreme-left parties as well as a small pro-monarchy party—too small to qualify for a ballot position. But unlike Portugal, Spain has several regional parties that reflect the ongoing importance of regional and autonomy issues in the country. The most important of these are in Catalonia and the Basque country. The regional parties are especially important in their home districts but, at the national level, with neither the PSOE nor the PP able to command a majority, they are often crucial partners in coalition governments, able to command just enough votes to give either of the larger parties a majority and garnering rewards (cabinet slots, a greater say on autonomy issues) for themselves.

Spain thus has a multiparty system that, like Portugal's, functions almost like a two-party system. Moreover, the party system is increasingly stable and institutionalized. In both countries in a relatively short period since the 1970s, the parties and the party systems have become important bases for democracy.

Italy threw off fascism (its defeat by the Allies in World War II immeasurably aided the process) in 1945 and established democracy shortly thereafter; democracy in Greece, Portugal, and Spain dates only from the mid-1970s. Democracy in all four countries is thus relatively new, yet it also seems firmly established. No other system of government seems possible or feasible. In this triumph of democracy across the board in Southern Europe for the first time, political parties and a stable party system have played a big role.

Yet the triumph of democracy and the important role of political parties in this achievement is not without its problems. The parties remain among the least respected institutions in all four countries. They are often corrupt, inefficient, and patronage-based. The parties are often dominated by their "barons" or chieftains rather than ruling of, by, and for all citizens. In addition, the real locus of power in these countries may no longer be in the party-election arena but in the nexus between the state bureaucracy, big business, and the European Union. We turn to that theme in the next section.

DECISION MAKING AND THE ROLE OF THE STATE

This section deals with government institutions, decision making, bureaucracy, and the role of the state. By the "state," we mean the vast web of government agencies, ministries, institutions, bureaucracy, kings (in old times, and in Spain still today), parliaments, prime ministers, and so forth, that is accorded a legitimate right to rule and that makes decisions affecting the polity. In Southern Europe, it is not just that the role and function of, let us say, the parliament is different in various particulars from the U.S. Congress; instead, the entire state system and the structure of state-society relations (the relations between government institutions and the various interest and functional groups that make up society) are different as well.

In Southern Europe, the state has long been strong in aspiration but often weak in its reach and ability to implement policy. For example, Southern Europe was *the* center of the notion of absolute monarchy, but that did not mean the kings who sought absolute power were always able to implement their policies effectively or to enforce their decrees in remote villages. "I obey but do not implement" was often the response of local officials to stupid or poorly informed decrees emanating from royal authority. That way, local officials could be in *formal compliance* with the authorities even while shielding their people at the grass roots from misbegotten policies.

Similarly with modern dictators: no one doubts that authoritarian leaders such as Franco, Salazar, Mussolini, and the Greek colonels were tough guys who ran strong-arm regimes. But one reason these dictatorships were so tough was because the regular government was so weak and unable to enforce its policies and will on society as a whole. Authoritarianism was often seen as a way to compensate for these other weaknesses, to utilize the instruments of dictatorship to make up, especially following particularly weak regimes or in times of crisis, for the ineffectiveness of the regular government institutions.

At the same time, Southern Europe has never had the same kind of strong societal or interest-group structure as has the United States, Great Britain, Germany, or other advanced industrial democracies. It lacks the "webs of associability" at the grassroots level (local Boy Scouts, Girl Scouts, PTAs, churches, community groups, etc.) that the perceptive French writer Alexis de Tocqueville found endemic in American society, and it has never (until recently) had the elaborate system of interest-group pluralism of other advanced democracies. So again to make up for the absence of a strong societal infrastructure, Southern Europe has frequently had to resort to inventing strong, authoritative states as a form of compensation. But even though "strong," the legitimacy and "reach" of these states have often been weak.

Southern Europe is, therefore, not just different from other modern democracies in the particularities of some of its institutions (presidentialism versus parliamentarism, for example), but also in the entire historical and philosophical bases of the state systems and their relations with the broader society.

Origins

The origins of the Southern European state systems and of state-society relations lie in the feudal past. The Southern European political systems, and those of Europe more generally, are thus fundamentally different from that of the United States, which had no feudal or medieval past. Recall that under feudalism and during much of the Middle Ages, society was decentralized and chaotic, the state system was weak, and national political systems were virtually nonexistent in most areas of Europe.

This situation began to change by the eleventh and twelfth centuries. More unified monarchies began to come into existence in Greece, Portugal, northern Spain, and the various regions of Italy. These monarchies gradually increased the territory under their control and their power within that territory.

As they did so, they often came into conflict with entrenched societal groups who sought similarly to enhance or protect their own rights and privileges. These groups included various religious orders and monasteries, several military orders (Hospitalers, Templars, Malta, etc.) left over from the crusades, towns and municipalities that had achieved some level of self-government, and economic groups organized in guilds of sheep herders, goldsmiths, coppersmiths, bankers, and the like. These groups sought to retain their powers, privileges, and right to govern their own affairs against the encroaching power of the central state.

These struggles waxed and waned and went on for hundreds of years, from the twelfth through the fifteenth centuries. Although the outcome was not always clear cut, in most areas the absolutist state and its absolutist monarchs won out. They curtailed the power of the local or corporate societal groups and in some cases snuffed them out altogether. Absolutism emerged triumphant from the sixteenth through the eighteenth century, and even beyond in some cases. But the triumph of absolutism also meant the end of societal pluralism and of the dynamic tension between a central authority seeking to enhance its power and societal groups seeking to maintain autonomy and self-government. When these two forces are in balance, in contrast, Southern Europe has traditionally thought of itself as being governed democratically.

The triumph of royal absolutism also meant that Southern Europe never developed until very recently the institutions of an independent legislature, an independent judiciary, or local government characteristic of democracies. Rather, power remained centralized and absolutist. Not only was societal pluralism snuffed out, but governmental pluralism was not allowed to develop either.

As it developed over the centuries, the Southern European state is very different from the U.S. conception of government. For one thing, the state is often viewed as "natural" and "good"; but if it is good and natural, there is little reason to check and balance it, limit it, and have separation of powers as in the U.S. system. Another difference is that citizens tend to look to the state, rather than historically to their own initiative, for protection, benefits, and social welfare. Even though often ineffective, the Southern European state is nevertheless viewed as a kind of "nanny state," taking care of people and responsible for the general well-being of its citizens.

By the nineteenth century, there were increased pressures for more liberal, republican, even democratic government. But in the face of these pressures, the established monarchies dug in their heels and refused to budge. They were backed by the traditional elite groups—army, church, and oligarchy—against the rising social forces of the middle and working classes. Unlike the situation in Northern Europe where the elites gradually accommodated to change, in Southern Europe they sought to block it altogether. To the earlier conflict over absolutism was thus added new elements: class struggle and social conflict. The result was not pluralism and democracy but polarization, conflict, and civil strife if not outright civil war.

The dictatorial regimes of Franco, Salazar, Mussolini, and Metaxas represented a continuation of this centuries-long struggle in new form. In the face of rising social and political change and the demands of new groups (labor, peasants, the middle class) for access to power and its benefits, these regimes clamped down and snuffed out the rising social forces or, under corporatism, subordinated them to state control. Absolutism was once again in the saddle but without some of the leavening effects of the monarchy; whatever vestiges remained of pluralism, local government, an independent parliament or court system, or societal group independence from the central state was eliminated.

Only since World War II in the case of Italy and the mid-1970s in Greece, Portugal, and Spain have democracy and societal and political pluralism returned. But that means (1) that democracy and pluralism are still new and not necessarily fully consolidated, and (2) that because of the delays, the political systems of Southern Europe still exhibit some unique features that mark them as different from other countries.

State-Society Relations

State-society relations in Southern Europe are still quite different from that of the United States or other Western democracies. For one thing, the number of groups in the system remains small. It is no longer limited to the nineteenth-century power triumvirate of church, army, and oligarchy, but it now includes trade unions, farmer groups, middle-class professional associations, business and banking interests, bureaucratic interests, and local and regional forces. But that still adds up to only ten or twelve major interest groups, compared to the fifty thousand registered national interest groups in the United States. Southern Europe is clearly more pluralist and democratic than before, but it still practices a form of limited pluralism, not the incredible hurly-burly of the American interest-group struggle.

Second, in a system of limited numbers of interest groups and of limited pluralism, there tend to be fewer moderating, crosscutting loyalties. It is often argued that in the United States, because we have so many interest groups and because each of us tends to belong to several of them at once—religious bodies, labor unions, tenants' associations, student groups, professional associations, parents' groups, political parties, school groups, and the like—our loyalty to any one single group or point of view is therefore moderated, tempered, and compromised, and tends to limit intense partisan or ideological commitment to any one single point of view, which is also good for centrist democracy. But this has not been true in the past in Southern Europe. There, people have tended to belong to and go all out for only one single group. Instead of the moderation of crosscutting loyalties, Southern Europe has featured absolute commitment to a single cause. Moreover, people tend to be stock-typed or stereotyped as *the* military officer, *the* bourgeoisie, *the* worker, *the* landowner, and so on, which reinforces extremist positions and causes people frequently to actually behave as the stereotypes call on them to do. Limited numbers of interest groups and the absence of crosscutting loyalties tend to reinforce the divisions and polarization that have long existed in Southern European society.

Third, given the long-standing weakness of civil society in Southern Europe, the state still leads. The state, and not so much private entrepreneurial groups, usually guides, directs, and manages the economy. The state doles out funds, projects, and programs so that investment and economic growth can take place. The state largely decides on priorities among pressing social as well as economic issues and directs the national budget in those directions. At the same time, people in Southern Europe tend to look to the state for guidance, direction, and benefits. The state in Southern Europe is looked on positively as the main source of goods, programs, jobs, patronage, and largesse. Hence, the state does not carry the negative connotations—"big government," "inside the Beltway," "bloated," "irrelevant," "inept"—that it often carries in the United States.

One reason the state had been strong in Southern Europe is that, historically, private groups have been weak. As indicated, Southern Europe has not long had the plethora of interest groups that the United States has. Nor does it have the vast web of neighborhood and community groups—PTAs, Boy Scouts, Girl Scouts, Rotary Clubs, lodges, bowling leagues, and so on—that the U.S. has and that is often pictured as the essential ingredient in American pluralist democracy. Nor in Southern Europe, until recently, has there been a dynamic, innovative, risk-taking, job-creating, private business sector capable by itself of launching new enterprises, putting people to work, and generating jobs as well as capital for investment. In the absence of this societal and entrepreneurial infrastructure, the state or government has often been required to step into the vacuum and provide the leadership, guidance, and investment that the private sector lacks.

A fourth feature of Southern European state-society relations is persistent corporatism or state-sponsored if not state-created, interest groups. If private interest groups are few and weak, then the state must create them. The issue is similar to that regarding capital and entrepreneurship: if the private sector is weak, then the state must step into the breach. This becomes particularly true in the age of industrialization when the state must harness all of its energies for a coordinated national development strategy. First, in the absence of much private investment capital, the state must provide the economic stimulus for growth; second, because interest groups are inchoate, unstable, and often disruptive, the state must coordinate, guide, and direct them as well. But as soon as you talk about business, labor, farmers, and other groups being "coordinated" or "guided" under government auspices, you are talking about corporatism, not liberal-pluralism. For that is precisely the definition of corporatism: state guidance, control, and co-optation of interest groups. It is important to remember, therefore, that corporatism in Southern Europe did not just disappear with the end of the Mussolini, Franco, Salazar, and Greek dictatorships. Instead, whenever interest groups are weak and the state has to guide them, assist them, and bring them into governmental decision making, both to get their viewpoint and in the process to pacify them, we are talking about corporatism. Corporatism has recently taken on new forms—more open, more pluralist, and more democratic—but it did not end with the fall of fascism.

Now, however, many of these features of Southern European state-society relations are changing. Interest groups are stronger and often more independent of the state, although many interest groups continue to receive subsidies from the state. The climate is now freer and more democratic in which these interest groups operate. And new, better organized, and more diverse interest groups continue to be formed. Southern Europe is gradually developing the civil society and the vast web of associational life that strengthens the grass roots that have long been lacking in the area. New forms of public-private partnerships have also emerged.

The introduction of a common European currency and of a single *European* monetary and central banking system, as distinct from local or national central banks, will also change the system. From now on, it will be harder for governments to subsidize their own interest groups through deficit financing because the European central bank may not permit that. For the same reason, it will be harder to give favors, vast government jobs, sinecures, and special treatment to favored interest groups. It will be harder to co-opt or buy off dissenting political groups. Although the precise implications of the movement toward a single currency governed by a single European central bank are still unknown, it is clear that these changes imply not just economic transformations but will have important political results as well.

Bureaucratic Politics

Most of the Southern European countries have comparatively large state sectors. The state may generate more than 30, 40, or 50 percent or more of the national economy. The state may own, subsidize, or have large shares in major industries, utilities, banks, construction, insurance, airlines, tourism, petrochemicals, and other major industries. Again, the state plays such a large and leading role in the economy because the private sector has tended to be weak and small.

The large state sector means the state has also been the largest employer, particularly of educated persons, in the country. Depending on the country, between one-third and one-half of the labor force may work for the state, either directly in the public bureaucracy or indirectly in one of the state's economic enterprises. Hence, in Southern Europe, the state sector, rather than the private sector, often offers the best opportunity for employment, for security in one's job, and for a comfortable pension as well as good health, educational, and other benefits.

Southern Europe has elaborate civil service laws and rules, but in the past these have not been consistently followed. In getting and keeping a government job and being promoted in the system, patronage, family connections, and political spoils count as least as much as merit and achievement. Individual persons tend to see their avenue for upward mobility through the state job system; at the same time, governments and political parties tend to reward their friends, supporters, cronies, and even foes by putting them all on the public payroll.

Americans are often used to hearing of individual government jobs being awarded on the basis of political connections, but in Southern Europe entire government programs and whole ministries or agencies are often turned over to well-connected interest groups or political parties for them to dole out patronage-style to their supporters. In Italy, for example, entire offices within the labor or social welfare ministries would be turned over to the Christian Democratic party for it to fill with its party loyalists; down the hall, and as a way of buying their loyalty, other offices would be turned over to the other main party, the Communists and their sympathizers. Such practices served important political and patronage functions; whether they served the interests of sound public policy may be another matter.

The state bureaucracy is also the agency through which most interest groups operate. Rather than dealing directly with each other, as for example in American-style collective bargaining between labor and employers, most interest groups in Southern Europe try to influence the state bureaucracy because it often determines wages, working conditions, rules, and benefits for the different categories of workers. As an interest group, you always concentrate your energies where power and decision making lie, and in Southern Europe that has long been the state rather than private employers. So you may demonstrate, stage strikes, march on the seat of government, or even try to close down the national economy, *all* in an effort to get the state to raise wages or decree improved benefits and working conditions. Or you may want to oust the labor or social welfare minister to bring in a new minister who is more amenable to your group's interests; alternatively, you may want the state to put pressure on private employers to grant your demands.

Note that this is really a system of *political bargaining,* through the state system, rather than direct collective bargaining between the affected parties as in the American system. The Southern European labor relations system is thus more bureaucratic, more indirect, and more politicized than is the American system. And it fits better a group of nations where the state sector is strong, the private sector historically weak, and where what we know as up-front, interest-group lobbying is still largely unknown. Southern Europe still largely prefers to handle these matters behind the scenes and bureaucratically, without direct confrontations.

But this system is changing in Southern Europe as well. First, the private sector, especially business, is growing and becoming more independent of the state. Second and related, direct collective bargaining between the affected interests, instead of their conflicts always being channeled through the state, is becoming more prevalent. Third, pressures for government streamlining and greater efficiency are making it harder for the state to be the employer of first resort and a large reservoir of patronage positions. Fourth, the civil bureaucracy is becoming more efficient, professional, less patronage-dominated, and more based on merit than personal, family, or political party connections. Finally, once again the coming of the euro and of European-wide monetary policy will make it harder to stuff the bureaucracy with sinecures or pay for vast new employment programs masquerading as public policies through deficit financing or the printing of more money.

Government Institutions

All four of the Southern European political systems are parliamentary systems. Power rests mainly in the parliament and in the government (cabinet and prime minister) that is selected from among its members. In this respect, the Southern European countries, and Western and Central Europe more generally, are fundamentally different from the presidential system and separation of powers of the United States.

In parliamentary systems, the executive and legislative branches are fused. Leaders of the government *must* come from the parliament and simultaneously be elected to represent their districts just like other members of parliament (MPs). Party leaders are chosen by their respective party conventions, and sometimes now in party primaries, to head the ticket and represent the party. If that party gains a majority in the election, then its leaders form a government. And, of course, the government will be able, unless there are extraordinary circumstances, to get its program passed by the parliament because, by definition, it has a majority there. If it had no majority, then it would not be able to form a government in the first place. The opposition, meanwhile, criticizes the government and chips away at its majority, hoping that *it* will win the next election and thus be able to form a government of its own. If there is anything comparable in the American system, it would be like, in the absence of a president and vice president, the speaker of the House of Representatives becoming prime minister and other House leaders of the same party becoming cabinet ministers.

This arrangement presumes a two-party system where one of the parties is guaranteed a majority, or a multiparty system where one of the parties is so strong that it gets more than 50 percent. But what if, as is the case in Southern Europe presently, there is a multiparty system and no one party gets a majority? Then the leading party, ordinarily, has to bargain with other, smaller parties to get enough parliamentary seats to form a majority, and thus to form a government. The cost of luring a small party into such a coalition arrangement is usually one or more cabinet seats going to that party, and other favors as well. The term of office in such parliamentary systems is usually five years, but if the balance of political power is close, a few MPs switch sides, and the government loses on a critical vote (a "vote of confidence"), then new elections must be called immediately and the process of organizing a government or of coalition formation begins all over again.

Now, suppose the two leading parties tie in the popular vote or are so close together electorally that little difference exists between them. Or suppose the leading party is unable to complete the coalition arrangements to lure in a second party to form a working coalition. Then trouble often arises in parliamentary systems. New elections may need to be called to resolve the impasse. Or perhaps the king (in Spain) or president (in Greece, Italy, or Portugal—usually a figurehead or ceremonial position but important in these circumstances) may step in to break the logjam. In those situations there may be the possibility of conflict, fragmentation, and breakdown—a remote possibility but not entirely inconceivable.

Greece For almost 150 years the question of whether Greece would be a monarchy or a republic—or perhaps some combination of these, a constitutional monarchy—often tore the country apart. The 1975 constitution adopted one year after the military dictatorship was overthrown finally resolved the issue in favor of a parliamentary republic.

Greece has both a president who is the head of state and a prime minister who is the head of government. The president's functions are largely ceremonial, although he may play a larger role if the government or party system are stalemated as described previously. The prime minister is the effective, day-to-day administrator of the country. For nearly half a century, interrupted by the military regime from 1967 to 1974, the prime ministership alternated between New Democracy leader Konstantinos Karamanlis and the two Papandreous: father Georgios and then son Andreas.

Greece is a parliamentary system, which by its very nature guarantees cooperation between the executive and legislative branches, because unless he has a majority in the Assembly or parliament, a prime minister cannot form a government. The prime minister is always the leader of the majority party in the Assembly.

Everyday governance in Greece is nevertheless conducted by three branches of government according to the principle of separation of powers but arranged according to the parliamentary system. That means an independent—at least in law and constitution—judiciary and an executive branch serving with the support and approval of the Assembly.

The executive branch of government consists of the cabinet led by the prime minister who is simultaneously the head of the majority party. The prime minister in Greece chooses cabinet secretaries both from the Assembly and from the outside. The cabinet must maintain the confidence of the Assembly; if it loses a vote of confidence, then new elections must immediately be held.

The Assembly in Greece is a unicameral body of three hundred deputies elected through direct, universal, and secret ballot. The term of office, unless the government loses a vote of confidence and new elections have to be held, is four years.

The judiciary in Greece is supposed to be independent, but it is often subject to strong political pressures. During the 1967–1974 dictatorship, civil and human rights were frequently violated. The legal system is a code law system derived from Roman law, modified by French and German influences, and infused with principles from classical Greece.

Greece has long been a centralized state, with most power concentrated in Athens; what there was of local government was usually dominated by regional or local oligarchies or elite families. But beginning in the 1980s, an effort was undertaken by a PASOK government to decentralize power. Elections were held at the local level; limited autonomy was also granted to Greece's nine regions and fifty-two provinces. These local government organizations provide larger opportunities for patronage and do have some useful functions, but in almost all policy areas, the central government in Athens still makes decisions.

The Greek civil service or bureaucracy is a mixture of high professionalism on the one hand and glaring inefficiency and partisan favoritism on the other. Once again, patronage is important: having a friend or relative or party colleague in the right office who can get you a job or cut through all the red tape and get your license, permit, or piece of paper processed expeditiously. Without such connections, the government business you need done may never get done.

This picture of the functioning of Greek government institutions is not very pretty. There are fine laws, constitutions, and formal institutions on the one hand; and then there is the real world of patronage, corruption, and insider connections on the other. If you are wealthy and well-connected, the system can work for you; if not, it can be endlessly frustrating.

Italy The Italian Republic came into existence in 1946, right after World War II. It is governed by a constitution written in 1946 and adopted in 1947 that proclaims Italy to be a unitary state with a parliamentary form of government. The republic has thus been functioning for just over half a century; whether it has gained full legitimacy, is an effective system of government, or has overcome Italy's past problems are still open questions.

According to the constitution, "the President of the Republic is the Head of State and represents the unity of the Nation." The president in Italy is largely a ceremonial figure but, like the president in Greece or Portugal or the king in Spain, he has some residual powers, especially in times of crisis or when the government is paralyzed. The Italian president is intermediary in power between the strong French president and the weak English crown.

Real power in Italy, as in other parliamentary systems, rests with the prime minister (PM). The PM is responsible for the overall direction and general policy of the government and for the promotion and coordination of the activities of the cabinet. Theoretically, the prime minister's office, almost always occupied by Christian Democrats during the first half century of the republic, is *the* focal point of the Italian political system; but the prime ministership has been so unstable during the life of the republic that effective leadership and long-range policy planning and implementation have often been lacking. Italy's prime ministers average about one year in office and then are forced to leave. It is usually not the parliament but the political parties, which give and then withdraw support for a government, that cause the rapid turnover.

While prime ministers come and go, cabinet ministers often stay on from one government to the next, giving the system some degree of stability. The bicameral parliament, consisting of a Senate and a Chamber of deputies, also provides a greater measure of stability to the system. But perhaps the main element of stability in the Italian system is the bureaucracy or civil service, whose members are unionized and enjoy long-term job stability.

High-level government jobs, however, are often determined on the basis of politics, patronage, and party affiliation. The system is shot through with corruption and spoils. At lower levels in the bureaucracy, low pay is often offset by government workers taking second (or third or fourth) jobs or accepting money in return for favoritism. Recall also that in many government offices the parties have "cannibalized" the positions and programs, using them for their own private advantage.

At the subnational level, Italy has three layers of government: the commune (a city, town, or village), the province, and the region. Although Italy is a centralized and unitary state, with almost all power concentrated in Rome, some individual taxing and policymaking authority has recently been devolved upon these lower-level units, especially the regions. Indeed, Italy's twenty regions have by now largely eclipsed the formal powers that once belonged to the provinces and the communes. As in so many things Italian, enormous differences exist between the northern (prosperous, more democratic, and participatory) regional governments and the southern (poorer, about the level of Greece, and more patronage-based) ones. Moreover, there is strong sentiment in the dynamic northern regions to break away from the slower-paced south, rather like Quebec in Canada.

Numerous studies have documented the scandals, inefficiency, corruption, vested interests, and patronage basis of Italian politics. In turn, survey data show that Italian citizens are apathetic, distrustful, and cynical toward government and government institutions, including political parties, elections, prime ministers, parliament, private business, and labor unions. These attitudes are often based on the negative experiences that Italians have had with public institutions. The result is a government system that is often ineffectual in dealing with serious public policy problems.

And yet, two things need to be said in closing this section. First, even though the formal government doesn't always work very well, Italians are extremely clever and innovative in devising informal channels (*sottogoverno*) to work around, over, or under the formal restrictions and frustrating bureaucratize. Second, even though politics in Italy are often chaotic, the Italian economy and private initiative are imaginative, dynamic, innovative, and booming. And, of course, with money, all kinds of things can be accomplished with or without the government.

Portugal Portugal has a parliamentary system and a president. The government is headed by a prime minister, the leader of the majority or top-ranking party, and, of course (as in all parliamentary systems), a member of the parliament. The presidency is usually a ceremonial, ribbon-cutting, and baby-kissing office, but if no party has a majority and cannot reach an agreement on a coalition, or if the government is paralyzed, then the president has the power to twist arms, dismiss the government, or call for new elections. In addition, the presidency in Portugal had been filled since the establishment of democracy in 1975 by unusually strong and capable individuals—Ramalho Eanes, Mario Soares, and Jorge Sampaio.

The winner of the democratic elections in 1975 was that same Mario Soares, who was then head of the Socialist Party. Soares and the Socialists dominated the first democratic governments in Portugal and were instrumental in consolidating the fledgling democracy. In the late 1970s and early 1980s, however, Portugal was governed by a series of weak, coalition governments in which no party had a majority and the leadership was generally ineffective. But by the mid-1980s, Portugal was reversing course and returned to a center-right government under Social-Democratic Party leader Anibal Cavaco Silva. For the first time ever, in the elections of 1987 and 1991, Portugal had a government that was able to command a majority; however, after ten years in power that saw a remarkable growth of the Portuguese economy, the center-right government lost support and gave way in the election of 1995 to a renewed Socialist Party headed by Antonio Guterres. But Guterres also followed a pragmatic, centrist policy course that kept Portugal close to the middle of the road, and he was re-elected in 1999.

Portugal is a small country, and it has been a unified and unitary one ever since the Middle Ages. Almost all political and governmental power, as well as economic, social, and cultural leadership, is concentrated in the capital city of Lisbon. There is, unlike Spain or Italy, little regional or separatist sentiment, except perhaps in the Azores Islands or the north of Portugal, both of which are more Catholic and conser-vative. That did not stop the government of Portugal, however, based on the Italian example, from launching a campaign to decentralize power and establish a new system of government at the regional level. But that effort was seen by most Portuguese as a ploy to create a new layer of regional patronage or an opportunity for the political parties (primarily the communists, who were strong at the local level) to compensate for their weakness nationally by qualifying for European subsidies given directly to local and

The goverment center, located in Lisbon, Portugal.

regional governments, without those going through the central ministries in Lisbon controlled by the government party. The initiative was killed in a popular referendum.

So even though Portugal's democracy is only one-quarter of a century old, it has become a stable, pragmatic, and centrist democracy, with alternation in government between the main parties, and a widespread consensus on democracy, economic development through a modern, mixed economy, and close adherence to stringent European financial (balanced budget, low inflation) requirements.

Spain Spain also has a parliamentary system. It was formally in place at the time dictator Franco died in 1975, but after the adoption of a new, democratic constitution in 1978, it acquired greater legitimacy.

The first post-Franco governments were dominated by center-right coalitions and prime ministers—Carlos Arias, Adolfo Suárez, and Leopoldo Calvo Sotelo—who had grown up within the Franco system. In 1982, however, and then again in 1986, Felipe González and the Socialist Workers Party (PSOE) won absolute majorities in the parliament (Cortes) and were then able to govern by themselves, without coalition partners. The success of the early governments in winning parliamentary (if not electoral) majorities was aided by the d'Hondt system of electoral vote counting, which awards additional seats to the leading party. Nevertheless, over time González lost popularity, several of his cabinet colleagues were accused of corruption and malfeasance, and his electoral vote count declined with the result that, after 1992, he was forced to govern in a coalition arrangement with the Basque and Catalan regional parties. In the 1996 election, González and the PSOE lost by one percentage point to José María Aznar and the Popular Party (PP); however, the PP captured only 38 percent of the vote and thus, like González toward the end, was forced to reach a coalition deal with the same two regional parties. Although the regional parties extracted a political price for this agreement, it did not prevent Aznar from enacting most of his program and steering the country back toward the center. In 2000, Aznar and the PP won again.

While Spain has a parliament and prime minister and is a parliamentary democracy, it also has a king. This setup is not a throwback to absolute monarchy, however, but a limited, constitutional monarchy like that of Great Britain. Franco had brought back the monarchy as a symbol of Spanish unity and cohesion; however, the young scion of the Bourbon royal family he chose as monarch, Juan Carlos, proved to be both more capable and more of a democrat than anyone had expected. He, along with Prime Minister Suárez, helped provide the impetus to democratization in the early post-Franco years, and in a notable showdown with right-wing extremists in the military in 1981, who tried to stage a coup, the king courageously came out for democracy and helped squelch the coup. Because of this episode and his overall regular-guy demeanor, the king and the royal family (his wife Sofia, the queen, is from the ousted

Greek royal family) have remained remarkably popular, and all the earlier talk of abolishing the monarchy (Juan Carlos was earlier jokingly called "Juan the Brief" because with democratization it was assumed he would not last very long) has for now been quieted. In fact, the Spanish monarch, in times of crisis, has powers by constitution that are remarkably parallel to those of the Italian or Portuguese president, to call for new elections or to break a political logjam.

Spain is a unitary and democratic republic but, unlike Portugal, it also has strong regionalist sentiment. The constitution of 1978 recognized these regional pressures and gave the regions the power to negotiate autonomy relations with the central state in Madrid. The constitution was later supplemented by enabling legislation under which seventeen of Spain's regions negotiated their own, varying autonomy relations with the central government. The central government is generally supreme in defense and foreign affairs, whereas the regional governments, with their own separate parliaments and presidents, have considerable latitude in domestic social, tourism, police, and other functions. But these relations between the central government and the regions are subject to virtually constant renegotiations over the respective powers and responsibilities of each and are also related to the election returns; that is, in recent years the need of the large national parties to form coalitions with some of the regional parties in order to get a working coalition. De facto, although it does not call it that, Spain has become, like Germany or the United States, a federal-type system, which also owes some of its indigenous origins to Spain's historic and unique system of center-region relations that go back a thousand years.

It is clear from the previous discussion that in a period of a quarter century (half a century in the case of Italy), Southern Europe has become a functioning, stable, democratic area. All four countries have traditional hangovers (like patronage or clan or family-based politics) from the past, as well as numerous internal tensions, but these aspects are not all that different from other, older democracies. The Southern European countries have all developed democratic institutions to go along with the more democratic political cultures and societies that had been growing there for many decades. Moreover, these are not just imported institutions, ill-fitting in the Southern European context. Rather, these are democratic institutions adapted to Southern European realities, and thus more likely to last. Moreover, in the case of such institutions as Spain's regional or autonomous governments and their relations with the central state, we have a development that is truly unique, indigenous, and possibly a model from which other divided countries can learn.

PUBLIC POLICY, DOMESTIC AND FOREIGN

Domestic Policy

Historically—that is, up until about the time of World War I—governments in Southern Europe were called on to provide few public policy programs or initiatives. In those days, prior to the onset of the modern welfare state, governments were generally quite small and had limited responsibilities; most governments had only four or five ministries—treasury, foreign affairs, war or military, and interior or public works—and did not feel responsible for a range of domestic social and economic programs. Care of the poor, the indigent, the unfortunate, the lame, the sick, and the insane was seen as the responsibility of the family and, if the family was unable, of the church: Roman Catholic in Italy, Portugal, and Spain and Orthodox in Greece. In this way, the government's role was kept modest and limited.

Toward the end of the nineteenth century and in the early decades of the twentieth, corresponding with the early stirrings of industrialization in Southern Europe, the "social question" began to be raised for the first time. The social question involved the issue of the rising power of organized labor as well as the debilitating social effects that the early phases of modern industrial capitalism often left in its wake: urban poverty, disease, unemployment, abandoned children, slum housing, and broken families. At first, families and the churches tried to deal with these rising problems in the traditional way, through charity, social programs, and good works. But with massive urbanization as well as frequent impoverishment of large numbers of peoples, the traditional charitable methods proved inadequate. The state or government began to be called on to provide the large-scale resources and programs that private groups were no longer able to provide. In Southern Europe, the pressures eventually gave rise in the inter-war period (1920s and 1930s) to authoritarian corporatism and corporatist regimes, whereas in Northern Europe during that period the same pressures laid the foundations for the modern welfare state. Hence, the inter-war period was a "critical juncture," spawning two of the main movements of the twentieth century: corporatism, on the one hand, and welfarism, on the other.

There are several useful explanations for Mussolini's fascism in Italy and the similar authoritarian-corporatism during this same inter-war period of Metaxas in Greece, Salazar in Portugal, and Franco in Spain. All of them represented, among other things, an attempt to respond to the "social question": what to do about organized labor as well as the legion of poor and unemployed? Marxism and bolshevism were unacceptable (remember, the Russian revolution also occurred during this period) and the other main alternative, liberalism, seemed to reflect more Anglo-Saxon traditions than the Catholic or Orthodox traditions of Southern Europe. Hence, corporatism was seen as a "third way," an alternative to both Marxism and liberalism, and one that was particularly attuned to the histories and sociologies of Southern Europe.

Under corporatism, labor was to be brought into the political process and given certain social benefits, but under state auspices and control. Labor would be obliged to give up its independence as a political movement as well as its revolutionary aspirations (Marxism and anarchism were particularly strong in Southern Europe) in return for being recognized and given legitimacy by the state, and for new social programs being showered upon it. To that end, all four countries enacted new labor, social security, and welfare programs in the 1920s and 1930s, meanwhile creating official, government-run unions for the workers.

Organized labor and the workers bore the brunt of government authoritarianism; and they were repressed by the regimes in power, which is why we often label them "fascist." Meanwhile, the unions that *did* accept what we may call the "corporatist compromise" (benefits in return for state regulation) often found that their organizations were rigidly controlled by the state and that the benefits promised in the way of advanced new social programs failed to materialize. In Southern Europe, therefore, the poor and the working class had the worst of all possible worlds: private and religious charity was coming to an end, their previously independent unions had lost their autonomy and were controlled by the government, and the government's promised social welfare, while drawn up on paper, failed to materialize.

This situation could not last indefinitely. In Italy, Mussolini and fascism were overthrown as World War II was drawing to a close; Italy then embarked on both a more democratic and a more socially progressive course. In Spain and Portugal, the authoritarian-corporatist regimes of Franco and Salazar hung onto power but floundered for the next thirty years, with only modest advances in the social policy area. Greece experienced civil war in the 1940s, a kind of chaotic and conflict-prone democracy in the 1950s and 1960s, and then a reversion to authoritarianism and corporatism again from 1967 to 1974. Only after these authoritarian regimes were overthrown or left power in the mid-1970s did Greece, Portugal, and Spain adopt the kind of modern social programs that Italy had adopted thirty years earlier and that most of Northern Europe had begun to adopt even earlier still.

Italy now has so many advanced social programs (at least on paper) in so many areas that it can be considered a kind of Mediterranean Sweden. But Greece, Portugal, and Spain still lag behind in many social program areas. In part, their retardation in the social field can be explained because these are still comparatively poorer countries than those of Northern Europe and they cannot afford all of the programs of the modern welfare state; in part, it is because their social program development was postponed so long by the persistence of old-fashioned social structures and authoritarian regimes. But now there is an explosion of new social programs in all of these countries, and a large, pent-up demand at the popular level for all of the programs and benefits that their northern neighbors have long enjoyed. Along with imitating all other things "European," Southern Europe is now rushing pell-mell toward Scandinavian-style welfare systems as well.

Greece During all of Greece's three-thousand-year history, the fundamental unit of society has been the nuclear family. Urbanization and Westernization have changed the family institution in recent decades, but the ties of kinship, patronage, and ritual kinship (godfathers, godchildren) still cut across all classes and affect both rural and urban Greeks. The Greek Orthodox church, especially in rural areas, has been an instrument for the preservation of traditional social values. Even as Greece has modernized since 1950 and become a more urban, educated, sophisticated, and European-oriented society, these ties of family, patronage, and personal connections have persisted and remain important.

The family or the church is still often expected to take care of widows, the sick, or the unemployed. While the Greek population has since World War II moved out of the traditional areas and into the cities, primarily Athens and Thessalonika, and while the government in the last two decades has expanded state-managed social programs, these programs have been underfunded and unevenly implemented. Government-run social programs look good on paper and make Greece appear like an advanced Scandinavian-style welfare state, but the benefits are often meager, insurance and delivery of services are fragmented among many agencies, and family or private contributions must be used to supplement the weak state programs. If a person is without personal funds or family support, state programs are generally inadequate. Once more, having a friend or family member or political party benefactor in the right state agency at the right time helps a lot.

Health care, education, welfare, social security benefits, pensions, unemployment insurance, and so on are all distributed unevenly in Greece. The same goes for pollution controls (the historic, twenty-five-hundred-year-old buildings on Athens' Acropolis are crumbling because of the pollution), for housing programs, and for other public policy programs. They are woefully underfunded, a confused mix of public and private, often ineffectively administered, and all have to be filtered through that labyrinthian, patronage-dominated Greek bureaucracy.

In the 1980s, the PASOK government sought to bring order and rationality out of this confusion. Its method of doing so was to increasingly centralize all social programs through state-run agencies. Its stated purpose was to transform Greece from a society with strong traditional practices and beliefs to a modern, secular, social-welfare state. A disguised agenda in all of these programs was to increase PASOK's own political support. PASOK's efforts achieved some successes, but many of the reform programs continued to face hostility and were often frustrated by corruption, the chaos of the Papandreou government, partisan bickering, and patronage considerations. The civil service is often inefficient and corrupt in the delivery of social programs, the state hospitals offer quite primitive care, and educational standards are slipping, but efforts to raise them set off strikes and protests by the students.

The problematic character of Greece's public policy and social welfare system reflects the larger Greek social and political context. Many elements of the traditional society in Greece are still present as the country has experienced modernization and Europeanization. In education, health care, environmental protection, women's rights, religion, and other public policy programs, the forces of change continue to erode old familiar institutions, even while the forces of traditional behavior remain powerful. The dilemma for Greece as for the other Southern European countries is how to find a formula for modernization that also considers the powerful forces of tradition.

Italy Italy's economic and industrial development began earlier than that of the other Southern European countries, was more sustained and thoroughgoing, with the result that today Italy is one of the world's wealthiest industrial nations. Italy can, therefore, afford a vast social welfare program that the other Southern European countries cannot. Despite the overall affluence, however, wealth is very unevenly distributed in Italy both on an individual basis and regionally (north and south), and many of the social programs that look so good on paper are only weakly implemented.

Italy's wealth is evident in the cosmopolitan northern regions.

Italy has long engaged in national economic planning, but the planning agencies lack clout and have not been successful. Much of Italy's economic development (maybe 50 percent or more) occurs in the underground or informal economy, which provides a means to avoid inconvenient government restrictions as well as taxes. In addition, for most of the post–World War II period, Italy's private economy has been so dynamic that central planning was deemed unnecessary.

Regional planning in contrast to national planning has been generally recognized as appropriate and necessary by a broad spectrum of public opinion. The main focus of regional planning has been the south—the *Mezzogiorno*—the six southernmost regions of Italy plus Sicily and Sardinia, which suffer from poor roads, poor agriculture, inefficient manufacturing, and economic poverty and stagnation. The per capita income of the south is only half that of the north, and the gap is widening further. Hence, the national government has showered the south with development projects through several plans, programs, and money transfers; however, these many programs have not erased the gap between north and south. In addition, the numerous transfer programs have now produced a backlash in the north, many of whose residents are

Southern Italy does not enjoy the same prosperity and wealth as the northern regions of Italy.

sick of seeing their tax money go down the south's "drain" and have formed a separatist political party—now one of Italy's four largest—whose program involves what would have been unthinkable a decade ago: dividing Italy, letting the south go its own way, and establishing a separate, obviously very affluent, European-oriented state in the north.

Italy has a wide array of state-run social services: health care, pension funds, workers' compensation, unemployment insurance, and family allowances. Many of these programs, on paper, look as advanced and generous as the welfare programs in the Scandinavian countries. To be fair, many of these services have improved over the years, but despite the impressive array of social services, discontent with them and their high cost is widespread. Italians complain that the programs look fine in law, but that the system is inefficient, cumbersome, and not very generous. Health care and education are inadequate. Social programs are burdened by the same levels of corruption, special favoritism, and patronage requirements as are other aspects of the Italian political system.

Recall from our earlier discussion how Italian political parties and interest groups have hived off whole sections of the social welfare ministry and other agencies to serve their own patronage needs and not the social needs of the public at large. Hence, while Italy looks "in theory" like an advanced welfare state, in practice few of these elaborate programs are ever implemented fully and are often used for purposes (graft, patronage) other than what the social legislation intends. Indeed, the implementation (or lack thereof) of social welfare tells us a lot about how the overall Italian political system operates: as much on the basis of patronage and clientelism as on formal law and constitution. Italians must look to the private sector, to their extended families, and to their own wit and imagination to do what the government frequently seems incapable of doing.

Portugal Throughout its history, Portugal was one of the poorest countries in Europe. The poverty stemmed from a lack of resources, from deep social and class cleavages, from political divisions, and from reactionary authoritarianism. Portugal's social problems were equally severe: malnutrition, high illiteracy, debilitating disease, and inadequate housing. The dictatorship of Antonio Salazar put in place the first advanced social programs in the 1950s and 1960s, but implementation was slow.

With its revolution in 1974, Portugal destroyed the old-fashioned political regime, but its economic underdevelopment persisted and was exacerbated for several years by chaotic political conditions. Not until a decade later in the mid-1980s, corresponding with the coming to power of a stable, business-oriented government as well as Portugal's joining the European Common Market and receiving massive European subsidies, did the economy take off. By now Portugal has reached a level of 70 percent of the EEC average: still poor by European standards but far better off than it was in the past. New highways, housing construction, as well as a new middle class make traditionally poor Portugal look like a boom area. Surprisingly, Portugal was one of the first countries to qualify under the Maastricht Agreement (balanced budget, low inflation) for the European Monetary Union. Rather than the divisive debates of the past, it is interesting that even the coming to power of a socialist government in Portugal in 1995 did not alter the fiscal restraint and tight monetary policy of its pro-business predecessor.

In the social field, Portugal has made equally impressive strides. Illiteracy has all but been eliminated, except among some in the older, passing generation. Urban as well as rural slums still exist, but overall the housing situation has greatly improved. Medical and health care have improved; the incidence of disease and malnutrition has declined greatly; and life expectancy is now close to European (rather than Third World) levels. At the same time, the government social programs that lagged for so long—pensions, welfare, unemployment, health insurance, and the like—are now finally being implemented. But it must also be remembered that Portugal is still not as wealthy as Scandinavia (or Italy or Spain) and, therefore, cannot afford the elaborate social programs that the advanced social welfare countries have. Nevertheless, major changes have occurred in the last twenty-five years so that Portugal now only has "pockets of poverty" rather than a society-wide "culture of poverty."

Economically, Portugal has also "taken off"; its major problems remain a lack of resources, a small internal market, the eventual reduction of its EU subsidies, and stiff competition in the larger EU and global economies.

Spain Spain's development is remarkably parallel to that of Portugal—except that its territory is five times larger with, correspondingly, more resources, greater wealth, and a bigger internal market. But for a long time Spain was similarly held back by a rigid, two-class social structure, disorganized and conflictual politics, and a reactionary dictatorship.

The big breakthrough economically for Spain came in the late 1950s when Generalissimo Franco reorganized his cabinet and committed the regime to a more open, less autarkic, growth-oriented policy. During the next two decades, investment poured in and the Spanish economy took off, achieving "miracle" economic growth, second in the world only to Japan during this period. The Spanish per capita income during this period doubled, then doubled again, lifting Spain out of the poverty in which it had long been mired. After a brief setback in the 1970s and early 1980s brought on by the OPEC oil cartel's quadrupling of petroleum prices, the Spanish economy took off again in the 1980s and 1990s, tripling and then quadrupling per capita income. During this second period, growth was further stimulated, as it was in Portugal, by mammoth EU subsidies. Interestingly, once again, a socialist government, that of González and the PSOE, was as pro-business as its conservative predecessor. By this point, Spain has become one of the major European economic actors, its per capita income is 80 percent of the European average, and its gross national product is now tenth in the world.

With economic prosperity, Spain can now afford the vast array of social programs it could never pay for in the past. Once again, Spain's story is much like Portugal's: economic backwardness historically, then the rising "social issue," and a corporatist regime (Franco's in Spain, Salazar's in Portugal) that tried, through authoritarian means and ultimately without great success, to bring harmony to labor-employer relations and a modicum of social welfare to the poor. The social programs were always limited, incomplete, and inadequately implemented, however, with the result that not until the post-Franco period did the government put some real flesh on these bones.

The results in Spain are extremely impressive. In a twenty-five-year period (since Franco died), Spain has moved from being one of the most regressive nations in Europe in the social field to one of its most progressive. Illiteracy has all but been eliminated. The entire educational system has been modernized and the number of universities quadrupled. Health care and nutrition are greatly improved so that, as one tours the Spanish countryside, one no longer sees the malnutrition, disease, malformed bodies, and bloated (from lack of food) bellies that one saw before. Life expectancy is now equal to that of the most prosperous areas of Europe, and young people are much taller than their elders—again a sign of better health care and nutrition. Like Portugal, Spain still has *pockets* of poverty and underdevelopment but no longer are these society-wide.

Spain must also face the facts that its European subsidies are running out, that many of its small firms are not competitive in either the EU or a global marketplace, and that many social and economic sectors still require modernization. Nevertheless, Spain is such a dynamic, vibrant, and ambitious society that it seems likely it will continue to forge ahead in the future.

Foreign Policy

There have been times in the past when *all* of the countries in Southern Europe were major players on the world's stage. Greece, after all, was one of the main cradles of Western civilization of whose philosophy, mathematics, political analysis, and general learning we are all products. The Roman Empire incorporated the entire circum-Mediterranean, reached into northern Europe (Roman coins and artifacts have been found in Scandinavia), and encompassed the entire then-known world. In the sixteenth century, both Spain and Portugal achieved the status of global powers with far-flung possessions in Africa, America, Asia, and the Middle East, and in Europe itself. In the twentieth century, however, none of these countries achieved the rank of great power, let alone superpower. Nevertheless, all four of them continued to play regional power roles, and in certain, specialized areas and regions they often aspired to larger global roles as well.

To begin, let us make some comparisons among these countries. Italy is a good-sized country, has a population of nearly sixty million, has an especially dynamic economy, is a member of the Group of Seven (of the world's largest economies), and, therefore, is a major player in European and even world affairs. Similarly, Spain has major resources, a population of forty million, a dynamic economy, and is increasingly a major player in Europe, the Mediterranean region, and Latin America. By contrast, Greece and Portugal are smaller countries, have populations of only ten million each, and, therefore, cannot be expected to be major global powers. Nevertheless, in the Eastern Mediterranean and the Balkans, Greece, a NATO member, is a force to be reckoned with, and in its perpetual conflicts with Turkey over Cyprus and other issues, Greece is capable of exercising strong leverage in all the hot issues of that region. Similarly with Portugal: it has fallen from major power status but, because of its colonial legacy in Africa, Asia, and Latin America (Brazil), it has proved to be a useful interlocutor or go-between in numerous conflicts in those areas. *All* of the Southern European countries have an influence worldwide that is larger than their size or resources would indicate.

A second fact to remember is that *all* of these countries are importers of oil, in some cases 100 percent dependent on imported oil, and almost all of that oil comes from North Africa and the Middle East. All four countries and their economies are *absolutely dependent* on a steady, reliable supply of petroleum at reasonable prices. Because of this oil dependency, all four of the Southern European countries are far closer to the Arab countries, far less close to Israel, and often at odds with U.S. policy in the Middle East.

During the Cold War, Southern Europe was thought of, and thought of itself, as peripheral to the Cold War's main conflict centers. Then, the heart of the Cold War was thought of as Berlin, divided Germany, the Iron Curtain between East and West. If there was to be a communist invasion of the West, the thinking was, it would come across the plains of Poland, through the Folda Gap, and on into Germany. Hence, Cold War defenses, including NATO, were concentrated there. If there was any Cold War danger in Southern Europe, it was thought to lie in these countries' *internal* politics: the large domestic communist parties and labor unions of Greece and Italy and the fear of what might happen in the unknown after the old regimes of Salazar in Portugal and Franco in Spain gave way.

But since the end of the Cold War, some new things have happened: some of NATO's major functions and the focus of security concerns have moved south. Since the Soviet Union and the Warsaw Pact collapsed, and since there is no longer a threat of an attack on Western Europe from the east, the strategic focus has shifted to Southern Europe. Now the Mediterranean has become the threat area, mainly focused on the possibility of a Greece-Turkey conflict, war in the Balkans, and a possible Arab-Israel conflagration.

But not just these hot spots have commanded attention; the issues have changed as well. The threat is no longer seen as an armed invasion of one country by another but another kind of "invasion": illegal immigrants, drugs, disease, crime, pollution, and social problems—all flowing across the Mediterranean into Southern Europe from North Africa and the Middle East. In this sense the Mediterranean is being viewed as the European Rio Grande, where the Third World meets the First World and where all the problems and conflicts of poor, underdeveloped countries coming face-to-face with affluent, developed ones are most intense. To reflect this changed strategic focus, NATO has also begun to shift several of its programs and resources away from Brussels and Northern Europe and toward Southern Europe and the Mediterranean.

To the Southern European countries, these Mediterranean-related issues are both international and domestic, what political scientists call "inter-mestic," because they combine the foreign and the local. All of the Southern European countries pay particular attention to the countries to the south and east across the Mediterranean because, to a degree unappreciated in the United States, they are strongly affected by what occurs in these countries. To the extent Morocco, Libya, Tunisia, Egypt, Lebanon, Turkey, the West Bank, and so forth are prosperous and stable, the Southern European countries can have good relations with them on such issues as oil, pollution, labor supplies, water rights, and so on. But to the extent these same countries become unstable and are unable to solve pressing social and economic problems, then—through large-scale immigration—these same problems plus terrorism, the peddling of drugs, transmittable disease, low skills and education levels, and so forth tend to become Southern Europe's *internal* problems.

That is why relations across the Mediterranean are often thought of as comparable to those between the United States and Mexico because if Mexico is stable and prosperous, our relations with that country are usually good; but to the degree Mexico remains poor and unstable, its problems have a way of becoming our problems. For those reasons the Southern European countries keep close tabs on both the internal situation and the foreign policy of those countries close to them across the Mediterranean.

All of the countries in Southern Europe seek to maintain good relations with the United States. After all, the United States is the world's only superpower, the world's most powerful economy, the guarantor (through NATO and the Mediterranean Fleet) of peace and stability in the Mediterranean, and the only trusted go-between and peacekeeper in the Balkans, between Greece and Turkey, and between Palestinians and Israelis. In addition, the United States has large communities of ethnic persons from all of the Southern European countries within its borders. The United States is trusted as a neutral peacemaker to the degree no other country in the region is trusted and, despite tensions and ups and downs in the relations, both national interest considerations, a shared Western heritage, and genuine friendliness and cooperation imply good relations between the United States and Southern Europe.

The most important relations of the Southern European countries at present, however, are with Europe. EUROPE writ large, with capital letters: the EU, NATO, the euro. For Europe is now coming together as a single economic, strategic, and perhaps ultimately political unit; and Southern Europe, excluded for so long, desperately wants to be part of that process. For being "European," recall, is not just a political and economic arrangement but a psychological and moral state as well. It means modernity, sophistication, democracy, acceptance, and being a part of what is arguably the world's most advanced area. Italy has been a member of this elite society for fifty years and is more blasé about it (although not without its lingering complexes); but Greece, Portugal, and Spain are new members and, therefore, are *eager* to be just as *European* as anyone. That is why Spain and Portugal surprised everyone by qualifying to be included in the European Monetary Union (EMU) far earlier than expected. Greece, however, has lagged behind.

We need to further distinguish among the separate countries and their various ties to Europe, but we need also to distinguish among the kinds of ties: economic, diplomatic, and strategic. Economically, all of the countries of Southern Europe want to be closely tied into the EU, but they differ in the degree they are prepared for it: Italy, most prepared; Spain, second; Portugal, third; Greece, fourth. Diplomatically, all of the countries must follow the common European foreign policy guidelines on most issues, even while retaining some degree of autonomy (Spain's special relationship with Latin America for example, or Greece and Turkey, Portugal and Southern Africa, Italy and North Africa) for themselves. Strategically, these countries are also working toward a common defense policy, although, as the Balkan wars indicate, it is difficult to forge a consensus on these issues. Eager to be a participant in European affairs, however, Spain has sent a peacekeeping force to the Balkans, while Italy has accepted refugees, and Greece, which may be a party to the conflict if it spreads to Macedonia, has followed its own policy.

Now let us look briefly at the foreign policies of the individual countries.

Greece Greece's geographic position fronting on the Mediterranean, Ionian, and Aegean seas and commanding a strategic location in the Eastern Mediterranean and Southeast Europe means, first of all, that it is inevitably and intimately involved in all of the conflicts past and present of that area; and, second, that the great powers—Britain in the nineteenth and early twentieth centuries and the United States during the entire Cold War era—take an intense interest in what happens in Greece and its neighborhood. Third, more than the other Southern European countries, Greek foreign policy looks both to the east (Turkey, the Near East) and to the west.

Greece is located in what is currently a very violent, conflict-prone, and dangerous neighborhood; it is one of the areas where the end of the Cold War did *not* usher in a new era of peace and harmony but unleashed forces that *increased* the dangers and instability in the region. As a result of all the dangers close to home, Greece has not been able to develop as close a relationship with Europe as its other

Greece put on a spectacular celebration to ring in the new millenium.

Southern European neighbors; at the same time, because of these neighborhood concerns, Greece's foreign policy has not been able to reach out to encompass broader, global goals as the other Southern European countries have done.

Greece's foreign policy is so complex and faces so many issues at once that it is almost impossible to present it in a few short paragraphs. First and most important, study a map! Probably the most explosive issue in Greek foreign policy is its relations with Turkey. Note that Greece consists not just of the mainland area but of thousands of islands, including many that are right on the Turkish shoreline. The most dangerous issue is Cyprus, which is presently unstably divided between Greece and Turkey. Because of religion (Orthodox versus Islam), history, past conflicts and occupations, long-simmering disputes over borders and territorial claims, past atrocities against each other's populations, and a host of other issues, Greeks and Turks hate each other with passion. That both countries are members of NATO, yet whose conflicts threaten to destroy the organization, does not help; and both countries are extremely sensitive to U.S. favoritism, real or imagined, toward one side or the other.

Next, look to Greece's north. There, the former Yugoslavia, now torn by war and conflict, was once Greece's friendly neighbor, a major trading partner, and its main overland route to connect with the rest of Western Europe. But now: (1) Albania is explosive, caught up in the Yugoslav civil wars, a Muslim country, a mean regime, home to a large expatriate Greek community whose rights it violates, and sending thousands of unwanted refugees southward into Greece. (2) Yugoslavia has split up; it is convulsed in warfare; it is also sending unwanted refugees into Greece; and it is no longer either a good trading partner or a safe passageway into Europe. (3) Macedonia, a former Yugoslav province, is now independent, but Greece refuses to recognize it in part because the name "Macedonia" is the same as Greece's northernmost province; again problems of instability, refugees, expatriate communities. (4) Bulgaria: very poor, the *least* successful politically and economically of the Eastern European former U.S.S.R. satellites; more refugees and expatriates. (5) Thrace: a Greek province but with sizable Turkish minorities, religious and ethnic conflicts, still more problems of disputed territories, refugees, expatriates, displaced persons. In other words, wherever one looks on Greece's immediate borders, there are problems, conflicts, dangers, war, revolution, religious and ethnic hatreds, jealousies, refugees, social issues, and economic disparities—all of which, singularly or in combination, are explosive. None of our other Southern European countries has anywhere near the amount of immediate, nearby foreign policy problems that Greece has.

These immediate dangers surrounding it and right on its borders mean that Greece has insufficient time or resources to deal with the larger, global, and long-term problems that the country also needs to worry about. Foremost among these is Europe: Greece's relations with the European Community have been more strained, tense, and conflicted than those of any other community member. Then, there is instability and conflict in the Middle East from which Greece, like the other Southern European countries, gets almost all of its sorely needed oil. Third, Greece, again like the other Southern European countries, needs to deal with North Africa on a variety of issues: immigration, drugs, terrorism, pollution, expatriate communities, and so on. Relations with the United States, although solid, are often testy, sensitive, and conflict-prone.

Finally, it needs to be said that all of these border and foreign policy problems are also costly in many ways, directly and indirectly, and deprive Greece of sorely needed funds for domestic, economic, and social development. In part because of its strategic and foreign policy preoccupations, Greece has not been able to devote the time and resources necessary for its own internal modernization.

Italy Italy was a charter member of NATO, the EEC, and the European Monetary Union. It has one of the most dynamic economies in the world, ranks sixth in the world in GNP, and is a charter member of the Group of Seven of the most advanced, industrial democracies. Italy is enormously proud of these accomplishments, especially since its earlier development was so slow, perverted (under Mussolini and fascism), and because outsiders have often made Italy, because of its political instability and earlier backwardness, the butt of cruel ethnic barbs.

Long isolated from and peripheral to the mainstreams of European history, Italy is now firmly anchored to the West, to Europe, and to the Western values of democracy, human rights, and a modern mixed economy. At one point, plagued by economic and political uncertainties and a major inferiority complex, which led under Mussolini to Italy attempting to become a world power (by conquering Ethiopia!), Italy has now taken its place as a bulwark of international stability and responsibility. As the Balkans and especially the former Yugoslavia exploded in conflict and civil war, as the Greek-Turkish conflict heated up again, as Middle East conflicts periodically threatened to break out, and as pressures from North Africa (instability, immigration, drugs, and terrorism) mounted, Italy has proven to be a rock of strength in a turbulent Mediterranean neighborhood. Indeed, as NATO has shifted many of its operations from northern to southern Europe, it has relocated to Italy.

For most of the period of the Cold War, Italy, unlike the north and center of Europe, saw the Soviet threat as distant, far away, and of little immediate importance. If the threat was not external, however, it was internal: the presence of the world's largest communist party outside of the Soviet Union. The Italian PCI was solidly entrenched in the trade unions, among peasants, intellectuals, and disaffected voters, and could regularly command 30–40 percent of the popular vote. The Christian Democratic Party, the Vatican, NATO, and the United States were all dedicated to keeping this large communist party out of power. But with the disintegration of the Soviet Union, the collapse of the Warsaw Pact (made up of the U.S.S.R. and its Eastern European satellites), and the end of the Cold War, the givens of this issue changed. First, it was no longer so crucial to keep the communists out of power; and, second, the communists themselves changed, losing strength and becoming more democratic.

The end of the Cold War also freed up Italian foreign policy to be more independent and aggressive in pursuing policies that it had long perceived to be in its interests. Italy has served as peacemaker and peacekeeper in the former Yugoslavia; it has absorbed numerous refugees from these areas as well as from Albania; and it has pioneered in reaching agreements with its Mediterranean neighbors over pollution controls, immigration, terrorism, and drugs. Italy is very much involved in seeking to cool down the Greek-Turkey conflict, in Middle East peace processes, and in the volatile situations in the Balkans and Eastern Mediterranean.

Like the other Southern European countries, Italy is strongly dependent on Middle East and North African oil and, therefore, stakes out positions in these areas sometimes at odds with U.S. policy. It has invested and is heavily involved in the peace processes in its former territories (Eritrea, Somalia, Ethiopia) along the Red Sea and in the Horn of Africa. Reflecting its booming economy, Italian firms are now investing in the Middle East, Africa, Asia, and Latin America.

Italy remains a close ally of the United States; at the same time, its membership in the EU and the EMU means that much of its foreign policy is tied to overall *European* foreign policy. But with its new wealth, power, self-confidence, and influence, Italy is also reaching out more independently to pursue broader foreign policy goals.

Portugal Portugal was once a global power with extensive colonies in Africa, Asia, and Latin America. But Portugal had gone into a centuries-long decline and by the 1970s had left only small enclaves in Asia (Macão, East Timor) as well as sizable territories in Southern Africa (Angola, Mozambique), which it was desperately trying to hang onto. However, national liberation armies in these African territories had fought the Portuguese to a draw, and in 1974, convulsed in a domestic revolution that the protracted colonial wars had helped bring on, Portugal granted independence to these last remnants of its once-great colonial empire.

Thereafter for several years, Portugal was so preoccupied with its debilitated economy and unstable domestic politics that it had virtually no foreign policy at all. Quite a few other countries and areas—the United States, Western Europe—helped Portugal with economic assistance and political advice during this difficult period, but Portugal was mainly passive internationally. As its political system stabilized in the 1980s and its economy began to take off, Portugal once again turned serious attention to international affairs.

Portugal's number-one priority was Europe. Portugal received massive aid and subsidies from Europe in the 1970s and 1980s, and in 1986 it joined the Common Market. Socially, economically, and politically, Portugal wanted desperately to be considered a "European country" (democratic, progressive, modern), and it bent all its resources in that direction. In 1999, it became a charter member of the European Monetary Union.

Meanwhile, Portugal reached out in other foreign policy directions, too. Its location at the entrance to the Mediterranean and its oil needs meant it kept close track of North African and Middle Eastern politics. It sought to form a Luso-phonic (Portuguese-speaking) confederation much like the British Commonwealth (Australia, New Zealand, etc.), but found that bigger, stronger (and former colony) Brazil also had ambitions along those lines. In Africa, Portugal served as a useful go-between to help solve the long civil wars in Angola and Mozambique. In Asia, it turned its former colony Macão over to China in 1999 and tried to pressure Indonesia into better human rights behavior in Portugal's former colony of East Timor and in securing its successful transition to independence.

In its relations with the United States, several issues are involved. Because of the Cold War, the United States has long had an interest in Portuguese stability and prosperity. Because of its location overlooking the Atlantic and the Mediterranean, and because of the Atlantic islands (Azores, Madeira) it possesses, the United States has historically had a strategic interest in the country. Considerable U.S. trade with and investment and tourism occurs in Portugal, and the Portuguese community in the United States is sizable and of growing political importance. The relations are good, solid, albeit sometimes distant; the tensions associated with the Portuguese revolution of the mid-1970s have waned.

Spain Spain was once, like Portugal, a major global power, but then it, too, went into a centuries-long decline culminating in the loss of its last colonial possessions (Cuba, Puerto Rico, the Philippines) to the "upstart" United States in the Spanish-American War of 1898. Spain retained small enclaves on the North African coast (Ceuta, Melilla), but in the twentieth century it was a greatly shrunken power. Moreover, during Franco's long dictatorship, Spain was barred from NATO and the EEC.

Perhaps even more than Portugal, Spain by the 1970s desperately wanted to be a "normal" European country. Culturally, socially, psychologically, and eventually politically (democracy), it wanted to become EUROPEAN. With its long economic boom, Spain began to come up to the European income level, and after Franco died in 1975 it also became a European-style democracy. Spain joined NATO in 1982, a decision that was ratified in a popular referendum in 1986, and that same year Spain joined the EC. Now Spain thinks of itself as a full and leading member of Europe, although its attitudes about Europe are more pragmatic than romantic. Nevertheless, Spain, like Portugal, was one of the first countries to qualify for EMU membership and was one of the few European countries to volunteer its forces for European peacekeeping duties in the former Yugoslavia.

As a bigger country than Greece or Portugal, Spain also has a more ambitious global agenda. Europe is its number-one priority, but it also keeps a close eye on North Africa and the Middle East. After all, most of the drugs, illegal immigration, and problems associated with North Africa enter Spain by way of British-owned Gibraltar on the Mediterranean tip of Spain and then are dispersed throughout Europe. In recent years, Spain has sought to expand its presence in Africa and Asia.

Because of ties of language, history, and culture, Spain feels especially close to Latin America. Its banks and multinational companies are very active in Latin America, and Spain has been the driving force behind the Ibero-American Summits, which meet regularly and include Spain, Portugal, and all of the countries of Latin America. Spain has also differed from the United States in its policy toward revolutionary movements in Central America during the 1980s and, contrary to the U.S. embargo, has rather consistently maintained good relations with communist Cuba. In all of these ways, Spain has tried to present itself not as an alternative (it lacks the global power to do that) but as a counter to the United States in Latin America.

Spain's relations with the United States are good and cordial but sometimes testy. The United States and Spain have many interests in common—democracy, human rights, trade, tourism, NATO, etc.—but there are lingering resentments as well. In some quarters Spain is still smarting from its defeat by the United States one hundred years ago in the Spanish-American

War; it still blames the United States for supporting the Franco dictatorship for many years, and Spain still sometimes sees its Hispanic civilization, in Latin America as well as Spain itself, as a rival to "Anglo-Saxon" (U.S.) civilization.

After what were, oftentimes, slow or delayed starts, all of the countries of Southern Europe have made it into the top ranks of the economically advanced nations. Among our four countries, Italy is first in GNP and per capita income; Spain, second; Greece, third; and Portugal, fourth. Italy and Spain are in the top-ten countries in the *world,* in terms of gross national product. In all four countries, the extreme poverty that once characterized them is in the process of being wiped out, although there are still pockets of poverty and sometimes immense regional differences as, for example, in Italy.

All four have similarly made immense strides in social policy. Starting from a weak economic base and with immense social and class differences among their people, Greece, Italy, Portugal, and Spain have vastly improved health care, nutrition, and life expectancy. Their educational systems, housing, social welfare, and pension and social security programs are now much better than in the past. Not only is the political will there to initiate such programs, but now, with economic development, so is the money to pay for them on a much larger scale. The countries of Southern Europe have not suddenly turned into Mediterranean Swedens or Denmarks, with their vast welfare states, but they have certainly closed the gap. In both the economic and social areas, the countries of Southern Europe are now among the world's leaders.

Their foreign policies are also interesting. None of these four countries is a global superpower—and we do need to further distinguish between larger Italy and Spain and smaller Greece and Portugal. But all of them are what we might call regional influentials—in Europe, in North Africa, and in the circum-Mediterranean. They also have interesting features and specialized foreign policy interests that make them worthy of further study: Greece-Cyprus-Turkey, Italy in the Horn of Africa, Portugal in Southern Africa, and Spain in Latin America. Their relations with the United States are good, solid, but sometimes complex.

REGIONALISM AND GLOBALIZATION

For most of the modern era, 1500–present, Southern Europe was peripheral to, and at the margins of, the European core. After the fall of the Roman Empire, Christendom split into its Eastern and Western blocs; meanwhile, the center of gravity in Europe gradually shifted to the north, while Southern or Mediterranean Europe was left behind. Southern Europe was bypassed or came late to all of the great "revolutions" that we associate with the making of the modern world: the Protestant Reformation, the Enlightenment, the Industrial Revolution, the scientific revolution, accelerated social change, and democratization. Many areas of Southern Europe remained feudal, medieval, and underdeveloped, while the north forged ahead.

The development of the north and the continued underdevelopment of the south bred in both areas a set of attitudes that persist, although now ameliorated, to this day. The north, because of its accomplishments and developed status, tended to feel superior to the south and to look down on it. The south, in turn, felt slighted by these attitudes, resented them, and often harbored a kind of inferiority complex toward the north. Even though the south for many centuries lagged considerably behind the north in economic, social, and political development, it often argued that its culture was superior to that of the north and that it didn't want to be like those "Anglo-Saxon countries" anyway. If Northern Europe insisted on making cruel, ethnic jokes at their expense and didn't really want them in European councils (the EEC or NATO), then Southern Europe had to insist publicly that it didn't really want to be in those organizations, even while privately maneuvering to be admitted. The issue of joining or being integrated into Europe was for the Mediterranean countries as much political and psychological as it was geographic or economic.

Italy was the first Southern European country to break out of this syndrome, ironically not because of its success but because of its defeat in World War II. Due to subsequent Cold War considerations, Italy became a charter member of both the EEC and NATO. Then Italy prospered, becoming over time the sixth-largest economy in the world, a reliable ally, and a democracy, with a standard of living on a par with several of the Northern European countries.

The other Southern European countries did not fare so well. Because of Cold War considerations, Greece was allowed to join NATO in 1952 and Portugal in 1953, but because of the long Franco dictatorship, Spain was kept out until 1982. In the economic sphere, because of their authoritarian regimes, Greece only joined the EEC in 1981 and Spain and Portugal in 1986, considerably later than the earlier European members. Keeping these countries out of the EEC not only prevented them from sharing in the full, post–World War II economic boom that Europe experienced; it also, because of this rejection, increased their anxiety, bitterness, and sense of inferiority vis á vis the rest of Europe. Hence, the campaign of these countries to join the EEC was not just economic; it was also tied in with their desires to be considered "normal" European countries with all the political (democracy), social (progressive), and psychological (developed, modern) characteristics that term implies. Virtually everything the Southern European countries have done over the last several decades has been directed at accomplishing this one, single, overriding goal: joining Europe in *all* its dimensions.

Once they were admitted to NATO and the EEC—"the Club"—the Southern European countries became among their most enthusiastic members. In part because they had been kept out so long, they participated enthusiastically in EEC councils, were energetic participants in the European Parliament, and were among the first to volunteer troops as part of a NATO peacekeeping mission in Bosnia. Three of the countries (Italy, Portugal, and Spain) qualified in the first round to be part of the European Monetary Union; these same three have been among the first to align their foreign policies with an overall *European* foreign policy. In contrast, Greece during the 1980s was more critical toward the EEC, failed to qualify in the first round for admission to the EMU, and, because of its ongoing conflict with fellow NATO member Turkey, maintains a more independent foreign policy. Nevertheless, Greece, too, wants strongly to be "in" Europe.

The Southern European countries have been so preoccupied over the last half century with joining Europe and being considered European that they may have neglected global trends occurring simultaneously. In their focus on European *regional* integration, they may have missed what is happening "out there" in the larger world. For the world is becoming a *global* marketplace, not just a regional one. Culture, ideas, trade, and technology are becoming increasingly global, not just local. The issues of drugs, immigration, terrorism, pollution, the environment, and so on are increasingly global issues not confined to just one region.

In their pell-mell rush to Europeanization, it may be that Greece, Italy, Portugal, and Spain have fallen behind somewhat in adapting to these global trends. An integrated Europe is the world's largest and richest market, but that does not mean one can ignore other global markets. It may be good to have a common European foreign policy, but the European countries, as they are finding out in Bosnia, Kosovo, Russia, and other areas, cannot act as if the rest of the universe didn't matter or didn't impose on their closed world. How should Europe or its individual countries react to all those aforementioned global problems and issues?

We will need more time to see how the New Europe, and specifically the Southern European countries, react to these global trends. The record so far is mixed. Europe's response to the fighting in Kosovo has generally been thought of as a failure. Nor did Europe and its supposedly common foreign policy react well to aggression and malfeasance by Saddam Hussein and Iraq. On the other hand, the EU has signed a trade agreement with MERCOSUR in South America, and its relations with other Third World areas have been at least as enlightened as those of the United States. Entering the twenty-first century, it will, in fact, be a major task for *all* nations to adjust their bilateral, regional, and global policies to all of these new trends.

Joining the EU will also have a major impact on the domestic politics of the Southern European nations. They now must conform to common European product standards, specifications, quality controls, health and environmental standards, and so on. Their policies on agriculture and in other economic areas are determined as much in Brussels as by their own economics ministries. In addition, because of the common financial policy that membership in the EMU obliges them to follow, the Southern European countries will no longer be able to finance costly social programs through deficit financing, extravagant borrowing abroad, or the tactic of cranking up the printing presses to produce more paper currency. These restrictions, in turn, will have a powerful negative effect on traditional Southern European patronage systems and clientelistic politics. No longer will it be so easy to stuff the government with friends and relatives or to dole out whole social programs to groups as a way of buying their loyalty. Instead, the emphasis will be on efficiency, rationality, and a streamlined public service. The European Union and particularly the common currency and monetary policy represent, therefore, not just a new economic program; they will have profound social and political consequences in Southern Europe as well.

CONCLUSION

For a long time, the countries of Southern Europe were referred to as "different"—and the term was not always meant as a compliment. It was not just the sun, tiled roofs, olive trees, Mediterranean cooking, and deep blue skies that marked them as different, however, but other, deeper forces as well. Socially, economically, culturally, politically, religiously, and even psychologically, Southern Europe seemed both backward and not a part of the European mainstream. The countries of Mediterranean Europe seemed to form a unique culture and society. These differences were summed up in the derogatory comments that "Europe stops at the Alps or Pyrenees," that "Greece lies beyond the pale," that Italy as a nation was a "figment of the imagination."

For many formative centuries, from approximately the sixteenth through the nineteenth, Southern European development appeared to diverge from that of the rest of Europe. The Southern European political systems were closed and authoritarian; there was no evolution toward democracy. Socially they remained rigid and two-class. From the height of wealth in the fifteenth and sixteenth centuries, they fell back into poverty and backwardness. Religious orthodoxy held back learning, science, and intellectual stimulation. Reactionary and backward looking in virtually all spheres, trapped in the Middle Ages, Southern Europe experienced little of the Enlightenment and Industrial Revolution that would lead to modernization. Its social and political systems were long dominated by traditional behavior, patronage, personalism, clientelism, inefficiency, family and clan-based politics, corruption, and

The Getty Museum in Bilbao, Spain, is one of the many cultural achievements in recent Spanish history.

authoritarianism. Backwardness in so many areas, in turn, produced national inferiority complexes and a sense that, if Europe did not want or respect them, they did not want Europe either.

When modernization finally began to come to Southern Europe in the nineteenth century, it was terribly disruptive and conflict-prone. The old guard and old oligarchies—the church, military, elites, and monarchy—tried to hang onto their power at all costs, while the often frustrated newer social forces turned to such revolutionary ideologies as Marxism and anarchism. The result during much of the nineteenth and early twentieth centuries was conflict, fragmentation, instability, and civil war, which held back development even more. Corporatism seemed to offer a "third way" for these paralyzed, conflict-prone societies and produced such dictators as Mussolini in Italy, Salazar in Portugal, Franco in Spain, and Metaxas and the colonels in Greece.

Hence, it was only in the post–World War II period—Italy first in the late 1940s but Greece, Portugal, and Spain two or three decades later—that Southern Europe began to join the modern world in *all* its dimensions. The economies of the area took off fueled by the general European and U.S. prosperity of the period; their social systems modernized and became more pluralist; and their political systems embraced parliamentary democracy. In the process, the Southern European countries also embraced Europe—the EC, NATO, and the EMU, to say nothing of European mores and behavior—and broke out of their historic international isolation. The changes in the last several decades in all areas of life have been nothing short of spectacular. This is not your father's or grandfather's poor, backward Greece, Italy, Portugal, or Spain any more. Instead, Southern Europe has become dynamic, alive, often on the frontier of change rather than, as in the past, lagging behind.

Now all of the countries of Southern Europe are democratic—for the first time ever—and this condition of democracy seems unlikely to change soon. All of the countries of Southern Europe will in all probability continue to develop economically as well as socially, and those conditions are unlikely to change either. All of the countries are thoroughly integrated into Europe, not just economically but culturally and psychologically as well. Southern Europe is now an integral part of Europe, no longer apart from it. In all of the countries of Southern Europe, however, a major task remains of reconciling the newer forces of democracy, modernization, and Europeanization with the older traditions of patronage, clientelism, and family and class privilege.

Now all of the Southern European countries have joined the European Monetary Union, although Greece lags somewhat. No one quite knows how this new financial community will all work out, how the common currency, the common financial policy, and—as we have seen here—the common foreign and strategic policies will all be harmonized. We do know that there will be economic and, hence, social and political tensions as the European subsidies to Southern Europe decline and as inefficient small firms prove unable to compete in the larger European and global markets. There will also be tensions caused by the European Central Bank's reluctance to allow member states to enact grandiose development strategies or to pay for elaborate patronage programs through deficit financing. The precise relations—and degrees of autonomy—between the individual countries and the central European institutions located in Brussels and Strasbourg have yet to be completely worked out, as do the relations between the regional European entities and the larger outside world. The outcome of all of these changes on Southern Europe is still uncertain.

While these uncertainties remain, no one doubts that Southern Europe in the last several decades has embarked on a new and very encouraging course that has produced vibrant democracy, accelerated economic development, vast social change, and full integration into Europe. It is clear that Europe no longer stops at the Alps or the Pyrenees. At the same time, Southern Europe has retained its own vibrancy, dynamism, culture, and special ways of doing things. We ought to celebrate both the differences and the progress made toward full integration into Europe.

SUGGESTED READINGS

General

Arrighi, Giovanni (ed.), *Semiperipheral Development: The Politics of Southern Europe in the Twentieth Century* (Beverly Hills, Sage, 1985).

Braudel, Fernand, *The Mediterranean and the Mediterranean World in the Time of Philip II* (New York, Harper Row, 1972).

Chilcote, Ronald, et al., *Transitions from Dictatorship to Democracy: Comparative Studies of Spain, Portugal, and Greece* (New York, Taylor and Francis, 1990).

Gellner, Ernest and John Waterbury (eds.), *Patrons and Clients in Mediterranean Societies* (London, Duckworth, 1977).

Gunther, Richard, et al., (eds.), *The Politics of Democratic Consolidation: Southern Europe in Comparative Perspective* (Baltimore, Johns Hopkins University Press, 1995).

Hamilton, Kimberly, *Migration and the New Europe* (Washington, DC, Center for Strategic and International Studies, 1994).

Kaplan, Lawrence S. et al., (eds.), *NATO and the Mediterranean* (Wilmington, Scholarly Resource, 1985).

Kohler, Beate, *Political Forces in Spain, Greece, and Portugal* (London, Butterworth, 1982).

Pomfret, Richard, *The Mediterranean Policy of the European Community* (New York, St. Martin's, 1986).

Sanders, Thomas G., *Secular Consciousness and National Conscience in Southern Europe* (New York, American Universities Field Staff, 1977).

Stuart, Douglas (ed.), *Politics and Security in the Southern Region of the Atlantic Alliance* (Baltimore, Johns Hopkins University Press, 1988).

Wiarda, Howard J. (ed.), Southern Europe and the Mediterranean—a special issue of the AEI *Foreign Policy and Defense Review,* VI, No. 2 (1986).

Williams, Allan (ed.), *Southern Europe Transformed: Political and Economic Change in Greece, Italy, Portugal, and Spain* (London, Harper Row, 1984).

Greece

Campbell, J. S., and P. Sherrard, *Modern Greece* (New York, Praeger, 1968).

Clogg, Richard, and G. Yannopoulos, *Greece Under Military Rule* (New York, Basic Books, 1972).

Curtis, Glenn E. (ed.), *Greece: A Country Study* (Washington, D.C., Government Printing Office, 1994).

Legg, Keith, *Politics in Modern Greece* (Stanford, Stanford University Press, 1969).

Macridis, Roy, *Greek Politics at the Crossroads* (Stanford, Hoover Institution Press, 1984).

Stearns, Monteagle, *Entangled Allies: U. S. Policy Toward Greece, Turkey, and Cyprus* (New York, Council on Foreign Relations, 1992).

Tsoucalas, C., *The Greek Tragedy* (Baltimore, Penguin, 1969).

Vatikiotis, P. J., *Greece: A Political Essay* (Beverly Hills, Sage, 1974).

Italy

Banfield, Edward, *The Moral Basis of a Backward Society* (New York, The Free Press 1958).

Barzini, Luigi, *The Italians* (Harmondsworth, Eng., Penguin, 1968).

Chubb, Judith, *Patronage, Power, and Poverty in Southern Italy* (Cambridge, Cambridge University Press 1982).

Furlong, Paul, *Modern Italy* (London, Routledge, 1994).

Gilbert, Mark, *The Italian Revolution: The End of Democracy Italian Style* (Boulder, Westview, 1995).

Haycraft, John, *Italian Labyrinth* (Harmondsworth, Eng., Penguin, 1985).

Hine, David, *Governing Italy* (Oxford, Clarendon Press, 1993).

Lange, Peter, and Sidney Tarrow (eds.), *Italy in Transition* (London, Frank Cass, 1980).

LaPalombara, Joseph, *Politics Italian Style* (New Haven, Yale University Press, 1987).

McCarthy, Patrick, *The Crisis of the Italian State* (New York, St. Martin's, 1995).

Putnam, Robert, *Making Democracy Work: Civic Traditions in Modern Italy* (Princeton, Princeton University Press, 1993).

Portugal

Bruneau, Thomas, et al. (eds.), *Portugal in Development: Emigration, Industrialization, and the European Community* (Ottawa, Can., University of Ottawa Press, 1984).

——— and Alex MacLeod, *Politics in Contemporary Portugal* (Boulder, Lynne Rienner, 1986).

——— *Political Parties and Democracy in Portugal.* (Boulder: Westview, 1997).

Magone, José M., *European Portugal: The Difficult Road to Sustainable Development.* (New York: St. Martin's, 1997).

Maxwell, Kenneth, *The Making of Portuguese Democracy* (New York, Cambridge University Press, 1995).

Opello, Walter C., *Portugal's Political Development* (Boulder, Westview, 1985).

Payne, Stanley, *A History of Spain and Portugal* (Madison, University of Wisconsin Press, 1973).

Pinto, Antonio Costa, *Salazar's Dictatorship and European Fascism* (New York, Columbia University Press, 1995).

Solsten, Eric (ed.), *Portugal: A Country Study* (Washington, D. C., Government Printing Office, 1994).

Wiarda, Howard J., *Corporatism and Development: The Portuguese Experience* (Amherst, University of Massachusetts Press, 1977).

——— *Iberia and Latin America: New Democracies, New Policies, New Models* (Lanham, MD, Rowman and Littlefield, 1996).

——— *Politics in Iberia: The Political Systems of Spain and Portugal* (New York, Harper Collins, 1993).

——— *Transitions to Democracy in Spain and Portugal* (Washington, D. C., American Enterprise Institute for Public Policy Research, 1989).

Spain

Abel, Christopher, and Nissa Torrents (eds.), *Spain: Conditional Democracy* (New York, St. Martin's, 1984).

Arango, E. Ramón, *Spain: Democracy Regained* (Boulder, Westview, 1995).

Bell, David S. (ed.), *Democratic Politics in Spain* (New York, St. Martin's, 1983).

Bonime-Blanc, Andrea, *Spain's Transition to Democracy: The Politics of Constitution Making* (Boulder, Westview, 1987).

Brennan, Gerald, *The Spanish Labyrinth* (Cambridge: Cambridge University Press, 1971).

Clark, Robert P., and Michael H. Haltzel (eds.), *Spain in the 1980s: The Democratic Transition and a New International Role* (Cambridge, Ballinger, 1987).

Coverdale, John F., *The Political Transformation of Spain After Franco* (New York, Praeger, 1979).

Crow, John A., *Spain: The Root and the Flower* (Berkeley, University of California Press, 1985).

Eaton, Samuel D., *The Forces of Freedom in Spain* (Stanford, Hoover Institution, 1981).

Gunther, Richard, *Politics and Culture in Spain* (Ann Arbor, Center for Political Studies, Institute of Social Research, University of Michigan, 1988).

―――― et al., *Spain After Franco: The Making of a Competitive Party System* (Berkeley, University of California Press, 1986).

Hooper, John, *The Spaniarda: A Portrait of the New Spain* (London, Penguin, 1986).

Maravall, José, *The Transition to Democracy in Spain* (New York, St. Martin's, 1982).

Marías, Julián, *Understanding Spain* (Ann Arbor, University of Michigan Press, 1990).

Michener, James, *Iberia: Spanish Travels and Reflections* (New York, Random House, 1978).

Payne, Stanley, *Franco's Spain* (New York, Crowell, 1967).

―――― *A History of Spain and Portugal* (Madison, University of Wisconsin Press, 1973).

Solsten, Eric, and Sandra W. Meditz (eds.), *Spain: A Country Study* (Washington, DC, Government Printing Office, 1990).

Wiarda, Howard J., and Margaret MacLeish Mott, *Catholic Roots and Democratic Flowers: The Political Systems of Spain and Portugal* (Westport, CT, Greenwood, 2001).

Wiarda, Howard J., *Iberia and Latin America: New Democracies, New Policies, New Models* (Lanham, MD, Rowman and Littlefield, 1996).

―――― *The Transitions to Democracy in Spain and Portugal* Washington, DC, (American Enterprise Institute for Public Policy Research, 1989).

8

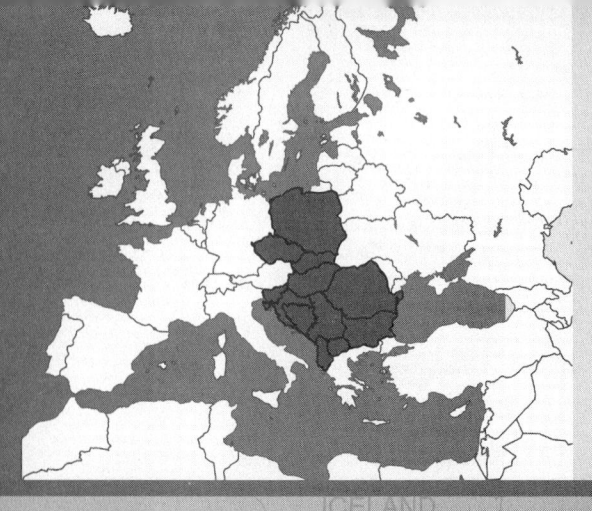

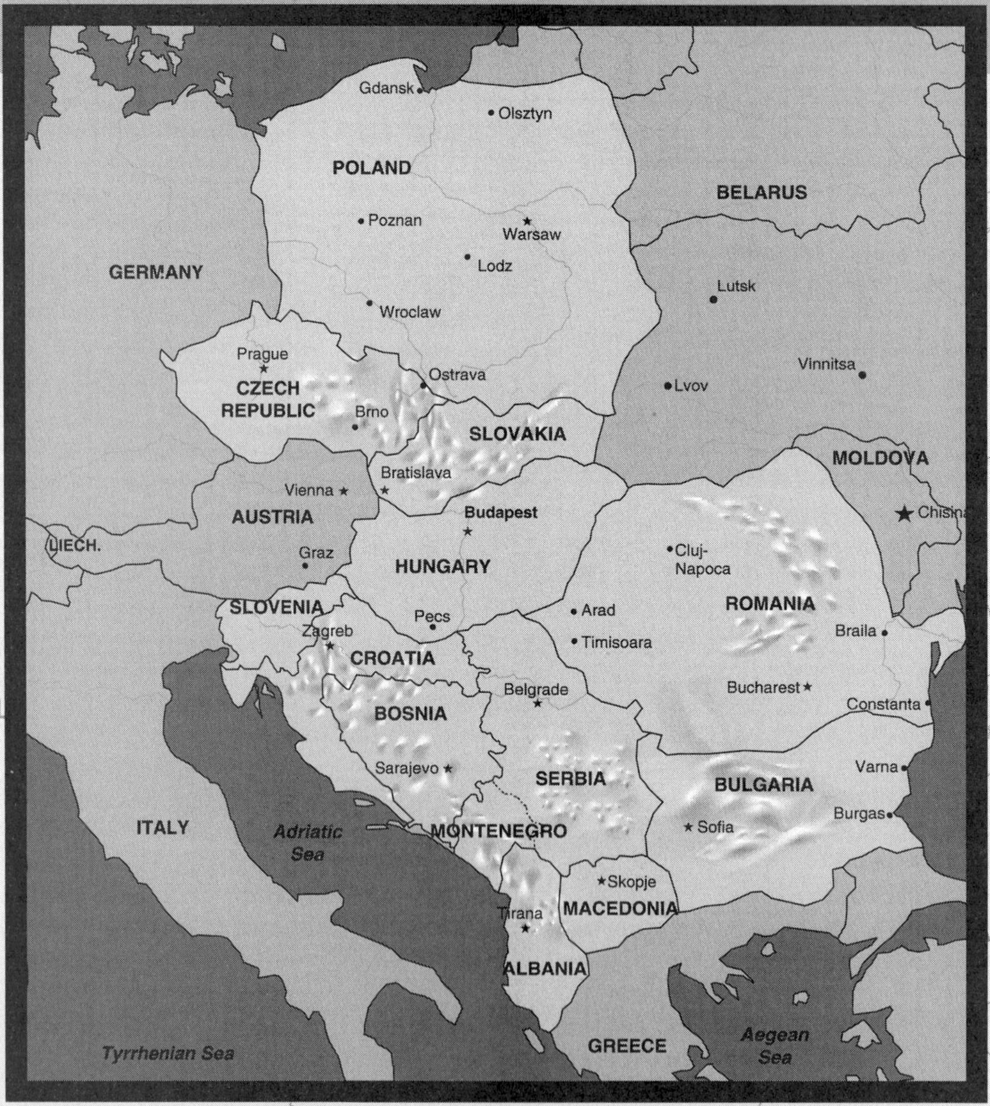

Gdansk
Olsztyn
POLAND
BELARUS
Poznan
Warsaw
Lodz
GERMANY
Lutsk
Wroclaw
Prague
Vinnitsa
CZECH
REPUBLIC
Ostrava
Lvov
Brno
SLOVAKIA
MOLDOVA
Bratislava
Vienna
Budapest
Chisinau
AUSTRIA
LIECH.
Graz
Cluj-
Napoca
HUNGARY
SLOVENIA
Arad
ROMANIA
Pecs
Zagreb
Timisoara
Braila
CROATIA
Belgrade
Bucharest
BOSNIA
Constanta
Sarajevo
Varna
SERBIA
BULGARIA
ITALY
Adriatic
Sea
MONTENEGRO
Sofia
Burgas
Skopje
Tirana
MACEDONIA
ALBANIA
Tyrrhenian Sea
GREECE
Aegean
Sea

Whither Eastern Europe?

Dale R. Herspring

COUNTRY PROFILES

	Pop.	Land Area (sq. km)	Pop. (sq. km)	GNP ($ billions)	Per Cap. Income	Rank	% Urban	Adult Lit.	Life Exp. Male	Life Exp. Female
ALBANIA	3,000,000	29,000	123	$ 2.7	$ 810	144	38	100%	69	75
BOSNIA AND HERZEGOVINA*	—	51,000	—	—	—	—	—	—	—	—
BULGARIA	8,000,000	111,000	75	$ 10.1	$ 1,230	131	69	98%	67	74
CROATIA	5,000,000	57,000	82	$ 20.7	$ 4,520	73	57	97%	68	77
CZECH REPUBLIC	10,000,000	79,000	133	$ 51.8	$ 5,040	69	66	100%	71	78
HUNGARY	10,000,000	93,000	110	$ 45.6	$ 4,510	74	66	99%	66	75
POLAND	39,000,000	323,000	127	$150.8	$ 3,900	79	65	100%	69	77
ROMANIA	22,000,000	238,000	98	$ 31.3	$ 1,390	125	57	98%	65	73
SERBIA*	—	—	—	—	—	—	—	—	—	—
SLOVENIA	2,000,000	20,000	99	$ 19.4	$ 9,760	52	52	100%	71	79
SLOVAKIA	5,000,000	49,000	112	$ 20.0	$ 3,700	80	66	100%	71	78

*Data unavailable because of war, conflict, nonreporting.

INTRODUCTION

With the possible exception of Russia, of all the areas covered in this book, Eastern Europe is one of the most diverse and difficult to deal with; it is also one of the most unstable and important areas. Two world wars started in this part of the world, and for years it served as a buffer between NATO and the communist world. In fact, it was part of the communist world, having suffered the imposition of that Russian-dictated system by the force of arms in the closing days of World War II and in the late 1940s.

Since the end of the Cold War, the twelve countries that make up what we now call Eastern Europe have all been struggling with the task of adapting to new circumstances—in most cases trying to create and nurture democratic institutions in an area where they never existed in the past. The key question is whether they can develop party structures and democratic forms of participation that will be both stable and enduring. After all, in every case they are starting from authoritarian systems and without much experience with free, open markets. Will the new executives be as authoritarian as the old ones, even though they may be called presidents or prime ministers? Will they be able to create a bureaucracy that will be supportive of a democratic polity? Will they be able to find a democratic means for resolving the difficult ethnic conflicts that plague that part of the world?

Then there is the question of economic decline. Will these new democratic countries be able to get their economies moving again? After all, in the vast majority of cases, the populace tends to identify economic success with democracy. Will the public be prepared to pay the price (belt-tightening, cutbacks) that goes with privatization, economic restructuring, and austerity that are part and parcel of this process? The bottom line is simple: if the economies do not begin to prosper, then public support of these new, democratic systems may suffer.

Creating new, democratic, and prosperous political systems will not be an easy task, as recent events in the Balkans have demonstrated. We no sooner appear to get developments in Bosnia under control—albeit with the aid of NATO troops—than another region, Kosovo, appears to threaten to destabilize the whole region and possibly lead to a major war.

Some of the countries in the area seem well on their way toward institutionalizing democratic polities. On the other hand, others are struggling. Indeed, in some cases, the polities that now exist seem to be even more authoritarian than was the case previously. They appear to have traded one form of autocracy (communism) for another (non-communist, but still authoritarian). Their economies also appear to be in serious trouble. The same point could be made with regard to dealing with ethnic issues. The situation with regard to human rights for minorities such as gypsies is only one of the most obvious examples.

In addition to the struggle to create democratic institutions and viable economies, many of the East European countries are working overtime to become part of the West. In some instances, this means officially becoming part of NATO, whereas in all cases it means an effort to develop ever closer economic ties with the European Union. In almost every instance, however, the elites running these countries believe that the best way to remain independent and free from the kind of Russian influence they were subjected to for more than forty years is to establish close ties with the West. For three of them (Poland, Hungary and the Czech Republic) this also meant becoming a member of NATO. Although others are waiting in line to join the Western alliance, all of them—including the three newly independent Baltic states of Latvia, Estonia, and Lithuania—recognize that the key to their economic development runs through Strasbourg, the home of the European Community. The question for many of them is how to convince Western Europe that it is in the latter's interest to have them as members.

The success or failure of the democratic experiment in Eastern Europe is critically important for the rest of Europe. To begin with, democratic polities are far less likely to begin wars. The fact that Serbia is now the main force behind conflict in the Balkans is at least in part a result of the dictatorship run by Slobodan Milosevic. Second, democratic polities tend to be more stable than dictatorships. One can never be certain when a dictatorship will topple, thereby creating major problems for all of the countries in the region. As a result, the rest of Europe is well-advised to foster the development of stable, properous, democratic systems in these former communist countries.

If the conflicts in Bosnia and Kosovo demonstrate nothing else, it is how fragile both peace and stability are in the region. The fact that neither of these conflicts has become more widespread by involving other countries in the region (e.g., Greece, Bulgaria, Turkey) is nothing short of a miracle. Should the conflict expand and escalate, it could easily develop into a major war; one that could upset the balance of power in Europe and lead to a much broader conflict. Needless to say, the idea of two NATO members (i.e., Turkey and Bulgaria) fighting each other creates nightmares in the minds of the Alliance's leadership.

Poland, Hungary, and the Czech Republic all seem to be well on their way toward creating democratic institutions, even if much still needs to be done to create the kind of economic prosperity and political stability characteristic of Britain or Germany. The fact that these three states have adopted democratic institiutions will have a major impact on the countries to the east. Belarus, Ukraine (one part of the Soviet Union), and even Russia cannot avoid paying careful attention to what is happening in these countries. If the democratic experiment succeeds, and all three countries become stable, prosperous, and functioning democracies, then others may decide to emulate them. Even if that does not happen, the fact that they appear to be less threatening could help calm fears and concerns in the region. The Russians may complain about NATO expansion, but stability and predictability in Eastern Europe are as much in their interest as in the interest of the United States and the rest of Europe.

Given where they started from, developments in Eastern Europe are also interesting because they show how important factors such as political culture are in the creation of democratic institutions. By this we mean the impact that things such as history, language, and culture have on the acceptability of democracy by the people living in the region. Those nations whose political culture is supportive of democratic institutions find the process of democratization easier to adopt to than those whose history, language, and culture argue against this new experiment. This does not mean that the latter cannot develop democratic institutions. Rather, it means that the process probably will be much longer and more difficult.

Finally, it is important to keep in mind that Eastern Europe led the way when it came to the collapse of communism. Gorbachev's denunciation of the Brezhnev doctrine was critical because it removed the danger that Moscow would utilize its troops to intervene if a country tried to get rid of its communist government.[1] But once it was clear that the Russians would not become involved, it is worth noting that the Eastern Europeans led the way in getting rid of communism. The Poles were the first to move toward the development of a democratic polity in 1989, and most of the East Europeans soon followed suit. Two years later, the Russians joined the democratic parade.

---

[1] In essence, the Brezhnev doctrine maintained that once a communist regime was established, Moscow was obliged to ensure that the country remained communist, even if that meant using the Soviet Army to ensure the survival of the regime.

Given the leading position the east Europeans occupied in getting rid of communism, this process can also tell us a lot about how democratization works in general. After all, we have twelve different countries, all of which are at different stages of political development. Questions such as what factors seem to be the most conducive to the creation of a democratic polity would seem to be of particular interest. Similarly, the Eastern European experiment may help us to better understand the relationship between economic development and the creation of democratic political institutions. By understanding the Eastern European experience, we may be better able to understand how this process works elsewhere. All of the former Russian republics claim to be working toward the creation of democratic polities, but all of them clearly have their problems. Is there something in the Eastern European experience that may offer lessons as these countries move forward?

The situation in Eastern Europe is also important because many Americans trace their origins back to these countries. One need only read a list of famous Americans to learn that millions of Americans trace their roots to this part of the world. To cite only one example, Hungarians never tire of pointing out the role played by their countrymen in developing the atomic bomb. "When Enrico Fermi left the room, the conversations switched into Hungarian because all of the other scientists were from Hungary," is the way one senior Hungarian official put it.

For many years, some people referred to Eastern Europe as the "forgotten region." Although this phrase may describe the situation during the post–World War II period under the communists, it is clearly no longer the case. Indeed, one could argue that Western eyes are focused on Eastern Europe to a degree unknown in the past. This attention is not only a result of the conflict in Kosovo, but a consequence of the fact that the situation in that beleaguered Serbian province occupies considerable attention in the Western media like the conflict in Bosnia did several years ago. Eastern Europe is also receiving an ever larger amount of attention for another, more positive reason. When it comes to transition from a totalitarian/authoritarian regime, the East Europeans are on the front line. How successful they are in making this transition will have a major impact not only on that region, but on Europe as well. Indeed, the success or failure of the democratic experiment in Eastern Europe may have important implications for the rest of the world.

HISTORY, GEOGRAPHY, BACKGROUND, AND POLITICAL CULTURE[2]

One of the main misconceptions about Eastern Europe on the part of Americans and West Europeans is the belief that all of these countries are more or less alike—that there really isn't much difference between them. If anything, the communist period and the domination of the region by the U.S.S.R. reinforced this belief. In looking at Eastern Europe, they were too often viewed as parts of the Soviet military, political, or economic machine. Although these countries have generally behaved as if they were part of the greater Soviet empire, important differences have always existed among the various peoples who inhabit this part of the world. Indeed, if the communist period succeeded in doing nothing else, it papered over these differences. Moscow would not allow the kind of individuality or autonomy that would have permitted these differences to show through. If ethnic feuds between countries like Romania and Hungary

---

[2]This section draws on this author's "Eastern Europe and the Search for a Democratic Political Culture," in Howard J. Wiarda, *Non-Western Theories of Development* (Orlando, Harcourt, Brace and Company, 1999), pp. 116–131.

got out of line, the Kremlin quickly suppressed them. If countries like Czechoslovakia or Hungary began to act independently, Moscow sent in troops to restore order or, as the Soviets called it, to "normalize" the situation. In short, all of the countries of Eastern Europe at one time or another lived under the threat of Soviet intervention, a situation that distorted the normal evolution of events in those countries.

If any one characteristic defines the countries of Eastern Europe, it is heterogeneity. Why? The reason is simple. All of these countries have very different political cultures—a result of very different cultures and historical experiences over the centuries. In some, like Poland, there is a highly individualistic orientation; in others, like Serbia, there is an equally strong collectivistic approach to political issues. As a result of these significant differences, the chances of developing democratic political institutions are much higher in some countries than in others. For example, countries like the Czech Republic appear to be well on their way toward creating a Western democratic political system, whereas others such as Bulgaria have a long way to go primarily because their indigenous political culture is less hospitable to democracy.

The primary result of the collapse of communism in Eastern Europe was that it permitted this heterogeneity in political culture to reemerge as an active political force. Long pent-up pressures for a multifaceted approach to dealing with the problems facing these countries again became part of the political landscape.

As used here, political culture "refers to the values, ideas, norms, belief systems, and patterns of behavior of a particular people or country."[3] History plays an important role in transmitting these values and beliefs, but so do other factors such as religion, language, economic development, political socialization, attitudes toward authority, and so on. What is important about this concept is that each polity develops its own, often unique political culture. Political culture changes, but generally only gradually. From a political standpoint this gradual change means that despite the major changes that have occurred in Eastern Europe over the past hundred years, important differences remain among these countries—differences that continue to influence the way political decisions are made as well as the prospects for democracy in these countries.

Let us now turn to a discussion of the factors that have led to the major differences in political culture on the part of the countries of Eastern Europe. First, there is the question of language. Languages are important because they underline the extent of diversity in the region while helping to determine an individual's cultural identity. Languages in Eastern Europe are divided among four main linguistic families: Slavic, Ural-Baltic, Romance, and Albanian. Within the Slavic language group, there are the Western Slavic languages (Polish, Slovak, and Czech) and the South Slavic group (Bulgarian, Serbo-Croatian, Macedonian, and Slovenian). The South Slavs (with the exception of the Croats and Slovenes) use the Cyrillic alphabet, the same one used by the Russians. The only Ural-Baltic language in the region is Hungarian. Romanian is a Romance language much closer to Latin in many ways than it is to the other languages in the region; it also includes some Slavic words. Finally, there are the Albanians. The Albanian language is part of an Indo-European language group, but it differs markedly from any other Indo-European languages in that group. Other languages are also spoken in the region, including Romani by Gypsies, Yiddish by Jews, German in parts of Romania, Greek by a minority in Albania, and Turkish by a minority in Bulgaria.

Linguistic factors affect political culture in Eastern Europe in two significant ways. First

---

[3] Howard J. Wiarda, *Introduction to Comparative Politics* (Belmont, CA: Wadsworth Publishing Co., 1993), p. 22.

and most obvious, tremendous linguistic differences exist among the various countries. If language is a key to how one interprets political phenomena, then each of these peoples tend to view reality somewhat differently.

The second and more important implication is that some of these languages tend to be Western oriented, whereas others are more focused on the East. For example, the Western Slavs tend to see themselves as Westerners speaking a Slavic language. As a Polish commentator stated, "Poles consider themselves to be Westerners who should be speaking English or French." The same Western orientation is evident among Czechs, Slovenes, and Croats.

The situation with regard to Hungarian is similar. German is the second most common language in Hungary, and Hungarians resent any suggestion that their Ural-Baltic languages make them un-Western. On the other hand, Albanians see little relationship between themselves and the West, whereas the Romanians often romanticize themselves as descendants of the Roman legions.

The situation is different when it comes to the Serbs and the Bulgarians. They tend to identify linguistically with the Russians. In fact, the languages are so similar that for many years Bulgarian students were not permitted to claim Russian as a foreign language.

As is the case with language, significant differences exist among Eastern Europeans when it comes to religion. Poles, for example, are almost all Roman Catholics. Protestants in Poland are assumed to be Germans, while Poles consider the Eastern Orthodox to be Russians. Indeed, for many years when the country was under external domination, the Catholic church served as the heart and soul of Polish national identity.

The Czech lands are the home of the Protestant Reformation. Jan Hus was burned at the stake for his Protestant heresies in Prague in the fifteenth century. Slovakia, meanwhile, is almost entirely Roman Catholic. Hungary is split sixty-forty between Roman Catholics and Protestants, while except for a Hungarian minority, Romania is primarily Orthodox. Bulgaria is also Orthodox, as are Serbia and Macedonia. Slovenia and Croatia are Roman Catholic, while many Bosnian Serbs are Muslim, as are many Albanians.

What is important about this situation is that it clearly parallels the situation in language. Poles, Czechs, Slovaks, Hungarians, Croats, and Slovenes tend to be Western oriented in both their language and their religion. Why is this critical? Because the concepts of democracy that these countries are trying to implement all come from the west and, to the degree that there is a proclivity to look to the west, there will be a greater willingness to accept the Western democratic experience.

Historically, of all the countries in Eastern Europe, the Czech Republic has long been the most advanced. In fact, prior to World War II, the Czech lands were among the most developed in all of Europe. Unfortunately, the communist system did much to undermine the vitality and efficiency of the Czech economy. The same is not true of Slovakia, however, which continues to lag behind Prague. Poland, on the other hand, has taken major strides toward the creation of a modern econony and is well on its way toward industrialization; however, it too maintains a large farm economy.

Romania is considerably less developed than Poland or the Czech and Slovak lands. Indeed, it is one of the most underdeveloped countries in the region. Hungary has made significant progress, especially in mechanizing agriculture, but it too lags far behind its Western neighbors. Bulgaria was the one country of Eastern Europe to benefit from Soviet domination, and even though still poor by European standards, it is far better off today economically than it was in 1945. For its part, Yugoslavia appeared to be making some economic progress in the late 1970s and 1980s, but then the country collapsed. The civil war in former Yugoslavia, together with Western sanctions imposed on Serbia, have almost totally destroyed the country's economy. While an end to hostilities would contribute significantly to improving the economic situation, so much has been destroyed and some areas were so underdeveloped even prior to the disintegration of Yugoslavia that rebuilding the economies of such former provinces and now independent countries as Serbia and Bosnia will take a long time. Finally, when it comes to economic development, Albania is Europe's "poor man." The end of communism only intensified the country's economic chaos. Indeed, the war in Kosovo has further strained matters.

Of all the areas discussed in this book, none has as many problems with ethnic minorities as does Eastern Europe. The presence of these minorities has not only led to irredentism[4]; in some cases popular feelings run so high that the central government has been forced to focus far more on resolving these issues than is appropriate—the drive toward democratization may become a victim of the battle over ethnicity. The existence of two different ethnic groups in the same country (as for example in Romania and Bulgaria) can lead to constant conflict. In nothing else, the continued existence of such a situation makes it difficult to create a democratic political system acceptable to all ethnic factions.

From a historical standpoint, it is important to keep in mind that the borders of Eastern Europe have shifted back and forth over the centuries. In fact, almost anyone in Eastern Europe could claim that some land somewhere in the region rightfully belongs to them. Poles, for example, are quick to point out that at one time in history they occupied all of Germany up to the Elbe. In fact, the name Berlin is not German, but Old Slavic. Often the movement of these boundaries led to intensified feelings of nationalism or a belief that one's country was wronged by history. This was especially true of Hungary. Almost one-third of Hungarians found themselves outside of Hungary as a result of what many consider to have been unequal treaties during the early part of this century. Meanwhile, Turks have been upset at their treatment at the hands of Bulgarian authorities. Albanians fret under what they consider to be Serbian and Macedonian repression, and Greeks object to Albanian dominance.

The Poles are among the few peoples in Eastern Europe whose ethnic makeup and political boundaries coincide. They inhabit a territory that is almost 100 percent Polish, without any ethnic minorities. At the same time, it is important to remember that Poland's borders have been moved back and forth over the past several centuries—indeed, at times Poland ceased to exist as a state. Only in the aftermath of World War II, with the movement of its eastern and western borders to the West, did the country really became homogeneous. The "purification" of Poland did not come without a price, however. Millions of Jews were exterminated and large numbers of Germans were expelled from what was once German territory.

World War II also helped solve the problem of the German minority in Czechoslovakia. The vast majority were expelled. The Czech Republic is now almost entirely Czech. The situation in Slovakia is different, however. It has a large Hungarian minority, and that issue is not only a problem internally, but also one that strains Hungarian-Slovak relations. With the exception of sizable minorities of Gypsies and Jews, Hungary itself is relatively "pure" from an ethnic standpoint. Meanwhile, Romania has about two million Hungarians. This minority has been a constant source of instability and conflict within Romania as the country has tried to decide how to treat its minority groups.

---

[4]Irredentism—one of Eastern Europe's most intractable problems—refers to claims staked out by one ethnic group on land occupied by another one. Two factors give rise to irredentism: The first is historical; Poles might argue that German land should be theirs because centuries previously it was Polish land. The second is demographic; Hungarians could claim Romanian land because significant parts of it is occupied primarily by ethnic Hungarians.

Thousands of Albanian refugees staying in shelters on the border of Blace Macedonia.

Given its tendency to try to assimilate the Hungarians by getting rid of their culture and language in favor of the Romanian language and culture, it is not surprising that the result has been conflict between Budapest and Bucharest.

While the issue is relatively unknown outside of Bulgaria, Sofia has had its own problems with its Turkish minority. Toward the end of the communist period, for example, Sofia made an attempt to Bulgarize the Turks by making them adopt Bulgarian names and by closing Turkish language schools.

Macedonia also has an important minority: 25 percent of the population is made up of Albanians. The government is concerned that if the situation in Kosovo gets out of hand it could spill over into Macedonia and upset the fragile political situation there. Not to be left out, Albania's small Greek population has also been a source of tension both within the country as well as in its relations with Athens. The Greeks in Albania seek autonomy and permission to retain their language and culture while Tirana (the capital of Albania) has from time to time pushed adoption of a more Albanian-oriented culture.

Finally, there is the former Yugoslavia. If nothing else, it is a "model" of what can happen when the minority problem gets out of hand. Except for Slovenia, all of the remaining republics have until recently had a large number of minorities. The government in Belgrade, for example, has been fighting a battle to keep Kosovo, which is about 90 percent Albanian, part of Serbia. Prior to the breakup of Yugoslavia, Croatia contained a large number of Serbs. With the destruction of the country and the resultant fighting, almost all of the Serbs were driven out of Croatia, thus helping to eliminate the country's minority problem.

Bosnia remains a headache not only for its own leadership but for the international community as well. The three ethnic groups—the

Serbs, Croats, and Bosnian Muslims—seem to get along only insofar as the Western military presence keeps the peace. The situation in that part of the world is far from resolved. There is fear that as soon as Western military forces withdraw, fighing will resume.

For most Americans, history is a subject to be studied in school. Things like the Civil War are events that happened a long time ago and that have only limited relevance for what is happening today. The situation in Eastern Europe is quite different. History is alive, and events that may have happened one thousand years ago are very much a part of the political culture of the various countries. People in this part of the world have long memories. They do not forget past wars, slights, or massacres. Take, for example, the situation in Kosovo. As already noted, Serbs make up less than 10 percent of the population. Yet, Kosovo remains an integral part of Serbia in the minds of almost all Serbians. Why? Because it contains the place where Serbia suffered the worst defeat in the country's history (at the hands of the Turks), as well as Serbia's first capital and Serbdom's most holy monastery. Regardless of whether or not they have ever seen it, Serbian children are raised reciting poems that stress the vital importance of this region to Serbian identity. Given this background, it is not a surprise that Belgrade has been unwilling to permit either autonomy or independence (as many Albanians want) to Kosovo. Giving up this land would be a negation of everything that is holy for Serbs and the fact that it is inhabited almost entirely by Albanians plays no role whatsoever.

Serbs also hold a grudge against Croats because the latter slaughtered Serbs during World War II. As a part of their own ethnic cleansing, Croats—who were allied with Germany—rounded up thousands of Serbs and slaughtered them. One of their favorite techniques was to appear in a village, round up the inhabitants, force them into the local (Orthodox) church, and then burn it down with everyone inside. This atrocity is one of the major reasons why the Serbs are so sensitive to the status of Serbs outside of Serbia proper. History has taught them that unless Serbs live under Serbian rule, they may be eliminated by other ethnic groups—a situation that legitimizes almost any kind of action to save them.

Not to be left out, Hungarians resent the way they have been treated historically by the Slovaks, the Romanians, and the Serbs (in the Vojvodina). Poles and Czechs still harbor concerns, even hatreds in some cases, about Germans. World War II may seem like a long time ago to you or perhaps a topic that you know only from movies like *Saving Private Ryan,* but for the average Pole or Czech who lost many close relatives in battles with the Germans, the war remains very real and very much in their conscience. Indeed, one of the main reasons why Czechoslovakia broke up was because of Slovak resentment over the discriminatory way they believed they had been treated by the Czechs over the years.

Before discussing the East European concept of politics, it is important to understand both the Western and the Russian ideas of government. Why? For the simple reason that the East Europeans (to varying degrees) fall somewhere between the two concepts. Some are closer to the West, whereas in others Russian influence has been stronger. First, let us say something about Western political culture.

When it comes to political culture, it is important to keep in mind that in the West, ideas such as pluralism are very much a part of everyday political life. The power of the ruler should never be absolute; it should always be limited. At the heart of the Western concept of political culture is the idea that the individual should always be permitted a certain amount of autonomy (how much varies by the country and time). The individual should always have a certain amount of private space—a situation that allows the individual to work out his or her problems without the direct intervention of the state. The individual may still have an obligation to God, but God and the state are not the same thing. In the aftermath of the Reformation, and even more important, the Renaissance, the idea of a theocratic state or one in which the government and religion were one was looked upon as absurd by the vast majority of people. The history of England and France was an effort to gradually and effectively limit the power of the king, and a king whose power was limited as in the United Kingdom had a difficult time arguing that he ruled by divine right.

There were good reasons for this situation. The king often depended on several independent cities where the guilds and the middle class were strong. He often found himself in a situation where he had to go to them for support, and most important of all, for money to finance his various activities, especially his armies. In time, this idea of several independent sources of power gave rise to the idea of a social contract; the idea that a deal was made between the rulers and the ruled. If rulers violated the social contract by violating the independent rights of the towns and other groups, they could be removed. These limits on sovereignty also gradually led to the idea of "rule by law." Law was autonomous, it was not a tool of the sovereign. Participation in the political system was accepted as legitimate, even if the idea of who had a right to participate gradually developed and changed over time. This concept helped provide the basis for democracy.

The Russian system, by contrast, was quite different. From the Russian standpoint, the idea of a balance of power was silly. Power was only effective if it was not fragmented; if it was held in the hands of a single individual with absolute power. Theologically, Russians believed that absolutism was a moral good. All groups in society should be controlled by the center, by the state. Besides, an absolute government could get more done quicker than a democratic one. Indeed, many Russians looked upon the latter as nothing more than a debating society.

As a result, Russians believed that the main purpose of political institutions was to carry out the sovereign's will. In such a situation, why worry about representative institutions? Participation did not mean the right to take part in decision making. Rather, it meant the right and obligation to carry out the orders of the sovereign.

For the most part, cities in Russia were not autonomous. The tsar took what he wanted from them. Nor were there any independent interest groups. This situation in turn made the idea of a social contract irrelevant. Leaders were not in power because they were chosen by the people. God put them there. Power went from the top down. The only social contract was between God and the tsar.

The situation was similar when it came to church-state relations. The main idea was that the church should be subordinate to the state. After all, the tsar was God's personal representative. Doing what the tsar commanded meant doing God's will. Not surprisingly, this meant that the belief in the tsar's divinity prevented the development of an autonomous law. The law was nothing more than the expression of the sovereign's will. Its purpose was twofold: first, to make the system run smoothly, and second, to help the populace understand how to carry out the sovereign's will.

Education was closely tied to the church. Little emphasis was placed on critical thinking. Instead, the primary focus was on rote learning. Education was collective. The main purpose was to learn how to behave in a manner that reinforced the collectivity and strengthened the state.

The key to understanding the East European system of politics is the idea of transition. Eastern Europe represented a transitional stage between Russia and the West. The region shared many Western experiences, but these factors were incorporated into Eastern Europe against the backdrop of Russian influence.

Take, for example, autonomous groups. Although most groups were not as tightly controlled in Eastern Europe as they were in Russia, they were far less autonomous than their counterparts in Western Europe. Native institutions tended to be weak because societal bonds were weak. This led to the rise of a bureaucratic state run by a relatively small elite. This elite in turn worked to marginalize regime opponents, although bureaucrats came to recognize that some limited autonomous entities had a right to exist. Nevertheless, none of these groups were strong enough to deal with the political center in the way that similar structures did in the West.

For their part, intellectuals tended to identify with the regime, and much of the opposition to governmental policies took place within the ruling elite. This meant that although there was far more governmental opposition than in Russia, the majority of the populace did not actively take part in politics. Participation was limited to a small elite, both for and against the regime.

Limited popular participation yielded a concept called the "discretionary power of the state." Under this idea, the state had the right to act in any area of politics unless expressly prohibited from doing so by law or custom. This formulation did not mean the same as rule by the will of the majority. Rather, it meant that the government could pretty much do what it wanted, with a few exceptions.

The state's discretionary power led to the creation of a "facade" of politics. There was outward respect for constitutional principles, and on many occasions the courts delivered objective decisions. In addition, several interest groups grew up and were active in the political process. The problem, however, was that the efficacy of courts, interest groups, and other factors depended on what concessions the elite was prepared to make.

Education was another area in which Eastern Europe was halfway between east and west. There was a strong difference, however, between the Balkans and the rest of the region. Central Europe (Poland, Hungary and the Czech lands) had a tradition of critical thought much like that which existed in Western Europe. In the case of the Balkans, the rote learning characteristics of Russia were more the rule.

Finally, unlike Russia, most of Eastern Europe—within limits—accepted the rule of law. The problem, however, was that the concept was not nearly as developed as in Western Europe. In fact, it was difficult to enforce laws if the country's ruler did not agree. The one exception was if laws covered either a custom or an area in which the sovereign was specifically prohibited from acting—a situation that provided more protection for the individual than was the case in Russia.

As far as church-state relations were concerned, they varied by country. In some places (Poland, Slovakia, Slovenia, and Croatia) the Roman Catholic church was relatively autonomous. In other cases (Romania, Bulgaria, and Serbia), the church was an obedient servant of the sovereign (as in Russia). In the Czech lands and Hungary, there was a mixture of Protestantism and Catholicism, while in Albania Islam was the primary religion.

It is difficult to evaluate the full impact of the communist experience. If anything, given the heavy-handed approach taken by the Russians, it reinforced the region's nondemocratic tendencies. For example, the new postcommunist elite was as authoritarian as its predecessors. After all, the communists believed they had a monopoly on knowledge and, like their tsarist predecessors, they proceeded from the assumption that the primary function of citizens, as well as those who ran the country, was to carry out the wishes of the rulers in the Kremlin.

Not surprisingly, the new elites paid little attention to public opinion and democratic trappings, as if the voting process was a sham. Participation in elections served primarily to show an individual's support for the system. As in the Russian case, the individual was invited to participate, but that meant carrying out the task the system had assigned to him. This failure to provide meaningful citizen involvement in politics meant that almost without exception, few East Europeans were ready for the post-communist experiment in democracy. The widespread acceptance of the status quo led many to look to the new regimes to solve most of their problems. In the main, this meant that few of them would be prepared to deal with the difficulties of capitalist and democratic development. If the new capitalist economy was not working, then it was clearly the regime's fault. Rather than holding themselves responsible for resolving issues, the people of some Eastern European states, frustrated with their countries' failures to move immediately from the darkness of Soviet domination to the dawn of post-communist affluence, tended to look to demagogic or xenophobic solutions, whether in the form of attacks on scapegoats or reliance on leaders with simple solutions to complex problems.

ETHNICITY

Whereas the other chapters in this book at this point now turn to a discussion of social and ethnic groups, class structure, interest groups, and political parties, this breakdown does not make much sense for the vast majority of the countries of Eastern Europe. Why? For the simple reason that these countries are all in the process of formation, of trying to develop things such as political parties and interest groups. It would be wrong to suggest that interest groups are totally lacking. In Poland, for example, workers are organized, albeit not as systematically and tightly as in the United States. Interest groups are also active in countries like Romania, even if their activities primarily take the form of demonstrations against the regime. Similarly, there are organizations of farmers in countries like Poland, the Czech Republic, and elsewhere, but in many cases they are still in their infancy from the standpoint of creating a politically relevant interest group. The same comment could be made about the army (all countries have one), and in some places the bureaucracy appears to have become the government. Students have also begun to organize. The key point, however, is that none of these groups (with the possible exception of the Roman Catholic church in Poland) are as well organized as their Western counterparts. In most cases, the government is able to ignore them when it comes to formulating and implementing policy.

Class structure is important in some countries, where it has begun to play a role. In most cases, however, class is much less important than in the west. One factor however, supersedes all others when it comes to Eastern Europe—and that is the issue of ethnicity. Indeed, this issue is so important that this entire section will be devoted to a discussion of it.

As noted previously, with the exception of Poland, all of the countries in the area are afflicted to one degree or another by ethnicity. The only reason that Poland has avoided the problem is because its borders were moved westward, thereby placing its Ukranian minority in Russia. In addition, the Germans were expelled, and the vast majority of the Jews were eliminated during the Holocaust.

Problems with ethnicity in Eastern Europe range from seemingly unimportant debates over what language should be used in a particular region to the full-scale warfare that has haunted Bosnia and Kosovo. The former is a reflection of how sensitive ethnic issues are in various parts of Eastern Europe, whereas the latter is indicative of how volatile such conflicts can become.

The Importance of Language

To many people in the West, disputes over language seem silly. In every one of the countries of Eastern Europe, there is a dominant language. Why not learn that language and use it in everyday business? After all, it makes more sense to use one language than two or three. If one wants to speak another language at home, so be it, but why exacerbate the situation by making matters more divisive? As we have learned in cases such as the debate over the relationship between French and English in a place like Quebec, language can be an explosive issue. The reason is simple. For many minorities, the ability to use their language, even if it involves only a small part of the population, is a sign of equality—an indication that the majority population accepts the minority population as equals—even if it causes all kinds of problems in everyday interactions (e.g., should all government documents be printed in several languages? What about street signs, especially when the two languages are very different?) In essence, language issues go to the heart of the problem of ethnicity.

Language is also about cultural identity. For those who value their cultural identity, recognition of their language is critical. If the country uses only one language, there is concern that in time the minority language will gradually be pushed aside and with it the minority culture. In fact, this is exactly what some countries have done in an effort to build a homogeneous political culture. Get rid of the minority language and force those who speak it to use the dominant language, and in time one will succeed in wiping out the minority culture in favor of the more dominant one. In the past, when Poland was partitioned between Russia, Prussia, and Austria, the first two conducted a vigorous campaign to substitute Russian and German for Polish. Only the dogged determination of the Poles to hold on to their language kept it alive—and with it their Polish culture.

Ruling elites in Eastern Europe learned long ago that it becomes difficult to integrate or assimilate ethnic minorities once they have become conscious and protective of their language and culture. Poles living in Lithuania continue to identify themselves as Poles, even though they share Lithuania's Roman Catholic religion; Gypsies continue to hold on to their culture and unique language; Hungarians in Slovakia and Romania have not given up their resistance to efforts to assimilate them into the dominant language and culture; and since the beginning of the war in former Bosnia-Herzegovina, Bosnian Muslims have started calling the Serbo-Croatian spoken there Bosnian, as a means of creating a separate and distinctive cultural identity. We now have the somewhat ridiculous situation where three different groups (Serbs, Croatians, and Bosnian Muslims) speak a mutually intelligible language, but in an effort to show their differences call it by three different names.

Concern for language as an identifying factor helps explain why Croatian students fought so hard in the aftermath of the breakup of Yugoslavia to distinguish Croatian as much as possible from Serbian (the two had previously been combined). Only if the Croatian language was significantly different from Serbian could the former legitimately proclaim that Croatia had the moral right to exist as a separate and independent nation/state. The same situation has prevailed in Serbia, where an effort has been made to get rid of as many Croatian and Turkish words as possible in order to "purify" the language. This has created the rather silly situation, however, where the Serbs must come up with new words for common items such as sugar, tobacco, cotton, soap, monkey, and brandy—words that are Turkish in origin—if they hope to get rid of all Turkish words. Such an exercise only makes sense when language and culture take precedence over ease of communication.

Linguistic nationalism is not a monopoly of the Balkans. Prior to the breakup of the country in 1993, Czechs and Slovaks spoke the same language—Czechoslovak. Once the split became reality, however, Slovakia began stressing the uniqueness of the Slovak language. For example, in 1995 a law was issued that stated that the Slovak language was the heart and soul of Slovak identity. The use of other languages was restricted, and the use of Slovak was required in official government business. The language law was aimed at the country's Hungarian minority, which makes up about 11 percent of the population. The Slovak government was obviously interested in making a statement that its Hungarian population (concentrated in the south along the Hungarian border) should not consider itself Hungarian but Slovak, and that the best way of showing its loyalty to the new Slovak state was by giving up Hungarian in favor of Slovak. The same was true of the Czech language. Despite its close similarities to Slovak, Bratislava has done its best to get rid of Czech words.

The situation in much of Eastern Europe has deteriorated to the point where fights are raging over such things as street signs. Should they be in two languages? For example, Serbia undertook a campaign to remove Hungarian signs in the Vojvodina, where a large Hungarian minority lives. Needless to say, the Hungarians were upset at what they perceived to be an effort to undermine their culture in favor of "Greater Serbian" culture. If the street signs go today, many of them fear that it will be only a matter of time before the legitimacy of the language itself will be challenged. Why should all Hungarians be forced to learn Serbian? Why should their street signs be in a foreign language in their own hometowns?

Gypsies

Before discussing some of the individual ethnic problems, something should be said about the one that impacts almost all countries, that of the Gypsies or Roma (as they call themselves). Eastern Europe used to have two other ethnic groups spread all over the region: the Germans and the Jews, but World War II eliminated the vast majority of Jews in the area. Most of the Germans were expelled, while the vast majority of Jews were horribly exterminated.

The Roma are an ancient people, and unlike the other ethnic minorities in Eastern Europe, they are not concentrated in any one country. While estimates vary, one specialist has suggested that approximately five million of them live in the region. Their communities range from an estimated seven thousand in Slovakia to close to two million in Romania.[5] What is even more important is that they are the fastest-growing ethnic group in the region. Unfortunately, when it comes to the Roma, the populace of all Eastern Europe—from Poland to Bulgaria—is united in its feeling of hatred toward them. Their unique language places them outside the cultural confines of even minority groups in these countries, and their refusal to adopt a sedentary lifestyle means that they live a life of poverty. Indeed, traditionally, the Roma had been the poorest ethnic group in all of Eastern Europe. During the communist era, most of them were employed as unskilled laborers because very few of them attend school and most are therefore illiterate. In addition to educational deficiencies, they also have problems with crime, juvenile delinquency, and low health standards.

To make matters worse, they have a reputation as thieves, beggars, and prostitutes. When traveling in Eastern Europe, visitors are constantly warned that Gypsies "are dirty and will steal anything." While some make their living as laborers or musicians, most are unemployed and have taken to a life of crime. The situation is further compounded by the discrimination they are subjected to. Stories of police brutality toward them are rampant. Any time an act of theft occurs, the police head for the nearest Roma settlement. The Roma are beaten, their

---

[5] Zoltan Barany, "Grim Realities in Eastern Europe," *Transition*, vol. 1. no. 4, 29 March 1995, p. 3.

A Gypsy or Roma encampment illustrating the poverty and poor conditions of their nomadic lifestyle.

dilapidated shacks are destroyed, and whatever possessions they may have are often seized because it is assumed that the only way they could have obtained them is through theft.

This situation raises the question—why care? What do Gypsies have to do with creating political security in Eastern Europe? The answer is clear. As long as this group is not integrated into Eastern European society (and many of them now move back and forth among the various countries), it will be difficult for these countries to develop stable democracies. As long as there is one group that the police—and public officials—feel free to treat as outcasts, lacking basic human rights, it will be difficult to establish the rule of law. Reports of acts of violence come from all over the region; from Slovakia, where stories of beatings by skinheads made the front pages of local newspapers, to Bulgaria, where some police officers seem to pride themselves on their ability to beat up Gypsies. There are also structural problems. For example, not only are the Roma not organized politically, but in some countries, such as Bulgaria, the law also prohibits the formation of political parties based on ethnicity. As a consequence, there is no organization to protect the interests of the eight hundred thousand Roma in Bulgaria. The situation is not much better in the Czech Republic with its higher standard of living and stronger democratic traditions. Between 1990 and 1993 skinheads murdered sixteen Roma.[6] In general, the tribal structure of the Roma militates against political action; they are so divided that the chances of them uniting to push for their rights are minimal.

At present, little is being done throughout the region to deal with the Roma problem, yet it will not go away. With the highest birth rate in Eastern Europe, the Gypsies are going to continue to haunt the region. Indeed, the situation is likely to get worse. At best, it is a ticking

---

[6]Ibid., p. 5.

time bomb, one that could well blow up in coming years. On the one hand, it is an issue that excites human rights groups, who will continue to heap criticism on the governments of the region for their failure to deal with the Roma problem. On the other hand, all of the governments of Eastern Europe seem to be primarily interested in finding a way to get rid of the Roma, rather than of finding ways to resolve these difficult problems. In many cases, governments seem to be in competition to provide the worst possible conditions for the Roma out of fear that if they improve conditions, it will only lead to an influx of more Roma from other parts of Eastern Europe. In the end, the Roma problem could not only destabilize many of these governments, but it could also lead to a popularly supported holocaust. While the latter eventuality seems unlikely under current conditions, the future is uncertain. In any case, in countries like Romania where the Roma population at two million is significant, failure to resolve this issue could contribute to the rise of a neofascist, nativist government, one that would use the presence of the Gypsies as a reason to introduce strong, authoritarian controls in the government, thereby undermining current efforts to create a democratic polity.

While the issue of Roma is a regionwide problem, and could become a major source of instability, the bilateral problems among the various countries have done the most to date to create problems for the creation of democratic polities in the region.

Hungarians in Romania

One of the most long-simmering ethnic problems has been the status of the Hungarian minority in Romania. The Hungarian minority, which numbers about 1.6 million or 7 percent of the total population, is the largest Hungarian minority outside the boundaries of Hungary. Under the iron, totalitarian rule of Romanian dictator Nicolae Ceausescu, the Hungarian minority suffered constantly. Ceausescu did not accept the idea of linguistic and cultural autonomy for the Hungarians and as a result countered every effort they made to gain acceptance of the Hungarian language and the right to educate their children in Hungarian language schools—up to and including a university in Cluj—which is located in Transylvania, the area where the vast majority of Hungarians are concentrated. It was a constant source of problems in Romanian-Hungarian relations.

On the positive side, it is worth noting that the post-communist Romanian and Hungarian governments have taken the need to resolve the Hungarian minority issue seriously. Budapest is primarily worried about the status of the Hungarians living in Romania and wants to ensure that their language and culture are protected. As a consequence, Hungarian authorities have long argued that the Council of Europe's statement on the protection of ethnic minorities should be part and parcel of any agreement between the two countries. As far as the more rational voices in Bucharest are concerned (there are also the more extreme nationalistic voices that want no rights for Hungarians), the key problem is to avoid a situation that would encourage separatism—the reunification of Transylvania with Hungary, of which it was a part in the period prior to World War I.

The Hungarian population's effort to gain its rights appeared to be on the way to realization at the end of 1996 when a new Romanian government was formed, which included the Democratic Alliance of Hungarians in Romania (RMDSZ). It looked as if at long last a serious effort would be made to resolve the ethnic issues, which in the case of the RMDSZ was restoration of ethnic minority rights in general and Hungarian language education in particular.

In fact, the new government came out in favor of the RMDSZ's demands. At long last it appeared that one of the region's longest and most bitter ethnic disputes was on its way to being resolved. Two ordinances were issued, which eliminated legal restrictions on Hungarian in education and the use of minority languages in local administration and Hungarian/Romanian signs in communities made up of both groups. Unfortunately, the more nationalist members of the Romanian party soon began to backtrack and to demand that these ordinances be rescinded. In fact, from all appearances, the leadership of the Romanian party does not have the power it needs to force its members to accept the coaliation agreement. The best hope for a resolution of this matter is Romania's fervent desire to join NATO. The Alliance will not accept that country into its ranks until its minority problems are resolved. In the meantime, the inability of the ruling coalition to resolve this issue creates the basis for more stability. If the RMDSZ withdraws from the coalition, then the country will face political instability and much of the good work that has been done in both the economic and political spheres could be lost.

Hungarians in Slovakia

The status of Hungarians in Slovakia has been a source of constant irritation both between the two capitals, Bratislava and Budapest, as well as between Slovaks and Hungarians within the country. At present, there are about six hundred thousand Hungarians living in Slovakia. Hungary ruled what is now the Slovak Republic for approximately one thousand years, until the creation of the state of Czechoslovakia in 1918. When World War II occurred, the Hungarians allied with Hitler's Germany and as a result, they were rewarded with control over the Hungarian lands in Slovakia.

In the immediate aftermath of the collapse of communism, Hungarian and Slovak parties seemed to be working well together. Then in October 1990, the Slovak parliament passed a law on language. The law allowed the use of the minority language in official documents, as long as Hungarians made up at least 20 percent of the population. The law satisfied neither side. Slovaks complained that it went too far in providing rights to minorities. For their part, the Hungarians argued that it did not go far enough. For example, employees of public institutions did not have to respond in the minority language, and they noted that the law prohibited the posting of bilingual signs.

Feeling that the government in Bratislava had not done enough, the Hungarian minority constantly called for the passage of legislation giving minorities more rights—something that the Slovak population opposed. This became a major issue when Slovakia applied to join the Council of Europe. The latter noted that Slovakia would only be permitted to become a member when it passed legislation permitting the posting of bilingual town and village signs, and repealed a 1950 Czechoslovak law preventing minorities from registering their names in birth registers in their native languages.

Then in 1995, Slovak President Vladimir Meciar and his Hungarian counterpart, Gyula Horn, signed a bilateral state treaty that guaranteed additional minority rights. Unfortunately, the treaty did not solve the problem. The following June, four Hungarian teachers were fired when they protested the government's plan to have certain subjects taught only in the Slovak language. The Hungarians feared that such a step would lead to a further assimilation of Hungarians. In addition, the Slovak government also made serious cuts in support of minority cultures. Then in 1995, parliament passed a new language law that took away the use of minority languages in official contacts.

The minority problem in Slovakia remains unresolved. The Hungarians continue to push for more autonomy and fear that the ultimate goal of the Slovak politicians is to wipe out the Hungarian minority as a definable and recognizable ethnic group. The key problem, however, is that the Slovaks are still trying to find their own identity. Not very long ago, they were part of Czechoslovakia. During that time, they believed that they were discriminated against constantly by the Czechs, who had traditionally held almost all of the key posts in the government. One result of the "velvet revolution"—the peaceful divorce that broke the country into two parts—was that it forced the Slovaks to come to grips with their own identity. Not only must they search for a new, non-Czech identity, but they also must find a way to deal with a recalcitrant and demanding Hungarian minority. Although this problem does not appear to be one that will lead to serious outbreaks of violence in the near future, until it is resolved it will continue to detract from the Slovaks' attempts to build a secure and stable political system.

Turks in Bulgaria

Before turning to the even larger ethnic issues—Bosnia and Kosovo—it is worth noting three other less pressing but important issues. The first concerns Bulgaria. From 1984–1989, Bulgarian communist leader Todor Zhivkov launched an assimiltation campaign. The key component of this program was a demand that all Turkish names be changed to Slavic-Christian names. His goal was nothing short of the elimination of Turks in Bulgaria. Needless to say, the Turks were up in arms, and in the summer of 1989, a mass exodus of Turks from Bulgaria began. Zhivkov went on TV and urged Turks to leave. Within a few months, one-half of the country's nine hundred thousand Turks had left. Relations with Ankara and the rest of the world were severely strained as mosques were closed and suggestions that the practice of Islam was not acceptable reverberated throughout the country.

In 1989, Zhivkov was forced to resign. The question of the Turkish minority quickly came to the fore again. Fortunately, rationality seems to have gained the upper hand. In December, the 1984 assimilationist decree was reversed. The response was widespread anti-Turkish demonstrations, especially in those areas where Turks and Bulgars lived together. It was as if the majority of the population—or at least a significant segment of it—was strongly in support of Zhivkov's policies.

Gradually, however, with the emergence of Turkish-Bulgarian politicians, as mayors or as parliamentary deputies, Bulgarians began to see that their greatest fear—Islamic fundamentalism—was not a major concern in their country. In fact, motivated in part by a desire to please the European Union, leaders of the country's most influential political party announced a plan in October 1998 to integrate minorities (including Turks) into local and district administration, the police and army, as well as other areas of Bulgarian society. In short, the problem seems to be on the way to resolution, although one suspects that in a crisis it could still be resurrected by those looking for a scapegoat. This is one of the reasons why it is so important for Bulgaria to stay out of the conflict in former Yugoslavia and for it to continue to enjoy political stability even if the economic outlook remains bleak.

Greeks in Albania

For many years, Albania has had problems with Greece, primarily because of its Greek minority. Greek officials have complained that Albanian officials have carried out a policy of intimidation against Greeks who live in Albania, hoping to drive them out so that their land can be given to Albanians. For its part, the government in Tirana has claimed that Greece is guilty because of its efforts to foment succession plots on the part of Greek-Albanians. As far as the minority itself is concerned, its primary demand is for an expansion of Greek language education to all parts of the country. For its part, the Albanian government appears to be trying to satisfy the demands for education in the Greek language. The problem, however, is that given how chaotic the situation is within the country, any attempt by the Albanian government to come up with a rational solution to any kind of a problem is difficult if not impossible.

In addition, with the end of communism, thousands of Albanians went to Greece in search of work, willing to do jobs that many Greeks found beneath them. Gradually, segments of the Greek population began to argue that these Albanian interlopers were taking jobs away from Greeks and that they were contributing to a rising crime rate. The result was large-scale deportations by the Greek government—a situation that led to charges of human rights violations by the Albanian government. With this kind of history, one has to wonder if these ethnic conflicts can ever be solved. They certainly won't disappear in the near term.

Albanians in Macedonia

Finally, there is Macedonia, a former province of Yugoslavia. About 25 percent of the population is Albanian, and the rest is Macedonian. The rise of Albanian nationalism in neighboring Kosovo has had an important impact on some Albanians in Macedonia. Almost all of them have friends and relatives in Kosovo. They see their colleagues fighting for their ethnic rights and ask why they should not enjoy greater autonomy, if not independence themselves. Clashes have occurred between Albanian separatists and the police, resulting in several killed and injured Albanians. To make matters worse, more and more Macedonian families are moving out of Albanian neighborhoods in the capital of Skopje—a situation that is ethnically dividing the city. Tensions between average Albanians and Macedonians are on the rise, and incidents on the border with Albania have also increased. Finally, several bombs have been set off around government buildings. Some people claim that the Albanian underground army is responsible, while others maintain that the violence is an attempt to destabilize the Macedonian government. The important factor is that as long as this ethnic tension goes on—not far from the conflict in Kosovo—it will be difficult for the Macedonian government to create the kind of political institutions that are critical to the country and the systems' stability over the long run.

Bosnia and Kosovo

This brings us to the most difficult, and to this point, the most intractable ethnic problems facing the states of Eastern Europe: Bosnia and Kosovo. Both countries are in part a result of the breakup of the former Yugoslavia, and both countries are sources of instability, not only in their own regions but also in the states that surround them. Until both issues are resolved—if that ever happens—there will remain a danger not only for neighboring states like Croatia, Serbia, Greece, Bulgaria, Turkey, and Macedonia, but for the entire continent of Europe as well. What is to guarantee that an incident in one of the conflicts will not unintentionally spill over into one of these other countries? If that should occur, what guarantee is there that such an action will not lead to an even wider conflict?

This is not the time nor the place to revisit the highly complex and dangerous conflicts in Bosnia and Kosovo. Nevertheless, something should be said about the ethnic basis of the problems in these areas because they show how dangerous such conflicts can be if they are not resolved and how destabilizing they can be to efforts to build stable and viable polities.

If one factor seems to motivate Serbs when it comes to ethnic questions, it is a fear that if Serbs are not under the control of Serbia, they will be persecuted to the point of being eliminated. Lest the reader get the impression that this is a case of paranoia, the Serbs have good reasons to be worried about the safety of their fellow countrymen. During World War II, for example, some six hundred

Damage from war and ethnic conflict in the former Yugoslavia.

thousand Serbs were killed by the Croatian Ustashi, who were allied with Hitler's Germany. Other examples could be given—cases of brutality and worse by the Hungarians and Turks—but the most recent experience with the Croatians did a lot to influence their behavior vis-à-vis the rest of Yugoslavia's ethnic groups when the country collapsed. What is also important to remember is that this fear is not just a concern on the part of the elite. Rather, it is a deep-seated fear in the hearts and minds of the average Serb.

During the communist period, the charismatic, tough-minded Marshal Josip Broz Tito carried out a policy aimed at controlling ethnic tensions. Any sign of ethnic nationalism was quickly put down by the government in Belgrade. Great efforts were made to forge interethnic relations. As long as Tito was alive, the situation seemed to be working. With a few exceptions, no one dared to light the fires of ethnic discord and hatred.

With Tito gone, Slobodan Milosevic came to rely heavily on ethnic fear in his rise to power. The speech he gave in Kosovo telling Serbs that they would not have to continue to put up with discrimination and second-class citizenship like Albanians in Kosovo hit home and helped propel him to the country's highest office. He continues to play the nationalist card in his efforts to solidify his power, and every time he is threatened he harps on it. The point made here, without going into a lot of detail, is that ethnic fear is a very real factor when it comes to motivating Serbs in dealing with other ethnic groups.

This is the main reason why the Belgrade government did almost nothing when Slovenia, another former Yugoslav province, declared its independence. After a few scuffles between the Yugoslav army and Slovenian forces, the former withdrew. There were almost no Serbs in Slovenia, so Belgrade's incentive to keep Slovenia from becoming independent was minimal. This was not the situation, however, when it came to Croatia. Approximately 12 percent of the population was Serbian. Given the past history of discrimination, not to mention brutality against Serbs by Croatians, the Serbs could not stand the idea of their people coming under Croatian rule. As a result, it was not long before Croatia and Serbia were locked in a full-scale war, which in the beginning cost the Croatians a considerable amount of territory.

The situation with regard to Bosnia is even more complex. Almost 32 percent of the populace in Bosnia was Serbian. During World War II, many Muslims had served in German SS units and, in any case, the Serbs thought they were anti-Serbian in the sense that they would ally with the Croatians against the Serbs when it came to governing the emerging state of Bosnia-Herzegovina. The situation was further complicated by external factors. While efforts were under way to find a formula that would protect the Serbian populace from being dominated by their Croatian/Bosnian neighbors (who, by the way, had a higher birth rate), the German government issued a statement offering international recognition to any of the three states (Slovenia, Croatia, and Bosnia) that asked for it by the end of the year. This led two-thirds of the Bosnian government (made up of Croatians, Bosnians, and Serbs) to declare independence. As a result, the Serbs—who also feared that they would become even more of a minority given the high Muslim birth rate—withdrew from the government and took up arms.

The story of the Bosnian war is too grisly and has been told too many times to repeat here. Suffice it to say that the Serbs were better armed because they were able to make use of weapons the Yugoslav army had hidden in the mountains many years before in the event of a Russian invasion, and that the Bosnian Serbs carried out a policy of ethnic cleansing. The latter was not a new idea in the Balkans, but it was an effective one. In order to ensure that a piece of territory remained Serbian, those who were not Serbs were removed, either by forcing them to leave or by eliminating them physically. As far as the high Muslim birth rate was concerned, Serbs went after it by systematically raping Muslim women, believing that having been defiled these women would not be acceptable as marriage partners in an Islamic society. It is also worth noting that the Bosnian Serbs had the support of the Serbian government in Belgrade—in some cases, the latter denied its involvement, but it was clear that Milosevic and his colleagues were encouraging the Bosnian Serbs, supplying them with weapons, and providing them with refuge when they needed it.

As the war waged on, the West, including the United States, inevitably became involved. All concerned realized the danger that this war represented. Aside from the obvious human rights issues, who could be sure that it would not spread, with all of the disastrous consequences such a development would have for peace in Europe? After lengthy discussions failed to produce a settlement, NATO forces entered the fray, and once it became clear to all three parties—and especially the Serbs—that the West meant business, they signed an agreement in Dayton, Ohio, on December 14, 1995, that was supposed to bring peace to the region. Unfortunately, the agreement had a serious flaw. The Serbian Bosnians were represented by Milosevic, who was charged with ensuring that they complied with the agreement. It was a case of placing the fox in charge of guarding the chicken coop because Milosevic had the task of enforcing a peace plan designed to correct some of the wrongs he helped create.

Despite efforts to create a unified Bosnian government, to resettle those who were removed from their homes, and to bring war criminals to justice, little has been done since December 1995. NATO troops occupy much of the land and ensure that peace is maintained. When it comes to building a meaningful government, however, little has been accomplished. For practical purposes, all three ethnic sectors seem to be self-governing. Indeed, one of the West's primary concerns was to take control of the local government away from the Serb leader Radovan Karadzic, who was an indicted war criminal. While there has been some success in this area, most observers believe that it will be many years before NATO troops can be successfully removed. Any decision to remove them in 2000 would most certainly lead to renewed violence and hostilities. In the meantime, some efforts are underway to build the basis for a meaningful system of government, but they are rudimentary at best.

The situation haunting Kosovo is both very different and much the same as Bosnia. It is similar in that it is at base also an ethnic issue. The region is officially a province of the rump, Yugoslavia, which today consists of Serbia and Montenegro. The problem, however, is that Kosovo is about 90 percent Albanian. Under normal circumstances this would mean that the region would be part of Albania; however, the situation in this part of the world is far from normal because of the role of history. For centuries, Kosovo has been the heart of Serbian culture. Its first capital was in Kosovo, the mother church for Serbian Orthodoxy is there, and many years ago the Serbs suffered their most serious military defeat at the hands of the Turks there. For these reasons—all of which are celebrated and repeated in Serbian songs and poems as well as in children's textbooks—it remains an integral part of Serbia in the minds of the majority of Serbs.

During Tito's reign, the region enjoyed considerable autonomy for both the Albanian language and culture. This changed, however, when Milosevic came to power. He revoked Kosovo's autonmous status and returned direct rule to the Belgrade government. Despite numerous efforts at peaceful dialogue, it soon became clear that Belgrade was unyielding on ethnic-related questions. Instead, Milosevic clamped down by sending in special Serbian police forces. Their brutality and Belgrade's refusal to accommodate Albanian desires for increased autonomy gradually led to the rise of a more radical group, the Kosovo Liberation Army (UCK). The latter group has resorted to violence and has been carrying on a campaign to oust the Serbs in order to either proclaim independence or become part of Greater Albania. Meanwhile, the Serbs have stated repeatedly that they will never agree to let Kosovo go. As a result of the fighting, more than ten thousand Albanians are homeless and thousands—including women, children, and old men—have been either wounded or killed.

As in the case of Bosnia, the West inevitably became involved. NATO threatened the use of air strikes as a means of keeping the Serbs in line, later it bombed Serbia as well as Serbs in Kosovo. As soon as the UCK decided that Serbian mobility was limited, it quickly seized on the situation to step up its own combat operations—a situation that was bound to lead to renewed hostilities between the two sides.

As this book goes to press, it appears that the Bosnian situation will remain under control—at least as long as NATO forces remain there. Kosovo and Serbia were heavily bombed and the area remains in conflict. The issue of ethnicity remains volatile and could spread into other countries in the region. It has already had a major impact on Albania. For years, these problems were swept under the rug largely because of Tito's strict handling of such matters. Belgrade certainly tried to ameliorate the matter, but the collapse of the Yugoslav government showed just how tenuous the situation was. If nothing else, both of these incidents should serve as a warning to other countries in Eastern Europe who have serious ethnic problems. Ignoring them (as appears to be the case with the Roma in many countries) will not make them go away. Indeed, as long as they exist, they will work against the creation of viable, democratic regimes. What is even more dangerous, however, is a situation when the regime is placed under stress as happened in former Yugoslavia. There will always be those leaders like Milosevic who are prepared to play the ethnic card in an effort to build up their own power, even if it costs thousands of people their lives.

Ethnicity is a primitive form of political conflict, and it makes it difficult to build a viable nation-state when ethnic tensions are so strong. In fact, the primary effect of sustained ethnic conflict is that it does more to tear the country apart than to build it into a unified state. Because these conflicts divide people along ethnic lines, it also makes it difficult to build interest groups, which normally cross ethnic lines. For example, members of a union or the armed forces in the West usually place their union or military identity ahead of their ethnic background. "We are Bavarians and Berliners and Rhinelanders, but most of all we are German soldiers," is a way one might put it. Given the problems that ethnicity places in the way of building viable interest groups, which are the heart of democratic polities, it should come as no surprise that ethnicity undermines movement toward democracy as well. It also makes it difficult to bring the idea of compromise into political discourse, another key aspect of any democratic political system. Until the day comes that ethnicity is no longer the divisive factor that it is at present, the creation of a well-functioning, democratic policy will remain a dream.

THE CHALLENGE OF CREATING DEMOCRATIC POLITICAL INSTITUTIONS

Ethnicity is not the only problem that stands in the way of the creation of democratic political institutions in Eastern Europe. As noted previously, most of these countries do not have a tradition of democracy, a situation that the communist experience only complicated further. In essence, the communist governments tried to create a situation in which the individual was under the direct control of the party-state. This meant the elimination of intermediary structures or institutions, regardless of whether that meant churches, civic clubs, interest groups, political parties, or the educational system. Everything was to be under the control of the party-state. The goal was a completely atomized, isolated population available to implement whatever policy the party elite decided was appropriate to deal with the issue at hand.

It would be wrong to suggest that communism in Eastern Europe was totally successful in achieving its goal. Total control is an ideal type, and the situation in Eastern Europe never reached the point that it did in the former Soviet Union. In Poland, for example, the Roman Catholic church never succumbed to total control. Indeed, most observers agree that the election of the Polish Cardinal Karol Wojtyla to become Pope John Paul II played a significant role in the collapse of communism not only in Poland, but in the region as a whole. Of interest is the fact that the church enjoys the confidence of the population in countries such as Poland, Romania, Slovakia, and Hungary.[7] Nevertheless, under communism it remained difficult and almost impossible to have independent political activity outside of the party's control.

Interest Groups

The problem with interest groups in most of the countries of Eastern Europe is that they are very poorly developed. Take labor, for example. During the communist era, unions served primarily as transmission belts for the party-states. It was not their job to represent workers,

---

[7] David G. Gibson, "High Public Confidence in the Church," *Transition*, vol. 2, no. 7, 5 April 1996, p. 29.

rather it was their task to ensure that the workers met their quotas on time. Now, however, they are being asked to assume a very different position as an advocate for the workers. While labor unions appear to be trying to do their best to represent the interests of the workers, they still have a long way to go before they will be in the same class with those in the West. They are generally poorly organized, underfunded, and led by leaders who are at a minimum paid by the government. Many are nothing more than offshoots of political parties (themselves poorly organized), and in several instances little more than an extension of government bureaucracies. Indeed, even in the case of the Solidarity Union in Poland, one can argue that it is far less influential than it was under the communists. The loss of a focused enemy like the communists has permitted the union to fragment.

One good sign for the development of democracy in Eastern Europe is that the militaries in all of the countries covered by this chapter appear to more or less accept the new rules of the democratic game. Compared with the situation under the communist governments, all of them are much smaller, and most of the military establishments say they welcome the new regimes. There are still problems with some of the senior officers—who were inherited from the old regime—and there is no doubt that the armed forces are being starved for resources. In the latter instance, this includes the Czech, Hungarian, and Polish militaries, all of which claim they are being restructured to meet NATO standards. It is also worth noting that in countries such as Poland, Hungary, Romania, and Bulgaria, the military enjoys considerable public support. In short, the military is not an interest group that should be feared by the elites of any of these countries. Even in the less democratic states such as Serbia, the regime has been engaged in a regular process of purging those who even give an appearance of opposing Milosevic or his policies.

Interest groups such as students, business leaders, women, the media, and educational institutions often enjoy little autonomy. Even when they do have some freedom of action, however, they are under constant attack from the government, which is often made up of former communists who do not understand why such groups should be autonomous to begin with. Even when that is not the case, however, members of such organizations often lack the skills and background necessary to permit them to operate effectively in these countries. Often, they stand around waiting for someone to tell them what to do, or they act in a manner that is certain to alienate the people whose support is critical to the success of their mission.

Having said that, the fact is, however, that the communists did a rather good job in politicizing almost all societal institutions, from political parties to the boy scouts. As a consequence, all of these countries were forced to start from the bottom in building autonomous political structures. Nowhere was this more obvious than when it came to political parties.

Political Parties

Political parties existed prior to the imposition of communist regimes by the Soviets, but with the exception of Czechoslovakia, the vast majority were elite parties staffed primarily by members of the elite who ruled in the name of the masses. As a consequence, almost all of Eastern Europe lacks the kind of historical experience with political parties that countries like Great Britain, France, Italy, and Germany had. In both of the latter instances, the parties were either subverted or kidnapped by the ruling regimes. Once fascist rule was over in Germany and Italy, however, they reappeared, and many people who had been members of the socialist, Christian Democratic, or liberal parties worked to revitalize them. In Eastern Europe, on the other hand, with the collapse of communism, in many instances the populace was forced to start anew.

It is also worth noting that in countries like Germany and Italy, the major parties represented key economic and political interests. They represented what American political scientists have referred to as "social cleavages" (e.g., British Conservatives representing those from the upper social-economic strata as contrasted to the Labour Party representing the working class). In the cases of Germany and Italy, once the parties were re-created, they quickly went back to playing the kind of role they had in the past—representing specific interests! Peasant parties existed for some time in most of the countries of Eastern Europe, but even in these cases, they almost always served as a vehicle for a particular politician or a group of politicians to influence the political process with little concern about the status of the peasants themselves. Furthermore, in several cases, these parties were taken over by the communists (e.g., East Germany and Poland), so that when communism collapsed, they carried with them the legacy of having been collaborators.

Lacking interest-oriented political parties, it is not surprising that once communism collapsed, these countries were faced with a plethora of new parties—from the Maoists to the Beer Drinker's Party. A lot of these parties lasted only a short time because many of the countries had in place a process similar to the West German 5 percent rule (if a party does not achieve at least 5 percent of the vote in an election, it may not sit in parliament; however, even though many parties have gone by the wayside, it is still worth noting that several countries have four or five viable political parties. It is also worth emphasizing that political parties come and go. Often they serve as ego-enhancing creations of individual politicians because many of these individuals find it both fun and profitable to head up their own party. As a result, many of these mini-parties lack a program, ideology or—most important—mass support. If we again use the West German case as an example, a new party (e.g., the Greens) may arise, but it is a rare event. In countries like Germany or Britain, the established parties tend to remain part of the political scene even if the amount of power they enjoy fluctuates.

Personalizing Power

Another problem that the Eastern European states have experienced has been the "personalization" of political power. In essence, this means that rather than voting for a party, voters elect an individual. This again is the exact opposite of what tends to occur in Western Europe. For awhile this was a problem in Poland in the person of Lech Walesa. It was also a problem in the Czech Republic (Vaclav Havel), and it remains a most serious problem in places like Serbia, although one could legitimately argue that if a free election were held in that country, Milosevic would not win. Nevertheless, the personalization continues to stand in the way of developing democratic institutions. There is evidence, for example, in the Balkans that the police see their primary loyalty to the *individual* in power.[8] Needless to say, this is not the way things are supposed to work in a democracy. By and large, most of the countries of Eastern Europe appear to have passed this point. Issues seem to be more important than personalities, at least to the degree they were in the early years.

Even the processes whereby political parties exert their influence has been suspect in most of Eastern Europe. Take the example of elections. Under communism, voting was a party/state requirement. Little association existed in the minds of the populace between the act of voting and resultant policy decisions. Why should the average citizen assume that casting a vote would impact on the

---

[8]Stafan Karuse, "Balkan Police Forces More Loyal to the Leaders than to the Laws," *Transition,* vol. 2, no. 5, 8 March 1996, p. 19.

decisions made by the government? It never had in the past.

Once competitive voting became a reality after communism's fall, there was another problem. Lacking the kind of long-term experience with voting, many voters assumed an almost direct relationship between voting and policy outcomes. To illustrate: Individuals might vote for privatization while assuming that once such a policy was passed the economy would improve immediately—a sort of political "instant gratification." In fact, as anyone who lives in a democratic polity understands, the relationship is much more tenuous. Privatization is part of an overall process of transiting from a command economy to a mixed, capitalist one. The process is not nearly as simple as many people in Eastern Europe assumed was the case. This is one of the main reasons why the former communists were put back in power in several of these countries shortly after the end of communism. Voters naively assumed that by casting their votes for a particular party they ensured that economic prosperity would follow. When it did not, many of them became impatient and voted for what they knew or thought they knew; that is, at least under the reborn communists the situation would be more stable and predictable.

Writing Constitutions

Another problem faced by all of the countries of Eastern Europe has been the creation of a constitution. On one level, this means the writing of a document acceptable to all of the major players, which is not as easily done as might appear. Poland has made significant progress, but there remain those who would argue that it still has not come up with a full constitution since the end of communism. Equally important is the question of what the constitution means. Take the debate that raged in Poland between Walesa and the Parliament. The former's reading of the constitution suggested that he was in charge of the armed forces, while the Sejm (the Polish parliament) maintained that the president's powers did not extend that far. Trying to define what the constitution meant was a difficult process that led to some acerbic exchanges at times. In practice, however, all of the countries of Eastern Europe (at least those that claim to be democratic) will have to go through this process. The practical meaning of a country's constitution is not intuitively obvious to those concerned. It is a matter of political power, one that will only be decided in the arena of internal political debate and battles.

Corruption

Corruption also remains a problem that these countries have to deal with. It was rampant under the communist governments, and it refuses to go away. This problem has been a concern not only in places like Albania, but in more stable polities like the Czech Republic as well. In Albania, for example, the prime minister was arrested in July 1993 for abusing his official position and misappropriating state funds in connection with the delivery of Italian humanitarian assistance. One year later he was sent to jail for twelve years, although he only served four years and maintained that the action was politically inspired. Other senior government officials have also been convicted of corruption and sentenced to jail. Despite such actions, however, corruption remains rampant. No one can even pay their bills without a bribe. The same is true of things like medical care, regardless of whether it is private or government.

While the democratic process is much better established in the Czech Republic, corruption has also been a problem there. In 1993, it was disclosed that sixteen parliamentary deputies had used their parliamentary immunity to import cars without paying custom duties. Senior government officials have also been accused of taking bribes from businessmen interested in influencing their actions, and the Interior Ministry has admitted that evidence suggests that some civil servants—including in some cases, policemen—are also taking bribes.

Separation of Powers

One of the key components of a Western democratic polity like the United States is the principle of the separation of powers. Unfortunately, this has also been a problem in some parts of Eastern Europe. The judiciary has not traditionally had the prestige that it has enjoyed in the United States, and to make matters worse, most judges are from the old communist regime—individuals who were not used to enjoying the kind of judicial independence that democratic systems assume as a given. In Albania, for instance, the biggest problem for the development of an independent judiciary has been the executive's constant interference in its internal affairs. Judges are subject to political pressure, while defendants are denied basic human rights. When attempts to reform the judicial system are made, they are primarily used to consolidate the ruling party's power and to eliminate political rivals.

The situation was similar under Vladimir Meciar in Slovakia. The idea of a fully independent judiciary never seemed to occur to him. Similarly, in 1992, the government of Croatia had a judge transferred to a less important court after he ordered the release of a Serbian prisoner, and in Romania in 1992, the minister of justice fired a judge who accepted a claim by the opposition party against the president's candidacy. Other examples could be given: for example, a judge who was dismissed in Bulgaria because the government considered him to be too independent. This is not to suggest that the courts are powerless in all of the countries of Eastern Europe. To the contrary, in some cases, they have done a respectable job. The problem, however, is that in many instances, especially in the Balkan region, the independence of the judiciary is being blocked, and until the day comes that they are able to function effectively as a separate arm of the regime, the dream of a democratic polity will be just that.

The Media

Of all of the areas of political life that proponents of democracy proclaim, few are more important than the media. Called the "fourth estate" by many who see it as one of the four key components of a democratic polity, it is not surprising that it has received considerable attention from Eastern European elites. In authoritarian states such as Serbia, the press has been harassed on a regular basis. Serbian strongman Milosevic seemed determined to muzzle the press in order to silence any criticism of his regime. Even democrats such as Poland's Lech Walesa have gotten into the act. In 1994, he took advantage of a loophole in the country's Broadcasting Act to unlawfully dismiss three members of the National Radio and Television Council who had offended him.

Another problem associated with the media has been the question of what role journalists should play in a democracy. On the one hand, some journalists have argued that now that they are freed from the shackles of communism, they should become advocates for particular ideological or policy preferences—in the way that many European journalists act. On the other hand, some maintain that they should follow the American example and to the greatest degree possible avoid partisanship—they should attempt to become independent observers taking neither one side nor the other. The problem for journalists is that either approach is dangerous. The first type presents problems because once journalists decide to push a particular policy, they both undermine their purported objectivity and open themselves up to charges that they are supporting a particular party or regime. As far as objective individuals are concerned, they run the risk of both alienating those who believe they should advocate certain policies and

Warsaw is a bustling modern city and the site of the legislative buildings, the Sejim.

facing the wrath of those like Milosevic who do not want an objective analysis of the news.

In order to provide the reader with a better "feel" for the situation in Eastern Europe, we will now turn to a brief analysis of the situation in each of these countries. As this overview will show, some appear to be well on the way toward developing democratic political systems, whereas others appear to have a long way—one might argue that the distance is too far—to go.

Poland

Of all the countries discussed in this chapter, Poland has done the best job in transiting from a communist, centrally planned economy to a democratic, mixed economy. One of the first steps taken by the post-communist government was the writing of a constitution. Despite the recognition of the importance of this document, it took until 1997 before one was finally adoped. There were deep divisions in the country. Questions such as what the role of the Church should be (i.e., should the special role played by Roman Catholicism in the country be specifically mentioned in the constitution?), what the relationship between the president and the Sejm should be in the area of national security, or how the Polish nation should be identified all had to be resolved. In the period up to 1997, Warsaw survived by making use first of the old Stalinist constitution and then after 1992 by utilizing the *Little Constitution*. The lack of a full-blown constitution led to constant arguments and disagreements, which was not surprising given the fact that the country's politicians were trying to work out a new set of rules for running the country.

As far as the actual arrangements that were worked out, the Parliament is far stronger in Poland than is the executive. The president is head of state and is elected directly. He has a variety of powers, but none of them place him in a position similar to that of the powerful French president. As far as the legislature is concerned, power is concentrated in the lower house—the Sejm. Contentious issues (abortion, the role of the Roman Catholic church) are openly debated, and political careers are made in the Sejm. The Sejm also decides who will be the country's prime minister and passes bills on major legislation. Indeed, it is no exaggeration to suggest that the Sejm is the heart of the Polish political system.

As far as the question of political stability is concerned, Poland has been relatively stable. Major disputes raged between the Sejm and President Walesa while the latter was in office, and there have been at least eight prime ministers since 1989. Deep personality differences and battles both within coalitions and among the ruling party(ies) have often complicated the policy process and made it anything but the rational procedure Westerners are used to. This is not to say that it is not effective, nor that considerable progress is not being made toward creating a more stable and viable political structure. Rather, it is to note that Warsaw is still undergoing a trial-and-error process of governing, a situation that one author called "institutional experimentation."[9] There has been restructuring—for example, the Defense Ministry and the armed forces have undergone major surgery and the same thing could be said for other parts of the political system—but many other arrangements remain to be worked out. For example, the educational system, transporation, communications, banking, finance, and the bureaucracy all show the legacies of the communist era, and all of these organizations are still desperately in need of being reformed.

Nowhere has institutional experimentation been more evident than with regard to political parties. In the 1989–1990 period, there were dozens of parties. Over time, however, power came to rest in the hands of the left-of-center parties—either the former communists known as the Alliance of the Democratic Left or a coalition of smaller parties known as the Solidarity Electoral Action. Smaller parties continued to exist, but these two were clearly the most important in determining the country's future.

The democratic process is far from perfect in Poland—far too few citizens vote, for example—suggesting a degree of alienation and unhappiness of the obligatory voting common to the communist era. Voters are at long last free not to vote. In addition, there are still too many occasions when the policy process seems to get sidetracked because of differences of opinion over what the constitution says or means. Furthermore, popular dissatisfaction with the costs involved in the transition process led to the election of a government made up of communist successor parties. Most important, however, is the fact that these actions, which are part of the growing process in any democracy, have not interfered with policymaking. Poland may not yet be the stable, viable, prosperous democratic polity that its citizens would prefer, but it has certainly come a long way and gives every indication of moving farther in that direction.

The Czech Republic

In June 1992, the Czechoslovak Republic broke into two parts—the Czech Republic and Slovakia—in a process that has often been referred to as the "Velvet Revolution." The breakup was amiable, and few harsh words were used by either side. In fact, one could argue that if the split had been based on public feelings, it would have never occurred. Even in Slovakia, where a lot of people believed they had been discriminated against by the Czechs—who had traditionally occupied most of the country's governing positions—there was no groundswell of support for an independent Slovakia. Rather, it was a result

---

[9]Ray Taras, "Politics in Poland," in Gabriel A. Almond, Russell J. Dalton, and G. Bingham Powell, Jr., *European Politics Today* (New York, Longman, 1999), p. 381.

The historic district of Prague in the Czech Republic.

of political differences, of the decision by the Slovaks to vote against the election of Vaclav Havel as president of the country. In response, the Czech parliament confirmed him as President of the Czech Republic, and each part of the country went its own way.

The Czech government adopted its constitution in 1992. The Czech Republic is a parliamentary government with two chambers. The president's role is largely ceremonial, and the executive, under the control of the Prime Minister and his cabinet, is ultimately responsible to the Parliament. The country's major parties are based on economic interests, making them more like traditional Western political parties than is the case in the rest of Eastern Europe. As a result, political stability in the Czech Republic has been the highest of anywhere in Eastern Europe.

This is not to suggest that Prague has not faced its own problems. There has been an ongoing debate over how to deal with nongovernmental organizations, and the government has been rocked by corruption scandals on more than one occasion. Environmental concerns—a major problem throughout Eastern Europe—have also been raised. The country, now enjoying full-fledged capitalism for the first time, is quickly developing a robber-baron mentality.

As far as the party structure itself is concerned, it is still being worked out. The main outlines of the main parties appear fairly clear, but each election brings with it new items that define their parameters more clearly. Furthermore, there is still a serious weakness when it comes to interest groups on one side and political parties on the other. As far as the actual governing process, the country has been run by a series of coalitions, which have included smaller parties. One unique aspect of the Czech political scene has been the absence of a strong left-wing, former communist party—something that has been part of the political landscape in the rest of Eastern Europe. This may be a result of the failure of the ex-communists to adapt well to the new political situation.

Although some problems still need to be overcome, the fact is that the Czech Republic is well on its way toward consolidating its democratic political system. Along with Poland, it receives substanial foreign capital investment and its economy is booming, which is always a good sign for stability and democracy. The problem of the Roma constantly pops up, regional pressures are evident, and the government is pressured to do something about it. Whether or not its actions will suffice is something that only time will determine. In the meantime, the Czech populace seems to have accepted the democratic rules of governance as their own.

Slovakia

The situation in Slovakia is quite different from that in the Czech Republic. To begin with, the country was severely hurt by the economic dislocations that accompanied the breakup of Czechoslovakia. This situation has been worsened by the outdated nature of its economic institutions and the resistance on the part of the country's elite to making the kind of economic reforms that are necessary to introduce a market economy. Privatization proceeded much slower than in the Czech Republic or Poland, and unemployment has been rampant. Furthermore, the country has been forced to deal with serious minority problems. Given the concern on the part of Slovak politicians that they not appear to be too pro-Hungarian (and therefore anti-Slovak), there has been a tendency to avoid cooperating with the Hungarian political parties. Although the problems inherent in dealing with this very large minority are formidable, more progress could have been made if the other political parties were more willing to work with the Magyars.

Slovakia's most serious problem, however, has been its failure thus far to develop the kind of political parties that Poland and the Czech Republic have. The primary reason for this situation has been the domination of the political scene by one individual—the country's former prime minister, Vladimir Meciar. He has dominated Slovak politics to a far greater degree since the end of communism than was the case even with such charismatic figures as Vaclav Havel or Lech Walesa in the Czech Republic or Poland, respectively. Up until very recently, all politics revolved around Meciar. There are few *institutional* safeguards.

The combination of what amounts to "personalistic politics" and the bitter hatred that Meciar felt toward the country's president (Michal Kovac) further destabilized Slovak politics. After Kovac came to power in February 1993, he turned down several of Meciar's appointments and called for a broad coalition in an effort to overcome the political instability that had haunted Slovakia since its creation. Needless to say, Meciar took great exception at Kovac's attempts to "interfere" in his running of the government, even if the constitution gave Kovac the right to approve appointments and to make such calls for cooperation. The result was a free for all. Indeed, what was most dangerous was that the fights that took place between Meciar and Kovac were not only "dirty" (involving at one point the kidnapping of Kovac's son by Meciar's security police), but their fights also had the effect of undermining the constitution itself. The actions Meciar took were aimed at getting rid of his opponents through administrative means, thereby avoiding the electoral process. By continually trying to change the basic rules of the constitutional game, Slovakia's rulers could not avoid undercutting public confidence in the democratic process. The rules were only there to be broken; there was nothing sacred about them. Furthermore, the public could not avoid coming away with the impression that the only way that Meciar could remain in power was by creating crisis and confrontation—situations that could only be dealt with by changing the constitution.

The country lacks general agreement on a routine approach to deal with political issues. There is no acceptance of the rules of the game when it comes to politics. Every confrontation or disagreement threatens to become a crisis, which is not the best way to run a democratic government. The idea of compromise appears foreign to opponents on both sides. The situation was made worse by Meciar's tendency to rely on patronage and authoritarianism as his ruling style. If he did not like something, he either tried to ignore it, sidestep it, or beat it up.

Another problem faced by post-communist Slovakia is that political parties appear to be rootless when it comes to structure. They are highly personalized and constantly beset with fragmenting disagreements, thereby providing "a constantly shifting political landscape for voters and political leaders alike."[10] In the main, since about 1990, political parties have been of two kinds: one that supports Meciar and the other that opposes him. While one can certainly understand why Slovaks might oppose the domineering Meciar, that is not sufficient basis for a political party. Besides, parties built on such a foundation generally tend to collapse once the primary reason for their existence or cooperation (e.g., Meciar or the communists) disappears and no longer serves as a focal point for their actions.

Finally, as noted previously, Slovakia is confronted with a major problem in trying to decide how to integrate its Hungarian minority into the country. Not only does this situation create problems for the government in Bratislava in its relations with Western Europe, but it also makes governing more difficult. As long as the country cannot figure out how to include the Hungarian parties in the government (cooperating with the Hungarians is seen by many Slovaks as a sign that the individual involved is anti-Slovak), the ability of any government to function in a democratic fashion will be undermined. No country can claim to be democratic until it has found a way to guarantee minority rights.

On the positive side, all parties concerned accept the principle of genuinely free and open elections, a process that permits the expression of different points of view. This process led to the defeat of Meciar in September 1998 and the election of a new government that appears interested in moving in the direction of a more stable, routine, democratic political system. The new government under prime minister Mikulas Dzurinda has its task cut out for it. The civil service system and the secret police need overhauling, as does the judiciary. The privatization process must be cleaned up, and the media, which Meciar tried to muzzle, must be dealt with in a more even-handed manner. Most important, however, Slovakia must become like other democratic countries, which will mean avoidance of the politics of division that characterized Meciar's rule.

Hungary

Hungary has made important strides toward the creation of a democratic polity. The parliament is the country's primary decision-making body. It has the power to elect both the prime minister and the president. The latter has little real power. His authority is primarily symbolic. The parliament institutionalized power and came up with a formal set of rules rather quickly despite what looked to many observers to be a somewhat incoherent and chaotic start. The result has been a very predictable policy procedure. In fact, Hungary was the first country in Eastern Europe to have its government finish its full parliamentary term without being forced to call early elections. In contrast to the situation in Slovakia, policy is seldom personalized, and debates and disagreements seldom lead to major confrontations.

---

[10]Carol Skalnik Leff, "Dysfunctional Democratization?" *Problems of Post-Communism,* September/October 1996, p. 41.

The key parliamentary body is the National Assembly, which decides basic policy issues and elects both the prime minister and the president. In addition, the prime minister enjoys considerable authority—so much so that he often does not consult members of his cabinet when making policy proposals. Interest groups are still in their infancy, but having said that, there are signs, especially among trade unions, that they are beginning to emerge and play a more important political role. Environmental groups and others representing minorities or women have also begun to spring up. It will be some time, however, before they have been sufficiently institutionalized to enable them to play an important role in the political process. The important factor, however, is that they are free to organize and have begun to do so.

As far as political parties are concerned, there were problems in the beginning. From 1990 to 1994, forty-eight Hungarian parliamentarians changed their party affiliations.[11] In recent years, however, the party structures have moved closer to becoming institutionalized. There are now two somewhat fragmented parties. On the one hand are the former communists who now call themselves the Hungarian Socialist Party. On the other hand, the major party is the Alliance of Young Democrats. Power has alternated between these two parties in recent years. At one point, the Hungarian populace seemed primarily concerned with the kind of social amenities that were present under the old regime, and the socialists found themselves in power. This situation changed, however, as voters began looking for an alternative.

The situation in Hungary is not too different from that in Poland or the Czech Republic when it comes to development of a viable, functioning democratic political system. Considerable progress has been made. There remain problems to be sure—party structure remains fluid and not always grounded in economic interests, for example. Having said that, the prognosis for the land of the Magyars appears positive. With more time and continued patience, the prospects for the future look good.

Romania

Unfortunately, the situation in Romania is much less optimistic than in the countries to the north. Part of the reason for the slowness of change in Romania comes from the fact that the revolution occurring in 1989 was less against the communist system and more aimed at the person of Ceausescu and his wife. As a consequence, the new regime that took over after their death was still firmly in the hands of the communists. Ion Illescu and his National Salvation Front augured for little change in policy. It was as if nothing of significance had changed. What was even more surprising was that most Romanians seemed to accept this situation as legitimate. Attempts were made to unseat Illescu, but he continued to win popular support and as a result, little changed in the economic, political, or social spheres. The various elections seemed to be arguments against significant change.

In the Romanian political system, the president is dominant, a situation that gave Illescu considerable power and authority. He names the prime minister and appoints the government and in effect, "can exercise strong influence over day-to-day operation of the government."[12] He is also commander-in-chief of the armed forces. One of the clearest signs of just how powerful the president is comes from his ability to call a public referendum if parliament votes to remove him.

The decision by the Romanian electorate in November 1996 to elect Emil Constantinescu as president marked a major break with the country's Leninist past. It was nothing short of

---

[11]As cited in Leff, *Dysfunctional Democratization,"* p. 41.

[12]Andrew A. Michta, *The Government and Politics of Postcommunist Europe* (Westport, Praeger, 1994), p. 78.

a change of the guard, giving the opposition a chance to rule in place of the corrupt excommunists headed by Illescu.

Constantinescu's election, however, was but a beginning. The country still lacked the kind of trust and commitment to the values of democracy necessary to complete its transition from an authoritarian to a democratic polity. While Romanian politicians talked of democracy and their support for it, the fact was that there was a contradiction between their commitment to democracy and their continued reliance on authoritarian approaches to governing a country such as Romania.

Turning to parliament, the fact is that the country's new president has a major challenge before him. From 1989 to 1996, Romania was ruled almost entirely by presidential decrees, not a genuinely democratic process. The government also freely dismissed government officials from the opposition parties or those who disagreed with its policies.[13]

Even more upsetting is the climate of fear and anxiety that prevails in present-day Romania. Racism appears to be on the rise. In fact, there are even attempts to resurrect the fascist Iron Guard, which played an active role during World War II. Similarly, there have been efforts to rehabilitate the pro-Nazi dictator Ion Antonescu, and dissent has not been tolerated. Judges are still appointed (and fired) by the government, thereby giving the executive effective control over the judiciary. In short, Illescu and his colleagues were not ready to take a look back at the communist experience with an eye toward making the kinds of reforms in the system that would be needed to create a genuinely democratic political system.

The situation facing the country's new president is not a good one. The country is in shambles. Indeed, the *Economist* probably put it best when it observed in the aftermath of the resignation of the prime minister, "New Romanian man, old mess."[14] The problem is that the ruling coalition is badly split and unwilling to take the kind of steps that will be necessary to make meaningful reforms in the country's economy. The country faces a very high inflation rate, a declining GDP, and deteriorating living standards, and the Social Democrats (many of whom are ex-communist *aparatachiks*) have threatened to leave the coalition because they do not like the way the regime is handling the question of economic reform.

On the positive side, the ouster of Illescu shows that many Romanians desire political change. The question, however, is just how strong the desire is to move toward a more democratic polity. The resignation of the country's prime minister in 1998 suggests that the ideas of compromise and mutual understanding are not well understood among those who ousted Illescu. Even if there were to be a desire for change, the country has a long way to go. Not only must it come to grips with its minority problems, including both Gypsies and Hungarians, but its political parties are also at best in their infancy, and the rules of governance and the ideas of a civil society and democracy are not well understood either by the populace or the governing elite. This is not surprising given the strict authoritarian nature of Illescu's time in office. Having noted that, however, the fact is that a lot of work must be done not only to build up parties, but also to ensure that they do not remain the kind of personalized organizations they have been in the past.

Bulgaria

In 1989, it appeared that the old regime was prepared to make the kind of concessions that would help move the country toward democracy. Petar Mladenov, who took over from long-time

---

[13] Vladimir Tismaneanu, "Tenuous Pluralism in the Post-Ceausescu Era," *Transition*, vol. 2, no. 26, 27 December 1996, p. 8.

[14] April 4, 1998.

communist boss Todor Zhivkov, quickly admitted that the communists had made mistakes. The new president then moved to end press censorship, stop persecuting Turks, and to call on those who had left for Turkey to return. He permitted the opposition to enter the political arena and stated that he would clip the wings of the country's secret police. Of particular importance was his decision to remove the clause in the constitution that gave the communist party special status.

Mladenov resigned the next year, but what was of critical importance was the fact that the country continued to be run by communists. The new government was clearly more liberal than the old one—and changed its name to the Bulgarian Socialist Party—but like Romania, those in power were from the old regime. The type of transfer of power that took place in Poland or Hungary was missing.

What was most surprising to Western observers was the outcome of the election in June. The "reformed" communists won more than 52 percent of the vote.[15] The communists were still running the country, while the opposition was heavily fragmented. In essence, what they tried to do was to reform the country's economy while maintaining most of the existing state structures. Unfortunately, the election of the communists had an important international effect because international institutions hesitated to give the government in Sofia significant amounts of economic assistance. Many people asked why they should provide aid to papered-over communists. The result was a downturn in the country's economic status.

By the following year, the country was in economic shambles, with Bulgarians standing in lines and clearly showing their discontent in demonstrations. The result was a major change in electoral fortunes in October 1991.

In this instance, the opposition (Union of Democratic Forces) won a majority of seats in the country's Parliament and began to introduce several democratizing procedures.

As far as the country's president is concerned, his power is limited. In fact, his role is largely symbolic, restricted primarily to representative functions. Unlike other countries in the Balkans, Bulgaria enjoys a free, independent judiciary. Likewise, the press and the media are also free.

Despite what might appear to be normal institutional structures, the fact is that the country has been very unstable politically. For example, between 1990 and 1997, Bulgaria had seven governments and three parliaments. All of them have tried and failed to deal with the country's economic problems, primarily because the populace does not seem prepared to pay the economic price that major reforms would entail. In fact, during that period, Bulgaria had more in common with the more often than not ineffective and outdated Italian political system than it did with those of Poland or Hungary. Many of the state structures remained in place from the communist period, standing in the way of government efficiency and undercutting its ability to introduce economic reforms. As far as the opposition is concerned, it remains fragmented, while the ruling socialists' response to the country's problems has been to ignore them by putting their heads in the sand like an ostrich.

The country's economy is in shambles and the populace is demoralized. The currency has collapsed, real wages have plummeted, inflation is up (200 percent by the end of 1996),[16] and poverty is widespread and corruption rampant. What future is there for the country? The political structure appears unable or unwilling to deal with these deep-seated eco-

---

[15]As cited in Andrew Michta, *The Government and Politics of Postcommunist Europe*, (London, Praeger, 1994), p. 93.

[16]Radek Sikorski, "The Death of Bulgaria," *The National Review*, November 25, 1996.

nomic problems. Indeed, the country's legacy is one of overcentralization in almost every sphere. How is one to build a democratic polity when a civil society is lacking? How can one expect Bulgarians not to look to Sofia to solve their problems when that is the way such matters have been handled for centuries? How can a political party that is really a coalition of fifteen other parties, held together primarily by its dislike for the former communists, be expected to accept the economic necessity of closing down factories, when such actions will mean the loss of thousands of jobs, including those of most of their supporters who were in the streets demonstrating for change? Furthermore, if Sofia does not deal with such issues effectively, the only alternative most Bulgarians see is to go to the streets and to demonstrate.

If there is a ray of hope, it is that the electoral process is open and is working (why else would the socialists have lost and accepted that fact?), and the IMF is pushing the Bulgarian government hard to decentralize and to introduce reforms in return for the outside assistance it so desperately needs. The task will not be easy, however. Bulgaria is not like Russia, which has a plethora of raw materials just waiting to be tapped. It has roses, which play a major role in making perfume, and it exports canned fruit. Furthermore, the entrepreneurial spirit so evident in countries like Poland and Hungary is missing in Bulgaria.

Meanwhile, the country's ethnic problem with the Turks remains unresolved. It is not as bad as is the case with Hungarians in Slovakia or Gypsies throughout the region, but it continues to stand in the way of democratic stability.

If there was ever an instance of political culture holding back the drive toward democracy, it is Bulgaria. Almost all factors seem to work against the creation of a civil society and the kinds of decentralization that will be critical if the country is to solve its political and economic problems.

Albania

If another example is needed to make the situation in Bulgaria look good, it is Albania. Long known as the "poor man" of Europe, since the collapse of communism, Albania has also gained the distinction of being one of the most unstable, corrupt, and unpredictable countries in the region. It seems to go from one crisis to another, while the danger that the crisis in Kosovo could slip over into its territory and lead to a war with Serbia remains very much a possibility.

Of all the countries of Eastern Europe, Albania was the most orthodox and rigidly Stalinist. Enver Hoxha ruled the country with an iron hand, effectively isolating it from the rest of Europe, while enforcing one of the strictest forms of centralized control known to modern politics on his people. Anything even remotely resembling independent groups were thoroughly penetrated and more often than not destroyed. To take just one example, in contrast to the strong Roman Catholic church in Poland, Hoxha declared that Albania was the world's finest atheist state. Priests and other religious leaders were quickly and effectively eliminated. In short, Albania went into the postcommunist period fearful of the ever-present secret police, while lacking the kind of associational tradition that was common to some other areas in Eastern Europe (the Czech Republic, for example). Furthermore, if the communists left any legacy, it was the arbitrary use of power. The idea that individuals can act within the political sphere only according to certain rules and regulations was an idea unknown to those who took over power when communism collapsed. Furthermore, from the public standpoint, the impact of this arbitrary form of rule was an attitude of political apathy and conformism. Why rock the boat? Better to behave oneself and leave politics alone.

The first free Albanian elections took place in March 1991. The communists won the cities, while the opposition was in the countryside. The results were similar to those in Bulgaria; the communists won two-thirds of the seats in parliament.[17] Throughout the remainder of the year, the country was beset with demonstrations—in fact, they deteriorated to the point where the communists (who now called themselves the Albanian Party of Labor) were forced to call new elections in 1992. In the event, the opposition Albanian Democratic Party won, placing the communists in the minority. Indeed, one of the most important accomplishments of the country's post-communist government was that the transfer of power was carried out with a minimum of violence, which was somewhat surprising given the brutal nature of communist rule under Hoxha. Few would have expected the communists to give up so easily and so peacefully.

During the early years, things appeared to be going well in Albania. By 1994, it was one of the more stable, if poorer, countries in Eastern Europe. Human rights appeared to be protected, and great efforts were being made to establish not only order but the rule of law as well. Despite this promising start, however, the evolution of politics in Albania since the end of communism has been nothing short of a disaster.

There are several reasons for the failure of the democratic experiment in Albania. First, there is the issue of corruption. By 1995, it had become almost impossible to get anything done in the country—from seeing a physician to getting a driver's license—without paying a bribe. The result was, despite claims by the country's leaders that they were tackling corruption, that the public had the impression that little had changed in this area. Corruption was a problem under the communists and it remained one today—What has changed? The situation was made worse by the disillusionment that many Albanians felt with regard to the economic reforms that were introduced. For many, it was like corruption—a means of enriching the country's privileged few.

Similarly, the governance process has been marked by constant upheavals. In one instance, within the space of one year, there were four different governments—not an action that is likely to build public confidence in the regime. Furthermore, rather than the kind of political parties that normally exist in democratic polities, Albania has seen a variety of coalitions—and in several instances, members of the coalition who have not gotten their way have resigned—thereby bringing down one government after another.

Then there is the question of the country's judicial system. From all appearances, it is far from the independent judiciary that a democratic polity assumes as a given. At least one senior politician was sent to jail for corruption. He has argued, however, that the real reason for his arrest and imprisonment was political—his opponents wanted him out of the way—while others have accused political leaders of trying to use the judicial system to further their own political careers.

Of the items that destabilized Albania during the post-communist period, none was more important than the so-called pyramid scheme. The scheme began operating in 1992. It offered high interest rates and, in the beginning, it appeared to be a successful venture. Albanians bought these "shares" thinking they were helping create capitalism, with an instant payoff. Wealth would now flow into their pockets automatically. In fact, the increasing numbers of investors who were attracted by this scheme had little or no idea of what capital investment meant. In the end, it was all a facade, a scheme sponsored by the government. They offered monthly interest rate returns of 25 percent or more. As you might expect, it was only a matter of time before the scheme collapsed. Soon Albanians were rioting in the streets—the worst riots since the fall of communism in 1991. The president and his government were accused of profiting from these schemes, and buildings were burned all over Albania. The Democratic Party chairman,

---

[17]As cited in Michta, *The Government and Politics of Postcommunist Europe*, p. 119.

Albanians protesting a failed Ponzi scheme ("get rich quick") launched by their own goverment.

Tritan Shehu, tried to calm a protest in a city south of Tirana and was badly beaten by the crowd. Feeling itself under siege, the government responded with force—an action that only further inflamed the situation as policemen were seized and beaten by angry crowds. The long-term result was a further deterioration of the country's economic status and a growing sense of cynicism on the part of most Albanians about their government. The then-existing government was forced to resign in March 1997.

By 1998, the situation had continued to worsen. In September 1997, for example, one of the opposition leaders was assassinated in the center of Tirana by assailants wearing police uniforms. The government was blamed, and opposition elements took to the streets burning a government building. Terrorist acts took place all over the country. In August 1998, one of the country's biggest hydroelectric power plants was blown up, while during the next month the headquarters of the socialist party in the northern town of Lezhe was also blown up. To make life even more difficult for the government, during the riots of early 1997 some seven hundred thousand firearms were stolen from army depots, and only one hundred thousand have been returned so far.[18] In fact, government control over the northern part of the country is questionable. Then there is the impact of events in Kosovo. The Serbian secret police have been active in these regions, and the Serbian army and police have from time to time crossed over the border in an attempt to control the Albanian Liberation Army. Refugees from Kosovo are also a problem. Thousands have already crossed into Albania, and others are likely to follow, thereby further straining the country's already seriously limited economic resources, not to mention its ability to control its own borders. There also remains the problem of the Greek minority in Albania.

As this book goes to press, Albania seems determined to self-destruct. In September 1998, for example, there was an attempted coup by one of the country's former leaders and the resignation of the country's prime minister. Meanwhile, the country still does not have a constitution despite efforts to draft one since 1991. It is possible that a constitution will be adopted in the near future, but what if

---

[18]Andi Bejtja, "Albania Spins Out of Control," *Transitions,* vol. 5, no. 10, October 1998, p. 45.

it is? With the country's economy in shambles, little progress made in the development of a democracy, and the danger that it will be increasingly enveloped in the conflict in Kosovo, the outlook for stability, let alone a democratic political system, is not good.

Former Yugoslavia

If there is one success story from former Yugoslavia, it is Slovenia, the former country's northernmost province. This small (population two million), picturesque country has been spared the horrors of war that has been a daily reality in areas such as Kosovo, Croatia, and Bosnia. Furthermore, considerable progress has been made in creating democratic political institutions.

Slovenia's first free election were held in 1990, and a constitution was adopted one year later. Primary power is in the hands of the parliament. The country has a president, but his power is largely ceremonial and representational. The status of the country's small minorities (Italians and Hungarians) is guaranteed and there have been few complaints, especially since Slovenia goes out of its way to permit them to use their own language whenever it makes sense.

Croatia is a somewhat different story. Born in the midst of a major war with Serbia, it has had an authoritarian form of government since its founding. Regardless of how desirable one may consider a democratic Croatia to be, it is hard to imagine a situation in which major democratic reforms will be introduced until the Bosnian situation is finally settled.

Croatia has a constitution that provides for a bicameral legislature and a president. The problem is that in the face of the problems the country has faced since its founding, the president has assumed special powers and is prepared to override the legislature by issuing emergency decrees because there is a war or national emergency. Only when matters return to normal in the region will it be reasonable to expect the country to get back on the road to developing democratic institutions, assuming of course that is what its leadership and populace decide they want for a government.

Finally, and most important, there is Serbia.[19] Proclaimed the "Third Yugoslavia" by the constitution of 1992, Serbia has made limited progress on the road to creating a democracy. In fact, it remained until 2000 a country controlled by one man—Slobodan Milosevic. The latter's position was consolidated in 1992 as the result of an election that many consider to have been rigged because there were widespread voting irregularities. In fact, a CSCE monitoring commission maintained that as many as 5 percent of the votes cast were not registered.[20] After that, Milosevic consolidated his position and ignored and manipulated the country's democratic constitution. For example, on July 15, 1998, Milosevic was elected president of Yugoslavia because the constitution of Serbia prohibited a president from serving more than two terms. He simply changed horses, but in practice the new position did nothing to weaken his hold on the country. Likewise, he had his rubberstamp parliament pass new election laws that ensured that elections could easily be manipulated in the future. For practical purposes, he controlled the state media and utilized it to his advantage. As far as the private media is concerned, he harassed it whenever he believed it was getting out of line. The idea of a free press was an anathema to him. When he became concerned about plots against him, he dismissed those he suspected—as happened in

---

[19] The situation in Macedonia and Bosnia will not be discussed here. In the case of the first, the situation is dominated at present by the ethnic issue, while in the latter, things are so fluid that there is little one could say that would not be out of date by the time this book is published. Suffice it to say that at the instigation of the West, efforts are being made to work out a reasonable arrangement between all three ethnic groups, although few observers realistically believe that it will ever be possible to create a viable, democratic, stable government comprising all three ethnic groups in the near future.

[20] As cited in Michta, *The Government and Politics of Postcommunist Europe*, p. 114.

the military. For a long time, the opposition was split and ineffective.

This is not to suggest that Milosevic did not have problems, because he certainly did. His country lived under sanctions imposed by the West, which had a serious negative impact on the country's economy. In a similar vein, he faced a challenge from President Milo Djukanovic, of Montenegro, another former Yugoslav province, who was an open critic of Milosevic's behavior. Milosevic refused to recognize Djukanovic's 1998 election victory and carried out an economic boycott of Montenegro in an effort to force him out of office.

Then there is the problem of Kosovo. Milosevic used this conflict for his own ends. The problem, however, was that he could not control it. He went beyond the bounds of acceptable behavior in carrying out ethnic cleansing. His thugs stole, raped, and killed at will. The United States and NATO retaliated with massive bombing, leaving both Serbia and Kosovo in shambles.

The fact of the matter is that although Serbia has formal, democratic institutions in place, nothing in the way of democracy could happen until Milosevic left the scene. When that happened in 2000, one could only hope that he would be replaced by someone from the opposition who was dedicated to democracy. The problem, however, is that the opposition is deeply split, and one cannot be certain that Milosevic will not be replaced by one of his lieutenants. What is even more worrisome is that there are those in Serbia who are even more nationalistic and further to the right. What if one of them were to come to power? As a result, the issue of democracy in Serbia must remain a question mark for the indefinite future. Many Serbs would like nothing better than to see the introduction of democracy. Unfortunately, there may be even greater numbers who would prefer to continue the kind of authoritarianism that has been Serbia's chosen form of government for many years.

Regardless of where one looks, problems abound when it comes to creating democratic institutions in the region; ones that will last for the indefinite future. One of the biggest problems is that while many in the region recognize the kinds of problems facing their particular country, it is not clear that they have either the will or the knowledge to do what is required to create viable democracies.

The situation is made worse by the deep-seated problems facing the area. This is not Scandinavia, a region rich in resources where strong economies are available to provide support for democratic experiments. Take, for example, social welfare. The populace in the area expect the government to take care of them, yet neither time nor money is available to provide such luxuries. The result is a combination of increased cynicism toward the various regimes (the government cannot deliver as the populace believes it is supposed to) and an increasingly more difficult task when it comes to creating democratic polities. For example, there is the legacy of communism. It may sound mundane, but communism continues to influence the thinking and behavior of large segments of the population in Eastern Europe. One most evident legacy is the presence of massive environmental damage throughout the area. Some areas have become almost uninhabitable, and it will take years before the scars left by the Soviet army and unrestrained economic development are removed.

To make matters worse, factors such as rampant corruption, patronage, and the lack of familiarity with the rules of democracy—the idea of compromise just to mention one—inhibit the development of democracy in the area. Then there is the tendency on the part of many segments of the population to identify democracy with economic affluence. Because the movement toward a more open economy has been difficult, and will take many years to complete, there has been a feeling on the part of some that democracy is a failure. Instead of bringing about instance economic affluence, it has often led to a drop in the living standard of much of the populace. Few in this part of the world understand that the construction of a viable capitalist economy is a long-term undertaking. It may be ten or twenty years or even longer before anything approaching economic affluence becomes a reality in the region. In the meantime, it will be increasingly difficult to convince the populace to stick with the experiment in democracy. Why should they?

POLICY CONCERNS

While each of these countries has its own particular policy concerns, whether that be the development of democracy, fighting corruption, improving its economy, or how to handle ethnic issues, one issue is overriding for all of these states—with the possible exception of Serbia—at the present time. That is the issue of ties with the West and, in particular, membership in the NATO Alliance. Getting NATO and Western Europe to accept them has been their overwhelming concern during the past five years, and it is likely to remain so for the indefinite future.

For the first time since prior to World War II, the countries of Eastern Europe found themselves alone—independent of the former U.S.S.R.—in 1989.[21] For awhile, it appeared that the northern three countries—Poland, Hungary, and Czechoslovakia—would join forces in an effort to improve their defense and political relationship in what came to be known as the Visegrad group. In fact, little came of what many people thought would be a positive, viable relationship, and what many Poles, Czechs, and Hungarians believed would develop into a means of increasing their influence when dealing with the countries of Western Europe.

Given the failure of the Visegrad relationship, it became increasingly clear to the leadership of all of the countries of Eastern Europe that if they hoped to avoid being stuck in what might be called a "never, never" land half way between Russia (with all of the instability and potential threat that country represented) and Western Europe, they would have to take steps to tie themselves to the west. The alliance—the Warsaw Pact—that had tied them to the east for almost forty years was gone! There was nothing readily available to replace it.

As far as the West was concerned, in the beginning only the Council of Europe appeared interested in embracing these countries. As far as NATO and the European Union were concerned, they adopted more of a "standoff" approach. NATO invited these countries to join NATO's parliamentary assembly, but only in 1994 were they asked to become members of NATO's Partnership for Peace program. By the end of 1995, NATO had begun to draw up the criteria for eventual membership but refused to provide a clear time table. The same was true of the EU. It has offered associate membership to several of the states but has failed to provide full membership or to even specify a firm date by which they would be admitted.

As a result of continued Eatsern European lobbying, as well as strong support from ethnic groups in the West, and especially the American Secretary of State, NATO began to take seriously expanding its membership to include countries from the region. At first, it appeared that five countries, including Poland, the Czech Republic, Hungary, Slovenia, and possibly Romania, might be included among the first installment. The latter two had especially strong support from France. From the beginning, Russia adopted the public stance of strong opposition to NATO's eastern expansion, arguing that it would both move NATO's border that much closer to Russia and increase the potential military threat the country faced.

---

[21]Some of the ideas in this section are taken from Ronald H. Linden, "The Age of Uncertainty: The New Security Environment in Eastern Europe." *Problems of Post-Communism,* September/October 1996, pp. 3–14.

In the end, however, NATO agreed to consider three countries—Poland, Hungary, and the Czech Republic. NATO took this action despite clear evidence that none of these countries was ready from a military standpoint. All three had armies that had serious deficiencies when it came to interoperability and modernization.[22] When and if the other countries will be permitted to join NATO remains an open question. There are those who fear that by including a second installment the Baltics would inevitably be a matter of concern. The Kremlin would clearly object strongly to including these additional countries in NATO, and such an action could have a major impact on East-West relations, a situation already made precarious by the uncertainty surrounding political and economic conditions within Russia.

As this book goes to press, it is hard to predict what will eventually happen when it comes to NATO or EU membership for these countries. The only thing that is certain is that all of them will continue to push as hard as possible to expand their ties to the West for political, economic, and strategic reasons.

CONCLUSION

In the first part of this chapter, it was suggested that the task of developing democratic institutions would be easier for some countries than for others. Based on the preceding discussion, it would appear that this is certainly the case. Countries in the north and those that have a stronger Western orientation and strong economies and institutions appear to be doing the best. Poland, the Czech Republic, Hungary, and Slovenia seem to be well on their way toward creating democratic polities. Slovakia is a bit of an exception, largely because of Meciar's seizure of power after Czechoslovakia broke up. His heavy-handed approach to running the country did little to advance the democratic agenda.

The situation in the southern countries, commonly known as the Balkans, including Romania, Bulgaria, Albania, and the former Yugoslavia (with the exception of Slovenia), has been quite different. In each instance, these countries have a long way to go before they can be considered to be on the road to developing stable, functioning democracies. As far as the various countries that made up the former Yugoslavia (with the exception of Slovenia) are concerned, that is understandable, both because of the political culture that has been hostile to the creation of democracy, as well as the civil war that has been raging in the area off and on for eight years. Romania and Bulgaria have some of the institutions of democracy, and the former has acted in a manner that suggests that it may begin to move in that direction. Having said that, however, the experiment with democracy in Romania remains fragile.

This brings us to the following question: What are the chances for democracy in Eastern Europe? Recognizing the difficulty of predicting events in that part of the world, I am optimstic with regard to the northern regions and Slovenia, mildly optimistic with regard to Romania, somewhat pessimistic about Bulgaria, and pessimistic with regard to Albania, Bosnia, Macedonia, Kosovo, and Serbia.

If there is hope for democracy in Eastern Europe, it comes from an outside source. In this regard, I have in mind external factors—the almost irresistible attraction of the West—in particular NATO and the European Union. All of the countries of Eastern Europe are highly desirous of membership in both bodies. They see one as the key to security and the other as indispensable to economic affluence. Both of these institutions impose strict democratizing criteria for membership. NATO, for example, will not accept a country if it does not have an effective form of civilian control over

---

[22]Dale R. Herspring, "After NATO Expansion: The East European Militaries," Problems of Post-Communism, January–February, 1998, pp. 10–20.

the military. Similarly, the EU requires members to guarantee minority rights. The point is that all of these countries will be under considerable pressure to conform to membership requirements, which puts a premium on the existence of a viable, functioning democracy.

Despite the importance of external stimuli, the ultimate decision of whether or not to democratize and whether to create the kind of political systems that many in this part of the world say they want will be an internal decision. The West cannot force these countries to become democratic, however many people would like to see this happen. There will have to be a general agreement on the part of the majority of the population and the ruling elite of each country in support of things like ending corruption, creating a separation of powers, establishing a free and open media, and the like. Just as one could argue that it will be increasingly difficult for a demagogue to stop the institutionalizing process that seems under way in Poland, it could just as well be argued that institutionalizing democracy in places like Bulgaria and Serbia will be equally difficult. Most of the prerequisites seem to be in place in countries like Poland, Slovenia, Hungary, and the Czech Republic. Although some of the structures are present in countries like Romania, Bulgaria, Croatia, and Albania, there is a serious lack of commitment to the process, and the effort to institutionalize democracy has not really begun.

The path to democracy in Eastern Europe will not be an easy one; indeed, it is by no means certain that all of the countries in the region will meet that goal. About the only thing that appears certain as this book goes to press is that change will be the one constant in the region, and the pace and direction of change will be different in each country. They all have different political cultures, and they are all at different stages of economic and political development. Some are more affluent and democratic, whereas others lag behind in both areas.

Looking ahead, it is clear that just as none of the countries are the same now as they were ten years ago, it is a safe bet that none of them will be in the situation in which they find themselves ten years from now. We can only hope that all of them will chose democracy and a more decentralized, capitalistic-type economy. Most important, however, is the hope that all of them will have the sustaining power necessary for them to reach those goals.

The frustrating part for those living outside the region is the realization that while we can support positive developments in this part of the world, when it comes down to it, there is little we can do to convince the people of Eastern Europe of the advantages of democracy and a more open economy. That belief will have to come from them.

SUGGESTED READINGS

Barany, Zoltan, and Ivan Volgyes, *The Legacies of Communism in Eastern Europe* (Baltimore, Johns Hopkins Press, 1995).

Cohen, Lenard J., *Broken Bonds,* 2nd ed. (Boulder, Westview, 1995).

Crawford, Keith, *East Central European Politics Today* (Manchester, Manchester University Press, 1996).

Fulbrook Mary, *Anatomy of a Dictatorship: Inside the GDR, 1949–1989* (Oxford, Oxford University Press, 1995).

Gros, Daniel, and Alfred Steinherr, *Winds of Change: Economic Transition in Central and Eastern Europe* (London, Longman, 1995).

Kaplan, Robert D., *Balkan Ghosts* (New York, St. Martins, 1993).

Leff, Carol, *The Czech and Slovak Republics* (Boulder, Westview, 1997).

Longworth, Philip, *The Making of Eastern Europe* (New York, St. Martins, 1997).

Michta, Andrew, *The Government and Politics of Postcommunist Europe* (New York, Praeger, 1994).

Taras, Raymond, *Consolidating Democracy in Poland* (Boulder, Westview, 1995).

White, Stephen, Judy Batt, and Paul Lewis (eds.), *Developments in East European Politics* (Durham, Duke University Press, 1993).

9

ICELAND
Norwegian Sea
Kirun
Rovaniemi
Lulea
Umea
FINLAND
SWEDEN
Vaasa
North Atlantic Ocean
NORWAY
Gulf of Bothnia
Tampere
Gavle
Helsinki
Stockholm
ESTONIA
Goteborg
Baltic Sea
Inverness
North Sea
LATVIA
DENMARK
IRELAND
Dublin
LITHUANIA
Leeds
Copenhagen
Cork
Leicester
Hamburg
U. K.
POLAND
NETHERLANDS
London
Amsterdam
Berlin
BELARUS
Brussels
GERMANY
Bonn
English Channel
BELGIUM
LUX.
Frankfurt
CZECH REPUBLIC
Paris
Stuttgart
SLOVAKIA
Nantes
MOLDOVA
AUSTRIA
FRANCE
LIECH.
Vaduz
HUNGARY
Clermont-Ferrand
Geneva
SWITZERLAND
SLOVENIA
ROMANIA
Bay of Biscay
Bordeaux
Lyon
Milan
Venice
CROATIA
Toulouse
BOSNIA
SERBIA
Marseille
Florence
Porto
MONACO
Valladolid
BULGARIA
ANDORRA
ITALY
Adriatic Sea
MONTENEGRO
Coimbra
Salamanca
Rome
PORTUGAL
Madrid
MACEDONIA
Barcelona
Lisbon
SPAIN
Valencia
Naples
ALBANIA
Palma
SARDINIA
Cordoba
GREECE
Aegean Sea
Sevilla
Tyrrhenian Sea
Malaga
Palermo

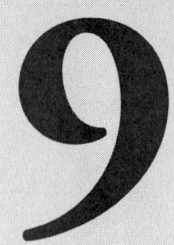

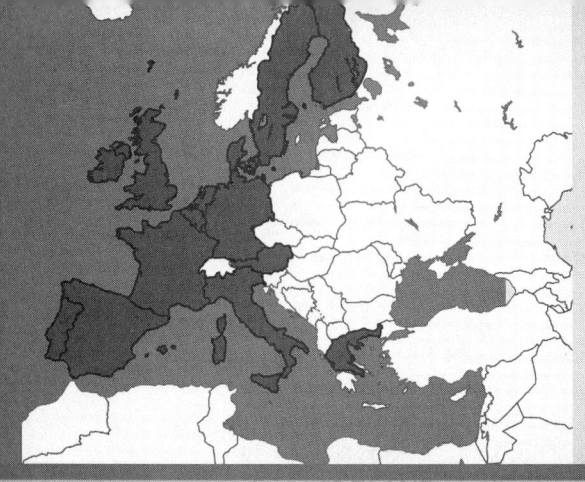

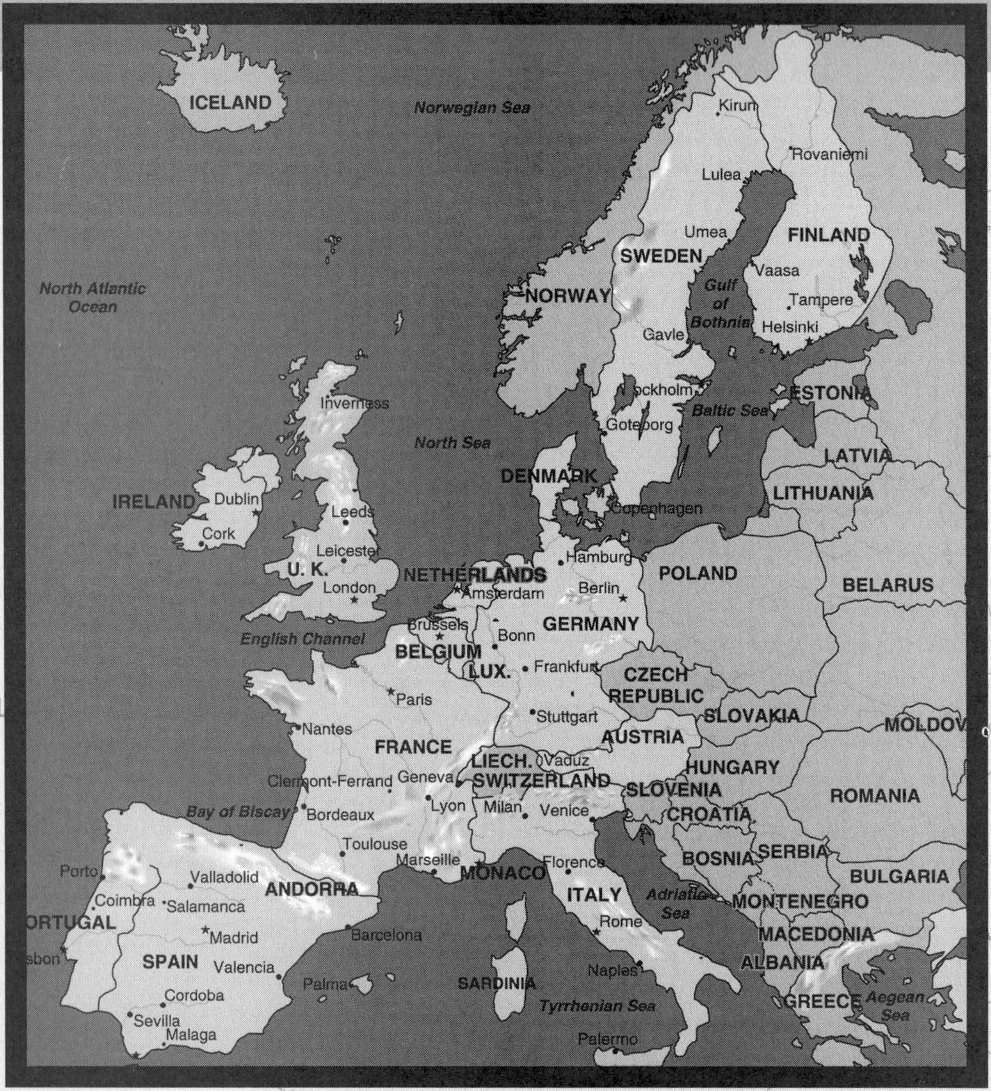

The European Union

Expanding and Deepening

John McCormick

THE EUROPEAN UNION*

Population: 373,300,000
Land Area: 3.14 million sq. km.
Gross National Product: $8 trillion

*Fifteen member states: Austria, Belgium, Denmark, Finland, France, Germany, Greece, Ireland, Italy, Luxembourg, The Netherlands, Portugal, Spain, Sweden, United Kingdom

INTRODUCTION

The other case studies in this book have focused on examples of independent sovereign states in Western Europe. This chapter focuses on an altogether different kind of political entity. At its most basic, the European Union (EU) is an international organization of which fifteen Western European states are members. However, the EU goes far beyond most conventional definitions of an international organization—it has much greater powers over its members, and its members have much greater obligations both to the rules of the EU and to each other. There are even some who see the EU as the forerunner of a European superstate—a United States of Europe—and argue that the study of government and politics in Western Europe must now be approached as much from a regional perspective as from the perspective of the individual states.

Just how far the EU has progressed along the road to political union is highly debatable. The member states have harmonized many of their laws, developed common policies in a variety of areas, worked increasingly in concert rather than in competition with each other, and have been transferring power to a new European level of authority. They have created a series of governing institutions and a common body of European law, they have built a single market in which there is almost completely free movement of people, money, goods, and services, and eleven EU member states are currently in the process of replacing their national currencies with a single European currency. However, Euroskeptics argue that the surrender of national sovereignty is a dangerous trend, and that economic integration is leading to a reduction in the powers of national governments and a dilution of national identity.

Developments such as these have important implications not just for the member states of the EU but for politics and economics in other parts of the world. The EU has become an economic superpower; it has just over 6 percent of the world's population but accounts for 28 percent of global gross national product (GNP) (compared to the U.S. share of 25 percent) and for more than 36 percent of global trade (compared to the U.S. share of about 15 percent).[1] The EU is likely to enlarge in the next few years to bring in several central and eastern European members, and it promises to be an important source of support as those countries continue their transition to democracy and free-market economics. Non-European states have already begun to reassess their relationships with the EU, the evolution of which is changing both the way the world sees Europe and the way Europeans see themselves.

The EU experience also stands as an important model for the other exercises in regional integration that are underway in different parts of the world. Americans, Canadians, and Mexicans are working on regional cooperation through the North American Free Trade Agreement (NAFTA), and although it is much looser and less ambitious than the European Union, it stands to learn much from the European experience. Similar exercises in regional cooperation and integration in Latin America, the Caribbean, south and southeast Asia, and southern and western Africa suggest that the days of the nation-state may be drawing to a close, and that the twenty-first century may see the world moving toward political and economic relations based instead on a network of regional groupings.

The European Union began life in 1952 as a limited experiment in the pooling of authority over national coal and steel industries by six countries: West Germany, France, Italy, and the three Benelux states (Belgium, the Netherlands, and Luxembourg). It then expanded in 1958 to become the European Economic Community (EEC), the main goal of which was to build a common European market. Nine more countries have since joined, so that all Western European states are now members, except for Iceland, Malta, Norway, and Switzerland. In

1992, the EEC became part of the European Union, a change of name that was intended to signify a sense of closer integration and cooperation on a wider variety of policies, including foreign policy and justice and home affairs.

The EU now has fifteen member states, covers a land area about one-third the size of the United States, and is home to 373 million people. It has a combined GNP of about eight trillion dollars (compared to seven trillion dollars in the United States),[2] although levels of wealth among its member states vary substantially. Generally speaking, the wealthiest parts are in the center or core, roughly in and around a triangle between London, Paris, and Hamburg, whereas the poorest parts are on the periphery and include Greece, southern Italy, Spain, Portugal, Ireland, and northern Britain. As membership expands over the next few years to take in Eastern Europe, the gap between rich and poor will expand.

In social terms, the EU is marked by significant divisions. The fifteen member states have histories that have constantly overlapped and intertwined as they have gone to war with each other, built alliances, and colonized neighboring territory. However, the dominance of the nation-state over the last three hundred years has encouraged Europeans to think more of their differences than their similarities. They are most obviously reminded of their social and cultural divisions by their multiple languages; Europeans speak at least thirty-six different languages[3] (although the EU recognizes only eleven as official languages). Although the vast majority of Europeans are white, there are significant ethnic minorities in many member states, including Turks in Germany, Algerians in France, and Indians in Britain. There are also significant religious differences, with several states (Italy, Ireland, Spain, and Portugal) being predominantly Catholic, while the rest follow varieties of Protestantism, and almost all European states have small Jewish and Muslim minorities.

One of the effects of European integration has been to open up borders within Europe and to make it much easier for countries to trade with one another, for corporations to merge and expand into the regional marketplace, and for individual Europeans to travel and to live and work in other countries. The distinctions among the member states of the EU have declined; they still retain their strong cultural identities, and their citizens still often have different norms and values, but an increase in personal mobility has promoted a greater intermingling of nationalities. Particularly in larger cities such as London, Paris, and Berlin, visitors from other countries are no longer simply tourists but have become permanent residents and have integrated themselves into the local community.

In political terms, the EU is difficult to categorize. It has gone far beyond the kind of cooperation that characterizes international organizations such as the United Nations or the Organization of American States, but it is still far short of a political union. The balance of power between the member states (on the one hand) and the EU institutions (on the other) has been changing in favor of the latter, but the EU institutions have only limited powers in selected areas, and the key decisions are still made as a result of bargaining among the governments of the member states. The EU is still far short of being a federation and is much closer to being a confederation, but even then it is a loose form of confederalism because the EU institutions have powers to speak on behalf of the member states only in selected areas. For example, the European Commission (the bureaucratic-executive arm of the EU) speaks on behalf of the member states on most trade issues, but the member states—especially the larger and more powerful ones—still largely go their own ways on foreign and defense policy. Similarly, although the EU now plays a strong role in the making of European policy on agriculture, competition, the environment, social issues, and transport, issues such as taxation, education, criminal law, and policing are still the preserve of the member states.

There is no European constitution in the sense that there is a single codified document, there is no European president or cabinet (although the commission comes close to providing these), citizens of Western Europe are still citizens of their home states rather than of the European Union, there is no European military, and the single European currency will not be fully in place until 2002 at the earliest. One of the goals of European integration is to build "an ever closer union," but it is debatable exactly what this means and what the EU eventually will become. The idea of a federal Europe is controversial, as is the idea of full political union.

The history of integration shows the member states taking cautious and often unwilling steps toward greater cooperation, moving opportunistically and incrementally rather than being driven by any kind of grand plan of European union. The most that can be said for now is that the EU is much more than a conventional international organization but still much less than a European superstate. Domestic politics within the member states is heavily influenced by the common policies of the European Union as a whole, but the EU is still ultimately an intergovernmental organization rather than a supranational authority.

BACKGROUND AND HISTORY

The European Union was born out of the ruins of World War II. Prior to the war, Europe had dominated global trade, banking, and finance; its empires had stretched across the world, and its military superiority had been unquestioned. However, Europeans had often gone to war with each other, and their conflicts and rivalries undermined the prosperity that cooperation might have brought. World War I (or the Great War) was often described as the war to end all wars, but it took one more conflagration finally to convince Europeans that the fundamental nature of the relationship among European states needed to be changed if a lasting peace was to be achieved.

World War II resulted in the deaths of more than forty million people and left behind numerous pockets of devastation. Cities lay in ruins, agricultural production was halved, food was rationed, and communications were disrupted by the destruction of bridges, railroads, and harbors. Every country involved sustained heavy casualties and widespread physical damage, and the war dealt a severe blow to European power and influence, clearing the way for the emergence of the United States and the Soviet Union as superpowers and creating a nervous new balance in the distribution of political influence in the world.

The priority for European leaders after the war was to create the conditions that would prevent Europeans from going to war with each other again. For many, the major internal threats to peace and security were nationalism and the nation-state, both of which had been discredited by the war. For many others, Germany was the core problem—peace was impossible, went the argument, unless Germany could be contained and its power diverted to constructive rather than destructive ends. It had to be allowed to rebuild its economic base and its political system, but to do so in ways that would not threaten European security. The mistakes that followed World War I, including the reparations imposed on Germany, had to be avoided.

Meanwhile, it was clear that Europe faced external threats arising out of the growing hostility between the two superpowers, and there were concerns that Europeans were becoming pawns in the emerging Cold War. There was clearly a need to protect Western Europe from the spread of Soviet influence, but there were also worries about the extent to which Western Europe and the United States could find common ground, and to which Western Europeans could rely on the U.S. protective shield.

TABLE 9.1		Key Dates in EU History
1947	September	Launch of Marshall Plan
1949	April	North Atlantic Treaty signed
1950	May	Publication of Schuman Declaration
1951	April	Treaty of Paris signed, creating the European Coal and Steel Community
1952	August	ECSC comes into operation
1954	October	Creation of Western European Union
1957	March	Treaties of Rome signed, creating Euratom and the European Economic Community
1958	January	Euratom and EEC come into operation
1960	May	Creation of European Free Trade Association
1968	July	Agreement of a common external tariff completes the creation of an EEC customs union; Common Agricultural Policy agreed
1973	January	Britain, Denmark, and Ireland join the Community, bringing membership to nine
1979	March	European Monetary System comes into operation
	June	First direct elections to the European Parliament
1981	January	Greece joins the Community, bringing membership to ten
1986	January	Spain and Portugal join the Community, bringing membership to twelve
	February	Single European Act signed in Luxembourg
1987	July	Single European Act comes into force
1990	October	German reunification brings the former East Germany into the Community
1992	February	Treaty on European Union signed
1993	November	Treaty on European Union come into force
1994	January	Creation of European Economic Area
1995	January	Austria, Sweden, and Finland join the European Union, bringing membership to fifteen
	March	Schengen Agreement comes into force
	July	Europol Convention signed
1997	October	Treaty of Amsterdam signed
1998	June	Establishment of the European Central Bank
1999	January	Adoption of single currency by eleven EU member states

Perhaps Europe would be better advised to take care of its own security. This, however, demanded a greater sense of unity and common purpose than Europe had ever been able to achieve before.

Opening Moves: 1951–1958

The idea of European integration has a history that dates back several centuries. As well as the attempts made by Charlemagne, Napoleon, Hitler, and others to extend political or military control over large swathes of Europe, many philosophers, diplomats, and even artists had mulled over the idea of voluntary cooperation or union and had outlined proposals talking variously of a confederal Christian republic, European assemblies and senates, and organized international systems for dispute resolution; among those who offered such suggestions were William Penn, Jean-Jacques Rousseau, Immanual Kant, Victor Hugo, and Winston Churchill.[4]

Their proposals were to remain no more than theories until the close of World War II, when the conditions were finally ripe for the practical application of plans for European cooperation. Among those who felt that a bold initiative was needed were the French businessman Jean Monnet (1888–1979) and

Robert Schuman (1880–1963), French foreign minister from 1948 to 1953. Both were enthusiastic Europeanists; both believed that decisive steps needed to be taken that would compel European governments to work together on practical cooperative projects, and both believed that the logical point of departure should be the perennial problem of Franco-German relations.

By 1950, it was clear to many that West Germany had to be allowed to rebuild its industry if it was to play a useful role in the western alliance, and that the threat historically posed by a powerful Germany to European peace had to be removed. One way of doing this was to let it rebuild under the auspices of a supranational organization, thereby tying it into the wider process of European reconstruction. Looking for a point of departure that was meaningful without being too ambitious, Monnet focused on the coal and steel industries, which offered strong potential for common European organization because coal and steel were the building blocks of industry, and integrating these two sectors would ensure that Germany became reliant on trade with the rest of Europe. This reliance would in turn underpin the economic reconstruction of Germany and help the French lose their fear of German industrial domination.[5]

Monnet felt that effective economic planning was beyond the ability of individual states working alone and knew from personal experience that intergovernmental organizations had a tendency to be hamstrung by the governments of their member states and to become bogged down in ministerial meetings. To avoid these problems, he proposed a new institutional structure that would be independent of national governments and would therefore be supranational rather than intergovernmental. After discussions with Monnet, Schuman took these ideas a step further at a press conference on May 9, 1950, a date now widely seen as marking the birth of the idea of a united Europe. He proposed that Franco-German production of coal and steel be placed "under a common High Authority, within the framework of an organization open to the participation of the other countries of Europe." This, he went on, would be "a first step in the federation of Europe," and would make war between France and Germany "not merely unthinkable, but materially impossible."[6]

Only six governments took up the invitation (West Germany, France, Italy, Belgium, the Netherlands, and Luxembourg), and negotiations among them led to the signing in April 1951 of the Treaty of Paris, creating the European Coal and Steel Community (ECSC). The new organization began work in August 1952 after ratification of the terms of the treaty in each of the member states. The ECSC was a small step in itself, but it represented the first time that European governments had given up significant powers to a supranational organization. It was allowed to pull down tariff barriers, abolish subsidies, fix prices, and generate income by imposing levies on steel and coal production. The ECSC showed that integration was feasible, and its very existence served to encourage "the Six" to work together.

While the ECSC went on to build modest but solid achievements, there were limits to its abilities, and Europeanists soon began to argue that something more needed to be done to provide the cause of integration with real momentum. Besides, it was increasingly difficult to develop the coal and steel sectors in isolation. A meeting of the foreign ministers of the Six in June 1955 resulted in a resolution that the time had come to "relaunch" the European idea on a more ambitious scale, and discussions led to the signing in March 1957 of the two Treaties of Rome, one creating the European Economic Community (EEC) and one the European Atomic Energy Community (Euratom).

Following member state ratification, both treaties came into force in January 1958. Under the terms of the EEC Treaty, the member states agreed to build a common market among themselves by the removal of all restrictions on internal trade, agreement of a common external tariff, the reduction of barriers to the free movement of people, services, and capital, the development of common agricultural and transport policies, and the eventual creation of European social and regional funds aimed at helping reduce economic and social disparities within and among the EEC member states. The Euratom Treaty, meanwhile, was designed to promote cooperation on atomic energy, an idea that was particularly supported by France.

As integration proceeded under the three treaties, the Community built a small group of governing institutions. The Brussels-based European Commission was a bureaucracy that was responsible for making new proposals for laws and policies, while the Council of Ministers brought together the relevant sets of national government ministers to make the final decisions on the adoption of those proposals. Meanwhile, the European Parliament was allowed to vet most proposals, although it did not begin to win significant powers over policymaking until 1979, when the first direct elections to the parliament were held. Finally, the European Court of Justice—based in Luxembourg—ensured that all laws met the letter and the spirit of the founding treaties and worked to build a body of European law that was consistently and equally applied throughout the member states.

Widening and Deepening: 1960–1987

Britain remained the most obvious absentee from the early efforts to integrate Europe. It still saw itself as a world power that enjoyed a special relationship with the United States, but its view of its role in the world began to change as it dismantled its empire during the 1950s, and British governments began reluctantly looking more toward cooperation with their European neighbors. However, Britain was uncomfortable with the closeness of the ties proposed by Monnet and Schuman, and so worked with several non-EEC members in the creation in January 1960 of the European Free Trade Association (EFTA), a body whose goal was free trade rather than economic and political integration.

Even while EFTA was being discussed, it had already become clear to Britain that real political influence in Europe lay not with EFTA, but with the EEC, that Britain risked political isolation if it stayed out of the EEC, and that the Community was actually working. Hence it applied for membership in August 1961, along with Ireland and Denmark, and they were joined in 1962 by Norway. The British application was vetoed twice by President Charles de Gaulle of France, mainly out of his belief that British membership would be a Trojan horse for U.S. influence in Europe.[7] The application was finally accepted in 1969 following de Gaulle's retirement. Membership negotiations took place in 1970–1971, and Britain, Denmark, and Ireland joined the EEC in January 1973. Norway would have joined as well, but a public referendum in September 1972 turned down membership.

An additional round of enlargements pushed the borders of the Community further south and west when Greece joined in 1981, and Spain and Portugal in 1986. By then, the EEC had become known simply as the European Community (EC), its twelve member states among them had a population of 322 million, and they accounted for just over one-fifth of all world trade. The Community had its own administrative structure and an independent body of law, and its citizens had direct (but limited) representation through the European Parliament, which also gave them a psychological and political stake in the evolution of the Community. However, progress on integration remained uneven. The creation of a common market had been one of the key goals of the Treaty of Rome, but nontariff barriers to the free movement of people and capital persisted, including different national technical, health, and quality standards, and varying levels of indirect taxation, such as value-added tax (VAT).

The term "Eurosclerosis" began to gain common currency in the 1970s, describing the economic stagnation, double-digit inflation, and high unemployment that afflicted Europe. European business was not competing well on the global market, scientists and industrialists were failing to collaborate, and there were concerns that progress on completion of the common market (or single market as it was now more usually known) was being handicapped by inflation and unemployment and by the temptation of member states to protect their home industries with nontariff barriers such as subsidies.[8] Competition from the United States and Japan was also growing. In response, Community governments decided to focus renewed attention on completing the single market and signed the Single European Act (SEA) in Luxembourg in February 1986. After ratification by national legislatures, it came into force in July 1987.[9]

The SEA was probably the most politically popular (or least controversial) of the changes made to the founding treaties. It had several goals, the most important of which was to achieve a border-free single market by midnight on December 31, 1992. This would be done by removing all remaining physical barriers (such as customs and passport controls at internal borders), fiscal barriers (mainly in the form of different levels of indirect taxation), and technical barriers (such as conflicting standards, laws, and qualifications). To achieve this, the Community would have to develop and adopt nearly three hundred specific pieces of law aimed at opening up intra-European trade.

The effects of the SEA were many and substantial: internal passport and customs controls were eased or lifted, banks could do business throughout the Community, companies could do business and sell their products throughout the Community, there was little to prevent EC residents from living, working, and opening bank accounts anywhere in the Community, protectionism became illegal, and monopolies on everything from electricity supply to telecommunications began to be broken down. The EC was also given powers over new policy areas, including the environment, research and development, and regional policy. It was a program with which even the most hardened Euroskeptics could live.

Maastricht and Further Enlargement: 1987–1995

The focus of European integration until the 1980s was on economic integration, and although the most enthusiastic pro-Europeans had also talked about the benefits of political integration, this idea was long left on the backburner of Community interests because of a prevailing feeling that there was little hope of building political union without first achieving economic union. False starts had been made with attempts in the 1950s and 1960s to outline the steps needed to achieve political union, but little was achieved beyond greater cooperation on foreign policy under a process known as European Political Cooperation (EPC). This worked well in some areas (such as EC policy toward developing countries), but it was more reactive than proactive, and a truly European foreign policy had not yet emerged.

Determined to reassert French leadership in the EC, President Francois Mitterrand focused on the theme of political union at a summit of EC leaders in 1984, with the result that a decision was taken to convene an intergovernmental conference on political union. The outcome was the Treaty of European Union, which was agreed at a summit of European leaders in Maastricht in the Netherlands in December 1991, and which came into force in 1992. The original wording of the draft treaty mentioned the goal of federal union, but Britain balked at this, so it was changed to read "an ever closer union among the peoples of Europe, in which decisions are taken as closely as possible to the citizen."

Although it was far from being an agreement on political union, the Maastricht treaty took the process of integration several steps further. As well as expanding EC powers into new policy areas such as consumer protection, public health policy, and transportation, it created a new legal entity known as the European Union. This label was meant to symbolize the next stage in the process of European integration and was based on three "pillars": a reformed and strengthened European Community, and two areas in which there was to be more regularized EC cooperation—a common foreign and security policy (CFSP), and home affairs and justice. Although the European Community still exists, one of the effects of Maastricht was to make the label "European Union" more popular. Maastricht also led to agreement on a timetable for the creation of a single European currency by January 1999, an idea that had been discussed by Community leaders as early as the 1970s but which had only begun to win political support in the late 1980s.

Meanwhile, the EC/EU had begun actively considering further enlargement, prompted by applications from several of its neighbors to the north, east, and south. Turkey has long been enthusiastically in favor of joining, but its applications have been turned down because of concerns about its human rights record and its poverty, and because of the opposition of Greece. Negotiations were instead opened at the turn of the 1990s with Austria, Sweden, Norway, and Finland, all of which were given the green light in early 1994. A referendum in Norway once again went against membership, but the other three countries joined in January 1995.

The spotlight has since shifted to the east, where the most realistic prospects for medium-term accession include states that have made a transition to free-market policies since the collapse of the Soviet Bloc in 1991. Negotiations opened in the spring of 1998 with Hungary, Poland, the Czech Republic, Slovenia, Estonia, and Cyprus, the expectation being that the next round of enlargement will take place in 2003–2006. Looking still further east, and further into the future, membership for the other Baltic states (Latvia and Lithuania) and for three former Soviet republics (Ukraine, Belarus, and Moldova) is not impossible, but this would depend on the resolution of questions over their relationship with Russia, and on how quickly they are able to make the transition to free-market policies. Latvia, Lithuania, Slovakia, Bulgaria, and Romania have all applied, with the first three having the strongest credentials, while the last two are unlikely to be seriously considered until after 2006.

The Single Currency and Beyond: 1997–present

In June 1997, EU leaders signed the Treaty of Amsterdam, a new set of revisions to the founding treaties of the EU, which came into force in 1999. It fell far short of its goal of agreeing to a political union to accompany the economic and monetary union promoted by the SEA and Maastricht, and the fifteen leaders were unable to agree to changes in the structure of EU institutions in preparation for a further expansion in membership. However, they were able to confirm the goals of launching the single European currency in January 1999, of enlarging the EU to the east, of further developing policies on asylum, immigration, unemployment, social policy, health protection, consumer protection, the environment, and foreign policy, and of making modest reforms to EU institutions. Amsterdam also provided an opportunity to take stock of progress since the signing of the Treaty of Paris.

First, the single market has been—by almost universal agreement—a great success. Not every piece of legislation aimed at removing the final barriers to trade has been agreed and implemented, but the EU has become one of the two biggest and richest markets in the world, intra-EU trade and competition has grown rapidly, and European multinational corporations have used the European market as a base from which to merge, set up joint ventures, and launch more aggressive competition on the global stage.

Second, while there is no common policy on immigration, visas, and asylum, there has been progress on the removal of border controls, and there are now almost no restrictions on travel around the EU. In 1985, France, Germany, and the Benelux states signed the Schengen Agreement, under which all border controls among them were to be removed. All EU member states except Britain and Ireland have since joined, along with two nonmembers, Iceland and Norway. The agreement came into force in 1995, and although its terms allow signatories to implement controls at any time, and not all countries have yet implemented truly passport-free travel, the agreement marked a substantial step toward the final removal of all border controls.

Third, in several policy areas the balance of decision-making power has shifted from the member states to the EU. Notable among these is agricultural policy, which has been the subject of a controversial system of subsidies since the Treaty of Rome: European farmers have been guaranteed payment for almost everything they have produced, and while this has encouraged a dramatic increase in production levels, it has also led to substantial overproduction of many commodities and the spread of intensive agriculture. Other areas in which the EU has made significant inroads include the development of Europe's poorer regions, social policies, the development of a European transport network, and environmental management.

Fourth, the EU still has no common foreign or defense policy, but it has made progress on some fronts. It has become a major actor on the world stage in terms of aid to eastern Europe, has signed preferential trade agreements with seventy-one African, Caribbean, and Pacific countries, and is helping to build a Mediterranean free-trade area (to be completed by 2010, and encompassing nearly seven hundred million people). However, the fifteen member states still pursue their own security interests and often take different positions on foreign policy problems, while several countries (including Ireland and Finland) insist on maintaining their neutrality. Organizational changes coming out of Amsterdam included an agreement to give more focus to foreign policy decision making and representation, although the EU still lacks the joint military that it needs in order to give substance to its foreign policy positions.

Finally, progress continues on the most ambitious project ever undertaken by the member states of the EU: the creation of the single European currency, the euro. A timetable agreed under Maastricht required participating states to take the preparatory step of fixing exchange rates in January 1999. This happened as projected, although only eleven of the fifteen EU members became part of the euro; Greece had not met the preconditions for entry, and public and political opinion in Britain, Denmark, and Sweden was hostile to the notion. Interest rates in "euroland" are now set by the European Central Bank, and—if all goes according to plan—a three-year gestation period will end in January 2002, when euro notes and coins will begin circulating, and national currencies will be completely replaced the following July.

POLITICAL CULTURE

It is usually easiest to identify the features of political culture in communities with a long history; they have had time to develop regular or consistent norms and values, and it is easier to see the link between political culture and political behavior. The same cannot be

The broad goals of policy in the European Union are set at meetings of the European Council. This brings together the leaders of the member states at summit meetings held 2 to 3 times each year, and is symbolic of the intergovermental nature of much that the EU does.

said of the European Union, however, because it is difficult to define the political character of the EU, and because its political culture is less a discreet set of norms than the cumulative culture created by the different norms and values of its member states and by the nature of European integration itself. Political culture is a moving target, the nature of which is influenced by changing political, economic, and social values. Having said this, the political culture of the process of European integration as it enters its sixth decade probably includes the following characteristics.

A Tension Between Intergovernmentalism and Supranationalism

One of the sharpest debates surrounding the process of European integration concerns the extent to which it is intergovernmental (that is, driven by bargains struck between the governments of the member states) and the extent to which it has developed a life of its own above and beyond the level of the member states.

Although key initiatives are launched by the European Council (the meeting place of the leaders of the member states) and the balance of power on decision making still rests with the Council of Ministers (the meeting place of national government ministers), many of the initiatives taken by the EU are part of the requirements of the treaties that are the basis of EU power. Furthermore, the member states among them have agreed on a body of EU law that has created its own requirements, and which is protected by the European Commission and the European Court of Justice, both supranational bodies.

This means that, just as the EU is something between a conventional international organization and a European superstate, so its political character is something between intergovernmental and supranational. Ironically—and this is something that worries opponents to European integration—the more decisions are taken by governments, the more the EU takes on a life and an authority of its own and becomes a supranational body.

Elitism and the Democratic Deficit

One of the most worrying structural weaknesses of the process of European integration is the extent to which the governments of the member states take key decisions without referring them to national electorates. The balance of decision-making power rests with political and economic elites, thereby creating a problem known as the democratic deficit, defined as the gap between the powers developed by the EU institutions and the ability of European citizens to hold those institutions accountable.

Although citizens can elect members of the European Parliament, it still has much more limited powers over European lawmaking than national legislatures have over national lawmaking. Furthermore, the people have little say (except through their national governments) in the appointment of the president of the European Commission, judges on the European Court of Justice, or other key posts such as president of the European Central Bank. Similarly, meetings of key decision-making bodies, such as the Council of Ministers and the Committee of Permanent Representatives, are closed to the public, and no records are available of their proceedings. Access to documents of the European Commission has improved but is still not easy, and important steps in the process of integration—such as agreement of the treaties of Maastricht and Amsterdam, and the decision to proceed with the single currency—were put to national referenda in very few of the member states.

The Knowledge Deficit

Related to the undemocratic nature of much of what happens at the European level is another problem that has so far received surprisingly little political or academic attention: the knowledge deficit. The average European knows remarkably little about how the EU works and what kind of effects it has had on his or her life. In recent surveys carried out by Eurobarometer, the EU opinion polling service, respondents have been asked how much they think they know about the EU, its policies and its institutions, and to give themselves a score out of ten, with ten meaning they know a great deal and one meaning they know little. About 75 percent of those polled give themselves failing scores (five or less), and a remarkable 13 percent admit they know nothing at all. On specific issues, about 70 percent of Europeans admit to being not very well or not at all informed about the single currency, and at the height of deliberations about the Treaty of Amsterdam in 1997, more than one-half of respondents said that they had not even heard of the treaty.[10]

Figures such as these are not encouraging. They suggest that Europeans still have a long way to go before they develop a sense of belonging to the European Union, and these high levels of ignorance perpetuate the democratic deficit and ensure that the process of European integration is driven more by the opinions and values of elites than of the average European. To be fair, the European Commission has long maintained a public information program about the EU and has tried to make its work more accessible through printed publications, videos, and the Internet, but the average European is still some distance from caring as much about what happens in Brussels as in his or her national capital.

REPRESENTATION AND PARTICIPATION

Most Europeans still think of themselves first and foremost as citizens of one state or another. That their states happen to be members of the European Union is a relatively minor factor in the way they approach social issues and their participation in politics. Except for the most mobile of Europeans, other member states are still "foreign," and politics is a matter still driven mainly by local and national priorities. However, "Europe" is playing an increasingly important role in local and national matters, and Europeans are slowly paying more attention to the impact of the EU on their

The new home of the European Parliament in Strasbourg, France, which was opened in 1999. The EP is the only directly elected institution in the EU system, but it has relatively few powers, and turnout at parliamentary elections is low.

lives. This has meant, in turn, that they are paying more attention to the channels they can use to influence the process by which European laws and policies are developed.

Elections and the Electoral System

The primary channel of direct political influence for EU citizens is offered by elections to the European Parliament (EP). These are held on a fixed rotation of five years, with every member state using multimember districts and variations on the theme of proportional representation (PR). Most member states treat their entire territory as a single electoral district, whereas Belgium, Ireland, and Italy have either four or five "Euro-constituencies," and Germany treats its sixteen *Länder* as separate constituencies.

PR has the advantage of accurately reflecting the proportion of the vote given to different parties. However, voters are represented by a group of Members of the European Parliament (MEPs) from different parties and may never get to know or develop ties with a particular representative. Furthermore, it spreads the distribution of seats so thinly that no one party has enough seats to form a majority. This process encourages legislators from different parties to work together and reach compromises, but it also makes it more difficult to get anything done.

Voters must be eighteen years of age and must be citizens of one of the EU member states. At one time, member states restricted voting to their own citizens, but since Maastricht, EU citizens have been allowed to vote in their country of residence and even to run for the EP wherever they live, regardless of their citizenship. They must register with the electoral authority of the member state in which they are living, and they must meet local qualifications if they want to vote and meet qualifications in their home state if they want to run. Member states have different rules on the minimum age for candidates, which ranges from eighteen to twenty-five, and they have different rules on how candidates qualify. Some do not allow independent candidates; some require candidates to pay deposits, and others require them to collect signatures, and so on.[11]

Turnout varies from one member state to another but is generally higher than voter turnout for elections in the United States; just over 56 percent of Europeans voted in 1994 and less than 50 percent in 1999, compared to 49 percent in the 1996 U.S. presidential election, and an average of 35 percent in midterm elections. Belgium and Luxembourg usually have the best turnout (90 percent or more), whereas in Britain, Finland, and the Netherlands, barely 23–30 percent of those eligible voted in 1999. There has been a tendency for turnout to fall in some of the poorer EU states (Portugal, Ireland, and Spain), to hold steady or decline slightly in the original six founder states (Italy excepted), and—ironically—to grow slightly in the two most skeptical members, Britain and Denmark.

Turnout at European elections is generally lower than that at national elections in the member states, and average turnout has fallen steadily from a high of more than 67 percent in 1979. There are several possible reasons for this trend.

- There is the sheer novelty of European elections, which have been a feature of the electoral calendar only since 1979.
- Few European voters really know what the EP does or what issues are at stake, and turnover among MEPs has been so high that few have developed the kind of transnational reputation that would encourage voters to take much interest in the politics of the EP. Even the president of the EP—the nearest equivalent to the Speaker of the U.S. House of Representatives—is almost unknown as a public figure. As a result, EU voters have developed few psychological ties to the European Parliament, which still seems anonymous and distant to most.
- No change of government is involved, as would be the case in a national election, so voters feel there is less to be lost or gained. The leadership of the commission bears no relation to the makeup of parliament; if it did, the stakes would be raised and there might be more voter interest.
- Party groups in the European Parliament are still learning how to coordinate their election campaigns across all of the member states, and campaigns still tend to be national rather than European. The Greens have so far been the only group to run EU-wide campaigns, running on a platform of issues such as opposition to nuclear power, disarmament, and more devolution of powers to the local level.
- The media and national governments still tend to downplay the significance of European elections, which are given relatively little coverage.
- Some voters have little interest in the EU or may be skeptical or hostile to the entire concept, making them disinclined to take part in European elections.
- Most voters still think European elections are a poll on their national governments rather than an opportunity to influence EU policies, about which many voters are still confused and uncertain. In 1994, for example, disgruntled Spanish voters used the European election to take seats away from the governing Socialist party of Felipe Gonzalez; British voters used it to state their disenchantment with the governing Conservative Party of John Major (the opposition Labour Party ended up with more than three times as many seats); and Italian voters used the election to make a statement about their disgust with the discredited leadership of the now defunct Christian Democrats.

As the influence of the European Union spreads, as more voters understand the stakes of European elections, and as the powers of the European Parliament grow, turnout may improve.

TABLE 9.2	Distribution of Seats in the European Parliament, January 2000								
	EUL	PES	ELDR	UEN	EPP	Greens	EDD	Ind	Total
Austria	–	7	–	–	7	2	–	5	21
Belgium	–	5	5	–	6	7	–	2	25
Denmark	1	3	6	1	1	–	4	–	16
Finland	1	3	5	–	5	2	–	–	16
France	11	22	–	12	21	9	6	6	87
Germany	6	33	–	–	53	7	–	–	99
Greece	7	9	–	–	9	–	–	–	25
Ireland	–	1	1	6	5	2	–	–	15
Italy	6	17	7	9	34	2	–	12	87
Luxembourg	–	2	1	–	2	1	–	–	6
Netherlands	1	6	8	–	9	4	3	–	31
Portugal	2	12	–	2	9	–	–	–	25
Spain	4	24	3	–	28	4	–	1	64
Sweden	3	6	4	–	7	2	–	–	22
United Kingdom	–	30	10	–	37	6	3	1	87
Total	42	180	50	30	233	48	16	27	626

EUL   Confederal group of the European United Left - Nordic Green Left
PES   Party of European Socialists
ELDR   Group of the European Liberal, Democratic and Reformist Party
UEN   Union for a Europe of Nations
EPP   European People's Party/European Democrats
Greens   Green Group in the European Parliament/European Free Alliance
EDD   The Europe of Democracies and Diversities Group
Ind   Independents and non-attached

Political Parties

MEPs do not sit in national blocs but come together in cross-national ideological groups with roughly similar goals and values. PR ensures that a substantial number of national parties are represented in the EP; following the arrival of MEPs from Austria, Finland, and Sweden in 1995, for example, more than seventy parties had seats in the chamber. Because many of these parties consist of as few as one or two members, they can achieve nothing by themselves, so they work to build party groups within parliament. Some of these groups are marriages of convenience, bringing together MEPs with different policies, but time has seen party groups developing more focus and consistency, and they now cover a wide array of ideologies and policies, from left to right, and from pro-European to anti-European.[12]

A minimum of twenty-nine MEPs is needed to form a group if they all come from one member state, twenty-three if they come from two member states, eighteen if they come from three states, and fourteen if they come from four or more states. No one party group has ever had enough seats to form a majority, so multipartisanship has been the order of business. The balance of power is also affected by changes in the number and makeup of party groups. Through all of those changes, three groups have developed a particular consistency: the Socialists (on the left), the Liberals (on the center-right), and the European People's Party (on the right).

Moving from left to right on the ideological spectrum (see Table 9.2), the party groups in parliament in 1999 were as follows:

- *European United Left (EUL).* This small group is all that remains from the game of musical chairs played on the left of the chamber since the mid-1980s.

Eurocommunists formed a Communist Group in 1973, but the collapse of the Soviet Union in 1989 encouraged Italian and Spanish communists to form their own European United Left, while more hard-line communists from France, Greece, and Portugal formed Left Unity. By 1994, only the EUL remained, made up mainly of Spanish, French, and Italian communists.

- *Party of European Socialists (PES)*. Until recently, socialists were the largest group in parliament, adding to the concerns of conservative Euroskeptics about the interventionist tendencies of the EU. PES finally slipped to second place in 1999 following elections which saw a shift to the right. The PES has shades of opinion ranging from ex-communists on the left to more moderate social democrats toward the center. It has members from every EU country, with those from Germany, Britain, Spain and France forming the biggest national blocs.

- *European Liberal Democratic and Reform Party (ELDR)*. The ELDR contains members from every EU member state except Germany, Greece, France, Austria and Portugal, but it is difficult to pinpoint in ideological terms. Most of its members fall in or around the center, and the group has suffered over the years from defections to the EPP.

- *European People's Party (EPP)*. This is the major group on the right and has consistently been one of the two largest party blocs in parliament. The group was once dominated by German and Italian Christian Democrats, but it changed its name to the EPP in 1976 and finally allowed the European Democrats (British and Danish conservatives) to join in 1992 on the condition that they accept the principles of the EPP, including federalism and a social Europe. The group is right of center and contains representatives from every EU member state, with the delegations from Germany, Britain and Italy being the largest.

- *The Greens*. usually associated with environmental issues, the Greens in fact pursue a much wider variety of interests related to social justice, and they refuse to be placed on the traditional ideological spectrum. Once part of the Rainbow Group, the Greens formed their own group after the 1989 elections increased their numbers.

In addition to the formal party groups, about 4-5 percent of MEPs sit as independents, describing themselves as nonattached. The number of nonattached legislators is usually high immediately after an election but begins to fall as they slowly join party groups. Cutting across the party groups are smaller *intergroups* tied to specific issues, such as joint stands on a foreign policy matter or a new initiative on European integration. One of the most famous of these intergroups was the Crocodile Club led by Italian Altiero Spinelli (a former European commissioner), which was behind a 1984 draft treaty on European Union that eventually provided one of the sparks that led to the 1991 Maastricht treaty.

Candidates for elections are chosen by their national parties, but they have an independent mandate and cannot always be bound by those parties.[13] Parliament was once seen as a haven for also-rans, but the quality of candidates competing in European elections is improving.

MEPs take their jobs more seriously and are kept much busier working on issues that have growing relevance and importance to the work of the EU. Until 1987, average attendance at plenaries was about 42 percent, since then it has grown to about 58 percent. It was once usual for MEPs to hold a dual mandate (sitting in both the EP and their home legislatures), but this is now very rare, and some member states (such as Spain and Belgium) have outlawed the dual mandate. This trend has not only weakened the links between national legislatures and the EP but has also given the EP greater independence and helped improve the credibility of MEPs.

Relatively speaking, women are well represented in the EP; the percentage has grown steadily from 16 percent in 1979 to 19 percent in 1989, to nearly 27 percent in 1996.[14] This proportion is above the average for liberal democracies (16 percent) and well above the figures for the United States (13 percent) and most EU member states (several of which are in single digits).[15]

Interest Groups

On a variety of issues, ranging from transport to the environment to regional issues, the member states of the EU have shifted increasingly from separate national approaches to common problems toward joint approaches. They have done this in part through strengthening pan-European institutions and policymaking, harmonizing policy goals and methods, and developing common goals and standards. While the member states have been the major actors in this process, it would be wrong to think that the process of integration has been unidimensional and that the EU has been built solely on the compromises worked out among the leaders of the member states. European integration has also led to the emergence of a European civil society, or a framework outside the formal structures of government in which people interact and associate with each other. While leaders have negotiated with their national interests to the fore, nongovernmental organizations—or interest groups—have cut across national frontiers to promote the shared sectoral interests of communities in multiple member states.

Several European bodies look much like interest groups but are part of the formal EU structure, including the Economic and Social Committee and the Committee of the Regions. Both are advisory bodies, each with 222 members appointed for renewable four-year terms and drawn from the member states roughly in proportion to population size. The former was set up under the Treaty of Rome to give employers, workers, and other sectional interests a forum in which they could meet, talk, and issue opinions to the commission, the Council of Ministers, and—more recently—the European Parliament. The latter was set up under the terms of Maastricht and met for the first time in 1994. It consists of representatives of regional and local bodies (including mayors and members of state or regional councils) and gives advice on issues that have an impact on local communities.

Beyond these, the last ten to fifteen years have seen the growth of hundreds of nongovernmental organizations that represent the views of a wide variety of sectional interests with a stake in the content of EU policy and law. Many are an outgrowth of preexisting national groups, others have been set up specifically to respond to European issues, and an increasing number have opened offices in Brussels so as to be close to the commission and the Council of Ministers.

The growth in interest group activity at the European level has followed the growth of the powers and influence of the EU institutions, or the "Europeanization" of policy areas that were previously the exclusive province of national governments.[16] Interest groups have not always simply followed the evolution of the EU, going wherever new opportunities for influence have presented themselves, but they have often been actively involved in pushing the EU in new directions. Business leaders, for example, were champions of the single market, arguing that competition among European corporations was a handicap to their ability to take on the Americans and the Japanese.

At the same time, the European Commission in particular has encouraged interest group activity, helping to open channels for the participation of Europe-wide groups at almost every stage of policymaking. This may have slowed down the policy process, but it has also reduced the commission's workload, provided a ready source of expertise, and helped the commission monitor the compliance records of member states. Studies indicate that nearly seven hundred groups are working to influence decisions taken at the European level, about two-thirds of which have been in existence since 1980 or earlier. Just over 60 percent are business groups, 21 percent deal with public interest issues, and 16 percent are professional organizations.[17]

Historically business and labor groups have dominated European-level interest representation, mainly because the process of integration has been driven for so long by economic issues.[18] As the EU has exerted greater power and influence since the mid-1980s over competition, mergers, the movement of workers, and related matters, so business and labor groups have turned their attention to activities in the commission and the Council of Ministers. Not only are individual corporations represented either directly or through lobbying firms in Brussels, but lobbying groups also represent broader sectors, such as the plastics, chemicals, and paper industries, and cross-sectoral federations have been created to represent wider memberships. Notable among these groups are the Union of Industrial and Employers' Confederations of Europe (UNICE), which was created in 1958 and now represents thirty-two national business federations from twenty-two countries. Meanwhile, the European Round Table of Industrialists brings together the chief executives of major European corporations, such as Fiat, Philips, ICI, and Siemens, and the EU Committee of the American Chamber of Commerce represents the interests of American firms that are active in Europe.

European labor is also represented in Brussels, most notably through groups such as the European Trade Union Confederation (ETUC), which was founded in 1972 and whose membership consists of a combination of European-level industry federations and national labor federations, such as Britain's TUC or Germany's DGB. At the same time, professional interests are represented by groups such as the Council of European Professional and Managerial Staff (EUROCADRES) and by associations representing everything from architects to dentists, journalists, opticians, and veterinarians. Several Brussels-based interest groups include member organizations from outside the EU, reflecting the extent to which the EU has come to matter to business and labor throughout Europe. Recent years have also seen a rise in the activities of groups representing public (or nonproducer) interests, such as consumer issues and human rights issues, as represented by the European Bureau of Consumer Unions and Amnesty International.

The environment provides a good example of an issue that has attracted growing attention from special interest groups as the EU has become more involved in matters about which they care. Particularly until the 1970s, most of the pressure for domestic environmental regulation in industrialized countries came from interest groups; they not only provided the pressure for policy change but also the ideas and the scientific data on which change was based.

Among EC member states, there was initially little inclination for those groups to lobby Community institutions because most environmental policy was still made at the national level, and the priorities varied from one member state to another. However, environmental groups have become increasingly active at the European level since the mid-1980s because the expanding body of European environmental laws and policies has made EU institutions (notably the commission) a more profitable target for interest group pressure. These institutions also lack the resources to collect information or to enforce laws, and welcome the input of interest groups.

The importance of European initiatives on the environment has been reflected in the opening of offices in Brussels since the second half of the 1980s by such groups as Friends of the Earth, Greenpeace, and the World Wide Fund for Nature, while many other groups have employed full-time lobbyists. It has also been reflected in the increased activities of groups representing the industrial perspective on environmental issues, such as the European Chemical Industry Council, Eurelectric, and the European Crop Protection Association.

Increased access to EU policymakers has led, in turn, to a more systematic approach among environmental groups to Euro-lobbying, and a clear trend toward approaching domestic environmental problems as EU-wide problems. The complexity of these problems has encouraged domestic groups to work more closely together and to form transnational coalitions, the best known of which is the European Environmental Bureau (EEB). Founded in 1974 with the encouragement of the commission, the EEB is an umbrella body for national interest groups in the EU and acts as a conduit for the representation of those groups in the EU institutions, particularly the commission. The bureau now claims to represent more than 130 national environmental groups with a combined membership of 23 million.

The methods that eurogroups use are similar to those used by groups at any level: promoting public awareness in support of their cause, building membership numbers in order to build influence and credibility, representing the views of their members, building networks with other interest groups, providing information to the EU institutions, meeting with EU lawmakers in an attempt to influence the content of law, and monitoring the implementation of EU law at the national level.

Aspinwall and Greenwood argue that the representation of interests at the European level has become more diversified and specialized, and that eurogroups are becoming protagonists, trying to influence policy rather than simply to monitor events, and using increasingly sophisticated means to attract allegiance.[19] Something of a symbiotic relationship has developed between the commission and interest groups, with the former actively supporting the work of many groups and giving them access to its advisory committee meetings, and the latter doing what they can to influence the content and development of policy and legislative proposals as they work their way through the commission.

The activities of interest groups have helped offset the problem of the democratic deficit by offering Europeans channels outside the formal structure of EU institutions that they can use to influence EU policy. They have also helped focus the attention of the members of interest groups on the expanding influence of the EU on the policies that affect their lives, have helped draw them more actively into the process by which the EU makes its decisions, and have encouraged them to bypass their national governments and to focus their attention on European responses to shared and common problems.

However, the work of interest groups does not disguise the problem of the democratic deficit, Franklin describes the lack of proper democratic accountability in the EU as "a crisis of legitimacy."[20] It is unlikely that the essential psychological link between EU institutions and EU citizens will be made until such time as the European Parliament becomes a true legislature, national political parties form pan-European federations and run as such, and the outcome of European elections has a direct effect on the content and performance of the commission and the Council of Ministers. This will not happen as long as the governments of the member states feel the need to use the Council of Ministers as the guarantor of national interests.

The Media

Partly because of language barriers, and partly because Europeans are only slowly beginning to take a more active interest in what is happening in other parts of the European Union, there is very little in the way of a European media system. All EU member states are dominated by national radio, television, and newspapers, and attempts to build pan-European media have so far had little success. For example, *The European* was launched in the mid-1980s as a daily European newspaper, but it was published in Britain and was in English; it subsequently became a weekly. The five-nation Europa-TV consortium, which hoped to transmit multilingual TV broadcasts to five million homes in the EC, collapsed in 1986 after amassing huge debts. More recently, Euronews was created in 1993 as a multilingual European response to CNN. Based in Lyon, France, it broadcasts twenty-four hours per day to cable and satellite viewers and shares some newsgathering operations with CNN, but it faces stiff competition from nationally based services in Britain, Germany, and France, as well as American channels such as NBC and CNN. It is owned jointly by eighteen European broadcasters, with Britain's Independent Television News holding a 49 percent stake.

In 1984, the European Commission developed a green paper entitled "Television Without Borders," and the Cockfield White Paper that was the basis of the Single European Act talked of the need to develop a single market in TV broadcasting, which the commission saw as an important element of the broader single market project. The commission subsequently tried to become involved in regulating satellite broadcasting, but the technology was developing faster than it could respond; its involvement was also criticized by several member states, which argued that it had no competence in this area.

A major concern for the commission has been controlling the cultural inroads made by Anglo-American broadcasting and trying to protect the European cinema and electronics industries from U.S. and Japanese competition. A directive was adopted on television broadcasting in 1989, which was aimed at making sure broadcasters—"where practicable"—used a majority of European programming. The attempt to impose quotas faces other problems as well: U.S. films and TV shows are more popular on the continent than is much locally produced material, and Europeans do not tend to much like each other's programming; for example, the French, the Germans, and the British have very different senses of humor. Finally, and most telling, there is the twin assault of U.S. programming provided by CNN and MTV and Anglo-American programming provided by British satellite companies such as Sky Television and British Satellite Broadcasting.

POLITICAL SYSTEM

As the European Union has grown, so has the body of laws and policies that drive its activities, and so have the powers and reach of the institutions that make, decide, and implement those laws and policies. Unfortunately, the concerns among the governments of the member states about loss of sovereignty have resulted in an institutional structure that is complex, confusing, and constantly changing. The powers and roles of the institutions have evolved slowly and unsteadily, often responding incrementally to short-term needs rather than according to any grand blueprint of what the governments of the member states want them eventually to become. The negotiations leading up to the treaty of Amsterdam were to have included major innovations but ended up doing little more than providing some light tinkering, so more changes are anticipated as the pressure for institutional reform grows and membership of the EU expands over the next few years.

The EU institutions cannot easily be compared with the conventional institutions of government at the national level. The comparisons can be made, but they must always be qualified: the College of Commissioners is something like a cabinet, but not entirely; the

European Parliament is a legislature but lacks many of the lawmaking powers of a true legislature; the European Commission is more than a bureaucracy, and so on. Furthermore, the institutions do not amount to a "government" in the conventional sense of the word because the member states still hold most of the decision-making powers and are still responsible for implementing EU policies; however, the institutions are becoming more powerful and significant, and their evolution is having the effect of slowly building a European government.

In brief, the five major institutions of the EU work as follows: the (1) European Commission is responsible for developing proposals for laws and policies, on which final decisions are taken by the (2) Council of Ministers in a complex interaction with the (3) European Parliament. Once a decision is made, the European Commission is then responsible for overseeing the implementation of laws and policies by the member states. Meanwhile, the (4) European Court of Justice works to build a common body of law for the EU and to make judgments on the correlation between EU law, national laws, and the EU treaties, while the (5) European Council brings the leaders of the member states together periodically to guide the overall direction of the European Union. Alongside these Big Five institutions is an expanding family of specialized bodies dealing with everything from regional policy to drug regulation, policing, and environmental research.

As with all systems of administration, this brief outline says nothing about the many subtle (and not so subtle) pressures that are brought to bear on European decision making, nor does it convey the many informal aspects of EU government: the different levels of influence exerted by member states; the political and economic pressures that drive the decisions of the member states; the roles played by interest groups, corporations, commission staff, and specialized working groups within the Council of Ministers; and all the muddling through that often characterizes policymaking in the EU, as in the member states.

The Constitution

The EU does not have a constitution in the sense that there is a single codified document that outlines the structure and powers of government and the rights of individuals. Instead, it has a complex body of treaties and laws that together amount to the functional equivalent of a constitution. The caution with which the member states have approached regional integration has so far discouraged them from calling a "constitutional convention" to combine and simplify all these documents. Instead, they have met occasionally at intergovernmental conferences (IGCs) where their representatives have agreed to amendments to the founding treaties.

The six major treaties are: Paris (1951), the two treaties of Rome (1957), the Single European Act (1987), the Maastricht treaty (1992), and the treaty of Amsterdam (1998). Each treaty has expanded and elaborated on the previous treaty, so that the sum of the agreements made by the EU can now be found in the text of the treaty of Amsterdam. The specific obligations of the member states can be found in the thousands of laws they have agreed on, many of which have undergone repeated amendment.

The European Commission

The EU decision-making process begins with the European Commission, which is the executive-bureaucratic arm of the EU. It develops proposals for new laws and policies, oversees the implementation of law, promotes the interests of the EU as a whole, manages the finances of the EU, and represents the member states collectively in negotiations with international organizations such as the United Nations and the World Trade Organization. It is the most supranational of the EU

The headquarters of the European Commission in Brussels, Belgium. Symbolically, it was closed for most of the 1990s for a major refurbishment, just as the goverments of the EU member states were rethinking the goals of European integration.

institutions and has long been at the heart of the process of European integration. It has not only encouraged member states to harmonize their laws, regulations, and standards, but it has also been the source of key policy initiatives, notably the completion of the single market.

Despite its importance, the commission is regularly the target of criticism, with Euroskeptics grumbling about waste and meddling by "Eurocrats" and complaints that the leaders of the commission are not elected and that its staff have little public accountability. For some, "Brussels" has become a codeword for some vague and threatening notion of government by bureaucracy, or "creeping federalism," and the need for institutional reform reached a head in March 1999 when the twenty-member College of Commissioners resigned following publication of a report cataloging instances of fraud and nepotism. However, the picture painted by the media is not entirely fair; the vast majority of commission employees are hard working and competent, and the commission has much less power than its detractors often suggest; it is not a decision-making body, and its powers are being reduced as those of other EU institutions grow. It is also very small given the size of its task; it has just over twenty-thousand staff, making it much smaller than many national government ministries.

The commission is headquartered in Brussels, its staff working in buildings around the city, in regional cities around the EU, and in national capitals around the world. It has three main elements: the College of Commissioners, the president of the commission, and the directorates-general.

The College of Commissioners The commission is led by a group of twenty commissioners, who serve five-year terms and function as something like a European cabinet. Each has a portfolio for which he or she is responsible, and one is appointed president. The twenty posts are distributed among the EU member states, with the five biggest countries (Germany, Britain, France, Italy, and Spain) having two each, and the rest one each.

Commissioners are appointed by their national governments but are not national representatives, and they must swear an oath of office saying that they will renounce any defense of national interests. There are no formal rules on appointments, but appointees usually must be acceptable to the other commissioners, to other governments, to the major political parties at home, and to the European Parliament[21]; they tend to be people who already have a national political reputation at home and can be appointed for a variety of reasons, including a reward for public service at home, political expediency, or the desire to remove someone from the domestic scene.

At the beginning of each term, all twenty commissioners are given portfolios, the distribution of which is done at the prerogative of the president; this has great political significance and is seen as an acid test of the abilities of the president to lead.[22] Despite regular claims of collegiality among commissioners, the college has its own internal hierarchy of positions: the key posts are those concerned with the budget, agriculture, and external relations.

The President The dominating figure in the commission hierarchy is the president, who is technically no more than a first among equals, but—like prime ministers in parliamentary systems—holds the trump card of the power of appointment. The president oversees meetings of the college, represents the commission in dealings with other EU institutions and national governments, and is responsible for making sure that the commission maintains the impetus of European integration. The president serves renewable five-year terms, but there are no formal rules regarding how the president is appointed. It has become normal for the leaders of the member states to decide the appointment at the European Council meeting held in the June before the term of the incumbent commission ends, settling on someone acceptable to all of them, to the commission itself, and to the European Parliament.

TABLE 9.3	Presidents of the European Commission
1958–67	Walter Hallstein (West Germany)
1968–69	Jean Rey (Belgium)
1970–72	Franco Maria Malfatti (Italy)
1972	Sicco Mansholt (Netherlands)
1973–76	Francois-Xavier Ortoli (France)
1977–80	Roy Jenkins (Britain)
1981–84	Gaston Thorn (Luxembourg)
1985–94	Jacques Delors (France)
1995-99	Jacques Santer (Luxembourg)
1999–present	Romano Prodi (Italy)

In recent years, the president has become a more important and visible figure. The job was given new prominence by Jacques Delors of France, who held the post in 1985–1994 and introduced a more presidential element to the government of the EU.[23] He had firm ideas about a strong, federal Europe asserting itself internationally and used this vision to push the EU in many new directions; during his term, for example, the Single European Act was developed and adopted, and the groundwork was laid for the development of the single European currency. His successor was Jacques Santer, former prime minister of Luxembourg, who launched fewer new initiatives and took a more relaxed approach to his job, thereby—according to his critics—creating the atmosphere that led to the corruption scandal of 1999. Santer was succeeded by Romano Prodi, former prime minister of Italy, who was charged with reforming the structure of the commission.

Directorates-General Below the college, the European Commission is divided into twenty-four directorates-general (DGs), which are the functional equivalent of national government ministries. Every DG is responsible for a particular area, has its own director-general, and is tied to a particular commissioner. Some DGs are more important (and bigger and wealthier) than others, the ranking being a reflection of the extent to which the EU is active in different policy areas; hence, those dealing with external affairs, industry, and agriculture are more powerful, whereas those dealing with fisheries, energy, and education are smaller and less influential.

About two-thirds of commission staff work on drawing up new laws and policies, or on overseeing implementation, about 20 percent are involved in research, and the rest are involved in translation and interpretation; the commission works mainly in English and French, but its documents must be translated into all eleven official EU languages.

The Council of Ministers

The Council of Ministers is the decision-making branch of the EU, the primary champion of national interests, and arguably the most powerful of the EU institutions. Once the commission has proposed a new law or policy, it is discussed and amended by the European Parliament, and the Council of Ministers is then responsible for the final decision on whether or not the proposal will become law. The council has three main elements: the ministers themselves, the permanent representatives, and the presidency.

The Ministers The Council of Ministers actually consists of multiple councils, with different groups of national ministers meeting according to the topic under discussion. Hence, agriculture ministers meet to take decisions on agricultural law and policy, the environment ministers to address new proposals for environmental law and policy, and so on. The number of meetings that each group holds varies and is a good reflection of the policy priorities of the EU: foreign, agriculture, and finance ministers meet monthly on average, fisheries and technology ministers every two months, and education and energy ministers only about twice each year. Most meetings last no more than one or two days and are usually held in Brussels.

When it comes to voting, the ministers have one of three options: a straight majority can be used on selected issues (notably matters relating to the single market), unanimity may be required if the council is considering a proposal that will move the EU into an entirely new policy area or substantially change an existing policy (but its use is now heavily restricted), and on all other matters it uses a qualified majority. Each minister is given several votes roughly in proportion to the population of his/her member state (while the Big Four countries have ten each, Luxembourg has just two) for a total of eighty-seven votes (see Table 9.4). To be successful, a proposal must win sixty-two of those votes; it can also be defeated by a blocking minority of twenty-six votes.

Permanent Representatives The main reason why the meetings of ministers are so short is because most of the key issues have already been discussed by specialists from national delegations consisting of about thirty to forty professional diplomats, who meet weekly with their counterparts in the powerful Committee of Permanent Representatives (COREPER). COREPER acts as a link between Brussels and the member states, represents the views of the governments of the member state, and ensures that the capitals are kept in touch with developments in Brussels. More important, representatives meet to discuss proposals for new laws and policies and to resolve as many differences as possible so that the workload of the ministers is reduced to a minimum. This gives them considerable power and influence.

The Presidency The presidency of the Council of Ministers (and of the European Council) is held not by a person but by a country. Every member state takes turns at holding the presidency for spells of six months each, beginning in January and July each year. The state holding the presidency sets the agenda for the EU as a whole, oversees EU foreign policy for six

TABLE 9.4 Representation in the Council of Ministers and the European Parliament

	Population (millions)	Votes in Council of Ministers	Seats in European Parliament
Germany	82.2	10	99
France	58.5	10	87
United Kingdom	58.2	10	87
Italy	57.2	10	87
Spain	39.7	8	64
Netherlands	15.7	5	31
Greece	10.5	5	25
Belgium	10.2	5	25
Portugal	9.8	5	25
Sweden	8.8	4	22
Austria	8.2	4	21
Denmark	5.2	3	16
Finland	5.1	3	16
Ireland	3.6	3	15
Luxembourg	0.4	2	6
Total	373.3	87	626

months, acts as the main voice of the EU on the global stage, represents the EU at meetings with the president of the United States, and hosts the biannual summit of the European Council (see following). Throughout, it mediates and bargains and is responsible for promoting cooperation among member states. The success of a presidency is measured according to the extent to which the incumbent member state is able to encourage compromise and agreement among the EU members, as well as by what is delayed, opposed, or promoted.[24]

Holding the presidency allows a member state to convene meetings and launch initiatives on issues of national interest, to try to bring those issues to the top of the EU agenda, and to earn prestige and credibility, assuming it does a good job. It allows the leaders of smaller states to negotiate directly with other world leaders and helps the process of European integration by making the EU more real to the citizens of the country holding the presidency; it helps them feel more involved and helps them see that they have a stake in the development of the EU.

European Commision President Romano Prodi (left), shown here meeting with Italian president Oscar Luigi Scalfaro in 1998 while Prodi was still prime minister of Italy. Prodi was widely expected to bring much-needed reforms to the culture of the commission.

The European Parliament

The European Parliament (EP) is the only directly elected institution in the EU system, but it has relatively few powers over how law and policy are made. It has many of the trappings of a conventional legislature but lacks three critical powers: it cannot introduce laws, enact laws, or raise revenues. It can suggest that the commission propose a new law or policy, it can amend laws as they go through the commission and the Council of Ministers, and it has equal powers with the council over the EU budget, but the commission and the council still hold most of the cards.

Despite its handicaps, the EP has used arguments about democratic accountability to win more responsibilities and to be taken more seriously. It has become less a body that reacts to commission proposals and council votes, and has increasingly launched its own initiatives and forced the other institutions to pay more attention to its opinions. Parliament has won more rights to amend laws and to check the activities of the other institutions, it has been a valuable source of ideas and new policy proposals, and it has acted as the conscience of the EU and the guardian of its democratic ideals[25]; however, it does these things mainly behind the scenes because it attracts much less public and media interest than the European Commission.

The EP consists of a single chamber, and its 626 members (MEPs) are directly elected by universal suffrage for fixed, renewable five-year terms. The number of seats is divided among the member states roughly on the basis of population, so that Germany has ninety-nine whereas Luxembourg has just six (see Table 9.4). Parliament's buildings are divided among three cities: the administrative headquarters are in Luxembourg, parliamentary committees meet in Brussels for about two to three weeks every month (except August), and the parliamentary chamber is situated in Strasbourg, France. Because committees are where most of the real bargaining and revising takes place, and because "additional" plenaries can be held in Brussels, the Strasbourg plenaries are relatively poorly attended, and MEPs tend to spend most of their time in Brussels.

Although it cannot introduce legislation, parliament's powers to influence and amend EU law have grown. As well as the advisory and supervisory powers set out in the treaties, Parliament has several essentially negative powers: the commission tries to anticipate the EP's position while drawing up a proposal, Parliament can delay or kill a proposal by sitting on it, and Parliament has the power to dismiss the commission.[26] Unfortunately, the concern of member states with preserving their powers over decision making in the Council of Ministers has created a complex legislative process under which parliament, depending on the kind of law under consideration, is asked to do anything from offering a nonbinding opinion to taking part in a give-and-take with the Council of Ministers that can involve a legislative proposal undergoing two readings (the "cooperation procedure") or even three readings (the "codecision procedure") in the EP. The latter process effectively gives the EP equal powers with the Council of Ministers over decisions on new laws.

Parliament also has joint powers with the council over fixing the EU budget, and it has several powers over the other EU institutions, including the right to debate the annual program of the commission, to take the commission or the council to the Court of Justice over alleged infringements of the treaties, and to approve the appointment of all the commissioners. The most potentially disruptive of Parliament's powers is its ability—with a two-thirds majority—to force the resignation of the College of Commissioners through a vote of censure. This is mainly a deterrent power, and has never been used, although the EP came close in January 1999 when it threatened to remove the college over allegations that several commissioners should be held accountable for fraud within their departments. The vote failed, but a committee was appointed, whose report led to the resignation of the College of Commissioners in March.

The European Court of Justice

The task of the Court of Justice is to build a body of common law for the EU which is equally, fairly, and consistently applied throughout the member states, to rule on the interpretation of the treaties and of EU laws, and to ensure that national and European laws—and international agreements being considered by the EU—meet the terms and the spirit of the treaties. It does this mainly by interpreting EU treaties and laws, and by giving rulings to national courts in cases where there are questions about the meaning of EU law. EU law takes precedence over the national laws of member states where the two conflict, but only in areas where the EU is active and where the member states have given up powers to the EU. Hence, the court has no powers over criminal law or family law but has made most of its decisions on the kind of economic issues in which the EU has been most actively involved.

The court made its most fundamental contribution to European integration in 1963 and 1964 when it declared that the Treaty of Rome was not just a treaty, but was also a constitutional instrument that imposed direct and common obligations on member states and took precedence over national law. Subsequent court rulings have confirmed the primacy of EU law, simplified completion of the single market by establishing the principle that a product made and sold legally in one member state cannot be barred from another, helped increase the powers of Parliament, strengthened individual rights, promoted free movement of workers, reduced gender discrimination, and helped the commission break down the barriers to competition.[27]

Based in Luxembourg, the court has four main elements: the judges, the president, the advocates general, and the Court of First Instance.

The Judges The Court of Justice has fifteen judges, each appointed for a six-year renewable term of office. About half come up for renewal every three years, so terms are staggered. The judges are theoretically appointed by common accord of the member state governments, but because every member state has the right to make one appointment, all fifteen are effectively national appointees. Apart from being acceptable to all of the other member states, judges must be legally competent and scrupulously independent, and they must avoid promoting the national interests of their home states. They are not allowed to hold administrative or political office while they are on the court, and while they can resign their positions, they can only be removed by other judges and the advocates general (not by member states or other EU institutions), and then only by unanimous agreement that they are no longer doing their job adequately.[28]

The President The judges elect one of their own by majority vote to be president for a three-year renewable term. The president presides over court meetings, is responsible for distributing cases among the judges and deciding the dates for hearings, and has considerable influence over the political direction of the court.

The Advocates General Copied from the French legal model, the nine advocates general are advisors who look at each of the cases as they come in, study the arguments, and deliver a preliminary opinion before the judges on what action should be taken and on which EU law applies. The judges are not obliged to agree with the opinion, or even to refer to it, but it gives them a point of reference from which to reach a decision. One is appointed by each of the Big Five member states, and the rest are appointed by the smaller states.

The Court of First Instance The Court of Justice has become much busier over time and now hears about 370 to 400 cases per year and makes about 200 to 300 judgments. As the volume of work grew during the 1970s and 1980s, it was taking the court up to two years to reach a decision on more complex cases. To clear the logjam, agreement was reached to create a subsidiary Court of First Instance in 1989. With fifteen members, its job is to be the first point of decision on less complicated cases. If cases are lost at this level, the parties involved may appeal to the Court of Justice.

The European Council

The European Council is the newest of the EU's five major institutions, although it is really more a process or a forum than an institution. It consists of the heads of government of EU member states, their foreign ministers, and the president and vice-presidents of the commission. This small group convenes at least twice per year at short summit meetings to provide strategic policy direction for the EU. The council is something like a steering committee or a board of directors for the EU; it sketches out the broad picture and leaves it to the other institutions to fill in the details.

The council was created in 1974 in response to a growing feeling among European leaders that the EEC needed stronger leadership to clear blockages in decision making and to give it a clearer sense of direction. Its existence was only finally given legal recognition with the Single European Act. Maastricht elaborated on its role but did not provide much clarity: it said that the Council would "provide the Union with the necessary impetus for its development and shall define the general political guidelines thereof." The council has been an important motor for integration and has launched major new initiatives (such as the European Monetary System in 1978, the Maastricht treaty in 1991, and the IGC that led to the Amsterdam treaty), issued major declarations on international crises, reached key decisions on EC institutional changes (such as the decision to begin direct elections to the European Parliament), and given new momentum to EU foreign policy. The council has also had its failures, however, including its inability to speed up agricultural or budgetary reform, or to agree on common EU responses to the Iraqi and Balkan crises.

The council normally meets every year in June and December, with special summits held as needed to deal with emergencies or particular problems. Summits are usually heralded by months of intensive preparation, so that most of the big decisions have already been agreed on before the heads of government come together. The summits themselves normally last just two days, are hosted by the country holding the presidency of the EU, and take place either in the capital of that country, or in a regional city or town. The goal of each summit is to agree to a set of conclusions, an advanced draft of which is usually awaiting the leaders at the beginning of the summit and that provides the focus for discussions. Council decisions are usually taken on the basis of unanimity, or at least of consensus, but the occasional lack of unanimity may force a formal vote, and some member states may want to attach conditions or reservations to the conclusions.

The summits are always major media events and are surrounded by extensive security. As well as the substantive political discussions that take place, enormous symbolism is attached to the outcomes of the summits, which are assessed according to the extent to which they represent breakthroughs or show EU leaders to be bogged down in disagreement. Failure and success reflect not only on the presidency but also on the whole process of European integration. The headline-making nature of the summits is enough in itself to concentrate the minds of participants and to encourage them to agree.

The European Council has more power over decision making than any other EU institution;

it can, in effect, set the agenda for the commission, override decisions reached by the Council of Ministers, and largely ignore parliament altogether. Certainty about the present and potential future role of the council is clouded by its ambiguities, and opinion remains divided over whether it is an integrative or a disintegrative body.²⁹

Other Institutions

As the powers and reach of the European Union have expanded, so an expanding group of specialized agencies has been founded to focus on specific elements of EU policy. These include the following:

- *European Investment Bank.* Based in Luxembourg, this autonomous institution was set up in 1958 to encourage "balanced and steady development" by making loans and giving guarantees. Its projects are designed to help poorer regions of the EU and to support modernization and improve the competitiveness of European industry, and they must be of common interest to several member states or the EU as a whole. Its biggest project to date has been the Channel Tunnel (Chunnel) linking Britain and France.

- *Court of Auditors.* Based in Luxembourg, this was set up in 1977 to act as an independent watchdog on EU financial affairs. It carries out annual audits of the accounts of EU institutions and has been active in drawing attention to financial mismanagement and fraud.

- *European Environment Agency.* Based in Copenhagen, this was set up in 1993 to collect information from the member states and neighboring non-EU states to help improve the quality of environmental protection policies. Among other things, it publishes a triennial report on the state of the European environment.

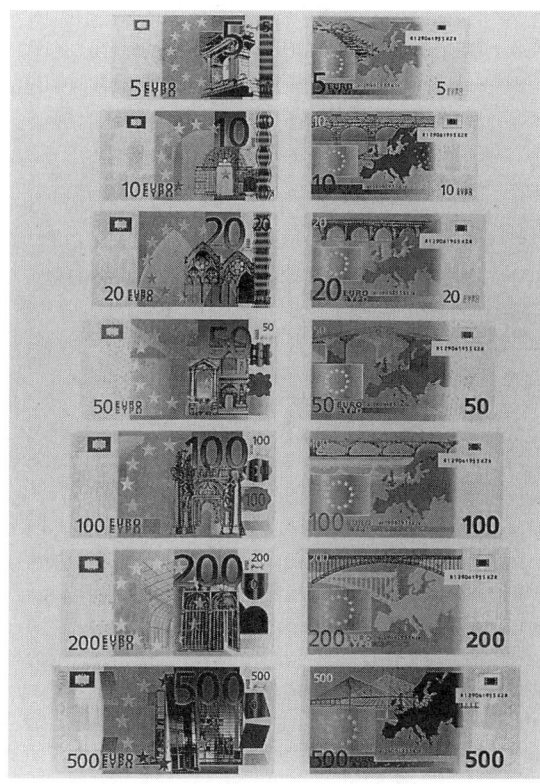

Designs for the new euro banknotes, which are set to replace most national currencies in the European Union in 2002. Since 1998, decisions on monetary policy in the euro-zone have been made by the European Central Bank.

- *European Agency for the Evaluation of Medicinal Products (EMEA).* Based in London, this was set up in 1995 to harmonize (but not replace) the work of national drug regulatory agencies, to help reduce the costs that drug companies incur by having to win separate approval from each member state, and to eliminate the protectionist tendencies of states that are unwilling to open their domestic drug markets to competition from other EU member states.

- *European Central Bank.* The most powerful of the specialized agencies, the bank is based in Frankfurt and was founded in

1998 to replace the European Monetary Institute (created 1994). Modeled on the famously independent German Bundesbank, its job is to ensure monetary stability by setting interest rates in relation to the euro. It has a governing body consisting of the central bank governors of the member states and a full-time executive board whose six members serve nonrenewable eight-year terms.

POLICIES AND POLICYMAKING

Debates have long raged about how policy is made and implemented at the national level in democracies, even though most have relatively predictable, stable, and institutionalized systems of government. Taken to the level of the European Union, those debates become more complicated. Not only is its governing structure very different from those found in conventional states, but the EU is still evolving, the balance of power among its institutions and member states is constantly changing, there is no EU constitution, and there are many ambiguities built into its major treaties. This complicates the task of defining and identifying the key sources of power and of describing (or at least predicting) how that power is used (Figure 9.1).

Although the sources and parameters of EU power are ambiguous, its authority has clearly deepened and broadened. From a time when the EU dealt only with coal and steel policy, the member states have transferred so many powers that the EU now touches (to varying degrees) on most aspects of economic, foreign, social, agricultural, and environmental policy. Despite this "Europeanization" of the policy process, however, and despite concerns about loss of sovereignty and complaints about the mythical monolith of "Brussels," the EU still has no direct powers of enforcement and implementation and has a very small budget (about $110 billion in 1999). The EU records in the fields of economic and foreign policy offer useful contrasts of the impact of integration on the powers of the member states. In the case of the former, the balance of power rests firmly with the EU and considerable progress has been made toward the development of common policies. In the case of the latter, the balance still rests with the member states, and while several smaller member states follow the lead of the EU, the larger states still pursue their own interests. Common policies exist in areas such as development cooperation, but there is still little in the way of a common EU defense policy.

Economic Policy

For most of its short life, the European Union has been driven mainly by the goal of economic integration. It was born in the early 1950s as a limited experiment in economic cooperation, grew in the 1960s to become a customs union, wrestled during the 1970s with attempts to build common economic policies and exchange rate stability, focused in the late 1980s on completing the single market, and is now working on the conversion to a single currency. The EU has made progress in other policy areas (such as agriculture, the environment, and development aid to poorer countries), but only since the late 1980s has it really paid more direct attention to issues outside the economic sphere.

Elements of the single market were built during the first ten to fifteen years, the Common Agricultural Policy was in place by the late 1960s (ensuring that farmers were paid guaranteed prices for their produce), and the customs union was completed in 1968. However, nontariff barriers persisted, including varying technical standards and quality controls and different levels of indirect taxation. In the mid-1970s, recession encouraged member

FIGURE 9.1 The European Union Policymaking Process

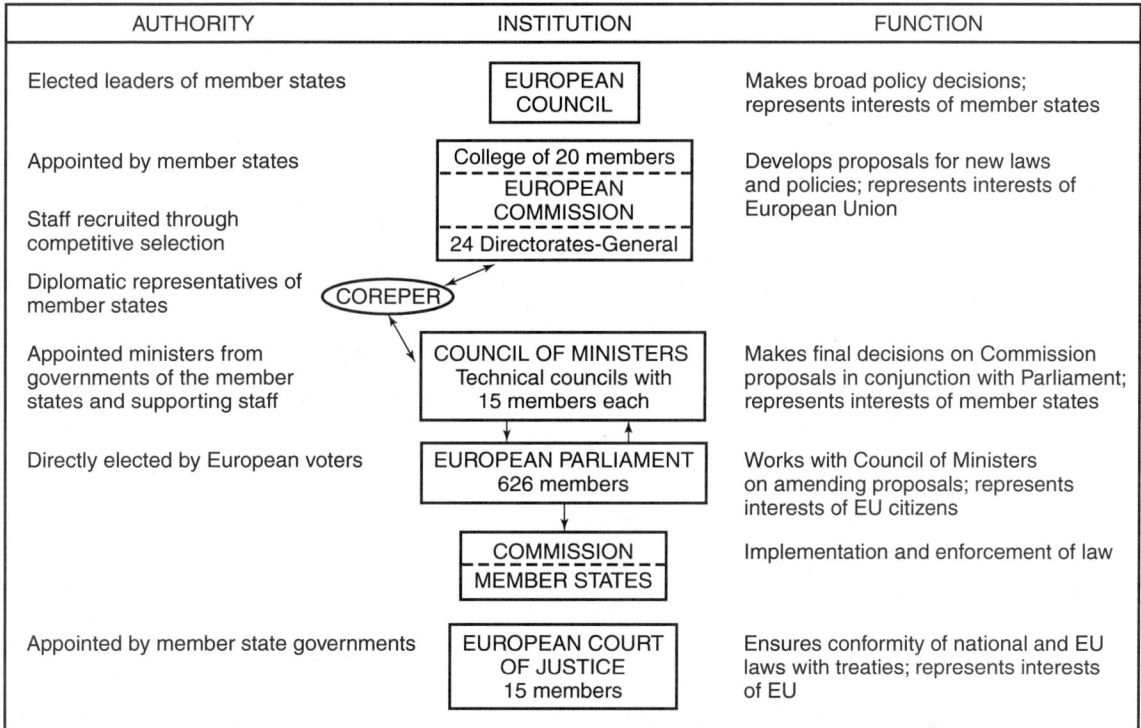

states to think more about protecting their national markets than about completing the single European market, and the process of building the European Community seemed to have become unstuck.

By the 1980s, there was a growing sense that something needed to be done to reverse the EC's relative economic decline and to exploit more fully the potential of the European marketplace, which had almost as many consumers as the United States and Japan combined. This change of thinking produced two landmark initiatives: the Single European Act (signed in 1986 with the goal of completing the single market by December 1992) and the plan for a single European currency, which led to eleven member states adopting the euro in January 1999.

The Single Market

The goal of the Single European Act (SEA) was to remove the remaining nontariff barriers to the free movement of people, goods, services, and capital between 1987 and 1992. Those barriers took three main forms: physical, fiscal, and technical.

The physical barriers consisted of customs and border checks at the EC's internal frontiers, which persisted because national governments wanted to control the movement of people (especially illegal immigrants), collect taxes and excises on goods being moved from one state to another, and enforce different health standards. Almost all of the internal checks were gradually removed in the late 1980s, a process that was accelerated by the signing in 1985 by France, Germany, and Benelux states of the Schengen Agreement. Named for the town in Luxembourg near which it was signed, it abolishes all border controls among its signatories, which now include all member states except Britain and Ireland; membership has even been extended to non-EU members Iceland and Norway. Its implementation has meant the end of checks at airports for flights among signatory states, the free circulation of people, common rules on asylum, the right of hot pursuit across frontiers, and moves toward a common policy on visas.

With the SEA opening up borders among member states, and Maastricht making justice and home affairs one of the three pillars of the European Union, some direction had to be given to the development of police cooperation. This realization led to the creation of the European Police Office, or Europol, which is charged with setting up an EU-wide system of information exchange targeted at combating terrorism, drug trafficking, vehicle smuggling, clandestine immigration networks, illegal nuclear material trafficking, money laundering, and other serious forms of international crime. Set up in 1993 as the European Drug Unit, its name changed with the signing in June 1996 of the Europol Convention, and it became fully operational in October 1998. Based in The Hague, Europol is not a law enforcement body in the mold of the FBI in the United States but is rather a criminal intelligence organization. Its job is to coordinate operations in its selected fields of responsibility among the national police forces of the EU. Because there is no common penal code or police law in the EU, it is unlikely that there will be a common European police force any time soon.[30]

Fiscal barriers included indirect taxation, which caused distortions of competition and artificial price differences among the member states and so posed a barrier to the single market. All fifteen member states have a value-added tax (VAT), but rates in the 1980s were as low as 12 percent in Luxembourg and as high as 22 percent in Denmark. Excise duties also varied, reflecting different levels of national concern about human health; for example, smokers in France paid nearly twice as much tax on cigarettes as those in Spain, smokers in Ireland paid four times as much, and smokers in Denmark paid six times as much.

Under the SEA, duty-free limits were gradually decreased and then were abolished altogether in January 1993. Agreement was reached in 1991 on a minimum rate of 15 percent VAT, with lower rates on basic necessities such as food, and in 1992 various minimum rates were agreed on excise duties. Agreement has since been reached on an EU-wide VAT system in which tax is collected only in the country of origin, the ultimate goal being a single rate of VAT, or at least variations within a very narrow band.

The technical barriers to the single market came mainly from regulations based on different safety, health, environmental, and consumer protection standards, and many seemed petty and inconsequential: different definitions of chocolate that prevented British chocolate from being sold in many other member states, for example, or the insistence by Germans that no beer could be sold in Germany that did not meet national "purity laws." At one level, technical standards were in the interests of consumer safety; at another, they amounted to economic protectionism. The Community had tried to remove technical barriers by developing EC standards and encouraging member states to conform, but this was a time-consuming and tedious task that did little to discourage the common image of interfering Eurocrats.

Three breakthroughs helped to simplify the process: (1) a 1979 decision by the European Court of Justice confirmed that all member states had to accept products from other states that meet domestic technical standards; (2) a 1983 mutual information directive required member states to tell the commission and the other member states if they planned to implement any new domestic technical regulations and to allow the others three months to respond if they felt these regulations would create new barriers to trade; and (3) the single market program included a "new approach" to technical regulation: instead of having the commission try to work out agreements on every rule and regulation, general objectives would be agreed on and detailed specifications would be drawn up as needed up by existing standards institutes, such as the European Standardization Committee.

These three arrangements helped the EC clear many bureaucratic and political hurdles, but free trade continues to be handicapped by technical differences that the marketplace is powerless to overcome. For example, everyone in the EU drives on the right side of the road except the British and Irish, who drive on the left. Similarly, television systems are different throughout the EU, obliging manufacturers to make eight different kinds of television sets. Most member states use the German PAL system of TV broadcasting, but the French use their own system, called SECAM. (Both of these systems are different from the U.S. standard, NTSC.) Finally, the design of electrical plugs and sockets differs from one member to another, forcing travelers to take an adapter with them wherever they go. In theory, all three problems could be resolved; in practice, only the development of a common plug has been seriously considered, and even that is likely to prove prohibitively expensive.

Effects of the Single European Act

In contrast to the often controversial decisions taken during the course of European integration, the passage of the SEA was widely welcomed. In addition to accelerating economic integration, it has also had several more tangible effects on the lives of Europeans.

Rights of Residence With only a few minor restrictions remaining, any resident of an EU member state can live and work in any other EU member state, open a bank account, take out a mortgage, transfer unlimited amounts of capital, and vote in local and European elections. With the removal of barriers to free movement, Europeans are now moving more freely around the EU, and an estimated 15 million EU citizens now live in another EU state.

Standardization of Professional Qualifications The EU has had to reach agreement on the standardization and recognition of professional qualifications. This has not been easy (it took seventeen years to harmonize the requirements for architects and sixteen years for pharmacists, for example), but progress was made in 1988 with agreement on the general systems directive, under which member states agreed to trust that for some jobs, professional standards in other member states are adequate.[31] The list of mutually recognized professions is growing and now includes accountants, librarians, architects, engineers, and lawyers.

Joint Ventures and Corporate Mergers European corporations have a long history of transnational mergers, which have produced such giants as Unilever and Royal Dutch Shell (both Anglo-Dutch). Despite this history, from 1950 to the early 1980s, European companies steadily lost markets at home and abroad to competition, first from the United States and then from Japan. The single market has helped to promote a rapid growth in trans-European cooperative ventures. Notable joint ventures include those between Thompson of France and Philips of the Netherlands on high-definition television, BMW and Rolls-Royce on aeroengines, among the fourteen member states of the European Space Agency, and among the twelve member states of Arianespace, a space-launch consortium that now controls more than one-half of the global market for launching commercial satellites.

An unprecedented surge of takeovers and mergers has occurred since the mid-1980s, notably in the chemicals, pharmaceuticals, and electronics industries. The annual number of mergers and acquisitions tripled between 1984 and 1990, when the number of intra-EC mergers overtook the number of national mergers for the first time.[32] The European mergers and acquisitions market is now about two-thirds the size of that of the United States and is likely to overtake the U.S. market in the next few years. European corporations have also become increasingly aggressive in pursuing mergers, takeovers, and joint ventures outside the EU. Examples include the development of British Airways as one of the world's most profitable airlines, and the 1998 merger between Daimler-Benz of Germany and Chrysler in the United States.

At the same time, care has been taken to ensure that the bigger corporations do not develop monopolies and overwhelm smaller business, so the EU has developed a controversial competition policy to avoid abuses such as price fixing, and to watch out for "abuses of dominant position" by bigger companies.[33] The 1998 merger regulation allows the European Commission to scrutinize all large mergers (even those involving companies based outside the EU that might have an effect on EU business), and the commission also keeps an eye on the effect of state subsidies on competition in trade.[34]

A Common Transport System Markets are only as close as the ties that bind them, and one of the priorities of economic policy in the EU has been to build a system of Trans-European Networks (TENs) aimed at integrating fifteen different transport, energy supply, and telecommunications systems, thereby pulling the EU together and promoting mobility. The development of TENs has been helped by a dramatic increase in tourism (Europe is the biggest tourist destination in the world, capturing nearly 60 percent of the world tourist trade[35]) and by the revitalization of the rail industry as a cost-efficient and environmentally friendly alternative to road and air transport. The development of TENs is now one of the priorities of the EU, which has proposed a program aimed at spending a projected 400 billion euros ($400 billion) by 2010 on 44,000 miles of railroad track and 9,300 miles of new roads, mainly on the outer edges of the EU.

Toward a Single Currency

Few aspects of European integration have been so controversial as the idea of a single currency, yet few barriers to the creation of a true single market are so fundamental as the existence of fifteen different currencies with fluctuating exchange rates. Perhaps the riskiest step in the history of European integration was taken in January 1999 when eleven EU member states locked in their exchange rates as a prelude to the final switch in July 2002 to a single European currency.

The issue of the single currency cuts to the heart of sovereignty and independence because a state that gives up control over its national currency effectively gives up control over all significant domestic economic policy choices, such as the freedom to be able to adjust interest rates. There are also concerns that the single currency will prevent member states from being able to take the measures needed to deal with national and local economic cycles, which may be different from those experienced by their neighbors. On the other hand, the single currency removes the need for travelers to exchange currencies, replaces the national currencies that stand as a constant reminder to Europeans of the differences among their countries, helps consumers compare prices across the member states, and may help the EU build a world-class currency that has the same credibility in global markets as the U.S. dollar and the Japanese yen.

Stable exchange rates were identified by European leaders as early as the 1950s as being central to the building of a common market, but the postwar system of fixed exchange rates took care of most of their concerns. Only when this system began to crumble in the late 1960s, and finally collapsed with the U.S. decision in 1971 to break the link between gold and the U.S. dollar, did European leaders pay more attention to the idea of monetary union.

The European Monetary System (EMS) was created in 1979 with the goal of creating a zone of exchange rate stability and of keeping inflation under control. Despite teething troubles (including its near collapse in 1992–1993 when Britain and Italy left the ERM and several other countries had to devalue their currencies), the basic principles behind the goal of monetary union were affirmed by the Maastricht treaty, which set a timetable for the switch to a single currency. EU member states wanting to take part had to meet four "convergence criteria" that were considered essential prerequisites, including low inflation and interest rates, a low national budget deficit, and a public debt of less than 60 percent of GDP.

In 1995, it was decided to call the new currency the euro, and in May 1998 it was decided that all but four member states would join the euro when it was launched in January 1999; Britain, Denmark, and Sweden opted to stay out, and Greece did not meet all four criteria. Since its launch, participating countries have fixed the exchange rates of their national currencies against the euro, and the European Central Bank has been overseeing the single monetary policy. All of the Bank's dealings with commercial banks and all of its foreign exchange activities are now transacted in euros, which are quoted against the yen and the U.S. dollar. The next step is due to be taken on January 1, 2002, when euro coins and notes will become available. Europeans will then be given six months to make the final transition from national currencies to the euro and to turn in all of their old banknotes and coins, and national currencies will cease to be legal tender by July 1, 2002, at the latest.

One of the main motives behind European integration has been the argument that Europe must create the conditions in which it can meet external economic threats without being undermined by internal divisions. Although the euro steadily lost value against the dollar and yen in 1999–2000, the switch to a single currency will represent the crowning achievement of fifty years of effort (1952–2002) aimed at removing the barriers to trade among Europeans and the construction of a single market designed to allow Europe to compete on the global stage from a position of strength. It has been argued that European monetary integration has been driven in large part by external forces and the pressures of an international monetary system dominated by the U.S. dollar.[36] While its implications for the domestic economies of Europe are debatable, the successful adoption of the euro will clearly make the EU a substantial new actor in that international system.

Foreign and Security Policy

The crisis that peaked in the Yugoslav province of Kosovo in the first half of 1998 dragged European foreign policy into the harsh light of day and—as had been the case so many times before—found it wanting. European leaders were quick to condemn the actions taken by Yugoslav leader Slobodan Milosevic to squelch an insurrection led by ethnic Albanians living in the province, but they did not back up their words with significant action. As Serbian forces battled the Kosovo Liberation Army (KLA), leading to the deaths of dozens and the expulsion of as many as two hundred thousand Kosovars from their homes, EU foreign ministers dithered. Lacking European armed forces that could be sent into Yugoslavia to back up their verbal disapproval, equivocating over whether to encourage talks between the Serbs and the KLA or to back the demands of the KLA for full independence, and undecided over which international forum to use to put pressure on the Milosevic government, the EU saw the most active initiatives for peace being taken by the United States. When military action was finally taken in March 1999, it was under the auspices of the North Atlantic Treaty Organization (NATO), with the United States providing the bulk of the personnel, aircraft, and weapons.

For many, the EU response to this new crisis on its doorstep was another illustration of how little progress it was making on the development of a common foreign policy. As more was expected from the Europeans, so their inability to agree on critical security problems had become more visible. The divisions had been most notable during the Gulf crisis of 1990–1991, when Iraq invaded Kuwait; while European leaders condemned the invasion, the levels of support they gave to the U.S.-led counter-invasion varied dramatically, from the substantial commitment made in arms and personnel by Britain and France, to Belgium's refusal to sell ammunition to Britain, to the insistence by Ireland that it maintain its neutrality.[37] The divisions became clear again in responses to crises in the Balkans during the 1990s and in the refusal of all but Britain to support renewed U.S. threats against Iraq in 1998.

While the various international security crises of the 1990s may have found the EU unprepared and lacking both political unanimity and military preparedness, in other respects the EU *has* made progress on external policies and has become an increasingly assertive influence on international affairs. As Christopher Hill, political scientist, put it, setbacks have produced renewed efforts at policy cooperation, which has followed a pattern of peaks and troughs along a gradual upward gradient, and "consensus has become more habit-forming."[38] The EU may not yet be a military power, but its economic power is no longer in any doubt: its fifteen member states constitute the biggest and richest market in the world, and the EU has become a force to be reckoned with in international trade negotiations.

Foreign policy was a latecomer to the agenda of European integration. It was not mentioned in the Treaties of Rome, and the Communities focused during the 1950s and 1960s on internal economic matters, although the logic of spillover implied that it would be difficult to long avoid developing common external economic and security policies. Not until 1970 was agreement reached on European Political Cooperation (EPC), a process under which there would be more cooperation on foreign policy. EPC was given formal recognition with the passage of the Single European Act, but it remained a loose and voluntary arrangement, with overall leadership provided by the European Council and continuity ensured by regular meetings of senior officials from all the foreign ministries.

Maastricht led to the launch of a new endeavor known as the Common Foreign and Security Policy (CFSP), which helped to push defense more squarely onto the EU agenda. Although decision making is still loosely structured, the CFSP gives more direction to foreign policy, committing the member states to defining and implementing a common policy that includes "all questions related to the security of the Union, including the eventual framing of a common defence policy, which might in time lead to a common defence." The goals of the CFSP are very loosely defined, with vague talk about defending "common values" and "fundamental interests," but the CFSP is based around systematic cooperation among the member states, with the European Council agreeing on common positions when necessary.

While the foreign policies of the smaller EU member states are now largely driven by EU policy, and while all of these developments have been part of a gradual movement toward greater coordination, the development of a European foreign policy still faces at least three major handicaps.

First, the member states have different agendas and priorities. The most fundamental division is that between Atlanticists such as Britain, the Netherlands, and Portugal, who argue in favor of a close security association with the United States through NATO, and Europeanists such as France and sometimes Germany, who look more toward European independence. Meanwhile, both Britain and France have special interests in their former colonies, Germany has given priority to building links with Eastern Europe, the Southern European countries are concerned with issues across the Mediterranean, and Ireland, Sweden, and Finland want to maintain their neutrality. Very few issues (other than trade) engage the common interest of all EU member states, and even where such issues exist, the fifteen states vary enormously in their abilities to respond.

Second, the EU lacks focus and leadership. Not only does the presidency of the Council of Ministers change every six months, but there also has been no one in the EU institutions until recently who could act as a focal point for discussions with other countries, which are obliged to switch their attention from one member state to another and to establish contacts with ministers and bureaucrats in fifteen capitals. As former U.S. Secretary of State Henry Kissinger once quipped, "When I want to speak to Europe, whom do I call?"

His concern was at least partly addressed by institutional changes made under the Treaty of Amsterdam. A Policy Planning and Early Warning Unit (PPEWU) was set up in Brussels to help the EU anticipate foreign crises. It consists of twenty members: one each from the member states, the Western European Union (see following), the European Commission, and three from the Council of Ministers. At the same time, the practice of distributing external relations portfolios in the commission among four different commissioners and the president was replaced with the creation of a new foreign policy position with the rank of vice-president.

Finally, and most important, no matter what institutional changes it agrees on, the EU will always work with one arm tied behind its back until it can back up its words with the threat of military force. Together, the fifteen member states amount to a formidable force; they have more than 2 million troops, 22,000 tanks, 21,000 artillery pieces, and 6,300 combat aircraft, which among them make up 85 to 95 percent of the NATO capability in Europe; however, the development of security arrangements in Western Europe since World War II has created a confusing mélange of commitments by different groups of countries to different organizations and at different levels.

Preeminent among these organizations is NATO, which was set up in 1949 in response to concerns about the Soviet threat. Then there is the Organization for Security and Cooperation in Europe (OSCE), which was born out of a reorganization in 1994 of the Conference on Security and Cooperation in Europe (CSCE). The OSCE, which includes the United States, is the only truly pan-European security organization, but it has so far restricted itself to conflict prevention and post-conflict rehabilitation, rather than to preparation for defense. The most likely prospects for the development of a joint European defense capability may lie with the Western European Union (WEU), a long moribund organization that was given new life by Maastricht. Founded by the Treaty of Brussels in 1954 in the wake of the collapse of the European Defence Community, the WEU was quickly overshadowed by NATO. Following the failure of a plan to give the EPC a security dimension, the WEU was revived in 1984 and passed its first modest test in 1987 when it coordinated minesweeping by its members in the Persian Gulf during the Iran-Iraq war.

With a secretariat in Brussels (to which it was moved from London in 1993) and a ministerial council and consultative assembly in Paris, the WEU hosts biannual meetings of the foreign and defense ministers of its ten member states: Belgium, France, Germany, Greece,

Italy, Luxembourg, the Netherlands, Portugal, Spain, and the United Kingdom (Austria, Denmark, Finland, Ireland, and Sweden are observers). As a possible foundation for the development of a European defense capability, the WEU has several advantages: it already exists; it could be used by the Europeans to develop their own defense policies independent of the United Sates; it can operate outside its member states (unlike NATO, which is technically limited to the territory of its member states); and not all EU member states are members of the WEU, so countries such as Ireland, Finland, and Sweden can be members of the EU while preserving their neutrality.

Although the leaders of the member states have disagreed over the development of European defense policy, the French and the Germans took the bull by the horns in May 1992 with the creation of Eurocorps, which grew out of an experimental Franco-German brigade set up in 1990. Headquartered in Strasbourg, the fifty-thousand-member Eurocorps has been operational since November 1995 and has been joined by contingents from Belgium, Spain, and Luxembourg. It was conceived as a step toward the development of a European army that was to give substance to the CFSP, give the EU an independent defense capability, and provide an insurance for Europe in the event that the United States decided to withdraw militarily from Europe. Germany insists that Eurocorps would complement NATO and that it would be placed under NATO "operational command" in the event of a threat to Western European security, but Britain, the Netherlands, and the United States suspect that France's objective is to displace the U.S. dominance of NATO.

External Economic Relations

If many questions remain about the EU's military power and global political influence, there are no such questions about its economic power. The common external tariff is in place, the single market is all but complete, the commission has new powers to represent the governments of all of the member states in negotiations on world trade, and it is now well understood by everyone that the EU is the most powerful actor in those negotiations. The establishment of the euro is designed to add to the economic weight of Europe by giving it a currency that can stand alongside the U.S. dollar and the Japanese yen in terms of its credibility and influence.

With just 6.4 percent of the world's population, the European Union now accounts for 28 percent of world gross national product (GNP), 36 percent of imports, and nearly 37 percent of exports. Given statistics such as these, the external economic policies of the EU have understandably moved to the top of the agendas of its major trading partners, not all of whom have liked what they have seen. Article 110 of the EEC Treaty outlined a Common Commercial Policy (CCP) based on the principle that the Community would contribute "to the harmonious development of world trade, the progressive abolition of restrictions on international trade, and the lowering of customs barriers." The CCP was not finally put in place until the completion of the single market; meanwhile, the EC's position on global trade negotiations and its focus on internal economic issues led to talk about a "Fortress Europe," particularly by U.S. political and corporate leaders concerned about both the implications of the single market and the EC's unwillingness to cut agricultural subsidies.

The concerns have been particularly visible during international trade negotiations held under the auspices of the World Trade Organization (WTO), which replaced the General Agreement on Tariffs and Trade (GATT, founded in 1948) in 1995. GATT oversaw several rounds of negotiations, the lengthiest and most contentious of which was the Uruguay Round, launched in 1986 by 105 countries and concluded in 1993. The Community had been involved in several earlier rounds of GATT negotiations, but the Uruguay Round was particularly controversial because it was expanded to include agricultural trade, thereby posing a direct challenge to the most protectionist of the Community policy areas.

Led by the United States, the Community's major trading partners insisted on cuts of 90 percent in export subsidies and of 75 percent in other farm support over a period of ten years, charging that such support gave EC farmers an unfair advantage. The EC initially agreed to only a 30 percent cut in farm subsidies and refused to reform the Common Agricultural Policy (CAP). After teetering several times on the brink of collapse, negotiations finally achieved a breakthrough in 1992, thanks in part to CAP reforms agreed on by the EC, including production and price reductions and a move away from subsidies to farmers based on production. When the next round of negotiations is launched the United States is keen to see agriculture at the top of the agenda again. However, the new role of the European Commission as a negotiator on behalf of all of the member states will give the EU significantly more influence than it had during the Uruguay Round.

Intra-European trade has grown enormously as a result of integration, but the record of EU trade with other parts of the world has been mixed. The United States remains the EU's single-largest trade partner, accounting for 19.7 percent of exports and 19.4 percent of imports, but the balance may change as the United States looks increasingly at building economic ties with the Pacific Rim. The Africa Caribbean Pacific (ACP) program has invested in building trade with developing countries, but it has had mixed results, and among them the seventy-one ACP states account for barely four percent of EU trade. India, China, Japan, and Australasia, meanwhile, are more likely to continue building links among themselves; Japan is the second-largest single source of imports to the EU but takes only five percent of EU exports. The greatest medium-term possibilities lie in Eastern Europe (with more than 127 million consumers and enormous productive potential), whereas longer-term possibilities lie with Russia and the other former Soviet republics (with about 220 million consumers, productive potential, and a wealth of largely untapped natural resources). Building ties with the East and both strengthening and expanding its own internal market are likely to remain the EU's major trade priorities for the foreseeable future.

CONCLUSIONS

The European Union was born out of the rubble of the most devastating war the world has ever known. It took its first tentative steps in an era that was divided by potentially fatal ideological tensions and that saw the end of colonialism and the construction of a global economy. Against a background of momentous change, Europeans embarked on an experiment in regional integration that obliged them to redefine both their place in the world and their attitudes toward one another. The experiment stumbled occasionally, made a few significant breakthroughs, sometimes seemed about to fulfill the prophecies of the skeptics, and at other times left them eating their words. The result was the creation of the European Union.

Fifty years later, much remains to be done and there is no certainty about what the EU will become. As the new millennium opens, Europeans find themselves faced with difficult choices that may give the EU more definition but may also detract from its past achievements. Many of those decisions are being forced on the EU by the need to adapt itself to eastward expansion and the growth of membership from fifteen countries to twenty or more. An organization designed around its six founding members must do some substantial rethinking in order to catch up with the changes it has seen since the Single European

Act. At least six major issues will be on the agenda as the new millennium progresses.

First, institutions will need to be reformed and the democratic deficit closed. The EU has bred five major institutions and a cluster of subsidiary bodies to deal with specific issues. None of these institutions has been static; their powers and character have changed as the process of integration has evolved, as the demands made on them have grown, and as the relationships among them have been reshaped. More change is to come as "the government of Europe" is given clearer definition:

- There will be pressure to make the commission more responsible and accountable by democratizing the process by which commissioners and the president are chosen and pressure to rethink the distribution of positions as more new member states join the EU.
- There will be a need to reconsider the place of the Council of Ministers and to make its deliberations more open, democratic, and representative; there will be pressure to rethink the Council's system of voting as the EU expands; the role of the presidency of the EU will also change as membership of the EU grows.
- The powers of the European Parliament will likely grow in light of increasing demands for accountability, the EP will become more like a true legislature, national political parties, will, it is hoped, become more adept at running European election campaigns, and the search for majority parties in the EP will continue; at the same time, the national quotas of seats will need to be recalculated.

One of the most glaring deficiencies of the European Union is the gap between popular will and the goals of the elites who have made most of the key decisions relating to European integration. As the EU becomes more real to more Europeans and its decisions more strongly affect their lives, popular pressure for more direct input into EU decision making will surely grow.

Second, adjustments will need to be made in light of eastward enlargement. There are twenty-four potential new members: three in Western Europe (Norway, Iceland, and Switzerland), three in the Mediterranean (Malta, Cyprus, and Turkey), twelve in Eastern Europe (including the five states of the former Yugoslavia), and six in the former Soviet Union. About half of these states have realistic short- to medium-term possibilities for membership. The next enlargement will focus on Poland, the Czech Republic, Hungary, Slovenia, Estonia, and Cyprus; this will change the economic, political, cultural, and geographic balance of the EU and make the need to reform the EU's institutions and decision-making processes more urgent.

Third, to give it a solid base from which to compete as a unit in the global market, the EU will need to continue to emphasize the building of European corporate, transport, and communication networks. This goal will mean anticipating more corporate mergers, liberalizing telecommunications, building a European data-transmission network, and creating a European energy generation and supply system.

Fourth, the construction of a true economic union remains high on the agenda of priorities. Eleven member states have now committed themselves to the single currency and have taken a leap into the unknown. At one level, a single currency makes good sense because it means the final completion of the single market; at another level, it has already caused problems as member states have tried to adjust to their inabilities to take independent action to deal with issues such as unemployment and inflation.

Fifth, the EU must begin to take care of its own security needs. As it becomes more assertive and confident, its relationship with the

United States and its place within NATO will change in a way that will reduce its dependence on the U.S. security blanket and compel it to build a "fourth pillar": common defense policies and a common defense force. The seeds of a security union have already been planted, and crises in the Middle East and the Balkans have emphasized both the policy fault lines in the European military capacity and the urgency of creating the ability to respond to future emergencies; however, a security union will not be developed without a resolution of several key problems:

- Policy differences among the EU member states, notably the neutrality of some, the independent nature of others, and the different spheres of influence and interest of the most powerful member states.
- Agreement on the role Germany will play. How long will it take for other Europeans to be comfortable with the prospect of German troops on their soil or of German troops being sent into neighboring trouble spots?
- Agreement on the relative contributions of the different member states. Will the bigger powers such as Britain, France, and Italy agree to bear the largest share of the burden?
- Agreement on the relationship between the EU and other preexisting security arrangements, notably NATO and the CSCE.
- Agreement on a new balance in the tripartite relationship among the EU, the United States, and Russia. What effect will Europe's failure always to agree with U.S. foreign and defense policy have on the transatlantic relationship?

Finally, there is the controversial issue of political union. In a sense, everything that has happened since the Schuman Declaration has been a preamble to this. Such a union is now virtually inevitable; the only questions concern the time it will take, the membership, and the structure of the union. It may be federal or confederal, or it may be an entirely new form of association tailored to meet the needs of what is, after all, a unique situation. It may be a true political union with all members moving together at the same speed, or it may be a multispeed Europe with its members moving toward the same ultimate goal but at a different pace. Some want Europe *à la carte,* with governments picking and choosing the policies they want to adopt, whereas others want an equal commitment by every member state.

Whatever form it takes, European political union *will* happen for at least four reasons: (1) The EU experiment has brought peace and prosperity, (2) Europeans have too much in common to allow their differences to act as an insurmountable barrier, (3) Europeans are tied with knots and bonds that are far too complex to be easily unraveled, and (4) European integration has developed an irresistible speed and momentum. The train left the station long ago, and even though the ride may be bumpy, the destination unclear, the design of the engine uncertain, and the relationship among the engineer, the guards, and the passengers still evolving, it is too late for anyone to leave the train.

INTERNET SITES

Europa: http//europa.eu.int
Home page of the European Union, with links to all its major institutions, to news about the EU, and to its legal data base.

European Commission:
http://europa.eu.int/comm/index_en.htm
The site on Europa for the European Commission, with useful information about its members and activities.

Council of Ministers: http://ue.eu.int/
Home page of the Council of Ministers, the major decisionmaking body in the EU structure.

European Parliament: http://www.europarl.eu.int/
Official home page of Parliament, containing much useful information on its membership and activities.

European Voice:
http://www.european-voice.com/
The Web site for a weekly English-language newspaper published in Brussels, and the best available source of news on developments in the EU.

NOTES/BIBLIOGRAPHY

1. GNP figures from World Bank, *World Bank Atlas 1996* (Washington, DC: World Bank, 1997); trade figures from International Monetary Fund, *Direction of Trade Statistics* (Washington, DC: International Monetary Fund), pp. 2–5.
2. World Bank, *ibid.*
3. Keegan, Victor, and Martin Kettle, *The New Europe* (London: Fourth Estate, 1993), p. 92.
4. For more details, see John McCormick, *Understanding the European Union* (New York: St Martin's Press, 1999), Chapter 2.
5. Monnet, Jean, *Memoirs* (Garden City, NY: Doubleday, 1978), p. 292.
6. Schuman, Robert, quoted in David Weigall and Peter Stirk (eds.), *The Origins and Development of the European Community* (London: Pinter, 1992), pp. 58–59.
7. For more details, see Derek W. Urwin, *The Community of Europe* (London and New York: Longman, 1995), pp. 120–129.
8. Pinder, John, *European Community: The Building of a Union* (Oxford: Oxford University Press, 1991), p. 65.
9. Urwin, *op cit.*, pp. 230–235.
10. Eurobarometer 48, Autumn 1997.
11. Westlake, Martin, *A Modern Guide to the European Parliament* (London and New York: Pinter and St. Martin's Press, 1994), pp. 84–85.
12. For details, see Simon Hix and Christopher Lord, *Political Parties in the European Union* (New York: St. Martin's Press, 1997), Chapter 2.
13. *Ibid.*, pp. 85–90.
14. Mackie, T. T., and F. W. S. Craig, *Europe Votes 2* (Chichester: Parliamentary Research Services, 1985), p. 242; T. T. Mackie (ed.), *Europe Votes 3* (Brookfield, VT: Dartmouth, 1990), pp. 5–16; Hix and Lord *ibid.*, p. 83.
15. Inter-Parliamentary Union (IPU), *Distribution of Seats Between Men and Women in National Parliaments* (Geneva: IPU, 1993).
16. Mazey, Sonia, and Jeremy Richardson, "The Logic of Organisation: Interest Groups," in Jeremy Richardson (ed.), *European Union: Power and Policy-Making* (London: Routledge, 1996), p. 200.
17. Aspinwall, Mark, and Justin Greenwood. "Conceptualising collective action in the European Union: An introduction," in Mark Aspinwall and Justin Greenwood (eds.), *Collective Action in the European Union: Interests and the New Politics of Associability* (London: Routledge, 1998).
18. Greenwood, Justin, *Representing Interests in the European Union* (Basingstoke: Macmillan, 1997), p. 101.
19. Aspinwall and Greenwood, *op cit.*
20. Franklin, Mark, "European elections and the European voter," in Jeremy Richardson (ed.), *European Union: Power and Policy-Making* (London: Routledge, 1996), p. 197.
21. For details on the process, see Michell Cini, *The European Commission: Leadership, Organization and Culture in the EU Administration* (Manchester: Manchester University Press, 1996), pp. 107–111.
22. de Bassompierre, Guy, *Changing the Guard in Brussels: An Insider's View of the EC Presidency* (New York: Praeger, 1988), p. 8.
23. Wallace, Helen, "The Council and the Commission After the Single European Act," in Leon Hurwitz and Christian Lequesne (eds.), *The State of the European Community: Policies, Institutions and Debates in the Transition Years* (Boulder, CO: Lynne Rienner, 1991).
24. Brewin, Christopher, and Richard McAllister, "Annual Review of the Activities of the European Community in 1990," in *Journal of Common Market Studies* 29:4, June 1991, pp. 385–430.
25. Lodge, Juliet, "EC Policymaking: Institutional Dynamics," in Juliet Lodge (ed.), *The European Community and the Challenge of the Future*, 2nd ed. (New York: St Martin's Press, 1993).
26. For details, see Westlake, *op cit.*, Chapter 3.
27. For examples, see Alain Van Hamme, "The European Court of Justice: Recent Developments," in Leon Hurwitz and Christian Lequesne (eds.), *The State of the European Community: Policies, Institutions and Debates in the Transition Years* (Boulder, CO: Lynne Rienner, 1991).
28. Lasok, K.P.E., *The European Court of Justice: Practice and Procedure* (London: Butterworths, 1984), pp. 7–8.
29. Johnston, Mary Troy, *The European Council: Gatekeeper of the European Community* (Boulder, CO: Westview, 1994), pp. 41–48.
30. *European Voice,* October 1–7, 1998, p. 18.

31. Orzak, Louis H., "The General Systems Directive and the Liberal Profession," in Leon Hurwitz and Christian Lequesne (eds.), *op cit.*

32. European Commission figures quoted in Loukas Tsoukalis, *The New European Economy Revisited: The Politics and Economics of Integration* (Oxford: Oxford University Press, 1997), p. 110.

33. Cini, Michelle, and Lee McGowan, *Competition Policy in the European Union* (Basingstoke: Macmillan Press, 1998).

34. Allen, David, "Competition Policy: Policing the Single Market," in Helen Wallace and William Wallace (eds.), *Policy-Making in the European Union* (Oxford: Oxford University Press, 1996).

35. World Trade Organization, *Compendium of Tourist Statistics 1989–94* (Madrid: WTO, 1996).

36. Loedel, Peter H., "Enhancing Europe's International Monetary Power: The Drive Toward a Single Currency," in Pierre-Henri Laurent and Marc Maresceau (eds.), *The State of the European Union Vol. 4: Deepening and Widening* (Boulder, CO: Lynne Rienner, 1998).

37. For details, see Stephanie B. Anderson, "Problems and Possibilities: The Development of the CFSP from Maastricht to the 1996 IGC," in Laurent and Maresceau, *ibid.*

38. Hill, Christopher, "EPC's Performance in Crises," in Reinhardt Rummel (ed.), *Toward Political Union: Planning a Common Foreign and Security Policy in the European Community* (Boulder, CO: Westview Press, 1992), pp. 135–136.

APPENDIX A

MAP A.1 The Roman Empire

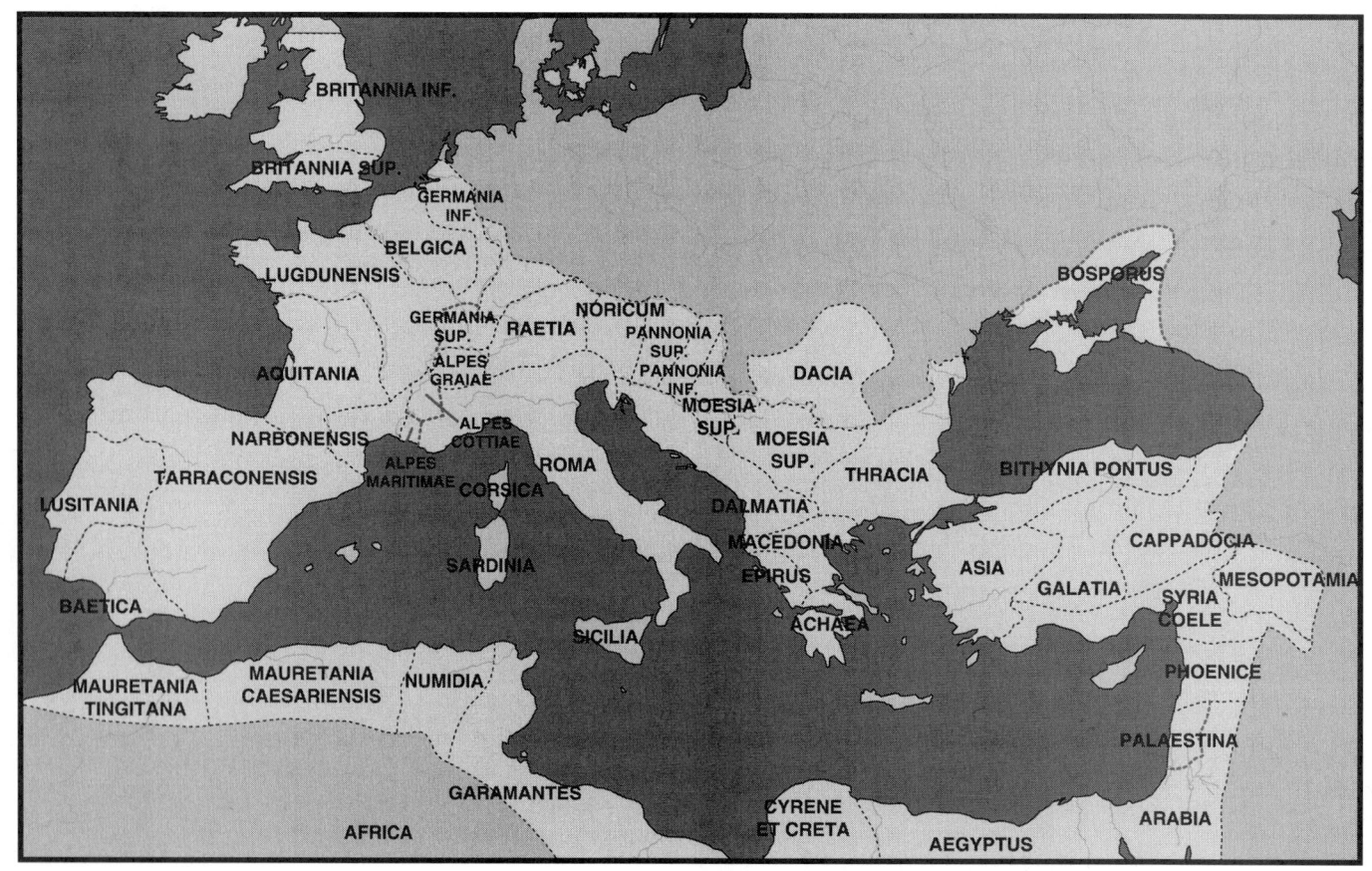

Maps

MAP A.2   The Iron Curtain

MAP A.3 Contemporary Europe

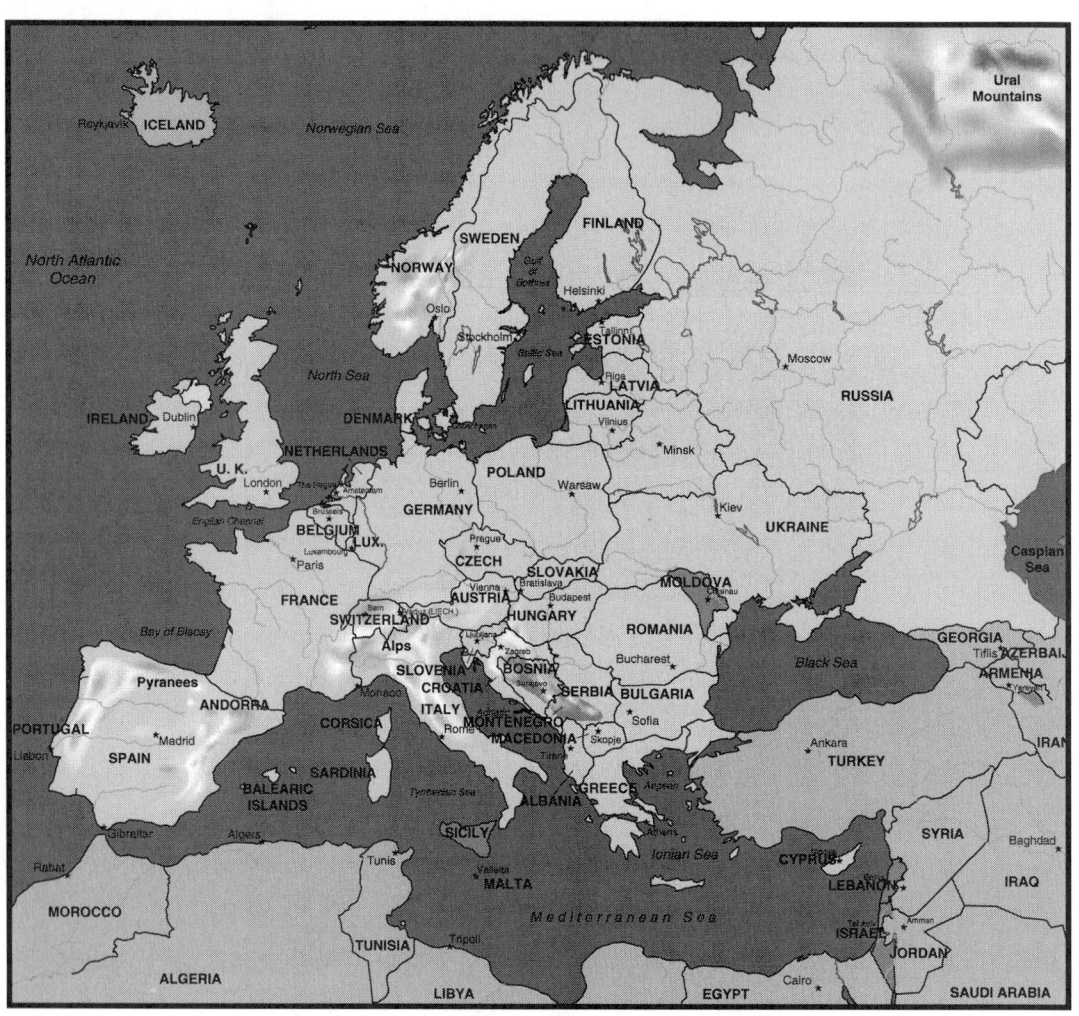

MAP A.4 Seventeenth-century France

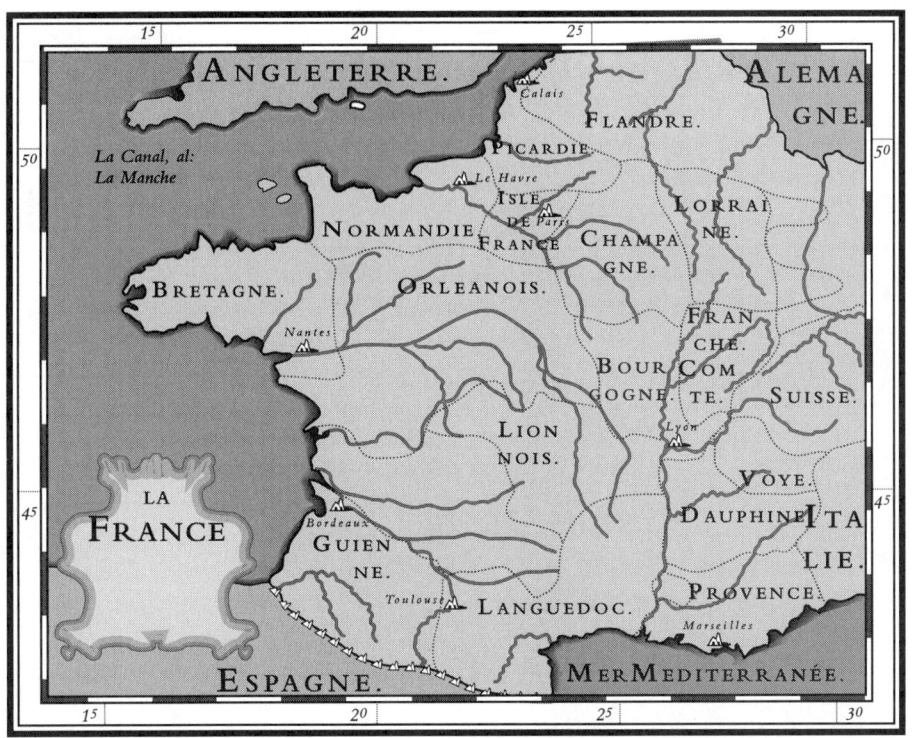

MAP A.5 Modern France

Index

A

Aasen, Ivar, 238
Adenauer, Konrad, 156
Africa Caribbean Pacific (ACP) program
    (European Union), 451
Age of Liberty (Sweden), 249
Agrarian Party of Russia, 193, 194, 196
Agriculture, France and, 101
Åland Islands, 235
Albania
    corruption in, 394, 405
    Greeks in, 386–387
    judiciary in, 395
    pyramid scheme, 405–406
    transition to democracy, 404–407
Albanian Democratic Party, 405
Albanian Liberation Army, 406
Albanian Party of Labor, 405
Alexander I, Tsar of Russia, 180
Alexander II, Tsar of Russia, 180
Allardt, Erik, 270
The Alliance (France), 119, 136–137
Alliance of the Democratic Left (Poland), 397
Alliance for Jobs, 155
Alliance of Young Democrats (Hungary), 401
Alsace-Lorraine, 99
Amin, Idi, 65
Amnesty International, 430
Ancher, Micheal, 220
Andersen, Bent Rold, 220
Andrew, Duke of York, 75
Antonescu, Ion, 402
Aquinas, Thomas, 19–20, 21
Arianespace, 445
Arias, Carlos, 347
Association of Greek Industrialists (SEV), 326
Auken, Kirsten, 289
Aznar, José Maria, 337, 347

B

Bagehot, Walter, 72–73, 74, 75
Baglai, Marat, 207
Barber, Benjamin, 106
Barre, Raymond, 133
Basic Law (Denmark), 253–254
Basic Law (Finland), 254, 258
Basic Law (Germany), 148, 158, 159–160,
    161, 162–163
    defense policy and, 171
    German unification and, 166
    political asylum and, 169–170
Basic Law (Norway), 254, 255
Basic Law (Sweden), 254–255
Battle of Stalingrad, 146
Baumgartner, Frank, 131
Belarus, post–Cold War era, 29
Bengtsson, Frans G., 293
Bergman, Ingmar, 222, 224
Berlin Wall, 149
Berlusconi, Silvio, 335
Bernadotte, King of Sweden, 242
Biörck, Gunnar, 288–289
Bismarck, Otto von, 24, 143, 144, 243
Bizonia, 148
Bjerregaard, Ritt, 286
Blair, Tony, 55, 73–74, 76–77, 85, 86, 135
    Britain/U.S. relationship under, 88
    election of 1997, 259
    European Monetary Union, 90
    Labour party and, 68–69
    Northern Ireland and, 60–62
    stance on EU, 34
    "Third Way" philosophy of, 54, 174
"Bloody Sunday," 181
Bogachev, Vladimir, 197
Bogdanor, Vernon, 73
Bohman, Gösta, 271

Boldyrev, Yuri, 198
Bolsheviks, 181
Bonaparte, Napoleon, 23, 100, 105, 143
    invasion of Russia, 180
Boothroyd, Betty, 79
Bosnia, ethnic conflict in, 371, 376–377, 387–390, 391
Brandt, Willy, 156, 159, 172
Braunthal, Gerard, 165
Brest-Litovsk Treaty, 181–182
Brezhnev doctrine, 371
Brezhnev, Leonid, 183
Britain, 52–90
    constitution of, 73–74
    democratization of, 40
    economic policy, 83–86
    electoral system, 65–67
    foreign policy, 86–89
    history of, 56–62
    interest groups, 70–72
    judiciary, 81–82
    legislature, 78–81
    local government, 82
    media, 72
    monarchy of, 74–75
    Parliament, 90
    political culture, 62–64
    political parties, 67–70
    political system, 72–78
    politics and policymaking, 82–89
    prime minister and cabinet, 75–78
    social and class structure, 64–65
    social policy, 86
British Broadcasting Corporation (BBC), 72
British Satellite Broadcasting, 432
Brundtland, Gro Harlem, 290
Bubis, Ignatz, 141
Bulgaria
    Post–Cold War era, 29
    transition to democracy, 402–404
    Turks in, 386, 404, 405
Bulgarian Socialist Party, 403
Bundesrat, 160, 161
Bundestag, 140, 160, 161, 165
    representation in, 157–158
Bureaucracy
    Britain, 82–83
    European Union, 419, 433–436
    France, 127–128
    Germany, 162–164
    Greece, 344–345
    Italy, 345
    Poland, 397
    Portugal, 346–347
    Russia, 203–204
    Southern Europe, 342–343, 344–345, 346–347, 348
    Spain, 348

C

Cable News Network (CNN), 432
Caetano, Marcello, 315, 317
Callaghan, James, 71
Canute the Great, King of Denmark, 241
Carl XVI Gustaf, King of Sweden, 257
Carlist Wars, 320
Catherine II (the Great), Empress of Russia, 180
Ceausescu, Nicolae, 384, 401
Center Party (CP) (Finland), 248, 258
Center Party (Germany), 144
Center Party (Sweden), 251
Central Association of German Industrialists, 154
Charlemagne, King of France, 19, 143, 309
Charles I, King of England, 57
Charles XII, King of Sweden, 292, 293
Charles, Prince of Wales, 75
Chechnya, 188, 190, 198, 202
Chernomyrdin, Viktor, 197, 204, 215
Chirac, Jacques, 98, 104, 118, 126
Christian Democratic Union (CDU), 150, 156, 161
    citizenship laws, 170
    economic issues, 167
    shifting constituencies of, 173
    unification issues, 166
Christian Democrats (DC) (Italy), 319, 334
Christian Democrats (CD) (Sweden), 251
Christian Social Union (CSU) (Germany), 156, 161

citizenship laws, 170
shifting constituencies of, 174
unification issues, 166
Chubais, Anatoly, 210
Church Act of 1686, 244
Church of England, 75
Church of Sacré Coeur, 109
Churchill, Winston, 31, 60, 147, 417
Civic political culture, 315
Clemenceau, Georges, 103
Climate of Europe, 15
Clinton, Bill, 54, 135
"Third Way" philosophy of, 174
Cockfield White Paper, 432
Cofindustria, 327
Cold War, 25, 26–28, 182–183, 212
end of, 28–30
Italy and, 358–359
Post–Cold War era, 28–30
Southern Europe, 355
Columbus, Christopher, 20
Committee of Permanent Representatives (COREPER), 436
Committee of the Regions (European Union), 429
Common Agricultural Policy (CAP) (European Union), 442
Common Commercial Policy (CCP) (European Union), 450
Common Foreign and Security Policy (CFSP) (European Union), 448
Commonwealth of Independent States (CIS), 214
Commune of 1871, 109
Communist Party (Germany), 162
Communist Party of Greece (KKE), 334
Communist Party (PCI) (Italy), 334, 335, 358–359
Communist Party of the Russian Federation (CPRF), 193, 194, 195–196
Communist Party of the Soviet Union (CPSU), 192, 215
Community of Eastern European Countries (COMECON), 35
Comparative politics, Europe's place in, 12–13

Confederation of British Industry (CBI), 71
Confederation of Employers Organization (CEOE) (Spain), 330
Conference on Security and Cooperation in Europe (CSCE), 449
Congress of Russian Communities (KRO), 194, 198
Congress of Vienna, 143
Conradt, David, 152
Conservative Party (Denmark), 250
Conservatives (Britain), 66, 69–70
Constantinescu, Emil, 401–402
Constitutional Council (France), 130–131, 132
Constitutional Court (Russia), 206
Cooperation procedure (European Parliament), 438
Core-periphery relations, Southern Europe and, 310–311
Corporatism, 24, 233, 279, 325, 329, 332, 341, 349–350
definition of, 46
Corsica, 99
Cossack election of 1928, 252
Council of Elders (Germany), 160
Council of Europe, 409
Council of European Professional and Managerial Staff (EUROCADRES), 430
Council for Foreign and Defense Policy (Russia), 213
Council of Ministers (European Union), 419, 433, 436–437
Court of Auditors (European Union), 441
Court of First Instance (European Union), 440
Cow trade of 1933, 266–267, 278
Cresson, Edith, 104
Cries and Whispers, 222–223
Croatia
ethnic conflict in, 389
transition to democracy, 407
Crocodile Club, 428
Cromwell, Oliver, 56, 57
Cunhal, Alvaro, 336
Czech Republic
corruption in, 394–395

government of, 398
post–Cold War era, 28–29
transition to democracy, 397–399

D

Dahl, Hans, 283
Dahl, Robert, 62–63
D'Alema, Massimo, 335
Dalgas, Enrico, 243
Deferre, Gaston, 117
de Gaulle, Charles, 97, 126
    Britain's EU membership and, 419
    challenges to governing France, 105
    EEC and, 33
    Gaullism, 118
    political parties and, 114, 115
    veto of British application to the EEC, 60
    view of political parties, 192
Delblanc, Sven, 285–286
Delors, Jacques, 34, 435
Democratic Alliance of Hungarians in Romania (RMDSZ), 384
Democratic deficit, 424
Democratic Party of the Left (Italy), 335
Democratization
    Albania, 404–407
    Bulgaria, 402–404
    Czech Republic, 397–399
    Eastern Europe, 371–372, 391–409, 410–411
    former Yugoslavia, 407–408
    Hungary, 400–401
    Poland, 396–397
    Romania, 400–401
    Slovakia, 399–400
    Southern Europe, 337
    Spain, 347–348
Denmark
    alcohol policy, 263
    geography, 235–236
    history, 241, 242, 243, 246–247, 249, 292, 294, 295–296
    political parties, 250, 251–252, 256–257, 281–282
    public policy, 229–230, 260, 263, 264–265, 267, 269, 275, 277, 278–279

d'Estaing, Valéry Giscard, 102, 118, 133
d'Hondt system, 347
Diana, Princess of Wales, 56, 75
Dicey, Albert Venn, 73
Dickens, Charles, 23
Diet of German Industry and Commerce, 155
Dirigisme, 100
Djukanovic, Milo, 408
Draskovic, Vuk, 171
Duma, 214
    lawmaking in, 205–206
    powers of, 203–204, 205
    presidency and, 201
    prime minister confirmation, 203
Dumont, René, 121
Dzurinda, Mikulas, 400

E

Eanes, Ramalho, 346
Eastern Europe, 368–411
    constitutions, writing of, 394
    corruption in, 394–395
    democracy, transition to, 371–372, 391–411
    development in, 374–375
    ethnic minorities, 375–377, 384–391
    ethnicity, 380–391
    gypsies in, 382–384
    interest groups, 391–392
    language, importance of, 380–382
    languages of, 373–374
    media, 395–396
    personalization of political power in, 393–394
    political culture, 372–380
    political parties, 392–393
    public policy concerns, 409–410
    religion, 374
    separation of powers in, 395
Eban, Abba, 215
Ecole Nationale d'Administration (ENA), 127
Ecole Polytéchnique (X), 127
Economic and Social Committee (European Union), 429
The Economist, 80

Ekelöf, Maja, 272
Ekman, Kerstin, 225–226
Elections
    Albania, 404–405
    Britain, 65–67
    Bulgaria, 403, 404
    Czech Republic, 398
    Eastern Europe, 379–380, 393–394
    European Union, 425–426
    France, 124
    Germany, 157–158, 159, 160, 161
    Greece, 333–334, 344
    Italy, 335
    Montenegro, 408
    Nordic countries, 282
    Poland, 397
    Portugal, 335, 346
    Romania, 401–402
    Russia, 202–203
    Serbia, 407
    Slovakia, 400
    Slovenia, 407
    Southern Europe, 343–344
    Spain, 336, 337, 347
Elizabeth II, Queen of England, 74–75
Enabling Act, 145
The English Constitution, 72–73
Engström, Albert, 263
Environment Party (Sweden), 251
Epsin-Andersen, Gøsta, 278
Erhard, Ludwig, 156
Erlander, Tage, 268, 269
Estonia, post–Cold War era, 29
Eurelectric, 431
Euro, 30, 34, 341, 422, 443, 446–447
    Britain and, 74, 85–86, 90
    France and, 134–135
Eurocorps, 450
Euronews, 432
Europa-TV Consortium, 432
Europe
    climate of, 15
    Cold War, 26–28
    comparative politics, 12–13, 43–50
    definition of, 9–12
    economy of, 3–8

    geography of, 15
    history of, 17–26
    integration of, 8–9, 30–38, 87, 412–453
    reasons to study, 13–14
    topography of, 15–17
    transition to democracy in, 39–43
    World War I and, 2–3
The European, 432
European Agency for the Evaluation of
    Medicinal Products (EMEA), 441
European Atomic Energy Community
    (Euratom), 32
    history of, 418–419
European Bureau of Consumer Unions, 430
European Central Bank (ECB), 134, 174–175,
    422, 441–442
European Chemical Industry Council, 431
European Coal and Steel Community (ECSC),
    32–33, 87
    history of, 418
European Commission, 419, 433–436
    authority of, 415
    College of Commissioners, 434–435
    Directorates-General (DGs), 435–436
    President of, 435
European Common Market, Southern
    Europe and, 322
European Community (EC), history of,
    419–420
European Convention on Human Rights, 74
European Council, 433, 440–441
European Court of Justice (ECJ), 81–82, 419,
    433, 439–440
    Advocates General, 439
    Court of First Instance, 440
    France and, 131
    President of, 439
European Crop Protection Association, 431
European Economic Community (EEC), 10,
    32, 33, 87, 414–415
    history of, 418–419
    Southern Europe and, 362
    Southern Europe's entrance into, 315
European Environment Agency, 441
European Environmental Bureau
    (EEB), 431

European Free Trade Association (EFTA), 10, 36, 419
European Investment Back (EIB), 441
European Liberal Democratic and Reform Party (ELDR), 427, 428
European Monetary System (EMS), 447
European Monetary Union (EMU)
    Portugal and, 353
    Southern Europe and, 362, 363, 365
European Parliament (EP), 419, 433, 438–439
European People's Party (EPP), 427, 428
European Police Office (Europol), 444
European Political Cooperation (EPC), 420, 448
European Round Table of Industrialists, 430
European Trade Union Confederation (ETUC), 430
European Union (EU), 8–9, 10, 30–36, 60, 412–453
    Britain and, 85–86, 87–88, 89–90
    Common Agricultural Policy (CAP), 155
    constitution of, 433
    Council of Ministers, 419, 433, 436–437
    Eastern Europe and, 409
    economic policy (external), 450–451
    economic policy (internal), 442–451
    elections, 425–426
    European Commission, 415, 419, 433–436
    European Council, 400, 433, 440–441
    European Court of Justice, 419, 433, 439–440
    European Parliament (EP), 419, 433, 438–439
    Finland's entrance into, 300
    foreign and security policy, 422, 447–450
    France and, 111, 129, 134–136
    Germany and, 168, 172
    history of, 31–36, 416–422
    interest groups, 429–431
    Italy and, 319
    media and, 431–432
    policies and policymaking, 442–451
    political culture, 422–424
    political parties and, 427–429
    political system, 432–442
    Southern Europe, 363
    Sweden's entrance into, 300
    terms of membership, 411
EU Committee of the American Chamber of Commerce, 430
European United Left (EUL), 427–428
Europol, 444
Eurosclerosis, 420

F

Fabius, Laurent, 134
Faeroe Islands, 235
Family of change (Greece), 318
Family of change (Italy), 318–319
Family of order (Greece), 318
Family of order (Italy), 318–319
Fascism, 332
Fatherland-All Russia Party, 195, 196, 198
Federal Assembly (Russia), 204–205
Federal Constitutional Court (Germany), 161, 162
Federal High Court (Germany), 162
Federal Republic of Germany (FRG), 140, 148
Federal Security Service (Russia), 297
Federalists, 50
Federation Council (Russia), 204–205
    lawmaking in, 205–206
Federation of German Employers' Association, 155
Federation of German Industry, 155
Federation Treaty, 189
Fermi, Enrico, 372
Fiat, 327
Fifth Republic (France), 98–99, 100, 113, 117, 136
    constitution of, 114, 115, 124
    presidentialization of politics in, 116
Finland
    Basic Law, 254, 258
    economy of, 284
    geography, 236
    history, 241, 242, 244, 245, 247–248, 296–297

political parties, 248, 256–257, 258
    Soviet Union and, 296–297
First Reich, 143
Fischer, Joschka, 172–173
Folk high schools, 246–247
Foreign Intelligence Service (SVR)
    (Russia), 207
Forza Italia, 335
Foster, Sir Norman, 142
France, 92–137
    agriculture in, 101
    bureaucracy, 127–128
    class structure, 109–111
    code law system, 130–131
    Constitutional Council, 130–131
    current trends in public policy,
        133–136
    decentralization reforms, 128–130
    executive legislative relations, 124–127
    history of, 97–105
    interests, 113–115, 125
    political institutions, 124–131
    political parties, 113, 115–123
    public policy formation, 123–133
    race and immigration, 105–108
    religion, 103, 111–113
    women's rights legislation, 132–133
Franco, Francisco, 39, 314, 315, 317, 332,
    347
    absolutism and, 339–340
    corporatism and, 349–350, 353
    growth-oriented policies of, 353
    policies under, 330
    restoration of traditional conservative
        society, 320
Frederick II the Great, King of Prussia, 143
Frederick III, Emperor of Germany, 144
Frederick William I, King of Prussia, 143
Frederick William III, King of Prussia, 143
Frederick William IV, King of Prussia, 143
Free Democratic Party (FDP) (Germany), 157
    citizenship laws, 170
    defense policy, 171
    economic issues, 167
    unification issues, 166
Free Enterprise Party (Finland), 248

French Communist Party (PCF), 115, 116,
    117, 136
French Revolution, 23, 97, 106, 114, 143
    effect on Southern Europe, 312, 316
Friends of the Earth, 431
Front National (FN) party (France), 113
Functional socialism, 266
Furet, François, 102

G

Gallen-Kallela, Akseli, 220
Garibaldi, Giuseppe, 313
General Agreement (Denmark), 267
General Agreement on Tariffs and Trade
    (GATT), 450–451
General Confederation of Greek Workers
    (GSEE), 326
General Confederation of Italian Industry,
    327
General Confederation of Portuguese
    Workers – National Intersendical
    (CGTP – IN), 329
General Union of Workers (GT) (Portugal),
    329
General Union of Workers (UGT) (Spain), 330
Generation Ecology (GE) party (France), 121
Geography of Europe, 15
German Democratic Republic (GDR), 140,
    149, 173
German Federation of Labor (DGB), 155
German People's Union, 157
Germany, 138–175
    bureaucracy, 163–164
    chancellor of, 159–160, 164–165
    citizenship laws, 170
    class structure, 154
    constitutional issues, 166
    defense policy, 170–172
    democratization of, 40–41
    economic issues, 166–168
    ethnic groups, 153–154
    European Union and, 172
    foreign workers in, 169
    geography, 150
    history of, 142–150
    interest groups, 154–155

legal system, 161–162
nuclear power issues, 168–169
occupation of, 147–148
parliament, 160–161
political asylum issues, 169–170
political culture, 151–152
political parties, 155–158
post–Cold War era, 28
president of, 159
public policy, 164–173
Second Reich, 144–145
social groups, 152–153
state, role of, 162–163
Third Reich, 145–147
unification of, 140, 149–150, 166, 171
Glasnost, 183
Glistrup, Mogens, 251
Glorious Revolution of 1688–1689, 57
Goebbels, Josef, 147
Goldhagen, Daniel, 141
González, Felipe, 337, 347, 353, 426
Gorbachev, Mikhail, 150, 183–184, 185, 186, 202
    denunciation of Brezhnev doctrine, 371
Government
    Albania, 404, 405
    Britain, 72–82
    Bulgaria, 403
    Croatia, 407
    Czech Republic, 398
    Denmark, 255
    European Union, 432–442
    Finland, 255, 258
    France, 124–131
    Germany, 158–164
    Greece, 344
    Hungary, 401–402
    Italy, 345–346
    Nordic countries, 252–255, 258–259, 261–262
    Norway, 255
    Poland, 396–397
    Portugal, 346–347
    Romania, 401, 402
    Russia, 201–202, 203–207
    Serbia, 407
    Slovakia, 399–400
    Slovenia, 407
    Southern Europe, 338–348
    Spain, 347–348
    Sweden, 255
Grandes Ecoles, 127
Grands Corps, 127–128
Great Britain. *See* Britain.
Great Reform Act of 1832, 58
Greater London Council, 82
Greece
    bureaucracy, 344–345
    democratization of, 41, 42–43
    domestic policy, 350–351
    foreign policy, 356–358
    government, 344
    interest groups, 326–327
    political culture, 317–318
    political parties, 333–334
    public policy, 350–351, 356–358
Green Front organization, 155
Green movement (France), 121–122
Green party (France), 121
Green taxes, 285
Greenland, 234–235, 295–296
Greenpeace, 431
Greens (European Union), 427, 428
Greens (Germany), 157
    citizenship laws, 170
    nuclear power issues, 169
    unification issues, 166
Grimsson, Ólafur Ragnar, 257
Grundtvig, N.F.S., 246–247, 287
Gustavus I, King of Sweden, 242, 243–245
Gustavus III, King of Sweden, 249, 292
Gustavus Adolphus, King of Sweden, 292
Guterres, Antonio, 336, 346
Gyllensten, Lars, 288
Gypsies, 382–384

H

Haakon, Crown Prince of Norway, 289–290
Hague, William, 70
Hallstein, Walter, 32
Halonen, Tarja, 257, 290
Hanseatic League, 154

Hansson, Per Albin, 259–260, 266, 294
Harald V, King of Norway, 257
Hart, Vivien, 62
Havel, Vaclav, 393, 398
Heath, Edward, 71
Hedborg, Anna, 290
Henry VIII, King of England, 57
Herzog, Roman, 159
Hill, Christopher, 448
Hindenburg, Paul von, 145
History
    Britain, 56–62
    Denmark, 241, 242, 243, 246–247, 249, 292, 294, 295–296
    Eastern Europe, 375–376, 377
    European Union, 416–422
    Finland, 241, 242, 244, 245, 247–248, 296–297
    France, 97–105
    Germany, 142–150
    Greece, 308–315
    Iceland, 239–240
    Italy, 308–315
    Nordic countries, 239–248
    Norway, 241, 242, 246, 294
    Portugal, 308–315
    Russia, 179–185
    Southern Europe, 308–315
    Spain, 308–315
    Sweden, 241, 242, 246, 249, 292–293
Hitler, Adolf, 2, 40–41, 141, 142, 145–146, 147
Hobbes, Thomas, 209
Holland, Jerome, 299
The Holocaust, 140–141
Holy Roman Empire, 143
Honecker, Erich, 149, 150
Horn, Gyula, 385
House of Commons, 76, 79–81
House of Lords, 62, 78–79
Hoxha, Enver, 404, 405
Hugo, Victor, 417
Hume, John, 61
Hungarian Socialist Party, 401
Hungary
    government of, 401–402
    interest groups, 401
    political parties, 401
    post–Cold War era, 28–29
    transition to democracy, 400–401
Huntford, Roland, 272
Hus, Jan, 374
Hussein, Saddam, 363

I
Ibsen, Henrik, 224
Iceland
    geography, 236–237
    history of, 239–240
    political culture, 240
    political parties, 256–257
Ideal types, 22
Illescu, Ion, 401, 402
Independent Television News, 432
Industrial Revolution, 23–24, 144
    Russia and, 180
Interest groups
    Britain, 70–72
    Eastern Europe, 380, 391–392
    European Union, 429–431
    France and, 113–115, 125
    Germany, 154–155
    Greece, 326–327
    Hungary, 401
    Italy, 327–329
    Nordic countries, 262–263
    Portugal, 329
    Russia, 192–195, 198–199, 209
    Southern Europe, 324–331, 338, 340, 341, 342
    Spain, 329–331
    Sweden, 279–280
Inter-mestic issues, 355
International Association for the Evaluation of Educational Achievement, 264
Irredentism, 375
Italian Communist Party (PCI), 319, 358–359
Italian Confederation of Small and Medium Industry, 327
Italian Socialist Party (PSI), 334, 335
Italy
    bureaucracy, 345

democratization of, 40
domestic policy, 351–352
foreign policy, 358–359
government, 345–346
interest groups, 327–329
political culture, 318–319
political parties, 334–335
public policy, 351–352, 358–359
Ivan III (the Great), Tsar of Russia, 179
Ivan IV (the Terrible), Tsar of Russia, 179

J

Jacobinisme, 100
Jacobins, 100, 114
Jacquet, Aimé, 95
James II, King of England, 57
John, King of England, 57
John Paul II, Pope, 391
Joint Constitutional Commission (Germany), 166
Jospin, Lionel, 95, 134
role of government, 96
"Third Way" philosophy of, 69
Juan Carlos, King of Spain, 347–348
Judiciary
Albania, 395, 405
Britain, 81–82
Bulgaria, 403
Eastern Europe, 379, 395
European Union, 419, 433, 439–440
France, 130–131
Germany, 161–162
Greece, 344
Nordic countries, 254
Romania, 402
Russia, 206–207
Southern Europe, 339
Junkers, 144

K

Kaase, Max, 151
Kampmann, Viggo, 269, 271
Kanslergade agreement, 264
Kant, Immanual, 417
Karadzic, Radovan, 390
Karamanlis, Konstantinas, 334, 344
Kauffmann, Henrik, 295
Kekkonen, Urho, 248, 255, 296–297
Kennedy, Charles, 70
Keynes, John Maynard, 265
Khasbulatov, Ruslan, 207
Khrushchev, Nikita, 182
Kierkegaard, Søren, 287
Kievan Rus, 179
Kirienko, Sergei, 197, 204, 205
Kissinger, Henry, 449
Kohl, Helmut, 156,
defense policy, 171
German unification, 166
nuclear power, 168–169
Kosovo, 407, 408
Albania and, 406
ethnic conflict in, 371, 376, 377, 387–390, 391
European Union and, 447–448
Kosovo Liberation Army (UCK), 390
Kovac, Michal, 399
Kristallnacht, 146
Krøyer, P.F., 220
Kulturkampf, 144
Kyoto Protocol, 285

L

Labour party (Britain), 66, 68–69
Lafontaine, Oskar, 157, 160, 167
Lalonde, Brice, 121
Länder, 150
Bundesrat and, 161
representation in, 158
Lapshin, Mikhail, 196
Latvia, post–Cold War era, 29
The Law of the Constitution, 73
League of Industrialists (Germany), 154
Lebed, Aleksandr, 198, 203
Left Democrats (Italy), 335
Left Party (Sweden), 252
Lenin, Vladimir, 181, 182
Le Pen, Jean-Marie, 95, 113
Front National party, 119, 120–121
Lewin, Leif, 233, 266, 274
Liberal Democracy (DL) party (France), 119

Liberal Democratic Party (LDP) (Russia), 193, 194, 197–198
Liberal Democrats (Britain), 66, 70
Liberalism, 24
Lind, Jenny, 293
Lindbeck, Assar, 260, 268, 271, 276
Linnaeus, Carl, 293
Lithuania, post–Cold War era, 29
Little Constitution, 396
Livingstone, Ken, 82
Locke, John, 54, 81
Lönnrot, Elias, 245
Louis XIV, King of France, 97
Louis-Napoleon, President of France, 100
Lundell, Ulf, 220
Luther, Martin, 20–21, 287–288
Luzhkov, Yuri, 205

M

Maastricht Treaty, 111, 420–421
Macedonia, Albanians in, 387
Mad cow disease, 87
Magna Carta, 40, 56, 57, 74
Major, John, 56, 67, 76, 78, 80
    1997 election, 69, 70, 81
    EU elections and, 426
    social conservatism, 63
    stance on EU, 34
Margrethe II, Queen of Denmark, 257
Marshall Plan, 149
Marx, Karl, 23, 109
Mauroy, Pierre, 134
Meciar, Vladimir, 385, 395, 399, 400, 410
Mediterranean Europe. *See* Southern Europe.
Mégret, Bruno, 120–121
Meidner, Rudolf, 272, 275
Mein Kampf, 146
Merkel, Angela, 156
Metaxas, Ionnis, 314, 317, 332, 339–340
    corporatism and, 349–350
Mill, John Stuart, 294
Milosevic, Slobodan, 371, 388, 389, 390, 395, 407
Ministry of Agriculture (Britain), 83

Ministry of Security (Russia), 207
Mitterand, François, 98, 126, 134
    European political union and, 420
    proportional representation, 116
    role in governmental affairs, 127
    Socialist Party, 117
Mladonov, Petar, 403
Moderate Coalition Party (Sweden), 250
Mommsen, Hans, 142
Mongol Conquest of 1480, 179
Mongols, 179
Monnet, Jean, 32, 417–418
Montenegro, 407
Morrison, Jim, 109
Moscow Regional Agency for Combating Organized Crime, 207
Muller, Pierre, 129
Munch, Edvard, 220
Murdoch, Rupert, 72
Mussolini, Benito, 2, 25, 40, 314, 317, 332, 338
    absolutism and, 339–340
    corporatism and, 325, 349–350
Myrdal, Gunnar, 265, 268, 276, 298

N

Nannenstad, Peter, 283
Napoleon, Emperor of France. *See* Bonaparte, Napoleon.
National Alliance (Italy), 335
National Assembly (France), 115, 124, 125, 126–127
National Assembly (Hungary), 401
National Association of German Industry, 154
National Coal Board (Britain), 84
National Coalition Party (NCP) (Finland), 248, 258
National Democratic Party (Germany), 157
National Farmers Union (NFU) (Britain), 83
National Front (FN) party (France), 115–116, 119–121
National Salvation Front (Romania), 401
National Union of Mineworkers (NUM) (Britain), 84
Nazi party, 145, 156

New Democracy (ND) Party (Greece), 317–318, 334
New Globalism
    Britain and, 87–88, 89–90
    Eastern Europe and, 409–410
    European Union and, 450–451
    France and, 96–97, 133–137
    Nordic countries and, 300
    Russia and, 213–214, 215
    Southern Europe and, 362–363, 365
Newly Industrialized Countries (NICs), 39
Nicholas II, Tsar of Russia, 180, 181
Niedermayer, Oskar, 151
Nielsen, Carl, 224
Njal's Saga, 222
Nokia, 283–284
Nordic countries, 218–301
    basic issues and patterns, 226–230
    culture, 285–286
    economy and society, 280–285
    education, 286–287
    foreign aid of, 298–299
    foreign and security policy, 291–301
    geography, 234, 235–237
    government, 261–262
    history, 239–248
    interest groups, 262–263
    languages, 238–239
    Nordic model, 230–234
    parties and constitutions, 248–259
    peoples, 237–238
    political culture, 220–230, 259–260, 281
    political parties, 256–257, 281–282
    public policy, 263–280, 291–301
    religion, 287–288
    values and temperaments, 220–226, 288–291
Nordic model, 230–234
North American Free Trade Agreement (NAFTA), 9, 414
North Atlantic Treaty Organization (NATO), 9, 10, 31, 36–38, 449
    Britain and, 88
    Eastern Europe and, 409–410
    Germany and, 172–173, 174–175
    Nordic countries and, 297–298
    peacekeeping efforts in Bosnia, 389–390
    peacekeeping efforts in Kosovo, 390
    Russia and, 214
    Southern Europe and, 308, 362
    Spain and, 315
    terms of membership, 410–411
Northern Ireland, 61
Norway
    Basic Law, 254, 255
    geography, 236
    history, 241, 242, 246, 294
    language, 238–239
    political parties, 250, 256–257
    public policy, 229, 280
November Manifesto of 1905, 248
Nuclear power, 168–169
Nurmeberg Laws, 146
Nuremberg Trial, 147
Nyerere, Julius, 298

O

Organization for Security and Cooperation in Europe (OSCE), 449
Ortega y Gassett, José, 330
Orthodox church, 327, 350
Ostpolitik, 172
Our Home is Russia (NDR) Party, 194, 195, 197
Overhang mandates, 160
Øverland, Arnulf, 288

P

Palme, Olof, 231, 260, 271, 275, 285, 299, 300
Panhellenic Socialist Movement (PASOK) (Greece), 317, 333, 334, 350–351
Pantouflage, 127
Papandreous, Andreas, 333, 334, 344
Papandreous, Georgios, 344
Papon, Maurice, 128
Paris Commune of 1871, 109
Parliamentary systems, 343
    definition of, 124
Parochial political culture, 315
Party of Democratic Socialism (PDS) (Germany), 157

Party of European Socialists (PES), 427, 428
Peace of Westphalia, 242
Penn, William, 417
People's home, 259–260, 261
People's Party (Sweden), 251
Père Lachaise, 109
Persson, Göran, 292
Peter I (the Great), Tsar of Russia, 179–180
Pierson, Paul, 278
Pinochet, Augusto, 78
Plaid Cymru, 70
Platini, Michel, 94
Plato, 286
Poland
    constitution of, 394, 396
    government of, 396–397
    post–Cold War era, 28–29
    religion in, 374
    transition to democracy, 396–397
Policy Planning and Early Warning Unit
    (PPEWU) (European Union), 449
Political culture
    Britain, 62–64
    definition of, 44
    Eastern Europe, 372–380
    European Union, 422–424
    France, 97–113
    Germany, 151–152
    Greece, 317–318
    Iceland, 240
    Italy, 318–319
    Nordic countries, 281
    Portugal, 319–320
    Russia, 187, 378
    Southern Europe, 315–321
    Spain, 320–321
Political parties
    Britain, 67–70
    Czech Republic, 398–399
    Denmark, 250, 251–252, 256–257, 281–282
    Eastern Europe, 392–393
    European Union, 427–429
    Finland, 248, 256–257, 258
    France, 113, 115–123
    Germany, 155–158
    Greece, 333–334
    Hungary, 401
    Iceland, 256–257
    Italy, 334–335
    Nordic countries, 250–252, 256–257, 259, 281–282
    Norway, 250, 256–257
    Poland, 397
    Portugal, 335–336
    Russia, 191–199
    Slovakia, 400
    Southern Europe, 331–338
    Spain, 336–337
    Sweden, 250–251, 252, 256–257, 282
Political Spring (PA) Party (Greece), 334
Pollution, 16–17
Pompidou, Georges, 118, 126
Pontoppidan, Henrik, 224
Popular Party (PP) (Portugal), 336
Popular Party (PP) (Spain), 337, 347
Portugal
    bureaucracy, 346–347
    democratization of, 41, 42–43
    domestic policy, 352–353
    foreign policy, 359–360
    government, 346–347
    interest groups, 329
    political culture, 319–320
    political parties, 335–336
    public policy, 352–353, 359–360
Portuguese Communist Party (PCP), 335–336
Portuguese Socialist Party (PSP), 336
Powell, Enoch, 65
Power ministries (Russia), 202
Prague, 2
Presidential systems, definition of, 124
Primakov, Yevgeny, 196, 198, 204
Prime Minister's Question Time, 80
Primo de Rivera, Miguel, 325
Prodi, Romano, 435
Progress Party (Denmark), 251
Protestant Reformation, 241–242
Przeworski, Adam, 277–278
Public policy
    Britain, 82–89

Denmark, 229-230, 260, 264-265, 267, 269, 275, 277, 278-279
Eastern Europe, 409-410
European Union, 442-451
France, 123-136
Germany, 164-173
Greece, 350-351, 356-358
Italy, 351-352, 358-359
Nordic countries, 230-234, 263-280, 291-301
Norway, 229, 280
Portugal, 352-353, 359-360
Russia, 210-214
Southern Europe, 348-361
Spain, 353-354, 360-361
Sweden, 229-230, 265-269, 271-273, 275, 279-280
Putin, Vladimir, 178, 190, 198, 203, 204, 210, 213, 214
Pyramid scheme in Albania, 405-406
Pytheas, 235

R
"Radical, Citizen, Green" group, 121
Radical Liberal party (Denmark), 253
Radicals Decree of 1972, 162
Ragnvald of Växjö, 242
Rally for the Republic (RPR) (France), 115, 118, 119
Rau, Johannes, 159
Reagan, Ronald, 54, 69, 133, 271
Rechtsstaat, 162
Regeringsform (RF) of 1974, 254-255
Rehn, Gösta, 267
Reichstag, 141-142
Renan, Ernest, 105-106
Republic, definition of, 55
Republicans (Germany), 157
Resorgimento, 312
Riefenstahl, Leni, 141
The Right (Norway), 250
Rivlin, Alice, 268
Roberts, Michael, 292, 293
Robespierre, 100, 114
Rocard, Michel, 117
Roma, 382-384
Roman Catholic church
  influence in Italy, 319, 328
  influence in Poland, 391
  influence in Portugal, 319, 329
  influence in Spain, 329
Romania
  government of, 401, 402
  Hungarians in, 384-385
  post-Cold War era, 29
  transition to democracy, 401-402
Romanov, Mikhail, 179
Roosevelt, Franklin D., 147
Roudy, Yvette, 132
Rousseau, Jean-Jacques, 100, 114, 417
Runeberg, J.L., 245
Russia, 176-215
  Cold War era, 182-183, 212
  Communist parties in, 195-196
  conservative/nationalist parties in, 197-199
  constitution of, 189, 199-201, 206, 207, 210
  crime in, 207-209
  democratization of, 41, 42-43, 185-186, 187
  economic reform in, 210-211
  economy of, 208
  elections in, 202-203
  ethnic and national groups, 188-191
  foreign policy, 212-214
  Gorbachev's reforms, 183-184
  government of, 203-204
  history of, 179-185
  lawmaking, 205-206
  legal system, 206-209
  legislature, 204-205
  political culture, 187, 378
  political parties, 191-199
  post-Cold War era, 29-30
  presidency of, 201-202, 206
  public policy, 210-214
  reformist parties in, 196-197
  Russian Revolution, 181-182
  socioeconomic background, 187-191
  state, role of, 209-210

Russian Communist Workers' Party (RCWP), 196
Russian Constitution, 189, 199–201, 206, 207, 210
Russian Constitutional Court, 206
Russian Revolution, 181–182
Russia's Choice party, 193, 194
Rutskoi, Aleksandr, 200
Rydberg, Carina, 285

S
Saint Augustine, 288
Salazar, Antonio, 39, 314, 315, 316, 317, 325, 332, 338
   absolutism and, 339–340
   corporatism and, 349–350, 353
   restoration of traditional conservative society, 319–320
   social programs under, 352
Saltsjöbaden agreement, 267, 268
Sami, 235
Sampaio, Jorge, 346
Santer, Jacques, 435
Saxo Grammaticus, 239
Scandinavia. *See* Nordic countries.
Scandinavism, 245–246
Schengen Agreement, 422, 444
Schindler's List, 140
Schmidt, Helmut, 156, 159
   defense policy, 170, 171
   nuclear power, 168
Schmidt, Vivien, 129–130
Schröeder, Gerhard, 140, 156–157
   campaign in 1998, 174
   economic and social policy, 168
   foreign policy, 172
   "Third Way" philosophy, 69
Schumacher, Kurt, 156
Schuman, Robert, 32, 418
Scotland
   local government, 82
   parliament, 82
Scottish National Party, 65
Scottish Nationalists, 66, 70
Second Reich, 144–145
   judiciary and, 161

Second Republic (France), 100
Sejm, 394, 397
Serbia
   democracy and, 407–408
   ethnic fears in, 387–389
Seven Weeks' War (1866), 143
Seven Years' War (1756–1763), 143
Shaw, George Bernard, 54
Shehu, Tritan, 406
Shippey, Tom, 239–240
Sibelius, Jean, 224
Silva, Anibal Cavaco, 336, 346
Single European Act (SEA), 420, 443–444
   effects of, 445–446
Sjöstrand, Östen, 301
Skokov, Yuri, 198
Sky Television, 432
Slovakia
   elections, 400
   Hungarians in, 385–386, 399, 400
   political parties, 400
   post–Cold War era, 28–29
   transition to democracy, 399–400
Slovenia
   independence of, 388–389
   transition to democracy, 407
Smith, Adam, 54
Snellman, J.V., 247
Soares, Mario, 336, 346
Social Democratic Center (CDS) (Portugal), 336
Social Democratic Labor Party (Russia), 181
Social Democratic Party (SPD) (Germany), 144, 148, 150, 156, 161
   citizenship laws, 170
   defense policy, 170
   economic issues, 167
   nuclear power issues, 169
   political asylum issues, 169–170
   shifting constituencies of, 173–174
   unification issues, 166
Social Democratic Party (PSD) (Portugal), 336
Social Democrats (Denmark), 253
Social Democrats (SSP) (Finland), 248, 258
Social Democrats (Romania), 402

Social Democrats (SAP) (Sweden), 250, 251, 259–260, 281
Social welfare models, 48–49
Socialism, 24
Socialist Party (PS) (France), 115, 117–118, 122
Socialist Party (PSI) (Italy), 318, 334, 335
Socialist Party (PSOE) (Spain), 330, 353
Socialist Reich Party, 162
Socialist Unity Party (SED) (Germany), 149, 157, 173
Socioeconomic background
  Britain, 64–65
  Eastern Europe, 380–391
  France, 105–113
  Germany, 152–154
  Greece, 321–324
  Italy, 321–324
  Portugal, 321–324
  Russia, 187–191
  Southern Europe, 321–324
  Spain, 321–324
Sofia, Queen of Spain, 347–348
Solidarity Electoral Action (Poland), 397
Solidarity Union (Poland), 392
Sotelo, Leopoldo Calvo, 347
Sottogoverno, 346
Southern Europe, 304–365
  bureaucracy, 342–343, 344–345, 346–347, 348
  bureaucratic politics, 342–343
  classes and social structure, 323–324
  development of, 306–308
  domestic policy, 348–354
  foreign policy, 354–361
  globalization, 362–363, 365
  government, 338–348
  government institutions, 343–348
  history of, 308–315
  interest groups, 324–331, 338, 340, 341, 342
  origin of the state, 338–340
  political culture, 315–321
  political parties, 331–338
  public policy, 348–361
  regionalism, 361–362
  socioeconomic background, 321–324
Spain
  bureaucracy, 348
  democratization of, 41, 42–43
  domestic policy, 353–354
  foreign policy, 360–361
  government, 347–348
  interest groups, 329–331
  political culture, 320–321
  political parties, 336–337
  public policy, 353–354, 360–361
  state-society relations, 340–341
Spanish Civil War of 1936–1939, 320
Spanish Communist Party (PCE), 330, 337
Spanish Socialist Workers Party (PSOE), 337, 338, 347
Spinelli, Altiero, 428
Stäel, Madame de, 114
Stalin, Josef, 147, 178, 182
Stalinism, 182
START II Treaty, 212
Stauning, Thorvald, 263
Steincke, K.K., 264–265
Stenhammar, Vilhelm, 224
Stepashin, Sergei, 204
Stone, Alec, 130
Stöss, Richard, 151
Sträng, Gunnar, 261, 269
Strindberg, August, 224
Strong society, 260, 261, 268–269
Suárez, Adolfo, 347
Subject political culture, 315
Supreme Arbitration Court of the Russian Federation, 207
Supreme Court of the Russian Federation, 207
Svalbard, 235
The swamp, 195
Sweden
  alcohol policy, 263–264
  Basic Law, 254–255
  constitution of, 249
  economy of, 280–281
  geography, 236
  history, 241, 242, 246, 249–250, 292–293

interest groups, 279–280
political culture, 259–260
political parties, 250–251, 252, 256–257, 282
public policy, 229–230, 263–264, 265–269, 271–273, 275, 279–280
Swedenborg, Emmanuel, 293
Synapismos, 334

T
Tapis, Bernard, 104
Tavsen, Hans, 241
Tegnér, Esaias, 243
Thatcher, Margaret, 54, 56, 68, 70, 76, 77–78, 80, 133
  Greater London Council, 82
  stance on EEC, 33, 34
  Thatcherism, 59–60, 84–85, 86, 89
Third Reich, 145–147
"Third Way" in politics, 69
Timbro group, 272
Tito, Marshal Josip Broz, 388
Tocqueville, Alexis de, 97, 338
Tokoi, Oskari, 248
Topography of Europe, 15–17
Tories, 66, 69–70
Trades Union Congress (TUC), 71
Trans-European Networks (TENs), 446
Treaty of Amsterdam (1997), 421
Treaty of European Union (TEU) (1991), 420–421
Treaty of Paris (1951), 418
Treaty of Versailles, 145, 146
Trimble, David, 61
Tuchman, Barbara, 24–25, 313
Tumanov, Vladimir, 207
Tyulkin, Viktor, 196

U
Ubozhko, Lev, 197
Ukraine, post–Cold War era, 29
Ulbricht, Walter, 149
Union of Democratic Forces (Bulgaria), 403
Union for French Democracy (UDF), 115, 118–119

Union of Industrial and Employers' Confederations of Europe (UNICE), 430
Union of Kalmar, 241
Union of the Left (France), 117
Union of Right Forces (SPS) (Russia), 195, 197, 205
Union of Soviet Socialist Republics (USSR), 182–185
  legal system of, 206, 207
Unionists, 50
Unitary state, definition of, 65
Unity Bloc (Russia), 195, 197, 205
Unity Party (Russia), 193, 195
Uruguay Round of GATT, 450–451

V
Varangians, 179
Velvet revolution, 386, 397–398
Venizelos, Eleuthérios, 314
Venstre, 250, 251
Versailles, Treaty of, 145, 146
Victoria, Queen of England, 24
Visegrad group, 409

W
Waldemar II, King of Denmark, 234
Wales
  local government, 82
  Senedd, 82
Walesa, Lech, 393, 394, 395, 397
Wallenberg, Raoul, 274–275
Walser, Martin, 141
War of Austrian Succession (1740–1749), 143
Warsaw Pact, 26
Washington, George, 331
Weber, Eugene, 105
Weber, Max, 274
Weimar Era, 145, 156
  chancellors in, 159
  judiciary and, 161
  presidency in, 159
Weizsäcker, Richard von, 159
Western European Union (WEU), 36, 449–450

Westminster model, 78
Westphalia, peace of, 242
Wigforss, Ernst, 265–266, 268
Wilde, Oscar, 109
William, Duke of Normandy (William the Conqueror), 57
William I, King of Prussia, 143, 144
William II, Emperor of Germany, 144
Wilson, Harold, 59, 68, 71
Wojtyla, Karol, 391
Women of Russia Party, 193, 194
Workers Commission (CCOO) (Spain), 330
World Trade Organization (WTO), 450
World War I, 24–25, 145
    effect on Southern Europe, 313–314
    Russia and, 181
World War II, 2–3, 140–141, 146–147
World Wide Fund for Nature, 431

Y

Yabloko party, 193, 194, 195, 197
Yalta Conference, 147
Yavlinsky, Grigory, 203
Yeltsin, Boris, 178, 184, 185, 186, 191, 192, 195, 200
    creation of The Russian Federation, 209
    dissolution of the Ministry of Security, 207
    economic reforms, 210–211
    foreign policy of, 212–213
    impeachment attempts against, 205
    legal reforms of, 206–207
    presidential decrees, 201
    presidential elections in 1996, 202–203, 209, 215
    prime ministers of, 204

Z

Zhirinovsky, Vladimir, 191, 193, 197–198, 202, 203
Zhivkov, Todor, 386, 403
Zidane, Zinedine, 95
Zorn, Anders, 220
Zyuganov, Gennady, 196, 202, 203, 209, 215

CREDITS

Chapter 1   Page 2: Keystone/Corbis; Page 3: B. Annebicque/Corbis; Page 11: SuperStock; Page 16: SuperStock; Page 27: D. Aubert/Corbis; Page 37: Juha Roininen/Corbis.

Chapter 2   Page 60: © Charles Gupton/Stock Boston; Page 61: Le Segretain/Corbis; Page 74: Tim Graham/Corbis; Page 79: SuperStock; Page 81: Tim Graham/Corbis.

Chapter 3   Page 108: DeLage/Sipa Press; Page 120: Bernard Bisson/Corbis; Page 125: Associated Press REUTERS; Page 135: François Poincet/Corbis.

Chapter 4   Page 142: Associated Press AP POOL; Page 147: SuperStock; Page 158: Pandis/Corbis; Page 167: Droese/Sipa Press.

Chapter 5   Page 184: Les Stone/Corbis; Page 191: SOVOFOTO/EASTFOTO; Page 199: Pandis/Corbis; Page 200: SuperStock; Page 212: AP Photo/Anatoly Maltsev.

Chapter 6   Page 236: SuperStock; Page 253: SuperStock; Page 270: D Van der Zwalm/Corbis; Page 289: Robert Maas/Sipa Press; Page 292: J.B. Vernier/Corbis; Page 295: SuperStock.

Chapter 7   Page 310: F. Pagani/Corbis; Page 328: Associate Press AP; Page 347: SuperStock; Page 351: SuperStock; Page 352: SuperStock; Page 357: Associated Press AP; Page 364: Jacques Pavlovsky/Corbis.

Chapter 8   Page 376: Yannis Kontos/Corbis; Page 383: J. Groch/Corbis; Page 388: Tomislav Peternek/Corbis; Page 396: SuperStock; Page 398: SuperStock; Page 406: Associated Press AP.

Chapter 9   Page 423: Corbis; Page 425: Yves Forestier/Corbis; Page 434: SuperStock; Page 437: Associated Press AP; Page 441: B. Bisson/Corbis.